APA
College
Dictionary
of Psychology

SECOND EDITION

AMERICAN PSYCHOLOGICAL ASSOCIATION

APA
College
Dictionary
of Psychology

SECOND EDITION

AMERICAN PSYCHOLOGICAL ASSOCIATION • *Washington, DC*

Published by
American Psychological Association
750 First Street, NE
Washington, DC 20002
www.apa.org

To order
APA Order Department
P.O. Box 92984
Washington, DC 20090-2984
Tel: (800) 374-2721; Direct: (202) 336-5510
Fax: (202) 336-5502; TDD/TTY: (202) 336-6123
Online: www.apa.org/pubs/books/
E-mail: order@apa.org

In the U.K., Europe, Africa, and the Middle East, copies may be ordered from
American Psychological Association
3 Henrietta Street
Covent Garden, London
WC2E 8LU England

Typeset in Aylesbury, England, by Market House Books, Ltd.
Printer: United Book Press, Baltimore, MD
Cover Designer: Naylor Design, Washington, DC

Library of Congress Cataloging-in-Publication Data
Names: VandenBos, Gary R., editor. | American Psychological Association.
Title: APA college dictionary of psychology / Gary R. VandenBos.
Other titles: American Psychological Association college dictionary of
  psychology | College dictionary of psychology
Description: Second edition. | Washington, DC : American Psychological
  Association, [2016] | Earlier edition: 2009. |
Identifiers: LCCN 2015043399| ISBN 9781433821585 (softcover) | ISBN
  9781433821592 (ebook) | ISBN 1433821583 (softcover) | ISBN 1433821591
  (ebook)
Subjects: LCSH: Psychology--Dictionaries.
Classification: LCC BF31 .A648 2016 | DDC 150.3--dc23 LC record available at http://lccn.loc.
gov/2015043399

British Library Cataloguing-in-Publication Data
A CIP record is available from the British Library.

Printed in the United States of America
Second Edition

http://dx.doi.org/10.1037/14944-000

The citation for this publication is American Psychological Association. (2016). *APA college dictionary of psychology* (2nd ed.). Washington, DC: Author.

Contents

Preface

Welcome to the *APA College Dictionary of Psychology, Second Edition.*

The parent reference for this new collegiate edition—the *APA Dictionary of Psychology, Second Edition*—was released in 2015 and has since met with strong critical endorsement and recognition from both the publishing and reference library communities. With the full dictionary's release, the decision to produce a second edition of our college dictionary was a natural one—not only because of the popularity of the first edition but also because there was so much new and revised material in the second edition of the parent dictionary to consider for inclusion in a collegiate update.

A bit of background on the revision process: For the first edition, APA Reference staff researched psychology texts in use at some three dozen institutions of higher learning in the United States with strong psychology curricula—from major public and private universities to small liberal arts and community colleges. Within this institutional spectrum, staff pinpointed the primary introductory undergraduate texts in general, personality and social, lifespan developmental, abnormal, and cognitive psychology, as well as any basic supporting texts in neuropsychology and methodology and statistics. That foundational first-edition research remained pertinent and valid as we began to prepare for the second edition.

As noted in the preceding paragraphs, with the recent release of a significantly updated, expanded, and revised edition of the parent APA dictionary, there was much new material from which to grow a second edition of the college dictionary. From the 1,000 new entries in the parent, we gleaned nearly 700 new entries for the college version. Editorial staff applied a fresh look at all of them—as well as at the recurring entries from the first edition—in some instances retaining definitions as they had appeared and in some amending text. In other words, the evaluation of each entry in this dictionary brought opportunities for updating and general textual improvement.

Thus, we are again pleased to offer a thoughtfully condensed, easily portable, and economically priced reference for the student of psychology —whether he or she is at the advanced placement level in high school, a college undergraduate enrolled in Intro Psych, or an undergraduate making psychology his or her major field of study. We hope our efforts have provided a usefully updated tool for these users as they navigate the basic lexicon of psychology.

Gary R. VandenBos, PhD
Editor in Chief

Editorial Staff

Editor in Chief
Gary R. VandenBos, PhD

Senior Editors (American Psychological Association)
Theodore J. Baroody
Julia Frank-McNeil
Kristen Knight
Patricia D. Mathis
Marion Osmun

Market House Books, Ltd., Editorial and Production
Amanda Garner-Hay
Anne Kerr
Jonathan Law

Editorial Consultants
Andrew C. Butler, PhD
Mary Beth M. Cresci, PhD
David C. Devonis, PhD
Donald A. Dewsbury, PhD
Leandre R. Fabrigar, PhD
Ingrid G. Farreras, PhD
Donelson R. Forsyth, PhD
Craig H. Kinsley, PhD
Maura Mitrushina, PhD
Harry T. Reis, PhD
Brian P. Yochim, PhD

Editorial Reviewers

Bernard J. Baars, PhD
John Bancroft, MD
Imants Baruš, PhD
Marlene Behrmann, PhD
Douglas A. Bernstein, PhD
Marian E. Berryhill, PhD
David F. Bjorklund, PhD
Paul H. Blaney, PhD
Robert F. Bornstein, PhD
Brian Bruya, PhD
Ann Kathleen Burlew, PhD

Gideon P. Caplovitz, PhD
Susan T. Charles, PhD
Philip J. Corr, PhD
Stephen L. Crites Jr., PhD
Jennifer Crocker, PhD
Jaine L. Darwin, PsyD
Michael Domjan, PhD
Perrin Elisha, PhD
Karla K. Evans, PhD
Todd J. Farchione, PhD
Shannon Foskett, MA

David C. Funder, PhD
Lisa Geraci, PhD
Meyer D. Glantz, PhD
Catherine A. Haden, PhD
Philip D. Harvey, PhD
Melissa J. Hawthorne, PhD
Gregory Hickok, PhD
Jennifer L. Hudson, PhD
Bryan A. Jones, PhD
Irene P. Kan, PhD
Robert J. Kastenbaum, PhD†
David A. S. Kaufman, PhD
John F. Kihlstrom, PhD
Frederick T. L. Leong, PhD
Jeffrey J. Magnavita, PhD
Rowland S. Miller, PhD
Brooke S. Parish, MD
Celine-Marie Pascale, PhD
Benton H. Pierce, PhD
Joseph H. Ricker, PhD

Damaris J. Rohsenow, PhD
Bennett L. Schwartz, PhD
Thomas F. Shipley, PhD
Karen Riggs Skean, PsyD
Anderson D. Smith, PhD
Jasper A. J. Smits, PhD
Stephen M. Stahl, MD, PhD
Craig E. L. Stark, PhD
William W. Stoops, PhD
George Stricker, PhD
William B. Swann Jr., PhD
Richard F. Thompson, PhD†
Matthew Walenski, PhD
Richard M. Warren, PhD
Elizabeth Weiss, PsyD
Thomas A. Widiger, PhD
Diane L. Williams, PhD
Sean H. Yutzy, MD

† deceased

Quick Guide to Format

Headword

causation *n.* the empirical relation between two events, states, or variables such that change in one (the cause) brings about change in the other (the effect). See also CAUSALITY. **—causal** *adj.*

Derived word

chronological age (CA) the amount of time elapsed since an individual's birth, typically expressed in terms of months and years. Compare BIOLOGICAL AGE.

Abbreviation

Cross-reference

counseling *n.* professional assistance in coping with personal problems, including emotional, behavioral, vocational, marital, educational, rehabilitation, and life-stage (e.g., retirement) problems. The **counselor** makes use of such techniques as ACTIVE LISTENING, guidance or advice, discussion, clarification, and the administration of tests.

Part-of-speech label

Hidden entry

Cross-reference

Plural form

crisis *n.* (*pl.* **crises**) **1.** a situation (e.g., a traumatic change) that produces significant cognitive or emotional stress in those involved in it. **2.** a turning point for better or worse in the course of an illness.

Sense number

Sense number

Cronbach's alpha a measure of the average strength of association between all possible pairs of items contained within a set of items. It is a commonly used index of the INTERNAL CONSISTENCY of a test and ranges in value from 0, indicating no internal consistency, to 1, indicating perfect internal consistency. Also called **alpha coefficient.** [Lee J. **Cronbach** (1916–2001), U.S. psychologist]

Etymology

cross-modal matching the ability to recognize an object initially inspected with one modality (e.g., touch) via another modality (e.g., vision). Also called **intermodal matching.**

Alternative name

Aa

A-B design the simplest SINGLE-CASE DESIGN, comprising a pretreatment or baseline phase (Phase A) followed by a treatment phase (Phase B). Although it allows for evaluation of the treatment's effect by comparing the DEPENDENT VARIABLE during the two phases, the design does not provide evidence of causality because it does not establish a repeated relationship between the introduction and removal of the treatment and a consequential change in the dependent variable, as occurs in an **A-B design**. See also PRETEST–POSTTEST DESIGN.

abducens nerve the sixth CRANIAL NERVE, carrying motor fibers for control of the lateral rectus muscle of the eye, which rotates the eyeball outward. Also called **abducent nerve**.

aberration *n.* **1.** any deviation, particularly a significant or undesirable one, from the normal or typical. See also MENTAL ABERRATION. **2.** in vision, the failure of light rays to converge at the same point, due to either distortion by a lens (**spherical aberration**) or the formation of colored fringes by a lens (**chromatic aberration**).

ability *n.* existing competence or skill to perform a specific physical or mental act. Although ability may be either innate or developed through experience, it is distinct from capacity to acquire competence (see APTITUDE).

ability test 1. a norm-referenced standardized test designed to measure competence to perform a physical or mental act. **2.** a test measuring achievement.

ablation *n.* the removal or destruction of part of a biological tissue or structure by a surgical procedure or a toxic substance, usually for treatment or to study its function. When the en-

tire tissue or structure is excised, the process is called **extirpation**.

ableism *n.* discrimination against individuals with disabilities or the tendency to be prejudiced against and to stereotype them negatively, for example, as less intelligent, nonproductive, or dependent on others. —**ableist** *adj.*

abnormal *adj.* relating to any deviation from what is considered typical, usual, or healthy, particularly if the deviation is considered harmful or maladaptive. In statistics, for example, abnormal scores are those that are outside the usual or expected range. The term, however, is most often applied to behavior that differs from a culturally accepted norm, especially when indicative of a mental disorder. —**abnormality** *n.* —**abnormally** *adv.*

abnormal psychology the branch of psychology devoted to the study, assessment, treatment, and prevention of maladaptive behavior. See also PSYCHOPATHOLOGY.

abortion *n.* the expulsion from the uterus of an embryo or fetus before it is able to survive independently. An abortion may be either spontaneous, in which case it occurs naturally and is also called a **miscarriage**, or induced, in which case it is produced deliberately by artificial means such as drugs or surgery and done for therapeutic reasons or as an elective decision. The latter practice is controversial and may involve **abortion counseling**, the provision of guidance, advice, information, and support on issues concerning termination of pregnancy and the alternatives of adoption or raising the child.

above-average effect the tendency to hold overly favorable views of one's own intellectual and social abilities relative to others. For example, students' predictions of their own final exam score in a particular college class often are based on their highest score received to that point, but their predictions of someone else's final exam score typically are based on that student's mean score. The above-average effect appears to be common and consistent across a variety of judgment domains. Also called **better-than-average effect**. Compare BELOW-AVERAGE EFFECT.

abreaction *n.* the therapeutic process of bringing forgotten or inhibited material (i.e., experiences, memories) from the unconscious into consciousness, with concurrent emotional release and discharge of tension and anxiety. See also CATHARSIS.

abscissa *n.* the horizontal coordinate in a graph or data plot; that is, the *x*-axis. See also ORDINATE.

absence seizure a type of GENERALIZED SEIZURE, formerly called a **petit mal seizure**, in which the individual abruptly ceases activity and cannot afterward remember the event. The absences usually last from 5 to 15 seconds, during which the individual is unresponsive and motionless, staring blankly. Seizures of this type typically begin between ages 4 and 12 and rarely persist into adulthood.

absenteeism *n.* unjustified absence from work or school, especially when regular or persistent. Although absenteeism has been linked to lack of job satisfaction, other factors may be more relevant, such as an **absence culture** in which employees regard sick leave as a benefit to be claimed rather than a provision to be utilized only when strictly necessary. Compare PRESENTEEISM.

absolute refractory period see REFRACTORY PERIOD.

absolute threshold the lowest or weakest level of stimulation (e.g., the slightest, most indistinct sound) that can be detected on 50% of trials. Although the name suggests a fixed level at which stimuli effectively elicit sensa-

tions, the absolute threshold fluctuates according to alterations in receptors and environmental conditions. Also called **absolute limen (AL)**.

absolute value a number considered without regard to its algebraic sign (i.e., whether it is positive or negative). For example, the absolute value of -1 is 1. Also called **modulus**.

absolutism *n.* the philosophical position that there are absolute ethical, aesthetic, or epistemological values. Phenomena are believed to have a fixed reality; thus, what is regarded as true in one circumstance will be regarded as true in all others as well. For example, a particular action will always be deemed immoral regardless of its outcome or any other individual or subjective considerations. Such a position involves a rejection (in whole or in part) of RELATIVISM.

abstinence *n.* the act of refraining from the use of something, particularly alcohol or drugs, or from participation in sexual or other activity. In most instances, abstinence from drugs or alcohol is the primary goal of substance abuse treatment. See also RELAPSE; SUBSTANCE WITHDRAWAL. —**abstinent** *adj.*

abstraction *n.* **1.** the formation of general ideas or concepts by extracting similarities from particular instances. The precise cognitive processes by which this occurs remain a subject of investigation. **2.** such a concept, especially a wholly intangible one, such as *goodness* or *truth.* —**abstract** *vb.*

abuse *n.* **1.** interactions in which one person behaves in a cruel, violent, demeaning, or invasive manner toward another person or an animal. The term most commonly implies physical mistreatment but also encompasses sexual and psychological (emotional) mistreatment. **2.** colloquially, the misuse of a substance to the extent that it causes the individual difficulty, whether or not it meets a formal diagnosis of SUBSTANCE ABUSE. —**abuser** *n.*

acalculia *n.* loss of the ability to perform simple arithmetic operations that results from brain injury or disease, usually to the PARIETAL LOBE. It is an acquired condition, whereas DYSCALCULIA is developmental.

acceleration *n.* **1.** an increase in speed of movement or rate of change. An important area of study in psychology is the range of forces sustained by the human body when it is in an accelerating vehicle, such as an automobile or aircraft, and the physical, physiological, and psychological consequences (e.g., disturbances of heart rhythm and blood pressure, disorientation and confusion, loss of consciousness). Compare DECELERATION. **2.** in mathematics and statistics, the rate of change in the SLOPE of a function or the rate of change in one variable as a function of an increase in a second variable.

accent *n.* phonetic features of an individual's speech that are associated with geographical region or social class. The standard version of a language is usually considered by native speakers to be unaccented. Compare DIALECT.

acceptance region the range of values for a test statistic that leads to acceptance of the NULL HYPOTHESIS, such that the ALTERNATIVE HYPOTHESIS is rejected as a valid explanation for observed data. Compare CRITICAL REGION.

accessible *adj.* **1.** receptive or responsive to personal interaction and other external stimuli. A client in psychotherapy, for example, is thought to be accessible if he or she responds to the therapist in a way that facilitates the development of rapport and, ultimately, fosters the examination of cognitive, emotional, and behavioral issues. **2.** retrievable through memory or other cognitive processes, as in ATTITUDE ACCESSIBILITY. **3.** denoting a building or other site that is easy to approach and enter, with facilities and fixtures that are easy to use, particularly by people with disabilities. —**accessibility** *n.*

accessory nerve the 11th CRANIAL NERVE, sometimes so named because one of its functions is to serve as an accessory to the 10th cranial nerve (the VAGUS NERVE). It innervates the sternomastoid and trapezius muscles in the neck.

accidental sampling see CONVENIENCE SAMPLING.

accommodation *n.* **1.** adjustment or modification. For example, regarding individuals with disabilities, it refers to REASONABLE ACCOMMODATIONS made to meet their needs. **2.** the process by which the focus of the eye is changed to allow near or distant objects to form sharp images on the retina. Accommodation is achieved mainly by contraction or relaxation of the CILIARY MUSCLES but also involves adjustments in the CONVERGENCE of the eyes and the size of the pupils. **3.** see PIAGETIAN THEORY. —**accommodate** *vb.*

acculturation *n.* the processes by which groups or individuals adjust the social and cultural values, ideas, beliefs, and behavioral patterns of their culture of origin to those of a different culture. **Psychological acculturation** is an individual's attitudinal and behavioral adjustment to another culture, which typically varies with regard to degree and type. Compare DECULTURATION; ENCULTURATION. —**acculturate** *vb.*

accuracy motive see SELF-ASSESSMENT MOTIVE.

acetaldehyde *n.* a toxic and volatile initial product of alcohol (ethanol) metabolism that is thought to be responsible for the ALCOHOL FLUSH REACTION and certain other physical sequelae of alcohol consumption, including unpleasant effects such as nausea, vomiting, and headache. Acetaldehyde is produced when alcohol is broken down by a liver enzyme called alcohol dehydrogenase. It is then broken down by another liver enzyme (acetaldehyde dehydrogenase) into acetate and, ultimately, into carbon dioxide and water. Acetaldehyde is also a major component of tobacco smoke. It may influence the development, progression, and persistence of alcohol use and of tobacco use. See also DISULFIRAM.

acetylcholine (ACh) *n.* a major, predominantly excitatory but also inhibitory, neurotransmitter both in the central nervous system, where it plays an important role in memory formation and learning, and in the peripheral nervous system, where it mediates skeletal, cardiac, and smooth muscle contraction.

acetylcholine receptor (AChR) any protein within a cell membrane that is stimulated by acetylcholine or acetylcholine-like substances. Located throughout the central and peripheral nervous system, AChRs have two main types: MUSCARINIC RECEPTORS and NICOTINIC RECEPTORS.

acetylcholinesterase (AChE) *n.* see CHOLINESTERASE.

acetylcholinesterase inhibitor (AChEI) see CHOLINESTERASE.

achievement *n.* **1.** the attainment of some goal, or the goal attained. See also NEED FOR ACHIEVEMENT. **2.** acquired knowledge (especially in a particular subject), proficiency, or skill. The term is most often used in this sense to mean academic achievement.

achievement motivation 1. the desire to perform well and be successful. In this sense, the term often is used synonymously with NEED FOR ACHIEVEMENT. **2.** the desire to overcome obstacles and master difficult challenges. High scorers in achievement motivation are likely to set higher standards and work with greater perseverance than equally gifted low scorers.

achievement test any norm-referenced standardized test intended to measure an individual's current level of skill or knowledge in a given subject. Often the distinction is made that achievement tests emphasize ability acquired through formal learning or training, whereas APTITUDE TESTS (usually in the form of intelligence tests) emphasize innate potential.

achromatic *adj.* **1.** without HUE and SATURATION. Thus, an **achromatic color** is black, white, or a shade of gray. **2.** able to refract light without splitting it into its constituent wavelengths. The term generally refers to lenses that do not distort the color of objects viewed through them. Compare CHROMATIC.

achromatism *n.* color blindness marked by the inability to perceive any color whatsoever: Everything is seen in different shades of gray. It is a congenital condition stemming from a lack of RETINAL CONES. Also called **achromatopsia**. See also DICHROMATISM; MONOCHROMATISM; TRICHROMATISM.

acoustic *adj.* associated with sound. The word is usually used to modify technical terms (e.g., ACOUSTIC REFLEX). **Acoustical** is used as a modifier in all other contexts (e.g., acoustical engineer).

acoustic encoding see VISUAL ENCODING.

acoustic nerve see AUDITORY NERVE.

acoustic reflex contraction of the middle ear muscles (the tensor tympani and stapedius muscle) elicited by intense sounds. This reflex restricts movement of the OSSICLES, thus reducing the sound energy transmitted to the inner ear and partially protecting it from damage.

acoustic store 1. a component of short-term memory that retains auditory information based on how items sound. Forgetting occurs when words or letters in the acoustic store sound alike. Compare ARTICULATORY STORE. **2.** see PHONOLOGICAL LOOP.

acquiescent response set see YEA-SAYING.

acquired immune deficiency syndrome see AIDS.

acquisition *n.* the attainment by an

individual of new behavior, information, or skills or the process by which this occurs. Although often used interchangeably with LEARNING, acquisition tends to be defined somewhat more concretely as the period during which progressive, measurable changes in a response are seen. —**acquire** *vb.*

acquisition curve see LEARNING CURVE.

actin *n.* see MUSCLE FIBER.

acting out 1. the behavioral expression of emotions that serves to relieve tension associated with these emotions or to communicate them in a disguised, or indirect, way to others. Such behaviors may include arguing, fighting, stealing, threatening, or throwing tantrums. **2.** in psychoanalytic theory, reenactment of past events as an expression of unconscious emotional conflicts, feelings, or desires—often sexual or aggressive—with no conscious awareness of the origin or meaning of these behaviors.

action *n.* **1.** a self-initiated sequence of movements, usually with respect to some goal. It may consist of an integrated set of component behaviors as opposed to a single response. **2.** the occurrence or performance of a process or function (e.g., the action of an enzyme).

action disorganization syndrome (**ADS**) a cognitive deficit resulting from damage to the FRONTAL LOBES of the brain and causing individuals to make errors on multistepped but familiar or routine tasks. Types of errors include omissions or additions of steps, disordered sequencing of steps, and object substitutions or misuse.

action potential (**AP**) the change in electric potential that propagates along the axon of a neuron during the transmission of a nerve impulse or the contraction of a muscle. It is marked by a rapid, transient DEPOLARIZATION of the cell's plasma membrane, from a RESTING POTENTIAL of about -70 mV

(inside negative) to about $+30$ mV (inside positive), and back again, after a slight HYPERPOLARIZATION, to the resting potential. Each action potential takes just a few milliseconds. Also called **spike potential**.

action research 1. research developed and carried out to address a social issue or problem, results of which are used to improve the situation. Investigating interventions to reduce the incidence and consequences of domestic violence is an example of action research. **2.** more generally, any research directed toward a practical goal, usually an improvement in a particular process or system. In organizational development, for example, action research involves not only systematically collecting data about an organization but also providing feedback to the organization, taking actions to improve the organization based on the feedback, and then evaluating the results of these actions.

action-specific energy in classical ETHOLOGY, a hypothetical supply of motivational energy within an organism that is associated with specific unlearned behavioral responses known as FIXED ACTION PATTERNS. Each response has its own energy supply, which builds up until the organism encounters the appropriate stimulus (see RELEASER) that triggers the response and thus depletes the energy supply. After the response and in the absence of the releaser, the action-specific energy begins to build up again.

activation *n.* **1.** in many theories of memory, an attribute of the representational units (such as NODES or LOGOGENS) that varies from weaker to stronger, with more strongly activated representations competing to control processing. **2.** the process of alerting an organ or body system for action, particularly arousal of one organ or system by another. An example is the pituitary gland's release of hormones that initiate specific activities within the ovaries

5

and testes in preparation for puberty. —**activate** *vb.* —**activational** *adj.*

activational effect a transient hormonal effect that typically causes a short-term change in behavior or physiological activity in adult animals. For example, increased testosterone in male songbirds during spring leads to increased aggression in territory defense and increased courtship behavior. Compare ORGANIZATIONAL EFFECT.

activation–synthesis hypothesis a hypothesis that explains dreams as a product of cortical interpretation of random neural activity arising from the brainstem (specifically the PONS).

active euthanasia direct action performed to terminate the life of a person (or animal) who is suffering greatly and is considered to have no chance for recovery. Administering a lethal injection is the most common method of active euthanasia today. This practice is distinguished from PASSIVE EUTHANASIA, in which treatments are withheld but no direct action to terminate the life is taken. See also ASSISTED DEATH.

active joy see JOY.

active listening a psychotherapeutic technique in which the therapist listens to a client closely, asking questions as needed, in order to fully understand the content of the message and the depth of the client's emotion. The therapist typically restates what has been said to ensure accurate understanding. Active listening is particularly associated with CLIENT-CENTERED THERAPY.

activities of daily living (ADLs) activities essential to an individual's personal care, such as getting into and out of bed and chairs, dressing, eating, toileting and bathing, and grooming. A person's ability to perform ADLs is often used as a measure of functional capabilities during the course of a disease or following an injury. See also INSTRUMENTAL ACTIVITIES OF DAILY LIVING.

activity theory 1. a school of thought, developed primarily by Soviet psychologists, that focuses on activity in general—rather than the distinct concepts of behavior or mental states—as the primary unit of analysis. The theory emphasizes a hierarchical structure of activity, object-orientedness, internalization and externalization, mediation (by tools, language, and other cultural artifacts or instruments), and continuous development. Also called **activity psychology**. **2.** a theory proposing that old age is a lively, creative experience characterized by maintaining existing social roles, activities, and relationships or replacing any lost ones with new ones. Compare CONTINUITY THEORY; DISENGAGEMENT THEORY.

actor–observer effect in ATTRIBUTION THEORY, the tendency for individuals acting in a situation to attribute the causes of their behavior to external or situational factors, such as social pressure, but for observers to attribute the same behavior to internal or dispositional factors, such as personality.

actualization *n.* the process of mobilizing one's potentialities and realizing them in concrete form. According to U.S. psychologist Carl Rogers (1902–1987), all humans have an innate **actualizing tendency** to grow and realize the self fully. See also SELF-ACTUALIZATION. —**actualize** *vb.*

actuarial *adj.* statistical: based on quantified experience and data. In medicine, the use of data about prior instances to estimate the likelihood or risk of a particular outcome is sometimes cited as an alternative to clinical predictions, which are open to human error.

acuity *n.* sharpness of perception. Whereas visual acuity is sharpness of vision and auditory acuity is sharpness of hearing, sensory acuity is the precision with which any sensory stimulation is perceived.

acupuncture *n.* a form of COMPLE-

MENTARY AND ALTERNATIVE MEDICINE in which fine needles are inserted into the body at specific points to relieve pain, induce anesthesia, or treat disease. It is based on the concept in traditional Chinese medicine that meridians, or pathways, conduct a life-force energy known as chi between places on the skin and the body's organ systems. Western scientists are unable to explain specifically how acupuncture produces its effects but theorize that the needling sites may be related to trigger points in the GATE-CONTROL THEORY of pain or may stimulate the release of ENDOGENOUS OPIOIDS. —**acupuncturist** *n.*

acute *adj.* **1.** denoting conditions or symptoms of sudden onset, short duration, and often great intensity. Compare CHRONIC. **2.** sharp, keen, or very sensitive (e.g., acute hearing).

acute stress disorder (**ASD**) a psychological condition that can occur immediately after exposure to a trauma. Symptoms such as intrusive thoughts, HYPERAROUSAL, and avoidance of situations that recall the traumatic event are the same as those of POSTTRAUMATIC STRESS DISORDER but do not last longer than 4 weeks. This disorder may also include elements of dissociation, such as DEPERSONALIZATION and DEREALIZATION.

acute stress response see HYPERAROUSAL.

adaptation *n.* **1.** adjustment of a sense organ to the intensity or quality of stimulation, resulting in a temporary change in sensory or perceptual experience, as in visual adaptation when the pupil of the eye adjusts to dim or bright light. **2.** reduced responsiveness in a sensory receptor or sensory system caused by prolonged or repeated stimulation. The adaptation may be specific, such as to the orientation of a particular stimulus. Also called **sensory adaptation**. **3.** modification to suit different or changing circumstances. In this sense, the term often refers to behavior that enables an individual to adjust to the environment effectively and function optimally in various domains, such as coping with daily stressors. Compare MALADAPTATION. **4.** adjustments to the demands, restrictions, and mores of society, including the ability to live and work harmoniously with others and to engage in satisfying social interactions and relationships. Also called **social adaptation**. **5.** the modification of an organism in structure or function that increases its ability to reproduce successfully and its offspring's ability to survive and reproduce successfully. **6.** in PIAGETIAN THEORY, the process of adjusting one's cognitive structures to meet environmental demands, which involves the complementary processes of assimilation and accommodation. —**adapt** *vb.* —**adaptational** *adj.* —**adaptive** *adj.*

adaptation level (**AL**) the theoretical baseline or zero point, which forms a standard against which new stimuli are evaluated. For example, a person who first lifts a 40 lb weight would then likely judge a 20 lb weight as light, whereas if that person first lifted a 4 lb weight he or she would then likely judge the 20 lb weight as heavy. Although it originated in studies of sensory perception, **adaptation-level theory** has since been applied in other fields, such as aesthetics and attitude change.

adaptation stage see GENERAL ADAPTATION SYNDROME.

addiction *n.* a state of psychological or physical dependence (or both) on the use of alcohol or other drugs. The term is often used as equivalent to SUBSTANCE DEPENDENCE and is sometimes applied to behavioral disorders, such as sexual, Internet, and gambling addictions. A chemical substance with significant potential for producing dependence is called an **addictive drug** (e.g., cocaine, heroin). —**addictive** *adj.*

addition rule a maxim of probability theory stating that the likelihood of observing a set of distinct events is equal to the sum of the probabilities of observing the individual events. Also called **addition law**. Compare MULTIPLICATION RULE.

additive effect the joint effect of two or more INDEPENDENT VARIABLES on a DEPENDENT VARIABLE where this is equal to the sum of their individual effects: The value of either independent variable is not conditional on the value of the other and there is no INTERACTION EFFECT.

additive gene a gene in which there are neither dominant nor recessive ALLELES, although gradations may exist between extremes. The resulting PHENOTYPE does not follow a pattern of MENDELIAN INHERITANCE but instead is determined by the combined effect of the alleles. Additive genes are responsible for such traits as height and skin color and are also believed to be the genetic component of some pathologies such as autism, Alzheimer's disease, and diabetes.

additive task a task or project that a group can complete by aggregating individual members' efforts or contributions. An example is a five-person team pulling together on a rope. Groups usually outperform individuals on such tasks, but overall group productivity rarely reaches its maximum potential owing to SOCIAL LOAFING. Compare COMPENSATORY TASK; CONJUNCTIVE TASK; DISJUNCTIVE TASK.

adenosine *n.* a compound in living cells that functions as a neuromodulator: By binding to special **adenosine receptors**, it influences the release of several neurotransmitters in the central nervous system. Combined with three phosphate units, adenosine becomes ATP (**adenosine triphosphate**), which functions as an energy source in metabolic activities.

adipose tissue connective tissue consisting largely of fat cells (**adipocytes**). Found beneath the skin and around major organs, it provides protection and insulation and functions as an energy reserve.

adjusted *R* the correlation between scores on a response or DEPENDENT VARIABLE and the values predicted by a set of INDEPENDENT VARIABLES, after accounting for the number of predictors and the number of observations involved in the calculation. See also MULTIPLE CORRELATION COEFFICIENT.

adjustment *n.* **1.** a change in attitude, behavior, or both by an individual on the basis of some recognized need or desire to change, particularly to account for the current environment or changing, atypical, or unexpected conditions. It may be assessed via a type of survey called an **adjustment inventory**, which compares a person's emotional and social adjustment with a representative sample of other individuals. A well-adjusted person is one who satisfies needs in a healthy, beneficial manner and demonstrates appropriate social and psychological responses to situations and demands. **2.** modification to match a standard. See METHOD OF ADJUSTMENT. —**adjust** *vb.*

adjustment disorder impairment in social or occupational functioning and severe emotional or behavioral symptoms occurring within 3 months after an individual experiences a specific identifiable stressful event, such as a divorce, business crisis, or family discord. The event is not as stressful as a trauma, which can lead to POSTTRAUMATIC STRESS DISORDER. Symptoms may include anxiety, depression, and conduct disturbances, and they tend to remit following elimination of the stressors.

adolescence *n.* the period of human development that starts with puberty (10–12 years of age) and ends with physiological maturity (approximately 19 years of age), although the exact age span varies across individuals. During this period, major changes occur at varying rates in physical characteristics, sexual characteristics, and sexual interest, resulting in significant effects on body image, self-concept, and self-esteem. Major cognitive and social developments take place as well: Most young people acquire enhanced abilities to think abstractly, evaluate reality hypothetically, reconsider prior experiences from altered points of view, assess data from multiple dimensions, reflect inwardly, create complex models of understanding, and project complicated future scenarios. Adolescents also tend to increase their peer focus and involvement in peer-related activities, place greater emphasis on social acceptance, and seek more independence and autonomy from parents. —**adolescent** *adj., n.*

adoption *n.* the legal process by which an infant or child is permanently placed with a family other than his or her birth family. An adoption may be private, in which a birth parent voluntarily plans for the placement of the child with adoptive parents through intermediaries, or public, in which a child who has been removed from his or her birth family because of neglect or abuse is placed with adoptive parents through public child welfare agencies. Adoptions may also be closed, allowing no contact between the birth and adoptive parents, or open, permitting varying degrees of pre- and postplacement contact and making possible a relationship between all three parties.

adoption study a research design that investigates the relationships among genetic and environmental factors in the development of personality, behavior, or disorder by comparing the similarities of biological parent–child pairs with those of adoptive parent–child pairs.

adrenal gland an endocrine gland adjacent to the kidney. Its outer layer, the **adrenal cortex**, secretes such hormones as ANDROGENS, GLUCOCORTICOIDS, and MINERALOCORTICOIDS. Its inner core, the **adrenal medulla**, se-

cretes the hormones EPINEPHRINE and NOREPINEPHRINE, both of which are CATECHOLAMINES and also serve as neurotransmitters.

adrenaline *n.* see EPINEPHRINE.

adrenergic *adj.* responding to, releasing, or otherwise involving EPINEPHRINE (adrenaline). For example, an **adrenergic neuron** is one that employs epinephrine as a neurotransmitter. The term often is used more broadly to include NOREPINEPHRINE as well.

adrenocorticotropic hormone (**ACTH**) see CORTICOTROPIN.

adult attachment see ATTACHMENT STYLE.

adulthood *n.* the period of human development in which full physical growth and maturity have been achieved and certain biological, cognitive, social, personality, and other changes associated with the aging process occur. Adulthood is sometimes divided into young adulthood (roughly 20 to 35 years of age); middle adulthood (about 36 to 64 years); and later adulthood (age 65 and beyond). The last is sometimes subdivided into young-old (65 to 74), old-old (75 to 84), and oldest old (85 and beyond). The oldest old group is the fastest growing segment of the population in many developed countries. See also EMERGING ADULTHOOD.

adult stem cell see STEM CELL.

advance directive a legal mechanism for individuals to specify their wishes and instructions about prospective health care in the event they later become unable to make such decisions. This can be achieved by means of a **durable power of attorney**, a legal document designating a **health care proxy** to make health care decisions on another person's behalf. Other advance directives include a **living will**, a legal document clarifying a person's wishes regarding future medical or, increasingly, mental health treatment; and a **do not resuscitate** (**DNR**) order stating that cardiopulmonary resuscitation (CPR) is not to be performed if the patient's heart or breathing stops. Federal law requires hospitals, nursing homes, and other institutions that receive Medicare or Medicaid funds to provide all patients on admission with written information regarding advance directives. See also INFORMED CONSENT.

advocacy *n.* the process whereby an individual speaks or acts to uphold the rights or explain the point of view of another person. An individual engaged in advocacy is called an **advocate**, of which there are two general types: A case advocate represents a single individual, and a class advocate represents a whole group of people. An example of a case advocate is a therapist who speaks for a client in court hearings or other situations involving decisions based on the client's mental health or related issues. An example of a class advocate is an individual in health care who represents consumers to protect their rights to effective treatment.

aerobic exercise physical activity, typically prolonged and of moderate intensity (e.g., walking, jogging, cycling), that involves the use of oxygen in the muscles to provide the needed energy. Aerobic exercise strengthens the cardiovascular and respiratory systems and is associated with a variety of health benefits, including increased endurance, reduction of body fat, and decreased depression and anxiety. Compare ANAEROBIC EXERCISE.

aesthesiometry *n.* see ESTHESI-OMETRY.

aesthetics *n.* the philosophical study of beauty and art, concerned particularly with the articulation of taste and questions regarding the value of aesthetic experience and the making of aesthetic judgments. —**aesthetic** *adj.*

affect *n.* any experience of feeling or emotion, ranging from suffering to elation, from the simplest to the most complex sensations of feeling, and from

the most normal to the most pathological emotional reactions. Along with COGNITION and CONATION, affect is one of the three traditionally identified components of the mind. See NEGATIVE AFFECT; POSITIVE AFFECT.

affective aggression see AGGRESSION.

affective concordance see CONCORDANCE.

affective discordance see DISCORDANCE.

affective disorder see MOOD DISORDER.

affective forecasting predicting one's own future emotional states, especially in connection with some event or outcome that one faces. People often "forecast" more extreme and lasting emotional reactions to events than they actually experience.

affective memory see EMOTIONAL MEMORY.

affective neuroscience a discipline that addresses the brain mechanisms underlying emotions. In seeking to understand the particular roles of major subcortical and cortical structures in the elicitation, experience, and regulation of emotion, affective neuroscience provides an important framework for understanding the neural processes that underlie psychopathology, particularly the mood and substance-related disorders.

affective well-being see SUBJECTIVE WELL-BEING.

affect theory the idea that feelings and emotions are the primary motives for human behavior, with people desiring to maximize their positive feelings and minimize their negative ones. Within the theory, affects are considered to be innate and universal responses that create consciousness and direct cognition. Eight primary affects are postulated: the positive ones of excitement and enjoyment; the negative ones of distress, fear, shame, disgust, and anger; and the relatively neutral one of interest. Despite their biological nature and triggering mechanisms, primary affects are subject to significant social modification and social causation. See also SCRIPT THEORY.

afferent *adj.* conducting or conveying from the periphery toward a central point. Compare EFFERENT.

affiliation *n.* a social relationship in which a person joins or seeks out one or more other individuals, usually on the basis of liking or a personal attachment rather than perceived material benefits. Some propose that the seeking of cooperative, friendly association with others who resemble or like one or whom one likes is a fundamental human desire, referring to it variously as the **affiliation motivation, affiliative drive, affiliative need,** or NEED FOR AFFILIATION. —**affiliative** *adj.*

affinity *n.* **1.** an inherent attraction to or liking for a particular person, place, or thing, often based on some commonality. **2.** relationship by marriage or adoption rather than blood. Compare CONSANGUINITY.

affordance *n.* in the theory of ECOLOGICAL PERCEPTION, any property of the physical environment that offers or allows an organism the opportunity for a particular physical action. An example is the location of a light switch in a room. When the switch is on the left-hand side of the doorway, it affords a left-hand reach-and-click movement.

aftercare *n.* **1.** a program of outpatient treatment and support services provided for individuals discharged from an institution, such as a hospital or mental health facility, to help maintain improvement, prevent relapse, and aid adjustment to life within the community. Aftercare may also refer to inpatient services provided for convalescent patients, such as those who are recovering from surgery. **2.** a form of day care, as in programs designed to care for children after school.

afterimage *n.* the image that remains after a stimulus ends or is removed. A positive afterimage occurs rarely, lasts a few seconds, and is caused by a continuation of receptor and neural processes following cessation of the stimulus; it has approximately the color and brightness of the original stimulus. A negative afterimage is more common, is often more intense, and lasts longer. It is usually complementary to the original stimulus in color and brightness; for example, if the stimulus was bright yellow, the negative afterimage will be dark blue.

age cohort see COHORT.

age dedifferentiation hypothesis see DIFFERENTIATION–DEDIFFERENTIATION HYPOTHESIS.

age differentiation hypothesis see DIFFERENTIATION–DEDIFFERENTIATION HYPOTHESIS.

age effect in research, any outcome associated with being a certain age. Such effects may be difficult to separate from COHORT EFFECTS and PERIOD EFFECTS.

ageism *n.* the tendency to be prejudiced against older adults, to negatively stereotype them (e.g., as unhealthy, helpless, or incompetent), and to discriminate against them, especially in employment and health care. —**ageist** *adj.*

agentic state a psychological condition that occurs when individuals, as subordinates to a higher authority in an organized status hierarchy, feel compelled to obey the orders issued by that authority. See BEHAVIORAL STUDY OF OBEDIENCE.

age regression a hypnotic technique in which the therapist helps the client recall a crucial experience by inducing amnesia for the present, then suggesting that he or she return, year by year, to the earlier date when a particular experience took place. This technique is also used in forensic contexts to help eyewitnesses and victims recall their experiences. The use of age regression in either context is controversial, given the potential for FALSE MEMORY and the debatable legitimacy of RECOVERED MEMORY.

aggregate data scores or observations that have been re-expressed by a SUMMARY STATISTIC. Calculating the arithmetic average of a set of test scores obtained over time for each individual in a group and then using each person's single average score as representative of his or her test performance would be an example of aggregating data.

aggression *n.* behavior aimed at harming others physically or psychologically. It can be distinguished from anger in that anger is oriented at overcoming the target but not necessarily through harm or destruction. When such behavior is purposively performed with the primary goal of intentional injury or destruction, it is termed **hostile aggression**. Other types of aggression are less deliberately damaging and may be instrumentally motivated (proactive) or affectively motivated (reactive). **Instrumental aggression** involves an action carried out principally to achieve another goal, such as acquiring a desired resource. **Affective aggression** involves an emotional response that tends to be targeted toward the perceived source of the distress but may be displaced onto other people or objects if the disturbing agent cannot be attacked (**displaced aggression**). In the classical psychoanalytic theory of Austrian neurologist Sigmund Freud (1856–1939), the aggressive impulse is innate and derived from the DEATH INSTINCT, but many non-Freudian psychoanalysts and most nonpsychoanalytically oriented psychologists view it as socially learned or as a reaction to frustration (see FRUSTRATION–AGGRESSION HYPOTHESIS). —**aggressive** *adj.*

aging *n.* the biological and psychological changes associated with chronological age. A distinction is often made between changes that arise from normal biological processes (see PRIMARY AGING) and changes that are caused by age-related pathologies (see SECONDARY AGING).

aging in place the ability of older individuals to live safely, independently, and comfortably in their own homes as they age and as their health-related and other needs change. Factors that influence whether an older individual can successfully age in place include environmental characteristics of the "place" itself (e.g., home, neighborhood, community), such as its physical suitability, safety, and access to appropriate support services if needed, and personal characteristics or circumstances that support an individual's independence, such as economic stability, positive relationships with family and friends, a sense of SELF-EFFICACY, and ability to manage ACTIVITIES OF DAILY LIVING.

agitation *n.* a state of increased but typically purposeless and repetitious activity, as in PSYCHOMOTOR AGITATION.

agnosia *n.* loss or impairment of the ability to recognize or appreciate the nature of sensory stimuli due to brain damage or disorder. Recognition impairment is profound and specific to a particular sensory modality. AUDITORY AGNOSIA, TACTILE AGNOSIA, and VISUAL AGNOSIA are the most common types, and each has a variety of subtypes.

agonist *n.* **1.** a drug or other chemical agent that binds to a particular receptor and produces a physiological effect, typically one similar to that of the body's own neurotransmitter at that receptor. There are PARTIAL AGONISTS, which stimulate the receptor only somewhat to produce the same physiological effect as the natural neurotransmitter but to a lesser degree, and **inverse agonists**, which act at the receptor to produce a physiological effect opposite to that produced by another agonist at that same receptor. **2.** a contracting muscle whose action generates force in the intended direction. Compare ANTAGONIST. **—agonism** *n.* **—agonistic** *adj.*

agoraphobia *n.* an excessive, irrational fear of being in open or unfamiliar places, resulting in the avoidance of public situations from which escape may be difficult, such as standing in line or being in a crowd. Agoraphobia may accompany PANIC DISORDER, in which an individual experiences unexpected panic attacks, or it may occur in the absence of panic disorder. **—agoraphobic** *adj.*

agrammatism *n.* a manifestation of APHASIA characterized by loss or impairment of the ability to use speech that conforms to grammatical rules, such as those governing word order. **—agrammatic** *adj.*

agranulocytosis *n.* a decline in the number of certain white blood cells (neutrophils) in the body, typically as a result of an immune reaction to a drug or other chemical or the toxic effect of this substance on the bone marrow, causing production of white blood cells to fall. The condition results in suppression of the immune response, rendering individuals vulnerable to opportunistic infections.

agraphia *n.* loss or impairment of the ability to write as a result of neurological damage or disorder. The specific forms of writing difficulties vary considerably but may include problems with spelling irregular or ambiguous words, writing numbers or particular letters, or performing the motor movements needed for handwriting. Also called **dysgraphia**. **—agraphic** *adj.*

aha experience the emotional reaction that typically occurs at a moment of sudden insight into a problem or other puzzling issue. It is the experience one would have on realizing, for example, how to fix a computer problem, master a dance step, or resolve some other difficulty. In psychotherapy, it is a client's sudden insight into his or her

motives for cognitions, affects, or behaviors. Also called **aha reaction**.

AIDS acquired immune deficiency syndrome: a clinical condition in which the immune system is so severely damaged from infection with human immunodeficiency virus (see HIV) as to allow serious opportunistic infections and diseases.

AIDS dementia complex (ADC) neuropsychological dysfunction directly attributable to HIV infection, found most commonly in those who have developed AIDS. It is marked by impairment in four areas: (a) cognition (e.g., memory loss, inability to concentrate); (b) behavior (e.g., inability to perform normal activities of daily living); (c) motor coordination (e.g., unsteady gait, loss of balance, incontinence); and (d) mood (e.g., severe depression, psychosis). Also called **HIV dementia**.

akathisia (**acathisia**) *n.* extreme restlessness characterized by an inability to sit or stand still and by fidgety movements or jitteriness, as well as a subjective report of inner restlessness.

akinesia *n.* loss or reduction of voluntary movement. Also called **akinesis**. **—akinetic** *adj.*

akinetopsia *n.* inability to see objects in motion as a result of damage to the visual cortex. Individuals with akinetopsia perceive moving stimuli as a series of stationary strobelike images and see visual trails behind moving objects. **—akinetopsic** *adj.*

alanine *n.* a nonessential amino acid found in plasma that has a role in the metabolism of sugar and acid and provides energy for various organs. Its consumption as a supplement in the form of beta-alanine may be associated with improved physical functioning (e.g., in athletes, older adults) by building muscle mass, and it also may have a role in alleviating depression, schizophrenia, and other disorders.

alarm reaction see GENERAL ADAPTATION SYNDROME.

alcohol *n*. short for ethyl alcohol (see ETHANOL).

alcohol dependence a pattern of repeated or compulsive use of alcohol despite significant behavioral, physiological, and psychosocial problems, plus indications of physical and psychological dependence—such as tolerance and characteristic withdrawal symptoms if use is suspended—that result in impaired control. It is differentiated from **alcohol abuse** by the preoccupation with obtaining alcohol or recovering from its effects and the overwhelming desire for its consumption. Alcohol dependence is known popularly as **alcoholism**.

alcohol flush reaction (AFR) reddening of the face, neck, or other parts of the body—sometimes accompanied by reduced blood pressure and increased heart rate, sweating, sleepiness, and nausea—following alcohol consumption. It is caused by the body's inability to metabolize alcohol efficiently due to a variation of the *ALDH2* gene, found in 40% to 50% of people of Asian descent. AFR is associated with an increased risk of cancer due to the carcinogenic properties of unmetabolized alcohol.

alcohol use disorder a catchall diagnostic categorization encompassing varying degrees of excessive use of alcohol. The disorder is characterized by such symptoms as alcohol craving, recurrent use of alcohol that interferes with the fulfillment of one's daily responsibilities, alcohol-seeking behavior, inability to control one's drinking, drinking despite potential hazards (e.g., drinking while driving), the need for increased amounts of alcohol to achieve its effects (tolerance), and withdrawal symptoms when one stops or reduces alcohol intake (e.g., hand tremors, nausea, agitation, hallucinations). The disorder is distinguished as mild, moderate, or severe, depending on the number and type of these symptoms an individual has.

aldosterone *n*. the principal MINERALOCORTICOID hormone secreted by the ADRENAL GLAND. It helps to regulate mineral and water metabolism by promoting potassium excretion and sodium retention in the kidneys. Excess secretion of aldosterone results in a pathological condition called **aldosteronism** (or **hyperaldosteronism**), marked by headaches, muscle weakness, fatigue, hypertension, and numbness.

alexia *n*. loss or impairment of the ability to comprehend written or printed words as a result of lesions, stroke, or other forms of neurological damage or disorder. It is generally seen in APHASIA but may occur in isolation, in which case it is called **pure alexia** (or **alexia without agraphia**) and characterized by reading impairment with preserved language production and auditory comprehension. See also DYSLEXIA.

alexithymia *n*. an inability to express, describe, or distinguish among one's emotions. It may occur in a variety of disorders, especially psychosomatic and some substance use disorders, or following repeated exposure to a traumatic stressor.

algesia *n*. the ability to experience the sensation of pain. Compare ANALGESIA. —**algesic** *adj*.

algorithm *n*. a well-defined procedure or set of rules that is used to solve a problem or accomplish a task or that is used for conducting a series of computations. An example is trying all the possible combinations in sequence to open a combination lock. Algorithms, which may be represented visually as flow charts, are essential to computer programming and information processing. Compare HEURISTIC. —**algorithmic** *adj*.

alienation *n*. **1.** estrangement from others, resulting in the absence of close or friendly relationships with people in one's social group (e.g., family, workplace, community). **2.** a deep-seated sense of dissatisfaction with one's personal existence and a lack of trust in one's social or physical environment or in oneself. **3.** the experience of being separated from reality or isolated from one's thoughts, feelings, or physical being, as in DEREALIZATION and DEPERSONALIZATION. **—alienated** *adj.*

alien limb syndrome a neurological disorder characterized by unintended hand, arm, or leg movements, often accompanied by a feeling that one has no control over the limb. The individual may not even recognize the limb as his or her own. The syndrome may be associated with lesions to the SUPPLEMENTARY MOTOR AREA or the motor regions of the CORPUS CALLOSUM.

allele *n.* an alternate form of a gene that occupies a given position on each of a pair of HOMOLOGOUS chromosomes. Each person typically has two alleles of each gene: One is inherited from the mother and the other from the father. Alleles may be alike (HOMOZYGOUS) or different (HETEROZYGOUS) and are responsible for variation in inherited characteristics, such as hair color or blood type. See also DOMINANT ALLELE; RECESSIVE ALLELE. **—allelic** *adj.*

allocentric *adj.* characterized by an orientation toward or focus on groups and connection to others. Compare IDIOCENTRIC. See also SOCIOCENTRISM. **—allocentrism** *n.*

allocortex *n.* those regions of the cerebral cortex that are phylogenetically older and have fewer than six main layers of cells. The allocortex is involved primarily in olfactory functions and limbic functions related to memory and emotion, and it comprises the three-layered **archicortex** (or **archipallium**), found mostly in the hippocampus, and the four- or five-layered **paleocortex** (or **paleopallium**), found mostly in the pyriform area and parahippocampal gyrus. Compare NEOCORTEX.

allogrooming *n.* behavior that involves two or more nonhuman animals picking through each other's fur, hair, or feathers. Often thought to have a solely hygienic function (i.e., the removal of dirt and parasites), allogrooming has been shown to have positive social effects as well, through production of ENDOGENOUS OPIOIDS in recipients. It is thus a mechanism that reinforces social relationships.

allomone *n.* a chemical signal that is released outside the body by members of one species and affects the behavior of members of another species. Compare PHEROMONE.

allonursing *n.* the provision by a female of nourishment for offspring that are not her own. Various explanations are offered for this behavior, including the parenting hypothesis, stating that the individual is practicing to improve her maternal skills; the reciprocity hypothesis, stating that the individual helps one who has helped her by sharing responsibility for nourishment; the milk evacuation hypothesis, stating that the individual nourishes others to get rid of surplus milk not consumed by her own offspring; and the kin selection hypothesis, stating that the individual obtains greater INCLUSIVE FITNESS by nourishing offspring to whom she is indirectly related. Allonursing may also have social benefits similar to those of ALLOGROOMING. Also called **communal nursing**.

all-or-none law the principle that the amplitude of the ACTION POTENTIAL in a neuron is independent of the magnitude of the stimulus. Thus, all stimuli above the neuron's threshold trigger action potentials of identical magnitude. Also called **all-or-none principle**.

all-or-none learning the theory that, in any given learning trial, learning occurs either completely and fully or not at all. This contrasts with a hypothesis of trial-by-trial **incremental learning**.

allostasis *n.* stability through change. Allostasis refers particularly to the idea that parameters of most physiological regulatory systems change to accommodate environmental demands. Although allostatic processes are critical for adaptive functioning, chronic or repeated activation of physiological systems in response to life's challenges is hypothesized to exact a toll on such systems.

alogia *n.* inability to speak because of dysfunction in the central nervous system. In a less severe form, it is sometimes referred to as **dyslogia**.

alpha (symbol: α) *n.* **1.** the probability of a TYPE I ERROR. **2.** a measure of RELIABILITY for a set of responses to a test or other assessment instrument. See CRONBACH'S ALPHA.

alpha coefficient see CRONBACH'S ALPHA.

alpha level see SIGNIFICANCE LEVEL.

alpha male the top-ranked or dominant male within a group, with primary access to resources, including food and mates. In many species, the alpha male prevents other males from mating or from mating during the peak time of female fertility. There are **alpha females** as well, with primary access to resources within their social groups and who, in some species, inhibit reproduction among other females.

alpha motor neuron see MOTOR NEURON.

alpha wave in electroencephalography, a type of low-amplitude BRAIN WAVE (frequency 8–12 Hz) that typically occurs when the eyes are closed or unfocused and no deliberate mental tasks are taking place; it is associated with a wakeful but relaxed state. There is evidence that the occurrence of alpha waves can be increased, as for example through meditation and **alpha-wave training**. Also called **alpha rhythm**.

altered state of consciousness (**ASC**) a state of psychological functioning that is significantly different from that experienced in ordinary states of CONSCIOUSNESS, being characterized by altered levels of self-awareness, affect, reality testing, orientation to time and place, wakefulness, responsiveness to external stimuli, or memorability or by a sense of ecstasy, boundlessness, or unity with the universe. In certain Eastern philosophies and TRANSPERSONAL PSYCHOLOGY, ASCs are regarded as higher states of consciousness and, often, as indicative of a more profound level of personal and spiritual evolution.

alter ego 1. a second identity or aspect of a person that exists metaphorically as his or her substitute or representative, with different characteristics. For example, an **avatar** is a digital alter ego that provides a virtual representation of a computer or Internet user in games, online discussion boards, or alternate online universes. **2.** an intimate, supportive friend with whom an individual can share all types of problems and experiences, as if he or she were "another self."

alternate form a set of test items that are developed to be similar to another set of test items, so that the two sets represent different versions of the same test. To demonstrate that one test is an alternate form of the other, a researcher usually must show that there is matching content (each test has the same number of each kind of item) and that factor loadings and MEASUREMENT ERRORS are approximately the same across the two versions. Also called **comparable form**.

alternate-forms reliability a measure of the consistency and freedom from error of a test, as indicated by a CORRELATION COEFFICIENT obtained from responses to two or more ALTERNATE FORMS of the test. Also called **comparable-forms reliability**.

alternating treatments design a type of study in which the experimental condition or treatment assigned to each participant changes from session to session or within sessions. For example, a researcher comparing two methods for eliminating the disruptive classroom behavior of a student might have the teacher use one method throughout the morning and the other method throughout the afternoon and then evaluate the student's behavior with each technique.

alternative hypothesis (AH; symbol: H_1, H_a) a statement that is contrasted with or contradicts the NULL HYPOTHESIS as an explanation for observed data. Generally, it is a scientific prediction of significant results in HYPOTHESIS TESTING; that is, an alternative hypothesis posits meaningful differences or relationships between the variables under investigation.

altruism *n.* an apparently unselfish behavior that provides benefit to others at some cost to the individual. In humans, it covers a wide range of behaviors, including volunteerism and martyrdom, but the degree to which such behaviors are legitimately without egoistic motivation is subject to debate. In animal behavior, it is difficult to understand how altruism could evolve in a species since NATURAL SELECTION operates on individuals. However, organisms displaying altruism can benefit if they help their relatives (see KIN SELECTION) or if an altruistic act is subsequently reciprocated. **—altruistic** *adj.* **—altruist** *n.*

Alzheimer's disease a progressive neurodegenerative disease characterized by cortical atrophy, neuronal death, synapse loss, and accumulation of AMYLOID PLAQUES and NEUROFIBRILLARY TANGLES, causing DEMENTIA and a significant decline in functioning. Early features include deficits in memory (e.g., rapid forgetting of new information, impaired recall and recognition), ANOMIA, executive dysfunction, depressive symptoms, and subtle personality changes such as social withdrawal, in-

difference, and impulsivity. As the disease progresses, there is global deterioration of cognitive capacities accompanied by intellectual decline, APHASIA, AGNOSIA, and APRAXIA. Behavioral features appear as well, including apathy, emotional blunting, delusions, decreased sleep and appetite, and increased motor activity (e.g., restlessness, wandering). [first described in 1907 by Alois **Alzheimer** (1864–1915), German neurologist]

amacrine cell any of a diverse class of neurons in the retina that connect RETINAL BIPOLAR CELLS and RETINAL GANGLION CELLS. Amacrine cells have no axons and do not contribute directly to the output of the retina.

ambiguity *n.* the property of a behavior, behavior pattern (including verbal or written communication), situation, or other stimulus that might lead to interpretation in more than one way. **—ambiguous** *adj.*

ambiguity tolerance the degree to which one is able to accept, and to function without distress or disorientation in, situations having conflicting or multiple interpretations or outcomes.

ambiguous figure a visual stimulus that can be interpreted in more than one way, such as an EMBEDDED FIGURE or a REVERSIBLE FIGURE. A well-known example is the young girl–old woman image, in which the black-and-white drawing sometimes appears to be of a young girl and sometimes of an old lady. This phenomenon is not restricted to the visual: An **ambiguous stimulus** is one of any sensory modality that can have multiple interpretations.

ambivalence *n.* the simultaneous existence of contradictory feelings and attitudes, such as friendliness and hostility, toward the same person, object, event, or situation. Swiss psychiatrist Eugen Bleuler (1857–1939), who first used the term in a psychological sense, regarded extreme ambivalence as a major symptom of schizophrenia. **—ambivalent** *adj.*

ambivalent attachment see INSE-CURE ATTACHMENT.

amblyopia *n.* poor vision caused by abnormal visual experience in early life rather than any physical defect of the eye. Common predisposing conditions include misalignment of the eyes (strabismus) and differing refractive powers of the eyes (anisometropia). Also called (colloquially) **lazy eye**. —**amblyopic** *adj.*

amenorrhea *n.* the absence of menstruation. When menstruation fails to begin after puberty, the condition is called primary amenorrhea. If menstrual periods stop, in the absence of pregnancy or menopause, the condition is known as secondary amenorrhea.

American Psychiatric Association (**APA**) a national medical and professional organization whose physician members specialize in the diagnosis, treatment, and prevention of mental disorders. It was founded in 1844 as the Association of Medical Superintendents of American Institutes for the Insane and renamed the American Medico-Psychological Association in 1892. The current name was adopted in 1922. Its objectives include the improvement of care for people with mental illnesses, the promotion of research and professional education in psychiatry, and the dissemination of psychological knowledge through nationwide public information, education, and awareness programs and materials. Its extensive publications include the *Diagnostic and Statistical Manual of Mental Disorders* (see DSM–5).

American Psychological Association (**APA**) a scientific and professional organization founded in 1892 that represents psychology in the United States and is the largest association of psychologists worldwide. Its mission is to advance the creation, communication, and application of psychological knowledge to benefit society and improve people's lives. Some of its specific goals are to encourage the development and application of psychology in the broadest manner; to promote research in psychology, the improvement of research methods and conditions, and the application of research findings; to improve the qualifications and usefulness of psychologists by establishing standards of ethics, conduct, education, and achievement; and to increase and disseminate psychological knowledge through meetings and a wide variety of scholarly material available through print and electronic media. Its major avenues of communication include more than 85 scholarly journals, the APA *Publication Manual*, some 80 books and videos per year, and seven electronic databases.

Ames room an irregularly shaped but apparently rectangular room in which cues for DEPTH PERCEPTION are manipulated to distort the viewer's perception of the relative size of objects within the room. Also called **Ames distorted room**. [Adelbert **Ames** Jr. (1880–1955), U.S. psychologist, inventor, and artist]

amino acid an organic compound that contains an amino group ($-NH_2$) and a carboxyl group ($-COOH$). Twenty amino acids are constituents of proteins; nine of these are **essential amino acids**, that is, they cannot be synthesized by the body and must be obtained from foods. Other amino acids are neurotransmitters or precursors to neurotransmitters.

amnesia *n.* partial or complete loss of memory. Either temporary or permanent, it may be due to physiological factors such as injury, disease, or substance use, or to psychological factors such as a traumatic experience. A disturbance in memory marked by inability to learn new information is called **anterograde amnesia**, and one marked by inability to recall previously learned information or past events is called **retrograde amnesia**. When severe enough to interfere markedly with social or occupational functioning or to represent a significant decline from a previous level of functioning, the memory loss is known as **amnestic disorder.** —**amnesiac** *adj., n.* —**amnesic** or **amnestic** *adj.*

amniocentesis *n.* a method of examining fetal chromosomes for any abnormality or for determination of sex. A hollow needle is inserted through the mother's abdominal wall into the uterus, enabling collection of amniotic fluid, which contains fetal cells.

amok (amuck) *n.* a CULTURE-BOUND SYNDROME observed among males in Malaysia, the Philippines, and other parts of southeast Asia. The individual experiences a period of social withdrawal and apathy, then makes a violent, unprovoked attack on nearby individuals. The aggressor eventually collapses from exhaustion and afterward has no memory of the event.

AMPA receptor see GLUTAMATE RECEPTOR.

amphetamines *pl. n.* a group of synthetic drugs that stimulate the RETICULAR FORMATION in the brain and cause a release of stored norepinephrine. The effect is a prolonged state of arousal and relief from feelings of fatigue. Introduced in 1932, amphetamines are prone to abuse and dependence, and tolerance develops with continued use. Although widely used in the past for weight loss, relief of depression, and other indications, modern use of amphetamines is more circumscribed because of their adverse effects. They are now used mainly to manage symptoms of attention-deficit/hyperactivity disorder and to treat certain cases of severe depression or narcolepsy.

amplitude *n.* magnitude or extent (e.g., of a stimulus) or peak value (e.g., of a sinusoid wave).

amplitude modulation see MODULATION.

amygdala *n.* an almond-shaped

structure in the TEMPORAL LOBE that is a component of the LIMBIC SYSTEM and considered part of the BASAL GANGLIA. It comprises two main groups of nuclei—the corticomedial group and the basolateral group—and through widespread connections with other brain areas has numerous viscerosensory and autonomic functions as well as an important role in memory, emotion, perception of threat, and fear learning. Also called **amygdaloid body; amygdaloid nuclei.** —**amygdaloid** *adj.*

amyloid *n.* a chemically diverse protein that accumulates abnormally between neural and other bodily cells, negatively affecting their functioning. There are various types, each associated with different pathological conditions. For example, beta-amyloid has received considerable attention for its detrimental influence on memory and cognition in Alzheimer's disease. —**amyloidal** *adj.*

amyloid plaque a clump of beta-amyloid protein surrounded by degenerated dendrites that is particularly associated with symptoms of Alzheimer's disease. Increased concentration of such plaques in the cerebral cortex of the brain is correlated with the severity of dementia. Also called **neuritic plaque; senile plaque.**

amyotrophic lateral sclerosis (**ALS**) a rapidly progressive adult-onset disease involving degeneration of both lower MOTOR NEURONS, responsible for muscle contraction, and upper motor neurons, responsible for MUSCLE SPINDLE sensitivity, and leading to death usually within 5 years of diagnosis. Symptoms include muscular atrophy and weakness, partial and complete paralysis, speech impairment, and difficulties swallowing or breathing. Also called **Lou Gehrig's disease.**

anabolism *n.* see METABOLISM. —**anabolic** *adj.*

anaclitic depression depression involving interpersonal dependency. It is characterized by intense fears of abandonment and feelings of helplessness and weakness. Compare INTROJECTIVE DEPRESSION.

anaerobic exercise strength-based physical activity, such as weight training and sprinting, that occurs in short, intense bursts with limited oxygen intake. The **anaerobic threshold** is the point at which energy use by the body is so great as to require the muscles to begin producing energy in the absence of adequate oxygen. Compare AEROBIC EXERCISE.

analgesia *n.* absence of or reduction in the sensation of pain. Compare ALGESIA. —**analgesic** *adj.*

analogies test a test of the participant's ability to comprehend the relationship between two items and then extend that relationship to a different situation: For example, paintbrush is to paint as pen is to ___.

analogue study an EXPERIMENTAL DESIGN in which the procedures or participants used are similar but not identical to the situation of interest. For example, if researchers are interested in the effects of therapist gender on client perceptions of therapist trustworthiness, they may use undergraduate students who are not clients and provide simulated counseling dialogues that are typed and identified as offered by a male or female therapist. The results of such studies are assumed to offer a high degree of experimental control.

analogy *n.* **1.** a similarity between two entities in certain limited respects. In biology, it refers to similarity of function in structures with different evolutionary origins, such as wings in bats and butterflies. **2.** a method of argument that relies on an inference that a similarity between two or more entities in some attributes justifies a probable assumption that they will be similar in other attributes. —**analogical** *adj.* —**analogous** *adj.*

anal stage in the classical psychoanalytic theory of Austrian neurologist Sigmund Freud (1856–1939), the second stage of PSYCHOSEXUAL DEVELOPMENT, typically occurring during the 2nd year of life, in which the child's interest and sexual pleasure are focused on the expulsion and retention of feces and the sadistic instinct is linked to the desire to both possess and destroy the OBJECT. Also called **anal phase**.

analysand *n.* in psychoanalysis, a patient who is undergoing treatment.

analysis *n.* **1.** the division of any entity into its component parts, typically for the purpose of investigation or study. **2.** see PSYCHOANALYSIS. —**analytic** or **analytical** *adj.*

analysis by synthesis any theory of information processing stating that both bottom-up processes and top-down processes interact in the recognition and interpretation of sensory input. According to such theories, which are associated particularly with speech perception and language processing, the person analyzes the physical attributes and constituent elements of a stimulus and then, guided by contextual information and knowledge acquired from previous experience or learning, extracts the significant information from this preliminary analysis of the stimulus and synthesizes it into an internal representation or interpretation of what the stimulus might be. This internal representation is compared to the stimulus input: If the two match, then the stimulus is recognized; if not, alternative representations are assembled for comparison until a match is found.

analysis of covariance (ANCOVA) a statistical method of studying the responses of different participant groups to a DEPENDENT VARIABLE that adjusts for the influence of a variable that is not being investigated but nonetheless is related to the dependent variable (see COVARIATE) and thus may influence the study results. For example, suppose a researcher analyzes whether there is a difference in learning among three types of instruction—in-class lecture, online lecture, and textbook only. He or she divides a random selection of adult students into three groups, implements the different instruction types, and administers the same test to all participants to determine how much they learned. If the researcher knows each participant's educational background, he or she could use an analysis of covariance to adjust the treatment effect (test score) according to educational level, which would reduce the observed variation between the three groups caused by variation in education levels rather than by the instruction itself.

analysis of variance (ANOVA) a statistical method of studying the variation across two or more groups of research participants in their responses on a DEPENDENT VARIABLE. ANOVAs test for significant differences among the mean response values of the groups and can be used to isolate both the joint INTERACTION EFFECTS and the separate MAIN EFFECTS of each INDEPENDENT VARIABLE on the dependent variable.

analyst *n.* generally, one who practices psychoanalysis. This is usually a PSYCHOANALYST in the tradition of Austrian neurologist Sigmund Freud (1856–1939), but the term is also applied to therapists adhering to the methods of various other theorists.

analytical intelligence in the TRIARCHIC THEORY OF INTELLIGENCE, the skills measured by conventional tests of intelligence, such as analysis, comparison, evaluation, critique, and judgment. Compare CREATIVE INTELLIGENCE; PRACTICAL INTELLIGENCE.

analytic psychology the system of psychoanalysis proposed by Swiss psychiatrist Carl Jung (1875–1961), in which the psyche is interpreted primarily in terms of philosophical values, primordial images and symbols, and a drive for self-fulfillment. Jung's basic concepts are (a) the EGO, which maintains a balance between conscious and

unconscious activities and gradually develops a unique self through INDIVIDUATION; (b) the PERSONAL UNCONSCIOUS, made up of memories, thoughts, and feelings based on personal experience; (c) the COLLECTIVE UNCONSCIOUS, made up of ancestral images, or ARCHETYPES, that constitute the inherited foundation of an individual's intellectual life and personality; and (d) dynamic polarities, or tension systems, which derive their psychic energy from the LIBIDO and influence the development and expression of the ego.

anchor *n.* a reference used when making a series of subjective judgments. For example, in an experiment in which participants gauge distances between objects, the experimenter introduces an anchor by informing the participants that the distance between two of the stimulus objects is a given value. That value then functions as a reference point for participants in their subsequent judgments.

anchoring bias the tendency, in forming perceptions or making quantitative judgments under conditions of uncertainty, to give excessive weight to the starting value (or ANCHOR) based on the first received information or one's initial judgment, and not to modify this anchor sufficiently in light of later information. For example, estimates of the product of $9 \times 8 \times 7 \times 6 \times 5 \times 4 \times 3 \times 2 \times 1$ tend to be higher than estimates of the product of $1 \times 2 \times 3 \times 4 \times 5 \times 6 \times 7 \times 8 \times 9$. Also called **anchoring effect**.

androgen *n.* any of a class of steroid hormones that act as the principal male SEX HORMONES, the major one being TESTOSTERONE. Androgens are produced mainly by the testes and influence the development of masculine SEX CHARACTERISTICS. They are also secreted in small quantities by the ADRENAL GLAND and can be produced synthetically. —**androgenic** *adj.*

androgen-insensitivity syndrome (AIS) an inherited condition affecting genital development and caused by varying degrees of insensitivity to androgens. There are three forms: complete, in which the insensitivity is total, resulting in external genitalia that are female; partial, in which some sensitivity to the hormones results in external genitalia that fall anywhere within the range of male to female; and mild, in which the external sex characteristics are male but there may be some breast growth at puberty. In all three forms, the internal organs are male (i.e., testes). Also called **testicular feminization syndrome**.

androgyny *n.* **1.** the presence of male and female characteristics in one individual. **2.** the state of being neither distinguishably masculine nor feminine in appearance, as in dress. —**androgyne** *n.* —**androgynous** *adj.*

anecdotal method an investigational technique in which informal verbal reports of incidents casually observed are accepted as useful information. The anecdotal method is scientifically inadequate but can offer clues as to areas of investigation that warrant more systematic, controlled research.

anencephaly *n.* congenital absence of the cranial vault (the bones forming the rear of the skull), with cerebral hemispheres completely missing or reduced to small masses. Infants born with anencephaly are usually blind, deaf, unconscious, and unable to feel pain. —**anencephalic** *adj.*

anesthesia *n.* the loss of sensitivity to stimuli, either in a particular area (local) or throughout the body and accompanied by loss of consciousness (general). It may be produced intentionally, for example, via the administration of drugs (called **anesthetics**) or the use of techniques such as ACUPUNCTURE or hypnotic suggestion, or it may occur spontaneously as a result of injury or disease. —**anesthetic** *adj.*

aneurysm (aneurism) *n.* an enlarge-

ment (swelling) at some point in an artery caused by the pressure of blood on weakened tissues, often at junctions where arteries split off from one another. —**aneurysmal** *adj.*

anger *n.* an emotion characterized by tension and hostility arising from frustration, real or imagined injury by another, or perceived injustice. It can manifest itself in behaviors designed to remove the object of the anger (e.g., determined action) or behaviors designed to express the emotion (e.g., swearing). Anger is distinct from, but a significant activator of, AGGRESSION, which is behavior intended to harm someone or something. Despite their mutually influential relationship, anger is neither necessary nor sufficient for aggression to occur.

angioma *n.* a tumor of the vascular system: an abnormal mass of blood vessels or lymph vessels.

angiotensin *n.* one of a family of peptides, including angiotensins I, II, and III, that are produced by the enzymatic action of renin on a precursor protein (**angiotensinogen**) in the bloodstream. Their effects include narrowing of blood vessels (VASOCONSTRICTION), increased blood pressure, thirst, and stimulation of ALDOSTERONE release from the adrenal gland.

angst *n.* **1.** fear or anxiety (German). **2.** in EXISTENTIALISM, a state of anguish or despair in which a person recognizes the fundamental uncertainty of existence and understands the significance of conscious choice and personal responsibility.

angular gyrus a ridge along the lower surface of the PARIETAL LOBE of the brain, formed by a junction of the superior and middle temporal gyri. This region has been proposed as the key area of reading and writing function. Lesions are associated with ALEXIA and AGRAPHIA, and structural abnormalities with DYSLEXIA.

anhedonia *n.* the inability to enjoy

experiences or activities that normally would be pleasurable. It is one of the defining symptoms of a MAJOR DEPRESSIVE EPISODE but is also seen in other disorders, including schizophrenia. **—anhedonic** *adj.*

animal model an animal whose characteristics are similar to those of humans, thus making it suitable for studying human behavior, processes, disorders or diseases, and so forth.

animism *n.* the belief that natural phenomena or inanimate objects are alive or possess lifelike characteristics, such as intentions, desires, and feelings. Animism was considered by Swiss child psychologist and epistemologist Jean Piaget (1896–1980) to be characteristic of the thought of children in the PREOPERATIONAL STAGE, later fading out and being replaced by the strong belief in the universal nature of physical causality. **—animistic** *adj.*

anomaly *n.* anything that is irregular or deviates from the norm, often referring to a congenital or developmental defect. **—anomalous** *adj.*

anomia *n.* loss or impairment of the ability to name objects. All individuals with APHASIA exhibit anomia, and the extent of naming difficulty is a good general measure of aphasia severity. **—anomic** *adj.*

anomie *n.* a sense of alienation and hopelessness in a society or group that is often a response to social upheaval. It also may be accompanied by changes in personal and social values. **—anomic** *adj.*

anorexia *n.* absence or loss of appetite for food or, less commonly, for other desires (e.g., sex), especially when chronic. It may be primarily a psychological disorder, as in ANOREXIA NERVOSA, or it may have physiological causes, such as hypopituitarism. **—anorectic** or **anorexic** *adj., n.*

anorexia nervosa an eating disorder, occurring most frequently in adolescent girls, that involves persistent refusal of food, excessive fear of weight gain, refusal to maintain minimally normal body weight, disturbed perception of body image, and amenorrhea (absence of at least three menstrual periods).

anosmia *n.* absence or loss of the ability to smell. General or total anosmia implies inability to smell all odorants on both sides of the nose, whereas partial anosmia implies an inability to smell certain odorants. **—anosmic** *adj.*

anosognosia *n.* a neurologically based failure to recognize the existence of a deficit or disorder, such as hearing loss, poor vision, or paralysis.

anoxia *n.* a decrease in the level of oxygen in the body tissues, including the brain. Consequences depend on the severity of the anoxia and the specific areas of the brain that are affected but can include generalized cognitive deficits or more focal deficits in memory, perception, or EXECUTIVE FUNCTIONS. Anoxia sometimes is used as a synonym of HYPOXIA. **—anoxic** *adj.*

Antabuse *n.* a trade name for DISULFIRAM.

antagonist *n.* **1.** a drug or other chemical agent that inhibits the action of another substance. For example, an antagonist may combine with the substance to alter and thus inactivate it (**chemical antagonism**); an antagonist may reduce the effects of the substance by binding to the same receptor without stimulating it, which decreases the number of available receptors (**pharmacological antagonism**); or an antagonist may bind to a different receptor and produce a physiological effect opposite to that of the substance (**physiological antagonism**). **2.** a contracting muscle whose action generates force opposing the intended direction of movement. This force may serve to slow the movement rapidly as it approaches the target or it may help to define the movement end point. Compare AGONIST. **—antagonism** *n.* **—antagonistic** *adj.*

antecedent *n.* an event or stimulus that precedes some other event or stimulus and often elicits, signals, or sets the occasion for a particular behavior or response. See also CONTINGENCY.

anterior *adj.* in front of or toward the front. In reference to two-legged upright animals, this term is sometimes used interchangeably with VENTRAL to mean toward the front surface of the body. Compare POSTERIOR. —**anteriorly** *adv.*

anterior cingulate cortex (ACC) the front, more curved part of the CINGULATE CORTEX, a structure in the forebrain that forms a collar around the CORPUS CALLOSUM. It is divided into two distinct areas believed to have essential roles in numerous activities. The **dorsal anterior cingulate cortex**, often considered the "cognition" division, is implicated in a range of EXECUTIVE FUNCTIONS. The **ventral anterior cingulate cortex**, often considered the "emotion" division, is thought to be involved in mediating anxiety, fear, aggression, anger, empathy, and sadness; in perceiving physical and psychological pain; and in regulating autonomic functions (e.g., blood pressure). The precise mechanisms by which these processes occur in the ACC remain unknown, but researchers theorize that a reciprocal relationship between the dorsal and ventral areas helps maintain a balance between cognitive and emotional processing so as to enable SELF-REGULATION. See also POSTERIOR CINGULATE CORTEX.

anterior commissure see COMMISSURE.

anterograde amnesia see AMNESIA.

anterograde memory the ability to retain events, experiences, and other information following a particular point in time. When this ability is impaired (i.e., by injury or disease), it becomes very difficult or even impossi-

ble to recall what happened from that moment forward, a condition known as anterograde AMNESIA. For example, an individual with deficits of anterograde memory resulting from a stroke might not remember the name of a new person introduced to him or her but would remember the name of a close childhood friend. Compare RETROGRADE MEMORY.

anthropocentrism *n.* the explicit or implicit assumption that human experience is the central reality and, by extension, the idea that all phenomena can be evaluated in terms of their relationship to humans. —**anthropocentric** *adj.*

anthropological linguistics the branch of linguistics that draws connections between the characteristics of a particular language and the cultural practices, social structures, and worldview of the society in which it is spoken (see LINGUISTIC DETERMINISM; LINGUISTIC RELATIVITY).

anthropology *n.* the study of human beings. This typically involves the description and explanation of similarities and differences among human groups in their languages, aesthetic expressions, belief systems, and social structures over the range of human geography and chronology. —**anthropological** *adj.* —**anthropologist** *n.*

anthropometry *n.* **1.** the scientific study of how the size and proportions of the human body are affected by such variables as age, sex, and ethnicity. **2.** the taking of measurements of the human body for purposes of comparison and study. —**anthropometric** *adj.* —**anthropometrist** *n.*

anthropomorphism *n.* **1.** the attribution of human characteristics to nonhuman entities such as deities, spirits, animals, plants, or inanimate objects. **2.** in COMPARATIVE PSYCHOLOGY, the tendency to interpret the behavior and mental processes of nonhuman animals in terms of human abilities. Compare ZOOMORPHISM. —**an-thropomorphic** *adj.*

antianxiety medication see ANXIOLYTIC.

antibody *n.* a modified protein molecule, produced by B LYMPHOCYTES, that interacts with an ANTIGEN and renders it harmless. Each type of antibody is designed to interact with a specific antigen and can be mass-produced by the body following exposure to that antigen. See IMMUNE SYSTEM.

anticholinesterase *n.* see CHOLINESTERASE.

anticonvulsant *n.* any drug used to reduce the frequency or severity of epileptic seizures or to terminate a seizure already underway. Until the advent of the hydantoins in the 1930s, which were developed specifically to control epileptic seizures, anticonvulsants consisted mainly of bromides (largely supplanted due to their toxicity and frequency of adverse side effects) and BARBITURATES. Also effective as antiseizure medications are the BENZODIAZEPINES. Also called **antiepileptic**.

antidepressant *n.* any drug administered in the treatment of depression. Most antidepressants work by increasing the availability of monoamine neurotransmitters such as norepinephrine, serotonin, or dopamine, although they do so by different routes. The MONOAMINE OXIDASE INHIBITORS (MAOIs) work by inhibiting monoamine oxidase, one of the principal enzymes that metabolize these neurotransmitters. Most of the other antidepressants, including the TRICYCLIC ANTIDEPRESSANTS (TCAs) and the selective serotonin reuptake inhibitors (see SSRI), inhibit the reuptake of serotonin or norepinephrine (and to a much lesser degree dopamine) into the presynaptic neuron. Either process leaves more of the neurotransmitter free to bind with postsynaptic receptors, initiating a series of events in the postsynaptic neuron that is thought to produce the actual therapeutic effect.

antidiuretic hormone (**ADH**) see VASOPRESSIN.

antigen *n.* any substance that is treated by the immune system as foreign and is therefore capable of inducing an immune response, particularly the production of ANTIBODIES that render it harmless. The antigen may be a virus, a bacterium, a toxin (e.g., bee venom), or tissue (e.g., blood) of another individual with different genetic characteristics. —**antigenic** *adj.*

antimanic drug see MOOD STABILIZER.

antioxidant *n.* a substance, such as beta-carotene, lutein, lycopene, selenium, and vitamins A, C, and E, that may protect cells against the effects of FREE RADICALS.

antipsychotic *n.* any pharmacological agent used to control the symptoms of schizophrenia and other disorders characterized by impaired reality testing, as evidenced by severely disorganized thought, speech, and behavior. Formerly called **major tranquilizers** and later **neuroleptics**, antipsychotics are commonly divided into two major classes: **conventional (first-generation) antipsychotics** and the newer **atypical (second-generation) antipsychotics**. The latter class has fewer adverse side effects than the former, particularly the neurologically based EXTRAPYRAMIDAL SYMPTOMS. However, the newer drugs have been associated with some serious metabolic and other issues, such as obesity, diabetes, and AGRANULOCYTOSIS.

antisocial *adj.* denoting or exhibiting behavior that sharply deviates from social norms and violates other people's rights. Arson and vandalism are examples of antisocial behavior. Compare PROSOCIAL.

antisocial personality disorder the presence of a chronic and pervasive disposition to disregard and violate the rights of others. Manifestations include repeated violations of the law, exploitation of others, deceitfulness, impulsivity, aggressiveness, reckless disregard for the safety of self and others, and irresponsibility, accompanied by lack of guilt, remorse, and empathy. The disorder has been known by various names, notably **psychopathic personality** and **sociopathic personality**. It is among the most heavily researched of the personality disorders and the most difficult to treat.

antithesis *n.* **1.** a THESIS, idea, or proposition that is opposite to or contradicts another. **2.** in philosophy, the second stage of a dialectical process based on proposition, contradiction, and the reconciliation of these (thesis, antithesis, and SYNTHESIS). —**antithetical** *adj.*

anxiety *n.* an emotion characterized by apprehension and somatic symptoms of tension in which an individual anticipates impending danger, catastrophe, or misfortune. The body often mobilizes itself to meet the perceived threat: Muscles become tense, breathing quickens, and heart beat accelerates. Anxiety may be distinguished from FEAR both conceptually and physiologically, although the two terms are often used interchangeably. Anxiety is considered a future-oriented, long-term response broadly focused on a diffuse threat, whereas fear is an appropriate, present-oriented, and short-lived response to a clearly identifiable and specific threat. —**anxious** *adj.*

anxiety disorder any of a group of disorders that have as their central organizing theme the emotional state of fear, worry, or excessive apprehension. They have a chronic course, albeit waxing and waning in intensity, and are among the most common mental health problems in the United States. The group includes PANIC DISORDER, various phobias (e.g., SPECIFIC PHOBIA, SOCIAL PHOBIA), and GENERALIZED ANXIETY DISORDER. OBSESSIVE-COMPULSIVE DISORDER and POSTTRAUMATIC STRESS DISORDER were traditionally considered

anxiety disorders but are now increasingly identified as separate, if still related, entities.

anxiety sensitivity fear of sensations associated with anxiety because of the belief that they will have harmful consequences. For example, an individual with high anxiety sensitivity is likely to regard feeling light-headed as a sign of impending illness or fainting, whereas an individual with low anxiety sensitivity would tend to regard this sensation as simply unpleasant. Research indicates that anxiety sensitivity is a traitlike risk factor linked to the development of PANIC ATTACKS and PANIC DISORDER.

anxiolytic *n.* a drug used in the treatment of anxiety, mild behavioral agitation, and insomnia. Formerly called **minor tranquilizers**, anxiolytics can also be used as adjunctive agents in the treatment of depression, panic disorder, and several other disorders. The most widely used are the BENZODIAZEPINES. Other drugs, such as certain SSRIs, have also been shown to have anxiolytic effects.

APA style guidelines and standards for writing (e.g., grammar) and formatting (e.g., data displays, headings) for students, instructors, researchers, and clinicians in the social and behavioral sciences, as collected in the PUBLICATION MANUAL OF THE AMERICAN PSYCHOLOGICAL ASSOCIATION.

apathy *n.* lack of motivation or goal-directed behavior and indifference to one's surroundings. Apathy is commonly associated with severe depression or schizophrenia, but it also is a major behavioral symptom in Alzheimer's disease, Parkinson's disease, and other neurodegenerative disorders. —**apathetic** *adj.*

Apgar score an evaluation of newborn infants on five factors: skin color, heart rate, respiratory effort, reflexes, and muscle tone. The evaluation is typically performed at 1 minute and again at 5 minutes after birth to assess the physical condition of the infant and to determine quickly if he or she needs immediate medical care. Each factor is scored 0, 1, or 2, with a maximum total of 10 points. A score below 3 indicates that the infant is in severe distress; a score of 4 to 7 indicates moderate distress; and a score of 7 to 10 indicates that the infant's condition is normal. [developed in 1952 by Virginia **Apgar** (1909–1974), U.S. anesthesiologist]

aphagia *n.* inability to swallow or eat. —**aphagic** *adj.*

aphasia *n.* an acquired language impairment that results from brain damage, typically from stroke, brain tumors, and cortical degenerative disorders (e.g., Alzheimer's disease). Traditionally, a distinction has been made between expressive and receptive forms of aphasia, whereby individuals with the former primarily have difficulty producing spoken and written language and those with the latter primarily have difficulty comprehending spoken and written language. A more contemporary distinction, however, is commonly made between **fluent aphasias**, characterized by plentiful verbal output consisting of well-articulated, easily produced, but inappropriate or meaningless utterances of relatively normal length and prosody (rhythm and intonation), and **nonfluent aphasias**, characterized by sparse, effortful utterances of short phrase length and disrupted prosody. Numerous types of aphasia exist, for example, BROCA'S APHASIA and WERNICKE'S APHASIA. —**aphasic** *adj.*

apnea *n.* temporary suspension of respiration. If the **apneic period** is long, the heart may slow and electroencephalogram changes may occur. Apnea can occur during sleep (see SLEEP APNEA) and is also found in many disorders, such as epilepsy and concussion. —**apneic** *adj.*

apoptosis *n.* see PROGRAMMED CELL DEATH. —**apoptotic** *adj.*

a posteriori denoting conclusions derived from observations or other manifest occurrences: reasoning from facts. Compare A PRIORI. [Latin, "from the latter"]

a posteriori comparison see POST HOC COMPARISON.

apparatus *n.* **1.** any instrument or equipment used in an experiment or other research. **2.** in biology, a group of structures—either microscopic or macroscopic—that perform a particular function.

apparent movement an illusion of motion or change in size of a visual stimulus. Several types have been identified and labeled with Greek letters, among them the familiar **beta movement**, in which successive presentations of stationary stimuli across the visual field produce the perception of a single, smoothly moving stimulus, and **gamma movement**, the seeming expansion of an object when it is suddenly presented and contraction when withdrawn. Also called **apparent motion**.

appearance–reality distinction the knowledge that the appearance of an object does not necessarily correspond to its reality. For example, a sponge shaped like a rock may look like a rock but it is really a sponge. Children younger than 3 may have difficulty making appearance–reality distinctions.

apperception *n.* **1.** the mental process by which a perception or an idea is assimilated into an individual's existing knowledge (his or her **apperceptive mass**). **2.** the act or process of perceiving something consciously. —**apperceive** *vb.* —**apperceptive** *adj.*

applied psychology the use of the theories, principles, and techniques of psychology to address practical concerns in such areas as problems of living or coping, education, vocational guidance, industry, ergonomics, consumer affairs, advertising, political

A

campaigns, and environmental issues. It may be contrasted with theoretical psychology or academic psychology, in which the emphasis is on understanding for its own sake rather than on the utility of the knowledge.

applied research studies conducted to solve real-world problems, as opposed to studies that are carried out to develop a theory or to extend basic knowledge. An example is ACTION RESEARCH. Compare BASIC RESEARCH.

applied science the use of scientific principles and theories to serve a practical human purpose rather than to extend knowledge for its own sake. Compare BASIC SCIENCE.

applied statistics the use of statistical methods and procedures to understand data in psychology, sociology, economics, and other disciplines. Compare THEORETICAL STATISTICS.

applied tension a technique in BEHAVIOR THERAPY that focuses on changing physiological responses (e.g., low blood pressure leading to fainting) by having the client practice muscle tensing and releasing during exposure to increasingly anxiety-evoking stimuli associated with a feared situation. The technique was developed and is still primarily used for blood, injury, and injection phobias.

appraisal *n.* the cognitive evaluation of the nature and significance of a phenomenon or event. In appraisal theories of emotion, such evaluations are seen as determinants of emotional experience. See COGNITIVE APPRAISAL THEORY. —**appraise** *vb.*

appraisal motive see SELF-ASSESSMENT MOTIVE.

apprehension *n.* **1.** uneasiness or dread about an upcoming event or the future generally. Also called **apprehensiveness.** **2.** the act or capability of grasping something mentally. Compare COMPREHENSION. —**apprehend** *vb.* —**apprehensible** *adj.* —**apprehensive** *adj.*

apprenticeship *n.* a means by which a novice gains practical experience in a trade or profession, often through a formal program of instruction and supervision from an experienced practitioner. See also MENTORING.

approach–approach conflict a situation involving a choice between two equally desirable but incompatible alternatives. See also APPROACH–AVOIDANCE CONFLICT; AVOIDANCE–AVOIDANCE CONFLICT.

approach–avoidance conflict a situation involving a single goal or option that has both desirable and undesirable aspects or consequences. The closer an individual comes to the goal, the greater the anxiety, but withdrawal from the goal then increases the desire. See also APPROACH–APPROACH CONFLICT; AVOIDANCE–AVOIDANCE CONFLICT.

apraxia *n.* loss or impairment of the ability to perform purposeful, skilled movements despite intact motor function and comprehension. The condition may be developmental or induced by neurological dysfunction and is believed to represent an impairment of the ability to plan, select, and sequence the motor execution of movements. There are several major types of apraxia, such as ideational apraxia, involving difficulty carrying out in the proper order a series of acts that comprise a complex task; ideomotor apraxia, involving difficulty imitating actions or gesturing to command; and speech (or verbal) apraxia, involving difficulty coordinating the movements necessary for speaking. —**apraxic** *adj.*

a priori denoting conclusions derived from premises or principles: deducing from prior assumptions. Compare A POSTERIORI. [Latin, "prior to"]

a priori comparison any examination in which two or more quantities are compared in accordance with plans established prior to conducting the research study. For example, even before data are collected, a researcher might hypothesize that two groups given personal instruction would show better mean performance on a task compared to those who receive only written instruction. Thus, he or she could decide in advance to compare the combined personal instruction groups to the written instruction group. Also called **planned comparison** (or **contrast**). Compare POST HOC COMPARISON.

aptitude *n.* the capacity to acquire competence or skill through training. Specific aptitude is potential in a particular area (e.g., artistic or mathematical aptitude); general aptitude is potential in several fields. Both are distinct from ABILITY, which is an existing competence.

aptitude test any assessment instrument designed to measure potential for acquiring knowledge or skill. Aptitude tests are thought of as providing a basis for making predictions for an individual's future success, particularly in an educational or occupational situation. In contrast, ACHIEVEMENT TESTS are considered to reflect the amount of learning already obtained.

aqueous humor see EYE.

arachnoid mater see MENINGES.

arachnophobia *n.* a persistent and irrational fear of spiders.

archetype *n.* in ANALYTIC PSYCHOLOGY, a structural component of the mind that derives from the accumulated experience of humankind. These inherited components are held in the COLLECTIVE UNCONSCIOUS and serve as a frame of reference with which individuals view the world and as one of the foundations on which the structure of personality is built. —**archetypal** *adj.*

archicortex *n.* see ALLOCORTEX.

archipallium *n.* see ALLOCORTEX.

archival research the use of books, journals, historical documents, and other existing records or stored data in scientific research. Archival research

allows for unobtrusive observation of human activity in natural settings and permits the study of phenomena that otherwise cannot easily be investigated. A persistent drawback, however, is that causal inferences are always more tentative than those provided by laboratory experiments.

arcuate fasciculus a bundle of nerve fibers linking the parts of the brain involved in the interpretation and control of speech (WERNICKE'S AREA and BROCA'S AREA, respectively).

arcuate nucleus 1. an arc-shaped collection of neurons in the hypothalamus that produce hormones. **2.** any of various small groups of gray matter on the bulge of the medulla oblongata. They are extensions of neurons in the basal PONS and project to the cerebellum.

argument *n.* a parameter on which the value of a mathematical FUNCTION depends.

arithmetic mean see MEAN.

arousal *n.* **1.** a state of physiological activation or cortical responsiveness, associated with sensory stimulation and activation of fibers from the RETICULAR ACTIVATING SYSTEM. **2.** a state of excitement or energy expenditure linked to an emotion. Usually, arousal is closely related to a person's appraisal of the significance of an event or to the physical intensity of a stimulus. —**arouse** *vb.*

arousal theory the theory that the physical environment can affect arousal levels by stimulation and by stress created when psychological or physical needs are not met. Arousal increases when personal space is diminished (see CROWDING) or when people are subjected to noise, traffic congestion, or other adverse conditions.

array *n.* any ordered arrangement of data, particularly a two-dimensional grouping of data into rows and columns. The following listing of students' scores on a test is an example of a simple array:

Student A	55
Student B	76
Student C	81
Student D	82
Student E	89
Student F	90
Student G	90
Student H	90
Student I	94
Student J	98

The concept may be extended to more than two dimensions.

arrhythmia *n.* any variation from the normal rhythm of the heartbeat. Kinds of arrhythmia include **tachycardia**, any rate above 100 beats per minute, and **bradycardia**, any rate of less than 60 beats per minute. —**arrhythmic** *adj.*

arteriosclerosis *n.* a group of diseases characterized by hardening and loss of elasticity of the walls of the arteries. A common type is ATHEROSCLEROSIS. —**arteriosclerotic** *adj.*

arthritis *n.* inflammation of joints, causing pain, swelling, and stiffness. The most severe and disabling form is rheumatoid arthritis, associated with the body attacking its own cells as foreign (see AUTOIMMUNITY). —**arthritic** *adj.*

articulation *n.* **1.** the shaping and production of the sounds required for intelligible speech. It is a complex process involving not only accurate movements of the vocal tract but also neural integration of timing, movement direction, force expenditure, and response speed. **2.** a joint between bones, which may be fixed or movable. —**articulate** *vb.*

articulatory control process see PHONOLOGICAL LOOP.

articulatory loop see PHONOLOGICAL LOOP.

articulatory rehearsal system see PHONOLOGICAL LOOP.

articulatory store 1. a component of short-term memory that retains auditory information based on the motor systems involved in pronouncing items, rather than on how they sound. Compare ACOUSTIC STORE. **2.** see PHONOLOGICAL LOOP.

artifact *n.* an experimental finding that is not a reflection of the true state of the phenomenon of interest but rather is the consequence of a flawed design or analytic error. For example, characteristics of the researcher (e.g., expectations, personality) or the participant (e.g., awareness of the researcher's intent, EVALUATION APPREHENSION) are common sources of artifacts. See also DEMAND CHARACTERISTICS.

artificial insemination (**AI**) the use of medical techniques to achieve conception by introducing sperm through the cervical opening and directly into the uterus. Artificial insemination may need to be done more than once for pregnancy to occur; to maximize success, it is usually scheduled to coincide with the days of ovulation.

artificial intelligence (**AI**) a sub-discipline of computer science that aims to produce programs that simulate human intelligence. There are many branches of AI, including robotics, computer vision, machine learning, game playing, and expert systems. AI has also supported research in other related areas, including COGNITIVE SCIENCE.

artificial selection human intervention in animal or plant reproduction to improve the value or utility of succeeding generations. Compare NATURAL SELECTION.

art therapy the use of artistic activities, such as painting and clay modeling, in psychotherapy and rehabilitation. The process of making art is seen as a means of symbolic communication and a vehicle for developing new insights and understandings, resolving conflicts, solving problems, and formulating new perceptions to achieve positive change and growth.

asceticism *n.* a character trait or life-style characterized by simplicity, renunciation of physical pleasures and worldly goods, social withdrawal, and extreme self-discipline. **—ascetic** *adj.*

Asch situation an experimental paradigm used to study conformity to group opinion. Participants make judgments as part of a group of confederates who make errors deliberately on certain trials. The extent to which participants publicly agree with the erroneous group judgment or resist the pressure to do so and remain independent provides a measure of conformity. [Solomon **Asch** (1907–1996), Polish-born U.S. psychologist]

Asperger's disorder a disorder associated with varying degrees of deficits in social and conversational skills, difficulties with transitions from one task to another or with changes in situations or environments, and preference for sameness and predictability. Obsessive routines and preoccupation with particular subjects of interest may be present, as may difficulty reading body language and maintaining proper social distance. Some people with Asperger's disorder have reported oversensitivity to sounds, tastes, smells, and sights, but the nature of such sensitivities is not well researched. In contrast to AUTISM, language skills develop, and there is no clinically significant delay in cognitive or adaptive functioning other than in social interactions. Also called **Asperger's syndrome**. [described in 1944 by Hans **Asperger** (1906–1980), Austrian psychiatrist]

assertiveness training a method of teaching individuals to change verbal and nonverbal signals and behavioral patterns and to enhance interpersonal communication generally through techniques designed to help them express emotions, opinions, and preferences—positive and negative—

clearly, directly, and in an appropriate manner. ROLE PLAY or behavior rehearsal is often used to prepare clients to be appropriately assertive in real-life situations.

assessment *n.* see PSYCHOLOGICAL ASSESSMENT.

assimilation *n.* **1.** the process of absorbing, incorporating, or making similar. For example, social assimilation is the process by which an immigrant to a new culture adopts the culture's beliefs and practices. **2.** see PIAGETIAN THEORY. **—assimilate** *vb.*

assisted death an action taken by one person to end the life of another, at the request of the latter. This action can take the form of either ASSISTED SUICIDE or ACTIVE EUTHANASIA. It is sometimes called **physician-assisted suicide**, which assumes a firm determination of the cause of death.

assisted living a form of congregate housing for older adults requiring long-term care services that include meals, personal care, and scheduled nursing care. Typically comprising private rooms or apartments, it encourages a degree of autonomy and independence in residents that is not provided for in nursing homes.

assisted reproductive technology (**ART**) any treatment for INFERTILITY in which both eggs and sperm are handled. In general, ART procedures involve surgically removing eggs from a woman's ovaries, combining them with sperm in a laboratory, and returning them to the woman's body or donating them to another woman. They do not include treatments in which only sperm are handled, as in ARTIFICIAL INSEMINATION, or procedures in which a woman takes drugs only to stimulate her egg production without the intention of having her eggs retrieved.

assisted suicide suicide in which the person ending his or her own life is provided the means to do so (e.g., a prescription) by another. See ASSISTED DEATH.

association *n.* **1.** a connection or relationship between items, particularly ideas, events, and feelings. Associations are established by experience and are fundamental to LEARNING THEORY and BEHAVIORISM. **2.** the degree of statistical dependence or relationship between two or more phenomena. —**associative** *adj.* —**associational** *adj.*

association analysis see CORRELATION ANALYSIS.

association cortex any of various areas of the CEREBRAL CORTEX that are not involved principally in sensory or motor representations but may be involved in integrative functions. Also called **association area**.

associative learning the process of acquiring new and enduring information via the formation of connections between elements. In different types of **associationistic learning theories**, these associated elements may be stimuli and responses, mental representations of events, or elements in neural networks.

assortative mating behavior in which mates are chosen on the basis of a particular trait or group of traits (e.g., attractiveness, similarity of body size). Also called **assortive mating**. Compare RANDOM MATING.

assumed similarity bias the tendency for perceivers to assume that other people possess the same qualities and characteristics that they have. This bias is thought to inflate the accuracy that perceivers attribute to their judgments about others.

assumption *n.* **1.** the premise or supposition that something is factual or true; that is, the act of taking something for granted. **2.** one or more conditions that need to be met for a statistical procedure to be fully justified from a theoretical perspective. For example, the ANALYSIS OF VARIANCE assumes HOMOGENEITY OF VARIANCE

and independence of observations, among other criteria. If the assumptions were to be violated to an extreme extent, the results would be invalid. See also ROBUSTNESS.

asthma *n.* a chronic disorder in which intermittent inflammation and narrowing of the bronchial passages produces wheezing, gasping, coughing, and chest tightness. Although the precipitating cause is usually an allergen, such as dust or pollen, environmental irritants, respiratory infection, anxiety, stress, and other agents may produce or aggravate symptoms. —**asthmatic** *adj.*

astigmatism *n.* a visual disorder in which the light rays of a visual stimulus do not all focus at a single point on the retina due to uneven curvature of the cornea or lens. The effect is an aberration or distortion of the visual image that makes it difficult to see fine detail. —**astigmatic** *adj.*

astrocyte *n.* a star-shaped central nervous system cell (GLIA) with numerous extensions that run in all directions. They provide structural support for the brain, are responsible for many homeostatic controls, and may isolate receptive surfaces. Recent research suggests that they may play a role in potassium neurotransmission as well. Also called **astroglia**.

asylum *n.* **1.** originally, a refuge for criminals (from Greek *asylon*, "sanctuary"). From the 19th century, the terms *asylum* or *insane asylum* were applied to mental institutions. These names are now obsolete, discarded because of their emphasis on refuge rather than treatment. **2.** the right to remain in a country, granted by the government of that country to individuals escaping oppression, war, or political unrest in their country of origin or allegiance.

asymmetry *n.* SKEWNESS: the condition in which the values of a data set are not arranged equally around a center point. Compare SYMMETRY. —**asymmetrical** *adj.*

ataxia *n.* inability to perform coordinated voluntary movements. It may be seen as a symptom of various disorders, such as multiple sclerosis or cerebral palsy, or it can occur in isolation. It can be heritable or acquired from injury or infection affecting the nervous system. When due to damage to the CEREBELLUM, it is called CEREBELLAR ATAXIA, and when due to loss of sensory feedback from the muscles and joints, it is called SENSORY ATAXIA. **—ataxic** *adj.*

atherosclerosis *n.* a common form of ARTERIOSCLEROSIS resulting from accumulations of lipids such as cholesterol on the inner walls of arteries and their hardening into **atherosclerotic** (or **atheromatous**) **plaques. —atherosclerotic** *adj.*

atonia *n.* lack of normal muscle tone. **—atonic** *adj.*

ATP *a*denosine *t*riphosphate: a nucleotide in living cells that is the source of chemical energy for biological processes. A bond between two of its three component phosphate groups is easily split by a particular enzyme, **ATPase** (**adenosine triphosphatase**), yielding energy when a cell requires it.

at risk vulnerable to a disorder or disease. Risk status for an individual is defined by genetic, physical, and behavioral factors or conditions. For example, children of people with schizophrenia may be considered at risk for schizophrenia, and heavy cigarette smokers are at risk for emphysema and lung cancer.

atrophy *n.* a wasting away of the body or a body part, as from lack of nourishment, inactivity, degenerative disease, or normal aging. **—atrophic** *adj.*

attachment *n.* the emotional bond between a human infant or a young nonhuman animal and its parent figure or caregiver; it is developed as a step in establishing a feeling of security and demonstrated by calmness while in the parent's or caregiver's presence. Attachment also denotes the tendency to form such bonds with certain other individuals in infancy as well as the tendency in adulthood to seek emotionally supportive social relationships.

attachment style the characteristic way people relate to others in the context of intimate relationships, which is heavily influenced by SELF-WORTH and interpersonal TRUST. Theoretically, the degree of attachment security in adults is related directly to how well they bonded to others as children. Four distinct categories of adult attachment style are typically identified: DISMISSIVE ATTACHMENT, FEARFUL ATTACHMENT, PREOCCUPIED ATTACHMENT, and SECURE ATTACHMENT. The two categories of attachment styles with respect to infant–mother relationships are SECURE ATTACHMENT and INSECURE ATTACHMENT, the latter characterized by various patterns (e.g., ambivalent attachment; avoidant attachment).

attachment theory a theory that (a) postulates an evolutionarily advantageous need, especially in primates, to form close emotional bonds with significant others: specifically, a need for the young to maintain close proximity to and form bonds with their caregivers; and (b) characterizes the different types of relationships between human infants and caregivers. These relationships have been shown to affect the individual's later emotional development and emotional stability. See also STRANGE SITUATION.

attention *n.* a state in which cognitive resources are focused on certain aspects of the environment and the central nervous system is in a state of readiness to respond to stimuli. Because it has been presumed that human beings do not have an infinite capacity to attend to everything—focusing on certain items at the expense of others— much research has been devoted to discerning which factors influence attention and to understanding the neural mechanisms that are involved in the selective processing of information. For example, past experience affects current perception (we notice things that have meaning for us), and some activities (e.g., reading) require conscious participation (i.e., voluntary attention). However, attention can also be captured (i.e., directed involuntarily) by qualities of stimuli in the environment, such as intensity, movement, repetition, contrast, and novelty.

attention-deficit/hyperactivity disorder (**ADHD**) a behavioral syndrome characterized by the persistent presence of six or more symptoms involving (a) inattention (e.g., failure to complete tasks or listen carefully, difficulty in concentrating, distractibility) or (b) impulsivity or hyperactivity (e.g., restlessness, fidgeting, difficulty in taking turns or staying seated, excessive talking, running about). The symptoms, which impair social, academic, or occupational functioning, start to appear before the age of 7 and are observed in more than one setting. ADHD has been given a variety of names over the years, including the still commonly used **attention-deficit disorder** (**ADD**).

attention network theory a theory holding that attention is dependent on three separate but interacting neural networks: an alerting or vigilance network, an orientation and selection network, and an executive and conflict network.

attenuation *n.* **1.** a lessening or weakening in the intensity, value, or quality of a stimulus. **2.** an underestimation of the size of an effect or relationship because of improper measurement or RESTRICTION OF RANGE.

attenuation theory a version of the FILTER THEORY of attention proposing that unattended messages are attenuated (i.e., processed weakly) but not entirely blocked from further processing. According to the theory, items in unattended channels of information have different thresholds of recognition depending on their significance to the

individual. Thus, a significant word (e.g., the person's name) would have a low threshold and, when mentioned, would be recognized even if that person's attention is concentrated elsewhere (e.g., in conversation with someone else). See also COCKTAIL-PARTY EFFECT.

attitude *n.* a relatively enduring and general evaluation of an object, person, group, issue, or concept on a dimension ranging from negative to positive. Attitudes provide summary evaluations of target objects and are often assumed to be derived from specific beliefs, emotions, and past behaviors associated with those objects. —**attitudinal** *adj.*

attitude accessibility the likelihood that an attitude will be automatically activated from memory on encountering the attitude object. Accessibility is assumed to depend on the strength of the associative link in memory between the representation of the object and the evaluation of the object: The stronger the memory link between the object and its evaluation, the more quickly the attitude will come to mind.

attitude strength the extent to which an attitude persists over time, resists change, influences information processing, and guides behavior. Strong attitudes possess all four of these defining features, whereas weak attitudes lack them.

attraction *n.* **1.** the feeling of being drawn to one or more individuals and desiring their company, usually but not necessarily because of a liking for them. Also called **interpersonal attraction**. **2.** in environmental psychology, a quality affecting proximity between individuals. Environmental influences, such as noise, heat, and humidity, decrease attraction between pairs of individuals. See PROXEMICS. —**attractive** *adj.*

attribution *n.* an inference regarding the cause of a person's behavior or an interpersonal event. Three dimensions are often used to evaluate people's **attri-**

butional styles, or characteristic tendencies when inferring such causes: the internal–external dimension (whether they tend to attribute events to the self or to other factors), the stable–unstable dimension (whether they tend to attribute events to enduring or transient causes), and the global–specific dimension (whether they tend to attribute events to causes that affect many events or just a single event).

attribution theory a theoretical proposition about the processes by which people ascribe motives to their own and others' behavior, specifying that ascribed motives may be either internal and personal (a DISPOSITIONAL ATTRIBUTION) or external and circumstantial (a SITUATIONAL ATTRIBUTION).

attrition *n.* the loss of study participants over time. Attrition may occur for a variety of reasons (e.g., the nature of the data being collected, participant relocation, aversive or costly data collection procedures) and can threaten the EXTERNAL VALIDITY and INTERNAL VALIDITY of research. It also creates the potential for BIAS—individuals who drop out may have unique characteristics that are relevant to the phenomenon of interest such that the remaining sample is no longer representative of the population—and may reduce the POWER of statistical analyses.

attunement *n.* the matching of affect between infant and parent or caregiver to create emotional synchrony. The parent's response can take the form of mirroring (e.g., returning an infant's smile) or be cross-modal (e.g., a vocal response "uh oh" to the infant's dropping cereal on the floor). Attunement communicates to the infant that the parent can understand and share the infant's feelings. Compare MISATTUNEMENT.

atypical antipsychotic see ANTIPSYCHOTIC.

audience effect the influence on a person's behavior of the presence of bystanders. Performance is often im-

proved when the action is simple and well learned (see SOCIAL FACILITATION) but may be inhibited when it is complicated, novel, or difficult to perform or when the person believes the behavior might incur the audience's disapproval (see SOCIAL INHIBITION). The audience effect has also been observed in fish, birds, nonhuman primates, and other animals.

audit *n.* an evaluation of a service, intervention, or outcome. For example, in health administration it refers to an examination of the care proposed or rendered by a provider, whereas in research it refers to an examination of the soundness of a study's findings.

audition *n.* hearing: the perception of sound.

auditory agnosia loss or impairment of the ability to recognize and understand the nature of verbal or nonverbal sounds. Subtypes are distinguished on the basis of the type of auditory stimulus the person has difficulty recognizing, for example, environmental sounds such as a dog barking or keys jingling (**nonverbal auditory agnosia** or **environmental sounds agnosia**), spoken words (PURE WORD DEAFNESS), or music (sensory amusia).

auditory canal see EXTERNAL AUDITORY MEATUS.

auditory cortex the sensory area for hearing, located on the upper side of the TEMPORAL LOBE of the cerebral cortex. It receives and processes sound input from the MEDIAL GENICULATE NUCLEUS in the thalamus. Its main subdivision is the **primary auditory cortex (A1)**, the first cortical region to receive this input. Surrounding A1 is the **secondary auditory cortex (A2)**, which provides additional auditory regulation to enhance A1 cortical processing. Also called **auditory projection area**.

auditory hallucination the perception of sound in the absence of an auditory stimulus. Hallucinations may, for example, be of accusatory or laudatory voices or of strange noises and other nonverbal sounds. They occur frequently in schizophrenia and other psychotic disorders but may be associated with other conditions as well (e.g., delirium, dementia).

auditory localization the ability to identify the position and changes in position of sound sources based on acoustic information. Also called **sound localization**.

auditory masking a reduction in the ability to detect, discriminate, or recognize one sound (the signal or target) due to the presence of another sound (the masker), measured as an increase in the detection threshold caused by the masker. The ability of one sound to mask another has been used extensively to assess the FREQUENCY SELECTIVITY of the auditory system.

auditory nerve the portion of the VESTIBULOCOCHLEAR NERVE concerned with the sense of hearing. It originates in the cochlea, from which nerve fibers pass through several layers of nuclei in the brainstem to terminate predominantly in the AUDITORY CORTEX. Also called **acoustic nerve**.

auditory projection area see AUDITORY CORTEX.

auditory system the biological structures and processes responsible for hearing. The peripheral auditory system, or auditory periphery, includes the external, middle, and inner ears and the AUDITORY NERVE. Auditory structures of the brain, including the AUDITORY CORTEX, constitute the central auditory system.

aural *adj.* pertaining to or perceived by the ear.

authoritarian parenting see PARENTING.

authoritarian personality a personality pattern characterized by strict adherence to highly simplified conventional values, an attitude of great deference to authority figures while demanding subservience from those regarded as lower in status, and hostility toward people who deviate from conventional moral prescriptions.

authoritative parenting see PARENTING.

autism *n.* **1.** a neurodevelopmental disorder characterized by markedly impaired social interactions and verbal and nonverbal communication; narrow interests; and repetitive behavior. Manifestations and features of the disorder appear before age 3 but vary greatly across children according to developmental level, language skills, and chronological age. They may include a lack of awareness of the feelings of others, impaired ability to imitate, absence of social play, abnormal speech, and a preference for maintaining environmental sameness. Also called **autistic disorder**. **2.** in schizophrenia, an abnormal preoccupation with the self and fantasy such that there is a lack of interest in or ability to focus on external reality. —**autistic** *adj.*

autism spectrum disorder (ASD) a group of disorders with an onset typically occurring during the preschool years and characterized by varying but often marked difficulties in communication and social interaction. ASD was formerly said to include such distinct disorders as the prototype AUTISM, ASPERGER'S DISORDER, CHILDHOOD DISINTEGRATIVE DISORDER, and RETT SYNDROME; it was synonymous with PERVASIVE DEVELOPMENTAL DISORDER but more commonly used, given its reflection of symptom overlap among the disorders. It is now the official term used in current psychiatric nomenclature, encompassing and subsuming these disorders as one diagnostic entity. Also called **autistic spectrum disorder**.

autobiographical memory vivid personal memories recalling experienced events or factual knowledge about oneself.

autohypnosis *n.* see SELF-HYPNOSIS. —**autohypnotic** *adj.*

autoimmunity *n.* a condition in which the body's immune system fails to recognize its own tissues as "self" and attempts to reject its own cells. It is a primary factor in the development of such diseases as rheumatoid arthritis and systemic lupus erythematosus (called **autoimmune disorders**). —**autoimmune** *adj.*

autokinesis *n.* any movement that is voluntary.

automaticity *n.* the quality of a behavior or mental process that can be carried out rapidly and without effort or explicit intention (an **automatic process**).

automatic thoughts instantaneous, habitual, and nonconscious thoughts that affect a person's mood and actions. Helping individuals to become aware of the presence and impact of negative automatic thoughts and then to test their validity is a central task of cognitive therapy.

automatization *n.* the development of a skill or habit to a point at which it becomes routine and requires little if any conscious effort or direction.

autonomic conditioning in CLASSICAL CONDITIONING, a procedure in which the conditioned response measured is an index of physiological arousal, usually an electrodermal measure such as SKIN CONDUCTANCE. The conditioned stimulus is usually a simple visual or auditory stimulus presented for 5 to 10 seconds, whereas the unconditioned stimulus is a mildly aversive stimulus such as an electric shock or a loud noise.

autonomic nervous system (**ANS**) the portion of the nervous system innervating smooth muscle and glands, including the circulatory, digestive, respiratory, and reproductive organs. It is divided into the SYMPATHETIC NERVOUS SYSTEM and PARASYMPATHETIC NERVOUS SYSTEM. **Autonomic responses** typically involve changes in involuntary bodily functions, such as heart rate, salivation, digestion, perspiration, pupil size, hormone secretion, bladder contraction, and engorgement of the penis and clitoris.

autonomous stage in the theory of moral development proposed by Swiss child psychologist and epistemologist Jean Piaget (1896–1980), the stage during which the child, typically 10 years of age or older, eventually understands that rules and laws are not permanent, fixed properties of the world but rather are flexible, modifiable entities created by people. The child gradually relies less on parental authority and more on individual and independent morality and learns that intentions, not consequences or the likelihood of punishment, are important in determining the morality of an act. Also called **autonomous morality**. See MORAL RELATIVISM. Compare HETERONOMOUS STAGE; PREMORAL STAGE.

autonomy *n.* **1.** a state of independence and self-determination in an individual, a group, or a society. **2.** the experience of acting from choice, rather than feeling pressured to act. This form of autonomy is considered a fundamental psychological need that predicts well-being.

autonomy versus shame and doubt the second of ERIKSON'S EIGHT STAGES OF PSYCHOSOCIAL DEVELOPMENT, between the ages of 1½ and 3 years. During this stage, children acquire a degree of self-reliance and self-confidence if allowed to develop at their own pace but may begin to doubt their ability to control themselves and their world if parents are overcritical, overprotective, or inconsistent.

autoreceptor *n.* a molecule in the membrane of a presynaptic neuron that regulates the synthesis and release of a neurotransmitter by that neuron by monitoring how much transmitter has been released and "telling" the neuron.

autoregression *n.* a pattern of relationship between repeated measures of a variable taken over time, such that the variable as observed at one point in time is predicted by the variable observed at one or more earlier points in time. See TIME-SERIES ANALYSIS.

autoshaping *n.* a form of conditioning in which a subject that has been given reinforcement following a stimulus, regardless of its response to that stimulus, consistently performs an irrelevant behavior. The classic example is a pigeon that receives food after a light goes on, then conditions itself to peck at the light even though the pecking is not necessary to receive the food.

autosome *n.* any chromosome that is not a SEX CHROMOSOME. A human normally has a total of 44 autosomes (arranged in 22 HOMOLOGOUS pairs) in the nucleus of each body cell. —**autosomal** *adj.*

autosuggestion *n.* the process of making positive suggestions to oneself for such purposes as improving morale, inducing relaxation, or promoting recovery from illness. Also called **self-suggestion**.

autotopagnosia *n.* a type of AGNOSIA involving loss or impairment of the ability to recognize (i.e., point to) parts of one's own body. Also called **autopagnosia**.

availability heuristic a common strategy for making judgments about likelihood of occurrence in which the individual bases such judgments on the salience of the information held in his or her memory about the particular type of event: The more available and relevant information there is, the more likely the event is judged to be. Compare REPRESENTATIVENESS HEURISTIC.

available-case analysis see PAIRWISE DELETION.

avatar *n.* see ALTER EGO.

average evoked potential (AEP) the summated electrical responses of the brain to repeated presentations of the same stimulus. Since any individual EVOKED POTENTIAL typically shows considerable random fluctuations, this technique is used to better distinguish the actual response from background "noise." Also called **average evoked response** (AER).

aversion *n.* a physiological or emotional response indicating dislike for a stimulus. It is usually accompanied by withdrawal from or avoidance of the objectionable stimulus (an **aversion reaction**). —**aversive** *adj.*

aversion conditioning the process by which a noxious or unpleasant stimulus is paired with an undesired behavior. This technique may be used therapeutically, for example, in the treatment of substance abuse, in which case it is called **aversion therapy**. Also called **aversive conditioning**.

aversive racism a form of racial PREJUDICE felt by individuals who outwardly endorse egalitarian attitudes and values but nonetheless experience negative emotions in the presence of members of certain racial groups, particularly in ambiguous circumstances. For example, if a White employer who supports equality nonetheless favors White candidates over Black candidates in job interviews when all the individuals' qualifications for the position are unclear, then he or she is demonstrating aversive racism. See also MODERN RACISM.

avoidance *n.* the practice or an instance of keeping away from particular situations, environments, individuals, or things because of either (a) the anticipated negative consequence of such an encounter or (b) anxious or painful feelings associated with them. Psychology brings several theoretical perspectives to the study of avoidance: its use as a means of coping; its use as a response to fear or shame; its existence as a personality style or predisposition; and its existence as a component in ANXIETY DISORDERS.

avoidance–avoidance conflict a situation involving a choice between two equally objectionable alternatives, such as when an individual must choose between unemployment and a salary cut. See also APPROACH–APPROACH CONFLICT; APPROACH–AVOIDANCE CONFLICT.

avoidance conditioning the establishment of behavior that prevents or postpones aversive stimulation. In a typical conditioning experiment, a buzzer is sounded, then a shock is applied to the subject (e.g., a dog) until it performs a particular act (e.g., jumping over a fence). After several trials, the dog jumps as soon as the buzzer sounds, avoiding the shock. Also called **avoidance learning**; **avoidance training**. See also ESCAPE CONDITIONING.

avoidant attachment see INSECURE ATTACHMENT.

avoidant personality disorder a personality disorder characterized by (a) hypersensitivity to rejection and disapproval, (b) a desire for uncritical acceptance, (c) social withdrawal in spite of a desire for affection and acceptance, and (d) low self-esteem. This pattern is long-standing and severe enough to cause objective distress and seriously impair the ability to work and maintain relationships.

awareness *n.* perception or knowledge of something. Accurate reportability of something perceived or known is widely used as a behavioral index of conscious awareness. However, it is possible to be aware of something without being explicitly conscious of it (e.g., see BLINDSIGHT). See also CONSCIOUSNESS; SELF-AWARENESS.

axis *n.* (*pl.* **axes**) **1.** an imaginary line that bisects the body or an organ in a particular plane. For example, the **long** or (**cephalocaudal**) **axis** runs in the median plane, dividing the body into right and left halves. **2.** a system made up of interrelated parts, as in the HYPOTHALAMIC–PITUITARY–ADRENAL AXIS. **3.** in *DSM–IV–TR*, any one of several dimensions for describing individual behavior and facilitating clinical assessment (e.g., Axis I, clinical disorders; Axis II, personality disorders and mental retardation). By contrast, *DSM–5* uses a nonaxial approach. **4.** a fixed reference line in a coordinate system. See also ABSCISSA; ORDINATE.

axon *n.* the long, thin, hollow, cylindrical extension of a NEURON that normally carries a nerve impulse away from the CELL BODY. An axon often branches extensively and may be surrounded by a protective MYELIN SHEATH. Each branch of an axon ends in a **terminal button** from which an impulse is transmitted, through discharge of a NEUROTRANSMITTER, across a SYNAPSE to a neighboring neuron. —**axonal** *adj.*

axonal transport the transportation of materials along the axon of a neuron via the flow of the jellylike fluid (**axoplasm**) it contains. Transport may be directed away from the CELL BODY (anterograde) or back toward the cell body (retrograde). Also called **axoplasmic flow**.

axon hillock a cone-shaped part of the CELL BODY of a neuron from which the axon originates. Depolarization must reach a critical threshold at the axon hillock for the axon to propagate a nerve impulse.

Bb

babbling *n.* prespeech sounds, such as *dadada*, made by infants from around 6 months of age. Babbling is usually regarded as practice in vocalization, which facilitates later speech development. —**babble** *vb.*

Babinski reflex the reflex occurring in a healthy infant in which the big toe extends upward and the other toes fan out when the sole of the foot is gently stimulated. This response is elicited in newborns to monitor central nervous system development. In adults, it is an indication of neurological disorder and called **Babinski's sign**. [Joseph F. **Babinski** (1857–1932), French neurologist]

baby talk the type of simplified speech used by adults and older children when talking to infants or very young children. See INFANT-DIRECTED SPEECH.

background variable see SUBJECT VARIABLE.

back-translation *n.* see TRANSLATION AND BACK-TRANSLATION.

backward conditioning a procedure in which an UNCONDITIONED STIMULUS is consistently presented before a NEUTRAL STIMULUS. Generally, this arrangement is not thought to produce a change in the effect of a neutral stimulus. Occasionally, however, the neutral stimulus may take on inhibitory functions, presumably because it consistently predicts the absence of the unconditioned stimulus. Also called **backward pairing**. Compare FORWARD CONDITIONING.

backward elimination a technique used in REGRESSION ANALYSIS to forecast an outcome or response variable using a subset of predictor variables narrowed down from a large initial set. In backward elimination, all available predictors are included originally and then examined one at a time, with any predictors that do not contribute in a statistically meaningful manner systematically dropped until a predetermined criterion is reached. Also called **stepdown selection**. See also STEPWISE REGRESSION.

balanced design any research design in which the number of observations or measurements obtained in each experimental condition is equal. For example, a health researcher interested in exercise and depression would be using a balanced design if he or she examined 50 people who exercise less than 30 minutes per day, 50 people who exercise between 30 and 60 minutes per day, and 50 people who exercise more than 60 minutes per day.

balanced scale a test or survey that has for each possible response a response that means the opposite. A rating scale with the four alternatives *very poor, poor, good,* and *very good* is an example, as is a set of survey questions in which half of the questions characterize a particular trait (e.g., perceived stress level) in one direction (e.g., low) and the other half characterize the trait in the opposite direction (e.g., high).

balance theory a theory specifying that people prefer elements within a cognitive system to be internally consistent with one another (i.e., balanced). Balanced systems are assumed to be more stable and psychologically pleasing than imbalanced systems. The theory has been primarily specified and tested within the context of systems involving three elements, which are sometimes referred to as P-O-X triads, in which P = person (i.e., self), O = other person, and X = some stimulus or event.

Bálint's syndrome a spatial and attentional disorder resulting from lesions in the parieto-occipital regions of the brain. It consists of inability to visually guide the hand to an object, inability to change visual gaze, and inability to recognize multiple stimuli in a scene and understand their nature as a whole. [first described in 1909 by Rudolf **Bálint** (1874–1929), Hungarian physician]

ballismus *n.* involuntary throwing or flinging movements of the limbs, caused by severe muscle contractions due to neurological damage. It may involve both sides of the body or, in the case of hemiballismus, one side only. Also called **ballism**.

ballistic *adj.* describing a movement (or part of a movement) in which the motion, once initiated, is not altered by feedback-based corrections. Ballistic is sometimes also used, incorrectly, to describe any rapid movement.

bandwagon effect the tendency for people in social and sometimes political situations to align themselves with the majority opinion and do or believe things because many other people appear to be doing or believing the same.

bandwidth *n.* **1.** a range of frequencies, usually expressed in hertz (cycles per second). In INFORMATION THEORY, it is a measure of the amount of information that a communication channel can transmit per unit of time. **2.** the range of information available from measuring instruments. Greater bandwidth is generally associated with lower accuracy (fidelity).

bandwidth selectivity see FREQUENCY SELECTIVITY.

barbiturate *n.* any of a family of drugs derived from barbituric acid that depress activity of the central nervous system. They typically induce profound tolerance and withdrawal symptoms and depress respiration. Their use became common in the 1930s, but they were rapidly supplanted in the 1970s by the BENZODIAZEPINES, which lack the lethality associated with overdose of the barbiturates. The prototype of the group, **barbital**, was introduced into medical practice in 1903.

bar graph a chart in which bars of varying height with spaces between them are used to display data for variables defined by qualities or categories. For example, to show the political affiliations of Americans, the different parties (e.g., Democrat, Republican, Independent) would be listed on the *x*-axis, and the height of the bar rising above each party would represent the number or proportion of people in that category. See also HISTOGRAM.

Barnum effect the tendency to believe that vague predictions or general personality descriptions, such as those offered by astrology, have specific applications to oneself.

basal age the highest MENTAL AGE level at which a participant can answer all items on a standardized test correctly. The concept of mental ages is used relatively rarely in current testing. Compare CEILING AGE.

basal forebrain a region of the ventral FOREBRAIN near the corpus callosum containing CHOLINERGIC neurons that project widely to the cerebral cortex and hippocampus. The basal forebrain is thought to be important in aspects of memory, learning, and attention. See BASAL NUCLEUS OF MEYNERT.

basal ganglia a group of nuclei (neuron cell bodies) deep within the cerebral hemispheres of the brain that includes the CAUDATE NUCLEUS, PUTAMEN, GLOBUS PALLIDUS, SUBSTANTIA NIGRA, and SUBTHALAMIC NUCLEUS. The putamen and globus pallidus are together known as the **lenticular** (or **lentiform**) **nucleus**, the lenticular nucleus and caudate nucleus are together known as the **corpus striatum**, and the caudate nucleus and putamen are together called the **striatum**. The basal ganglia are involved in the generation of goal-directed voluntary movement. Also called **basal nuclei**.

basal metabolism the minimum energy expenditure required to maintain the vital functions of the body while awake but at rest and not expending energy for thermoregulation. **Basal metabolic rate (BMR)** is measured in kilojoules (or calories) expended per kilogram of body weight or per square meter of body surface per hour.

basal nucleus of Meynert a collection of neurons in the BASAL FOREBRAIN that modulates the activity of many areas of the neocortex by providing CHOLINERGIC innervation. It is implicated in Alzheimer's disease. Also called **basal magnocellular nucleus; Meynert's nucleus.** [Theodor H. **Meynert** (1833–1892), Austrian neurologist]

baseline functioning see PREMORBID FUNCTIONING.

base rate the naturally occurring frequency of a phenomenon in a population. An example is the percentage of students at a particular college who have major depressive disorder. This rate is often contrasted with the rate of the phenomenon under the influence of some changed condition in order to determine the degree to which the change influences the phenomenon.

base-rate fallacy a decision-making error in which information about the rate of occurrence of some trait in a population (the base-rate information) is ignored or not given appropriate weight. For example, given a choice of the two categories, people might categorize a man as an engineer, rather than a lawyer, if they heard that he enjoyed physics at school—even if they knew that he was drawn from a population consisting of 90% lawyers and 10% engineers. See REPRESENTATIVE-NESS HEURISTIC.

basic anxiety in EGO PSYCHOLOGY, a feeling of being helpless, abandoned, and endangered in a hostile world. It is theorized to arise from the infant's helplessness and dependence on his or her parents or from parental indiffer-

ence. Defenses against basic anxiety and hostility may produce NEUROTIC NEEDS.

basic-level category a category formed at the level that people find most natural and appropriate in their normal, everyday experience of the things so categorized. A basic-level category (e.g., *bird, table*) will be broader than the more specific subordinate categories into which it can be divided (e.g., *hawk, dining table*) but less abstract than the superordinate category into which it can be subsumed (e.g., *animals, furniture*). Also called **basic category; natural category.**

basic need see PHYSIOLOGICAL NEED.

basic research research conducted to obtain greater understanding of a phenomenon, explore a theory, or advance knowledge, with no consideration of any direct practical application. Compare APPLIED RESEARCH.

basic science scientific research or theory that is concerned with knowledge of fundamental phenomena and the laws that govern them, regardless of the potential applications of such knowledge. Also called **pure science.** Compare APPLIED SCIENCE.

basic trust versus mistrust the first of ERIKSON'S EIGHT STAGES OF PSYCHOSOCIAL DEVELOPMENT, between birth and 18 months of age. During this stage, the infant either comes to view other people and himself or herself as trustworthy or comes to develop a fundamental distrust of his or her environment. The growth of basic trust, considered essential for the later development of self-esteem and healthy interpersonal relationships, is attributed to a primary caregiver who is responsively attuned to the infant's individual needs while conveying the quality of trustworthiness, whereas the growth of basic mistrust is attributed to neglect, lack of love, or inconsistent treatment.

basilar membrane a fibrous membrane within the COCHLEA that supports the ORGAN OF CORTI. In response to sound, the basilar membrane vibrates; this leads to stimulation of the HAIR CELLS—the auditory receptors within the organ of Corti.

battered-child syndrome (BCS) the effects on a child of intentional and repeated physical abuse by parents or other caregivers. In addition to sustaining physical injuries, the child is at increased risk of experiencing longerterm problems, such as depression, posttraumatic stress disorder, substance abuse, decreased self-esteem, and sexual and other behavioral difficulties. See also CHILD ABUSE.

battered-woman syndrome (**BWS**) the psychological effects of being physically abused by a spouse or domestic partner. The syndrome includes LEARNED HELPLESSNESS in relation to the abusive spouse, as well as symptoms of posttraumatic stress. The incidence of domestic violence toward women played a role in the origins of this term; however, it is now understood that men may be the victims of violence by a domestic partner and may also exhibit the effects of this syndrome.

Bayesian *adj.* denoting an approach to statistical inference and probability that enables previously known (a priori) information about a population characteristic of interest to be incorporated into the analysis. In Bayesian methods, estimated quantities are based in part on empirical data (i.e., what was actually observed in a sample) and in part on collective or individual knowledge about what to expect in the population. [Thomas **Bayes** (1702–1761), British mathematician and theologian]

Bayes theorem a formula for calculating the probability that an event will occur that allows for the acquisition of new information regarding that event. For example, consider the probability that an individual will have a stroke

within the next year. Using Bayes theorem, one could take an estimate of this probability based on general population data for that individual's age group and revise it to account for the results of that person's stress tests and other cardiological markers. [Thomas **Bayes**]

Bayley Scales of Infant and Toddler Development scales for assessing the developmental status of infants and young children ages 1 month to 42 months. Test stimuli, such as form boards, blocks, shapes, household objects (e.g., utensils), and other common items, are used to engage the child in specific tasks of increasing difficulty and elicit particular responses. The Bayley scales were originally published in 1969 and subsequently revised in 1993; the most recent version is the **Bayley–III**, published in 2005. [developed by U.S. psychologist Nancy **Bayley** (1899–1994)]

B cell see LYMPHOCYTE.

Bedlam *n.* the popular name for the Hospital of Saint Mary of Bethlehem in Bishopsgate, London, founded as a monastery in 1247 and converted into an asylum for the insane by Henry VIII in 1547. Many of the inmates were in a state of frenzy, and as they were shackled, starved, beaten, and exhibited to the public for a penny a look, general turmoil prevailed. The word itself thus became synonymous with wild confusion or frenzy. Sometimes the term **bedlamism** was used for psychotic behavior, and the term **bedlamite** for a psychotic individual.

before–after design see PRETEST–POSTTEST DESIGN.

behavior *n.* **1.** an organism's activities in response to external or internal stimuli, including objectively observable activities, introspectively observable activities, and nonconscious processes. **2.** more restrictively, any action or function that can be objectively observed or measured in response to controlled stimuli. Historically, behaviorists contrasted objective behavior with mental activities, which were considered subjective and thus unsuitable for scientific study. See BEHAVIORISM. —**behavioral** *adj.*

behavioral activation an intervention that explicitly aims to increase an individual's engagement in valued life activities through guided goal setting to bring about improvements in thoughts, mood, and quality of life.

behavioral approach system (**BAS**) in REINFORCEMENT SENSITIVITY THEORY, the physiological mechanism believed to control appetitive motivation. It is theorized to be sensitive to signals of reward, nonpunishment, and escape from punishment. Activity in this system causes the individual to begin (or to increase) movement toward goals. It has also been held that this system is responsible for the experience of positive feelings such as hope, elation, and happiness in response to these signals and that having a strong or chronically active BAS tends to result in extraversion. Also called **behavioral activation system**. Compare BEHAVIORAL INHIBITION SYSTEM.

behavioral assessment the systematic study and evaluation of an individual's behavior using a wide variety of techniques, including direct observation, interviews, and self-monitoring. When used to identify patterns indicative of disorder, the procedure is called **behavioral diagnosis** and is essential in deciding on the use of specific behavioral or cognitive behavioral interventions.

behavioral cardiology see CARDIAC PSYCHOLOGY.

behavioral contract see BEHAVIOR CONTRACT.

behavioral couples therapy a COUPLES THERAPY that focuses on interrupting negative interaction patterns through instruction, modeling, rehearsal, feedback, positive behavior exchange, and structured problem solving. This therapy can be conducted with individual couples or in a couples group format. When practiced with legally married partners, it is called **behavioral marital therapy**. See also INTEGRATIVE BEHAVIORAL COUPLES THERAPY.

behavioral economics an interdisciplinary field concerned with understanding how problem-solving strategies, biases, and other psychological variables influence economic behavior. In contrast to the standard view within traditional economics that people are rational actors who always make choices to maximize their well-being, behavioral economists view human rationality as limited and subject to personal, social, and situational influences. Thus, they seek to devise more realistic, psychologically plausible models of economic behavior to account for a variety of decision-making anomalies and market inconsistencies that have been observed, such as loss aversion (the tendency to go to disproportionately great lengths to avoid perceived losses) and temporal discounting (the tendency to prefer small rewards received sooner to larger ones received later).

behavioral endocrinology the study of the relationships between the functioning of the endocrine glands and neuroendocrine cells and behavior. For example, gonadal secretion of sex hormones influences sexual behavior, and secretion of corticosteroids by the adrenal glands influences physiological and behavioral responses to stress.

behavioral genetics the study of familial or hereditary behavior patterns and of the genetic mechanisms of behavior traits. Also called **behavior genetics**.

behavioral inhibition a temperamental predisposition characterized by restraint in engaging with the world combined with a tendency to scrutinize the environment for potential threats and to avoid or withdraw from unfamiliar situations or people.

behavioral inhibition system

(**BIS**) in REINFORCEMENT SENSITIVITY THEORY, the physiological mechanism believed to control aversive motivation. It is theorized to be sensitive to signals of punishment and nonreward. Activity in this system suppresses behavior that may lead to negative or painful outcomes and inhibits movement toward goals. It has also been held that this system is responsible for the experience of negative feelings such as fear, anxiety, frustration, and sadness in response to these signals and that having a strong or chronically active BIS tends to result in introversion. Compare BEHAVIORAL APPROACH SYSTEM.

behavioral medicine a field that

applies behavioral theories and methods to the prevention and treatment of medical and psychological disorders. Areas of application include chronic illness, lifestyle issues (e.g., substance abuse, obesity), SOMATOFORM DISORDERS, and the like. Behavioral medicine is an interdisciplinary field in which physicians, psychologists, psychiatrists, social workers, and others work together in patient care.

behavioral mimicry see MIMICRY.

behavioral model a conceptualiza-

tion of psychological disorders in terms of overt behavior patterns produced by learning and the influence of REINFORCEMENT CONTINGENCIES. Treatment techniques, including SYSTEMATIC DESENSITIZATION and MODELING, focus on modifying ineffective or maladaptive patterns.

behavioral neuropsychology a

subspecialty of CLINICAL NEUROPSYCHOLOGY that integrates behavior therapy techniques into the treatment of individuals with brain damage.

behavioral neuroscience a

branch of NEUROSCIENCE and BIOLOGICAL PSYCHOLOGY that seeks to understand and characterize the specific neural circuitry and mechanisms underlying behavioral propensities or capacities.

behavioral psychotherapy see
BEHAVIOR THERAPY.

behavioral science any of various

disciplines that use systematic observation and experimentation in the scientific study of human and nonhuman animal actions and reactions. Psychology, sociology, and anthropology are examples.

behavioral sleep medicine

(**BSM**) a clinical specialty area combining aspects of health psychology and sleep disorders medicine. Practitioners include psychologists, physicians, nurse practitioners, and other health care professionals certified in the discipline who seek to understand the cognitive and behavioral factors that contribute to the development and maintenance of adult and pediatric sleep disorders and who use this knowledge to provide empirically validated, nonpharmacological interventions.

behavioral study of obedience

the experimental analysis, especially as carried out by U.S. social psychologist Stanley Milgram (1933–1984) in the 1960s, of individuals' willingness to obey the orders of an authority. In Milgram's experiment, each participant played the role of a teacher who was instructed to deliver painful electric shocks to other "participants" for each failure to answer a question correctly. The latter were in fact CONFEDERATES who did not actually receive shocks for their many deliberate errors. Milgram found that a substantial number of participants (65%) were completely obedient, delivering what they believed were shocks of increasing intensity despite the protestations and apparent suffering of the victims.

behavior analysis the decomposi-

tion of behavior into its component parts or processes. This approach to psychology emphasizes interactions between behavior and the environment.

behavior coding a method of re-

cording observations in which defined labels are used by specially trained individuals to denote specific qualities and characteristics of behaviors as they are witnessed. For example, a developmental researcher might use the following coding scheme for infant vocalizations: (a) vowels; (b) syllables (i.e., consonant–vowel transitions); (c) babbling (a sequence of repeated syllables); and (d) other (e.g., crying, laughing, vegetative sounds such as cooing). Behavior coding systems typically are specific to a given study and the behaviors under investigation.

behavior contract an agreement between therapist and client in which the client agrees to carry out certain behaviors, usually between sessions but sometimes during the session as well. Also called **behavioral contract**.

behavior disorder any persistent and repetitive pattern of behavior that violates societal norms or rules or seriously impairs a person's functioning. The term is used in a very general sense to cover a wide range of disorders or syndromes.

behavior genetics see BEHAVIORAL GENETICS.

behaviorism *n.* an approach to psychology, formulated in 1913 by U.S. psychologist John B. Watson (1878–1958), based on the study of objective, observable facts rather than subjective, qualitative processes, such as feelings, motives, and consciousness. To make psychology a naturalistic science, Watson proposed to limit it to quantitative events, such as stimulus–response relationships, effects of conditioning, physiological processes, and a study of human and animal behavior, all of which can best be investigated through laboratory experiments that yield objective measures under controlled conditions. Historically, behaviorists held that mind was not a proper topic for scientific study because mental events are subjective and not independently verifiable. See also NEOBEHAVIORISM; RADICAL BEHAVIORISM.

behavior modification the use of OPERANT CONDITIONING, BIOFEEDBACK, MODELING, AVERSION CONDITIONING, RECIPROCAL INHIBITION, or other learning techniques as a means of changing human behavior. For example, behavior modification is used in clinical contexts to improve adaptation and alleviate symptoms and in organizational contexts to encourage employees to adopt safe work practices. The term is often used synonymously with BEHAVIOR THERAPY.

behavior observation the recording or evaluation of the ongoing behavior of one or more research participants by one or more observers. Behavior observation may be carried out live or through video media and often involves the use of rating scales, checklists, or charts.

behavior shaping see SHAPING.

behavior theory the assumption that behavior, including its acquisition, development, and maintenance, can be adequately explained by stimuli- and response-based principles of learning. Behavior theory attempts to describe environmental influences on behavior, often using controlled studies with laboratory animals.

behavior therapy a form of psychotherapy that applies the principles of learning, OPERANT CONDITIONING, and CLASSICAL CONDITIONING to eliminate symptoms and modify ineffective or maladaptive patterns of behavior. The focus of this therapy is on the behavior itself and the contingencies and environmental factors that reinforce it, rather than exploration of the underlying psychological causes of the behavior. A wide variety of techniques are used in behavior therapy, such as BIOFEEDBACK, MODELING, and SYSTEMATIC DESENSITIZATION. Also called **behavioral psychotherapy**.

belief *n.* **1.** acceptance of the truth, reality, or validity of something (e.g., a phenomenon, a person's veracity), particularly in the absence of substantiation. **2.** an association of some characteristic or attribute, usually evaluative in nature, with an object (e.g., this car is reliable).

belief bias the tendency to be influenced by one's knowledge about the world in evaluating conclusions and to accept them as true because they are believable rather than because they are logically valid. Belief bias is most often assessed with syllogistic reasoning tasks in which the believability of the conclusion conflicts with logical validity. For example, given the syllogisms *All flowers have petals; roses have petals; therefore, roses are flowers* and *All fish can swim; tuna are fish; therefore, tuna can swim*, an individual is more likely to rely on prior knowledge and personal beliefs and to accept both conclusions as valid when in fact only the second is logically valid.

belief in a just world see JUST-WORLD HYPOTHESIS.

belief perseverance the tendency to maintain a belief even after the information that originally gave rise to it has been refuted or otherwise shown to be inaccurate.

belief system a set of two or more beliefs or attitudes that are associated with one another in memory.

bell curve the characteristic shape obtained by graphing a NORMAL DISTRIBUTION. With a large rounded central peak tapering off on either side, it resembles a cross-sectional representation of a bell.

Bell–Magendie law the principle that the VENTRAL ROOTS of the spinal cord are motor in function and the DORSAL ROOTS are sensory. [Charles **Bell** (1774–1842), Scottish surgeon and anatomist; François **Magendie** (1783–1855), French physiologist]

below-average effect the tendency of a person to underestimate his or her intellectual and social abilities relative to others. The below-average effect is common when the skill in question is

relatively hard (e.g., sculpting human figures from clay), whereas the opposite ABOVE-AVERAGE EFFECT generally occurs when the skill in question is relatively easy (e.g., operating a computer mouse). Also called **worse-than-average effect**.

Bender Visual–Motor Gestalt Test a test used to assess visual–motor functioning and perceptual ability, as well as to diagnose neurological impairment. The participant copies line drawings of geometric figures onto blank pieces of paper (Copy Phase) and then redraws them from memory (Recall Phase). All reproductions are scored on a 5-point scale, ranging from 0 (*no resemblance*) to 4 (*nearly perfect*). Originally developed in 1938, the test (often shortened to **Bender–Gestalt**) is now in its second edition (published in 2003). [Lauretta **Bender** (1897–1987), U.S. psychiatrist]

benign *adj.* **1.** in health care, denoting a disorder or illness that has a favorable prognosis. **2.** denoting a condition that is relatively mild, transient, or not associated with serious pathology. Compare MALIGNANT.

benzodiazepine *n.* any of a family of drugs that depress central nervous system activity and also produce sedation and relaxation of skeletal muscles. Benzodiazepines are commonly used in the treatment of generalized anxiety and insomnia and are useful in the management of acute withdrawal from alcohol and in seizure disorders. Clinically introduced in the 1960s, they rapidly supplanted the barbiturates, largely due to their significantly lower toxicity in overdose. Prolonged use can lead to tolerance and psychological and physical dependence.

bereavement *n.* the experience of having had a loved one die. The bereaved person may feel emotional pain and distress (see GRIEF) and may or may not express this distress to others (see MOURNING; DISENFRANCHISED GRIEF). Indeed, individual grief and

B

mourning responses vary widely. —**bereaved** *adj.*

Bereitschaftspotential (**BP**) *n.* see READINESS POTENTIAL.

Bernoulli trial a single experiment in which the only two possible outcomes are success or failure. Usually a value of 0 is used to denote a failure (i.e., the item of interest does not occur) and a value of 1 is used to denote a success (i.e., the item does occur). A sequence of Bernoulli trials is known as a **Bernoulli process**. [Jacques **Bernoulli** (1654–1705), Swiss mathematician and scientist]

beta (symbol: β) *n.* **1.** the likeliness of committing a TYPE II ERROR in research. **2.** the effect of a predictor variable on an outcome variable, such as in REGRESSION ANALYSIS or STRUCTURAL EQUATION MODELING.

beta coefficient the multiplicative constant in a REGRESSION ANALYSIS that indicates the change in an outcome variable associated with the change in a predictor variable after each has been standardized to have a distribution with a mean of 0 and a STANDARD DEVIATION of 1. A beta coefficient controls for the effect of other predictors included in the analysis and thus allows for direct comparison of the individual variables despite differences in measurement scales (e.g., salary measured in dollars and educational degree measured in years of schooling). Also called **beta weight**.

beta movement see APPARENT MOVEMENT.

beta wave in electroencephalography, the type of BRAIN WAVE (frequency 13–30 Hz) associated with alert wakefulness and intense mental activity. Also called **beta rhythm**.

beta weight see BETA COEFFICIENT.

better-than-average effect see ABOVE-AVERAGE EFFECT.

between-groups variance the variation in experimental scores that is attributable only to membership in different groups and exposure to different experimental conditions. It is reflected in the ANALYSIS OF VARIANCE by the degree to which the several group means differ from one another and is compared with the WITHIN-GROUPS VARIANCE to obtain an F RATIO. Also called **between-subjects variance**.

between-subjects design a study in which individuals are assigned to only one treatment or experimental condition and each person provides only one score for data analysis. For example, in a between-subjects design investigating the efficacy of three different drugs for treating depression, one group of depressed individuals would receive one of the drugs, a different group would receive another one of the drugs, and yet another group would receive the remaining drug. Thus, the researcher is comparing the effect each medication has on a different set of people. Also called **between-groups design**; **independent-groups design**. Compare WITHIN-SUBJECTS DESIGN.

between-subjects factor in an ANALYSIS OF VARIANCE, an INDEPENDENT VARIABLE with multiple levels, each of which is assigned to or experienced by a distinct group of participants. In a study examining weight loss, for example, the different amounts of daily exercise under investigation would be a between-subjects factor if each was undertaken by a different set of people. Also called **between-subjects variable**.

between-subjects variance see BETWEEN-GROUPS VARIANCE.

bias *n.* **1.** partiality: an inclination or predisposition for or against something. See also PREJUDICE. **2.** any tendency or preference, such as a RESPONSE BIAS. **3.** systematic error arising during SAMPLING, data collection, data analysis, or data interpretation. **4.** any deviation of a measured or calculated quantity from its actual (true) value, so that the measurement or calculation is unrepresentative of the item of interest. —**biased** *adj.*

bigamy *n.* the act of marrying someone when already married to someone else. In cultures that permit individuals to have more than one spouse, this practice should be referred to as POLYGAMY and not bigamy. Compare MONOGAMY. —**bigamist** *n.* —**bigamous** *adj.*

Big Five personality model a model of the primary dimensions of individual differences in personality. The dimensions are usually labeled extraversion, neuroticism, agreeableness, conscientiousness, and openness to experience, although the labels vary somewhat among researchers. See also FIVE-FACTOR PERSONALITY MODEL.

bigram *n.* any two-letter combination. In PSYCHOLINGUISTICS research, the term typically refers to a within-word consecutive character sequence (e.g., *paper* contains the bigrams *pa, ap, pe,* and *er*), whereas in learning and memory research, it generally refers to a freestanding nonword (e.g., TL, KE).

bilateral *adj.* denoting or relating to both sides of the body or an organ. For example, **bilateral symmetry** is the symmetrical arrangement of an organism's body such that the right and left halves are approximately mirror images of one another; **bilateral transfer** is the TRANSFER OF TRAINING or patterns of performance for a skill from one side of the body, where the skill (e.g., handwriting) was originally learned and primarily used, to the other side of the body. —**bilaterally** *adv.*

bilingual education instruction in two languages, typically in one's native language and in the dominant language of the country in which one is educated. In transitional bilingual education, as students gain fluency, they shift to instruction solely in their non-native language, usually within 2 to 3 years. In total immersion bilingual programs, the emphasis is solely on

second-language acquisition for both native and nonnative speakers.

bilingualism *n.* the regular use of two or more languages by a person or within a group of people. —**bilingual** *adj.*

bimodal distribution a set of scores with two peaks or MODES around which values tend to cluster, such that the frequencies at first increase and then decrease around each peak. For example, when graphing the heights of a sample of adolescents, one would obtain a bimodal distribution if most people were either 5′7″ or 5′9″ tall. See also UNIMODAL DISTRIBUTION.

binaural cue any difference in the sound arriving at the two ears from a given sound source (i.e., an interaural difference) that acts as a cue to permit AUDITORY LOCALIZATION. The common cues are interaural level differences, interaural time differences, and interaural phase differences.

binding problem the theoretical issue of how the brain perceives and represents different features, or conjunctions of properties, as one object or event. This problem arises because different attributes of a stimulus (e.g., hue, form, spatial location, motion) are analyzed by different areas of the cerebral cortex yet are experienced in consciousness as a unity; the binding problem is relevant in all areas of knowledge representation, including such complex cognitive representations as THEORY OF MIND.

binge-eating disorder an eating disorder marked by recurring discrete periods of uncontrolled consumption of large quantities of food and by distress associated with this behavior. There is an absence of inappropriate compensatory behaviors (e.g., vomiting, laxative misuse, excessive exercise, fasting). Compare BULIMIA NERVOSA.

binocular cue see DEPTH CUE.

binocular disparity the slight difference between the right and left retinal images. When both eyes focus on an object, the different position of the eyes produces a disparity of visual angle, and a slightly different image is received by each retina. The two images are automatically compared and fused, providing an important cue to depth perception. Also called **retinal disparity**.

binocular rivalry the failure of the eyes to fuse stimuli. For example, if horizontal bars are viewed through the left eye and vertical bars through the right eye, the perception is a patchy and fluctuating alternation of the two patterns, rather than a superimposition of the patterns to form a stable checkerboard.

binomial distribution the PROBABILITY DISTRIBUTION for each possible sequence of results on a variable that has only two possible outcomes, with the likeliness of obtaining each outcome remaining constant. For example, a binomial distribution of the results of trying to predict the outcomes of 10 coin tosses would display the probability of observing each possible set of results, including one success and nine failures, two successes and eight failures, and so forth. This distribution is often denoted by $b(n,\theta)$.

bioecological model see ECOLOGICAL SYSTEMS THEORY.

biofeedback *n*. **1.** information about bodily processes and systems provided by an organism's receptors to enable it to maintain a physiologically desirable internal environment and make adjustments as necessary. **2.** the use of an external monitoring device (e.g., electrocardiograph) to provide an individual with information regarding his or her physiological state. When used to help a person obtain voluntary control over autonomic body functions, such as heart rate or blood pressure, the technique is called **biofeedback training**. It may be applied therapeutically to treat various conditions, including chronic pain and hypertension.

biogenic *adj*. **1.** produced by living organisms or biological processes. **2.** necessary for the maintenance of life.

biogenic amine any of a group of amines (chemical compounds that contain one or more amino groups [-NH2]) that affect bodily processes and nervous system functioning. Biogenic amines are divided into subgroups (e.g., CATECHOLAMINES, INDOLEAMINES) and include the neurotransmitters dopamine, epinephrine, histamine, norepinephrine, and serotonin.

bioinformatics *n*. the use of INFORMATICS in medicine and other life sciences, as in the analysis of public health, genomics, and biomedical research data. Also called **biomedical informatics**.

biological age age as determined by changes in bodily structure and performance that are normative at specific times during the lifespan. Compare CHRONOLOGICAL AGE.

biological clock the mechanism within an organism that controls the periodicity of BIOLOGICAL RHYTHMS, even in the absence of any external cues. A biological clock in mammals is located in the SUPRACHIASMATIC NUCLEUS of the hypothalamus.

biological determinism the concept that psychological and behavioral characteristics are entirely the result of constitutional and biological factors. Environmental conditions serve only as occasions for the manifestation of such characteristics. Compare ENVIRONMENTAL DETERMINISM.

biological marker a variation in the physiological processes of an organism that accompanies a disorder, irrespective of whether it directly causes the disorder. Also called **biomarker**.

biological perspective an approach to abnormal psychology that emphasizes physiologically based causative factors, such as the AMYLOID PLAQUES in Alzheimer's disease, and consequently tends to focus primarily on BIOLOGICAL THERAPIES.

biological psychology the science that deals with the biological basis of behavior, thoughts, and emotions and the reciprocal relations between biological and psychological processes. It also addresses topics such as behavior-changing brain lesions, chemical responses in the brain, and brain-related genetics. It includes such fields as BEHAVIORAL NEUROSCIENCE, CLINICAL NEUROSCIENCE, COGNITIVE NEUROSCIENCE, BEHAVIORAL ENDOCRINOLOGY, and PSYCHONEUROIMMUNOLOGY. Also called **biopsychology; physiological psychology; psychobiology**.

biological rhythm any periodic variation in a living organism's physiological or psychological function, such as energy level, sexual desire, or menstruation. Such rhythms can be linked to cyclical changes in environmental cues, such as daylength or passing of the seasons, and tend to be daily (see CIRCADIAN RHYTHM) or annual (see CIRCANNUAL RHYTHM). They can vary with individuals and with the period of the individual's life. Also called **biorhythm**. See also INFRADIAN RHYTHM; ULTRADIAN RHYTHM.

biological therapy any form of treatment for mental disorders that is intended to alter physiological functioning, including drug therapies, ELECTROCONVULSIVE THERAPY, and PSYCHOSURGERY. Also called **biomedical therapy**.

biomarker *n.* see BIOLOGICAL MARKER.

biomedical informatics see BIOINFORMATICS.

biomedical therapy see BIOLOGICAL THERAPY.

biopsychology *n.* see BIOLOGICAL PSYCHOLOGY.

biopsychosocial *adj.* denoting a systematic integration of biological, psychological, and social approaches to the study of mental health and specific mental disorders.

biorhythm *n.* **1.** a synonym of BIOLOGICAL RHYTHM. **2.** according to pseudoscientific belief, any one of three basic cycles (physical, emotional, and intellectual) that can be charted like a sine wave and with which every individual is said to be programmed at birth. It is maintained that these cycles continue unaltered until death and that good and bad days for various activities can be calculated accordingly.

biosocial *adj.* pertaining to the interplay or mingling of biological and social factors, as with human behavior that is influenced simultaneously by complex neurophysiological processes and social interactions.

bioterrorism *n.* a form of TERRORISM in which biological agents such as viruses and bacteria are deliberately released into air, water, or food to cause illness and death. Anthrax, for example, has been used in bioterrorism.

bipolar *adj.* denoting something with two opposites or extremities, such as a BIPOLAR NEURON or the BIPOLAR DISORDERS. **—bipolarity** *n.*

bipolar disorder any of a group of mood disorders in which symptoms of mania and depression alternate. A distinction is made between **bipolar I disorder**, in which the individual fluctuates between episodes of mania or hypomania and MAJOR DEPRESSIVE EPISODES or experiences a mix of these, and **bipolar II disorder**, in which the individual fluctuates between major depressive and hypomanic episodes. The former official name for bipolar disorders, **manic-depressive illness**, is still in frequent use. See also CYCLOTHYMIC DISORDER.

bipolarity *n.* a construct of mutual exclusion and, by implication, a strong negative correlation between opposite dimensions. It typically is applied to affect or mood (e.g., happiness vs. sadness; enjoyment vs. irritation), but it also may be used to describe INDIVIDUAL DIFFERENCES (e.g., introversion vs. extraversion).

bipolar neuron a neuron with only two extensions—an AXON and a DENDRITE—that run from opposite sides of the CELL BODY. Cells of this type are found primarily in the retina (see RETINAL BIPOLAR CELL) as well as elsewhere in the nervous system. Also called **bipolar cell**. Compare MULTIPOLAR NEURON; UNIPOLAR NEURON.

birth cohort see COHORT.

birth defect see CONGENITAL DEFECT.

birth order the ordinal position of a child in the family (first-born, second-born, youngest, etc.). There has been much psychological research into how birth order affects personal adjustment and family status, but the notion that it has strong and consistent effects on psychological outcomes is not supported. Current family-structure research sees birth order not so much as a causal factor but rather as an indirect variable that follows in importance more process-oriented variables (e.g., parental discipline, sibling interaction, genetic and hormonal makeup).

birth trauma in psychoanalytic theory, the psychological shock of being born, due to the sudden change from the security of the womb to the experience of multiple, varied stimuli from the external world. Austrian neurologist Sigmund Freud (1856–1939) viewed birth as the child's first anxiety experience and the prototype of separation anxiety. To Austrian psychoanalyst Otto Rank (1884–1939), who first proposed the idea, it was the crucial factor in causing neuroses. The theory was subsequently disproven by infant research.

bisection *n.* the act of splitting something into two equal parts. In psychophysics, it refers to a scaling method in which a participant adjusts a stimulus until it is perceived as halfway between two other stimuli with respect to a particular dimension.

biserial correlation coefficient (symbol: r_b; r_{bls}) a measure of the degree or strength of association between a variable whose values may span a range (e.g., grade point average) and a variable with only two discrete values (e.g., pass or fail). It is distinct from the POINT BISERIAL CORRELATION COEFFICIENT in assuming that there is a NORMAL DISTRIBUTION underlying most characteristics. Also called **biserial** *r*.

bisexuality *n.* sexual attraction to or sexual behavior with both men and women. Although much psychological research demonstrates the existence of a continuum of sexual attraction within most individuals, equal responsiveness to both sexes over the lifespan is relatively rare, appearing to be more common in women than in men and varying across cultures. —**bisexual** *adj., n.*

bisphenol A (BPA) a chemical compound used to produce polycarbonate plastics, such as plastic water and baby bottles, and the epoxy resins found in the lining of food cans, water supply pipes, and other metal products. The U.S. Food and Drug Administration has "some concern" (on a scale of "negligible concern" to "serious concern") about the effects of BPA exposure on the brain and behavior of fetuses, infants, and children; it is working to limit exposure and, with the Environmental Protection Agency and other agencies, to evaluate further BPA's health consequences. See also ENDOCRINE DISRUPTOR.

bit *n.* **1.** in computing, a variable that can take only the values of zero or one. [bi(nary) + (digi)t] **2.** in information theory, the quantity of information that decreases uncertainty or the germane alternatives of a problem by one half. For example, if a dollar bill has been placed in one of 16 identical books standing side by side on a shelf, and one has to identify this book by asking a minimum number of questions that can be answered only by "yes" or "no," the best way to begin would be to ask if the book is to the right (or to the left) of center. The answer to this question would provide one bit of information.

bivariate *adj.* characterized by two variables or attributes. For example, a set of height and weight measurements for each participant in a study would be bivariate data. Compare UNIVARIATE. See also MULTIVARIATE.

black box a system in which both the input and output are observable but the processes that occur between them are unknown or not observable. Such internal processes must be hypothesized on the basis of known relationships between external factors and the resulting effects. For example, in the relationship between leadership ability (input) and on-the-job performance as a project manager (output), the role of the organizational climate could be considered a black box if it is not understood.

black box warning see BOXED WARNING.

blackout *n.* **1.** total loss of consciousness produced, for example, by sudden lowering of the blood supply to the brain or by decreased oxygen supply. **2.** amnesia produced by alcoholic intoxication.

black sheep effect the tendency to evaluate a disreputable or disliked person more negatively when that person is a member of one's own group rather than of some other group. Although an apparent contradiction of INGROUP BIAS, the black sheep effect is explained by SOCIAL IDENTITY THEORY: People respond negatively to those who act in ways that threaten their group's identity, particularly when they affiliate strongly with their group.

blaming the victim a social psychological phenomenon in which individuals or groups attempt to cope with the bad things that have happened to others by assigning blame to the victim of the trauma or tragedy. Victim blaming serves to create psychological distance between the blamer and the victim, may rationalize a failure to

intervene if the blamer was a bystander, and creates a psychological defense for the blamer against feelings of vulnerability.

blastocyst *n.* the mammalian EMBRYO at a very early stage of development. It consists of a tiny hollow sphere containing an inner cell mass, enclosed in a thin layer of cells that help implant the blastocyst in the uterine lining.

blended family see STEPFAMILY.

blind *adj.* **1.** denoting a lack of sight. See BLINDNESS. **2.** denoting a lack of awareness. In research, a blind procedure may be employed deliberately to enhance experimental control: A **single blind** is a procedure in which participants are unaware of the experimental conditions under which they are operating; a **double blind** is a procedure in which both the participants and the experimenters interacting with them are unaware of the particular experimental conditions; and a **triple blind** is a procedure in which the participants, experimenters, and data analysts are all unaware of the particular experimental conditions.

blindness *n.* profound, near-total, or total impairment of the ability to perceive visual stimuli, with legal blindness defined in the United States as visual acuity of 20/200 or less in the better eye with best correction or a visual field of 20° or less in the widest meridian of the better eye. Major causes include inoperable CATARACT, uncontrolled GLAUCOMA, age-related MACULAR DEGENERATION, diabetes, rubella, and brain injury. —**blind** *adj.*

blindsight *n.* the capacity of some individuals with damage to the STRIATE CORTEX to detect and even localize visual stimuli presented to the blind portion of the visual field. Discrimination of movement, flicker, wavelength, and orientation may also be present. However, these visual capacities are not accompanied by conscious awareness. The causes of blindsight are the subject of some debate. See also DEAF HEARING; NUMBSENSE.

blind spot 1. the area of the monocular visual field in which stimulation cannot be perceived because the image falls on the site of the OPTIC DISK. **2.** a lack of insight or awareness—often persistent—about a specific area of one's behavior or personality, typically because recognition of one's true feelings and motives would be painful.

block design a type of research study in which participants are divided into relatively homogeneous subsets (blocks) from which they are assigned to the experimental or treatment conditions. For example, in a simple block design to evaluate the efficacy of several antidepressants, participants with similar pretest depression scores might be grouped into homogeneous blocks and then assigned to receive different medications. The purpose of a block design is to ensure that a characteristic of the study participants that is related to the target outcome (i.e., a COVARIATE) is distributed equally across treatment conditions.

blocking *n.* **1.** a process in which one's flow of thought or speech is suddenly interrupted. The individual is suddenly aware of not being able to perform a particular mental act, such as finding the words to express something that he or she wishes to say. **2.** the process of grouping research participants into relatively homogeneous subsets on the basis of a particular characteristic. Such blocking helps adjust for preexisting patterns of variation between experimental units. See BLOCK DESIGN.

blood alcohol concentration (**BAC**) the amount of ETHANOL in the bloodstream after alcohol consumption, measured as a percentage. In the United States, the limit at which it becomes a crime to drive after drinking is generally 0.08% (i.e., 0.08 g of alcohol per 100 mL of blood). Also called **blood alcohol level** (**BAL**).

blood–brain barrier a semipermeable barrier formed by cells lining the blood capillaries that supply the brain and other parts of the central nervous system. It prevents large molecules, including many drugs, from passing from the blood to the fluid surrounding brain cells and to the cerebrospinal fluid, thus protecting the brain from potentially harmful substances. Ions and small molecules, such as water, oxygen, carbon dioxide, and alcohol, can cross relatively freely. Entry is also possible for lipid-soluble compounds, such as anesthetics, which diffuse through plasma membranes.

blood phobia a persistent and irrational fear of blood, specifically of seeing blood. An individual confronting blood experiences a subjective feeling of disgust and fears the consequences of the situation, such as fainting.

blood pressure the pressure exerted by the blood against the walls of blood vessels, especially arteries. It varies with the strength of the heartbeat, the elasticity of the artery walls and resistance of the arterioles, and the person's health, age, and state of activity. See also HYPERTENSION.

bodily-kinesthetic intelligence in the MULTIPLE-INTELLIGENCES THEORY, the skills involved in forming and coordinating bodily movements, such as dancing, playing a violin, or playing basketball.

body *n.* **1.** the entire physical structure of an organism, such as the human body. **2.** the main part of a structure or organ, such as the body of the penis. **3.** a discrete anatomical or cytological structure, such as the MAMMILLARY BODY.

body dysmorphic disorder (**BDD**) a SOMATOFORM DISORDER characterized by excessive preoccupation with an imagined defect in physical appearance or markedly excessive concern with a slight physical anomaly. The preoccupation is typically accompanied by frequent checking of the defect.

body image the mental picture one forms of one's body as a whole, including its physical characteristics (**body percept**) and one's attitudes toward these characteristics (**body concept**).

body language the expression of feelings and thoughts, which may or may not be verbalized, through posture, gesture, facial expression, or other movements. For example, anger is usually indicated by a facial expression in which there are downward lines in the forehead, cheeks, and mouth, and the hands may be clenched. Body language is often called NONVERBAL COMMUNICATION.

body mass index (**BMI**) a widely used measure of adiposity or obesity based on the following formula: weight (kg) divided by height squared (m²).

bonding *n.* the process in which ATTACHMENTS or other close relationships are formed between individuals, especially between mother and infant. An early, positive relationship between a mother and a newborn child is considered by some theorists to be essential in establishing unconditional love on the part of the parent, as well as security and trust on the part of the child. In subsequent development, bonding establishes friendship and trust.

Bonferroni *t* test see DUNN–BONFERRONI PROCEDURE. [Carlo Emilio **Bonferroni** (1892–1960), Italian mathematician]

boomerang effect a situation in which a persuasive message produces attitude change in the direction opposite to that intended. Boomerang effects occur when recipients generate counterarguments substantially stronger than the arguments contained in the original message.

bootstrapping *n.* **1.** any process or operation in which a system uses its initial resources to develop more powerful and complex processing routines, which are then used in the same fashion, and so on cumulatively. In LAN-

GUAGE ACQUISITION, for example, the term describes children's ability to learn complex linguistic rules, which can be endlessly reapplied, from extremely limited data. **2.** a statistical technique to estimate the variance of a PARAMETER when standard assumptions about the shape of the data set (e.g., it follows a NORMAL DISTRIBUTION) are not met. In this procedure, a subset of values is taken from the data set, a quantity (e.g., the mean) is calculated, and the values are reinserted into the data; this sequence is repeated a given number of times. From the resulting set of calculated values (e.g., the set of means), the summary value of interest is calculated (e.g., the standard deviation of the mean). —**bootstrap** *vb.*

borderline 1. *adj.* pertaining to any phenomenon difficult to categorize because it straddles two distinct classes, showing characteristics of both. Thus, **borderline intelligence** is supposed to show characteristics of both the average and subaverage categories. **2.** *n.* an informal or shorthand designation for someone with BORDERLINE PERSONALITY DISORDER or its symptoms.

borderline personality disorder a personality disorder characterized by a long-standing pattern of instability in mood, interpersonal relationships, and self-image that is severe enough to cause extreme distress or interfere with social and occupational functioning. Symptoms include impulsive behavior (e.g., gambling, indiscriminate sex, overeating, substance abuse); intense but unstable relationships; uncontrollable temper outbursts; combativeness; DELIBERATE SELF-HARM; and chronic feelings of emptiness and boredom.

bottom-up processing INFORMATION PROCESSING in which incoming stimulus data initiate and determine the higher level processes involved in their recognition, interpretation, and categorization. For example, in vision, features would be combined into objects, and objects into scenes, recognition of which would be based only on the information in the stimulus input. Typically, perceptual or cognitive mechanisms use bottom-up processing when information is unfamiliar or highly complex. Compare TOP-DOWN PROCESSING. See also SHALLOW PROCESSING.

box-and-whisker plot a graphical display of the central value, variance, and extreme values in a data set. A rectangle (box) is drawn along the vertical y-axis of the plot, which shows the range of data values. The length of the box indicates the middle 50% of scores and its two ends indicate the upper and lower HINGES. Lines (whiskers) extending outward from the box denote variation in the upper and lower 25% of scores, while a separate line within the box indicates the score that falls in the very middle of the set (i.e., the MEDIAN). Stars or other single points indicate extreme scores. A box-and-whisker plot can be used to compare data sets when large numbers of observations are involved. Also called **boxplot**.

boxed warning an alert strongly recommended by the U.S. Food and Drug Administration to be included in the LABELING of medications that have been found to have particularly serious or life-threatening side effects or that should be prescribed only under certain circumstances or to certain patient populations. The warning must be prominently displayed and in bold type. Also called **black box warning**.

bradycardia n. see ARRHYTHMIA.

bradykinesia n. abnormal slowness in the execution of voluntary movements. Also called **bradykinesis**. Compare HYPOKINESIS. —**bradykinetic** adj.

brain n. the enlarged, anterior part of the CENTRAL NERVOUS SYSTEM within the skull. The brain develops by differentiation of the embryonic NEURAL TUBE along an anterior–posterior axis to form three main regions—the FOREBRAIN, MIDBRAIN, and HINDBRAIN—that can be further subdivided on the basis

of anatomical and functional criteria. The cortical tissue is concentrated in the forebrain, and the midbrain and hindbrain structures are often considered together as the BRAINSTEM. Also called **encephalon**.

brain-based learning see NEUROEDUCATION.

brain–computer interface (BCI) a system that translates the electrical activity of the brain into signals controlling external displays and devices, such as cursors on computer screens, Internet browsers, robotic arms, switches, or prostheses. This muscle-independent arrangement aims to help people with motor functions severely limited by injuries, progressive neurodegenerative diseases, or other conditions to communicate, manipulate objects in the environment, and otherwise enhance their independence and quality of life. Also called **brain–machine interface** (BMI).

brain concussion see CONCUSSION.

brain damage injury to the brain. It can have various causes, including prenatal infection, birth injury, head injury, toxic agents, brain tumor, brain inflammation, severe seizures, certain metabolic disorders, vitamin deficiency, intracranial hemorrhage, stroke, and surgical procedures. Brain damage is manifested by impairment of cognitive, motor, or sensory skills mediated by the brain.

brain localization theory any of various theories that different areas of the brain serve different functions. Since the early 19th century, opinion has varied between notions of highly precise localization and a belief that the brain, or large portions of it, functions as a whole. Many modern techniques, including localized electrical stimulation of the brain, electrical recording from the brain, and brain imaging, have added information about localization of function. For many investigators, however, the concept of extreme parcellation of functions has given way to concepts of distributed control by collective activity of different regions.

brain–machine interface (BMI) see BRAIN–COMPUTER INTERFACE.

brainstem *n.* the part of the brain that connects the cerebrum with the spinal cord. It includes the MIDBRAIN, PONS, and MEDULLA OBLONGATA and is involved in the autonomic control of visceral activity, such as salivation, respiration, heartbeat, and digestion.

brain stimulation the use of ELECTRICAL STIMULATION, TRANSCRANIAL MAGNETIC STIMULATION, or other methods to stimulate specific areas of the brain as a means of determining their functions and their effects on behavior and as a therapeutic technique.

brainstorming *n.* a problem-solving strategy in which ideas are generated spontaneously and uninhibitedly, usually in a group setting, without any immediate critical judgment about their potential value. —**brainstorm** *vb.*

brainwashing *n.* a broad class of intense and often coercive tactics intended to produce profound changes in attitudes, beliefs, and emotions. Targets of such tactics have typically been prisoners of war and members of religious cults.

brain waves spontaneous, rhythmic electrical impulses emanating from different areas of the brain. According to their frequencies, brain waves are classified as ALPHA WAVES (8–12 Hz), BETA WAVES (13–30 Hz), DELTA WAVES (1–3 Hz), GAMMA WAVES (31–80 Hz), or THETA WAVES (4–7 Hz).

breakthrough *n.* a significant, sometimes sudden, forward step in therapy, especially after an unproductive plateau.

Brief Psychiatric Rating Scale (**BPRS**) a system of evaluating the presence and severity of clinical psychiatric signs on the basis of 24 factors, such as bizarre behavior, hostility, emotional withdrawal, and disorientation. Each factor is rated on a 7-point scale

ranging from *not present* to *extremely severe*, based on the judgments of trained observers.

brief psychodynamic psychotherapy a set of time-limited PSYCHODYNAMIC PSYCHOTHERAPY approaches intended to enhance client self-awareness and understanding of the influence of the past on present behavior. One particularly important issue is identified as the central focus for the treatment, thus creating a structure and establishing a goal for the sessions. Rather than allowing the client to associate freely and discuss seemingly unconnected issues, the brief psychodynamic therapist is expected to be fairly active in keeping the session focused on the main issue. The number of sessions varies from one approach to another, but the therapy is typically considered to involve no more than 25 sessions. Also called **short-term psychodynamic psychotherapy**.

brief psychotherapy any form of psychotherapy intended to achieve positive change during a short period (generally 10–20 sessions). Brief psychotherapies rely on active techniques of inquiry, focus, and goal setting and tend to be symptom specific. They may be applied on an individual or group level and are used in the treatment of a variety of behavioral and emotional problems. There are numerous different types, such as brief COGNITIVE BEHAVIOR THERAPY, brief PLAY THERAPY, BRIEF PSYCHODYNAMIC PSYCHOTHERAPY, FOCAL PSYCHOTHERAPY, and INTERPERSONAL PSYCHOTHERAPY. Also called **short-term psychotherapy**.

brief psychotic disorder a disturbance involving the sudden onset of at least one psychotic symptom (e.g., incoherence, delusions, hallucinations, grossly disorganized or catatonic behavior). The condition lasts no longer than a month, with complete remission of all symptoms and a full return to previous levels of functioning.

brightness *n.* the perceptual correlate of light intensity. The brightness of a stimulus depends on its amplitude (energy), wavelength, the ADAPTATION state of the observer, and the nature of any surrounding or intervening stimuli.

brightness constancy the tendency to perceive a familiar object as having the same brightness under different conditions of illumination. For example, a piece of white paper has a similar brightness in daylight as it does at dusk, even though the energy it reflects may be quite different. Brightness constancy is one of the PERCEPTUAL CONSTANCIES. Also called **lightness constancy**.

Broca's aphasia one of eight classically identified APHASIAS, characterized by nonfluent conversational speech and slow, halting speech production. Auditory comprehension is relatively good for everyday conversation, but there is considerable difficulty with complex syntax or multistep commands. The ability to write is impaired as well. It is associated with injury to Broca's area. [Paul **Broca** (1824–1880), French physician and anthropologist]

Broca's area a region of the posterior portion of the inferior frontal convolution of a CEREBRAL HEMISPHERE that is associated with the production of speech. [discovered in the 1860s and studied and researched by Paul **Broca**]

Brodmann's area an area of cerebral cortex characterized by variation in the occurrence and arrangement of cells (see CYTOARCHITECTURE) from that of neighboring areas. These areas are identified by numbers and in many cases have been associated with specific brain functions, such as area 17 (STRIATE CORTEX, or primary visual cortex), areas 18 and 19 (PRESTRIATE CORTEX), and area 6 (PREMOTOR AREA). [Korbinian **Brodmann** (1868–1918), German neurologist]

brood parasitism a practice in which a female bird lays its eggs in the nest of another species, leaving the other parents to rear its chicks. The parasitic species may eject some of the eggs of the host species, and the young of the parasitic species often hatch earlier and beg more intensively than the surviving host brood, successfully competing for food against the foster parents' own offspring.

buffering *n.* the protection against the effects of stressful experiences that is afforded by an individual's social support. —**buffer** *vb.*

bulimia *n.* insatiable hunger for food. It may have physiological causes, such as a brain lesion or endocrine disturbance, or be primarily a psychological disorder. —**bulimic** *adj., n.*

bulimia nervosa an eating disorder involving recurrent episodes of binge eating (i.e., discrete periods of uncontrolled consumption of abnormally large quantities of food) followed by inappropriate compensatory behaviors (e.g., self-induced vomiting, misuse of laxatives, fasting, excessive exercise). Compare BINGE-EATING DISORDER.

bullying *n.* persistent threatening and aggressive physical behavior or verbal abuse directed toward other people, especially those who are younger, smaller, weaker, or in some other situation of relative disadvantage. **Cyberbullying** is verbally threatening or harassing behavior conducted through such electronic technology as websites, e-mail, and text messaging.

burnout *n.* physical, emotional, or mental exhaustion accompanied by decreased motivation, lowered performance, and negative attitudes toward oneself and others. It results from performing at a high level until stress and tension, especially from extreme and prolonged physical or mental exertion or an overburdening workload, take their toll. Burnout is most often observed in professionals who work in service-oriented vocations (e.g., social workers, teachers, correctional officers) and experience chronic high levels of stress.

buspirone *n.* an anxiolytic that produces relief of subjective symptoms of
anxiety without the sedation, behavioral disinhibition, and risk of dependence associated with the BENZODIAZ-
EPINES. Its use has been limited,
however, by its relative lack of efficacy
compared with benzodiazepines.

butyrophenone *n.* any of a class of
ANTIPSYCHOTICS used primarily in the
treatment of schizophrenia, mania, and
severe agitation. They are associated
with TARDIVE DYSKINESIA and numerous EXTRAPYRAMIDAL SYMPTOMS.

butyrylcholinesterase (BuChE)
n. see CHOLINESTERASE.

bystander effect a phenomenon in
which people fail to offer needed help in
emergencies, especially when other
people are present in the same setting.
Research on this tendency has identified a number of psychological and
interpersonal processes that inhibit
helping, including misinterpreting
other people's lack of response as an
indication that help is not needed,
CONFUSION OF RESPONSIBILITY, and
DIFFUSION OF RESPONSIBILITY.

Cc

caffeine *n.* a central nervous system stimulant found in coffee, tea, cola, cocoa, chocolate, and certain prescribed and over-the-counter medications. Its effects include rapid breathing, increased pulse rate and blood pressure, and diminished fatigue. Precise effects vary with the amount ingested and the tolerance of the individual. Moderate doses produce an improved flow of thought and clearness of ideas, together with increased respiratory and vasomotor activity; large doses may make concentration or continued attention difficult and cause insomnia, headaches, and confusion in some individuals.

calcium-channel blocker any of a class of drugs used in the treatment of hypertension and abnormal heart rhythms (arrhythmias). Calcium-channel blockers inhibit the flow of calcium ions into the smooth-muscle cells of blood vessels and the cells of heart muscle, which need calcium to contract, thus inducing prolonged relaxation of the muscles.

canalization *n.* **1.** the containment of variation of certain characters within narrow bounds so that expression of underlying genetic variation is repressed. It is a developmental mechanism that maintains a constant PHENOTYPE over a range of different environments in which an organism might normally occur. **2.** the hypothetical process by which repeated use of a neural pathway leads to greater ease of transmission of impulses and hence its establishment as permanent.

cancer *n.* any one of a group of diseases characterized by the unregulated, abnormal growth of cells to form malignant tumors (see NEOPLASM), which invade neighboring tissues; the abnormal cells generally are capable of spreading via the bloodstream or lymphatic system to other body areas or organs by the process of metastasis. Causes of cancer are numerous but commonly include viruses, environmental toxins, diet, and inherited genetic variations. Cancers generally are classified as carcinomas if they involve the epithelium (e.g., lungs, stomach, or skin) and sarcomas if the affected tissues are connective (e.g., bone, muscle, or fat). More than 150 different kinds of cancer have been identified in humans, based on cell types, rate of growth, and other factors. —**cancerous** *adj.*

cannabidiol (CBD) *n.* a CANNABINOID that lacks the psychoactive properties of delta-9-TETRAHYDROCANNABINOL but shares its antiinflammatory and other medical properties. Its potential roles in the management of a wide range of medical conditions are being studied.

cannabinoid *n.* any of a class of about 60 substances in the CANNABIS plant that includes those responsible for the psychoactive properties of the plant. The most important cannabinoid is TETRAHYDROCANNABINOL.

cannabis *n.* any of three related plant species (*Cannabis sativa, C. indica,* or *C. ruderalis*) whose dried flowering or fruiting tops or leaves are widely used as a recreational drug, known as **marijuana**. When smoked, the principal psychoactive agent in these plants, delta-9-TETRAHYDROCANNABINOL (THC), is rapidly absorbed into the blood and almost immediately distributed to the brain, causing the rapid onset of subjective effects that last 2 to 3 hours. These effects include a sense of euphoria or well-being, easy laughter, perceptual distortions, impairment of concentration and short-term memory, and craving for food. Tolerance to the effects of THC develops with repeated use, and a withdrawal syndrome has been identified.

Cannon–Bard theory the theory that emotional states result from the influence of lower brain centers (the hypothalamus and thalamus) on higher ones (the cortex), rather than from sensory feedback to the brain produced by peripheral internal organs and voluntary musculature. According to this theory, the thalamus controls the experience of emotion, and the hypothalamus controls the expression of emotion, both of which occur simultaneously. [proposed in the 1920s and early 1930s by Walter B. **Cannon** (1871–1945) and Philip **Bard** (1898–1977), U.S. physiologists]

canonical analysis any of a class of statistical procedures used to assess the degree of relationship between sets of variables via interpretation of a limited number of linear combinations of specific values of those variables. The overall objective of such procedures is to reduce the DIMENSIONALITY of the data under investigation. Examples include MULTIPLE REGRESSION and MULTIVARIATE ANALYSIS OF VARIANCE, among others.

capacity *n.* the maximum ability of an individual to receive or retain information and knowledge or to function in mental or physical tasks. Capacity in turn determines his or her potential for intellectual or creative development or accomplishment.

carcinogen *n.* any substance that initiates the development of CANCER (**carcinogenesis**) when exposed to living tissue. Tobacco smoke, which induces lung cancer, is an example. —**carcinogenic** *adj.*

cardiac muscle the specialized muscle tissue of the heart. It consists of striated fibers that branch and interlock and are in electrical continuity with each other. This arrangement permits ACTION POTENTIALS to spread rapidly

from cell to cell, allowing large groups of cells to contract in unison.

cardiac psychology a subspecialty of BEHAVIORAL MEDICINE that studies how behavioral, emotional, and social factors influence the development, progression, and treatment of CORONARY HEART DISEASE (CHD). Among the psychosocial factors linked to the onset and exacerbation of CHD are anger, hostility, anxiety, depression, psychological stress, job stress, and lack of social support. Contextual factors, including socioeconomic status and ethnicity, may also contribute to CHD. **Cardiac psychologists** design interventions to prevent the disease or improve the prognosis and quality of life of those who already have it. These interventions focus on the nonphysical aspects of adopting and maintaining healthier lifestyles (e.g., learning relaxation, time management, and stress management skills). Also called **behavioral cardiology**; **psychocardiology**.

cardiovascular (**CV**) *adj.* relating to the heart and blood vessels or to blood circulation.

cardiovascular disease any disease, congenital or acquired, that affects the heart and blood vessels. Cardiovascular diseases include HYPERTENSION, congestive heart failure, ARTERIOSCLEROSIS, and CORONARY HEART DISEASE.

caregiver *n.* a person who attends to the needs of and provides assistance to someone else who is not fully independent, such as an infant or an ill adult. A person who does the majority of the work is called the **primary caregiver**. —**caregiving** *n.*, *adj.*

caregiver burden the stress and other psychological symptoms experienced by family members and other nonprofessional caregivers in response to looking after individuals with mental or physical disabilities, disorders, or diseases.

carrier *n.* **1.** an individual who is infected with a pathogen for a disease and is capable of infecting others but does not develop the disease. **2.** an individual who has a mutation in a gene that conveys either increased susceptibility to a disease or other condition or the certainty that the condition will develop.

carrier wave see MODULATION.

carryover effect the effect on the current performance of a research participant of the experimental conditions that preceded the current conditions. For example, in a crossover design in which a particular drug is administered to nonhuman animals in the first experimental condition, a carryover effect would be evident if the drug continued to exert an influence on the animals' performance during a subsequent experimental condition. Also called **holdover effect**.

CART analysis classification and regression tree analysis: a method of classifying data into successively smaller and more homogeneous subgroups according to a set of PREDICTOR VARIABLES. CART analysis is similar to but distinct from REGRESSION ANALYSIS in its homogeneity of case subsets. The results of a CART analysis may be displayed in a diagram resembling a tree—subsets of data, based on values of the outcome variable, are shown to branch off from higher level subsets of data.

Cartesian dualism the position taken by French philosopher and mathematician René Descartes (1596–1650) that the world comprises two distinct and incompatible classes of substance: *res extensa*, or extended substance, which extends through space; and *res cogitans*, or thinking substance, which has no extension in space. The body (including the brain) is composed of extended and divisible substance, whereas the mind is not. Descartes accepted that there is interaction between mind and body, holding that in some activities the mind operates independently of bodily influences, whereas in others the body exerts an influence. Similarly, in some bodily activities there is influence from the mind, whereas in others there is not. To the question of how such incompatible substances can interact at all, Descartes had no answer. See DUALISM; MIND–BODY PROBLEM.

case history a record of information relating to a person's psychological or medical condition. Used as an aid to diagnosis and treatment, it usually contains test results; interview transcripts; professional evaluations; and sociological, occupational, and educational data. See also PATIENT HISTORY.

case study an in-depth investigation of a single individual, family, event, or other entity. Multiple types of data (psychological, physiological, biographical, environmental) are assembled, for example, to understand an individual's background, relationships, and behavior. Although case studies allow for intensive analysis of an issue, they are limited in the extent to which their findings may be generalized.

castration anxiety fear of injury to or loss of the genitals. As posited in classical psychoanalytic theory, the various losses and deprivations experienced by the infant boy may give rise to the fear that he will also lose his penis.

castration complex in classical psychoanalytic theory, the whole combination of the child's unconscious feelings and fantasies associated with being deprived of the PHALLUS, which in boys means the loss of the penis and in girls the belief that it has already been removed. It derives from the discovery that girls have no penis and is closely tied to the OEDIPUS COMPLEX.

catabolism *n.* see METABOLISM. `—**catabolic** *adj.*

catalepsy *n.* a state of unresponsiveness in which a fixed body posture or physical attitude is maintained over a long period of time. It is seen in CATATONIC SCHIZOPHRENIA, EPILEPSY, and other disorders. —**cataleptic** *adj.*

cataplexy *n.* a sudden loss of muscle tone that may be localized, causing (for example) loss of grasp or head nodding, or generalized, resulting in collapse of the entire body. It is a temporary condition usually precipitated by an extreme emotional stimulus. —**cataplectic** *adj.*

cataract *n.* a progressive clouding (opacification) of the lens of the eye that eventually results in severe visual impairment if untreated. Central vision in particular is impaired, with symptoms including dim or fuzzy vision, sensitivity to glare, and difficulty seeing at night. Cataract is frequently associated with the degenerative processes of aging, but it may also be congenital or due to disease or injury.

catastrophe theory a mathematical theory regarding discontinuous (discrete) changes in one variable as a function of continuous change in some other variable or variables. It proposes that a small change in one factor may cause an abrupt and large change in another. An example is the dramatic change in the physical properties of water as the temperature reaches 0 °C or 100 °C (32 °F or 212 °F).

catatonia *n.* a state of muscular rigidity or other disturbance of motor behavior, such as CATALEPSY, extreme overactivity, or adoption of bizarre postures. —**catatonic** *adj.*

catatonic schizophrenia a relatively rare subtype of schizophrenia characterized by motor immobility interspersed with excessive motor activity. Other common features include extreme negativism (apparently motiveless resistance to all instructions), MUTISM, ECHOLALIA, or ECHOPRAXIA.

catecholamine *n.* any of a class of BIOGENIC AMINES formed by a catechol molecule and an amine group. Derived from tyrosine, catecholamines include dopamine, epinephrine, and norepinephrine, which are the predominant neurotransmitters in the SYMPATHETIC NERVOUS SYSTEM.

categorical data information that consists of counts or observations in specific categories rather than measurements. Categorical data that have a meaningful order are referred to more specifically as ORDINAL DATA, whereas categorical data without a meaningful order are known as NOMINAL DATA.

categorical perception in speech perception, the phenomenon in which a continuous acoustic dimension, such as VOICE-ONSET TIME, is perceived as having distinct categories with sharp discontinuities at certain points. Whereas discrimination is much more accurate between categories, individuals tested often are unable to discriminate between acoustically different stimuli that fall within the same categorical boundaries. Categorical perception is crucial in the identification of PHONEMES.

categorical scale a sequence of numbers that identify items as belonging to mutually exclusive categories. For example, a categorical scale for the political party affiliation of a group of Americans might use 1 to denote Republican, 2 to denote Democrat, and 3 to denote Independent. When the number sequence has a meaningful order a categorical scale is more precisely called an ORDINAL SCALE; when it is devoid of such meaningful order it is known as a NOMINAL SCALE.

categorical variable a variable that is defined by a set of two or more categories. Examples include a person's sex, marital status, or rankings of particular stimuli (such as the relative loudness of different sounds).

categorization *n.* the process by which objects, events, people, or experiences are grouped into classes on the basis of (a) characteristics shared by members of the same class and (b) features distinguishing the members of one class from those of another. Also called **classification**. —**categorize** *vb.*

catharsis *n.* in psychoanalytic theory, the discharge of previously repressed affects connected to traumatic events that occurs when these events are brought back into consciousness and reexperienced. This is understood, more generally, as the release of strong, pent-up emotions. See also ABREACTION. [from Greek, literally: "purgation," "purification"] —**cathartic** *adj.*

cathexis *n.* in psychoanalytic theory, the investment of PSYCHIC ENERGY in an OBJECT of any kind, such as a wish, fantasy, person, goal, idea, social group, or the self. Such objects are said to be **cathected** when an individual attaches emotional significance (positive or negative affect) to them.

Cattell–Horn theory of intelligence a theory proposing that there are two main kinds of intellectual abilities nested under general intelligence: *g-c*, or **crystallized intelligence** (or **ability**), which is the sum of one's knowledge and is measured by tests of vocabulary, general information, and so forth; and *g-f*, or **fluid intelligence** (or **ability**), which is the set of mental processes that is used in dealing with relatively novel tasks and is used in the acquisition of *g-c*. [British psychologist Raymond B. **Cattell** (1905–1998) originally developed the theory in the 1940s; John L. **Horn** (1928–2006), a U.S. psychologist, subsequently contributed to the theory beginning in the 1960s]

caudal *adj.* **1.** pertaining to a tail. **2.** situated at or toward the tail end of an organism. Compare ROSTRAL.

caudate nucleus one of the BASAL GANGLIA, so named because it has a long extension, or tail.

causality *n.* in philosophy, the position that all events have causes, that is, that they are consequences of antecedent events. Traditionally, causality has been seen as an essential assumption of NATURALISM and all scientific explanation, although some have questioned whether causality is a necessary assumption of science. See also CAUSATION; DETERMINISM. —**causal** *adj.*

causal variable see INDEPENDENT VARIABLE.

causation *n.* the empirical relation between two events, states, or variables such that change in one (the cause) brings about change in the other (the effect). See also CAUSALITY. —**causal** *adj.*

cautious shift a CHOICE SHIFT in which an individual making a decision as part of a group adopts a more cautious approach than the same individual would have adopted had he or she made the decision alone. Studies suggest that such shifts are rarer than the opposite RISKY SHIFT.

ceiling age the lowest MENTAL AGE level at which a participant on a standardized test answers all the items incorrectly. The concept of mental ages is used relatively rarely in current testing. Compare BASAL AGE.

ceiling effect a situation in which the majority of values obtained for a variable approach the upper limit of the scale used in its measurement. For example, a test whose items are too easy for those taking it would show a ceiling effect because most people would achieve or be close to the highest possible score. In other words, the test scores would exhibit SKEWNESS and have little VARIANCE, thus prohibiting meaningful analysis of the results. Compare FLOOR EFFECT.

cell *n.* **1.** the basic unit of organized tissue, consisting of an outer plasma membrane, the NUCLEUS, and various organelles (specialized membrane-bound structures) in a watery fluid together comprising the **cytoplasm**. **2.** a combination of two or more characteristics represented by the intersection of a row and a column in a statistical table. A tabular display resulting from a study of handedness in men and women, for instance, might consist of four cells: left-handed females, left-handed males, right-handed females, and right-handed males.

cell assembly a group of neurons that are repeatedly active at the same time and develop as a single functional unit, which may become active when any of its constituent neurons is stimulated. This enables, for example, a person to form a complete mental image of an object when only a portion is visible or to recall a memory from a partial cue. Cell assembly is influential in biological theories of learning and memory.

cell body the part of a NEURON (nerve cell) that contains the nucleus and most organelles. Also called **soma**.

cell death see PROGRAMMED CELL DEATH.

cellular respiration see RESPIRATION.

censor *n.* in psychoanalytic theory, the mental agency, located in the PRE-CONSCIOUS, that is responsible for REPRESSION. The censor is posited to determine which of one's wishes, thoughts, and ideas may enter consciousness and which must be kept unconscious because they violate one's conscience or society's standards or are in conflict with other wishes or perceptions, or because the affect associated with them is disturbing or overwhelming. The idea was introduced in the early writings of Austrian neurologist Sigmund Freud (1856–1939), who later developed it into the concept of the SUPEREGO. —**censorship** *n.*

censoring *n.* the situation in which some observations are missing from a set of data. Censoring is common in studies of survival time, in which the research often ends before the event of interest occurs for all study units.

centile *n.* a shortened name for PERCENTILE.

central canal the channel in the center of the spinal cord, which contains CEREBROSPINAL FLUID.

central dyslexia an acquired DYS-

LEXIA characterized by difficulties with the pronunciation and comprehension of written words. Unlike in VISUAL WORD-FORM DYSLEXIA, the visual analysis system of the brain is intact, and the damage is to other, higher level brain pathways and systems involved in reading (e.g., the semantic system).

central executive a component of WORKING MEMORY that manages the activities of the PHONOLOGICAL LOOP and VISUOSPATIAL SKETCHPAD. The central executive thus performs such varied functions as focusing attention on and switching attention between different tasks, dividing attention between simultaneous tasks, and initiating long-term memory ENCODING and RETRIEVAL. Despite its crucial role, however, the central executive is of limited capacity and does not have any storage ability of its own.

central fissure see CENTRAL SULCUS.

central gray see PERIAQUEDUCTAL GRAY.

central limit theorem (**CLT**) the statistical principle that the sum of independent values from any distribution will approach a NORMAL DISTRIBUTION as the number of values in the distribution increases. In other words, the larger the sample size, the more closely the sampling distribution approximates a normal distribution. The central limit theorem is used to justify the use of certain data analysis methods that rely on an assumption of normality.

central nervous system (**CNS**) the entire complex of NEURONS, AXONS, and supporting tissue that constitute the brain and spinal cord. The CNS is primarily involved in mental activities and in coordinating and integrating incoming sensory messages and outgoing motor messages. Compare PERIPHERAL NERVOUS SYSTEM.

central pattern generator any of the sets of neurons in the spinal cord capable of producing oscillatory behavior and thought to be involved in the control of locomotion and other tasks.

central processes see EXECUTIVE FUNCTIONS.

central route to persuasion the process by which attitudes are formed or changed as a result of carefully scrutinizing and thinking about the central merits of attitude-relevant information. See also ELABORATION-LIKELIHOOD MODEL. Compare PERIPHERAL ROUTE TO PERSUASION.

central sulcus a major cleft that passes roughly vertically along the lateral surface of each CEREBRAL HEMISPHERE from a point beginning near the top of the cerebrum. It marks the border between the FRONTAL LOBE and the PARIETAL LOBE. Also called **central fissure**.

central tendency the middle or center point of a set of scores. The central tendency of a sample data set, for instance, may be estimated by a number of different statistics (e.g., MEAN, MEDIAN, MODE).

centration *n.* in PIAGETIAN THEORY, the tendency of children in the PREOPERATIONAL STAGE to attend to one aspect of a problem, object, or situation at a time, to the exclusion of others. Compare DECENTRATION.

cephalocaudal *adj.* from head to tail, as in the long axis of the body. The term typically refers to the maturation of an embryo or infant, wherein the greatest development takes place at the top of the body (i.e., the head) before the lower parts (i.e., the arms, trunk, legs). Compare PROXIMODISTAL.

cerebellar ataxia poor muscular coordination due to damage in the cerebellum. Individuals cannot integrate voluntary movements and therefore find it difficult to stand or walk, feed themselves, and perform complex activities (e.g., playing the piano).

cerebellar cortex the GRAY MATTER, or unmyelinated nerve cells, covering the surface of the CEREBELLUM.

cerebellum *n.* (*pl.* **cerebella**) a portion of the HINDBRAIN dorsal to the rest of the BRAINSTEM, to which it is connected by the cerebellar peduncles. The cerebellum modulates muscular contractions to produce smooth, accurately timed BALLISTIC movements; it helps maintain equilibrium by predicting body positions ahead of actual body movements. [Latin, literally: "little brain," diminutive of CEREBRUM]

cerebral aqueduct a passage containing CEREBROSPINAL FLUID that extends through the MIDBRAIN to link the third and fourth cerebral VENTRICLES.

cerebral blindness see CORTICAL BLINDNESS.

cerebral cortex the layer of GRAY MATTER that covers the outside of the CEREBRAL HEMISPHERES in the brain and is associated with higher cognitive functions, such as language, learning, perception, and planning. It consists mostly of NEOCORTEX, which has six main layers of cells; regions of cerebral cortex that do not have six layers are known as ALLOCORTEX. Differences in the CYTOARCHITECTURE of the layers led to the recognition of distinct areas, called BRODMANN'S AREAS, many of which are known to serve different functions.

cerebral dominance the controlling or disproportionate influence on certain aspects of behavior by one CEREBRAL HEMISPHERE (e.g., language is typically left dominant in right-handed people). See HEMISPHERIC LATERALIZATION.

cerebral hemisphere either half (left or right) of the cerebrum. The hemispheres are separated by a deep LONGITUDINAL FISSURE, but they are connected by commissural, projection, and association fibers so that each side of the brain normally is linked to functions of tissues on either side of the body. See also HEMISPHERIC LATERALIZATION.

cerebral lateralization see HEMI-SPHERIC LATERALIZATION.

cerebral palsy (**CP**) a set of non-progressive movement and posture disorders that results from trauma to the brain occurring prenatally, during the birth process, or before the age of 5. Symptoms include spasticity, paralysis, unsteady gait, and speech abnormalities but these may be accompanied by disorders of any other brain function, resulting in cognitive changes, seizures, visual defects, tactile impairment, hearing loss, and intellectual disability.

cerebrospinal fluid (**CSF**) the fluid within the CENTRAL CANAL of the spinal cord, the four VENTRICLES of the brain, and the subarachnoid space of the brain. It serves as a watery cushion to protect vital tissues of the central nervous system from damage by shock pressure, and it mediates between blood vessels and brain tissue in exchange of materials, including nutrients.

cerebrovascular accident (**CVA**) a disorder of the brain arising from pathologies of its blood vessels, such as cerebral HEMORRHAGE, EMBOLISM, or THROMBOSIS, resulting in temporary or permanent alterations in cognition, motor and sensory skills, or levels of consciousness. This term is often used interchangeably with STROKE.

cerebrovascular disease a pathological condition of the blood vessels of the brain. It may manifest itself as symptoms of STROKE or a TRANSIENT IS-CHEMIC ATTACK.

cerebrum *n.* the largest part of the brain, forming most of the FOREBRAIN and lying in front of and above the cerebellum. It consists of two CEREBRAL HEMISPHERES bridged by the CORPUS CALLOSUM. Each hemisphere is divided into four main lobes: the FRONTAL LOBE, OCCIPITAL LOBE, PARIETAL LOBE, and TEMPORAL LOBE. The outer layer of the cerebrum—the CEREBRAL CORTEX—is intricately folded and composed of GRAY MATTER. Also called **telencephalon**. [Latin, literally: "brain"]

cesarean section (**caesarean section; C-section**) a surgical procedure in which incisions are made through a woman's abdominal and uterine walls to deliver a baby under circumstances in which vaginal delivery is inadvisable.

change agent a specific causative factor or element or an entire process that results in change, particularly in the sense of improvement. In psychotherapy research, a change agent may be a component or process in therapy that results in improvement in the behavior or psychological adaptation of a patient or client.

change blindness a failure to notice changes in the visual array appearing in two successive scenes. This is surprisingly common whenever the brief movement (the transient) that usually accompanies a change is somehow masked or interrupted. For example, experimental participants shown a picture of an airplane, then a blank screen, and then another picture of the same plane have difficulty detecting that in the second picture the plane is missing an engine. Such failures have also been documented in such real-world situations as automobile accidents, eyewitness identifications, military operations, and everyday interpersonal interactions.

chaos theory an area of mathematical theory that deals with nonlinear systems that are profoundly affected by their initial conditions, tiny variations in which can produce complex, unpredictable, and erratic effects. It has been applied by some psychological researchers to the study of human behavior. See COMPLEXITY THEORY; DYNAMIC SYSTEMS THEORY.

character strength a positive trait, such as kindness, teamwork, or hope, that is morally valued in its own right and contributes to the fulfillment of the self and others. See POSITIVE PSYCHOLOGY.

charisma *n.* the special quality of personality that enables an individual to attract and gain the confidence of others, particularly of large numbers of people. It is exemplified in outstanding political, social, and religious leaders. —**charismatic** *adj.*

chemical antagonism see ANTAGONIST.

chemical synapse a type of specialized junction through which a signal is transmitted from one neuron to another across the narrow gap (SYNAPTIC CLEFT) separating them through the release and diffusion of NEUROTRANSMITTER. Although slower than ELECTRICAL SYNAPSES, chemical synapses are more flexible and comprise the majority of neuronal junctions within the body. Because of this prevalence, the qualifier generally is omitted and SYNAPSE used alone to denote a chemical junction.

chemoaffinity hypothesis the notion that each neuron has a chemical identity that directs it to form synapses on the proper target cell during development.

chemoreceptor *n.* a sensory nerve ending, such as any of those in the TASTE BUDS or OLFACTORY EPITHELIUM, that is capable of reacting to certain chemical stimuli. In humans, there are hundreds of different taste receptor proteins and a total of about 300,000 TASTE CELLS. Humans also have about 1,000 types of OLFACTORY RECEPTORS and about 1,000 receptors of each type. Other mammals (e.g., dogs) may have ten times that number.

child abuse harm to a child caused by a parent or other caregiver. The harm may be physical (violence), sexual (violation or exploitation), psychological (causing emotional distress), or neglectful (failing to provide needed care). See also BATTERED-CHILD SYNDROME.

child advocacy any organized and structured interventions on behalf of children by professionals or institutions, often in relation to such issues as

special parenting needs, child abuse, and adoption or foster care.

child development the sequential changes in the behavior, cognition, and physiology of children as they grow from birth through adolescence. See DEVELOPMENTAL TASK.

child-directed speech the specialized REGISTER of speech that adults and older children use when talking to young children. It is simplified and often more grammatically correct than adult-directed speech. See also INFANT-DIRECTED SPEECH.

childhood *n.* the period between the end of infancy (about 2 years of age) and the onset of puberty (10–12 years of age). This period is sometimes divided into (a) early childhood, from 2 years through the preschool age of 5 or 6 years; (b) middle childhood, from 6 to 8–10 years of age; and (c) late childhood, or preadolescence, which is identified as the 2-year period before the onset of puberty and the beginning of ADOLESCENCE.

childhood amnesia the commonly experienced inability to recall events in one's life prior to about 3 years of age. Childhood amnesia has been attributed to the facts that (a) cognitive abilities necessary for encoding events for the long term have not yet fully developed and (b) parts of the brain responsible for remembering personal events have not yet matured. Also called **infantile amnesia**.

childhood disintegrative disorder a disorder characterized by a significant loss of two or more of the following: previously acquired language skills, social skills or adaptive behavior, bowel or bladder control, play, or motor skills. This regression in functioning follows a period of normal development and occurs between the ages of 2 and 10. Impairments in social interaction and communication are also evident.

child neglect the denial of attention,

care, or affection considered essential for the normal development of a child's physical, emotional, and intellectual qualities, usually due to indifference from, disregard by, or impairment in the child's caregivers.

chi-square (symbol: χ^2) *n.* a statistic that is the sum of the squared differences between the observed scores in a data set and the EXPECTED VALUE. That is, to obtain the chi-square one finds the difference between each observed score and the expected score, squares that difference, and divides by the expected score; finally, one adds the resulting values for each score in the set. The smaller the chi-square, the more likely it is that the model from which the expected score is obtained provides a legitimate representation of the phenomenon being measured.

chi-square distribution (χ^2 **distribution**) a distribution of the sums of independent squared differences between the observed scores in a data set and the expected score for the set. If a random sample is repeatedly drawn from a normal population and measured on some variable and the obtained scores transformed via STANDARDIZATION, multiplied by themselves, and then added, the result will be a chi-square distribution with DEGREES OF FREEDOM equal to the size of the samples drawn.

chi-square test any of various procedures that use a CHI-SQUARE DISTRIBUTION to evaluate how well a theory fits a set of observed data. Unless otherwise specified, this term usually refers to the **chi-square test for independence**, used to determine whether there is a relationship between two variables whose values are categories. For example, it may be used to test whether sex (male vs. female) is unrelated to having a household pet (yes vs. no). It compares observed data to the data that would be expected in each cell of a CONTINGENCY TABLE if the two variables were entirely independent. This discrepancy between observed and expected counts is then used to compute the CHI-SQUARE statistic.

chlorpromazine (**CPZ**) *n.* the first synthesized ANTIPSYCHOTIC agent, effective in managing the acute symptoms of schizophrenia, acute mania, and other psychoses. Associated with a number of unwanted adverse effects, including TARDIVE DYSKINESIA, chlorpromazine has been largely supplanted by newer antipsychotic agents but is still used as a referent for dose equivalency of other antipsychotics. U.S. trade name: **Thorazine**.

choice reaction time the total time that elapses between the presentation of a stimulus and the occurrence of a response in a task that requires a participant to make one of several different responses depending on which one of several different stimuli is presented. In other words, the participant must make a conscious decision before responding. Also called **complex reaction time**; **compound reaction time**. Compare SIMPLE REACTION TIME.

choice shift any change in an individual's choices or decisions that occurs as a result of group discussion, as measured by comparing his or her prediscussion and postdiscussion responses. In many cases, a RISKY SHIFT is seen within the group as a whole. See also CAUTIOUS SHIFT.

cholecystokinin (**CCK**) *n.* a PEPTIDE HORMONE that is released from the duodenum and may be involved in the satiation of hunger. It also serves as a NEUROTRANSMITTER at some locations in the nervous system.

cholinergic *adj.* responding to, releasing, or otherwise involving ACETYLCHOLINE. For example, a **cholinergic neuron** is one that employs acetylcholine as a neurotransmitter.

cholinesterase (**ChE**) *n.* an enzyme that splits ACETYLCHOLINE into choline and acetic acid, thus inactivating the neurotransmitter after its release at a synaptic junction. Cholinesterase occurs in two forms: **acetylcholinesterase** (**AChE**), found in nerve tissue and red blood cells; and **butyrylcholinesterase** (**BuChE**, or **pseudocholinesterase** [**PChE**]), found in blood plasma and other tissues. Drugs that block the ability of this enzyme to degrade acetylcholine are called **cholinesterase inhibitors** (**ChEIs**, or **acetylcholinesterase inhibitors** [**AChEIs**] or **anticholinesterases**).

chorea *n.* irregular and involuntary jerky movements of the limbs and facial muscles. Chorea is associated with various disorders, including HUNTINGTON'S DISEASE. —**choreal** *adj.* —**choreic** *adj.*

chromatic *adj.* **1.** in vision, possessing both HUE and SATURATION. Thus, a **chromatic color** is any color other than black, white, or gray. Compare ACHROMATIC. **2.** in music, pertaining to an octave scale in which each note differs from the preceding note by one semitone.

chromatic aberration see ABERRATION.

chromosome *n.* a strand or filament composed of nucleic acid (mainly DNA in humans) and proteins that carries the genetic, or hereditary, traits of an individual. The normal human complement of chromosomes totals 46, or 23 pairs (44 AUTOSOMES and 2 SEX CHROMOSOMES), which contain an estimated 20,000 to 25,000 genes (see GENOME). Each parent contributes one chromosome to each pair, so a child receives half its chromosomes from its mother and half from its father. —**chromosomal** *adj.*

chronic *adj.* denoting conditions or symptoms that persist or progress over a long period of time and are resistant to cure. Compare ACUTE.

chronic fatigue syndrome (**CFS**) an illness characterized by often disabling fatigue, decrease in physical activity, and flulike symptoms, such as muscle weakness, swelling of the lymph nodes, headache, sore throat, and sometimes depression. The condition is typically not diagnosed until symptoms have been ongoing for several months, and it can last for years. The cause is unknown, although certain viral infections can set off the illness.

chronic stress the physiological or psychological response to a prolonged internal or external stressful event (i.e., a STRESSOR). The stressor need not remain physically present to exert its effects; recollections of it can substitute for its presence and sustain chronic stress.

chronobiology *n.* the branch of biology concerned with BIOLOGICAL RHYTHMS, such as the sleep–wake cycle.

chronological age (**CA**) the amount of time elapsed since an individual's birth, typically expressed in terms of months and years. Compare BIOLOGICAL AGE.

chronosystem *n.* in ECOLOGICAL SYSTEMS THEORY, changes and continuities occurring over time that influence an individual's development. These influences include normative life transitions (e.g., school entry, marriage, retirement), nonnormative life transitions (e.g., divorce, winning the lottery, relocation), and the cumulative effects of the entire sequence of transitions over the life course. Compare EXOSYSTEM; MESOSYSTEM; MACROSYSTEM.

chunking *n.* the process by which the mind divides large pieces of information into smaller pieces (**chunks**) that are easier to retain in SHORT-TERM MEMORY. As a result of this recoding, one item in memory (e.g., a keyword or key idea) can stand for multiple other items (e.g., a short list of associated points). The capacity of short-term memory is believed to be constant for the number of individual units it can store (seven plus or minus two), but the units themselves can range from simple chunks (e.g., individual letters or numbers) to complex chunks (e.g., words or phrases).

ciliary muscle smooth muscle behind the iris of the eye that changes the shape of the lens to bring objects into focus on the retina. The ciliary muscle regulates the tension of the delicate elastic fibers connected to the lens, causing the lens to flatten (which lessens its power and allows focus of distant objects) or become more curved (which increases the power of the lens and allows focus of near objects). The action of the ciliary muscle is a large component of ACCOMMODATION.

cingulate cortex a long strip of CE-REBRAL CORTEX on the medial surface of each cerebral hemisphere in the prefrontal lobe. The cingulate cortex arches over and generally outlines the location of the CORPUS CALLOSUM, from which it is separated by the callosal SULCUS. It is a component of the LIMBIC SYSTEM and has a role in emotion, memory, and motor planning.

circadian rhythm any periodic variation in physiological or behavioral activity that repeats at approximately 24-hour intervals, such as the sleep-wake cycle. Compare INFRADIAN RHYTHM; ULTRADIAN RHYTHM.

circannual rhythm a BIOLOGICAL RHYTHM of behavior, growth, or some other physiological variable that recurs yearly.

circular reaction in PIAGETIAN THE-ORY, repetitive behavior observed in children during the SENSORIMOTOR STAGE, characterized as primary, secondary, or tertiary circular reactions. The primary phase involves ineffective repetitive behaviors; the secondary phase involves repetition of actions that are followed by reinforcement, typically without understanding causation; and the tertiary phase involves repetitive object manipulation, typically with slight variations among subsequent behaviors.

cisgender *adj.* having or relating to a GENDER IDENTITY that corresponds to the culturally determined gender roles for one's birth sex (i.e., the biological sex one was born with). A **cisgender man** or **cisgender woman** is thus one whose internal gender identity matches, and presents itself in accordance with, the externally determined cultural expectations of the behavior and roles considered appropriate for one's sex as male or female. Also called **cisgendered**. Compare TRANSGENDER. **—cisgenderism** *n.*

civil commitment a legal procedure that permits a person who is not charged with criminal conduct to be certified as mentally ill and to be institutionalized involuntarily.

clairvoyance *n.* in parapsychology, the alleged ability to see things beyond the normal range of sight, such as distant or hidden objects or events in the past or future. See also EXTRASENSORY PERCEPTION. **—clairvoyant** *n., adj.*

classical conditioning a type of learning in which an initially neutral stimulus—the CONDITIONED STIMULUS (CS)—when paired with a stimulus that elicits a reflex response—the UNCONDI-TIONED STIMULUS (US)—results in a learned, or conditioned, response (CR) when the CS is presented. For example, the sound of a tone may be used as a CS and food in a dog's mouth as an US. After repeated pairings, namely, the tone followed immediately by food, the tone, which initially had no effect on salivation (i.e., was neutral with respect to it), will elicit salivation even if the food is not presented. Also called **Pavlovian conditioning; respondent conditioning.** [discovered in 1903 by Russian physiologist Ivan Pavlov (1849–1936)]

classical psychoanalysis 1. psychoanalytic theory in which major emphasis is placed on the LIBIDO, the stages of PSYCHOSEXUAL DEVELOPMENT, and the ID instincts or drives. The prototypical theory of this kind is that of Austrian neurologist Sigmund Freud (1856–1939). **2.** psychoanalytic treatment that adheres to Sigmund Freud's basic procedures, using dream interpretation, free association, and analysis of RESISTANCE, and to his basic aim of developing insight into the patient's unconscious life as a way to restructure personality.

classical test theory (**CTT**) the theory that an observed score (e.g., a test result) that is held to represent an underlying attribute (e.g., intelligence) may be divided into two quantities—the true value of the underlying attribute and the error inherent to the process of obtaining the observed score. The theory serves as the basis for models of test RELIABILITY and assumes that individuals possess stable characteristics or traits that persist through time. Compare ITEM RESPONSE THEORY.

classification n. 1. in cognitive psychology, see CATEGORIZATION. 2. in clinical psychology and psychiatry, the grouping of mental disorders on the basis of their characteristics or symptoms. —**classify** vb.

classification and regression tree analysis see CART ANALYSIS.

class inclusion the concept that a subordinate class (e.g., dogs) must always be smaller than the superordinate class in which it is contained (e.g., animals). According to PIAGETIAN THEORY, understanding the concept of class inclusion represents an important developmental step. Children progress from classifications based on personal factors, perceptual features, and common function to classifications based on hierarchical relationships; for example, a monkey is a primate, a mammal, and a vertebrate animal.

class interval a range of numerical values that constitute one segment or class of a variable of interest. For example, individual weights can be placed into class intervals such as 100 lb–120 lb, 121 lb–140 lb, 141 lb–160 lb, and so forth. Class intervals often are used in FREQUENCY DISTRIBUTIONS and HISTOGRAMS to present a large data set in a simpler manner that is more easily interpreted.

claustrophobia n. a persistent and irrational fear of enclosed places (e.g., elevators, closets, tunnels) or of being confined (e.g., in an airplane or the backseat of a car). The focus of fear is typically on panic symptoms triggered in these situations, such as feelings of being unable to breathe, choking, sweating, and fears of losing control or going crazy. —**claustrophobic** adj.

claustrum n. (pl. **claustra**) a thin layer of gray matter in the brain that separates the white matter of the lenticular nucleus from the INSULA. The claustrum forms part of the BASAL GANGLIA and its function is unknown (from Latin: "barrier"). —**claustral** adj.

Clever Hans the "thinking horse," reputed to be able to solve mathematical problems, spell words, distinguish colors, and identify coins, that became famous in Berlin around 1900. It signaled its answers by tapping its foot. However, German psychologist Oskar Pfungst (1874–1932), using experimental methods, demonstrated that the horse was responding to minimal cues in the form of involuntary movements on the part of its owner.

client n. a person receiving treatment or services, especially in the context of counseling or social work. See PATIENT–CLIENT ISSUE.

client abuse see PATIENT ABUSE.

client-centered therapy a form of psychotherapy developed by U.S. psychologist Carl Rogers (1902–1987) in the early 1940s. According to Rogers, an orderly process of client self-discovery and actualization occurs in response to the therapist's consistent empathic understanding of, acceptance of, and respect for the client's FRAME. The therapist reflects and clarifies the ideas of the client, who begins to see himself or herself more clearly, to resolve conflicts, and to interpret his or her thoughts and feelings, consequently changing behavior that he or she considers problematic. It was originally known as **nondirective therapy**, although this term is now used more broadly to denote any approach to psychotherapy in which the therapist establishes an encouraging atmosphere but avoids giving advice, offering interpretations, or engaging in other actions to actively direct the therapeutic process. Also called **person-centered therapy**.

climacteric *n.* the biological stage of life in which reproductive capacity declines and finally ceases. In women this period, which results from changes in the levels of estrogens and progesterone and is known as **menopause**, typically occurs between 45 and 55 years of age and lasts 2 to 7 years. During this time, menstrual flow gradually decreases in occurrence, duration, and volume (a transitional phase called **perimenopause**) and finally ceases altogether, and various physical and potentially psychological changes, such as hot flashes, night sweats, joint pain, emotional lability, and depression, may occur in varying combinations and degrees. Some men undergo a similar period about 10 years later than is typical for women (see MALE CLIMACTERIC).

clinical *adj.* of or relating to the diagnosis and treatment of psychological, medical, or other disorders. Originally involving only direct observation of patients, clinical methods have now broadened to take into account biological and statistical factors as well.

clinical depression among mental health professionals, a synonym for MAJOR DEPRESSIVE DISORDER. Within the general public, however, the term is often used more broadly to encompass any DEPRESSIVE DISORDER requiring therapeutic intervention.

clinical geropsychology an interdisciplinary field of research and practice that addresses the mental health needs and services of older adults. It interfaces with geriatric medicine and clinical psychotherapy, focusing not only on the processes of normal aging but also on adverse experiences in later life, such as depression, anxiety disorders, misuse of alcohol and other substances, suicidal behavior, and mild cognitive impairment and dementia.

clinical hypnosis see HYPNOTHERAPY.

clinical interview a type of directed conversation initially used with children but now applied in a variety of contexts, including HUMAN FACTORS research, diagnostic evaluation, and treatment planning for patients by mental health professionals. In a clinical interview, the investigator may utilize certain standard material but essentially determines which questions to ask based on the responses given by the patient to previous ones. This technique is largely spontaneous and enables the interviewer to adapt questions to the patient's comprehension and ask additional questions to clarify ambiguities and enhance understanding.

clinical method the process by which a health or mental health professional arrives at a conclusion, judgment, or diagnosis about a client or patient.

clinical neuropsychology a specialty of clinical psychology that represents the applied practice of NEUROPSYCHOLOGY and is concerned with assessment of and rehabilitation from brain injury that impairs an individual's ability to function.

clinical neuroscience a field in which basic neuroscience data and the scientific method are coupled to such fields as clinical psychology, psychiatry, and neurology to better understand the neural underpinnings of mental and nervous system disorders and to improve their diagnosis and treatment.

clinical practice providing health or mental health services to patients or clients. In mental health, clinical practice includes services (e.g., psychological assessment, diagnosis, treatment) provided by a clinical psychologist, psychiatrist, or other mental health care provider who works directly with clients or patients to relieve distress or dysfunction caused by emotional and behavioral problems. Clinical practice typically refers to work in health and mental health clinics or in group or independent practices.

clinical psychology the branch of psychology that specializes in the research, assessment, diagnosis, evaluation, prevention, and treatment of emotional and behavioral disorders. **Clinical psychologists** are doctorate-level professionals who have received training in research methods and techniques for the diagnosis and treatment of various psychological disorders. They work primarily in health and mental health clinics, in research, in academic settings, or in group and independent practices. They also serve as consultants to other professionals in the medical, legal, social-work, and community-relations fields.

clinical significance the extent to which a study result is judged to be meaningful in relation to the diagnosis or treatment of disorders. An example of a clinically significant result would be an outcome indicating that a new intervention strategy is effective in reducing symptoms of depression. See also PRACTICAL SIGNIFICANCE; STATISTICAL SIGNIFICANCE.

clinical trial a research study designed to compare a new treatment or drug with an existing standard of care or other control condition (see CONTROL GROUP). Trials generally are designed to answer scientific questions and to find better ways to treat individuals who have a specific disease or disorder. See also RANDOMIZED CLINICAL TRIAL.

clique *n.* a status- or friendship-based subgroup within a larger group or organization. Cliques are particularly common during adolescence, when they are often used to raise social standing, strengthen friendship ties, and reduce feelings of isolation and exclusion.

clone 1. *n.* an organism that is genetically identical to another, whether because both organisms originate from a single common parent as a result of asexual reproduction or because one is derived from genetic material taken from the other. **2.** *vb.* to produce genetically identical copies of a particular organism or cell. —**clonal** *adj.*

clonic *adj.* of, relating to, or characterized by **clonus**, a type of involuntary movement caused by a rapid succession of alternate muscular contractions and relaxations. Although some forms of clonus, such as hiccups, are considered normal, most such movements are abnormal; for example, clonus occurs as part of a TONIC–CLONIC SEIZURE.

closed question see FIXED-ALTERNATIVE QUESTION.

closure *n.* **1.** the act, achievement, or sense of completing or resolving something. In psychotherapy, for example, a client achieves closure with the recognition that he or she has reached a resolution to a particular psychological issue or relationship problem. **2.** one of the GESTALT PRINCIPLES OF ORGANIZATION. It states that people tend to perceive incomplete forms (e.g., images, sounds) as complete, synthesizing the missing units so as to perceive the image or sound as a whole. Also called **law of closure**; **principle of closure**.

cluster analysis a method of multivariate data analysis in which individuals or units are placed into distinct subgroups based on their strong similarity with regard to specific attributes. For example, one might use cluster analysis to form groups of individual children on the basis of their levels of anxiety, aggression, delinquency, and cognitive difficulties so as to identify useful typologies that could increase understanding of co-occurring mental disorders and lead to more appropriate treatments for specific individuals.

clustering *n.* the tendency for items to be consistently grouped together in the course of recall. This grouping typically occurs for related items. It is readily apparent in memory tasks in which items from the same category, such as nonhuman animals, are recalled together. —**cluster** *n., vb.*

cluster suicide a statistically high occurrence of suicides within a circumscribed geographic area, social group, or time period. Cluster suicides have been identified involving adolescents, factory workers, and dispersed individuals who imitated the suicide of an admired role model.

coacting group a group consisting of two or more individuals working in one another's presence on tasks and activities that require little or no interaction or communication (**coaction tasks**), such as clerical staff working at individual desks in an open-design office. Researchers often create coacting groups in laboratory studies to determine the effect of the mere presence of others on performance.

coarticulation *n.* a phenomenon in which the performance of one or more actions in a sequence varies according to the other actions in the sequence. This is particularly important in speech, where the formation of certain PHONEMES varies according to the speech sounds that immediately precede or follow: For example, the aspirated [p] sound in *pin* differs slightly from the unaspirated [p] in *spin*.

cocaine *n.* a drug, obtained from leaves of the coca shrub, that stimulates the central nervous system, with the effects of reducing fatigue and increasing well-being, followed by a period of depression as the initial effects diminish. The drug acts by blocking the reuptake of the neurotransmitters dopamine, serotonin, and norepinephrine.

cochlea *n.* the bony fluid-filled part of the inner ear that is concerned with hearing. Shaped like a snail shell, it

forms part of the bony LABYRINTH. Along its length run three canals: the SCALA VESTIBULI, SCALA TYMPANI, and SCALA MEDIA, or cochlear duct. The floor of the scala media is formed by the BASILAR MEMBRANE; the ORGAN OF CORTI, which rests on the basilar membrane, contains the HAIR CELLS that act as auditory receptor organs. —**cochlear** *adj.*

cochlear implant an electronic device designed to enable individuals with complete deafness to hear and interpret some sounds, particularly those associated with speech. It consists of a microphone to detect sound, a headpiece to transmit sound, a processor to digitize sound, and a receiver to signal electrodes that are surgically implanted in the cochlea to stimulate the auditory nerve. In contrast to a hearing aid, which amplifies sound, it directly stimulates the auditory nerve.

cochlear nucleus a mass of cell bodies of second-order auditory neurons in the brainstem. The principal subdivisions are the ventral, dorsal, and anterior cochlear nuclei.

cocktail-party effect the ability to attend to one of several speech streams while ignoring others, as when one is at a cocktail party. Research in this area in the early 1950s suggested that the unattended messages are not processed, but later findings indicated that meaning is identified in at least some cases. For example, the mention of one's name is processed even if it occurs in an unattended speech stream. See also ATTENUATION THEORY.

codeine *n.* a morphine-derived OPIATE that is used as an analgesic (alone or in combination with other analgesics, e.g., aspirin) and as a cough suppressant. It also induces euphoria; however, its addiction potential is substantially less than that of heroin.

code of ethics a set of standards and principles of professional conduct, such as the *Ethical Principles of Psychologists and Code of Conduct* of the

American Psychological Association. See ETHICS.

coefficient *n.* **1.** a quantity or value that serves as a measure of some property. For example, the CORRELATION COEFFICIENT is a measure of linear relatedness. **2.** in algebra, a scalar that multiplies a variable in an equation. For example, in the equation $y = bx$, the scalar quantity b is said to be a coefficient.

coefficient of determination (symbol: r^2) a numerical index that reflects the proportion of variation in an outcome or response variable that is accounted for by its relationship with a predictor variable. Obtained by multiplying the value of the CORRELATION COEFFICIENT (r) by itself, the coefficient of determination ranges in value from 0 to 1. Low values indicate the outcome is relatively unrelated to the predictor, whereas values closer to 1 indicate that the two variables are highly related. For example, if $r = .30$, then the coefficient of determination is $.30^2 = .09$ and interpreted to mean 9% of the variance between the two variables is common or overlapping. Also called **squared correlation coefficient**.

coefficient of multiple determination (symbol: R^2) a numerical index that reflects the degree to which variation in a response or outcome variable (e.g., workers' incomes) is accounted for by its relationship with two or more predictor variables (e.g., age, gender, years of education). Obtained by multiplying the value of the MULTIPLE CORRELATION COEFFICIENT (R) by itself, the coefficient of multiple determination ranges in value from 0 to 1. Low values indicate that the outcome is relatively unrelated to the predictors, whereas values closer to 1 indicate that the outcome and the predictors are highly related. For example, if $R = .40$, then the coefficient of multiple determination is $.40^2 = .16$ and interpreted to mean 16% of the variance in outcome is explainable by the set of predictors.

coevolution *n.* the concurrent evolution of two or more species that mutually affect each other's existence.

cognition *n.* **1.** all forms of knowing and awareness, such as perceiving, conceiving, remembering, reasoning, judging, imagining, and problem solving. Along with AFFECT and CONATION, it is one of the three traditionally identified components of mind. **2.** an individual percept, idea, memory, or the like. —**cognitional** *adj.* —**cognitive** *adj.*

cognitive appraisal theory the theory that cognitive evaluation is involved in the generation of each and every emotion. This concept is elaborated in the **cognitive–motivational–relational theory**, which recognizes that cognition is one of three simultaneously operating processes that contribute to the generation of any emotion.

cognitive behavior therapy (**CBT**) a form of psychotherapy that integrates theories of cognition and learning with treatment techniques derived from COGNITIVE THERAPY and BEHAVIOR THERAPY. CBT assumes that cognitive, emotional, and behavioral variables are functionally interrelated. Treatment is aimed at identifying and modifying the client's maladaptive thought processes and problematic behaviors through COGNITIVE RESTRUCTURING and behavioral techniques to achieve change.

cognitive coping any strategy in which a person uses mental activity to manage a stressful event or situation. A variety of different forms exist, such as putting the experience into perspective, thinking about pleasant experiences instead of the current difficulty (positive refocusing), redefining the situation to emphasize potential benefits (positive reappraisal), exaggerating the negative consequences of the event (catastrophizing), blaming oneself or others for the occurrence of the event, and dwelling on the negative emotions associated with the event (rumination). Some of these strategies (e.g., positive reappraisal, positive refocusing, putting things into perspective) are considered more effective than others, being associated with more positive psychological outcomes.

cognitive development the growth and maturation of thinking processes of all kinds, including perceiving, remembering, concept formation, problem solving, imagining, and reasoning.

cognitive disorder any disorder that involves impairment of the EXECUTIVE FUNCTIONS, such as organization, regulation, and perception. Impairments in these fundamental processes can affect performance in many cognitive areas, including processing speed, reasoning, planning, judgment, decision making, emotional engagement and regulation, perseveration, impulse control, awareness, attention, language, learning, memory, and timing.

cognitive dissonance an unpleasant psychological state resulting from inconsistency between two or more elements in a cognitive system. It is presumed to involve a state of heightened arousal and to have characteristics similar to physiological drives (e.g., hunger).

cognitive dissonance theory a theory proposing that people have a fundamental motivation to maintain consistency among elements in their cognitive systems. When inconsistency occurs, people experience an unpleasant psychological state that motivates them to reduce the dissonance in a variety of ways.

cognitive enhancer a type of drug used to improve cognitive function, usually in the treatment of progressive dementias such as Alzheimer's disease but also of cognitive dysfunction due to traumatic brain injury. Cognitive enhancers do not reverse the course of the dementia but are reported to slow its progress in mild to moderate forms. Many of these drugs work by inhibiting

the activity of acetylcholinesterase in the central nervous system, thereby counteracting the disruption of CHOLINERGIC neurotransmission observed in patients with Alzheimer's disease. Also called **memory-enhancing drug**; and, formerly, **nootropic**.

cognitive ergonomics a specialty area of ERGONOMICS that seeks to understand the cognitive processes and representations involved in human performance. Cognitive ergonomics studies the combined effect of information-processing characteristics, task constraints, and task environment on human performance and applies the results of such studies to the design and evaluation of work systems.

cognitive functioning the performance of the mental processes of perception, learning, memory, understanding, awareness, reasoning, judgment, intuition, and language.

cognitive impairment any impairment in perceptual, learning, memory, linguistic, or thinking abilities. Multiple significant cognitive impairments in memory plus one or more other cognitive defects are characteristic of DEMENTIA.

cognitive learning theory any theory postulating that learning requires central constructs and new ways of perceiving events. Cognitive learning theories are usually contrasted with behavioral learning theories, which suggest that behaviors or responses are acquired through experience.

cognitive load the relative demand imposed by a particular task, in terms of mental resources required. See also COGNITIVE OVERLOAD.

cognitive map a mental understanding of an environment, formed through trial and error as well as observation. Human beings and other animals have well-developed cognitive maps that contain spatial information enabling them to orient themselves and find their way in the world.

cognitive model a theoretical view of thought and mental operations, which provides explanations for observed phenomena and makes predictions about an unknown future. People are continually creating and accessing internal representations (models) of what they are experiencing in the world for the purposes of perception, comprehension, and behavior selection (action).

cognitive neuropsychology the study of the structure and function of the brain as it relates to perception, reasoning, remembering, and all other forms of knowing and awareness. Cognitive neuropsychology focuses on examining the effects of brain damage on thought processes—typically through the use of single-case or small-group designs—so as to construct models of normal cognitive functioning.

cognitive neuroscience a branch of NEUROSCIENCE and BIOLOGICAL PSYCHOLOGY that focuses on the neural mechanisms of cognition. Although overlapping with the study of the mind in COGNITIVE PSYCHOLOGY, cognitive neuroscience, with its grounding in such areas as experimental psychology, neurobiology, physics, and mathematics, is more concerned with the specific neural mechanisms by which mental processes occur in the brain. Also called **neurocognition**.

cognitive overload the situation in which the demands placed on a person by mental work (the COGNITIVE LOAD) are greater than the person's mental abilities can cope with.

cognitive process any of the mental functions assumed to be involved in the acquisition, storage, interpretation, manipulation, transformation, and use of knowledge. These processes encompass such activities as attention, perception, learning, and problem solving and are commonly understood through several basic theories, including the SERIAL PROCESSING approach,

the PARALLEL PROCESSING approach, and a combination theory, which assumes that cognitive processes are both serial and parallel, depending on the demands of the task.

cognitive psychology the branch of psychology that explores the operation of mental processes related to perceiving, attending, thinking, language, and memory, mainly through inferences from behavior. The cognitive approach, which developed in the 1940s and 1950s, diverged sharply from contemporary BEHAVIORISM in (a) emphasizing unseen knowledge processes instead of directly observable behaviors and (b) arguing that the relationship between stimulus and response was complex and mediated rather than simple and direct. Its concentration on the higher mental processes also contrasted with the focus on instincts and other unconscious forces typical of psychoanalysis. More recently, cognitive psychology has been influenced by approaches to INFORMATION PROCESSING and INFORMATION THEORY developed in computer science and ARTIFICIAL INTELLIGENCE. See also COGNITIVE SCIENCE.

cognitive reserve a capacity of the adult brain to sustain the effects of disease or injury without manifesting clinical symptoms of dysfunction and to draw on the active acquisition and differential use of numerous sophisticated cognitive strategies to process information, solve problems, and perform tasks. In other words, individuals with high cognitive reserve have developed a variety of efficient NEURAL NETWORKS and NEURAL PATHWAYS to cope with brain pathology such that they can have a greater degree of underlying neurological damage than individuals with low cognitive reserve before becoming symptomatic. The size of this hypothesized supply of mental abilities and mechanisms, and thus the degree of protection against dementia and other neurological disorders it conveys, is believed to depend on the intellectual challenges a person experiences throughout life: More mental stimulation creates more reserve.

cognitive restructuring a technique used in COGNITIVE THERAPY and COGNITIVE BEHAVIOR THERAPY to help the client identify his or her self-defeating beliefs or cognitive distortions, refute them, and then modify them so that they are adaptive and reasonable.

cognitive science an interdisciplinary approach to understanding the mind and mental processes that combines aspects of cognitive psychology, philosophy of mind, epistemology, neuroscience, anthropology, psycholinguistics, and computer science.

cognitive-social learning theory see SOCIAL-COGNITIVE THEORY.

cognitive style a person's characteristic mode of perceiving, thinking, remembering, and problem solving. Cognitive styles might differ in preferred elements or activities, such as visual versus verbal ENCODING, and along various dimensions, such as FIELD DEPENDENCE versus field independence. Some sources use the term **learning style** interchangeably with cognitive style, whereas others use the former more specifically to mean a person's characteristic cognitive, affective, and psychological behaviors that influence his or her preferred instructional methods and interactions with the learning environment.

cognitive theory any theory of mind that focuses on mental activities, such as perceiving, attending, thinking, remembering, evaluating, planning, language, and creativity, especially a theory that suggests a model for the various processes involved.

cognitive therapy (**CT**) a form of psychotherapy based on the concept that emotional and behavioral problems in an individual are, at least in part, the result of maladaptive or faulty ways of thinking and distorted attitudes toward oneself and others. The objective of the therapy is to identify

these faulty cognitions and replace them with more adaptive ones, a process known as COGNITIVE RESTRUCTURING. The therapist takes the role of an active guide who attempts to make the client aware of these distorted thinking patterns and who helps the client correct and revise his or her perceptions and attitudes by citing evidence to the contrary or by eliciting it from the client. See also COGNITIVE BEHAVIOR THERAPY.

cognitive triad a set of three beliefs thought to characterize MAJOR DEPRESSIVE EPISODES. These are negative beliefs about the self, the world, and the future. Also called **negative triad**.

cognitive unconscious unreportable mental processes such as implicit percepts, memories, and thoughts. There are many sources of evidence for a cognitive unconscious, including regularities of behavior due to habit or AUTOMATICITY, inferred grammatical rules, the details of sensorimotor control, and implicit knowledge after brain damage. Compare EMOTIONAL UNCONSCIOUS.

cognitive well-being see SUBJECTIVE WELL-BEING.

cohabitation *n.* the state or condition of living together as sexual and domestic partners without being married. —**cohabit** *vb.* —**cohabitee** *n.*

Cohen's *d* a measure of EFFECT SIZE based on the standardized difference between two means: It indicates the number of STANDARD DEVIATION units by which the means of two data sets differ. For example, a mentoring intervention associated with a Cohen's *d* of +0.25 indicates an increase of 0.25 standard deviation units for the average child who received mentoring relative to the average child who did not receive mentoring. The metric is used to represent effect sizes in META-ANALYSES as well as in the determination of POWER, with values of 0.20, 0.50, and 0.80 representing small, medium, and large effect sizes, respectively. See also

GLASS'S D. [Jacob **Cohen** (1923–1998), U.S. psychologist and statistician]

Cohen's kappa (symbol: κ) a numerical index that reflects the degree of agreement between two raters or rating systems classifying data into mutually exclusive categories, corrected for the level of agreement expected by chance alone. Values range from 0 (*no agreement*) to 1 (*perfect agreement*), with kappas below .40 generally considered poor, .40 to .75 considered fair to good, and more than .75 considered excellent. In accounting for chance, Cohen's kappa avoids overestimating the true level of agreement as might occur through simply determining the number of times that two raters agree relative to the total number of ratings. [Jacob **Cohen**]

cohesion *n.* see GROUP COHESION.

cohort *n.* a group of individuals who share a similar characteristic or experience. The term usually refers to an **age** (or **birth**) **cohort**, that is, a group of individuals who are born in the same year and thus of similar age.

cohort effect any outcome associated with being a member of a group whose members all undergo similar experiences. Cohort effects may be difficult to separate from AGE EFFECTS and PERIOD EFFECTS in research.

cohort study see LONGITUDINAL DESIGN.

collapsing *n.* the process of combining multiple response options or categories to form a smaller number of responses or categories. For example, a researcher could collect demographic data for students at a particular college by each year of matriculation (i.e., freshman, sophomore, junior, and senior) and then collapse the information from four to two categories (e.g., lower division and upper division).

collective memory shared recollection: mental representations of past events that are common to members of a social group. For example, mine workers may collectively remember the accidental death of a coworker differently than the general public, just as younger and older people may remember significant historical events differently. Collective memory is expressed in numerous forms—including oral and written narratives, monuments and other memorials, commemorative rituals, and symbols—and serves a range of functions, such as establishing and maintaining relationships, teaching or entertaining others, and supporting group identity. Also called **cultural memory**; **social memory**.

collective monologue a form of speech in which children talk among themselves without apparently communicating with each other in a meaningful way; that is, the statements of one child seem unrelated to the statements of the others.

collective unconscious the part of the UNCONSCIOUS that, according to Swiss psychiatrist Carl Jung (1875–1961), is common to all humankind and contains the inherited accumulation of primitive human experiences in the form of ideas and images called ARCHETYPES. It is the deepest and least accessible part of the unconscious mind. See also PERSONAL UNCONSCIOUS.

collectivism *n.* a social or cultural tradition, ideology, or personal outlook that emphasizes the unity of the group or community rather than each person's individuality. Collectivist societies tend to stress cooperation, communalism, constructive interdependence, and conformity to cultural roles and mores. Compare INDIVIDUALISM. —**collectivist** *adj.*

colliculus *n.* (*pl.* **colliculi**) a small elevation. Two pairs of colliculi are found on the dorsal surface of the MIDBRAIN. The rostral pair (the **superior colliculi**) receive and process visual information and help control eye movements. The caudal pair (the **inferior colliculi**) receive and process auditory information. [from Latin, "small hill"]

collinearity *n.* in REGRESSION ANALYSIS, the situation in which two INDEPENDENT VARIABLES are so highly associated that one can be closely or perfectly predicted by the other. For example, collinearity likely is present if a researcher examines how height and age contribute to children's weight, since the two predictors are highly interrelated (i.e., as children grow older they get taller). Collinearity requires the use of PARTIALING procedures to distinguish the unique influences of the independent variables. See also MULTICOLLINEARITY. —**collinear** *adj.*

colonialism *n.* see POSTCOLONIALISM.

color *n.* the quality of visible light that corresponds to wavelength as perceived by retinal receptors. It is thus the subjective experience of a physical entity. Color is characterized by the three separate attributes of HUE, SATURATION, and BRIGHTNESS, but in general usage the term refers to hue only.

color agnosia see VISUAL AGNOSIA.

color blindness the inability to discriminate between colors and to perceive color hues. Color blindness may be caused by disease, drugs, or brain injury (acquired color blindness), but most often it is an inherited trait (congenital color blindness) that affects about 10% of men (it is rare in women). The most common form of the disorder involves the green or red receptors of the cone cells in the retina, causing a red–green confusion. Total color blindness (ACHROMATISM) is rare. See also DICHROMATISM; MONOCHROMATISM; TRICHROMATISM.

color constancy the tendency to perceive a familiar object as having the same color under different conditions of illumination. For example, a red apple will be perceived as red in well-lit or poorly illuminated surroundings. Color constancy is an example of PERCEPTUAL CONSTANCY.

color contrast the effect of one color on another when they are viewed in proximity. In simultaneous contrast, complementary colors, such as yellow and blue, are enhanced by each other: The yellow appears yellower, and the blue appears bluer. In successive contrast, the complement of a color is seen after shifting focus to a neutral surface.

color vision the ability to distinguish visual stimuli on the basis of the wavelengths of light they emit or reflect.

column *n.* in anatomy, a structure that resembles an architectural pillar. An example is the SPINAL COLUMN. —**columnar** *adj.*

coma *n.* a profound state of unconsciousness in which a person is unaware of the self or environment; does not engage in any voluntary activity; and does not respond to light, sound, touch, or other stimuli. He or she cannot be roused, his or her eyes remain closed, and normal sleep and wake cycles cease. Causes are numerous but commonly include head injury or other trauma, blockage or rupture of cerebral blood vessels, infection, oxygen deprivation (from cardiac arrest, hypoxia, etc.), seizures, strokes, and metabolic disturbances. Comas typically last 10 to 14 days, with affected individuals often progressing to a MINIMALLY CONSCIOUS STATE or a VEGETATIVE STATE. —**comatose** *adj.*

combination *n.* the selection of r objects from among n objects without regard to the order in which the objects are selected. The number of combinations of n objects taken r at a time is often denoted as $_nC_r$. A combination is similar to a PERMUTATION but distinguished by the irrelevance of order.

commissure *n.* a structure that forms a bridge or junction between two anatomical areas, particularly the two cerebral hemispheres or the halves of the spinal cord. Examples include the two key landmarks in brain mapping: the **anterior commissure**, a bundle of myelinated fibers that joins the TEMPORAL LOBES and contains fibers of the olfactory tract; and the **posterior com-**

missure, a bundle of myelinated fibers that connects regions in the midbrain and DIENCEPHALON. See also CORPUS CALLOSUM. —**commissural** *adj.*

commissurotomy *n.* a surgical procedure involving a partial cutting of a commissure, especially that between the two cerebral hemispheres, the CORPUS CALLOSUM. A complete sectioning of the corpus callosum also severs its large forward portion, the anterior commissure, but this is now avoided if possible, in favor of partial transections. This surgery has been used to treat severe and intractable epilepsy, and it also has enabled researchers to study the isolated functions of each hemisphere. See SPLIT BRAIN.

commitment *n.* confinement to a mental institution by court order following certification by appropriate mental health authorities. The process may be voluntary but is generally involuntary.

common factor 1. any of several variables that are common to various types of psychotherapy, such as the THERAPEUTIC ALLIANCE, and that promote therapeutic success regardless of the different approaches used; common factors can thus be contrasted with factors that are unique to a particular therapy, such as the use of interpretation. THERAPEUTIC FACTORS are similar but typically apply to therapies with groups. **2.** see SPECIFIC FACTOR.

common fate one of the GESTALT PRINCIPLES OF ORGANIZATION, stating that objects functioning or moving in the same direction appear to belong together, that is, they are perceived as a single unit (e.g., a flock of birds). Also called **law of common fate**; **principle of common fate**.

common metric a unit or scale of measurement that is applied to data from different sources. In a META-ANALYSIS, for instance, the results from multiple studies may need to be placed on a common metric so that they may be meaningfully compared.

common region a recently introduced GESTALT PRINCIPLE OF ORGANIZATION, stating that objects sharing a common bounded region of space appear to belong together and tend to be perceived as a distinct group. For example, animals in a fenced-in enclosure are more likely to be seen as a group than are the same distribution of animals arrayed in open space. Also called **law of common region**; **principle of common region**.

communal nursing see ALLONURSING.

communal relationship a relationship in which interaction is governed primarily by consideration of the other's needs and wishes. This contrasts with an **exchange relationship**, in which the people involved are concerned mainly with receiving as much as they give.

communication *n.* the transmission of information, which may be by verbal (oral or written) or nonverbal means (see NONVERBAL COMMUNICATION). Humans communicate to relate and exchange ideas, knowledge, feelings, and experiences and for many other interpersonal and social purposes. Nonhuman animals likewise communicate vocally or nonvocally for a variety of purposes, such as to convey intentions to one another or to manage or manipulate the behavior of others.

community mental health activities undertaken in the community, rather than in institutional settings, to promote mental health. The community approach focuses on the total population of a single geographic area and involves overall planning and demographic analyses of the area's mental health needs. It emphasizes preventive services and seeks to provide a continuous, comprehensive system of services designed to meet the mental health needs in the community.

community mental health center (CMHC) a community-based facility providing prevention, treatment, and rehabilitation mental health services, including full diagnostic evaluation; outpatient individual and group therapy; emergency inpatient treatment; substance abuse treatment; and vocational, educational, and social rehabilitation programs.

community psychology a branch of psychology that encourages the development of theory, research, and practice relevant to the reciprocal relationships between individuals and the social systems that constitute the community context. It intersects with other branches of psychology (e.g., social psychology) and with other disciplines, such as sociology and public health. It emphasizes social welfare, community mental health, and prevention. Its research findings and methods are applied with regard to poverty, substance abuse, violence, school failure, and other social issues.

comorbidity *n.* the simultaneous presence in an individual of more than one physical or mental illness, disease, or disorder. —**comorbid** *adj.*

companionate love a type of love characterized by strong feelings of intimacy and affection for another person rather than strong emotional arousal in the other's presence. In these respects, companionate love is distinguished from PASSIONATE LOVE. See also TRIANGULAR THEORY OF LOVE.

comparable form see ALTERNATE FORM.

comparable-forms reliability see ALTERNATE-FORMS RELIABILITY.

comparative cognition a subfield of comparative psychology that investigates the origins and mechanisms of cognition in various species and studies the differences and similarities in cognitive processes (e.g., perception, spatial learning and memory, problem solving, social cognition) across a range of animals, including humans, dolphins, elephants, chimpanzees, parrots, and bees.

comparative psychology the study of nonhuman animal behavior with the dual objective of understanding the behavior for its own sake and furthering the understanding of human behavior. Comparative psychology usually involves laboratory studies (compare ETHOLOGY) and typically refers to research involving nonhuman species whether or not it involves comparing their behavior with that of humans. Some **comparative psychologists** engage in both field and laboratory studies.

comparative trial see CONTROLLED TRIAL.

comparison *n.* any appraisal of two or more groups to identify differences, such as that between the mean of a variable in one population and its mean in another. Comparisons may be planned in advance (a priori comparisons) or decided on after data analysis has already begun (post hoc comparisons). Also called **contrast**.

comparison level (CL) in INTERDEPENDENCE THEORY, a standard by which an individual evaluates the quality of any social relationship in which he or she is currently engaged. The CL represents the average outcomes one expects to receive in one's dealings with others based on one's prior relationships. In most cases, individuals whose prior relationships yielded positive rewards with few costs will have higher CLs than those who experienced fewer rewards and more costs in prior relationships. If the reward-to-cost ratio of the current relationship falls below the CL, the individual will experience dissatisfaction.

compassionate love a form of love that emphasizes the well-being of another person. Compassionate love is affectionate and giving, focused on reducing the other's suffering and promoting the other's flourishing. Originally used to define a type of selfless caring described by several religious traditions, the concept is now applied broadly to romantic partners, family members, social groups, and humanity as a whole. See also COMPANIONATE LOVE; PASSIONATE LOVE.

compensation *n.* **1.** substitution or development of strength or capability in one area to offset real or imagined deficiency in another. This may be referred to as **overcompensation** when the substitute behavior exceeds what might actually be necessary in terms of level of compensation for the deficiency. In classical psychoanalytic theory, it is described as a DEFENSE MECHANISM that protects the individual against the conscious realization of such deficiencies. However, many psychologists emphasize the positive aspects of compensation. For example, it can be regarded as an important component of successful aging because it reduces the negative effects of cognitive and physical decline associated with the aging process. See SELECTIVE OPTIMIZATION WITH COMPENSATION. **2.** in neuroscience, the recruitment of brain areas to substitute for the loss, due to injury or disease, of neural activity in other areas. **3.** in PIAGETIAN THEORY, a mental process in which one realizes that for any operation there exists another operation that compensates for the effects of the first; that is, a change in one dimension can compensate for changes in another. Also called **reciprocity**. —**compensate** *vb.* —**compensatory** *adj.*

compensatory task a task or project that a group can complete by averaging individual members' solutions or recommendations. Groups often outperform individuals on such tasks when the members are equally proficient at the task and do not share common biases that produce systematic tendencies toward overestimation or underestimation. Compare ADDITIVE TASK; CONJUNCTIVE TASK; DISJUNCTIVE TASK.

competence *n.* **1.** the ability to exert control over one's life, to cope with specific problems effectively, and to make changes to one's behavior and one's environment, as opposed to the ability to adjust or adapt to circumstances as they are. Affirming, strengthening, or achieving a client's competence is often a basic goal in psychotherapy. **2.** one's developed repertoire of skills, especially as it is applied to a task or set of tasks. **3.** in linguistics, the nonconscious knowledge of the underlying rules of a language that enables individuals to speak and understand it. In this sense, competence is distinct from the actual linguistic **performance** of any particular speaker, which may be constrained by such nonlinguistic factors as memory, attention, or fatigue. **4.** in law, the capacity to comprehend the nature of a transaction and to assume legal responsibility for one's actions. Also called **competency**. Compare INCOMPETENCE. —**competent** *adj.*

competition *n.* any performance situation structured in such a way that success depends on performing better than others. Interpersonal competition involves individuals striving to outperform each other; intergroup competition involves groups competing against other groups; intragroup competition involves individuals within a group trying to best each other. Compare COOPERATION. —**compete** *vb.* —**competitive** *adj.*

complementary and alternative medicine (**CAM**) a group of therapies and health care systems that fall outside the realm of conventional Western medical practice. Among many forms are ACUPUNCTURE, MEDITATION, and the use of certain dietary supplements. Complementary medicine is used as an adjunct to conventional treatment; alternative medicine stands alone and replaces conventional treatment.

completion test a type of test in which for each item the participant is required to supply a missing phrase, word, number, or symbol.

complex *n.* a group or system of related ideas or impulses that have a common emotional tone and exert a strong but usually unconscious influence on the individual's attitudes and behavior. The term, introduced by Swiss psychiatrist Carl Jung (1875–1961) to denote the contents of the PERSONAL UNCONSCIOUS, has taken on an almost purely pathological connotation in popular usage, which does not necessarily reflect usage in psychology.

complex cell a neuron in the cerebral cortex that responds to visual stimulation of appropriate contrast, orientation, and direction anywhere in its receptive field. Compare SIMPLE CELL.

complex emotion any emotion that is an aggregate of two or more others. For example, hate may be considered a fusion of anger, fear, and disgust, whereas love blends tenderness, pleasure, devotion, and passion. By contrast, **simple emotions** are those that are irreducible by analysis to any other emotion. They are pure, unmixed states and include anger, fear, and joy, among others.

complexity theory a field that studies nonlinear systems with very large numbers of interacting variables using mathematical modeling and computer simulation. In general, it proposes that such systems are too complex to be accurately predicted but are nevertheless organized and nonrandom. Complexity theory has important applications in such fields as ecology, epidemiology, finance, and information science. See also CHAOS THEORY; DYNAMIC SYSTEMS THEORY.

complex reaction time see CHOICE REACTION TIME.

compliance *n.* **1.** submission to the demands, wishes, or suggestions of others, often involving a change in a person's behavior in response to a direct request. **2.** adherence to a medical treatment regime, especially one involving prescribed drug treatment. —**compliant** *adj.* —**comply** *vb.*

compound reaction time see CHOICE REACTION TIME.

comprehension *n.* the act or capability of understanding something, especially the meaning of a communication. Compare APPREHENSION. —**comprehend** *vb.*

compulsion *n.* a type of behavior or a mental act engaged in to reduce anxiety or distress. Typically, the individual feels driven or required to perform the compulsion to reduce the distress associated with an OBSESSION or to prevent a dreaded event or situation. For example, individuals with an obsession about contamination may wash their hands repetitively until their skin is cracked and bleeding. Such compulsions do not provide pleasure or gratification, although the individual may experience temporary relief from engaging in them. They are disproportionate or irrelevant to the feared situation that they are used to neutralize. —**compulsive** *adj.*

compulsive personality disorder see OBSESSIVE-COMPULSIVE PERSONALITY DISORDER.

computational model any account of cognitive or psychobiological processes that assumes that the human mind functions like a digital computer, specifically in its ability to form representations of events and objects and to carry out complex sequences of operations on these representations.

computed tomography (**CT**) a radiographic technique for quickly producing detailed, three-dimensional images of the brain or other soft tissues. An X-ray beam is passed through the tissue from many different locations, and the different patterns of radiation absorption are analyzed and synthesized by a computer. Also called **computerized axial tomography** (**CAT**); **computerized tomography**. See also MAGNETIC RESONANCE IMAGING.

computer addiction see INTERNET ADDICTION.

computer-assisted instruction (**CAI**) a sophisticated offshoot of programmed learning, in which the memory-storage and retrieval capabilities of the computer are used to provide drill and practice, problem solving, simulation, and gaming forms of instruction. It is also useful for relatively individualized tutorial instruction. Also called **computer-assisted learning (CAL)**.

computerized assessment the process of using a computer to obtain and evaluate psychological information about a person. The computer presents questions or tasks and then makes diagnoses and prognoses based on a comparison of the participant's responses or performance to databases of previously acquired information on many other individuals.

conation *n.* the proactive (as opposed to habitual) part of motivation that connects knowledge, emotions, drives, desires, and instincts to behavior. Along with AFFECT and COGNITION, conation is one of the three traditionally identified components of mind.

concentration *n.* the act of bringing together or focusing, such as bringing one's thought processes to bear on a central problem or subject. —**concentrate** *vb.*

concept *n.* an idea that represents a class of objects or events or their properties, such as *cats, walking, honesty, blue,* or *fast.* —**conceptual** *adj.*

concept formation the process by which a person abstracts a common idea from one or more particular examples and learns the defining features or combination of features that are characteristic of a class (e.g., those describing a bird) or that are necessary and sufficient to identify members of a class of objects, relations, or actions (e.g., the concepts *triangle, above,* or *move*).

concept hierarchy a collection of objects, events, or other items with common properties arranged in a multilevel structure. Concepts on the higher levels have broad meanings, whereas those at lower levels are more

specific. For example, a concept hierarchy of ANXIETY DISORDERS would place that term on top, with PHOBIAS lower, and specific types of phobia (e.g., CLAUSTROPHOBIA) on the bottom.

conceptual replication see REPLICATION.

concordance *n.* **1.** the state or condition of being in harmony or agreement. **Affective concordance** is said to exist, for instance, when facial gestures mirror internal states of feeling, such as frowning when perplexed or annoyed, or when two or more individuals related through some condition or activity experience the same or similar emotional reactions. **2.** in TWIN STUDIES, the presence of a given trait or disorder in both members of the pair. Evidence for genetic factors in the production of the trait or disorder comes from the comparison of concordance rates between identical and fraternal twins. Compare DISCORDANCE.

concrete operational stage in PIAGETIAN THEORY, the third major stage of cognitive development, occurring approximately from 7 to 12 years of age, in which children can decenter their perception (see DECENTRATION), are less egocentric, and can think logically about physical objects and about specific situations or experiences involving those objects. See also FORMAL OPERATIONAL STAGE; PREOPERATIONAL STAGE; SENSORIMOTOR STAGE.

concurrent validity the extent to which one measurement is supported by a related measurement obtained at about the same point in time. In testing, the VALIDITY of results obtained from one test (e.g., self-report of job performance) can often be assessed by comparison with a separate but related measurement (e.g., supervisor rating of job performance) collected simultaneously. See also CRITERION VALIDITY.

concussion *n.* mild injury to the brain, due to trauma or jarring, that disrupts brain function and usually involves at least brief unconsciousness.

Symptoms may include memory loss, headache, irritability, inappropriate emotional reactions, and changes in behavior.

conditional positive regard an attitude of acceptance and esteem that others express toward an individual on a conditional basis, that is, depending on the acceptability of the individual's behavior in accordance with the others' personal standards. Conditional regard works against sound psychological development and adjustment in the recipient. Compare UNCONDITIONAL POSITIVE REGARD.

conditional probability the likeliness that an event will occur given that another event is known to have occurred. Conditional probability plays an important role in statistical theory. The probability of observing a particular outcome given that another outcome is known to have occurred can be derived from a CONTINGENCY TABLE. Also called **conditional likelihood**.

conditioned aversion a tendency or desire to avoid one stimulus that results from its pairing with another stimulus that is experienced as unpleasant. Such an aversion may arise after a single pairing of the stimuli (see CONDITIONED TASTE AVERSION) or as part of a process of deliberate repeated pairings (as in AVERSION CONDITIONING). For example, a person who is trying to stop nail biting may paint her fingernails with a bitter substance, such that the foul taste experienced each time she chews a nail eventually leads to cessation of the behavior.

conditioned reinforcement see SECONDARY REINFORCEMENT.

conditioned reinforcer see NATURAL REINFORCER; SECONDARY REINFORCEMENT.

conditioned response (**CR**) in CLASSICAL CONDITIONING, the learned or acquired response to a conditioned stimulus. Also called **conditioned reflex**.

conditioned stimulus (**CS**) a neutral stimulus that is repeatedly associated with an UNCONDITIONED STIMULUS until it acquires the ability to elicit a response that it previously did not. In many cases, the response elicited by the conditioned stimulus is similar to that elicited by the unconditioned stimulus. A light, for example, by being repeatedly paired with food (the unconditioned stimulus), eventually comes to elicit the same response as food (i.e., salivation) when presented alone.

conditioned stimulus–unconditioned stimulus interval (**CS–US interval**) the time period between a participant's exposure to a stimulus for which there has been response training (i.e., conditioning) and the participant's exposure to a stimulus for which there has been no training.

conditioned taste aversion the association of the taste of a food or fluid with an aversive stimulus (usually gastrointestinal discomfort or illness), leading to a very rapid and long-lasting aversion to, or at the least a decreased preference for, that particular taste. Conditioned taste aversion challenges traditional theories of associative learning, since very few pairings between the food and illness are needed to produce the effect (often one pairing will suffice), the delay between experiencing the taste and then feeling ill can be relatively long, and the aversion is highly resistant to EXTINCTION.

conditioning *n.* the process by which certain kinds of experience make particular actions more or less likely. See CLASSICAL CONDITIONING; INSTRUMENTAL CONDITIONING; OPERANT CONDITIONING.

conditions of worth the state in which an individual considers love and respect to be conditional on meeting the approval of others. This belief derives from the child's sense of being worthy of love on the basis of parental approval: As the individual matures, he or she may continue to feel worthy of affection and respect only when expressing desirable behaviors. See CONDITIONAL POSITIVE REGARD.

conduct disorder (CD) a persistent pattern of behavior that involves violating the basic rights of others and ignoring age-appropriate social standards. Some examples are lying, theft, arson, running away from home, truancy, burglary, cruelty to animals, and fighting. The individual may display callousness, lack of guilt, and shallow affect. CD is distinguished from OPPOSITIONAL DEFIANT DISORDER by the increased severity of the behaviors and their occurrence independently of an event occasioning opposition.

conduction aphasia a form of APHASIA characterized by difficulty in repeating words and phrases accurately, even though language comprehension may be intact. Spontaneous speech tends to be grammatically correct but with frequent errors in the sounds of words and in finding the correct words to convey meaning. Contemporary research indicates that a lesion centered around the ridge on the inferior PARIETAL LOBE and the PLANUM TEMPORALE is responsible.

conduction deafness see DEAFNESS.

cone *n.* see RETINAL CONE.

confabulation *n.* the falsification of memory in which gaps in recall are filled by fabrications that the individual accepts as fact. It is not typically considered to be a conscious attempt to deceive others. Confabulation occurs most frequently in KORSAKOFF'S SYNDROME and to a lesser extent in other conditions associated with neurologically based amnesia (e.g., Alzheimer's disease). In forensic contexts, eyewitnesses may resort to confabulation if they feel pressured to recall more information than they can remember.
—**confabulate** *vb.*

confederate *n.* **1.** in experimentation, an aide of the experimenter who poses as a participant but whose behavior is rehearsed prior to the experiment. **2.** in parapsychology, an individual who assists a supposed PSYCHIC by covertly providing him or her with information about a client's concerns, preferences, background, or situation, thus creating or strengthening the illusion of the psychic's paranormal abilities.

confidence interval (CI) a range of values for a population PARAMETER that is estimated from a sample with a preset, fixed probability (the CONFIDENCE LEVEL) that the range will contain the true value of the parameter. The width of the confidence interval provides information about the precision of the estimate, such that a wider interval indicates relatively low precision and a narrower interval indicates relatively high precision. For example, a confidence interval for the population mean could be calculated with data obtained from a sample and would provide an estimated range of values within which the actual population mean is believed to lie. A confidence interval is often reported in addition to the POINT ESTIMATE of a population parameter.

confidence level a value expressing the frequency with which a given CONFIDENCE INTERVAL contains the true value of the parameter being estimated. For example, a 95% confidence level associated with a confidence interval for estimating a population mean indicates that in 95% of all estimates based on a random sample of a given size the confidence interval will contain the true value of the population mean. The particular confidence level used is up to the researcher but generally is 95% or 99%.

confidentiality *n.* a principle of professional ethics requiring providers of mental health care or medical care to limit the disclosure of a patient's identity, his or her condition or treatment, and other data entrusted to professionals during assessment, diagnosis, and treatment. Similar protection is given to research participants and survey respondents against unauthorized access to information they reveal in confidence. See also TARASOFF DECISION. —**confidential** *adj.*

configural learning learning to respond to two or more stimuli on the basis of their combination rather than on the individual experience of any of those stimuli alone. For example, if neither a tone nor a light presented separately is followed by food, but a tone–light combination is, configural learning has occurred when a conditioned response is elicited by the tone–light combination.

confirmation bias the tendency to gather evidence that confirms preexisting expectations, typically by emphasizing or pursuing supporting evidence while dismissing or failing to seek contradictory evidence.

confirmatory factor analysis (**CFA**) any method of testing A PRIORI hypotheses specifying that the relationships among a set of observed variables are due to a particular set of unobserved variables. Unlike EXPLORATORY FACTOR ANALYSIS, in which all measured (manifest) variables are examined in relation to all underlying (latent) variables, confirmatory factor analysis imposes explicit theoretical restrictions so that observed measures relate with some (often just one) latent factors but not others.

conflict *n.* the occurrence of mutually antagonistic or opposing forces, including events, behaviors, desires, attitudes, and emotions. In psychoanalytic theory, the term refers to the opposition between incompatible instinctual impulses or between incompatible aspects of the mental structure (i.e., the ID, EGO, and SUPEREGO) that may be a source of NEUROSIS if it results in the use of defense mechanisms other than SUBLIMATION. In interpersonal relations, conflict denotes the disagreement, discord, and friction that occur when the actions or beliefs of one or

more individuals are unacceptable to and resisted by others.

conformity *n.* the adjustment of one's opinions, judgments, or actions so that they become more consistent with (a) the opinions, judgments, or actions of other people or (b) the normative standards of a social group or situation. Conformity includes temporary outward acquiescence (COMPLIANCE) as well as more enduring private acceptance (CONVERSION).

confound *n.* in an experiment, an independent variable that is conceptually distinct but empirically inseparable from one or more other independent variables. **Confounding** makes it impossible to differentiate that variable's effects in isolation from its effects in conjunction with other variables. For example, in a study of high-school student achievement, the type of school (e.g., private vs. public) that a student attended prior to high school and his or her prior academic achievements in that context are confounds. Also called **confounding variable**.

confusion of responsibility the tendency for bystanders to refrain from helping in both emergencies and nonemergencies to avoid being blamed by others for causing the problem. This is a contributing factor in the BYSTANDER EFFECT. See also DIFFUSION OF RESPONSIBILITY.

congenital *adj.* denoting a condition or disorder that is present at birth.

congenital adrenal hyperplasia (**CAH**) an inherited disorder caused by mutations that encode for enzymes involved in one of the various steps of steroid hormone synthesis in the adrenal gland. These defects result in the absence or decreased synthesis of CORTISOL from its cholesterol precursor and a concomitant abnormal increase in the production of androgens. Symptoms in females include ambiguous genitalia and masculinization of secondary sex characteristics; in males, they include premature puberty.

congenital defect any abnormality present at birth, regardless of the cause. It may be caused by faulty fetal development (e.g., spina bifida, cleft palate), hereditary factors (e.g., Huntington's disease), chromosomal aberration (e.g., Down syndrome), maternal conditions affecting the developing fetus (e.g., fetal alcohol syndrome), metabolic defects (e.g., phenylketonuria), or injury to the brain before or during birth (e.g., some cases of cerebral palsy). A congenital defect may not be apparent until several years after birth (e.g., an allergy or a metabolic disorder) or even until after the individual has reached adulthood (e.g., Huntington's disease). Also called **birth defect**.

congruence *n*. in phenomenological personality theory, (a) the need for a therapist to act in accordance with his or her true feelings rather than with a stylized image of a therapist or (b) the conscious integration of an experience into the self. —**congruent** *adj*.

conjunctive task a group task or project that cannot be completed successfully until all members of the group have completed their portion of the job (e.g., a factory assembly line). This means that the speed and quality of the work are determined by the least skilled member. Compare ADDITIVE TASK; COMPENSATORY TASK; DISJUNCTIVE TASK.

connectionism *n*. **1.** an approach that views human cognitive processes in terms of massively parallel cooperative and competitive interactions among large numbers of simple neuronlike computational units. Although each unit exhibits nonlinear spatial and temporal summation, units and connections are not generally to be taken as corresponding directly to individual neurons and synapses. **2.** the concept that learning involves the acquisition of neural links, or connections, between stimulus and response. —**connectionist** *adj*.

connectionist model any of a class of theories hypothesizing that knowledge is encoded by the connections among representations stored in the brain rather than in the representations themselves. Connectionist models suggest that knowledge is distributed rather than being localized and that it is retrieved through SPREADING ACTIVATION among connections. The connectionist model concept has been extended to artificial intelligence, particularly to its NEURAL NETWORK models of problem solving.

connector neuron see INTERNEURON.

connotative meaning see DENOTATIVE MEANING.

consanguineous family see EXTENDED FAMILY.

consanguinity *n*. a biological relationship between two or more individuals who are descended from a common ancestor. Compare AFFINITY.

conscience *n*. an individual's sense of right and wrong or of transgression against moral values. In psychoanalysis, conscience is the SUPEREGO, or ethical component of personality, which acts as judge and critic of one's actions and attitudes. More recent biological approaches suggest that the capacity of conscience may be neurologically based, whereas psychosocial approaches emphasize the role of learning in the development of conscience and its influence in the formation of groups and societies.

conscious (Cs) 1. *adj*. relating to or marked by awareness or consciousness. **2.** *n*. in the classical psychoanalytic theory of Austrian neurologist Sigmund Freud (1856–1939), the region of the psyche that contains thoughts, feelings, perceptions, and other aspects of mental life currently present in awareness. The content of the Cs is thus inherently transitory and continuously changing as the person shifts the focus of his or her attention. Compare PRECONSCIOUS; SUBCONSCIOUS; UNCONSCIOUS.

consciousness *n.* **1.** the state of being conscious. **2.** an organism's AWARENESS of something either internal or external to itself. **3.** the waking state. **4.** in medicine and brain science, the distinctive electrical activity of the waking brain, as recorded via electroencephalography, that is commonly used to identify conscious states and their pathologies.

Beyond these succinct senses of the term, there are intricate philosophical and research controversies over the concept of consciousness and multiple perspectives about its meaning. Broadly, these interpretations divide along two (although not always mutually exclusive) major lines: (a) those proposed by scholars on the basis of function or behavior (i.e., consciousness viewed "from the outside"—the observable organism); and (b) those proposed by scholars on the basis of experience or subjectivity (i.e., consciousness viewed "from the inside"—the mind).

Functional or behavioral interpretations tend to define consciousness in terms of physical, neurobiological, and cognitive processes, such as the ability to discriminate stimuli, to monitor internal states, to control behavior, and to respond to the environment. Experiential or subjective interpretations, however, tend to define consciousness in terms of mental imagery; intuition; subjective experience as related to sensations, perceptions, emotions, moods, and dreams; self-awareness; awareness of awareness itself and of the unity between the self and others and the physical world; STREAM OF CONSCIOUSNESS; and other aspects of private experience. See also ALTERED STATE OF CONSCIOUSNESS.

consciousness studies a multidisciplinary field that combines approaches from cognitive science, neurophysiology, and philosophy of mind to investigate the nature of consciousness. Major concerns include the relationship of the mind to the body (see MIND–BODY PROBLEM), the difficulty of explaining the emergence of subjective experience on the basis of the physical nature of the brain, the significance of ALTERED STATES OF CONSCIOUSNESS, and the possibility of consciousness in computers or other manmade systems.

consensual validation the process by which a therapist helps a client check the accuracy of his or her perception or the results of his or her experience by comparing it with those of others, often in the context of GROUP THERAPY.

consensus *n.* general agreement among the members of a group, especially when making an appraisal or decision.

consent *n.* voluntary assent or approval given by an individual: specifically, permission granted by an individual for medical or psychological treatment, participation in research, or both. Individuals should be fully informed about the treatment or study and its risks and potential benefits (see INFORMED CONSENT).

conservation *n.* the awareness that physical quantities do not change in amount when they are altered in appearance, such as when water is poured from a wide, short beaker into a thin, tall one. According to PIAGETIAN THEORY, children become capable of this mental operation in the CONCRETE OPERATIONAL STAGE. See also REVERSIBILITY.

conservation psychology a subfield of psychology that seeks to understand the attitudes and behavior of individuals and groups toward the natural environment so as to promote their use of environmentally sustainable practices. Because of the highly diverse categories of behavior being studied, **conservation psychologists** generally focus on specific actions, such as paper recycling, rather than general tendencies. Although related to ENVIRONMENTAL PSYCHOLOGY, conservation psychology is distinct in its orientation toward protecting ecosystems and preserving resources while ensuring quality of life for humans and other species.

consistency motive the desire to confirm one's current beliefs about one's self. Self-consistency strivings are thought to minimize discomfort associated with disjunctions between different aspects of self-knowledge. Compare SELF-ASSESSMENT MOTIVE; SELF-ENHANCEMENT MOTIVE.

consolidation *n.* the neurobiological processes by which a permanent memory is formed following a learning experience. See PERSEVERATION–CONSOLIDATION HYPOTHESIS.

conspecific 1. *adj.* belonging to the same species. **2.** *n.* a member of the same species.

constant *n.* a fixed quantity that remains unchanged during a specified operation or series of operations. For example, the element *a* in the REGRESSION EQUATION $y = a + bx + e$ is a constant. Compare VARIABLE.

constitution *n.* the basic psychological and physical makeup of an individual, due partly to heredity and partly to life experience and environmental factors. **—constitutional** *adj.*

construal *n.* a person's perception and interpretation of attributes and behavior of the self or of others. See also INDEPENDENT SELF-CONSTRUAL; INTERDEPENDENT SELF-CONSTRUAL.

construct *n.* **1.** a complex idea or concept formed from a synthesis of simpler ideas. **2.** an explanatory model based on measurable, verifiable events or processes (an empirical construct) or on processes inferred from data of this kind but not themselves directly observable (a hypothetical construct). Many of the models used in psychology are hypothetical constructs.

constructionism *n.* see CONSTRUCTIVISM.

constructive coping any instrumental approach to stress management that is generally considered to be adap-

tive or otherwise positive. Examples include planning and strategizing, seeking help and support from others, REFRAMING the situation, and meditating. Research suggests that constructive coping is likely to be used when stressors are of high intensity or when there is little negative emotional arousal generated in the context of the stressful experience or event.

constructive memory a form of remembering marked by the use of general knowledge stored in one's memory to construct a more complete and detailed account of an event or experience. See RECONSTRUCTIVE MEMORY; REPEATED REPRODUCTION.

constructive play a form of play in which children manipulate materials in order to create or build objects, for example, making a sand castle or using blocks to build a house. Constructive play facilitates creativity, learning, and the development of motor and other skills.

constructivism *n.* the theoretical perspective that people actively build their perception of the world and interpret objects and events that surround them in terms of what they already know. Thus, their current state of knowledge guides processing, substantially influencing how (and what) new information is acquired. Also called **constructionism**. See also SOCIAL CONSTRUCTIVISM. **—constructivist** *adj.*

construct validity the degree to which a test or instrument is capable of measuring a concept, trait, or other theoretical entity. For example, if a researcher develops a new questionnaire to evaluate respondents' levels of aggression, the construct validity of the instrument would be the extent to which it actually assesses aggression as opposed to assertiveness, social dominance, and so forth. A variety of factors can threaten construct validity, including various forms of BIAS and various EXPERIMENTER EFFECTS.

consultant *n.* a mental health care

contiguity

or medical specialist called on to provide professional advice or services in terms of diagnosis, treatment, or rehabilitation.

consumer neuroscience see NEUROMARKETING.

consumer psychology the branch of psychology that studies the behavior of individuals as consumers and the marketing and communication techniques used to influence consumer decisions. **Consumer psychologists** investigate the psychological processes underlying consumer behavior and responses to both for-profit and not-for-profit marketing.

contact comfort the positive effects experienced by infants or young animals when in close contact with soft materials. The term originates from experiments in which young rhesus monkeys exposed both to an artificial cloth mother without a bottle for feeding and to an artificial wire mother with a bottle for feeding spent more time on the cloth mother and, when frightened, were more readily soothed by the presence of the cloth mother than the wire mother.

contact hypothesis the proposition that interaction among people belonging to different groups will reduce intergroup prejudice. Research indicates that the prejudice-alleviating effects of contact are robust across many situations, but that they are strengthened when the people from the different groups are of equal status, are not in competition with each other, and do not readily categorize the others as very different from themselves.

contamination *n.* in testing and experimentation, the situation in which prior knowledge, expectations, or other factors relating to the variable under study are permitted to influence the collection and interpretation of data about that variable.

content analysis a systematic procedure for coding the themes in qualitative material, such as projective-test responses, propaganda, or fiction. For example, content analysis of verbally communicated material (e.g., articles, speeches, films) is done by determining the frequency of specific ideas, concepts, or terms.

content-referenced test see CRITERION-REFERENCED TEST.

content validity the extent to which a test measures a representative sample of the subject matter or behavior under investigation. For example, if a test is designed to survey arithmetic skills at a third-grade level, content validity indicates how well it represents the range of arithmetic operations possible at that level. Modern approaches to determining content validity involve the use of EXPLORATORY FACTOR ANALYSIS and other multivariate procedures.

content word in linguistics, a word with an independent lexical meaning, that is, one that can be defined with reference to the physical world or abstract concepts and without reference to any sentence in which the word may appear. Nouns, verbs, adjectives, and many adverbs are considered to be content words. Compare FUNCTION WORD.

context *n.* the conditions or circumstances in which a particular phenomenon occurs, especially as this influences memory, learning, judgment, or other cognitive processes. —**contextual** *adj.*

contextual analysis any method of evaluating data that takes into account the characteristics of the environment in which the information was collected and their influence on study units. For example, a contextual analysis of data gathered from an experimental study conducted in a laboratory would take into account the effects of the laboratory itself on study participants (e.g., behavior), whereas one conducted in a public setting would account for the effects of that environment on the participants.

contiguity *n.* the co-occurrence of

93

stimuli in time or space. Learning an association between two stimuli is generally thought to depend at least partly on the contiguity of those stimuli. —**contiguous** *adj.*

contingencies of self-worth particular areas of life in which people invest their SELF-ESTEEM, such that feedback regarding their standing or abilities in these domains has a strong effect on their SELF-CONCEPT. Research indicates that people choose to stake their self-esteem in different domains, so that for some people material or professional success is vital to their sense of self-worth, whereas for others this is much less important than being well liked or sexually attractive, for example.

contingency *n.* a conditional, probabilistic relation between two events. When the probability of Event B given Event A is 1.0, a perfect positive contingency is said to exist. When Event A predicts with certainty the absence of Event B, a perfect negative contingency is said to exist. Probabilities between −1.0 and 1.0 define a continuum from negative to positive contingencies, with a probability of 0 indicating no contingency.

contingency management in BEHAVIOR THERAPY, a technique in which a reinforcement, or reward, is given each time the desired behavior is performed. This technique is particularly common in substance abuse treatment.

contingency table a two-dimensional table in which frequency values for categories of different variables are presented in the rows and columns. For example, the sex and geographical locations of a sample of individuals applying for a particular job may be displayed in a contingency table. Thus, the number of women from Los Angeles would be given in one CELL, the number of men from Los Angeles would be given in another, the number of women from New York City would be given in yet another, and so on. Also called **cross-classification table**.

continuity *n.* the quality or state of being unending or connected into a continuous whole. For example, the traditional concept of continuity of care implies the provision of a full range of uninterrupted medical and mental health care services to a person throughout his or her lifespan, from birth to death, as needed.

continuity hypothesis the assumption that successful DISCRIMINATION learning or problem solving results from a progressive, incremental, continuous process of trial and error. Responses that prove unproductive are extinguished, whereas every reinforced response results in an increase in associative strength, thus producing the gradual rise of the LEARNING CURVE. Problem solving is conceived as a step-by-step learning process in which the correct response is discovered, practiced, and reinforced. Compare DISCONTINUITY HYPOTHESIS.

continuity theory a theory proposing that people generally maintain the same personality style, activity level, interests, and social roles as they age. Compare ACTIVITY THEORY; DISENGAGEMENT THEORY.

continuous *adj.* describing a variable, score, or distribution that can take on any numerical values within its range. Compare DISCONTINUOUS; DISCRETE. See also CONTINUOUS VARIABLE.

continuous reinforcement (**CRF**) in operant and instrumental conditioning, the REINFORCEMENT of every correct (desired) response. It is identical to a fixed-ratio 1 schedule of reinforcement (see FIXED-RATIO SCHEDULE). Also called **continuous reinforcement schedule**.

continuous variable a variable that may in theory have an infinite number of possible values. For example, time is a continuous variable because accurate instruments will enable it to be measured to any subdivision of a unit (e.g., 1.76 seconds). By contrast, number of children is not a continuous variable because it is not possible to have 1.76 children. Compare DISCONTINUOUS VARIABLE.

continuum of care provision over a period of time of continuous, comprehensive, and integrated care that involves health, mental health, and social services—in the home, a health care setting, or the community—at the appropriate level of intensity. The wide range and levels of available services in a continuum of care allow for adjustments to be made in treatment when the patient or client improves (e.g., during successful drug addiction treatment) or worsens (e.g., as the health of a terminally ill patient declines).

contraction *n.* a shortening or tensing of a group of MUSCLE FIBERS.

contralateral *adj.* situated on or affecting the opposite side of the body. For example, motor paralysis occurs on the side of the body contralateral to the side on which a brain lesion exists. Compare IPSILATERAL. —**contralaterally** *adv.*

contrast *n.* **1.** that state in which the differences between one percept, thing, event, or idea and another are emphasized by a comparison of their qualities. This may occur when the stimuli are juxtaposed (simultaneous contrast) or when one stimulus immediately follows the other (successive contrast). **2.** in statistics, see COMPARISON.

contrast sensitivity a measure of spatial RESOLUTION based on an individual's ability to detect subtle differences in light and dark coloring or shading in an object of a fixed size. Detection is affected by the size of contrasting elements and is usually tested using a grating of alternating light and dark bars, with sensitivity being defined by the minimum contrast required to distinguish that there is a bar pattern rather than a uniform screen.

contributing cause a cause that is not sufficient to bring about an end or event but that helps in some way to bring about that end or event. A contributing cause may be a necessary condition or it may influence events more indirectly by affecting other conditions that make the event more likely.

control *n.* **1.** authority, power, or influence over events, behaviors, situations, or people. **2.** the regulation of all extraneous conditions and variables in an experiment so that any change in the DEPENDENT VARIABLE can be attributed solely to manipulation of the INDEPENDENT VARIABLE and not to any other factors.

control group a comparison group in a study whose members receive either no intervention at all or some established intervention. The responses of those in the control group are compared with the responses of participants in one or more EXPERIMENTAL GROUPS that are given the new treatment or condition being evaluated.

controlled trial a study in which patients with a particular condition, disease, or illness are assigned either to a treatment group, which receives the new intervention under investigation, or to a CONTROL GROUP, which receives either no intervention or some standard intervention already in use. If individuals are allocated to the different groups at random, then the design is a RANDOMIZED CLINICAL TRIAL. Also called **comparative trial**.

control processes those processes that organize the flow of information in an INFORMATION-PROCESSING system.

control variable a variable that is considered to have an effect on the response measure in a study but that itself is not of particular interest to the researcher. To remove its effects a control variable may be held at a constant level during the study or managed by statistical means (e.g., a PARTIAL CORRELATION).

convenience sampling any process for selecting a sample of individuals or cases that is neither random nor systematic but rather is governed by chance or ready availability. Interviewing the first 50 people to exit a store is an example of convenience sampling. Data obtained from convenience sampling do not generalize to the larger population; there may be significant SAMPLING BIAS, and SAMPLING ERROR cannot be estimated. Also called **accidental** or **opportunity sampling**.

conventional antipsychotic see ANTIPSYCHOTIC.

conventional level in KOHLBERG'S THEORY OF MORAL DEVELOPMENT, the intermediate level of moral reasoning, characterized by an individual's identification with and conformity to the expectations and rules of family and society: The individual evaluates actions and determines right and wrong in terms of other people's opinions. Also called **conventional morality**. See also PRECONVENTIONAL LEVEL; POSTCONVENTIONAL LEVEL.

convergence *n.* the rotation of the two eyes inward toward a light source so that the image falls on corresponding points on the foveas. Convergence enables the slightly different images of an object seen by each eye to come together and form a single image.

convergent thinking critical thinking in which an individual uses linear, logical steps to analyze a number of already formulated solutions to a problem to determine the correct one or the one that is most likely to be successful. Compare DIVERGENT THINKING.

conversation analysis a specialty within DISCOURSE ANALYSIS that focuses on casual discussions as well as other more formal, extended verbal exchanges between two or more speakers.

conversion *n.* **1.** an unconscious process in which anxiety generated by psychological conflicts is transformed into physical symptoms. **2.** actual change in an individual's beliefs, attitudes, or behaviors that occurs as a result of SOCIAL INFLUENCE. Unlike COMPLIANCE, which is outward and temporary, conversion occurs when the targeted individual is personally convinced by a persuasive message or internalizes and accepts as his or her own the beliefs expressed by other group members. Also called **private acceptance**. See also CONFORMITY. —**convert** *vb.*

conversion disorder a SOMATOFORM DISORDER in which patients present with one or more symptoms or deficits affecting voluntary motor and sensory functioning that suggest a physical disorder but for which there may be evidence of psychological involvement. These **conversion symptoms** can include paralysis, loss of voice, blindness, seizures, disturbance in coordination and balance, and loss of pain and touch sensations. There must be clear incompatibility of symptoms with recognized neurological pathology before a diagnosis can be made. Also called **functional neurological symptom disorder**.

convolution *n.* a folding or twisting, especially of the surface of the brain.

convulsion *n.* an involuntary, generalized, and violent muscular contraction, in some cases tonic (contractions without relaxation) and in others clonic (alternating contractions and relaxations of skeletal muscles).

Cook's distance (**Cook's *D***) in an analysis of the relationship between a response variable and one or more predictor variables, a measure of the difference that is made to the result when a single observation is dropped from the analysis. Cook's *D* thus indicates the degree of influence of a particular data value. An observation typically is considered influential if it has a Cook's *D* larger than $4/(n - k - 1)$, where n is the sample size and k is the number of terms in the model. [R. Dennis **Cook** (1944–), U.S. statistician]

Coolidge effect increased sexual vigor when a human or nonhuman animal mates with multiple partners. The phenomenon is named for U.S. President Calvin Coolidge, alluding to a visit that he and his wife made to a farm where Mrs. Coolidge observed a rooster mating frequently.

cooperation *n.* a process whereby two or more individuals work together toward the attainment of a mutual goal or complementary goals. This contrasts with COMPETITION, in which an individual's actions in working toward a goal lessen the likelihood of others achieving the same goal. —**cooperate** *vb.* —**cooperative** *adj.*

coparenting *n.* the coordination by parents of their child-rearing practices. It can be supportive in nature, with partners reinforcing one another in child-rearing activities, but it may also be antagonistic, whereby partners are either inconsistent in parenting (e.g., show discrepant levels of parent–child engagement) or undermine each other's child-rearing efforts (e.g., compete for their children's attention). Also called **parental alliance**.

coping *n.* the use of cognitive and behavioral strategies to manage the demands of a situation when these are appraised as taxing or exceeding one's resources or to reduce the negative emotions and conflict caused by such demands. —**cope** *vb.*

coping strategy an action, a series of actions, or a thought process used in meeting a stressful or unpleasant situation or in modifying one's reaction to such a situation. Coping strategies typically involve a conscious and direct approach to problems, in contrast to DEFENSE MECHANISMS. See also EMOTION-FOCUSED COPING; PROBLEM-FOCUSED COPING.

coping style the characteristic manner in which an individual confronts and deals with stress, anxiety-provoking situations, or emergencies.

coprolalia *n.* spontaneous, unprovoked, and uncontrollable use of obscene or profane words and expressions, particularly those related to feces. It is a symptom that may be observed in individuals with a variety of neurological disorders, particularly TOURETTE'S DISORDER.

core knowledge the psychological and neural mechanisms underlying human cognition. Typically, each mechanism is characterized as having four properties. First, it is domain specific and functions to represent a particular kind of entity (e.g., individual objects, places in the environment). Second, it is task specific and uses its representations to track and recognize objects and locations. Third, it uses only a subset of the information delivered by the organism's input systems (e.g., visual perception) and sends information only to a subset of its output systems. Fourth, it is relatively automatic and impervious to explicitly held beliefs. Infants and young children are thought to possess core knowledge in areas (relating, e.g., to people and social relations, objects, numbers, and quantities) that have been important throughout human evolutionary history. Its mechanisms are considered to be shared with many nonhuman species.

cornea *n.* the transparent part of the outer covering of the eye, through which light first passes. It is continuous laterally with the SCLERA. The cornea provides the primary refractive power of the eye. —**corneal** *adj.*

coronal plane the plane that divides the front (anterior) half of the body or brain from the back (posterior) half.

coronary heart disease (CHD) a cardiovascular disorder characterized by restricted flow of blood through the coronary arteries supplying the heart muscle. The cause is usually ATHEROSCLEROSIS of the coronary arteries and often leads to fatal myocardial infarction (heart attack). Behavioral and psychosocial factors are frequently involved in the development and prognosis of the disease. Also called **coronary artery disease**. See CARDIAC PSYCHOLOGY.

corpus callosum a large tract of nerve fibers running across the LONGITUDINAL FISSURE of the brain and connecting the cerebral hemispheres: It is the principal connection between the two sides of the brain and the largest of the interhemispheric COMMISSURES.

corpus striatum see BASAL GANGLIA.

correlation *n.* the degree of relationship (usually linear) between two variables, which may be quantified as a CORRELATION COEFFICIENT.

correlational research a type of study in which relationships between variables are simply observed without any control over the setting in which those relationships occur or any manipulation by the researcher. FIELD RESEARCH often takes this form. For example, consider a researcher assessing teaching style. He or she could use a correlational approach by attending classes on a college campus that are each taught in a different way (e.g., lecture, interactive, computer aided) and noting any differences in student learning that arise. Compare EXPERIMENTAL RESEARCH.

correlation analysis any of various statistical procedures for identifying relationships among variables and determining their strength or degree. CANONICAL ANALYSIS and FACTOR ANALYSIS are examples. Correlation analyses make no inferences about causality. Also called **association analysis**.

correlation coefficient a numerical index reflecting the degree of linear relationship between two variables. It is scaled so that the value of +1 indicates a perfect positive relationship (such that high scores on variable *x* are associated with high scores on variable *y*), −1 indicates a perfect negative relationship (such that high scores on variable *x* are associated with low

scores on variable *y*, or vice versa), and 0 indicates no relationship. The most commonly used type of correlation coefficient is the Pearson PRODUCT-MOMENT CORRELATION COEFFICIENT.

correlation matrix a symmetrical matrix displaying the degree of association (as indexed by a CORRELATION COEFFICIENT) between all possible pairs of variables contained in a set.

correspondence bias see FUNDAMENTAL ATTRIBUTION ERROR.

correspondent inference theory a model describing how people form inferences about other people's stable personality characteristics from observing their behavior. Correspondence between behaviors and traits is more likely to be inferred if the actor is judged to have acted (a) freely, (b) intentionally, (c) in a way that is unusual for someone in the situation, and (d) in a way that does not usually bring rewards or social approval. See also ATTRIBUTION THEORY.

cortex *n.* (*pl.* **cortices**) the outer or superficial layer or layers of a structure, as distinguished from the central core. In mammals, the cortex of a structure is identified with the name of the gland or organ, for example, the CEREBELLAR CORTEX or CEREBRAL CORTEX. Compare MEDULLA. —**cortical** *adj.*

cortical blindness blindness, with normal pupillary responses, that is due to complete destruction of the OPTIC RADIATIONS or the STRIATE CORTEX. Because the subcortical structures (white matter) of the visual system are involved, it is also called **cerebral blindness**. Typically caused by a stroke affecting the occipital lobe of the brain, cortical blindness can also result from traumatic injury or HYPOXIA.

cortical deafness deafness that is caused by damage to auditory centers in the cerebral cortex of the brain. The peripheral auditory system (which includes the retrocochlear neural pathways terminating in the brainstem) can be intact in this condition.

corticospinal tract see VENTROMEDIAL PATHWAY.

corticosteroid *n.* any of the steroid hormones produced by the ADRENAL GLAND. They include the GLUCOCORTICOIDS (e.g., CORTISOL), which are involved in carbohydrate metabolism, and the MINERALOCORTICOIDS (e.g., ALDOSTERONE), which have a role in electrolyte balance and sodium retention.

corticotropin *n.* a hormone secreted by the anterior pituitary gland, particularly when a person experiences stress. It stimulates the release of various other hormones (primarily CORTICOSTEROIDS) from the adrenal gland. Also called **adrenocorticotropic hormone (ACTH)**; **adrenocorticotropin**.

cortisol *n.* a major GLUCOCORTICOID hormone whose activity increases blood sugar levels. Cortisol is considered the primary STRESS HORMONE: In response to stress or injury, blood cortisol levels, and therefore glucose levels, increase, whereas activity of the immune system decreases and release of inflammatory substances in the body is contained. Cortisol thus improves the body's ability to manage stress and to repair itself. Exposure to prolonged stress, however, can lead to excessive levels of cortisol, which can have deleterious effects on the body (e.g., hyperglycemia).

cosleeping *n.* a practice in which one or both parents sleep in the same room with their infant, near enough for them to touch. Cosleeping arrangements may include three-sided bassinets that attach to the adult bed or cribs placed next to the bed. These arrangements are thought to promote BONDING, encourage breast-feeding, and improve infant sleep.

counseling *n.* professional assistance in coping with personal problems, including emotional, behavioral, vocational, marital, educational, rehabilitation, and life-stage (e.g., retirement) problems. The **counselor** makes use of such techniques as ACTIVE LISTENING, guidance or advice, discussion, clarification, and the administration of tests.

counseling psychology the branch of psychology that specializes in facilitating personal and interpersonal functioning across the lifespan. Counseling psychology focuses on emotional, social, vocational, educational, health-related, developmental, and organizational concerns—such as improving well-being, alleviating distress and maladjustment, and resolving crises—and addresses issues from individual, family, group, systems, and organizational perspectives. In contrast to a clinical psychologist (see CLINICAL PSYCHOLOGY), who usually emphasizes origins of maladaptations, a **counseling psychologist** emphasizes adaptation, adjustment, and more efficient use of the individual's available resources.

counterbalancing *n.* arranging a series of experimental conditions or treatments in such a way as to minimize the influence of extraneous factors, such as practice or fatigue, on experimental results. In other words, counterbalancing is an attempt to reduce or avoid CARRYOVER EFFECTS and ORDER EFFECTS. A simple form of counterbalancing would be to administer experimental conditions in the order A-B to half of the participants and in the order B-A to the other half; a LATIN SQUARE would be a more complex form.

counterconditioning *n.* an experimental procedure in which a nonhuman animal, already conditioned to respond to a stimulus in a particular way, is trained to produce a different response to the same stimulus that is incompatible with the original response. This same principle underlies many of the techniques used in BEHAVIOR THERAPY to eliminate unwanted behavior in people.

counterculture *n.* a social movement that maintains its own alternative mores and values in opposition to prevailing cultural norms. The term is historically associated with the hippie movement and attendant drug culture of the late 1960s and early 1970s, which rejected such societal norms as the work ethic and the traditional family unit. See also SUBCULTURE. —**countercultural** adj.

counterfactual thinking imagining ways in which events in one's life might have turned out differently. This often involves feelings of regret or disappointment (e.g., *If only I hadn't been so hasty*) but may also involve a sense of relief, as at a narrow escape (e.g., *If I had been standing 3 feet to the left*).

counterproductive work behavior (**CWB**) undesirable employee behavior that can undermine the goals of an organization or its members and can negatively affect the organization's financial well-being. CWBs cover a wide range of behavior, such as sabotage, theft, absenteeism, bullying, sexual harassment, discrimination, workplace violence, drug and alcohol abuse, and violation of confidentiality agreements.

countershock phase see GENERAL ADAPTATION SYNDROME.

countertransference n. the therapist's unconscious (and often conscious) reactions to the patient and to the patient's TRANSFERENCE. These thoughts and feelings are based on the therapist's own psychological needs and conflicts and may be unexpressed or revealed through responses to patient behavior. The term was originally used to describe this process in psychoanalysis but has since become part of the common lexicon in other forms of psychodynamic psychotherapy and in other therapies. In CLASSICAL PSYCHO-ANALYSIS, countertransference was viewed as a hindrance to the analyst's understanding of the patient, but to modern analysts and therapists, it may serve as a source of insight into the patient's effect on other people.

couples therapy therapy in which both partners in a committed relationship are treated at the same time by the same therapist or therapists. Couples therapy is concerned with problems within and between the individuals that affect the relationship. For example, one partner may have undiagnosed depression that is affecting the relationship, or both partners may have trouble communicating effectively with one another. Individual sessions may be provided separately to each partner, but most of the course of therapy is provided to both partners together. Couples therapy for married couples is known as **marital therapy**.

covariance n. a scale-dependent measure of the relationship between two variables such that corresponding pairs of values on the variables are studied with regard to their relative distance from their respective means. A positive covariance results when values of one variable that lie above the mean of that variable tend to be paired with values of the second variable that also lie above the mean of that variable. A negative covariance results when values of one variable that lie above the mean tend to be paired with values of the second variable that lie below the mean.

covariance matrix a square matrix that represents how variance in each variable in a set is related to variance in all other variables in the set. The covariances between pairs of variables are located at the intersection of the row and column that correspond to the two variables. The quantities along the diagonal of the matrix are variances rather than covariances. Also called **dispersion matrix**.

covariate n. a variable that exhibits COVARIATION with a measured outcome or DEPENDENT VARIABLE: It is often included in an analysis so that its effect may be taken into account when interpreting the effects of the INDEPENDENT VARIABLES of interest. For example, covariates are used in ANALYSES OF COVARIANCE to statistically adjust groups so that they are equivalent with regard to these variables; they may also be used in MULTIPLE REGRESSION to minimize error that may arise from omitting any noncentral but potentially influential variables.

covariation *n.* a relationship between two quantitative variables such that as one variable tends to increase (or decrease) in value, the corresponding values of the other variable tend to also increase (or decrease). For example, if a person's weight consistently rises as he or she grows older, then the two variables would be exhibiting covariation. —**covary** *vb.*

covert *adj.* denoting anything that is hidden or that is not directly observable, open to view, or publicly known, whether by happenstance or by deliberate design. Compare OVERT.

covert sensitization a BEHAVIOR THERAPY technique for reducing an undesired behavior in which the client imagines performing the undesired behavior (e.g., overeating) and then imagines an unpleasant consequence (e.g., vomiting).

crack *n.* a dried mixture of COCAINE and baking soda that can be smoked. It produces a rapid, short-lived high. It is less pure than freebase cocaine (a highly concentrated and chemically altered form) and therefore less expensive and more accessible. The term **crack baby** is slang for an infant whose mother used crack cocaine during pregnancy. In utero exposure to cocaine has been associated with negative effects on learning and functioning.

Cramér's *V* (symbol: *V*; φ_c) a measure of the degree of association between two variables that have two or more unordered response categories. More specifically, it is an omnibus EFFECT SIZE that quantifies the overall association among the rows and columns in a CONTINGENCY TABLE. Also called **Cramér's phi**. [Harald **Cramér** (1893–1985), Swedish mathematician]

cranial nerve any of the 12 pairs of nerves that arise directly from the brain and are distributed mainly to structures in the head and neck. Some of the cranial nerves are sensory, some are motor, and some are mixed (i.e., both sensory and motor). Cranial nerves are designated by Roman numerals, as follows: I, OLFACTORY NERVE; II, OPTIC NERVE; III, OCULOMOTOR NERVE; IV, TROCHLEAR NERVE; V, TRIGEMINAL NERVE; VI, ABDUCENS NERVE; VII, FACIAL NERVE; VIII, VESTIBULOCOCHLEAR NERVE; IX, GLOSSOPHARYNGEAL NERVE; X, VAGUS NERVE; XI, ACCESSORY NERVE; and XII, HYPOGLOSSAL NERVE.

craving *n.* an unrelenting desire, urge, or yearning. It is often a criterion for the diagnosis of drug addiction or alcoholism.

creative intelligence in the TRIARCHIC THEORY OF INTELLIGENCE, the set of skills used to create, invent, discover, explore, imagine, and suppose. This set of skills is alleged to be relatively (although not wholly) distinct from analytical and practical skills. Compare ANALYTICAL INTELLIGENCE; PRACTICAL INTELLIGENCE.

creativity *n.* the ability to produce or develop original work, theories, techniques, or thoughts. A creative individual typically displays originality, imagination, and expressiveness, but analyses have failed to ascertain why one individual is more creative than another. See also DIVERGENT THINKING. —**creative** *adj.*

creole *n.* a language that has evolved from profound and prolonged contact between two or more languages and that both shares features of the present languages and evolves altogether novel features. Although typically developing from a PIDGIN, a creole becomes stable over time and will usually have a fully developed grammatical system.

Creutzfeldt–Jakob disease (CJD) a rapidly progressive neurological disease caused by abnormal prion proteins and characterized by DEMENTIA, involuntary muscle movements, muscular incoordination (ataxia), visual disturbances, and seizures. Vacuoles form in the gray matter of the brain and spinal cord, giving it a spongy appearance. Classical CJD occurs sporadically worldwide and typically affects individuals who are middle-aged or older. Variant CJD (vCJD) causes similar symptoms but typically affects younger people, who are believed to have acquired the disease by eating meat or meat products from cattle infected with bovine spongiform encephalopathy. [Hans Gerhard **Creutzfeldt** (1885–1964) and Alfons **Jakob** (1884–1931), German neuropathologists]

criminal responsibility a defendant's ability to formulate criminal intent at the time of the crime with which he or she is charged; it must be proved in court before the person can be convicted. Criminal responsibility may be excluded for reason of INSANITY or mitigated for a number of other reasons.

crisis *n.* (*pl.* **crises**) **1.** a situation (e.g., a traumatic change) that produces significant cognitive or emotional stress in those involved in it. **2.** a turning point for better or worse in the course of an illness.

crisis intervention 1. the brief ameliorative, rather than specifically curative, use of psychotherapy or counseling to aid individuals, families, and groups who have undergone a highly disruptive experience, such as an unexpected bereavement or a disaster. **2.** psychological intervention provided on a short-term, emergency basis for individuals experiencing mental health crises, such as attempted suicide.

crista (**crysta**) *n.* the structure within the ampulla at the end of each SEMICIRCULAR CANAL that contains hair cells sensitive to the direction and rate of movements of the head.

criterion *n.* (*pl.* **criteria**) a standard against which a judgment, evaluation, or comparison can be made. For exam-

ple, a well-validated test of creativity might be used as the criterion to develop new tests of creativity.

criterion group a group tested for traits its members are already known to possess, usually for the purpose of demonstrating that responses to a test represent the traits they were intended to represent. For example, a group of children with diagnosed visual disabilities may be given a visual test to assess its validity as a means of evaluating the presence of visual disabilities.

criterion-referenced test an exam from which decisions are made about an individual's absolute level of accomplishment (i.e., mastery or nonmastery) of the material covered in that exam according to some standard reference point. For example, if a student obtains a score of 70% on a reading exam and a passing score is 65%, then he or she has done acceptably well. Also called **content-referenced test**. See also NORM-REFERENCED TEST.

criterion validity an index of how well a test correlates with an established standard of comparison (i.e., a CRITERION). Criterion validity is divided into three types: predictive validity, concurrent validity, and retrospective validity. For example, if a measure of criminal behavior is valid, then it should be possible to use it to predict whether an individual (a) will be arrested in the future for a criminal violation, (b) is currently breaking the law, and (c) has a previous criminal record. Also called **criterion-referenced validity**.

critical flicker frequency (CFF) the rate at which a periodic change, or flicker, in an intense visual stimulus fuses into a smooth, continuous stimulus. A similar phenomenon can occur with rapidly changing auditory stimuli. Also called **flicker fusion frequency**.

critical period 1. an early stage in life when an organism is especially open to specific learning, emotional, or socializing experiences that occur as part of normal development and will not recur at a later stage. For example, the first 3 days of life are thought to constitute a critical period for IMPRINTING in ducks, and there may be a critical period for language acquisition in human infants. See also SENSITIVE PERIOD. **2.** in vision, the period of time after birth, varying from weeks (in cats) to months (in humans), in which full, binocular visual stimulation is necessary for the structural and functional maturation of the VISUAL SYSTEM.

critical region a range of values that may be obtained from a statistical procedure that would lead to rejecting a specific claim about a population. More specifically, it is the portion of a PROBABILITY DISTRIBUTION containing the values for a test statistic that would result in rejection of a NULL HYPOTHESIS in favor of its corresponding ALTERNATIVE HYPOTHESIS. Compare ACCEPTANCE REGION.

critical thinking a form of directed, problem-focused thinking in which the individual tests ideas or possible solutions for errors or drawbacks. It is essential to such activities as examining the validity of a hypothesis or interpreting the meaning of research results.

critical value a value used to make decisions about whether a test result is statistically meaningful. For example, to evaluate the result of a T TEST to determine whether a sample mean is significantly different from the hypothesized population mean, a researcher would compare the obtained test statistic to the values from a T DISTRIBUTION at a given PROBABILITY LEVEL. If the statistic exceeds the critical value within that distribution, the NULL HYPOTHESIS is rejected and the result is considered significant. See also CRITICAL REGION.

Cronbach's alpha a measure of the average strength of association between all possible pairs of items contained within a set of items. It is a commonly used index of the INTERNAL CONSISTENCY of a test and ranges in value from 0, indicating no internal consistency, to 1, indicating perfect internal consistency. Also called **alpha coefficient**. [Lee J. **Cronbach** (1916–2001), U.S. psychologist]

cross-adaptation *n.* the change in sensitivity to one stimulus caused by adaptation to another.

cross-classification table see CONTINGENCY TABLE.

cross-correlation *n.* a measure of the degree of association between corresponding values from a series of values for two or more variables.

cross-cultural psychology a branch of psychology that studies similarities and variances in human behavior across different cultures and identifies the different psychological constructs and explanatory models used by these cultures. It has been influenced by anthropology and emphasizes social psychological analyses of international differences. See also CULTURAL PSYCHOLOGY.

crossing over in genetics, see RECOMBINATION.

cross-lagged panel design a study of the relationships between two or more variables across time in which one variable measured at an earlier point in time is examined with regard to a second variable measured at a later point in time, and vice versa. For example, suppose an organizational researcher measures job satisfaction and job performance at the beginning of one fiscal year and at the beginning of a second fiscal year. Examining the correlations between satisfaction and performance at the different times provides information about their possible causal association.

cross-modal matching the ability to recognize an object initially inspected with one modality (e.g., touch) via another modality (e.g., vision). Also called **intermodal matching**.

cross-modal perception see INTERSENSORY PERCEPTION.

cross-modal transfer recognition of an object through a sense other than the sense through which the object was originally encountered.

cross-sectional analysis the examination of data that have been collected at a single point in time. For example, a researcher might conduct a cross-sectional analysis after measuring the income of people in different professions at the end of a particular year. Compare TIME-SERIES ANALYSIS.

cross-sectional design a research design in which individuals, typically of different ages or developmental levels, are compared at a single point in time. An example is a study that involves a direct comparison of 5-year-olds with 8-year-olds. Given its snapshot nature, however, it is difficult to determine causal relationships using a cross-sectional design. Moreover, a cross-sectional study is not suitable for measuring changes over time, for which a LONGITUDINAL DESIGN is required.

cross-sequential design a study in which two or more groups of individuals of different ages are directly compared over a period of time. It is thus a combination of a CROSS-SECTIONAL DESIGN and a LONGITUDINAL DESIGN. For example, an investigator using a cross-sequential design to evaluate children's mathematical skills might measure a group of 5-year-olds and a group of 10-year-olds at the beginning of the research and then subsequently reassess the same children every 6 months for the next 5 years.

cross-tolerance *n.* a condition in which TOLERANCE to one drug results in a lessened response (i.e., increased tolerance) to a related drug. Cross-tolerance may be seen with amphetamines, benzodiazepines, hallucinogens, and opiates, among other drugs.

cross-validation *n.* a procedure used to assess the utility or stability of a statistical model. A data set is randomly divided into two subsets, the first of

which (the **derivation sample**) is used to develop the model and the second of which (the **cross-validation sample**) is used to test it. In regression analysis, for example, the first subset would be analyzed in order to develop a REGRESSION EQUATION, which would then be applied to the remaining subset to see how well it predicts the scores that were actually observed.

crowding *n.* psychological tension produced in environments of high population density, especially when individuals feel that the amount of space available to them is insufficient for their needs. Crowding may have a damaging effect on mental health and may result in poor performance of complex tasks and increased physiological stress. Two key mechanisms underlying crowding are lack of control over social interaction (i.e., lack of privacy) and the deterioration of socially supportive relationships.

crowd psychology 1. the mental and emotional states and processes unique to individuals when they are members of street crowds, mobs, and other such collectives. **2.** the scientific study of these phenomena.

cryptomnesia *n.* an IMPLICIT MEMORY phenomenon in which people mistakenly believe that a current thought or idea is a product of their own creation when, in fact, they have encountered it previously and then forgotten it. Cryptomnesia can occur in any creative enterprise, as for example when an investigator develops a research idea that he or she believes is original whereas it can be documented that he or she saw or heard the idea at some earlier point in time. Also called **unconscious plagiarism**.

crystallized intelligence (crystallized ability) see CATTELL–HORN THEORY OF INTELLIGENCE.

CSI effect a presumed phenomenon in which popular television crime shows are thought to raise jurors' expectations about forensic science and influence their verdicts if the evidence they hear at trial does not meet those expectations. This effect, according to observations from attorneys, judges, and journalists, is manifested as jurors tending to believe they understand the manner in which investigators collect, analyze, and interpret crime scene evidence; to insist on large amounts of often highly technical evidence in determining defendant guilt; and to overvalue the conclusiveness of DNA testing—that is, to have forensic presumptions of the sort that are the stock and trade of popular crime dramas on television. [coined from *CSI: Crime Scene Investigation*, a popular U.S. forensics-based television program that began in 2000]

cue *n.* a stimulus, event, or object that serves to guide behavior, such as a RETRIEVAL CUE, or that signals the presentation of another stimulus, event, or object.

cue-dependent forgetting forgetting caused by the absence at testing of a stimulus (or cue) that was present when the learning occurred. See also MOOD-DEPENDENT MEMORY; STATE-DEPENDENT LEARNING.

cultural absolutism see CULTURAL UNIVERSALISM.

cultural bias the tendency to interpret and judge phenomena in terms of the distinctive values, beliefs, and other characteristics of the society or community to which one belongs. This sometimes leads people to form opinions and make decisions about others in advance of any actual experience with them (see PREJUDICE). Cultural bias has become a significant concern in many areas, including PSYCHOMETRICS, ERGONOMICS, and CLINICAL PSYCHOLOGY. See also CULTURE-FAIR TEST; CULTURE-FREE TEST.

cultural determinism the theory or premise that individual and group characteristics and behavior patterns are produced largely by a given society's economic, social, political, and religious organization. See also SOCIAL DETERMINISM.

cultural diversity the existence of societies, communities, or subcultures that differ substantially from one another, in particular those that function within a larger society while maintaining their distinct culture traits.

cultural memory see COLLECTIVE MEMORY.

cultural neuroscience an emerging discipline that uses brain-imaging technology to show how environment and beliefs can shape mental function. Research suggests that even as people perceive the same stimulus, their brains may activate differently, showing neural responses that reflect their cultural values. See also SOCIAL NEUROSCIENCE.

cultural psychology an interdisciplinary extension of general psychology concerned with those psychological processes that are inherently organized by culture. It is a heterogeneous class of perspectives that focus on explaining how human psychological functions are culturally constituted through various forms of relations between people and their social contexts. As a discipline, cultural psychology relates to cultural anthropology, sociology, semiotics, language philosophy, and culture studies. See also CROSS-CULTURAL PSYCHOLOGY.

cultural relativism the view that attitudes, behaviors, values, concepts, and achievements must be understood in the light of their own cultural milieu and not judged according to the standards of a different culture. In psychology, the relativist position questions the universal application of psychological theory, research, therapeutic techniques, and clinical approaches, because those used or developed in one culture may not be appropriate or applicable to another. Compare CULTURAL UNIVERSALISM.

cultural tailoring adapting a questionnaire, intervention, or the like for the particular cultural population in which it will be used, with an awareness of the population's values, attitudes, history, and other influences on behavior. Cultural tailoring is intended to maximize rates of participant recruitment for studies, increase rates of completion for surveys and other instruments, enhance accuracy in language and understanding in communications, and increase positive outcomes from treatment.

cultural universalism the view that the values, concepts, and behaviors characteristic of diverse cultures can be viewed, understood, and judged according to universal standards. Such a view involves the rejection, at least in part, of CULTURAL RELATIVISM. Also called **cultural absolutism**.

culture *n.* **1.** the distinctive customs, values, beliefs, knowledge, art, and language of a society or a community. These values and concepts are passed on from generation to generation, and they are the basis for everyday behaviors and practices. **2.** the characteristic attitudes and behaviors of a particular group within society, such as a profession, social class, or age group. See also COUNTERCULTURE; SUBCULTURE. —**cultural** *adj.*

culture-bound syndrome a pattern of mental illness and abnormal behavior that is unique to a specific ethnic or cultural population and does not conform to standard Western classifications of psychiatric disorders. Culture-bound syndromes include, among many others, AMOK and VOODOO DEATH. Also called **culture-specific syndrome**.

culture-fair test a test based on common human experience and considered to be relatively unbiased with respect to special background influences. Unlike some standardized intelligence assessments, which may reflect predominantly middle-class experience, a culture-fair test is designed to apply across social lines and to per-

mit equitable comparisons among people from different backgrounds. Nonverbal, nonacademic items are used, such as matching identical forms, selecting a design that completes a given series, or drawing human figures.

culture-free test an intelligence test designed to eliminate cultural bias completely by constructing questions that contain either no environmental influences or no environmental influences that reflect any specific culture. However, the creation of such a test is probably impossible, and psychometricians instead generally seek to develop CULTURE-FAIR TESTS.

culture of honor a cultural norm in a region, nation, or ethnic group prescribing immediate, definitive retribution as the preferred reaction to an insult or other transgression, particularly one that threatens a person's reputation. A related concept is the subculture of violence, used to explain the relatively high rates of violent crime among certain minority populations in impoverished urban areas.

cumulative frequency (**CF**) a running total of how often specific values occur. Cumulative frequencies are used in DESCRIPTIVE STATISTICS when listing the number of participants who fall into each of several categories of a variable that can be ordered from low to high. For example, if test scores in a particular classroom are 1 F, 2 Ds, 4 Cs, 3 Bs, and 2 As, the cumulative frequency is obtained by successively adding the number of students at each score from an F to an A. Thus, the cumulative frequency values from the lowest to the highest would be 1, 3, 7, 10, and 12 for F, D, C, B, and A, respectively.

cumulative record a continuous tally or graph to which new data are added. In CONDITIONING, for example, a cumulative record is a graph showing the cumulative number of responses over a continuous period of time. It is often used in such contexts to display performance of a freely occurring behavior under a SCHEDULE OF REINFORCEMENT and provides a direct and continuous indicator of the rate of response.

curvilinear *adj.* describing an association between variables that does not consistently follow an increasing or decreasing pattern but rather changes direction after a certain point (i.e., it involves a curve in the set of data points). For example, the relationship between anxiety and achievement often has a curvilinear pattern of increasing achievement with increasing anxiety (i.e., worry about not doing well on an upcoming test) up to a certain point when there is so much anxiety that achievement tends to decrease. Thus, individuals who are not at all anxious and those who are extremely anxious would both be expected to have poor performance, whereas moderately anxious individuals would be expected to have reasonably high performance. See also NONLINEAR.

cutaneous *adj.* relating to or affecting the skin. For example, a cutaneous receptor, such as a PACINIAN CORPUSCLE, is a specialized cell in the skin that detects and responds to specific external stimuli.

cyberbullying *n.* see BULLYING.

cybernetics *n.* the scientific study of communication and control as applied to machines and living organisms. It includes the study of self-regulation mechanisms, as in thermostats or feedback circuits in the nervous system, as well as transmission and self-correction of information in both computers and human communications. Cybernetics was formerly used to denote research in ARTIFICIAL INTELLIGENCE. —**cybernetic** *adj.*

cyclic AMP (**cAMP**; **cyclic adenosine monophosphate**) a SECOND MESSENGER that is involved in the activities of DOPAMINE, NOREPINEPHRINE, and

SEROTONIN in transmitting signals at nerve synapses.

cyclic GMP (**cGMP**; **cyclic guanosine monophosphate**) a SECOND MESSENGER that is common in postsynaptic neurons.

cyclothymic disorder a mood disorder characterized by periods of hypomanic symptoms and periods of depressive symptoms that occur over the course of at least 2 years. The number, duration, and severity of these symptoms do not meet the full criteria for a MAJOR DEPRESSIVE EPISODE or a HYPOMANIC EPISODE. It often is considered to be a mild BIPOLAR DISORDER. Also called **cyclothymia**.

cytoarchitecture *n.* the arrangement of cells in organs and tissues, particularly those in the NEOCORTEX. The different types of cortical cells are organized in layers and zones. The number of layers varies in different brain areas, but a typical section of neocortex shows six distinct layers. Differences in cytoarchitecture have been used to divide the neocortex into 50 or more regions, many of which differ in function. The scientific study of the cytoarchitecture of organs is called **cytoarchitectonics**. See also BRODMANN'S AREA. —**cytoarchitectural** *adj.*

cytochrome oxidase blob (**CO blob**) a small patch of neurons in the STRIATE CORTEX with greater than background levels of activity of **cytochrome oxidase**, an enzyme in the inner membrane of MITOCHONDRIA that is important in aerobic respiration. Neurons in the CO blobs are sensitive to the wavelength of a visual stimulus.

cytokine *n.* any of a variety of small proteins or peptides that are released by cells as signals to those or other cells. Each type stimulates a target cell that has a specific receptor for that cytokine. Cytokines mediate many responses of the IMMUNE SYSTEM, including inflammation, allergies, fever, and the proliferation of lymphocytes.

cytoplasm *n.* see CELL. —**cytoplasmic** *adj.*

cytoskeleton *n.* an internal framework or "scaffolding" present in all CELLS. Composed of a network of filaments and MICROTUBULES, it maintains the cell shape and plays an important role in cell movement, growth, division, and differentiation, as well as in intracellular transport (e.g., the movement of VESICLES).

Dd

dark adaptation the ability of the eye to adjust to conditions of low illumination by means of an increased sensitivity to light. The bulk of the process takes 30 minutes and involves expansion of the pupils and retinal alterations, specifically the regeneration of RHODOPSIN and IODOPSIN. Compare LIGHT ADAPTATION.

data *pl. n.* (*sing.* **datum**) observations or measurements, usually quantified and obtained in the course of research. For example, a researcher may be interested in collecting data on health-related behaviors such as frequency and amount of exercise, number of calories consumed per day, number of cigarettes smoked per day, number of alcoholic drinks per day, and so forth.

data analysis the process of applying graphical, statistical, or quantitative techniques to a set of observations or measurements in order to summarize it or to find general patterns. For example, a very basic data analysis would involve calculating DESCRIPTIVE STATISTICS and possibly graphing the observations with a HISTOGRAM or BAR GRAPH.

data collection a systematic gathering of information for research or practical purposes. Examples include mail surveys, interviews, laboratory experiments, and psychological testing.

data mining the automated (computerized) examination of a large set of observations or measurements, particularly as collected in a complex database, to discover patterns, correlations, and other regularities that can be used for predictive purposes. For example, retailers often use data mining to predict the buying trends of customers or to design targeted marketing strategies, whereas clinicians may use it to determine variables predicting hospitalization for psychological disorders.

data set a collection of individual but related observations or measurements considered as a single entity. For example, the entire range of scores obtained from a class of students taking a particular test would constitute a data set.

daydream *n.* a waking fantasy, or reverie, in which wishes, expectations, and other potentialities are played out in imagination. Part of the stream of thoughts and images that occupy most of a person's waking hours, daydreams may be unbidden and apparently purposeless or may reflect simple, spontaneous desires. Researchers have identified at least three ways in which individuals' daydreaming styles differ: positive-constructive daydreaming, guilty and fearful daydreaming, and poor attentional control. These styles are posited to reflect the daydreamer's overall emotion and personality tendencies.

day hospital a nonresidential facility where individuals with mental disorders receive treatment and support services during the day and return to their homes at night. Specific service offerings vary across facilities but generally include psychological evaluation, individual and group psychotherapy, social and occupational rehabilitation, and SOMATIC THERAPY. Staff members are multidisciplinary, comprising psychiatrists, psychologists, social workers, vocational counselors, and others.

deaf hearing the capacity of some people with total deafness to detect and localize sounds without any conscious awareness of doing so. Studies suggest that this capacity is involuntary and is not accompanied by any ability to identify or interpret sounds. It has been proposed that such individuals may have a heightened sense of feeling that enables them to respond to the vibrations in sound waves. See also BLINDSIGHT; NUMBSENSE.

deafness *n.* the partial or complete absence or loss of the sense of hearing. The condition may be hereditary or acquired by injury or disease at any stage of life, including in utero. The major kinds are **conduction deafness**, due to a disruption in sound vibrations before they reach the nerve endings of the inner ear, and **sensorineural deafness**, caused by a failure of the nerves or brain centers associated with the sense of hearing to transmit or interpret properly the impulses from the inner ear. —**deaf** *adj.*

death education learning activities or programs designed to educate people about death, dying, coping with grief, and bereavement. Death education is typically provided by certified thanatologists from a wide array of mental and medical health personnel, educators, clergy, and volunteers.

death instinct in psychoanalytic theory, a drive whose aim is the reduction of psychical tension to the lowest possible point, that is, death. It is first directed inward as a self-destructive tendency and is later turned outward in the form of the aggressive instinct. In the dual instinct theory of Austrian neurologist Sigmund Freud (1856–1939), the death instinct, or THANATOS, stands opposed to the LIFE INSTINCT, or EROS, and is believed to underlie such behaviors as aggressiveness, sadism, and masochism.

debriefing *n.* the process of giving participants in a completed research project a fuller explanation of the study in which they participated than was possible before or during the research.

decay theory the theory that learned material leaves in the brain a trace or impression that autonomously recedes and disappears unless the material is practiced and used. Decay

theory is a theory of forgetting. Also called **trace-decay theory**.

deceleration *n.* a decrease in speed of movement or rate of change. For example, a medical researcher may be interested in a deceleration in the progression of an illness or symptom as evidence that a treatment is working effectively. Compare ACCELERATION.

decentration *n.* in PIAGETIAN THEORY, the gradual progression of a child away from egocentrism toward a reality shared with others. Occurring during the CONCRETE OPERATIONAL STAGE, decentration includes understanding how others perceive the world, knowing in what ways one's own perceptions differ, and recognizing that people have motivations and feelings different from one's own. It can also be extended to the ability to consider many aspects of a situation, problem, or object, as reflected, for example, in the child's grasp of the concept of CONSERVATION. Also called **decentering**. Compare CENTRATION. —**decenter** *vb.*

deception *n.* any distortion of or withholding of fact with the purpose of misleading others. For example, a researcher who has not disclosed the true purpose of an experiment to a participant has engaged in deception, as has an animal that has given a false alarm call that disperses competitors and thus allows him or her to gain more food. —**deceive** *vb.* —**deceptive** *adj.*

decibel (symbol: dB) *n.* a logarithmic unit used to express the ratio of acoustic or electric power (intensity). An increase of 1 bel is a 10-fold increase in intensity; a decibel is one tenth of a bel and is the more commonly used unit, partly because a 1 dB change in intensity is just detectable (approximately and under laboratory conditions).

decision making the cognitive process of choosing between two or more alternatives. Psychologists have adopted two converging strategies to understand decision making: (a) statistical analysis of multiple decisions involving complex tasks and (b) experimental manipulation of simple decisions, looking at the elements that recur within these decisions.

decision rule in HYPOTHESIS TESTING, a formal statement of the set of values of the test statistic that will lead to rejection of the NULL HYPOTHESIS that there is no significant effect in the study being examined. For example, a common decision rule is to reject the null hypothesis when the value of a z TEST statistic exceeds 1.96.

decision theory a broad class of presumptions in the quantitative, social, and behavioral sciences that aim to explain a process and identify optimal ways of arriving at conclusions so that prespecified criteria are met.

declarative memory memory of facts or events that is retained over a significant period of time and that can be consciously recalled, typically in response to a specific request to remember. It generally is divided into two subtypes: EPISODIC MEMORY and SEMANTIC MEMORY. See also EXPLICIT MEMORY. Compare NONDECLARATIVE MEMORY.

decoding *n.* the process of translating coded information back into its source terms or symbols. Decoding is used in information processing, communication, and computer science. —**decode** *vb.*

decompensation *n.* a breakdown in an individual's DEFENSE MECHANISMS, resulting in progressive loss of normal functioning or worsening of psychiatric symptoms.

deconditioning *n.* a technique in BEHAVIOR THERAPY in which learned responses, such as phobias, are "unlearned" (deconditioned). For example, a person with a phobic reaction to flying might be deconditioned initially by practicing going to the airport and using breathing techniques to control anxiety. See also DESENSITIZATION.

deconversion *n.* **1.** loss of one's

faith in a religion, as in a Catholic of many years who becomes an atheist or agnostic. Compare CONVERSION. **2.** less commonly, regression from a more complex belief system to a simpler one.

decortication *n.* surgical removal of the outer layer (cortex) of an anatomical structure, especially the outer layer of the cerebrum of the brain (i.e., the CEREBRAL CORTEX).

deculturation *n.* the processes, intentional or unintentional, by which traditional cultural beliefs or practices are suppressed or otherwise eliminated as a result of contact with a different, dominant culture. Compare ACCULTURATION. —**deculturate** *vb.*

deduction *n.* **1.** a conclusion derived from formal premises by a valid process of DEDUCTIVE REASONING. **2.** the process of inferential reasoning itself. Compare INDUCTION. —**deductive** *adj.*

deductive reasoning the form of logical reasoning in which a conclusion is shown to follow necessarily from a sequence of premises, the first of which stands for a self-evident truth or agreed-upon data. In the empirical sciences, deductive reasoning underlies the process of deriving predictions from general laws or theories. Compare INDUCTIVE REASONING. See also LOGIC.

deep brain stimulation (DBS) a neurosurgical procedure used most commonly to treat the disabling neurological symptoms of Parkinson's disease (e.g., tremor, rigidity, stiffness). An insulated wire passed under the skin of the head, neck, and shoulder connects an electrode implanted in the brain to a neurostimulator that is usually implanted near the collarbone. Electrical signals from the neurostimulator trigger the electrode to begin emitting small pulses of electricity to areas in the brain that control movement, blocking abnormal nerve signals that cause tremor and other neurological symptoms. DBS is also used for people with highly treatment-resistant major depression if multiple medications, psychotherapy, and electroconvulsive therapy have failed.

deep dyslexia a form of acquired DYSLEXIA characterized by semantic errors (e.g., reading *parrot* as *canary*), difficulties in reading abstract words (e.g., *idea*, *usual*) and function words (e.g., *the*, *and*), and an inability to read pronounceable nonwords. See also PHONOLOGICAL DYSLEXIA; SURFACE DYSLEXIA.

deep processing cognitive processing of a stimulus that focuses on its meaningful properties rather than its perceptual characteristics. It is considered that processing at this semantic level, which usually involves a degree of ELABORATION, produces stronger, longer-lasting memories than SHALLOW PROCESSING.

deep structure in TRANSFORMA-TIONAL GENERATIVE GRAMMAR, an abstract base form of a sentence in which the logical and grammatical relations between the constituents are made explicit. The deep structure generates the SURFACE STRUCTURE of a sentence through transformations, such as changes in word order or the addition or deletion of elements.

Deese–Roediger–McDermott paradigm a laboratory memory task used to study false recall. It is based on a report in 1959 that, after presentation of a list of related words (e.g., *snore, rest, dream, awake*), participants mistakenly recalled an unpresented but strongly associated item (e.g., *sleep*). Called the **Deese paradigm** after its original investigator, U.S. psychologist James **Deese** (1921–1999), it has since been renamed to reflect renewed research into the technique by U.S. cognitive psychologists Henry L. **Roediger** III (1947–) and Kathleen B. **McDermott** (1968–).

defense mechanism in classical psychoanalytic theory, an unconscious reaction pattern employed by the EGO to protect itself from the anxiety that arises from psychic conflict. Such

mechanisms range from mature to immature, depending on how much they distort reality. In more recent psychological theories, defense mechanisms are seen as normal means of coping with everyday problems and external threats, but excessive use of any one, or the use of immature defenses (e.g., DE-NIAL, DISPLACEMENT, or REPRESSION), is still considered pathological. See also AVOIDANCE; PROJECTION; RATIONALIZA-TION; REGRESSION; SUBLIMATION; SUBSTITUTION. [proposed in 1894 by Austrian neurologist Sigmund Freud (1856–1939)]

defensive attribution a bias or error in attributing cause for some event such that a perceived threat to oneself is minimized. For example, people might blame an automobile accident on the other driver's mistake, because this attribution lessens their perception that they themselves are responsible for the accident.

deferred imitation imitation of an act minutes, hours, or days after viewing the behavior. Research indicates that deferred imitation of simple tasks can be initially observed in infants late in their first year.

deficiency motivation in the humanistic psychology of U.S. psychologist Abraham Maslow (1908–1970), the type of motivation operating on the lower four levels of his hierarchy of needs (see MASLOW'S MOTIVATIONAL HIERARCHY). Deficiency motivation is characterized by the striving to correct a deficit that may be physiological or psychological in nature. Compare METAMOTIVATION.

degeneration *n.* **1.** deterioration or decline of organs or tissues, especially of neural tissues, to a less functional form. **2.** deterioration or decline of moral values. —**degenerate** *vb.*

degradation *n.* **1.** in neurophysiology, the process by which NEUROTRANS-MITTER molecules are broken down into inactive metabolites. **2.** more generally, the process or result of declining or reducing in value, quality, level, or status.

degrees of freedom 1. (symbol: *df*) the number of elements that are allowed to vary in a statistical calculation, or the number of scores minus the number of mathematical restrictions. If the MEAN of a set of scores is fixed, then the number of degrees of freedom is one less than the number of scores. For example, if four individuals have a mean IQ of 100, then there are three degrees of freedom, because knowing three of the IQs determines the fourth IQ. **2.** in motor control, the various joints that can move or the various muscles that can contract to produce a movement.

dehumanization *n.* any process or practice that is thought to reduce human beings to the level of mechanisms or nonhuman animals, especially by denying them autonomy, individuality, and a sense of dignity. —**dehumanize** *vb.*

deindividuation *n.* an experiential state characterized by loss of self-awareness, altered perceptions, and a reduction of inner restraints that results in the performance of unusual and sometimes antisocial behavior. It can be caused by a number of factors, such as a sense of anonymity or submersion in a group.

deinstitutionalization *n.* the joint process of moving people with developmental or psychiatric disabilities from structured institutional facilities to their home communities and developing comprehensive community-based residential, day, vocational, clinical, and supportive services to address their needs. —**deinstitutionalize** *vb.*

déjà vu the feeling that a new event has already been experienced or that the same scene has been witnessed before (French, "already seen"). The feeling of familiarity may be due to a neurological anomaly, to resemblance between the present and the past scenes, or to a similar scene having been pictured in a daydream or night dream. The feeling may occur even though the person experiencing it cannot consciously recollect the earlier event or scene. See FALSE MEMORY.

delay conditioning in CLASSICAL CONDITIONING, a procedure in which the CONDITIONED STIMULUS is presented, and remains present, for a fixed period (the delay) before the UNCONDITIONED STIMULUS is introduced. Compare SIMULTANEOUS CONDITIONING.

delayed matching to sample (**DMTS**) a procedure in which the participant is shown a sample stimulus and then, after a variable time, a pair of test stimuli and is asked to select the test stimulus that matches the earlier sample stimulus. In **delayed non-matching to sample**, the participant must choose the stimulus that was not presented in the sample phase.

delayed response a response that occurs some time after its DISCRIMINATIVE STIMULUS has been removed. The most common **delayed response task** for nonhuman animals is one in which the animal is required to recall the location of a reward after a delay period has elapsed.

deliberate self-harm (**DSH**) the intentional, direct destruction of body tissue (most commonly by cutting, burning, scratching, hitting, or biting oneself or by head banging) without conscious suicidal intent but resulting in injury severe enough for tissue damage to occur. Typically associated with BORDERLINE PERSONALITY DISORDER, DSH has also been found to occur at high rates among nonclinical populations of adolescents. It is seen as well in individuals with intellectual and developmental disabilities, in whom it is usually known by its older synonym **self-injurious behavior**.

delinquency *n.* behavior violating social rules or conventions. The term is often used to denote the misbehavior of children or adolescents. See JUVENILE DELINQUENCY. —**delinquent** *adj., n.*

delirium *n.* a disturbed mental state in which attention cannot be sustained, the environment is misperceived, and the stream of thought is disordered. The individual may experience such symptoms as disorientation, memory impairment, disturbance in language, hallucinations, illusions, and misinterpretation of sounds or sights. Delirium may be caused by a variety of conditions, such as infections, cerebral tumors, substance intoxication and withdrawal, head trauma, and seizures.

delirium tremens (DTs) a potentially fatal alcohol withdrawal syndrome involving extreme agitation and anxiety, paranoia, visual and tactile hallucinations, disorientation, tremors, sweating, and increased heart rate, body temperature, and blood pressure.

delta (symbol: Δ) *n.* **1.** a measure of the change in a PARAMETER. For example, ΔR^2 indicates how much of the change in R^2 (the COEFFICIENT OF MULTIPLE DETERMINATION) was caused or explained by a given step (e.g., adding a specific variable to an analysis). **2.** see GLASS'S D.

delta wave the lowest frequency BRAIN WAVE recorded in electroencephalography. Delta waves are large, regular-shaped waves that have a frequency between 1 and 3 Hz. They are associated with deep sleep (**delta-wave sleep**).

delusion *n.* an often highly personal idea or belief system, not endorsed by one's culture or subculture, that is maintained with conviction in spite of irrationality or evidence to the contrary. Common types include DELUSIONS OF GRANDEUR, DELUSIONS OF PERSECUTION, and DELUSIONS OF REFERENCE.

delusional disorder any of a group of psychotic disorders with the essential feature of one or more delusions that are not due to an ingested substance, a medical condition, or another mental disorder that can be associated with firmly held delusional beliefs (e.g., obsessive-compulsive disorder, body dysmorphic disorder).

delusion of grandeur the false attribution to the self of great ability, knowledge, importance or worth, identity, prestige, power, accomplishment, or the like.

delusion of persecution the false conviction that others are threatening or conspiring against one.

delusion of reference the false conviction that the actions of others and events occurring in the external world have some special meaning or significance (typically negative) in relation to oneself.

demand characteristics in an experiment or research project, cues that may influence or bias participants' behavior, for example, by suggesting the outcome or response that the experimenter expects or desires.

dementia *n.* **1.** a generalized, pervasive deterioration of memory and at least one other cognitive function, such as language and an EXECUTIVE FUNCTION; there are a variety of causes, commonly including Alzheimer's disease, Pick's disease, and cerebrovascular disease. The loss of intellectual abilities is severe enough to interfere with an individual's daily functioning and social and occupational activity. When occurring after the age of 65, it is termed **senile dementia**, and when appearing before 65, it is called **presenile dementia**, although these distinctions are becoming obsolete because its manifestations are the same no matter the age of onset. Dementia should not be confused with age-associated memory impairment or mild cognitive impairment, which have a much less deleterious effect on day-to-day functioning. **2.** historically, loss of ability to reason due to mental illness, diseases such as neurosyphilis, or advanced age (senility). [Latin, "out of mind"]

dementia of the Alzheimer's

type (**DAT**) another name for ALZHEIMER'S DISEASE.

dementia praecox a progressively deteriorating psychotic disorder marked by severe, incurable cognitive disintegration beginning in early adulthood (Latin, "premature dementia"). The term, now obsolete, was formalized in the 1890s as a taxonomic concept by German psychiatrist Emil Kraepelin (1856–1926), who defined it as one of two major classes of mental illness (the other being manic-depressive illness; see BIPOLAR DISORDER) and distinguished it from the "senile dementia" of advanced age. The concept was replaced after Swiss psychiatrist Eugen Bleuler (1857–1939) deemphasized its characterization as an early dementia with an irreversible disease course and renamed it "schizophrenia" in 1908.

dementia syndrome of depression see PSEUDODEMENTIA.

demography *n.* the statistical study of human populations in regard to various factors and characteristics, including geographical distribution, sex and age distribution, size, structure, and growth trends. —**demographer** *n.* —**demographic** *adj.*

dendrite *n.* a branching, threadlike extension of the CELL BODY that increases the receptive surface of a neuron. The full arrangement of the dendrites of a single neuron is termed a **dendritic tree**, and the specific pattern and quality of that arrangement is termed **dendritic branching**. —**dendritic** *adj.* [from Greek *dendron*, "tree"]

dendritic spine a mushroom-shaped outgrowth along the dendrite of a neuron, which forms a SYNAPSE with the axon terminals of neighboring neurons.

denial *n.* a DEFENSE MECHANISM in which unpleasant thoughts, feelings, wishes, or events are ignored or excluded from conscious awareness. It may take such forms as refusal to ac-

knowledge the reality of a terminal illness, a financial problem, an addiction, or a partner's infidelity. Denial is an unconscious process that functions to resolve emotional conflict or reduce anxiety. —**deny** *vb.*

denotative meaning the objective or literal meaning of a word or phrase as opposed to its **connotative meaning**, which includes the various ideas and emotions that it suggests within a particular culture. For example, the word *father* denotes "male parent" but may connote a range of ideas involving protection, authority, and love.

density *n.* a measure of the amount of physical space per individual. High density can produce crowding, the feeling of having insufficient space. Interior indices of density (e.g., people per room) are consistently related to negative psychological consequences, whereas external indices (e.g., people per square mile) are not. —**dense** *adj.*

dentate gyrus a strip of gray matter that connects the ENTORHINAL CORTEX with the HIPPOCAMPUS. It includes a narrow layer of cells called the **subgranular zone**, which is one of only two currently known areas in the adult brain in which new neurons are formed (NEUROGENESIS); the other area is the SUBVENTRICULAR ZONE in the lateral ventricles.

deoxyribonucleic acid see DNA.

dependence *n.* **1.** the state of having some reliance on or association with another entity or event, as when one variable is formed from another variable in an analysis. For example, dependence would be seen if a researcher included IQ, formed from mental age over actual age, in an analysis that already has age as a variable. **2.** a state in which assistance from others is expected or actively sought for emotional or financial support, protection, security, or daily care. Whereas some degree of dependence is natural in interpersonal relations, excessive, inappropriate, or misdirected reliance on others is often a focus of psychological treatment. **3.** see SUBSTANCE DEPENDENCE. **4.** in OPERANT CONDITIONING, a causal relation between a response and a consequence, which results in a CONTINGENCY. Also called **dependency.** —**dependent** *adj.*

dependency ratio a measure of the portion of a population that is composed of people who are not in the work force and depend on others for support versus people who are in the work force and are self-sufficient. The dependency ratio is often defined in terms of age groups, with those who either are too young to work or are retired being set against those who are in their prime earning years; it is then calculated as the number of individuals aged below 15 or above 64 divided by the number of individuals aged 15 to 64.

dependent events in probability theory, events that have a relationship such that the outcome of one affects the outcome of the other. For example, overeating and being overweight are dependent events, whereas shoe size and political party preference are most likely not. Compare INDEPENDENT EVENTS.

dependent personality disorder a personality disorder manifested in a long-term pattern of passively allowing others to take responsibility for major areas of life and of subordinating personal needs to the needs of others.

dependent samples sets of data that are related, owing to their having been collected from the same group on two or more occasions (as with a pre- and posttest) or from two or more sets of individuals who are closely associated (e.g., parents and their children). Also called **dependent groups**; **related samples.** Compare INDEPENDENT SAMPLES.

dependent variable (**DV**) the outcome that is observed to occur or change after the occurrence or variation of the INDEPENDENT VARIABLE in an experiment, or the effect that one wants

to predict or explain in CORRELATIONAL RESEARCH. Dependent variables may or may not be related causally to the independent variable. Also called **outcome variable**; **response variable**.

depersonalization *n.* a state of mind in which the self appears unreal. Individuals feel estranged from themselves and usually from the external world, and thoughts and experiences have a distant, dreamlike character.

depersonalization disorder a DISSOCIATIVE DISORDER characterized by one or more episodes of depersonalization severe enough to impair social and occupational functioning. Onset of depersonalization is rapid and usually manifested in a feeling that one's extremities are changed in size, a perception of oneself as if from a distance, and, in some cases, a feeling that the external world is unreal (DE-REALIZATION).

deployment psychology a branch of MILITARY PSYCHOLOGY devoted to understanding and addressing the unique mental and behavioral health needs of members of the armed forces and their families during and after members' posting to combat zones and other operational environments. Research in this area focuses on the psychosocial effects of combat exposure and of injuries sustained in combat; barriers to accessing mental health care in the military; the psychology of trauma and promotion of RESILIENCE among military personnel and their families; and the process of readjusting to civilian life for returning military personnel. Clinical services focus on treating mental health disorders common among returning military personnel (e.g., posttraumatic stress disorder); mitigating the negative effects of these disorders on the families of those affected; teaching effective coping skills (e.g., anger management) to returning soldiers and their families to better prepare them to handle interpersonal difficulties; and using STRESS-INOCULATION TRAINING and other strategies during deployment to enhance the psychological well-being of soldiers and thus prevent the subsequent development of serious problems.

depolarization *n.* a reduction in the electric potential across the plasma membrane of a cell, especially a neuron, such that the inner surface of the membrane becomes less negative in relation to the outer surface. Depolarization occurs when the membrane is stimulated and sodium ions (Na+) flow into the cell. If the stimulus intensity exceeds the excitatory threshold of the neuron, an ACTION POTENTIAL is created and a nerve impulse propagated. Compare HYPERPOLARIZATION.

depressant 1. *adj.* having the quality of diminishing or retarding a function or activity of a body system or organ. **2.** *n.* any agent that has this quality, especially a drug that depresses activity in the central nervous system (i.e., a CNS depressant).

depression *n.* **1.** a negative affective state, ranging from unhappiness and discontent to an extreme feeling of sadness, pessimism, and despondency, that interferes with daily life. Various physical, cognitive, and social changes also tend to co-occur, including altered eating or sleeping habits, lack of energy or motivation, difficulty concentrating or making decisions, and withdrawal from social activities. It is symptomatic of a number of mental health disorders. **2.** in psychiatry and psychology, any of the DEPRESSIVE DISORDERS. —**depressed** *adj.*

depressive disorder any of the mood disorders that typically have sadness as the predominant symptom. They primarily include MAJOR DEPRESSIVE DISORDER and DYSTHYMIC DISORDER.

depressive personality disorder a controversial personality diagnosis characterized by glumness, pessimism, a lack of joy, the inability to experience pleasure, and low self-esteem. Some clinicians attempt to

differentiate this disorder from MAJOR DEPRESSIVE DISORDER and DYSTHYMIC DISORDER.

deprivation *n.* the removal, denial, or unavailability of something needed or desired. In CONDITIONING, deprivation refers specifically to the reduction of access to or intake of a REINFORCER. —**deprive** *vb.*

depth cue any of a variety of means used to inform the visual system about the depth of a target or its distance from the observer. **Monocular cues** require only one eye and include signals about the state of the CILIARY MUSCLES, the nearness or distance of objects based on their clear or indistinct appearance, the LINEAR PERSPECTIVE of objects, and the occlusion of distant objects by near objects. **Binocular cues** require integration of information from the two eyes and include signals about the CONVERGENCE of the eyes and BINOCULAR DISPARITY.

depth interview an interview designed to reveal an individual's deep-seated feelings, attitudes, opinions, and motives by encouraging him or her to express them freely without fear of disapproval or concern about the interviewer's reactions. Such interviews may be conducted, for example, in counseling and as part of qualitative market research. They tend to be relatively lengthy, unstructured, one-on-one conversations.

depth-of-processing hypothesis the theory that the strength of memory depends on the degree of cognitive processing the material receives. Depth has been defined variously as ELABORATION, the amount of cognitive effort expended, and the distinctiveness of the MEMORY TRACE formed. This theory evolved from an expanded empirical investigation of the LEVELS-OF-PROCESSING MODEL OF MEMORY.

depth perception awareness of three-dimensionality, solidity, and the distance between the observer and the object. Depth perception is achieved through such cues as visual ACCOMMODATION, BINOCULAR DISPARITY, and CONVERGENCE. See also VISUAL CLIFF.

depth psychology a general approach to psychology and psychotherapy that focuses on unconscious mental processes as the source of emotional disturbance and symptoms, as well as of personality, attitudes, creativity, and lifestyle. Typical examples are CLASSICAL PSYCHOANALYSIS and PSYCHODYNAMIC PSYCHOTHERAPY, but others include the ANALYTIC PSYCHOLOGY of Swiss psychiatrist Carl Jung (1875–1961) and the INDIVIDUAL PSYCHOLOGY of Austrian psychiatrist Alfred Adler (1870–1937).

depth therapy any form of psychotherapy, brief or extended, that involves identifying and working through unconscious conflicts and experiences that underlie and interfere with behavior and adjustment. Compare SURFACE THERAPY.

derealization *n.* a state characterized by a diminished feeling of reality; that is, an alteration in the perception or cognitive characterization of external reality so that it seems strange or unreal ("This can't be happening"), often due to trauma or stress. It may also occur as a feature of schizophrenia or of dissociative disorders. See also DEPERSONALIZATION.

derivation sample see CROSS-VALIDATION.

descriptive norm any of various consensual standards (SOCIAL NORMS) that describe how people typically act, feel, and think in a given situation. These standards delineate how most people actually do behave, whereas INJUNCTIVE NORMS prescribe how they should behave.

descriptive research an empirical investigation designed to test prespecified hypotheses or to provide an overview of existing conditions, and sometimes relationships, without manipulating variables or seeking to establish cause and effect. For example, a survey undertaken to ascertain the political party preferences of a group of voters would be a descriptive study because it is intended simply to identify attitudes rather than systematically infer or analyze influencing factors.

descriptive science see NORMATIVE SCIENCE.

descriptive statistics procedures for depicting the main aspects of sample data, without necessarily inferring to a larger population. Descriptive statistics usually include the MEAN, MEDIAN, and MODE to indicate the midpoint of the data, as well as the RANGE and STANDARD DEVIATION, which reveal how widely spread the scores are within the sample. Descriptive statistics might also include HISTOGRAMS and other graphs. Compare INFERENTIAL STATISTICS.

desensitization *n.* a reduction in emotional or physical reactivity to stimuli that is achieved by such means as DECONDITIONING techniques. See also IN VIVO DESENSITIZATION; SYSTEMATIC DESENSITIZATION.

design *n.* the format of a research study, describing how it will be conducted and the data collected. For example, an EXPERIMENTAL DESIGN involves an INDEPENDENT VARIABLE and at least two groups, a treatment or experimental group and a control group, to which participants are randomly assigned and then assessed on the DEPENDENT VARIABLE. A variety of other design types exist, including CORRELATIONAL RESEARCH, QUASI-EXPERIMENTAL DESIGNS, LONGITUDINAL DESIGNS, NATURAL EXPERIMENTS, and OBSERVATIONAL STUDIES, among others.

determinism *n.* the philosophical position that all events, physical or mental, are the necessary results of antecedent causes or other forces. Determinism, which requires that both the past and the future are fixed, manifests itself in psychology as the position that all human behaviors result from specific, efficient causal antecedents, such as biological structures or processes, environmental conditions, or past experiences. This view contrasts with belief in FREE WILL, which implies that individuals can choose to act in some ways independent of antecedent events and conditions. Those who advocate free-will positions often adopt a position of SOFT DETERMINISM, which holds that free will and responsibility are compatible with determinism. Others hold that free will is illusory, a position known as HARD DETERMINISM. Of contemporary psychological theories, BEHAVIORISM takes most clearly a hard determinist position. Compare INDETERMINISM. See also CAUSALITY. —**determinist** *adj., n.* —**deterministic** *adj.*

deterministic model a mathematical function in which the outcome can be exactly established. In other words, the model explains all of the variance in a DEPENDENT VARIABLE and no ERROR TERM is needed. This contrasts with a STOCHASTIC MODEL, from which a range of possible values may result.

deterministic process see STOCHASTIC PROCESS.

detoxification *n.* a therapeutic procedure, popularly known as **detox**, that reduces or eliminates toxic substances (e.g., alcohol, opioids) in the body. The procedure may be metabolic (by converting the toxic substance to a less harmful agent that is more easily excreted), or it may require induced vomiting, gastric lavage (washing), or dialysis. Detoxification typically occurs in a clinic, hospital unit, or residential rehabilitation center devoted to treating individuals for the toxic effects of alcohol or drug overdose and to managing their acute withdrawal symptoms.

development *n.* the progressive series of changes in structure, function, and behavior patterns that occur over

the lifespan of a human being or other organism. —**developmental** *adj.*

developmental coordination disorder a motor skills disorder characterized by marked impairment in the development of motor coordination, with performance of motor activities (e.g., walking, handwriting) well below that expected for the child's chronological age. Significant impairment of academic performance or daily living activities is also observed. However, the difficulties are not due to intellectual disability or to a neurological disorder affecting movement (e.g., cerebral palsy).

developmental disability a developmental level or status that is attributable to a cognitive or physical impairment, or both, originating before the age of 22. Such an impairment is likely to continue indefinitely and results in substantial functional or adaptive limitations. Examples of developmental disabilities include intellectual disability, autism, and learning disorders. Also called **developmental disorder**.

developmental dysgraphia see DISORDER OF WRITTEN EXPRESSION.

developmental norm the typical skills and expected level of achievement associated with a particular stage of development.

developmental psychology the branch of psychology that studies the physical, mental, and behavioral changes that occur from conception to old age and investigates the various biological, neurobiological, genetic, psychological, social, cultural, and environmental factors that affect development throughout the lifespan. Since its emergence as a formal discipline in the late 19th century, the field has broadened its focus from one that largely emphasized infant, child, and adolescent development to one, beginning in the 1920s, that also accounted for adult development and the aging process and, more recently, prenatal development. The term is now often considered virtually synonymous with LIFESPAN DEVELOPMENTAL PSYCHOLOGY. See also GENETIC PSYCHOLOGY.

developmental psychopathology the scientific study of the origins and progression of psychological disorders as related to the typical processes of human growth and maturation. Central to this field is the belief that studying departures from developmental NORMS will enhance understanding of those norms, which will in turn enhance the conceptualization and treatment of mental illness.

developmental science the interdisciplinary study of changes in the biopsychosocial dimensions of individuals over their lifespan and into successive generations.

developmental systems approach the view that development is the result of bidirectional interaction between all levels of biological and experiential variables, from the genetic through the cultural.

developmental task any of the fundamental physical, social, intellectual, and emotional achievements and abilities that must be acquired at each stage of life for normal and healthy development. Because development is largely cumulative, the inability to master developmental tasks at one stage is likely to inhibit development in later stages.

developmental theory any theory based on the continuity of human development and the importance of early experiences in shaping personality. Examples are the psychoanalytic theory of PSYCHOSEXUAL DEVELOPMENT, ERIKSON'S EIGHT STAGES OF PSYCHOSOCIAL DEVELOPMENT, learning theories that stress early conditioning, and role theories that focus on the gradual acquisition of different roles in life.

deviation *n.* a significant departure or difference. This conceptually broad term has a variety of applications in psychology and related fields but most commonly refers to behavior that is significantly different from the accepted standard or norm, or to the arithmetical difference between one of a set of values and some fixed amount, generally the MEAN of the set or the value predicted by a model. See STANDARD DEVIATION.

deviation IQ the absolute measure of how far an individual differs from the MEAN on an individually administered IQ test. This is the approach now most commonly used in standard IQ tests. A reported deviation IQ is a standard score on an IQ test that has a mean of 100 and a standard deviation specific to that of the test administered, usually 15 or 16 for intelligence tests. The test scores represent a deviation from the mean score rather than a quotient, as was typical in the early days of IQ testing.

deviation score the difference between an observation or value *x* and the MEAN value (i.e., *x* – mean) in a set of data. The sum of the deviation scores for a given data set will equal zero, as approximately half of the values will be less than the mean and half will be greater than the mean. Also called **deviation value**.

diagnosis (**Dx**) *n.* (*pl.* **diagnoses**) **1.** the process of identifying and determining the nature of a disease or disorder by its signs and symptoms, through the use of assessment techniques (e.g., tests and examinations) and other available evidence. **2.** the classification of individuals on the basis of a disease, disorder, abnormality, or set of characteristics. Psychological diagnoses have been codified for professional use, notably in the DSM–5. **3.** the decision or statement itself that results from this process or classification, as in "She was given a diagnosis of schizoaffective disorder." —**diagnostic** *adj.*

Diagnostic and Statistical Man-

ual of Mental Disorders see DSM—5.

diagnostic test any examination or assessment measure that may help reveal the nature and source of an individual's physical, mental, or behavioral problems or anomalies.

dialect *n.* a variety of a language that is associated with a particular geographical region, social class, or ethnic group and that has its own characteristic words, grammatical forms, and pronunciation. Dialects of a language are generally mutually intelligible. Compare ACCENT; REGISTER. **—dialectal** *adj.*

dialectical behavior therapy (DBT) a flexible, stage-based therapy that combines principles of BEHAVIOR THERAPY, COGNITIVE BEHAVIOR THERAPY, and MINDFULNESS. It establishes a "dialectic" between helping individuals to accept the reality of their lives and their own behaviors on the one hand and helping them learn to change their lives, including dysfunctional behaviors, on the other. Its underlying emphasis is on helping individuals learn both to regulate and to tolerate their emotions. DBT is designed for especially difficult-to-treat patients, such as those with BORDERLINE PERSONALITY DISORDER.

diary method a technique for compiling detailed data about an individual who is being observed or studied by having the individual record his or her daily behavior and activities. Also called **diary survey**.

diaschisis *n.* a loss or deficiency of function in brain regions surrounding or connected to an area of localized damage.

diathesis *n.* any susceptibility to or predisposition for a disease or disorder.

diathesis–stress model the theory that mental and physical disorders develop from a genetic or biological predisposition for that illness (diathesis) combined with stressful conditions

that play a precipitating or facilitating role.

dichotic listening the process of receiving different auditory messages presented simultaneously to each ear. Listeners experience two streams of sound, each localized at the ear to which it is presented, and are able to focus on the message from one ear while ignoring the message from the other ear.

dichotomized variable an item or score that initially had a set of continuous values (e.g., age) but was then separated into two possible values (e.g., younger and older). It may be useful to create a dichotomized variable when certain data values have been deliberately excluded from study, such as when an investigator conducting workforce research excludes from examination those individuals who have not yet begun working and those who have retired.

dichotomous thinking the tendency to think in terms of polar opposites—that is, in terms of the best and worst—without accepting the possibilities that lie between these two extremes. The term has been used to characterize the tendency of people with MAJOR DEPRESSIVE DISORDER to view mildly negative events as extremely negative, but the potential role of such thinking in other conditions (e.g., eating disorders, personality disorders) is under investigation.

dichotomous variable a variable that can have only one of two values (typically, 0 or 1) to designate membership in one of two possible categories, such as female versus male or agree versus disagree. Also called **binary variable**.

dichromatism (**dichromatopsia**) *n.* partial color blindness in which the eye contains only two types of cone PHOTOPIGMENT instead of the typical three: Lack of the third pigment leads to confusion between certain colors. Red–green color blindness is the most common, whereas the blue–green variety is relatively rare. Another type, yellow–blue, has been proposed, but its existence has yet to be firmly established. See also ACHROMATISM; MONOCHROMATISM; TRICHROMATISM. **—dichromatic** *adj.*

diencephalon *n.* the posterior part of the FOREBRAIN that includes the THALAMUS, EPITHALAMUS, and HYPOTHALAMUS. **—diencephalic** *adj.*

difference score (symbol: *D*) an index of dissimilarity or change between observations from the same individual across time, based on the measurement of a construct or attribute on two or more separate occasions. For example, it would be helpful to calculate a difference score for a person's weight at the beginning of a diet and exercise program and the final weight 6 months later.

difference threshold the smallest difference between two stimuli that can be consistently and accurately detected on 50% of trials. Also called **difference limen (DL); just noticeable difference (JND; jnd)**. See also WEBER'S LAW.

differential diagnosis 1. the process of determining which of two or more diseases or disorders with overlapping symptoms a particular patient has. **2.** the distinction between two or more similar conditions by identifying critical symptoms present in one but not the other.

differential item functioning (**DIF**) the circumstance in which two individuals of similar ability do not have the same probability of answering a question in a particular way. This often is examined to assess whether men and women or individuals of different ethnicity are likely to provide disparate answers on a test. If so, the fairness of the test can be called into question.

differential psychology the branch of psychology that studies the nature, magnitude, causes, and consequences of psychological differences between individuals and groups, as well as the methods for assessing these differences. See also INDIVIDUAL DIFFERENCES.

differentiation *n.* **1.** sensory discrimination of differences among stimuli. For example, wines that at first taste are identical may, with experience, be readily distinguished. **2.** a conditioning process in which a limited range of behavior types is achieved through selective REINFORCEMENT of only some forms of behavior. **3.** in embryology, the process whereby cells of a developing embryo undergo the changes necessary to become specialized in structure and function.

differentiation–dedifferentiation hypothesis two complementary proposals about the development of intelligence. One (the **age differentiation hypothesis**) proposes that intelligence begins as a fairly unified, general ability that then differentiates into separate, albeit related, abilities as children develop. According to the other proposal (the **age dedifferentiation hypothesis**), a process occurs after age 65 during which the separate abilities developed in childhood become increasingly intercorrelated as a result of decreasing fluid intelligence (see CATTELL–HORN THEORY OF INTELLIGENCE); at this time, intelligence dedifferentiates and returns to a single factor of general ability. Both proposals have garnered much debate over the years, but the evidence for each remains limited.

diffusion of responsibility the diminished sense of responsibility often experienced by individuals in groups and social collectives. This diffusion has been proposed as a possible mediator of a number of group-level phenomena, such as the BYSTANDER EFFECT and SOCIAL LOAFING. See also CONFUSION OF RESPONSIBILITY.

digital divide any significant gap between groups of individuals in their access to and skilled use of computers, the Internet, smartphones, and other information and communication technologies. For example, there is a digital divide between older adults and younger people: Because the former have been without computers for most of their lives, they tend to be less knowledgeable about the use of such technology than the latter, who have grown up with the technology.

digit span the number of random digits from a series that a person can recall following a single auditory presentation. A span of 5 to 9 digits is considered typical for an adult.

diglossia *n.* the situation in which two varieties of a language coexist and have distinct social functions within a community; these are usually characterized by high (H) and low (L) uses, H being associated with formality and literacy, and L with everyday colloquial usage.

dimensionality *n.* the number of factors applied in measuring a construct. In FACTOR ANALYSIS and PRINCIPAL COMPONENTS ANALYSIS, it is important to assess the dimensionality of a set of items on a scale in order to form cohesive subscales that each describe a similar set of items.

dimorphism *n.* the existence among members of the same species of two distinct forms that differ in one or more characteristics, such as size, shape, or color. See also SEXUAL DIMORPHISM. —**dimorphic** *adj.*

diploid *adj.* denoting or possessing the normal number of chromosomes, which in humans is 46: the 22 HOMOLOGOUS pairs of AUTOSOMES plus the male or female set of XY or XX SEX CHROMOSOMES. Compare HAPLOID.

direct correlation see POSITIVE CORRELATION.

directional hypothesis a scientific prediction stating (a) that an effect will occur and (b) whether that effect will specifically increase or specifically de-

crease, depending on changes to the INDEPENDENT VARIABLE. For example, a directional hypothesis could predict that depression scores will decrease following a 6-week intervention, or conversely that well-being will increase following a 6-week intervention. Also called **one-tailed hypothesis**. Compare NONDIRECTIONAL HYPOTHESIS.

directional test a statistical test of a DIRECTIONAL HYPOTHESIS. Also called **one-tailed test**. Compare NONDIRECTIONAL TEST.

direction circular see LABELING.

directive counseling an approach to counseling and psychotherapy in which the therapeutic process is directed along lines considered relevant by the counselor or therapist. Directive counseling is based on the assumption that the professional training and experience of the counselor or therapist equip him or her to manage the therapeutic process and to guide the client's behavior. Also called **directive therapy**.

direct observation a method of collecting data in which a researcher simply views or listens to the subjects of the research, without asking specific questions or manipulating any variables. The method of direct observation is useful in FIELD RESEARCH. See also NATURALISTIC OBSERVATION.

direct replication the process of repeating a study with different data under similar conditions, or of conducting several different studies with the same data. Direct replication is useful for establishing that the findings of the original study are reliable (see RELIABILITY). In contrast, SYSTEMATIC REPLICATION uses a different data set and also adjusts the conditions in specific ways.

disability *n.* a lasting physical or mental impairment that significantly interferes with an individual's ability to function in one or more central life activities, such as self-care, ambulation, communication, social interaction, sexual expression, or employment. For example, an individual who cannot see has a visual disability. See also HANDICAP. —**disabled** *adj.*

disability adjusted life years (**DALYs**) a measure of the influence of disease or injury on the length and quality of a person's life. It takes into account the potential loss of years due to premature mortality and the value of years lived with disability. One DALY represents one lost year of "healthy" life.

disaster psychology the specialized domain of training, research, and service provision applied to individuals, communities, and nations exposed to a disaster. A key goal is to reduce initial distress and foster short- and long-term adaptive functioning following a disaster. Within this domain, **disaster mental health** is the term most widely used in the United States to describe the psychological component in overall disaster response. See also CRISIS INTERVENTION.

discontinuity effect the markedly greater competitiveness of intergroup interactions relative to the competitiveness of interpersonal interactions. DIFFUSION OF RESPONSIBILITY and IN-GROUP BIAS have been proposed as contributing factors to this effect.

discontinuity hypothesis in GESTALT PSYCHOLOGY, the viewpoint that emphasizes the role of sudden insight and perceptual reorganization in successful DISCRIMINATION learning and problem solving. According to this view, a correct answer is only recognized when its relation to the issue as a whole is discovered. Compare CONTINUITY HYPOTHESIS.

discontinuous *adj.* intermittent or disconnected. For example, a string of numbers indicating nonsequential ranks is discontinuous because it does not have a smooth flow from one value to the next. See also DISCRETE. Compare CONTINUOUS.

discontinuous variable a variable that has distinct, DISCRETE values but no precise numerical flow. For example, gender can be thought of as a discontinuous variable with two possible values, male or female. In contrast, a CONTINUOUS VARIABLE involves numerically precise information, such as height, weight, and miles per hour. Also called **discrete variable**.

discordance *n.* **1.** the state or condition of being at variance. **Affective discordance** may be observed, for example, when a person relates a particularly disturbing experience without any facial or vocal indication of distress. **2.** in TWIN STUDIES, dissimilarity between a pair of twins with respect to a particular trait or disease. Compare CONCORDANCE. —**discordant** *adj.*

discourse *n.* the areas of written, spoken, and signed communication, whether formal (debate) or informal (conversation). The term is most often used in LINGUISTICS, where **discourse analysts** focus on both the study of language (sentences, speech acts, and lexicons) as well as the rhetoric, meanings, and strategies that underlie social interactions.

discourse analysis the study of linguistic structures that extend beyond the single sentence, such as conversations, narratives, or written arguments. Discourse analysis is particularly concerned with the ways in which a sequence of two or more sentences can produce meanings that are different from or additional to any found in the sentences considered separately. The norms and expectations that govern conversation are a major concern of discourse analysis, as is the structure of conversational language generally.

discovery learning learning that occurs through solving problems, by formulating and testing hypotheses, and in actual experience and manipulation in attempting solutions.

discrete *adj.* separate or distinct; often

referring to data that have names or ranks as values. In contrast, CONTINUOUS data have a potentially infinite flow of precise numerical information. See also DISCONTINUOUS.

discrete variable see DISCONTINUOUS VARIABLE.

discriminant analysis a MULTIVARIATE method of data analysis that uses a linear combination of values from a set of quantitative variables to predict differences among a set of predefined categories or groups of another variable. For example, a researcher might use a discriminant analysis to determine whether several measures of personality can differentiate those who pursue different majors in college.

discriminant function 1. any of a range of statistical techniques used to situate an item that could belong to any of two or more variables in the correct set, with minimal probability of error. **2.** in DISCRIMINANT ANALYSIS more specifically, a linear combination of predictor variables that is used to categorize items into distinct groups.

discrimination *n.* **1.** the ability to distinguish between stimuli or objects that differ quantitatively or qualitatively from one another. In conditioning, this meaning is extended to include the ability to respond in different ways in the presence of such different stimuli. **2.** differential treatment of the members of different ethnic, religious, national, or other groups. Discrimination is usually the behavioral manifestation of PREJUDICE and therefore involves negative, hostile, and injurious treatment of the members of rejected groups. **—discriminate** *vb.*

discrimination training a procedure in which an OPERANT RESPONSE is reinforced in the presence of a particular stimulus but not in the absence of that stimulus. For example, a rat's lever-press response might be reinforced when a stimulus light is on but not when the light is off. The rat will eventually learn to press the lever only when the light is on.

discriminative stimulus (symbol: S^D) in OPERANT CONDITIONING, a stimulus that increases the probability of a response because of a previous history of differential REINFORCEMENT in the presence of that stimulus. For example, if a pigeon's key pecks are reinforced when the key is illuminated red but not when the key is green, the red stimulus will come to serve as a S^D and the pigeon will learn to peck only when the key is red.

discursive psychology the study of social interactions and interpersonal relationships with a particular focus on understanding the ways in which individuals construct events via written, spoken, or symbolic communication.

disease *n.* a definite pathological process with organic origins, marked by a characteristic set of symptoms that may affect the entire body or a part of the body and that impairs functioning.

disease management an integrated treatment approach for patients with chronic health conditions that seeks to minimize the effects of their condition through illness-specific management, education, and patient support.

disease model any of several theories concerning the causes and course of a pathological condition or process.

disenfranchised grief grief that society (or some element of it) limits, does not expect, or may not allow a person to express. Examples include the grief of parents for stillborn babies and of teachers for the death of students. Disenfranchised grief may isolate the bereaved individual from others and thus impede recovery. See also GRIEF COUNSELING; GRIEF WORK; MOURNING.

disengagement *n.* the act of withdrawing from an attachment or relationship or, more generally, from an unpleasant situation. **—disengaged** *adj.*

disengagement theory a theory proposing that old age involves a gradual withdrawal of the individual from society and of society from the individual. According to this theory, those happiest in old age have turned their attention inward toward the self and away from involvement in the outside world. Empirical research has shown, however, that this mutual withdrawal is not an inevitable component of old age. Compare ACTIVITY THEORY; CONTINUITY THEORY.

disgust *n.* a strong aversion, for example, to the taste, smell, or touch of something deemed revolting, or toward a person or behavior deemed morally repugnant. **—disgusting** *adj.*

dishabituation *n.* the reappearance or enhancement of a habituated response (i.e., one that has been weakened following repeated exposure to the evoking stimulus) due to the presentation of a new stimulus. It is a useful method for investigating perception in nonverbal individuals or nonhuman animals. Compare HABITUATION.

disidentification *n.* **1.** a protective mechanism whereby one removes a potentially harmful characteristic or experience (e.g., one that causes STEREOTYPE THREAT) from one's self-identity as insulation from anxiety or failure. **2.** in meditation, a benign separation from one's sense of self in order to gain self-knowledge. It is a stepping away from self-identity as an attempt to observe oneself objectively.

disinhibition *n.* diminution or loss of the normal control exerted by the cerebral cortex, resulting in poorly regulated or poorly restrained emotions or actions.

disintegration *n.* a breakup or severe disorganization of some structure or system of functioning, for example, of psychic and behavioral functions.

disjunctive task a group task or project, such as solving a complex problem, that is completed when a single solution, decision, or group member's recommendation is adopted by the group. This means that the group's performance tends to be determined by the most skilled member. Compare ADDITIVE TASK; COMPENSATORY TASK; CONJUNCTIVE TASK.

dismissive attachment an adult attachment style that combines a positive INTERNAL WORKING MODEL OF ATTACHMENT of oneself, characterized by a view of oneself as competent and worthy of love, and a negative internal working model of attachment of others, characterized by one's view that others are untrustworthy or undependable. Individuals with dismissive attachment are presumed to discount the importance of close relationships and to maintain rigid self-sufficiency. Compare FEARFUL ATTACHMENT; PREOCCUPIED ATTACHMENT; SECURE ATTACHMENT.

disorder of written expression a LEARNING DISORDER in which writing skills are substantially below those expected for a person's chronological age, education, and measured intelligence. The writing difficulties (e.g., grammatical errors, spelling errors, poor handwriting) significantly interfere with academic achievement and activities of daily living that require writing skills. Also called **developmental dysgraphia**.

disorganization *n.* loss or disruption of orderly or systematic structure or functioning. For example, thought disorganization is an inability to integrate thought processes; behavior disorganization manifests as self-contradictory or inconsistent behavior.

disorganized attachment a form of INSECURE ATTACHMENT in which infants show no coherent or consistent behavior during separation from and reunion with their parents.

disorganized schizophrenia a subtype of schizophrenia characterized primarily by random and fragmented speech and behavior and by flat or inappropriate affect. Also called **hebephrenia**.

disorientation *n.* impaired ability to identify oneself or to locate oneself in relation to time, place, or other aspects of one's surroundings. Long-term disorientation can be characteristic of neurological and psychological disorders; temporary disorientation can be caused by alcohol or drugs or can occur in situations of acute stress. —**disoriented** *adj.*

dispersion *n.* the degree to which a set of scores deviate from the mean. Also called **spread**. See also RANGE; STANDARD DEVIATION; VARIANCE.

dispersion matrix see COVARIANCE MATRIX.

displaced aggression see AGGRESSION.

displacement *n.* the transfer of feelings or behavior from their original object to another person or thing. In psychoanalytic theory, displacement is considered to be a DEFENSE MECHANISM in which the individual discharges tensions associated with, for example, hostility and fear by taking them out on a less threatening target. Thus, an angry child might break a toy or yell at a sibling instead of attacking the father; a frustrated employee might criticize his or her spouse instead of the boss; or a person who fears his or her own hostile impulses might transfer that fear to knives, guns, or other objects that might be used as a weapon. —**displace** *vb.*

display *n.* specific stereotyped actions (i.e., actions repeated with little variation) that bring about a response in another individual: an integral part especially of animal communication. Display behavior may be a physical or vocal signal, usually involving stimulation of the visual or auditory senses. It may include body language that would convey a message of courtship to a member of the opposite sex (e.g., a show of plumage or color) or a suggestion that would be interpreted by an opponent as threatening (e.g., bared teeth or hissing noises).

display rule a socially learned standard that regulates the expression of emotion. Display rules vary by culture; for example, the expression of anger may be considered appropriate in some cultures but not in others.

disposition *n.* a recurrent behavioral, cognitive, or affective tendency that distinguishes an individual from others.

dispositional attribution the ascription of one's own or another's actions, an event, or an outcome to internal or psychological causes specific to the person concerned, such as traits, moods, attitudes, decisions and judgments, abilities, or effort. Also called **internal attribution; personal attribution**. Compare SITUATIONAL ATTRIBUTION.

dissociation *n.* a DEFENSE MECHANISM in which conflicting impulses are kept apart or threatening ideas and feelings are separated from the rest of the psyche.

dissociative amnesia a DISSOCIATIVE DISORDER characterized by failure to recall important information about one's personal experiences, usually of a traumatic or stressful nature, that is too extensive to be explained by normal forgetfulness. Recovery of memory often occurs spontaneously within a few hours and is usually connected with removal from the traumatic circumstances with which the amnesia was associated.

dissociative disorders any of a group of disorders characterized by a sudden or gradual disruption in the normal integrative functions of consciousness, memory, or perception of the environment. Such disruption may last for minutes or years, depending on the type of disorder. Typically included in this category are DISSOCIATIVE AMNESIA, DISSOCIATIVE IDENTITY DISORDER, and DEPERSONALIZATION DISORDER.

dissociative fugue a potential feature of DISSOCIATIVE AMNESIA in which the individual suddenly and unexpectedly travels away from home or a customary place of daily activities and is unable to recall some or all of his or her past. Symptoms also include either confusion about personal identity or assumption of a new identity. The fugue state can last from hours to months, and there may be no memory of travel once the individual is brought back to the prefugue state.

dissociative identity disorder (**DID**) a DISSOCIATIVE DISORDER characterized by the presence in one individual of two or more distinct identities or personality states that each recurrently take control of the individual's behavior. It is believed to be associated with severe physical and sexual abuse, especially during childhood. DID remains the subject of considerable controversy, however, with many disputing its validity as a diagnosis and citing the incidences of childhood abuse reported by diagnosed individuals or their therapists as cases of FALSE MEMORY. It is still commonly known as **multiple personality disorder**. See also SPLIT PERSONALITY.

dissonance *n.* see COGNITIVE DISSONANCE.

distal *adj.* **1.** situated or directed toward the periphery of the body or toward the end of a limb. **2.** remote from or mostly distantly related to the point of reference or origin. Compare PROXIMAL.

distal stimulus in perception, the actual object in the environment that stimulates or acts on a sense organ. Compare PROXIMAL STIMULUS.

distance *n.* the disparity between two values or entities. In statistics, the term often refers to the difference or DEVIA-TION between a RAW SCORE and a mean score.

distance cue any of the auditory or visual cues that enable an individual to judge the distance of the source of a stimulus. Auditory distance cues include intensity of familiar sounds (e.g., voices), intensity differences between the ears, and changes in spectral content. In vision, distance cues include the size of familiar objects and ACCOMMODATION.

distance therapy any type of psychotherapy in which sessions are not conducted face to face because of problems of mobility, geographical isolation, or other limiting factors. Distance therapy includes interventions by telephone, audioconference, or videoconference (known collectively as **telepsychotherapy**) and the Internet (see E-THERAPY).

distress *n.* the negative stress response, often involving negative affect and physiological reactivity: a type of stress that results from being overwhelmed by demands, losses, or perceived threats. It has a detrimental effect by generating physical and psychological maladaptation and posing serious health risks for individuals. This generally is the intended meaning of the word STRESS. Compare EUSTRESS. —**distressing** *adj.*

distress tolerance the level of either (a) one's unwillingness to experience emotional distress as part of pursuing desired goals or (b) one's inability to engage in goal-directed behaviors when experiencing distress. Low distress tolerance is related to a range of disorders, including borderline personality disorder, substance abuse, and eating disorders.

distributed cognition a model for intelligent problem solving in which either the input information comes from separated and independent sources or the processing of this input information takes place across autonomous computational devices.

distributed practice a learning procedure in which practice periods for a particular task are separated by lengthy rest periods or lengthy periods of practicing different activities, rather than occurring close together in time. In many learning situations, distributed practice is found to be more effective than MASSED PRACTICE. Also called **spaced practice**. See also SPACING EFFECT.

distributed-practice effect see SPACING EFFECT.

distribution *n.* the relation between the values that a variable may take and the relative number of cases taking on each value. A distribution may be simply an empirical description of that relationship or a mathematical (probabilistic) specification of the relationship. For example, it would be helpful in examining the distribution of scores for a college exam to view the frequency of students who achieved various percentages correct on the exam. In a NORMAL DISTRIBUTION, most of the scores would fall in the middle (i.e., about 70% correct or a score of C), with fewer students achieving a D (i.e., 60%–69% correct) or a B (i.e., 80%–89% correct) and even fewer earning 59% or less (i.e., an F) or 90% to 100% (e.g., an A). See also FREQUENCY DISTRIBUTION; PROBABILITY DISTRIBUTION.

distribution-free test see NONPARAMETRIC TEST.

distributive justice the belief that rules can be changed and punishments and rewards distributed according to relative standards, specifically according to equality and equity. Developing in children by the age of 11 or older, the belief makes allowances for subjective considerations, personal circumstances, and motive. Compare IMMANENT JUSTICE.

disulfiram *n.* a drug used as an aversive agent in managing alcohol abuse or dependence. Disulfiram inhibits the activity of acetaldehyde dehydroge-

nase, an enzyme responsible for the metabolism of alcohol (ethanol) in the liver. Consumption of alcohol following administration of disulfiram results in accumulation of acetaldehyde, a toxic metabolic product of ethanol, with such unpleasant effects as nausea, vomiting, sweating, headache, a fast heart rate, and palpitations. U.S. trade name: **Antabuse**.

diurnal *adj.* **1.** daily; that is, recurring every 24 hours. **2.** occurring or active during daylight hours. Compare NOCTURNAL. **—diurnality** *n.*

divergence *n.* the rotation of the two eyes outward when shifting fixation from a nearby target object to one that is far away. **—divergent** *adj.*

divergent thinking creative thinking in which an individual solves a problem or reaches a decision using strategies that deviate from commonly used or previously taught strategies. This term is often used synonymously with LATERAL THINKING. Compare CONVERGENT THINKING.

diversity *n.* the wide range of variation of living organisms in an ecosystem. When describing people and population groups, diversity can include such factors as age, gender, sexuality, race, ethnicity, nationality, and religion, as well as education, livelihood, and marital status.

divided attention attention to two or more channels of information at the same time, so that two or more tasks may be performed concurrently. It may involve the use of just one sense (e.g., hearing) or two or more senses (e.g., hearing and vision).

dizygotic twins (**DZ twins**) twins, of the same or different sex, that have developed from two separate ova fertilized by two separate sperm. DZ twins are genetically as much alike as ordinary full siblings born separately. On average, DZ twins are approximately half as genetically similar to one another as MONOZYGOTIC TWINS. Also called **fraternal twins**.

DNA *d*eoxyribo*n*ucleic *a*cid: one of the two types of nucleic acid found in living organisms; it is the principal carrier of genetic information in chromosomes. Certain segments of the DNA molecules constitute the organism's genes, with each gene specifying the manufacture of a particular protein or ribosome. Structurally, DNA consists of two intertwined, helically coiled strands of nucleotides—the double helix. The nucleotides each contain one of four bases: adenine, guanine, cytosine, or thymine. Each base forms hydrogen bonds with the adjacent base on the other, sister strand, producing consecutive base pairs arranged rather like the "rungs" on a helical ladder. Because of DNA's ability to conserve its base sequence when replicating, the genetic instructions it carries are also conserved, both during cell division within a single organism and for that organism's offspring following reproduction. Compare RNA.

dogmatism *n.* a personality trait characterized by the tendency to act in a blindly certain, assertive, and authoritative manner in accordance with a strongly held set of beliefs that are resistant to change. The beliefs often contain elements that are isolated from one another and thus may contradict one another. —**dogmatic** *adj.*

domestic violence any action by a person that causes physical harm to one or more members of his or her family unit. For example, it can involve battering of one partner by another, violence against children by a parent, or violence against elders by younger family members.

dominance *n.* **1.** the exercise of influence or control over others. **2.** an older term for the tendency for one hemisphere of the cerebral cortex to exert greater influence than the other over certain key functions, such as speech production or manual tasks. See

HEMISPHERIC LATERALIZATION. **3.** in genetics, the ability of one allele to determine the PHENOTYPE of a HETEROZYGOUS individual. See DOMINANT ALLELE. —**dominant** *adj.*

dominance hierarchy 1. a system of stable linear variations in prestige, status, and authority among group members. It is the PECKING ORDER of the group, which describes who is influential and who submits to that influence. **2.** any ordering of motives, needs, or other psychological or physical responses based on priority or importance. An example is MASLOW'S MOTIVATIONAL HIERARCHY.

dominant allele the version of a gene (see ALLELE) whose effects are manifest in preference to another version of the same gene (the RECESSIVE ALLELE) when both are present in the same cell. Hence, the trait determined by a dominant allele (the **dominant trait**) is apparent even when the allele is carried on only one of a pair of HOMOLOGOUS chromosomes.

door-in-the-face technique a two-step procedure for enhancing compliance in which an extreme initial request is presented immediately before a more moderate target request. Rejection of the initial request makes people more likely to accept the target request than would have been the case if the latter had been presented on its own. See also FOOT-IN-THE-DOOR TECHNIQUE; LOW-BALL TECHNIQUE; THAT'S-NOT-ALL TECHNIQUE.

dopa (DOPA) *n.* 3,4-*d*ihydroxyphenyl-*a*lanine: an amino acid that is a precursor to DOPAMINE and other catecholamines.

dopamine (DA) *n.* a CATECHOLAMINE neurotransmitter that has an important role in motor behavior and is implicated in numerous mental conditions and emotional states. For example, destruction of the DOPAMINERGIC neurons in the SUBSTANTIA NIGRA in the midbrain is responsible for the symptoms of Parkinson's disease (e.g., rigidity, tremor), and blockade of the actions of dopamine in other brain regions accounts for the therapeutic activities of many antipsychotic drugs. Dopamine is synthesized from the dietary amino acid tyrosine, and in nondopaminergic neurons and the adrenal medulla, it is further metabolized to form NOREPINEPHRINE and EPINEPHRINE, respectively.

dopamine hypothesis the influential theory that schizophrenia is caused by an excess of dopamine in the brain, due either to an overproduction of dopamine or a deficiency of the enzyme needed to convert dopamine to norepinephrine (adrenaline). There is some supporting pharmacological and biochemical evidence for this hypothesis, and it is still widely discussed and promoted, particularly in a revised form that postulates the involvement in schizophrenia of both increased mesolimbic and decreased prefrontal dopaminergic activity. See also GLUTAMATE HYPOTHESIS.

dopaminergic *adj.* responding to, releasing, or otherwise involving dopamine. For example, a **dopaminergic neuron** is any neuron in the brain or other parts of the central nervous system for which dopamine serves as the principal neurotransmitter. Four major tracts (called **dopaminergic pathways**) of dopamine-containing neurons are classically described: the mesocortical system, damage to which is associated with depression and attention-deficit/hyperactivity disorder; the mesolimbic system, in which excess dopamine activity is hypothesized to be associated with positive and negative symptoms of schizophrenia; the nigrostriatal tract, which is involved in motor functions and Parkinson's disease; and the tuberoinfundibular tract, a local circuit from the hypothalamus to the pituitary that is involved in the regulation of the pituitary hormone prolactin.

Doppler effect the apparent increase or decrease in wavelength or frequency observed when a source of electromagnetic radiation or sound approaches or recedes from the observer or listener, which produces a change in hue or pitch. [Christian Andreas **Doppler** (1803–1853), Austrian mathematician]

dorsal *adj.* denoting the hind region or the back surface of the body. In reference to the latter, this term sometimes is used interchangeably with POSTERIOR. Compare VENTRAL. —**dorsally** *adv.*

dorsal anterior cingulate cortex see ANTERIOR CINGULATE CORTEX.

dorsal column any of various tracts of sensory nerve fibers that run through the white matter of the spinal cord on its dorsal (back) side.

dorsal horn either of the upper regions of the H-shaped pattern formed by the PERIAQUEDUCTAL GRAY in the spinal cord. The dorsal horns extend toward the dorsal roots and mainly serve sensory mechanisms. Compare VENTRAL HORN.

dorsal posterior cingulate cortex see POSTERIOR CINGULATE CORTEX.

dorsal root any of the SPINAL ROOTS that convey sensory nerve fibers and enter the spinal cord dorsally, on the back surface of each side. Compare VENTRAL ROOT.

dorsal stream a series of cortical maps that originate in the STRIATE CORTEX (primary visual cortex) of the occipital lobe and project forward and upward into the parietal lobe. Known informally as the "where" or "how" pathway, the dorsal stream is involved in processing object motion and location in space. Compare VENTRAL STREAM.

dorsolateral *adj.* located both dorsally (toward the back) and laterally (toward the side). —**dorsolaterally** *adv.*

dorsolateral prefrontal cortex (**DLPFC**) a region of the brain located near the PREFRONTAL CORTEX in humans, involved in WORKING MEMORY, voluntary attentional control, and speech production. Damage to this region results in an inability to select task-relevant information and to freely shift attention based on external cues.

dorsoventral *adj.* oriented or directed from the back (dorsal) region of the body to the front (ventral) region. Compare VENTRODORSAL. —**dorsoventrally** *adv.*

dose–response relationship a principle relating the potency of a drug to its efficacy in affecting a target symptom or organ system. **Potency** refers to the amount of a drug necessary to produce the desired effect; **efficacy** refers to the drug's ability to act at a target receptor or organ to produce the desired effect. Dose–response curves may be graded, suggesting a continuous relationship between dose and effect, or quantal, wherein the desired effect is an either–or phenomenon, such as prevention of arrhythmias.

dot plot see SCATTERPLOT.

double bind a situation in which an individual receives contradictory messages from another person. For example, a parent may respond negatively when his or her child approaches or attempts to engage in affectionate behavior but then, when the child turns away or tries to leave, reaches out to encourage the child to return. Double-binding communication was once considered a causative factor in schizophrenia.

double blind see BLIND.

double dissociation a research process for demonstrating the action of two separable psychological or biological systems, such as differentiating between types of memory or the function of brain areas. One experimental variable is found to affect one of the systems, whereas a second variable affects the other. The differentiating variables may be task related, pharma-

cological, neurological, or individual differences.

double standard the hypocritical belief that a code of behavior is permissible for one group or individual but not for another. For example, a double standard is held by the father who insists on his daughter's virginity while encouraging his son's philandering.

Down syndrome a chromosomal disorder characterized by an extra chromosome 21 and by distinct facial features (e.g., round flat face, slanted eyes) and below-average brain size and weight. Affected individuals usually have mild to severe intellectual disability, and their muscular movements tend to be slow, clumsy, and uncoordinated. Their lifespan is reduced compared with that in the general population, and they typically show early onset of Alzheimer's disease. Down syndrome is one of the most common physiological causes of intellectual disability. [described in 1866 by John Langdon Haydon **Down** (1828–1896), British physician]

d prime (symbol: d') a measure of an individual's ability to detect signals; more specifically, a measure of sensitivity or discriminability derived from SIGNAL DETECTION THEORY that is unaffected by response biases. It is the difference (in standard deviation units) between the means of the NOISE and signal + noise distributions. A value of $d' = 3$ is close to perfect performance; a value of $d' = 0$ is chance ("guessing") performance.

dream *n.* a physiologically and psychologically conscious state that occurs during sleep and is often characterized by a rich array of endogenous sensory, motor, emotional, and other experiences. Dreams occur most often, but by no means exclusively, during periods of REM SLEEP. Those that occur during NREM SLEEP are characterized primarily by thoughts and emotions, whereas REM dreams are characterized primarily by (a) visual imagery along with a sense of motion in space; (b) intense emotion, especially fear, elation, or anger; (c) belief that the dream content is real; and (d) sudden discontinuities in dream characters, situations, and plot elements. REM dream reports are optimally obtained immediately after waking an individual, whereas individuals awakened during NREM sleep report fewer dreams. Diverse theories about the nature, meaning, and function of dreams have arisen from varied sources throughout history. These range from the suggestion of Greek physician Hippocrates (c. 460–c. 377 BCE) that dreams provide early evidence of disease, to the view of Austrian neurologist Sigmund Freud (1856–1939) that dreams are symbolic condensations of conflicting impulses rejected from waking consciousness to avoid emotional distress, to various hypotheses (e.g., ACTIVATION–SYNTHESIS HYPOTHESIS) that have emerged in recent years from the scientific study of dreaming as a neurocognitive process. **—dream** *vb.* **—dreamlike** *adj.* **—dreamy** *adj.*

dream analysis a technique in which the content of dreams is interpreted to reveal underlying motivations or symbolic meanings and representations (i.e., LATENT CONTENT). Also called **dream interpretation**.

dream-work *n.* in psychoanalytic theory, the transformation of the LATENT CONTENT of a dream into the MANIFEST CONTENT experienced by the dreamer. This transformation is effected by such processes as SYMBOLIZATION and DISPLACEMENT.

drift *n.* **1.** a reduction in variation in genetic traits that can occur when sampling from continually smaller groups, such that some traits ultimately become excluded from possibility. **2.** a reduction in the reliability of technical instruments or in the accuracy of observers over time.

drive *n.* **1.** a generalized state of readiness precipitating or motivating an activity or course of action. Drive is hypothetical in nature, usually created by deprivation of a needed substance (e.g., food), the presence of negative stimuli (e.g., pain, cold), or the occurrence of negative events. **2.** in the classical psychoanalytic theory of Austrian neurologist Sigmund Freud (1856–1939), a concept used to understand the relationship between the psyche and the soma (mind and body); drive is conceived as having a somatic source but creating a psychic effect. Freud identified two separate drives as emerging from somatic sources: LIBIDO and AGGRESSION.

drive-reduction theory a theory of learning in which the goal of motivated behavior is a reduction of a drive state. It is assumed that all motivated behavior arises from drives, stemming from a disruption in homeostasis, and that responses that lead to reduction of those drives tend to be reinforced or strengthened.

drug *n.* a substance, other than food, that influences motor, sensory, cognitive, or other bodily processes. Drugs generally are administered for experimental, diagnostic, or treatment purposes but also tend to be used recreationally to achieve particular effects.

drug abuse see SUBSTANCE ABUSE.

drug addiction see ADDICTION; SUBSTANCE DEPENDENCE.

drug court an alternative to the usual legal processing and penalties for nonviolent drug offenders. Drug court focuses on treatment and rehabilitation rather than punishment.

drug dependence see SUBSTANCE DEPENDENCE.

drug therapy see PHARMACOTHERAPY.

drug tolerance see TOLERANCE.

drug withdrawal see SUBSTANCE WITHDRAWAL.

DSM–5 the fifth edition of the *Diag-*

nostic and Statistical Manual of Mental Disorders, prepared by the American Psychiatric Association and published in 2013. It uses a nonaxial approach to psychiatric diagnosis, with separate notations for psychosocial and contextual factors and disability; organization of diagnoses according to the period (i.e., childhood, adolescence, adulthood, later life) during which they most frequently first manifest; clustering of disorders according to internalizing factors (e.g., anxiety, depression) and externalizing factors (e.g., impulsive, disruptive conduct); and consolidation of separate diagnostic areas into spectra (e.g., AUTISM SPECTRUM DISORDER).

dual coding theory the theory that linguistic input can be represented in memory in both verbal and visual formats. Concrete words that readily call to mind a picture, such as *table* or *horse*, are remembered better than abstract words, such as *honesty* or *conscience*, which do not readily call to mind a picture, because the concrete words are stored in two codes rather than one.

dualism *n.* the position that reality consists of two separate substances, defined by French philosopher and mathematician René Descartes (1596–1650) as thinking substance (mind) and extended substance (matter). In the context of the MIND–BODY PROBLEM, dualism is the position that the mind and the body constitute two separate realms or substances. Dualistic positions raise the question of how mind and body interact in thought and behavior. Compare MONISM. See also CARTESIAN DUALISM. —**dualist** *adj., n.* —**dualistic** *adj.*

dual process theory of color vision see OPPONENT PROCESS THEORY OF COLOR VISION.

dual-store model of memory the concept that memory is a two-stage process, comprising SHORT-TERM MEMORY, in which information is retained for a few seconds, and LONG-TERM MEMORY, which permits the retention of information for hours to many years. Also called **dual memory theory**.

dual trace hypothesis a restatement of the PERSEVERATION–CONSOLIDATION HYPOTHESIS of memory formation specifying that short-term memory is represented neurally by activity in reverberating circuits and that stabilization of these circuits leads to permanent synaptic change, reflecting the formation of long-term memory. See HEBBIAN SYNAPSE.

dummy variable 1. in REGRESSION ANALYSIS, a numerical variable that is created to represent a qualitative fact, which is done by giving a variable a value of 1 or 0 to indicate the presence or absence of a categorical trait. A dummy variable usually represents a DICHOTOMOUS VARIABLE, that is, one that can have only two categories. For example, gender could be coded as a 1 to represent female and a 0 to represent male. **2.** in mathematics and computer science, a variable that can stand for or be bound to any element from its domain. Also called **indicator variable**.

dummy variable coding a method of assigning numerical values to a CATEGORICAL VARIABLE in such a way that the variable reflects class membership. The values of 0 and 1 often are used, with 0 typically representing nonmembership and 1 typically representing membership. Compare EFFECT CODING.

Dunn–Bonferroni procedure a statistical method for assessing whether multiple pairs of samples are significantly different from each other, while protecting the overall TYPE I ERROR rate by dividing the alpha or SIGNIFICANCE LEVEL by the number of comparisons made. For example, if a researcher wants to investigate whether three samples are significantly different using an alpha of .05, three T TESTS could be conducted (i.e., between groups 1 and 2, 2 and 3, and 1 and 3) using an alpha level of .05/3 = .0167 for each comparison; this approach would hold the overall Type I error rate at .05. Also called **Bonferroni *t* test**; **Dunn's multiple comparison test**. [Olive Jean **Dunn**, U.S. mathematician; Carlo Emilio **Bonferroni** (1892–1960), Italian mathematician]

Dunnett's multiple comparison test a statistical method for assessing whether a CONTROL GROUP is significantly different from each of several treatment groups. It is similar to the DUNN–BONFERRONI PROCEDURE but not as stringent in that it does not require the SIGNIFICANCE LEVEL per comparison to be as small. The index of difference that is obtained from this test is called **Dunnett's *t***. [Charles W. **Dunnett** (1921–2007), Canadian statistician]

Dunn's multiple comparison test see DUNN–BONFERRONI PROCEDURE.

durable power of attorney see ADVANCE DIRECTIVE.

dura mater see MENINGES.

dwarfism *n.* a condition of underdeveloped body structure due to a developmental defect, a hereditary trait, hormonal or nutritional deficiencies, or disease. Some forms of dwarfism, such as that due to thyroid-hormone deficiency, are associated with intellectual disability.

dyad (**diad**) *n.* a pair of individuals in an interpersonal situation, such as mother and child, husband and wife, or patient and therapist. —**dyadic** *adj.*

dynamic formulation the ongoing attempt to organize the clinical material elicited about a client's behavior, traits, attitudes, and symptoms into a structure that helps the therapist understand the client and plan his or her treatment effectively.

dynamic psychology a theory of psychology emphasizing causation and motivation in relation to behavior, specifically the stimulus–organism–response chain in which the stimulus–response relationship is regarded as the mechanism of behavior and the drives

of the organism are the mediating variable.

dynamic psychotherapy see PSYCHODYNAMIC PSYCHOTHERAPY.

dynamic systems theory a theory that attempts to explain behavior and personality in terms of constantly changing, self-organizing interactions among many organismic and environmental factors that operate on multiple timescales and levels of analysis. See CHAOS THEORY; COMPLEXITY THEORY.

dynamometry *n.* the measurement of force expended or power, especially muscular effort or strength. A **dynamometer** usually consists of a spring that can be compressed by the force applied. For example, a hand dynamometer is a device for measuring manual grip strength by the amount of force applied to a spring by the hands. —**dynamometric** *adj.*

dysarthria *n.* a motor speech disorder characterized by difficulty speaking coherently because of impairment in the central or peripheral nervous system. There are four main types usually described: dyskinetic, spastic, peripheral, and mixed. —**dysarthric** *adj.*

dyscalculia *n.* an impaired ability to perform simple arithmetic operations that results from a congenital deficit. It is a developmental condition, whereas ACALCULIA is acquired.

dysexecutive syndrome (**DES**) a collection of symptoms that involve impaired executive control of actions, caused by damage to the frontal lobes of the brain. Individuals have difficulty in initiating and switching actions; for example, they cannot prevent an inappropriate but highly automated action from occurring or change their actions to appropriate ones.

dysfunction *n.* any impairment, disturbance, or deficiency in behavior or operation. —**dysfunctional** *adj.*

dysgraphia *n.* see AGRAPHIA. —**dysgraphic** *adj.*

dyslexia *n.* a neurologically based learning disability manifested as severe difficulties in reading, spelling, and writing words, resulting from impairment in the ability to make connections between written letters and their sounds. It can be either acquired (in which case it is often referred to as ALEXIA) or developmental, is independent of intellectual ability, and is unrelated to disorders of speech and vision that may also be present. Although it is often subdivided into two general classes—VISUAL WORD-FORM DYSLEXIA and CENTRAL DYSLEXIA—and various other subtypes of dyslexia have also been proposed, there is no universally accepted system of classification. —**dyslexic** *adj.*

dyslogia *n.* see ALOGIA.

dysmenorrhea *n.* difficult or painful menstruation. —**dysmenorrheic** *adj.*

dysnomia *n.* a SEMANTIC MEMORY deficit that impairs word retrieval and object naming, as seen in individuals with Alzheimer's disease and temporal lobe epilepsy.

dyspareunia *n.* painful sexual intercourse, particularly in women.

dysphoria *n.* a mood characterized by generalized discontent and agitation. —**dysphoric** *adj.*

dysregulation *n.* any excessive or otherwise poorly managed mechanism or response. For example, emotional dysregulation is an extreme or inappropriate emotional response to a situation (e.g., temper outbursts, DELIBERATE SELF-HARM); it may be associated with bipolar disorders, borderline personality disorder, autism spectrum disorder, psychological trauma, or brain injury.

dysrhythmia *n.* any rhythmic abnormality, as might be detected in speech or in brain waves.

dyssemia *n.* difficulty in interpreting (decoding) or producing (encoding) nonverbal information (e.g., facial, postural, gestural, and paralinguistic expressions).

dyssomnia *n.* any of various disorders marked by abnormalities in the amount, quality, or timing of sleep. NARCOLEPSY is an example. See also PARASOMNIA.

dysthymia *n.* any depressed mood that is mild or moderate in severity. Also called **minor depression**. —**dysthymic** *adj.*

dysthymic disorder a mood disorder characterized by symptoms that are less severe but more enduring than those in MAJOR DEPRESSIVE DISORDER. Also called **persistent depressive disorder**.

Ee

ear *n.* the organ of hearing and balance. In humans and other mammals, the ear is divided into external, middle, and inner sections. The PINNA of the EXTERNAL EAR collects sounds that are then funneled through the EXTERNAL AUDITORY MEATUS to the TYMPANIC MEMBRANE. The sounds are vibrations of air molecules that cause the tympanic membrane to vibrate, which in turn vibrates the OSSICLES, three tiny bones in the MIDDLE EAR. The motion of the last of these bones produces pressure waves in the fluid-filled COCHLEA of the INNER EAR. The motion of the fluid in the cochlea is converted by specialized receptors called HAIR CELLS into neural signals that are sent to the brain by the AUDITORY NERVE.

ear canal see EXTERNAL AUDITORY MEATUS.

eardrum *n.* see TYMPANIC MEMBRANE.

early intervention a collection of specialized services provided to children from birth to 3 years of age with identified conditions placing them at risk of developmental disability or with evident signs of developmental delay. Services are designed to minimize the impact of the infant's or toddler's condition, and in addition to stimulatory, social, and therapeutic programs, they may include family training, screening, assessment, and health care.

early-selection theory any theory of attention proposing that selection of stimuli for processing occurs prior to stimulus identification. According to early-selection theory, unattended stimuli receive only a slight degree of processing that does not encompass meaning, whereas attended stimuli proceed through a significant degree of deep, meaningful analysis. Compare LATE-SELECTION THEORY.

eating disorder any disorder characterized primarily by a pathological disturbance of attitudes and behaviors related to food, including ANOREXIA NERVOSA, BULIMIA NERVOSA, and BINGE-EATING DISORDER. Other eating-related disorders include PICA and RUMINATION disorder.

echoic memory the retention of auditory information for a brief period (2–3 seconds) after the end of the stimulus.

echolalia *n.* mechanical repetition of words and phrases uttered by another individual. It is often a symptom of a neurological or developmental disorder, particularly catatonic schizophrenia or autism.

echolocation *n.* the ability to judge the direction and distance of objects or obstacles from reflected echoes made by acoustic signals. For example, both bats and marine mammals (e.g., dolphins) can locate objects by emitting high-pitched sounds that are reflected from surfaces of the physical environment and prey objects.

echopraxia *n.* mechanical repetition of another person's movements or gestures. It is often a symptom of a neurological disorder, particularly catatonic schizophrenia.

eclecticism *n.* a theoretical or practical approach that blends, or attempts to blend, diverse conceptual formulations or techniques into an integrated approach. —**eclectic** *adj.*

ecological niche the function or position of an organism or a population within a physical and biological environment.

ecological perception an organism's detection of the AFFORDANCES and INVARIANCES within its natural, real-world environment, as mediated and guided by its immersion in and movement through that environment.

ecological systems theory an evolving body of theory and research concerned with the processes and conditions that govern the course of human development in the actual environments in which human beings live. Originally focused on the environment as a context for child development (in terms of nested systems ranging from micro- to macro-), the theory is now known as the **bioecological model**, denoting a broader conception of human development as a process that is affected, across the lifespan and across successive generations, by both environmental context and individual biopsychological characteristics.

ecological validity the degree to which research results are representative of conditions in the wider world. For example, psychological research carried out exclusively among university students might have a low ecological validity when applied to the population as a whole.

ecology *n.* the study of relationships between organisms and their physical and social environments. —**ecological** *adj.* —**ecologist** *n.*

ecopsychology *n.* **1.** a field that promotes a less egocentric mode of thinking in favor of a more ecocentric one. By encouraging humans to rethink their position in the natural world, some psychologists believe they can influence people to be more responsible stewards of nature. **2.** an occasional synonym of ENVIRONMENTAL PSYCHOLOGY.

Ecstasy *n.* the popular name for MDMA.

edema *n.* an accumulation of fluid in body cells, organs, or cavities, resulting in swelling. —**edematous** *adj.*

educational neuroscience see NEUROEDUCATION.

educational psychology a branch of psychology dealing with the application of psychological principles and theories to a broad spectrum of teaching, training, and learning issues in educational settings.

EEG biofeedback see NEUROFEEDBACK.

effect *n.* in ANALYSIS OF VARIANCE, a statistically significant relationship between variables, such that one variable is held to be an outcome of another (or some combination of others). See MAIN EFFECT; INTERACTION EFFECT.

effect coding in REGRESSION ANALYSIS, a procedure in which values of 1 or −1 are assigned to represent the categories of a DICHOTOMOUS VARIABLE. The results obtained for the group indicated by values of 1 are then interpreted relative to the larger group comprising all participants. For example, a researcher could assign values of 1 to individuals in an EXPERIMENTAL GROUP and values of −1 to those in a CONTROL GROUP. He or she could conclude that there is a treatment effect if the experimental group has a mean different from the GRAND MEAN across all of the individuals. Compare DUMMY VARIABLE CODING.

effective stimulus see FUNCTIONAL STIMULUS.

effect size any of various measures of the magnitude or meaningfulness of a relationship between two variables. For example, COHEN'S D shows the number of STANDARD DEVIATION units between two means. Often, effect sizes are interpreted as indicating the practical significance of a research finding. Additionally, in META-ANALYSES, they allow for the computation of summary statistics that apply to all the studies considered as a whole. See also STATISTICAL SIGNIFICANCE.

efferent *adj.* conducting or conveying away from a central point. Compare AFFERENT.

efficacy *n.* in pharmacology, see DOSE–RESPONSE RELATIONSHIP.

effortful processing mental activity that requires deliberation and control and involves a sense of effort or overcoming resistance. Compare AUTOMATICITY.

effort justification a phenomenon whereby people come to evaluate a particular task or activity more favorably when it involves something that is difficult or unpleasant. Because expending effort to perform a useless or unenjoyable task, or experiencing unpleasant consequences in doing so, is cognitively inconsistent (see COGNITIVE DISSONANCE), people are assumed to shift their evaluations of the task in a positive direction to restore consistency.

ego *n.* **1.** the SELF, particularly the conscious sense of self (Latin, "I"). In its popular and quasi-technical sense, ego refers to all the psychological phenomena and processes that are related to the self and that comprise the individual's attitudes, values, and concerns. **2.** in psychoanalytic theory, the component of the personality that deals with the external world and its practical demands. More specifically, the ego enables the individual to perceive, reason, solve problems, test reality, and adjust the instinctual impulses of the ID to the demands of the SUPEREGO.

ego analysis psychoanalytic techniques directed toward discovering the strengths and weaknesses of the EGO and uncovering its defenses against unacceptable impulses. See also EGO STRENGTH; EGO WEAKNESS.

egocentric speech speech in which there is no attempt to exchange thoughts or take into account another person's point of view.

egocentrism *n.* **1.** the tendency to emphasize one's own needs, concerns, and outcomes rather than those of others. Also called **egocentricity**. See also IDIOCENTRIC. Compare SOCIOCENTRISM. **2.** in PIAGETIAN THEORY, the tendency to perceive the situation from one's own perspective, believing that others see things from the same point of view as oneself. —**egocentric** *adj.*

ego defense in psychoanalytic theory, the use of DEFENSE MECHANISMS to protect the EGO against anxiety arising from threatening impulses and conflicts as well as external threats.

ego-ideal *n.* in psychoanalytic theory, the part of the EGO that is the repository of positive identifications with parental goals and values that the individual genuinely admires and wishes to emulate, such as integrity and loyalty, and that acts as a model of how he or she wishes to be. In his later theorizing, Austrian neurologist Sigmund Freud (1856–1939) incorporated the ego-ideal into the concept of the SUPEREGO. Also called **self-ideal**.

egoism *n.* a personality characteristic marked by selfishness and behavior based on self-interest with disregard for the needs of others. See also EGOTISM. —**egoistic** *adj.*

ego psychology in psychoanalysis, an approach that emphasizes the functions of the EGO in controlling impulses, planning, and dealing with the external environment. Compare ID PSYCHOLOGY.

ego strength in psychoanalytic theory, the ability of the EGO to maintain an effective balance between the inner impulses of the ID, the SUPEREGO, and outer reality. An individual with a strong ego is thus one who is able to tolerate frustration and stress, postpone gratification, modify selfish desires when necessary, and resolve internal conflicts and emotional problems before they lead to NEUROSIS. Compare EGO WEAKNESS.

egotism *n.* excessive conceit or a preoccupation with one's own importance. See also EGOISM. —**egotistic** *adj.*

ego weakness in psychoanalytic theory, the inability of the EGO to control impulses and tolerate frustration, disappointment, or stress. The individual with a weak ego is thus one who suffers from anxiety and conflicts, makes excessive use of DEFENSE MECHANISMS or uses immature defense mechanisms, and is likely to develop neurotic symptoms. Compare EGO STRENGTH.

eidetic image a clear, specific, high-quality mental image of a visual scene that is retained for a period (seconds to minutes) after the event. Individuals who experience eidetic imagery (called **eidetikers**) continue to see a visual scene and are able to report on its details even though they know the stimulus is no longer there. This type of imagery is more common in children than in adults.

eigenvalue (symbol: λ) *n.* a numerical index, commonly used in FACTOR ANALYSIS and PRINCIPAL COMPONENTS ANALYSIS, that indicates the portion of the total variance among several correlated variables that is accounted for by a more basic, underlying variable or construct. Eigenvalues are of central importance in linear algebra (i.e., matrix algebra).

Einstellung *n.* an expectation or readiness associated with particular stimuli. It may foster a degree of mental inflexibility by instilling a tendency to respond to a situation in a certain way. For example, a person who successfully solves a series of problems using one formula may apply that same formula to a new problem solvable by a simpler method. The contemporary term for this concept is MENTAL SET. [German, "attitude"]

ejaculation *n.* the automatic expulsion of semen and seminal fluid through the penis resulting from involuntary and voluntary contractions of various muscle groups, normally associated with ORGASM. See also PREMATURE EJACULATION. **—ejaculatory** *adj.*

elaborated code a linguistic REGISTER typically used in formal situations (e.g., academic discourse), characterized by a wide vocabulary, complex constructions, and unpredictable collocations of word and idea. This contrasts with the **restricted code** used in much informal conversation, which is characterized by a narrow vocabulary, simple constructions, and predictable ritualized forms, with much reliance on context and nonverbal communication to convey meaning.

elaboration *n.* **1.** the process of interpreting or embellishing information to be remembered or of relating it to other material already known and in memory. The LEVELS-OF-PROCESSING MODEL OF MEMORY holds that the level of elaboration applied to information as it is processed affects both the length of time that it can be retained in memory and the ease with which it can be retrieved. See also DEEP PROCESSING. **2.** the process of scrutinizing and thinking about the central merits of attitude-relevant information. This process includes generating inferences about the information, assessing its validity, and considering the implications of evaluative responses to the information. **—elaborate** *vb.*

elaboration-likelihood model (**ELM**) a theory of PERSUASION postulating that attitude change occurs on a continuum of elaboration and thus, under certain conditions, may be a result of relatively extensive (see CENTRAL ROUTE TO PERSUASION) or relatively little (see PERIPHERAL ROUTE TO PERSUASION) scrutiny of attitude-relevant information. The theory postulates that ATTITUDE STRENGTH depends on the amount of elaboration on which the attitude is based.

elaborative rehearsal an ENCODING strategy to facilitate the formation of memory by linking new information to what one already knows. For instance, when trying to remember that someone is named George, one might think of five other things one knows about people named George. See DEPTH-OF-PROCESSING HYPOTHESIS.

elder abuse harm to an adult aged 65 or older caused by another individual. The harm can be physical (violence), sexual (nonconsensual sex), psychological (causing emotional distress), material (improper use of belongings or finances), or neglect related (failure to provide needed care).

elderspeak *n.* adjustments to speech patterns, such as speaking more slowly or more loudly, shortening sentences, or using limited or less complex vocabulary, that are sometimes made by younger people when communicating with older adults.

Electra complex the female counterpart of the OEDIPUS COMPLEX, involving the daughter's love for her father, jealousy toward the mother, and blame of the mother for depriving her of a penis. Austrian neurologist Sigmund Freud (1856–1939) rejected the phrase, using the term *Oedipus complex* to refer to both boys and girls, but many modern textbooks of psychology propagate the mistaken belief that *Electra complex* is a Freudian term. [defined by Swiss psychiatrist Carl Jung (1875–1961)]

electrical stimulation the stimulation of neurons by electrical energy, as in, for example, the intracranial stimulation that occurs when electrodes are implanted in a region of the brain.

electrical synapse a type of connection in which neurons are not separated by a cleft but instead are joined by a GAP JUNCTION so that the nerve impulse is transmitted across without first being translated into a chemical message.

electric potential see POTENTIAL.

electrocardiogram (ECG; EKG) *n.* a wavelike tracing, either printed or displayed on a monitor, that represents the electrical impulses of the conduction system of the heart muscle as it passes through a typical cycle of contraction and relaxation. The electrical currents are detected by electrodes attached to specific sites on the patient's chest, legs, and arms and recorded by an instrument, the **electrocardiograph**. In the procedure, which is called **electrocardi-**

ography, the wave patterns of the electrocardiogram reveal the condition of the heart chambers and valves to provide an indication of possible cardiac problems.

electroconvulsive therapy (ECT) a controversial treatment in which a seizure is induced by passing a controlled, low-dose electric current (an **electroconvulsive shock**) through one or both temples. ECT is most often used to treat patients with severe endogenous depression who fail to respond to antidepressant drugs. Benefits are temporary, and the mechanisms of therapeutic action are unknown. Also called **electroconvulsive shock** (or **electroshock**) **therapy** (EST).

electrode *n.* an instrument with a positive-pole cathode and a negative-pole anode used to stimulate biological tissues electrically or record electrical activity in these tissues. See also MICROELECTRODE.

electroencephalography (EEG) *n.* a method of studying BRAIN WAVES using an instrument (**electroencephalograph**) that amplifies and records the electrical activity of the brain through electrodes placed at various points on the scalp. The resulting record (**electroencephalogram**, or **EEG**) of the brain-wave patterns is used both in diagnosing epilepsy and other neurological disorders and in studying normal brain function.

electromyography (EMG) *n.* the recording (via an instrument called an **electromyograph**) of the electrical activity of muscles through electrodes placed in or on different muscle groups. This procedure is used in the diagnosis of neuromuscular diseases, such as myasthenia gravis or amyotrophic lateral sclerosis. A record of the electric potentials is called an **electromyogram** (EMG).

electronic health record (EHR) a digital record of an individual's health-related information that is created, gathered, managed, and consulted by authorized health care staff. The use of health information technology to maintain health records allows for improved patient care by facilitating care coordination and widespread data exchange among providers and by enhancing patients' access to their own records.

electroshock therapy (EST) see ELECTROCONVULSIVE THERAPY.

embarrassment *n.* a SELF-CONSCIOUS EMOTION in which a person feels awkward or flustered in other people's company or because of the attention of others, as, for example, when being observed engaging in actions that are subject to mild disapproval from others. —**embarrassed** *adj.*

embedded figure a type of AMBIGUOUS FIGURE in which one or more images blend into a larger pattern and so are not immediately obvious.

emblem *n.* a bodily movement that substitutes for a spoken word or phrase and that can be readily comprehended by most individuals in a culture. Examples are shaking the head back and forth to signify *no* and nodding the head up and down to indicate *yes.* —**emblematic** *adj.*

embolism *n.* the interruption of blood flow due to blockage of a vessel by an **embolus**, material formed elsewhere and carried by the bloodstream to the site of obstruction. The embolus may be a blood clot, air bubble, fat globule, or other substance. In a coronary artery, it may cause a fatal heart attack, and in the brain, an embolic STROKE.

embryo *n.* an animal in the stages of development between cleavage of the fertilized egg and birth or hatching. In human prenatal development, the embryo comprises the products of conception during the first 8 weeks of pregnancy; thereafter, it is called a FETUS. —**embryonic** *adj.*

embryonic stem cell see STEM CELL.

emergent property a characteristic of a complex system that is not predictable from an analysis of its components

and that thus often arises unexpectedly. For example, it has frequently been claimed that conscious experience is not predictable by analysis of the neurophysiological and biochemical complexity of the brain.

emerging adulthood a developmental stage that is neither adolescence nor young adulthood but is theoretically and empirically distinct from them both, spanning the late teens through the twenties, with a focus on ages 18 to 25. Emerging adulthood is distinguished by relative independence from social roles and from normative expectations. Having left the dependency of childhood and adolescence, and having not yet taken on the responsibilities that are normative in adulthood, emerging adults engage in identity exploration, a process of trying out various life possibilities (e.g., in love, work, and worldviews) and gradually moving toward making enduring decisions.

emic *adj.* denoting an approach to the study of human cultures that interprets behaviors and practices in terms of the system of meanings created by and operative within a particular cultural context. Such an approach would generally be of the kind associated with ETHNOGRAPHY rather than ETHNOLOGY. Compare ETIC.

emitted behavior a natural response to a circumstance; that is, behavior that is not influenced by, or dependent on, any external stimuli. Compare RESPONDENT BEHAVIOR.

emotion *n.* a complex reaction pattern, involving experiential, behavioral, and physiological elements, by which an individual attempts to deal with a personally significant matter or event. The specific quality of the emotion (e.g., FEAR, SHAME) is determined by the specific significance of the event. For example, if the significance involves threat, fear is likely to be generated; if the significance involves disapproval from another, shame is likely to be generated. Emotion typically involves FEELING but differs from feeling in having an overt or implicit engagement with the world. —**emotional** *adj.*

emotional abuse nonphysical abuse: a pattern of behavior in which one person deliberately and repeatedly subjects another to nonphysical acts that are detrimental to behavioral and affective functioning and overall mental well-being. Researchers have yet to formulate a universal, mutually agreeable definition of the concept, but they have identified a variety of forms that emotional abuse may take, including verbal abuse; intimidation and terrorization; humiliation and degradation; exploitation; harassment; rejection and withholding of affection; isolation; and excessive control. Also called **psychological abuse**.

emotional disorder 1. any psychological disorder characterized primarily by maladjustive emotional reactions that are inappropriate or disproportionate to their cause. **2.** loosely, any mental disorder.

emotional intelligence the ability to process emotional information and use it in reasoning and other cognitive activities. It comprises four abilities: to perceive and appraise emotions accurately; to access and evoke emotions when they facilitate cognition; to comprehend emotional language and make use of emotional information; and to regulate one's own and others' emotions to promote growth and well-being. The **emotional intelligence quotient** is an index of these abilities; it is sometimes abbreviated **EQ** (for **emotional quotient**, nominally similar to IQ).

emotional memory memory for events that evoke an emotional response. Emotional memories can be implicit, as when nonhuman animals demonstrate such phenomena as conditioned fear (see AVOIDANCE CONDITIONING), or they can be explicit, as when individuals reexperience the original emotions engendered by an event

(e.g., terror when describing an accident, joy when describing a close family member's wedding). Emotional memory is distinct from the more general phenomenon of enhanced storage and retrieval of emotional stimuli, which for example is seen when experimental participants recall aversive nouns from a word list better than they recall neutral items. Also called **affective memory**.

emotional processing theory a theory proposing a hypothetical sequence of changes that is evoked by emotional engagement with the memory of a significant event, particularly a trauma. The theory is based on the concept of a mental framework ("fear structure") for reacting to threat that includes information about a feared stimulus (e.g., a snake), about physiological and behavioral responses (e.g., rapid heartbeat, sweating), and about the meaning of these elements (e.g., the snake is poisonous and will bite me and I am afraid of it). For some individuals, these fear structures become distorted, so that even harmless stimuli become seen as dangerous and act to trigger excessive physiological reactions, deliberate avoidance of memories of the event, emotional withdrawal, and other maladaptive behaviors. The theory was proposed in response to the difficulties of traditional learning theories in explaining intrusion symptoms and fear in POSTTRAUMATIC STRESS DISORDER.

emotional quotient (**EQ**) see EMOTIONAL INTELLIGENCE.

emotional unconscious that aspect of the nonconscious mind that consists of unreportable emotional or motivational states. It is suggested that such states may influence thought and action without the individual becoming consciously aware of them. The extent to which an individual can be said to have emotions without being conscious of them, however, is controversial. Compare COGNITIVE UNCONSCIOUS.

emotional valence the value associated with a stimulus as expressed on a continuum from pleasant to unpleasant or from attractive to aversive. In FACTOR ANALYSIS and MULTIDIMENSIONAL SCALING studies, emotional valence is one of two axes (or dimensions) on which an emotion can be located, the other axis being arousal (expressed as a continuum from high to low). For example, happiness is typically characterized by pleasant valence and relatively high arousal, whereas sadness or depression is typically characterized by unpleasant valence and relatively low arousal.

emotion-focused coping a stress-management strategy in which a person focuses on regulating his or her negative emotional reactions to a stressor rather than taking actions to change the stressor itself. The strategy may use a variety of cognitive and behavioral tools to regulate emotion, such as meditation, positive REFRAMING, wishful thinking or other avoidance techniques, and seeking social support, or conversely engaging in social withdrawal. Emotion-focused coping may be used primarily when a person appraises a stressor as beyond his or her capacity to change. Compare PROBLEM-FOCUSED COPING.

emotion regulation the ability of an individual to modulate an emotion or set of emotions. Explicit emotion regulation requires conscious monitoring, using techniques such as construing situations differently in order to manage them better, changing the target of an emotion (e.g., anger) in a way likely to produce a more positive outcome, and recognizing how different behaviors can be used in the service of a given emotional state. Implicit emotion regulation operates without deliberate monitoring; it modulates the intensity or duration of an emotional response without the need for awareness. Emotion regulation typically increases across the lifespan. Also called **emotional regulation**.

emotive *adj.* related to or arousing emotion.

empathic failure 1. a lack of understanding of another person's feelings, perceptions, and thoughts. **2.** in psychoanalysis, a situation in which a patient feels misunderstood by the therapist or analyst. Compare ATTUNEMENT; MISATTUNEMENT.

empathy *n.* understanding a person from his or her frame of reference rather than one's own, or vicariously experiencing that person's feelings, perceptions, and thoughts. In psychotherapy, therapist empathy for the client can be a path to comprehension of the client's cognitions, affects, motivations, or behaviors. **—empathic** or **empathetic** *adj.* **—empathize** *vb.*

empirical *adj.* **1.** derived from or denoting experimentation or systematic observations as the basis for conclusion or determination, as opposed to speculative, theoretical, or exclusively reason-based approaches. Many forms of research attempt to gain **empirical evidence** in favor of a hypothesis by manipulating an INDEPENDENT VARIABLE and assessing the effect on an outcome or DEPENDENT VARIABLE. **2.** based on experience.

empiricism *n.* **1.** an approach to EPISTEMOLOGY holding that all knowledge of matters of fact either arises from experience or requires experience for its validation. In particular, empiricism denies the possibility of ideas present in the mind prior to any experience, arguing that the mind at birth is like a blank sheet of paper. Although there is a strong emphasis on empiricism in psychology, this can take different forms. Some approaches to psychology hold that sensory experience is the origin of all knowledge and thus, ultimately, of personality, character, beliefs, emotions, and behavior. BEHAVIORISM is the purest example of empiricism in this sense. Advocates of other theoretical approaches to psychology, such as PHENOMENOLOGY, argue that the definition of experience as only sensory experience is too narrow. **2.** the view that experimentation is the most important, if not the only, foundation of scientific knowledge and the means by which individuals evaluate truth claims or the adequacy of theories and models. **—empiricist** *adj., n.*

empowerment *n.* **1.** the promotion of the skills, knowledge, and confidence necessary to take greater control of one's life. In psychotherapy, the process involves helping clients become more active in meeting their needs and fulfilling their desires. **2.** the delegation of increased decision-making powers to individuals or groups in a society or organization. **—empower** *vb.*

empty nest the family home after the children have reached maturity and left, often creating an emotional void (**empty nest syndrome**) in the lives of the parents (**empty nesters**).

encapsulation *n.* **1.** the process of separating or keeping separate, particularly the ability of some people experiencing delusions to maintain high levels of functioning and prevent their delusions from pervading everyday behavior and cognitive states (hence called **encapsulated delusions**). **2.** enclosure, as in a sheath or other covering.

encephalitis *n.* inflammation of the brain, typically caused by viral infection. The symptoms may be mild, with influenza-like characteristics, or severe and potentially fatal, with fever, vomiting, confusion or disorientation, drowsiness, seizures, and coma or loss of consciousness. **—encephalitic** *adj.*

encephalon *n.* see BRAIN.

encoding *n.* the conversion of a sensory input into a form capable of being processed and deposited in memory. Encoding is the first stage of memory processing, followed by RETENTION and then RETRIEVAL.

encoding specificity the principle that RETRIEVAL of memory is optimal

when the retrieval conditions (such as context or cues) duplicate the conditions that were present when the memory was formed.

encopresis *n.* repeated defecation in inappropriate places (clothing, floor, etc.) that occurs after the age of 4 and is not due to a substance (e.g., a laxative) or to a general medical condition. Encopresis may or may not be accompanied by constipation and is often associated with poor toilet training and stressful situations.

encounter group a group of individuals in which constructive insight, sensitivity to others, and personal growth are promoted through direct interactions on an emotional and social level. The leader functions as a catalyst and facilitator rather than as a therapist and focuses on here-and-now feelings and interaction rather than on theory or individual motivation.

enculturation *n.* the processes, beginning in early childhood, by which particular cultural values, ideas, beliefs, and behavioral patterns are instilled in the members of a society. Compare ACCULTURATION. **—enculturate** *vb.*

endocannabinoid *n.* see ENDOGENOUS CANNABINOID.

endocrine disruptor a natural or synthetic chemical that blocks, stimulates, mimics, or otherwise affects hormones in the endocrine system (e.g., sex hormones, thyroid hormones). Natural endocrine disruptors include, for example, phytoestrogens (i.e., ESTROGENS produced by some plants). Examples of synthetic endocrine disruptors are industrial chemicals, plastics such as BISPHENOL A, and certain pharmaceutical agents. Effects of exposure to endocrine disruptors may include infertility, birth defects, and cancer.

endocrine gland any ductless gland that secretes hormones directly into the bloodstream to act on distant targets. Such glands include the PITUITARY GLAND, ADRENAL GLAND, THYROID

GLAND, gonads (TESTES and OVARIES), and ISLETS OF LANGERHANS. Together, they comprise the **endocrine system**. Compare EXOCRINE GLAND.

endogamy *n.* the custom or practice of marrying within one's KINSHIP NETWORK, caste, or other religious or social group. Compare EXOGAMY. —**endogamous** *adj.*

endogenous *adj.* originating within the body as a result of normal biochemical or physiological processes (e.g., ENDOGENOUS OPIOIDS) or of predisposing biological or genetic influences (e.g., ENDOGENOUS DEPRESSION). Compare EXOGENOUS. —**endogenously** *adv.*

endogenous cannabinoid (eCB) any of several CANNABIS-like substances produced within the bodies of vertebrates. Although widely distributed throughout the body, endogenous cannabinoids are concentrated particularly within the central nervous system, where they function as NEUROMODULATORS, regulating communication between neurons by influencing the release of GAMMA-AMINOBUTYRIC ACID, GLUTAMATE, and other neurotransmitters at SYNAPSES. They also play an important role in other processes, including those related to immune function, pain perception, learning and memory, energy expenditure and metabolism, appetite control, nausea and vomiting, mood, responses to stress, facilitation of motor behavior, and the motivational and rewarding aspects of numerous behaviors and stimuli (including several recreational drugs). Also called **endocannabinoid.**

endogenous depression depression that occurs in the absence of an obvious psychological stressor and in which a biological or genetic cause is implied. Compare REACTIVE DEPRESSION.

endogenous opioid a substance produced in the body that has the analgesic and euphoric effects of morphine. Three families of endogenous opioids are well known: the enkephalins, EN-

DORPHINS, and dynorphins. All are NEUROPEPTIDES that bind to OPIOID RECEPTORS in the central nervous system; they are mostly inhibitory, acting like opiates to block pain. Three other endogenous opioid peptides have been identified: nociception/orphanin FQ and endomorphins 1 and 2.

endogenous variable a DEPENDENT VARIABLE whose values are determined, caused, or explained by factors within the model or system under study. Compare EXOGENOUS VARIABLE.

endolymph *n.* the fluid contained in the membranous labyrinth of the inner ear, that is, within the SCALA MEDIA, SEMICIRCULAR CANALS, SACCULE, and UTRICLE. —**endolymphatic** *adj.*

endophenotype *n.* a type of BIOLOGICAL MARKER that is simpler to detect than genetic sequences and that may be useful in researching vulnerability to a wide range of psychological and neurological disorders. Endophenotypes may be a useful link between genetic sequences and their external emotional, cognitive, or behavioral manifestations.

endoplasmic reticulum (ER) a network of membranous tubules and sacs extending from the nucleus to the outer membrane of a typical animal or plant cell. It is responsible for the processing and modification of proteins and lipids, both for distribution within the cell and for secretion.

endorphin *n.* any of a class of NEUROPEPTIDES, found mainly in the pituitary gland, that function as ENDOGENOUS OPIOIDS. The best known is beta-endorphin; the others are alpha-endorphin and gamma-endorphin. The production of endorphins during intense physical activity is one explanation for the so-called runner's high or exercise high.

endowment effect the tendency of people to place a higher value on items once they own them or once these have been associated with the self in some other way. The endowment effect is characterized by increased positive emotions toward the object.

end plate a specialized region of a muscle-cell membrane that faces the terminus of a motor neuron within a NEUROMUSCULAR JUNCTION. The depolarization that is induced in this muscular region when stimulated by a neurotransmitter released from the adjacent motor neuron terminus is called the **end-plate potential**.

energy drink any of a group of widely available liquids that may contain large quantities of caffeine as well as sugar, taurine, ginseng, ginkgo biloba, B vitamins, antioxidants, and artificial sweeteners and that are used to increase energy, alertness, and endurance. Overuse has been associated with agitation, anxiety, insomnia, and arrhythmias.

engineering psychology a subfield of HUMAN FACTORS PSYCHOLOGY concerned with identifying the psychological principles that govern human interaction with environments, systems, and products and applying these principles to issues of engineering and design. See also HUMAN ENGINEERING.

engram *n.* the hypothetical MEMORY TRACE that is stored in the brain. The nature of the engram, in terms of the exact physiological changes that occur to encode a memory, is as yet unknown.

enmeshment *n.* a condition in which two or more people, typically family members, are involved in each other's activities and personal relationships to an excessive degree, thus limiting or precluding healthy interaction and compromising individual autonomy and identity.

enrichment *n.* **1.** enhancement or improvement by the addition or augmentation of some desirable property, quality, or component. For example, job enrichment policies are designed to enhance quality of worklife and thus employees' interest in and attitude toward work tasks; and marriage-enrichment

groups are intended to enhance the interpersonal relationships of married couples. **2.** the provision of opportunities to increase levels of behavioral or intellectual activity in an otherwise unstimulating (i.e., impoverished) environment. For example, the provision of play materials and opportunities for social contacts has been shown to enhance the development of young children.

entitativity *n.* the extent to which a group or collective is considered by others to be a real entity having unity, coherence, and internal organization rather than a set of independent individuals. In general, groups whose members share a common fate, are similar to one another, and are located close together are more likely to be considered a group rather than a mere aggregation.

entity theory see IMPLICIT SELF THEORY.

entorhinal cortex a region of cerebral cortex in the ventromedial portion of the temporal lobe. It has reciprocal connections with various other cortical and subcortical structures and is an integral component of the medial temporal lobe memory system. It is also involved in spatial navigation.

entrainment *n.* the process of activating or providing a timing cue for a BIOLOGICAL RHYTHM. For example, the production of gonadal hormones in seasonally breeding animals can be a result of entrainment to increasing day length.

entrapment *n.* **1.** a process in which one makes increasing commitments to a failing course of action or an unattainable goal in order to justify the amount of time and effort already invested, feeling helpless to do otherwise. An example is provided by a company that proceeds with the design and construction of a new building for its employees after economic and other changes significantly reduce profits, halt business growth, and result in staff layoffs that make the new space not only financially burdensome but also no longer necessary. **2.** a pathological condition in which swelling of surrounding tissue places excessive pressure on a nerve. Fibers located on the surface of the nerve usually bear the brunt of the compression, whereas interior fibers tend to be less affected. Repeated or long-term entrapment can cause nerve damage and muscle weakness.

entrepreneurship *n.* the assumption of all the risks of the creation, organization, and management of a business venture for the reward of future profits. **Social entrepreneurship** is the use of an entrepreneurial approach with similar assumed risks to create, organize, and manage a venture whose profits are used primarily to promote a positive return to society by effecting social change.

enuresis *n.* repeated involuntary urination in inappropriate places (clothing, floor, etc.) that occurs after the chronological age when continence is expected (generally 5 years old) and that is not due to a substance (e.g., a diuretic) or to a general medical condition. Enuresis is frequently associated with delayed bladder development, poor toilet training, and stressful situations.

envelope *n.* in acoustics, a slowly varying or "smoothed" change in amplitude. Usually it refers to temporal changes, such as those produced by amplitude MODULATION, but it can also refer to the shape of a spectrum or to spatial changes. Temporal and spectral envelopes are important in auditory perception.

environment *n.* the aggregate of external agents or conditions—physical, biological, social, and cultural—that influence the functions of an organism. See also ECOLOGY. **—environmental** *adj.*

environmental agnosia the inability of individuals with some brain injuries to recognize familiar places and

surroundings, including their homes and neighborhoods.

environmental determinism the view that psychological and behavioral characteristics are largely or completely the result of environmental conditions. Biological factors are considered to be of minor importance, exerting little if any influence. Compare BIOLOGICAL DETERMINISM.

environmentalism *n.* **1.** the concept that the environment and learning are the chief determinants of behavior and thus are the major cause of interpersonal variations in ability and adjustment; accordingly, behavior is largely modifiable. Compare HEREDITARIANISM. See also NATURE–NURTURE. **2.** a social movement and position that emphasizes the ecological relationship between humans and the natural environment and strives to protect the environment as an essential resource. **—environmentalist** *n.*

environmental press–competence model a model of stress and adaptation in which adaptive functioning in the environment depends on the interaction between stimuli in a person's physical and social environment that place demands on that individual (**environmental press**) and the individual's competence in meeting these demands, which is shaped by such personal characteristics as physical health and cognitive and perceptual abilities.

environmental psychology a multidisciplinary field that investigates the effects of the physical environment on human behavior and welfare. Influences studied may include environmental stressors (e.g., noise, crowding, air pollution, temperature); design variables (e.g., lighting); the design of technology (see ERGONOMICS); and larger, more ambient qualities of the physical environment, such as floorplan layouts, the size and location of buildings, and proximity to nature.

environmental sounds agnosia see AUDITORY AGNOSIA.

environmental stress theory the concept that autonomic and cognitive factors combine to form an individual's appraisal of stressors in the environment as threatening or nonthreatening.

enzyme *n.* a protein that acts as a biological catalyst, accelerating the rate of a biochemical reaction without itself becoming permanently altered. Many enzymes require other organic molecules (coenzymes) or inorganic ions (cofactors) to function normally. Most enzymes are named according to the type of reaction they catalyze; for example, acetylcholinesterase (see CHOLINESTERASE) splits and inactivates molecules of the neurotransmitter acetylcholine.

ependymal cell a type of nonneuronal central nervous system cell that lines the brain VENTRICLES and the CENTRAL CANAL of the spinal cord and that helps circulate cerebrospinal fluid.

epidemiology *n.* the study of the frequency and distribution of specific diseases and disorders. The **epidemiologist** also seeks to establish relationships to such factors as heredity, environment, nutrition, or age at onset. Results of epidemiological studies are intended to find clues and associations rather than necessarily to show causal relationships. See also INCIDENCE; PREVALENCE. —**epidemiologic** or **epidemiological** *adj.*

epigenesis *n.* **1.** the theory, now accepted, that prenatal development is a gradual, complex, and cumulative process involving successive differentiation of morphological structures from fertilized ovum to embryo to fetus. **2.** the theory that characteristics of an organism, both physical and behavioral, arise from an interaction between genetic and environmental influences rather than from one or the other. See also NATURE–NURTURE. **3.** in genetics, the occurrence of a heritable change in gene function that is not the result of a change in the base sequence of the organism's DNA. See also EPIGENETICS. —**epigenetic** *adj.*

epigenetics *n.* the study of heritable chemical modifications to DNA that alter gene activity without changing nucleotide sequence. Such modifications instead typically involve the attachment of additional material to the DNA molecule itself or the structural alteration of its associated proteins, which disrupt the normal development and functioning of cells by influencing gene activation, deactivation, transcription, and so forth. Epigenetic mechanisms have been proposed as the means by which environmental and psychosocial factors such as toxins and early childhood experiences interact with physiology: They affect neural function through changes in gene expression that lead to individual differences in cognition and behavior (e.g., learning, memory, aggression, affect).

epilepsy *n.* a group of chronic brain disorders associated with disturbances in the electrical discharges of brain cells and characterized by recurrent seizures, with or without clouding or loss of consciousness. Some forms of epilepsy are due to brain inflammation, brain tumor, vascular disturbances, structural abnormality, brain injury, or degenerative disease, whereas other forms are of unknown origin or due to nonspecific brain defects. Types of seizure vary depending on the nature of the abnormal electrical discharge and the area of the brain affected. —**epileptic** *adj.*

epinephrine *n.* a CATECHOLAMINE neurotransmitter and adrenal hormone that is the end product of the metabolism of the dietary amino acid tyrosine. It is synthesized primarily in the adrenal medulla by methylation of norepinephrine, which itself is formed from DOPAMINE. As a hormone, it is secreted in large amounts when an individual is stimulated by fear, anxiety, or a similar stress-related reaction. As a neurotransmitter, it increases the heart rate and force of heart contractions, relaxes bronchial and intestinal smooth muscle, and produces varying effects on blood pressure as it acts both as a vasodilator and vasoconstrictor. Also called **adrenaline**.

epiphenomenon *n.* (*pl.* **epiphenomena**) a mere by-product of a process that has no effect on the process itself. The term is used most frequently to refer to mental events considered as products of brain processes. Thus, although mental events are real in some sense, they are not real in the same way that biological states and events are real, and not necessary to the explanation of mental events themselves. Epiphenomena are conceived of as having no causal power. —**epiphenomenal** *adj.*

episodic buffer a component of WORKING MEMORY that is a subsidiary of the CENTRAL EXECUTIVE. It is a temporary multimodal store that combines information from the PHONOLOGICAL LOOP and VISUOSPATIAL SKETCHPAD subsystems of working memory with information about time and order to form and maintain an integrated, detailed representation of a given stimulus or event that can then be deposited into long-term memory as necessary. It is "episodic" in the sense that it holds integrated episodes or scenes, and it is a "buffer" in the sense of providing a limited capacity interface between systems using different representational codes.

episodic memory the ability to remember personally experienced events associated with a particular time and place. Episodic memory supplements SEMANTIC MEMORY as a form of DECLARATIVE MEMORY. The hippocampus plays a key role in episodic memory formation and retrieval. Atrophy of this area and structures in the associated hippocampal formation is a hallmark feature of Alzheimer's disease, although episodic memory also declines considerably with normal aging.

epistemology *n.* the branch of philosophy concerned with the nature, origin, and limitations of knowledge. It is also concerned with the justification of truth claims. In psychology, interest in epistemology arises from two principal sources. First, as the study of the behavior of human beings, psychology has long had interest in the processes of knowledge acquisition and learning of all sorts. Second, as a science, psychology has an interest in the justification of its knowledge claims. In connection with this concern, most work on epistemology in psychology has concentrated on the scientific method and on the justification of scientifically derived knowledge claims. In general, the guiding epistemology of psychology has been EMPIRICISM, although some approaches to the subject, such as psychoanalysis, the developmental psychology of Swiss child psychologist and epistemologist Jean Piaget (1896–1980), and the humanistic psychology of U.S. psychologist Carl Rogers (1902–1987), are heavily influenced by RATIONALISM. —**epistemological** *adj.*

epithalamus *n.* a portion of the DIENCEPHALON that is immediately above and behind the THALAMUS. It includes the PINEAL GLAND and the posterior COMMISSURE.

equilibration *n.* in PIAGETIAN THEORY, the process by which an individual uses assimilation and accommodation to restore or maintain a psychological equilibrium, that is, a cognitive state devoid of conflicting SCHEMAS.

equilibrium *n.* a state of physical or mental balance or stability (e.g., in posture, physiological processes, psychological adjustment). See HOMEOSTASIS; VESTIBULAR SYSTEM.

equilibrium potential the state in which the tendency of ions (electrically charged particles) to flow across a cell membrane from regions of high concentration is exactly balanced by the opposing potential difference (electric charge) across the membrane.

equipotentiality *n.* the hypothesis of U.S. neuropsychologist Karl S. Lashley (1890–1958) that large areas of cerebral cortex have similar potential to perform particular functions, including learning and other complex processes, so that intact cortical areas may take over functions of damaged or destroyed areas. Proposed in 1929 following experimental observations of the effects of different brain lesions on rats' ability to learn a complex maze, the concept has been challenged by subsequent research showing that areas of cortex have relatively specific functions. Brain plasticity (adaptive shifting of function) is commonly observed after local cortical damage, however. See also MASS ACTION.

equity theory a theory of justice regarding what individuals are likely to view as a fair return from activities involving themselves and a number of other people. The theory posits that people compare the ratio of the outcome of the activity (i.e., the benefits they receive from it) to their inputs (e.g., effort, skills) with the outcome-to-input ratios of those engaged in a comparable activity.

erectile dysfunction (ED) the lack or loss of ability to achieve an erection; that is, IMPOTENCE. Causes of erectile dysfunction may be psychological or physical, including the effects of medications or drug abuse. If a man normally experiences a nocturnal erection or is able to induce an erection by masturbation but cannot achieve or maintain an erection during sexual intercourse, the dysfunction is assumed to be due largely or solely to psychological factors. See MALE ERECTILE DISORDER.

ergonomics *n.* the discipline that applies a knowledge of human abilities and limitations drawn from physiology, biomechanics, anthropometry, and other areas to the design of systems, equipment, and processes for safe and efficient performance. The term is often used synonymously with HUMAN FAC-TORS. See also HUMAN SYSTEMS INTEGRATION. —**ergonomic** *adj.*

Erikson's eight stages of psychosocial development the theory proposed by German-born U.S. psychologist Erik Erikson (1902–1994) that a sense of continuity, worth, and integration is gradually achieved by facing goals and challenges during eight stages of development across the lifespan. The stages are (a) infancy: BASIC TRUST VERSUS MISTRUST; (b) toddler: AUTONOMY VERSUS SHAME AND DOUBT; (c) preschool age: INITIATIVE VERSUS GUILT; (d) school age: INDUSTRY VERSUS INFERIORITY; (e) adolescence: IDENTITY VERSUS IDENTITY CONFUSION; (f) young adulthood: INTIMACY VERSUS ISOLATION; (g) middle age: GENERATIVITY VERSUS STAGNATION; and (h) older adulthood: INTEGRITY VERSUS DESPAIR.

erogenous zone an area or part of the body sensitive to stimulation that is a source of erotic or sexual feeling or pleasure. Among the primary zones are the genitals, buttocks and anus, the breasts (especially the nipples), and the mouth.

Eros *n.* the god of love in Greek mythology (equivalent to the Roman Cupid), whose name was chosen by Austrian neurologist Sigmund Freud (1856–1939) to designate a theoretical set of strivings oriented toward sexuality, development, and increased life activity (see LIFE INSTINCT). In Freud's dual instinct theory, Eros is seen as involved in a dialectic process with THANATOS, the striving toward reduced psychical tension and life activity (see DEATH INSTINCT). See also LIBIDO.

error *n.* **1.** in experimentation, any change in a DEPENDENT VARIABLE not attributable to the manipulation of an INDEPENDENT VARIABLE. **2.** in statistics, a deviation of an observed score from a true score, where the true score is often defined by the mean of the particular group or condition in which the score being assessed for error occurs, or from the score predicted by a model.

error term the element of a statistical equation that indicates the amount of change in the DEPENDENT VARIABLE that is unexplained by change in the INDEPENDENT VARIABLES.

error variance the element of variability in a score that is produced by extraneous factors, such as measurement imprecision, and is not attributable to the INDEPENDENT VARIABLE or other controlled experimental manipulations. Error variance usually indicates how much random fluctuation is expected within scores and often forms part of the denominator of test statistics, such as the F RATIO in an ANALYSIS OF VARIANCE. Also called **residual variance**.

escape conditioning the process by which a subject acquires a response that results in the termination of an aversive stimulus. For example, if a monkey learns that pulling a lever eliminates a loud noise, escape conditioning has occurred. Also called **escape learning**; **escape training**. See also AVOIDANCE CONDITIONING.

ESP cards see ZENER CARDS.

essential amino acid see AMINO ACID.

essentialism *n.* in philosophy, the position that things (or some things) have "essences"; that is, they have certain necessary properties without which they could not be the things they are. In Marxism, POSTMODERNISM, POSTSTRUCTURALISM, and certain feminist perspectives, essentialism is the rejected position that human beings have an essential nature that transcends such factors as social class, gender, and ethnicity. See also UNIVERSALISM.

esteem need any desire for achievement, reputation, or prestige that is necessary for a sense of personal value and SELF-ESTEEM. Comprising the fourth level of MASLOW'S MOTIVATIONAL HIERARCHY, esteem needs depend on the admiration and approval of others.

esthesiometry (aesthesiometry) *n.*

the measurement of sensitivity to touch. Classically, two different versions of an instrument called an **esthesiometer** (or **aesthesiometer**) have been used. One consists of bristles of different lengths and thicknesses that are applied to determine the minimum pressure intensity required to produce a sensation. The other is a compasslike device to determine the smallest separation distance at which two points of stimulation on the skin are perceived as one. More sophisticated techniques have now been developed, such as those involving electrodes.

estimator *n.* a quantity calculated from the values in a sample according to some rule and used to give an approximation of the value in a population. For example, the sample mean or average is an estimator for the population mean; the value of the sample mean is the estimate.

estrogen *n.* any of a class of STEROID HORMONES that are produced mainly by the ovaries and act as the principal female SEX HORMONES, inducing estrus in female mammals and secondary female sexual characteristics in humans. The estrogens occurring naturally in humans are estradiol (the most potent), estrone, and estriol, which are secreted variously by the ovarian follicle, corpus luteum, placenta, testes, and adrenal cortex.

estrous cycle the cyclical sequence of reproductive activity shown by female mammals (except humans and other primates; see MENSTRUAL CYCLE). Animals that experience one estrous cycle per year are called monestrous; those that have multiple estrous cycles annually are polyestrous.

ethanol *n.* a substance formed naturally or synthetically by the fermentation of glucose and found in beverages such as beers, wines, and distilled liquors. It is the most frequently used and abused DEPRESSANT in many cultures. When consumed, it primarily affects the central nervous system, mood, and cognitive functions. In small doses, it can produce feelings of warmth, well-being, and confidence. As more is consumed, there is a gradual loss of self-control, and speech and control of limbs become difficult; at high consumption levels, nausea and vomiting, loss of consciousness, and even fatal respiratory arrest may occur. Also called **ethyl alcohol**.

e-therapy *n.* an Internet-based form of DISTANCE THERAPY used to expand access to clinical services typically offered face-to-face. This therapy can be conducted via webcam, in real-time messaging, in chat rooms, and in e-mail messages.

ethical code see CODE OF ETHICS.

ethics *n.* **1.** the branch of philosophy that investigates both the content of moral judgments (i.e., what is right and what is wrong) and their nature (i.e., whether such judgments should be considered objective or subjective). **2.** the principles of morally right conduct accepted by a person or a group or considered appropriate to a specific field. In psychological research, for example, proper ethics requires that participants be treated fairly and without harm and that investigators report results and findings honestly. —**ethical** *adj.*

ethnic *adj.* denoting or referring to a group of people having a shared social, cultural, linguistic, and sometimes religious background.

ethnic group any major social group that possesses a common identity based on history, culture, language, and often religion.

ethnic identity an individual's sense of being a person who is defined, in part, by membership in a specific ethnic group. This sense is usually considered to be a complex construct involving shared social, cultural, linguistic, religious, and often racial factors but identical with none of them.

ethnic psychology a branch of psychology that studies how the culture,

language, and related phenomena of different ethnic groups within a nation or region affect the attitudes, experiences, and behaviors of group members. Influenced by sociology, the field focuses on the unique sociocultural attributes of those of different races and ethnicities within each society, particularly as related to social class distinctions. Also called **ethnopsychology**; **racial and ethnic minority psychology**.

ethnic socialization the transmission by parents, caregivers, or others of information, values, and perspectives about their ethnic group to the next generation, with the goals of instilling children with pride in their ethnic heritage and providing them with strategies for coping with ethnic discrimination and other barriers to success in mainstream society. See also RACIAL SOCIALIZATION.

ethnocentrism *n.* **1.** the practice of regarding one's own ethnic, racial, or social group as the center of all things. Just as EGOCENTRISM is a sense of self-superiority, so ethnocentrism is the parallel tendency to judge one's group as superior to other groups. **2.** the tendency, often unintentional, to base perceptions and understandings of other groups or cultures on one's own. Also called **ethnocentricity**. See also INGROUP BIAS; SOCIOCENTRISM. —**ethnocentric** *adj.*

ethnography *n.* the descriptive study of cultures or societies based on direct observation and (ideally) some degree of participation. Compare ETHNOLOGY. See also EMIC. —**ethnographer** *n.* —**ethnographic** *adj.*

ethnology *n.* the comparative, analytical, or historical study of human cultures or societies. Compare ETHNOGRAPHY. See also ETIC. —**ethnologist** *n.* —**ethnological** *adj.*

ethnomethodology *n.* the analysis of the underlying conventions and systems of meaning that people use to make sense of commonplace social interactions and experiences. —**ethno-methodological** *adj.* —**ethnomethodologist** *n.*

ethnopsychology *n.* see ETHNIC PSYCHOLOGY.

ethogram *n.* a detailed listing and description of the behavior patterns of a nonhuman animal in its natural habitat. The description is objective rather than interpretative. For example, a vocalization given in response to a predator would be described in terms of its acoustic properties rather than its apparent function of alarm call.

ethology *n.* the comparative study of the behavior of nonhuman animals, typically in their natural habitat but also involving experiments both in the field and in captivity. Ethology is often associated with connotations of innate or species-specific behavior patterns, in contrast with COMPARATIVE PSYCHOLOGY. The theory and methods from both areas are now closely interrelated, and **animal behavior** is a more neutral and more broadly encompassing term. Increasingly, ethology is used to describe research involving observation and detailed descriptions of human behavior as well. —**ethological** *adj.* —**ethologist** *n.*

ethyl alcohol see ETHANOL.

etic *adj.* denoting an approach to the study of human cultures based on concepts or constructs that are held to be universal and applicable cross-culturally. Such an approach would generally be of the kind associated with ETHNOLOGY rather than ETHNOGRAPHY. Compare EMIC.

etiology *n.* **1.** the causes and progress of a disease or disorder. **2.** the branch of medical and psychological science concerned with the systematic study of the causes of physical and mental disorders. —**etiological** *adj.*

eugenics *n.* a social and political philosophy that seeks to eradicate genetic defects and improve the genetic makeup of populations through selec-tive human breeding. The eugenic position is groundless and scientifically naive, in that many conditions associated with disability or disorder, such as syndromes that increase risk of intellectual disability, are inherited recessively and occur unpredictably.

euphoria *n.* extreme happiness and an elevated sense of well-being. An exaggerated degree of euphoria that does not reflect the reality of one's situation is common in MANIC EPISODES and HYPOMANIC EPISODES. —**euphoric** *adj.*

eustachian tube a slender tube extending from the middle ear to the pharynx (which connects the mouth and nostrils to the esophagus), with the primary function of equalizing air pressure on both sides of the tympanic membrane (eardrum). [Bartolommeo **Eustachio** (1524–1574), Italian anatomist]

eustress *n.* the positive stress response, involving optimal levels of stimulation: a type of stress that results from challenging but attainable and enjoyable or worthwhile tasks (e.g., participating in an athletic event, giving a speech). It has a beneficial effect by generating a sense of fulfillment or achievement and facilitating growth, development, mastery, and high levels of performance. Compare DISTRESS.

euthanasia *n.* the act or process of terminating a life, usually to prevent further suffering in an incurably or terminally ill individual. Euthanasia is distinguished from the much more widely accepted practice of forgoing invasive treatments, as permitted under natural-death laws throughout the United States. Traditionally, a distinction between PASSIVE EUTHANASIA (withholding treatment) and ACTIVE EUTHANASIA (taking directly lethal action) has been made. In current practice, however, the term *euthanasia* typically is used to mean active euthanasia only. See also ASSISTED DEATH. —**euthanize** *vb.*

evaluation *n.* a careful examination

or overall appraisal of something, particularly to determine its worth, value, or desirability. For example, the evaluation of a particular therapeutic technique refers to a determination of its success in achieving defined goals.

evaluation apprehension uneasiness or worry about being judged by others, especially worry experienced by participants in an experiment as a result of their desire to be evaluated favorably by the experimenter or by others observing their behavior.

event-related potential (ERP) a specific pattern of electrical activity produced in the brain when a person is engaged in a cognitive act, such as discriminating one stimulus from another. There are a number of different ERP components, and different cognitive operations have been associated with the amplitude and latency of each. Because ERPs provide specific information about the precise timing and (given appropriate caveats) location of mental events, they serve as an important bridge between psychological function and neural structures. Although the terms are sometimes used synonymously, ERPs are distinct from EVOKED POTENTIALS, which are associated with more elementary sensory stimulation.

event sampling a strategy commonly used in DIRECT OBSERVATION that involves noting and recording the occurrence of a carefully specified behavior whenever it is seen. For example, a researcher may record each episode of apnea that occurs within a 9-hour period overnight while a person sleeps.

evidence-based practice (EBP) the integration of the best available scientific research from laboratory and field settings with clinical expertise so as to provide effective psychological services that are responsive to a patient's culture, preferences, and characteristics (e.g., functional status, level of social support, strengths). Clinical decisions should be made in collaboration with the patient, based on relevant data, and with consideration for the probable costs, benefits, and available resources and options. The ultimate goal of EBP is to promote empirically supported principles that can be used to enhance public health.

evoked potential (EP) a specific pattern of electrical activity produced in a particular part of the nervous system, especially the brain, in response to external stimulation, such as a flash of light or a brief tone. Different modalities and types of stimuli produce different types of sensory potentials, and these are labeled according to their electrical polarity (positive or negative) and their timing (e.g., milliseconds). Although the terms are sometimes used synonymously, EPs are distinct from EVENT-RELATED POTENTIALS, which are associated with higher level cognitive processes. Also called **evoked response (ER)**.

evolution *n.* the process of gradual change in the appearance of populations of organisms that takes place over generations. Such changes are widely held to account for the present diversity of living organisms originating from relatively few ancestors since the emergence of life on earth. **—evolutionary** *adj.*

evolutionary psychology an approach to psychological inquiry that views human cognition and behavior in a broadly Darwinian context of adaptation to evolving physical and social environments and new intellectual challenges. It differs from SOCIOBIOLOGY mainly in its emphasis on the effects of NATURAL SELECTION on INFORMATION PROCESSING and the structure of the human mind.

exacerbation *n.* an increase in the severity of a disease or disorder or of its symptoms.

exact replication see REPLICATION.

exact test any statistical test in which the probability of finding a result as extreme or more extreme than the one obtained, given the NULL HYPOTHESIS, can be calculated precisely rather than approximated.

exchangeability *n.* the ability to be used in different circumstances or situations. For example, in measurement and statistics, items that are equally appropriate on different versions of a test and methods or parameters that work well under different conditions show exchangeability.

exchange relationship see COMMUNAL RELATIONSHIP.

exchange theory see SOCIAL EXCHANGE THEORY.

excitation *n.* the electrical activity elicited in a neuron or muscle cell in response to an external stimulus, specifically the propagation of an ACTION POTENTIAL.

excitation-transfer theory the theory that emotional responses can be intensified by AROUSAL from other stimuli not directly related to the stimulus that originally provoked the response. According to this theory, when a person becomes aroused physiologically, there is a subsequent period of time when the person will experience a state of residual arousal yet be unaware of it. If additional stimuli are encountered during this time, the individual may mistakenly ascribe his or her residual response from the previous stimuli to those successive stimuli.

excitatory neurotransmitter see NEUROTRANSMITTER.

excitatory postsynaptic potential (EPSP) a brief decrease in the difference in electrical charge across the membrane of a neuron that is caused by the transmission of a signal from a neighboring neuron across the synapse (specialized junction) separating them. EPSPs increase the probability that the postsynaptic neuron will initiate an ACTION POTENTIAL and hence fire a nerve impulse. Compare INHIBITORY POSTSYNAPTIC POTENTIAL.

excitatory synapse a specialized type of junction at which activity from one neuron (in the form of an ACTION POTENTIAL) facilitates activity in an adjacent neuron by initiating an EXCITATORY POSTSYNAPTIC POTENTIAL. Compare INHIBITORY SYNAPSE.

excoriation (skin-picking) disorder a psychiatric diagnosis characterized by recurrent picking at one's own skin, leading to lesions and causing significant distress or impairment.

executive functions higher level cognitive processes of planning, decision making, problem solving, action sequencing, task assignment and organization, effortful and persistent goal pursuit, inhibition of competing impulses, flexibility in goal selection, and goal-conflict resolution. These often involve the use of language, judgment, abstraction and concept formation, and logic and reasoning. They are frequently associated with neural networks that include the frontal lobe, particularly the prefrontal cortex. Deficits in executive functioning are seen in various disorders, including Alzheimer's disease and schizophrenia. Also called **central processes**; **higher order processes**.

exercise psychology see SPORT AND EXERCISE PSYCHOLOGY.

exhaustion stage see GENERAL ADAPTATION SYNDROME.

exhibitionism *n.* a PARAPHILIA in which a person exposes his or her genitals to an unsuspecting stranger as a means of achieving sexual excitement. —**exhibitionist** *n.*

existential anxiety 1. in EXISTENTIALISM, the angst associated with one's freedom as a human being to make choices, with one's responsibility for the consequences of those choices, and with the sense that one's existence is devoid of absolute meaning and purpose given that such choices occur in the absence of rational certainty or structure. **2.** a general sense of anguish or despair associated with an individual's recognition of the inevitability of death.

existential–humanistic therapy a form of psychotherapy that focuses on the entire person rather than solely on behavior, cognition, or underlying motivations. Emphasis is placed on the client's subjective experiences, free will, and ability to decide the course of his or her own life. Also called **humanistic–existential therapy**.

existentialism *n.* a philosophical and literary movement that emerged in Europe in the period between the two World Wars and became the dominant trend in Continental thought during the 1940s and 1950s. In the immediate postwar years, French philosopher and author Jean-Paul Sartre (1905–1980), who is usually seen as the existentialist thinker *par excellence*, popularized both the term *existentialism* and most of the ideas now associated with it. Existentialism represents a turning away from systematic philosophy, with its emphasis on metaphysical absolutes and principles of rational certainty, toward an emphasis on the concrete existence of a human being "thrown" into a world that is merely "given" and contingent. Such a being encounters the world as a subjective consciousness, "condemned" to create its own meanings and values in an "absurd" and purposeless universe. The human being must perform this task in the absence of any possibility of rational certainty. Various forms of EXISTENTIAL PSYCHOLOGY have taken up the task of providing explanations, understandings of human behavior, and therapies based on existentialist assumptions about human existence. They have emphasized such constructs as alienation, authenticity, and freedom, as well as the difficulties associated with finding meaning and overcoming anxiety. —**existential** *adj.* —**existentialist** *n., adj.*

existential neurosis a pathological condition characterized by feelings of despair and anxiety that arise from living inauthentically, that is, from failing to take responsibility for one's own life and to make choices and find meaning in living.

existential psychology a general approach to psychological theory and practice that derives from EXISTENTIALISM. It emphasizes the subjective meaning of human experience, the uniqueness of the individual, and personal responsibility reflected in choice.

existential psychotherapy a form of psychotherapy that deals with the here and now of the client's total situation rather than with his or her past or underlying dynamics. It emphasizes the exploration and development of meaning in life, focuses on emotional experiences and decision making, and stresses a person's responsibility for his or her own existence.

exocrine gland any gland that secretes a product onto the outer body surface or into body cavities through a duct. Examples are the tear-producing lacrimal (or lachrymal) gland and the salivary gland. Compare ENDOCRINE GLAND.

exogamy *n.* the custom or practice of marrying outside one's KINSHIP NETWORK or other religious or social group. Compare ENDOGAMY. —**exogamous** *adj.*

exogenous *adj.* originating outside the body, referring, for example, to drugs (exogenous chemicals) or to phenomena, conditions, or disorders resulting from the influence of external factors. Compare ENDOGENOUS. —**exogenously** *adv.*

exogenous depression see REACTIVE DEPRESSION.

exogenous variable an INDEPENDENT VARIABLE whose value is determined by factors outside the model or system under study. Compare ENDOGENOUS VARIABLE.

exosystem *n.* in ECOLOGICAL SYSTEMS THEORY, those societal structures that function largely independently of the individual but nevertheless affect the immediate context within which he or she develops. They include the government, the legal system, and the media. Compare CHRONOSYSTEM; MACROSYSTEM; MESOSYSTEM.

expectancy effect the effect of one person's expectation about the behavior of another person on the actual behavior of that other person (interpersonal expectancy effect), or the effect of a person's expectation about his or her own behavior on that person's actual subsequent behavior (intrapersonal expectancy effect).

expectancy-value model the concept that motivation for an outcome depends largely on the significance of that outcome and the probability of achieving it.

expected value the value of a random variable or one of its functions as derived by mathematical calculation rather than observation. It is symbolized by $E(x)$, with x varying according to the specific item of interest that is being calculated. Usually, the expected value is a mean or weighted average.

experience-dependent process in brain development, changes in neurochemistry, anatomy, electrophysiology, and neuronal structure following various experiences that are unique to an individual and may occur at any time during the lifespan. The experience of training in certain behavioral and cognitive tasks, for example, has been shown to increase the length of dendrites and spine density, the primary sites of excitatory SYNAPSES, on individual neurons, effectively increasing the amount of space available for synaptic connections. Such changes are thought to be among the primary mechanisms by which the brain adapts to environmental demands and thus may represent an important component of the neural substrate of learning and memory.

experience-expectant process in brain development, a predetermined maturational process in which SYNAPSES are formed and maintained only when an organism has undergone expected species-typical experiences during a particular CRITICAL PERIOD. Such functions as vision will develop for all members of a species if given species-typical environmental stimulation (e.g., light).

experiment n. a series of observations conducted under controlled conditions to study a relationship with the purpose of drawing causal inferences about that relationship. An experiment involves the manipulation of an INDEPENDENT VARIABLE, the measurement of a DEPENDENT VARIABLE, and the exposure of various participants to one or more of the conditions being studied. RANDOM SELECTION of participants and their RANDOM ASSIGNMENT to conditions are also necessary in experiments. —**experimental** adj.

experimental condition a level of the INDEPENDENT VARIABLE that is manipulated by the researcher in order to assess the effect on a DEPENDENT VARIABLE. Participants in an experimental condition receive some form of TREATMENT or experience whereas those in a CONTROL condition do not. For example, patients in an experimental condition may receive a new drug, whereas those in a control condition may receive a pill that looks like the new drug but is only a PLACEBO containing some inert substance.

experimental control see CONTROL.

experimental design an outline or plan of the procedures to be followed in scientific experimentation in order to reach valid conclusions, with consideration of such factors as participant selection, variable manipulation, data collection and analysis, and minimization of external influences.

experimental group a group of participants in a research study who are exposed to a particular manipulation of the INDEPENDENT VARIABLE (i.e., a particular treatment or TREATMENT LEVEL). The responses of the experimental group are compared with the responses of a CONTROL GROUP, other experimental groups, or both.

experimental hypothesis a premise that describes what a researcher in a scientific study hopes to demonstrate if certain conditions are met, such as RANDOM SELECTION of participants, RANDOM ASSIGNMENT to EXPERIMENTAL GROUPS or CONTROL GROUPS, and manipulation of an INDEPENDENT VARIABLE.

experimental manipulation in an experiment, the manipulation of one or more INDEPENDENT VARIABLES in order to investigate their effect on a DEPENDENT VARIABLE. An example would be the assignment of a specific treatment or PLACEBO to participants in a research study in order to control possible CONFOUNDS and assess the effect of the treatment.

experimental method a system of scientific investigation, usually based on a design to be carried out under controlled conditions, that is intended to test a hypothesis and establish a causal relationship between independent and dependent variables.

experimental neuropsychology the use of empirical methods to study the physiological structures and processes of the nervous system and their relationships to cognition and behavior. For example, an **experimental neuropsychologist** might examine how different probes affect memory performance in individuals with and without schizophrenia in order to identify which memory processes are most vulnerable to disruption in schizophrenia and to determine how people with the disorder can best remember.

experimental neurosis a pathological condition induced in a nonhuman animal during conditioning experiments requiring discriminations between nearly indistinguishable

stimuli or involving punishment for necessary activities (e.g., eating). Experimental neurosis may be characterized by a range of behavioral abnormalities, including agitation, irritability, aggression, regressive behavior, escape and avoidance, and disturbances in physiological activity such as pulse, heart, and respiration rates.

experimental philosophy 1. in the late 17th and 18th centuries, a name for the new discipline of experimental science then emerging. Use of the term often went with an optimism about the ability of experimental science to answer the questions that had been posed but unsolved by "natural philosophy." The systematic work of British physicist and mathematician Isaac Newton (1642–1727) is often given as a defining example of experimental philosophy. **2.** a late 20th-century movement holding that modern experimental science, particularly neuroscience, will ultimately uncover the biological foundations of thought and thereby provide a material answer to the questions of EPISTEMOLOGY. In other words, experimental philosophy holds that answers to philosophical questions regarding the mind and its activities can, and likely will, be reduced to questions of how the brain functions. See REDUCTIONISM.

experimental psychology the scientific study of behavior, motives, or cognition in a laboratory or other controlled setting to predict, explain, or influence behavior or other psychological phenomena. Experimental psychology aims at establishing quantified relationships and explanatory theory through the analysis of responses under various controlled conditions and the synthesis of adequate theoretical accounts from the results of these observations.

experimental realism the extent to which a controlled study is meaningful and engaging to participants, eliciting responses that are spontaneous and natural. See also MUNDANE REALISM.

experimental research research utilizing randomized assignment of participants to conditions and systematic manipulation of variables with the objective of drawing causal inferences. It is generally conducted within a laboratory or other controlled environment, which in reducing the potential influence of extraneous factors increases INTERNAL VALIDITY but decreases EXTERNAL VALIDITY. Compare CORRELATIONAL RESEARCH.

experimental treatment 1. in research, the conditions applied to one or more groups that are expected to cause change in some outcome or DEPENDENT VARIABLE. **2.** an intervention or regimen that has shown some promise as a cure or ameliorative for a disease or condition but is still being evaluated for efficacy, safety, and acceptability.

experimental variable an INDEPENDENT VARIABLE that is manipulated by the researcher to determine its relationship to or influence on some outcome or DEPENDENT VARIABLE.

experimenter bias any systematic errors in the research process or the interpretation of its results that are attributable to a researcher's behavior, preconceived beliefs, expectancies, or desires about results. For example, a researcher may inadvertently cue participants to behave or respond in a particular way.

experimenter effect any influence a researcher may have on the results of his or her research, derived from either interaction with participants or unintentional errors of observation, measurement, analysis, or interpretation. In the former, the experimenter's personal characteristics (e.g., age, sex, race), attitudes, and expectations directly affect the behavior of participants. In the latter, the experimenter's procedural errors (often arising from his or her expectations about results) have no effect on participant responses

but indirectly distort the research findings.

explanatory variable see INDEPENDENT VARIABLE.

explicit attitude a relatively enduring and general evaluative response of which a person is consciously aware. Compare IMPLICIT ATTITUDE.

explicit memory long-term memory that can be consciously recalled: general knowledge or information about personal experiences that an individual retrieves in response to a specific need or request to do so. This term is used interchangeably with DECLARATIVE MEMORY but typically with a performance-based orientation—that is, a person is aware that he or she possesses certain knowledge and specifically retrieves it to complete a task overtly eliciting that knowledge (e.g., a multiple-choice exam). Compare IMPLICIT MEMORY.

exploratory factor analysis (**EFA**) a method for finding a small set of underlying dimensions from a large set of related measures. The observed data are freely explored in order to discover the underlying (latent) variables that explain the interrelationships among a larger set of observable (manifest) variables. For example, exploratory factor analysis has been conducted to assess whether there are one, two, or more dimensions underlying items used to assess intelligence. Compare CONFIRMATORY FACTOR ANALYSIS.

exponential curve a graph of a rapidly growing FUNCTION in which the increase is proportional to the size of an x variable and the SLOPE is equal to the value of the y variable.

exposure therapy a form of BEHAVIOR THERAPY that is effective in treating anxiety disorders. It involves systematic and repeated confrontation with a feared stimulus, either in vivo (live) or in the imagination, and may encompass any of a number of behavioral interventions, including DESENSI-

TIZATION, FLOODING, IMPLOSIVE THERAPY, and extinction-based techniques. It works by (a) HABITUATION, in which repeated exposure reduces anxiety over time by a process of EXTINCTION; (b) disconfirming fearful predictions; and (c) increasing feelings of self-efficacy and mastery.

expressed emotion (EE) negative attitudes, in the form of criticism, hostility, and emotional overinvolvement, demonstrated by family members toward a person with a mental disorder. High levels of expressed emotion have been shown to be associated with poorer outcomes in mood, anxiety, and schizophrenic disorders and an increased likelihood of relapse.

expressive language disorder a developmental disorder characterized by impairment in acquiring the ability to use language effectively for communicating with others despite normal language comprehension. Manifestations include below-average vocabulary skills, difficulty producing complete sentences, and problems recalling words.

extended family 1. a family unit consisting of parents and children living in one household with other individuals united by kinship (e.g., grandparents, cousins). **2.** in modern Western societies, the NUCLEAR FAMILY together with various other relatives who live nearby and keep in regular touch. **3.** most generally, any family members beyond the nuclear family (e.g., grandparents, cousins, aunts, uncles). Also called **consanguineous family**.

extension *n.* the straightening of a joint in a limb (e.g., the elbow joint) so that two parts of the limb (e.g., the forearm and upper arm) are drawn away from each other.

extensor *n.* a muscle whose contraction extends a part of the body; for example, the triceps muscle group extends, or straightens, the arm. Compare FLEXOR.

external attribution see SITUATIONAL ATTRIBUTION.

external auditory meatus the canal that conducts sound through the external ear, from the pinna to the tympanic membrane (eardrum). Also called **auditory canal; ear canal**.

external capsule a thin layer of myelinated nerve fibers separating the CLAUSTRUM from the PUTAMEN. See also INTERNAL CAPSULE.

external ear the part of the ear consisting of the PINNA, the EXTERNAL AUDITORY MEATUS, and the outer surface of the eardrum (see TYMPANIC MEMBRANE). Also called **outer ear**.

external genitalia see GENITALIA.

externalization *n.* **1.** a DEFENSE MECHANISM in which one's thoughts, feelings, or perceptions are attributed to the external world and perceived as independent of oneself or one's own experiences. A common expression of this is PROJECTION. **2.** the process of learning to distinguish between the self and the environment during childhood.

external locus of control see LOCUS OF CONTROL.

external reliability the extent to which a measure is consistent when assessed over time or across different individuals. External reliability calculated across time is referred to more specifically as RETEST RELIABILITY; external reliability calculated across individuals is referred to more specifically as INTERRATER RELIABILITY.

external respiration see RESPIRATION.

external validity the extent to which the results of research or testing can be generalized beyond the sample that generated them. For example, if research has been conducted only with male participants, it cannot be assumed that similar results will apply to female participants. The more specialized the sample, the less likely will it be that the results are highly generalizable to other individuals, situations, and time periods. Compare INTERNAL VALIDITY.

exteroception *n.* sensitivity to stimuli that are outside the body, resulting from the response of specialized sensory cells called **exteroceptors** to objects and occurrences in the external environment. Exteroception includes the five senses of sight, smell, hearing, touch, and taste, and exteroceptors thus take a variety of forms (e.g., photoreceptors—retinal rods and cones—for sight; cutaneous receptors—Pacinian corpuscles, Meissner's corpuscles, Merkel's tactile disks—for touch). Compare INTEROCEPTION.

extinction *n.* **1.** in CLASSICAL CONDITIONING, (a) a procedure in which pairing of stimulus events is discontinued, either by presenting the CONDITIONED STIMULUS alone or by presenting the conditioned stimulus and the UNCONDITIONED STIMULUS independently of one another; or (b) the result of this procedure, which is a gradual decline in the probability and magnitude of the CONDITIONED RESPONSE. **2.** in OPERANT CONDITIONING, (a) a procedure in which reinforcement is discontinued, that is, the reinforcing stimulus is no longer presented; or (b) the result of this procedure, which is a decline in the rate of the formerly reinforced response. —**extinguish** *vb.*

extirpation *n.* see ABLATION.

extraneous variable a measure that is not under investigation in an experiment but may potentially affect the outcome or DEPENDENT VARIABLE and thus may influence results. Such potential influence often requires that an extraneous variable be controlled during research. See also CONFOUND.

extrapolation *n.* the process of estimating or projecting unknown score values on the basis of the known scores obtained from a given sample. For example, a researcher might estimate how well students will do on an achievement test on the basis of their current performance, or estimate how

well a similar group of students might perform on the same achievement test.

extrapsychic *adj.* pertaining to that which originates outside the mind or that which occurs between the mind and the environment. Compare INTRAPSYCHIC.

extrapunitive *adj.* referring to the punishment of others: tending to direct anger, blame, or hostility away from the self toward the external factors, such as situations and other people, perceived to be the source of one's frustrations. Compare INTROPUNITIVE.

extrapyramidal symptoms (**EPS**) a group of adverse drug reactions attributable to dysfunction of the extrapyramidal tract of the central nervous system, which regulates muscle tone and body posture and coordinates opposing sets of skeletal muscles and the movement of their associated skeletal parts. Manifestations of EPS include rigidity of the limbs, tremor, and other Parkinson-like signs; dystonia (abnormal facial and body movements); and akathisia (restlessness). These symptoms are among the most common side effects of the high-potency conventional ANTIPSYCHOTICS. Also called **extrapyramidal syndrome** (**EPS**).

extrasensory perception (**ESP**) alleged awareness of external events by other means than the known sensory channels. It includes TELEPATHY, CLAIRVOYANCE, and PRECOGNITION. Despite considerable research, the existence of any of these modalities remains highly controversial. See PARAPSYCHOLOGY.

extrastriate cortex see PRESTRIATE CORTEX.

extraversion (**extroversion**) *n.* one of the elements of the BIG FIVE and FIVE-FACTOR PERSONALITY MODELS, characterized by an orientation of one's interests and energies toward the outer world of people and things rather than the inner world of subjective experience. Extraversion is a broad personality trait and, like INTROVERSION, exists on a continuum of attitudes and behaviors. Extraverts are relatively outgoing, gregarious, sociable, and openly expressive. —**extraversive** *adj.* —**extraverted** *adj.* —**extravert** *n.*

extremely low birth weight (**ELBW**) see LOW BIRTH WEIGHT.

extrinsic motivation an external incentive to engage in a specific activity, especially motivation arising from the expectation of punishment or reward (e.g., completing a disliked chore in exchange for payment). Compare INTRINSIC MOTIVATION.

ex vivo referring to procedures taking place outside of a living organism. For example, during surgery an organ may be removed, treated ex vivo, and returned to the body. Ex vivo research uses living cells or tissue in a laboratory setting soon after their removal from the organism. These ex vivo cells or tissue are not necessarily cultured, as in IN VITRO experiments. Compare IN VIVO. [Latin, literally: "out of life"]

eye *n.* the organ of sight. The human eye has three layers: (a) the outer corneoscleral coat, which includes the transparent CORNEA and the fibrous SCLERA; (b) the middle layer, called the uveal tract, which includes the IRIS, the ciliary body, and the choroid layer; and (c) the innermost layer, the RETINA, which is sensitive to light. RETINAL GANGLION CELLS communicate with the central nervous system through the OPTIC NERVE, which leaves the retina at the OPTIC DISK. The eye also has three chambers. The anterior chamber, between the cornea and the iris, and the posterior chamber, between the ciliary body, LENS, and posterior aspect of the iris, are filled with a watery fluid, the **aqueous humor**, and are connected by the PUPIL. The third chamber, the vitreous body, is the large cavity between the lens and the retina and is filled with a thick, transparent fluid, the **vitreous humor**.

eye contact a direct look exchanged between two people who are interacting. Research on eye contact has shown that that people look more at the other person when listening to that person than when they themselves are talking; that people tend to avoid eye contact when they are embarrassed; and that the more intimate the relationship, the greater the eye contact.

eye-movement desensitization and reprocessing (**EMDR**) a treatment to reduce the emotional impact of trauma-based symptoms such as anxiety, nightmares, flashbacks, or intrusive thought processes. The therapy asks clients to visualize the traumatic event while simultaneously concentrating on the rapid lateral movements of a therapist's finger.

eye movements movements of the eyes caused by contraction of the extrinsic eye muscles. These include movements that allow or maintain the visual fixation of stationary targets; SMOOTH-PURSUIT EYE MOVEMENTS; VERGENCE movements; SACCADES; and reflexive movements of the eyes, such as the OPTOKINETIC REFLEX and VESTIBULO-OCULAR REFLEX.

eyewitness memory an individual's recollection of an event, often a crime or accident of some kind, that he or she personally saw or experienced. The reliability of eyewitness memory is a major issue in FORENSIC PSYCHOLOGY.

Eysenck Personality Inventory (**EPI**) a self-report test originally comprising 57 yes–no questions designed to measure two major personality dimensions, extraversion and neuroticism. The EPI was revised and expanded following its initial publication in 1963 to become the **Eysenck Personality Questionnaire** (**EPQ**), the most recent version of which (the **EPQ–R**) includes 90 questions and measures the additional personality dimension of psychoticism. [German-born British psychologist Hans **Eysenck** (1916–1997) and British psychologist Sybil B. G. **Eysenck**]

Ff

fabulation *n.* random speech that includes the recounting of imaginary incidents by a person who believes these incidents are real. See also DELUSION.

face validity the apparent soundness of a test or measure. The face validity of an instrument is the extent to which the items or content of the test appear to be appropriate for measuring something, regardless of whether they actually are.

facework *n.* in social interactions, a set of strategic behaviors by which people attempt to maintain both their own dignity ("face") and that of the people with whom they are dealing. Facework strategies include politeness, deference, tact, avoidance of difficult subjects, and the use of half-truths and "white lies." The conventions governing facework differ widely between cultures.

facial affect program a hypothetical set of central nervous system structures that accounts for the patterning of universal, basic facial expressions of emotion in humans. Such a program could provide the link between a specific emotion and a given pattern of facial muscular activity.

facial electromyography a technique for measuring the endogenous electrical activity of any muscle or muscle group in the face by the appropriate placement of electrodes (see ELECTROMYOGRAPHY). This procedure is usually carried out to detect subtle facial movements related to emotion or speech.

facial expression a form of nonverbal signaling using the movement of facial muscles. An integral part of communication, facial expression also reflects an individual's emotional state. Cross-cultural research indicates that certain facial expressions are spontane-ous and universally correlated with such primary emotions as surprise, fear, anger, sadness, and happiness. DISPLAY RULES, however, can modify or even inhibit these expressions.

facial feedback hypothesis the hypothesis that sensory information provided to the brain from facial muscle movements is a major determinant of intrapsychic feeling states, such as fear, anger, joy, contempt, and so on.

facial nerve the seventh CRANIAL NERVE, which innervates facial musculature and some sensory receptors, including those of the external ear and the tongue.

facilitation *n.* in neuroscience, the phenomenon in which the threshold for propagation of the action potential of a neuron is lowered because of repeated signals at a synapse or the SUMMATION of subthreshold impulses. —**facilitate** *vb.*

facilitator *n.* a professionally trained or lay member of a group who fulfills some or all of the functions of a group leader. The facilitator encourages discussion among all group members, without necessarily entering into the discussion.

factitious disorder a disorder in which the patient intentionally produces or feigns physical or psychological symptoms solely so that he or she may assume the SICK ROLE (compare MALINGERING) or imposes the same deceptions or harm on others (e.g., a dependent). See also MÜNCHAUSEN SYNDROME.

factitious disorder by proxy see MÜNCHAUSEN SYNDROME BY PROXY.

factor *n.* anything that contributes to a result or has a causal relationship to a phenomenon, event, or action. In ANALYSIS OF VARIANCE, for example, a factor is an independent variable, whereas in FACTOR ANALYSIS, it is an underlying, unobservable LATENT VARIABLE thought (together with other factors) to be responsible for the interrelations among a set of observed variables.

factor analysis (FA) a broad family of mathematical procedures for reducing a set of interrelations among MANIFEST VARIABLES to a smaller set of unobserved LATENT VARIABLES or factors. For example, a number of tests of mechanical ability might be intercorrelated to enable factor analysis to reduce them to a few factors, such as fine motor coordination, speed, and attention. See CONFIRMATORY FACTOR ANALYSIS; EXPLORATORY FACTOR ANALYSIS.

factorial design an experimental study in which two or more CATEGORICAL VARIABLES are simultaneously manipulated or observed to study their joint influence (INTERACTION EFFECT) and separate influences (MAIN EFFECTS) on a separate DEPENDENT VARIABLE. For example, a researcher could use a factorial design to investigate treatment type (e.g., new exercise procedure vs. traditional procedure) and age (younger than 40 vs. older than 40). See also TWO-BY-TWO FACTORIAL DESIGN.

factor rotation in FACTOR ANALYSIS, the repositioning of LATENT VARIABLES (factors) to a new, more interpretable configuration by a set of mathematically specifiable TRANSFORMATIONS. Factors initially are extracted to meet a mathematical criterion of maximal variance explanation, which often does not result in a scientifically meaningful representation of the data. Indeed, for any one factor solution that fits the data to a specific degree, there will exist an infinite number of equally good mathematical solutions. Thus, rotation is required to obtain a solution that is both mathematically viable and logically sound. See OBLIQUE ROTATION; ORTHOGONAL ROTATION.

fading n. in conditioning, the gradual changing of one stimulus to another, which is often used to transfer STIMULUS CONTROL. Stimuli can be faded out (gradually removed) or faded in (gradually introduced).

failure to thrive (FTT) significantly inadequate gain in weight and height by an infant. It reflects a degree of growth failure due to inadequate release of growth hormone and, despite an initial focus on parental neglect and emotional deprivation, is currently believed to have multifactorial etiology, including biological, nutritional, and environmental contributors. The condition is associated with poor long-term developmental, health, and socioemotional outcomes.

faith healing 1. the treatment of physical or psychological illness by means of religious practices, such as prayer or "laying on of hands." **2.** any form of unorthodox medical treatment whose efficacy is said to depend on the patient's faith in the healer or the healing process (see PLACEBO EFFECT). In such cases, any beneficial effects may be attributed to a psychosomatic process rather than a paranormal or supernatural one.

faking n. the practice of some participants in an evaluation or psychological test who either (a) "fake good" by choosing answers that create a favorable impression, as may occur, for example, when an individual is applying for admission to an educational institution; or (b) "fake bad" by choosing answers that make them appear disturbed or incompetent, as may occur, for example, when an individual wishes to be exonerated in a criminal trial. —**fake** vb.

fallopian tube either of the slender fleshy tubes in mammals that convey ova (egg cells) from each ovary to the uterus and where fertilization may occur. [Gabriele **Fallopius** (1523–1562), Italian anatomist]

false-consensus effect the tendency to assume that one's own opinions, beliefs, attributes, or behaviors are more widely shared than is actually the case. A robustly demonstrated phenomenon, the false-consensus effect is often attributed to a desire to view one's thoughts and actions as appropriate, normal, and correct. Compare FALSE-UNIQUENESS EFFECT.

false memory a distorted recollection of an event or, most severely, recollection of an event that never actually happened. False memories are errors of commission, because details, facts, or events come to mind, often vividly, but the remembrances fail to correspond to prior events. Even when people are highly confident that they are remembering "the truth" of the original situation, experimental evidence shows that they can be wrong. The phenomenon is of particular interest in legal cases, specifically those involving eyewitness memories and **false memory syndrome (FMS)**, in which adults seem to recover memories of having been physically or sexually abused as children, with such recoveries often occurring during therapy. The label is controversial, as is the evidence for and against recovery of abuse memories; false memory syndrome is not an accepted diagnostic term, and some have suggested using the more neutral phrase RECOVERED MEMORY. Also called **paramnesia**.

false-uniqueness effect the tendency to underestimate the extent to which others possess the same beliefs and attributes as oneself or engage in the same behaviors, particularly when these characteristics or behaviors are positive or socially desirable. It is often attributed to a desire to view one's thoughts and actions as unusual, arising from personal, internal causes. Compare FALSE-CONSENSUS EFFECT.

falsifiability *n.* the condition of admitting falsification: the logical possibility that an assertion, hypothesis, or theory can be shown to be false by an observation or experiment. The most important properties that make a state-ment falsifiable in this way are (a) that it makes a prediction about an outcome or a universal claim of the type "All Xs have property Y" and (b) that what is predicted or claimed is observable. Austrian-born British philosopher Karl Popper (1902–1994) argued that falsifiability is an essential characteristic of any genuinely scientific hypothesis. —**falsifiable** *adj.*

familiarity *n.* a form of remembering in which a situation, event, place, person, or the like provokes a subjective feeling of recognition and is therefore believed to be in memory, although it is not specifically recalled.

familism *n.* a cultural value common in collectivist or traditional societies that emphasizes strong interpersonal relationships within the EXTENDED FAMILY, together with interdependence, collaboration, and the placing of group interests ahead of individual interests. —**familistic** *adj.*

family intervention **1.** a synonym for FAMILY THERAPY. **2.** an intervention taught by a therapist to one family member (e.g., parent) who then delivers the intervention to another family member (e.g., child) in the home. It is frequently used as an early intervention for a variety of disorders, such as autism, attention-deficit/hyperactivity disorder, speech and language pathology, and disruptive behavior disorders.

family mythology the shared stories, norms, and beliefs within a family system. The mythology can be used to deny trauma or pathology within the family or to ascribe meaning to events in ways that suggest their inevitability or importance.

family study research conducted among siblings, parents, or children to assess evidence for genetic links for characteristics or outcomes, often related to health or disease. For example, a family study might be conducted to assess whether individuals from the same family who share a similar genetic structure also have similar responses to a health-promotion intervention, such as diet, exercise, or medication. The extent to which performance on a given measure varies as a function of genetic similarity is used as an indication of the HERITABILITY of that measure.

family systems theory a broad conceptual model underlying various family therapies that focuses on the relationships between and among interacting individuals in a family. Combining core concepts from GENERAL SYSTEMS THEORY, OBJECT RELATIONS THEORY, and SOCIAL LEARNING THEORY, the model stresses that therapists must see the family as a whole, rather than work only with individual members, to create constructive, systemic, and lasting changes in the family.

family therapy a form of psychotherapy that focuses on the improvement of interfamilial relationships and behavioral patterns of the family unit as a whole, as well as among individual members and groupings, or subsystems, within the family. Family therapy includes a large number of treatment forms with diverse conceptual principles, processes and structures, and clinical foci. Some family therapy approaches (e.g., that based on OBJECT RELATIONS THEORY) reflect extensions of models of psychotherapy with individuals in the interpersonal realm, whereas others (e.g., STRUCTURAL FAMILY THERAPY) evolved in less traditional contexts.

fantasy *n.* **1.** any of a range of mental experiences and processes marked by vivid imagery, intensity of emotion, and relaxation or absence of logic. Fantasizing is normal and common and often serves a healthy purpose of releasing tension, giving pleasure and amusement, or stimulating creativity. It can also be indicative of pathology, as in delusional thinking or significant disconnection from reality. **2.** in psychoanalytic theories, a figment of the imagination: a mental image, night

dream, or daydream in which a person's conscious or unconscious wishes and impulses are fulfilled. —**fantasize** *vb.*

farsightedness *n.* see HYPEROPIA.

fast mapping the ability of young children to learn new words quickly on the basis of only one or two exposures to these words.

father surrogate a substitute for a person's biological father, who performs typical paternal functions and serves as an object of identification and attachment. Father surrogates may include such individuals as adoptive fathers, stepfathers, older brothers, teachers, and others.

fatigue effect a decline in performance on a prolonged or demanding research task that is generally attributed to the participant becoming tired or bored with the task. The fatigue effect is an important consideration when administering a lengthy survey or test in which participants' performance may worsen simply due to the challenges of an extended task.

***F* distribution** a theoretical PROBABILITY DISTRIBUTION widely used in the ANALYSIS OF VARIANCE, MULTIPLE REGRESSION, and other statistical tests of hypotheses about population variances. It is the ratio of the variances of two independent random variables each divided by its DEGREES OF FREEDOM. In an analysis of variance, for example, the *F* distribution is used to test the hypothesis that the variance between groups is significantly greater than the variance within groups, thus demonstrating evidence of some differences among the means. See F RATIO; F TEST.

fear *n.* a basic, intense emotion aroused by the detection of imminent threat, involving an immediate alarm reaction that mobilizes the organism by triggering a set of physiological changes. These include rapid heartbeat, redirection of blood flow away from the periphery toward the gut, tensing of the muscles, and a general mobilization of the organism to take action (see FIGHT-OR-FLIGHT RESPONSE). Fear differs from ANXIETY in that the former is considered an appropriate short-term response to a present, clearly identifiable threat, whereas the latter is a future-oriented, long-term response focused on a diffuse threat. Whatever their precise differences in meaning, however, the terms are often used interchangeably in common parlance.

fearful attachment an adult attachment style characterized by a negative INTERNAL WORKING MODEL OF ATTACHMENT of oneself and of others. Individuals with fearful attachment doubt both their own and others' competence and efficacy and are presumed not to seek help from others when distressed. Compare DISMISSIVE ATTACHMENT; PREOCCUPIED ATTACHMENT; SECURE ATTACHMENT.

fear of failure persistent and irrational anxiety about failing to measure up to the standards and goals set by oneself or others. Fear of failure may be associated with PERFECTIONISM and is implicated in a number of psychological disorders, including eating disorders and some anxiety disorders.

fear of success a fear of accomplishing one's goals or succeeding in society, or a tendency to avoid doing so. Fear of success was originally thought to be experienced primarily by women, because striving for success was held to place a woman in conflict between a general need for achievement and social values that tell her not to achieve "too much." It is now thought that men and women are equally likely to experience fear of success.

feature detector any of various hypothetical or actual mechanisms within the human information-processing system that respond selectively to specific distinguishing features. For example, the visual system has feature detectors

for lines and angles of different orientations as well as for more complex stimuli, such as faces. Feature detectors are also thought to play an important role in speech perception, where their function would be to detect those features that distinguish one PHONEME from another.

feature-integration theory (FIT) a two-stage theory of visual ATTENTION. In the first (preattentive) stage, basic features (e.g., color, shape) are processed automatically, independently, and in parallel. In the second (attentive) stage, other properties, including relations between features of an object, are processed serially, one object (or group) at a time, and are "bound" together to create a single object that is consciously perceived.

Fechner's law a mathematical formula relating subjective experience to changes in physical stimulus intensity: Specifically, the sensation experienced is proportional to the logarithm of the stimulus magnitude. It is derived from WEBER'S LAW and expressed as $\Psi = k \log S$, where Ψ is the sensation, k is a constant, and S is the physical intensity of the stimulus. See also STEVENS LAW. [Gustav Theodor **Fechner** (1801–1887), German physician and philosopher]

feedback *n.* information about a process or interaction provided to the governing system or agent and used to make adjustments that eliminate problems or otherwise optimize functioning. It may be stabilizing NEGATIVE FEEDBACK or amplifying POSITIVE FEEDBACK. The term's origins in engineering and cybernetics lend it a distinct connotation of input–output models that is not as strictly applicable to the wide variety of usages found in psychology, such as BIOFEEDBACK, information feedback, and social feedback.

feedback loop in cybernetic theory, a self-regulatory model that determines whether the current operation of a system is acceptable and, if not, attempts to make the necessary changes. Its operation is summarized by the acronym TOTE (test-operate-test-exit). The two test phases compare the current reality against the goal or standard. The operate phase involves any processes or interventions designed to resolve unacceptable discrepancies between the reality and the standard. In the exit phase, the supervisory feedback loop is closed down because the circumstances have been brought into agreement with the standard. Also called **TOTE model**.

feeling *n.* **1.** a self-contained phenomenal experience. Feelings are subjective, evaluative, and independent of the sensations, thoughts, or images evoking them. They are inevitably evaluated as pleasant or unpleasant, but they can have more specific intrapsychic qualities as well. The core characteristic that differentiates feelings from cognitive, sensory, or perceptual intrapsychic experiences is the link of AFFECT to APPRAISAL. Feelings differ from EMOTIONS in being purely mental, whereas emotions are designed to engage with the world. **2.** any experienced sensation, particularly a tactile or temperature sensation (e.g., pain, coldness).

female ejaculation expulsion of a lubricating fluid by the vestibular glands of a woman during sexual stimulation and orgasm. The fluid may reach peak flow before orgasm, often increasing when stimulation is prolonged.

female genitalia see GENITALIA.

female Oedipus complex see OEDIPUS COMPLEX.

female orgasmic disorder a condition in which a woman recurrently or persistently has difficulty obtaining orgasm or is unable to reach orgasm at all following sexual stimulation and excitement, causing marked distress or interpersonal difficulty.

female sexual arousal disorder a condition in which a woman recurrently or persistently is unable to attain or maintain adequate vaginal lubrication and swelling during sexual excitement, causing marked distress or interpersonal difficulty. It is a prevalent sexual problem for women and has a complex etiology involving a variety of physiological and psychological factors.

female sexual dysfunction (FSD) any of various conditions experienced by women that involve sexual difficulties and associated distress significant enough to interfere with participation in sexual relationships. Although specific definitional criteria vary, female sexual dysfunction generally is categorized into four groups of symptoms: persistent absence of desire, inability to get or stay excited, difficulty achieving orgasm, and pain associated with stimulation or intercourse. Among the particular problems often included as FSD are DYSPAREUNIA, FEMALE ORGASMIC DISORDER, FEMALE SEXUAL AROUSAL DISORDER, VAGINISMUS, and sexual difficulties from underlying medical causes.

feminism *n.* any of a number of perspectives that take as their subject matter the problems and perspectives of women or the nature of biological and social phenomena related to gender. Although some feminist perspectives focus on issues of fairness and equal rights, other approaches emphasize what are taken to be inherent and systematic gender inequities in Western society (see PATRIARCHY). In psychology, feminism has focused attention on the nature and origin of gender differences in psychological processes. —**feminist** *adj., n.*

fertilization *n.* the fusion of a sperm and an egg cell to produce a ZYGOTE. In humans, fertilization occurs in a FALLOPIAN TUBE.

fetal alcohol syndrome (FAS) a group of adverse fetal and infant health effects associated with heavy maternal alcohol intake during pregnancy. It is characterized by low birth weight and retarded growth, craniofacial anomalies (e.g., microcephaly), neurobehavioral problems (e.g., hyperactivity), and cognitive abnormalities (e.g., language acquisition deficits); intellectual disability may be present. Children showing some but not all features of this syndrome are described as having **fetal alcohol effects (FAE).**

fetal programming during prenatal development, a fetus's physiological adaptation in utero to changing environmental conditions or stimuli (e.g., maternal stress, poor maternal nutrition, environmental toxins) and the long-term consequences of this adaptation on the child's postnatal development into adulthood. It is believed that the effects of fetal programming may predispose individuals to later health and mental health disorders.

fetishism *n.* a type of PARAPHILIA in which inanimate objects—commonly undergarments, stockings, rubber items, shoes, or boots—are repeatedly or exclusively used in achieving sexual excitement. Objects designed for use in stimulating the genitals (e.g., vibrators) are not considered to be involved in fetishism. Fetishism occurs primarily among males and may compete or interfere with sexual contact with a partner. —**fetishistic** *adj.*

fetus *n.* an animal EMBRYO in the later stages of development. In humans, the fetal period is from the end of the 8th week after fertilization until birth. —**fetal** *adj.*

field *n.* **1.** a defined area or region of space, such as the VISUAL FIELD. **2.** a complex of personal, physical, and social factors within which a psychological event takes place. See FIELD THEORY. **3.** somewhere other than a laboratory, library, or academic setting in which experimental work is carried out or data collected. See FIELD EXPERIMENT.

field dependence a COGNITIVE

STYLE in which the individual consistently relies more on external referents (environmental cues) than on internal referents (bodily sensation cues). The opposite tendency, relying more on internal than external referents, is **field independence.** Both were discovered during experiments conducted in the 1950s to understand the factors that determine perception of the upright in space.

field experiment a study that is conducted outside the laboratory in a "real-world" setting. Participants are exposed to one of two or more levels of an INDEPENDENT VARIABLE and observed for their reactions; they are likely to be unaware of the research. It often is conducted without RANDOM SELECTION or RANDOM ASSIGNMENT of participants to conditions and without deliberate experimental manipulation of the independent variable by the researcher.

field research studies conducted outside the laboratory, in a "real-world" setting, which typically involve observing or interacting with participants in their typical environments over an extended period of time. Field research has the advantage of ECOLOGICAL VALIDITY and affords the opportunity to understand how and why behavior occurs in a natural social environment; it has the disadvantages of loss of environmental control and ability to do precise experimental manipulations. Thus, field research is often said to have more EXTERNAL VALIDITY and less INTERNAL VALIDITY than laboratory-based research.

field survey an assessment that involves collecting information on specific individuals or entities, usually in their natural environment. For example, a field survey could be conducted on a sample of students from underrepresented groups to assess their attitudes, experience, and performance regarding quantitative methods, before providing an intervention to increase their quantitative reasoning.

field theory a systematic approach describing behavior in terms of patterns of dynamic interrelationships between individuals and the psychological, social, and physical situation in which they exist. This situation is known as the **field space** or LIFE SPACE, and the dynamic interactions are conceived as forces with positive or negative valences (subjective values).

field work a less common name for FIELD RESEARCH.

fight-or-flight response a pattern of physiological changes elicited by activity of the SYMPATHETIC NERVOUS SYSTEM in response to threatening or otherwise stressful situations that leads to mobilization of energy for physical activity (e.g., attacking or avoiding the offending stimulus), either directly or by inhibiting physiological activity that does not contribute to energy mobilization. Specific sympathetic responses include increased heart rate, respiratory rate, and sweat gland activity; elevated blood pressure; decreased digestive activity; pupil dilation; and a routing of blood flow to skeletal muscles.

figure *n.* a graph, drawing, or other depiction used to convey the essential findings from a research study. Common figures used in psychological research include BAR GRAPHS, which show the frequency of endorsement for several categories of a variable (e.g., the number of individuals who have various diseases), and VENN DIAGRAMS, which use overlapping circles to show how much shared variance there is between two or more variables.

figure–ground *adj.* relating to the principle that perceptions have two parts: a figure or object that stands out in good contour and an indistinct, homogeneous background.

file-drawer problem the fact that a large proportion of all studies actually conducted are not available for review because they remain unpublished in "file drawers," having failed to obtain positive results. Thus, the results of a meta-analysis may not yield reliable EFFECT SIZE estimates because only studies that have been published or otherwise are widely available to researchers can be included in the analysis.

filter theory an early theory of attention proposing that unattended channels of information are filtered prior to identification. This theory continues to be influential in the form of its successor, the ATTENUATION THEORY.

fine motor describing activities or skills that require coordination of small muscles to control small, precise movements, particularly in the hands and face. Examples of **fine motor skills** include handwriting, drawing, cutting, and manipulating small objects. Compare GROSS MOTOR.

first-generation antipsychotic see ANTIPSYCHOTIC.

first-impression bias see PRIMACY EFFECT.

Fisher least significant difference test a statistical procedure to compare pairs of means, conducted after an F TEST has revealed that at least one pair of means is significantly different. The test calculates the smallest value that would be significantly different from chance when subtracting one mean from another mean. If the absolute value of the actual difference between a pair of means is larger than this **least significant difference** (**LSD**), a researcher can reject a NULL HYPOTHESIS that the means are equal and conclude that they are significantly different. Also called **protected** *t* **test**. [Ronald Aylmer **Fisher** (1890–1962), British statistician and geneticist]

Fisher's r to z transformation a statistical procedure that converts a Pearson PRODUCT-MOMENT CORRELATION COEFFICIENT to a standardized Z SCORE to assess whether the correlation is significantly different from zero. The test is useful in providing a normally distributed statistic (called the **Fisher transformed value** or **Fisher's z**) that can be used in HYPOTHESIS TESTING or in forming a CONFIDENCE INTERVAL. Also called **Fisher z transformation; z transformation**. [Ronald Aylmer Fisher]

fissure *n.* a cleft, groove, or indentation in a surface, especially any of the deep grooves in the cerebral cortex. See also SULCUS.

fit 1. *n.* the degree to which values predicted by a model correspond with empirically observed values. For example, in STRUCTURAL EQUATION MODELING, a researcher may want to see how well his or her hypothesized model of the relationships among a set of variables actually fits the VARIATION and COVARIATION in the data. **2.** *adj.* see FITNESS.

fitness *n.* **1.** a set of attributes that people have or are able to achieve relating to their ability to perform physical work and to carry out daily tasks with vigor and alertness, without undue fatigue, and with ample energy to enjoy leisure pursuits. **2.** in biology, the extent to which an organism or population is able to produce viable offspring in a given environment, which is a measure of that organism's or population's adaptation to that environment. See also INCLUSIVE FITNESS; REPRODUCTIVE SUCCESS. —**fit** *adj.*

five-factor personality model (FFM) a model of personality in which five dimensions of individual differences—extraversion, neuroticism, conscientiousness, agreeableness, and openness to experience—are viewed as core personality structures. Unlike the BIG FIVE PERSONALITY MODEL, which views the five personality dimensions as descriptions of behavior and treats the five-dimensional structure as a taxonomy of individual differences, the FFM views the factors as psychological entities with causal force. The two models are frequently and incorrectly conflated in the scientific litera-

ture, without regard for their distinctly different emphases.

fixation *n.* **1.** an obsessive preoccupation with a single idea, impulse, or aim, as in an IDÉE FIXE. **2.** a shortened name for visual fixation, that is, the orientation of the eyes so that the image of a viewed object falls on the FOVEA CENTRALIS of the retina. **3.** in psychoanalytic theory, the persistence of an early stage of PSYCHOSEXUAL DEVELOPMENT or the inappropriate attachment to an early psychosexual object or mode of gratification, such as anal or oral activity. —**fixate** *vb.*

fixed action pattern (FAP) in classical ethology, a stereotyped, genetically preprogrammed, species-specific behavioral sequence that is evoked by a RELEASER stimulus and is carried out without sensory feedback. In contemporary ethology, the term MODAL ACTION PATTERN is more often used.

fixed-alternative question a test or survey item in which several possible responses are given and participants are asked to pick the correct response or the one that best matches their preference. An example of a fixed-alternative question is "Which of the following most closely corresponds to your age: 12 or younger, 13 to 19, 20 to 39, 40 to 59, 60 to 79, or 80 or older?" A fixed-alternative question is sometimes referred to as a **closed question**, although this can also refer to any inquiry requesting a short definite answer (e.g., "How old are you?"). Also called **fixed-choice question; forced-choice question**. Compare FREE-RESPONSE QUESTION; OPEN QUESTION.

fixed effect an INDEPENDENT VARIABLE whose levels are specified by the researcher rather than randomly chosen within some level of permissible values. For example, a health researcher who specifically chose to examine the effect on weight loss of no exercise, 1 hour of exercise, or 3 hours of exercise per week would be treating time spent exercising as a fixed effect.

All levels of interest are included in the design, and thus anyone wanting to replicate the study would have to use the same levels of exercise as in the original. Also called **fixed factor**. Compare RANDOM EFFECT.

fixed-interval schedule (FI schedule) in conditioning, an arrangement in which the first response that occurs after a set interval has elapsed is reinforced. For example, "FI 3 min" means that reinforcement is given to the first response occurring at least 3 minutes after a previous reinforcement. Often, experience with FI schedules results in a temporal pattern of responding, characterized by little or no responding at the beginning of the interval, followed by an increased rate later on as reinforcement becomes more imminent. This pattern is often referred to as the **fixed-interval scallop**.

fixed parameter a specific value assigned (as opposed to estimated) by a researcher when testing a statistical model. For example, in STRUCTURAL EQUATION MODELING, researchers may use a fixed parameter of 1.0 for one of the factor loadings or variances of each LATENT VARIABLE in a model.

fixed-ratio schedule (FR schedule) in conditioning, an arrangement in which reinforcement is given after a specified number of responses. "FR 1" means that reinforcement is given after each response, "FR 50" means that reinforcement is given after every 50 responses, and so on.

fixed variable a variable whose value is specified by a researcher or otherwise predetermined and not the result of chance. Compare RANDOM VARIABLE.

flashback n. 1. the reliving of a traumatic event after at least some initial adjustment to the trauma appears to have been made. Memories may be triggered by words, sounds, smells, or scenes that are reminiscent of the original trauma (as in a backfiring car

triggering a flashback to being in combat). Flashbacks may be associated with posttraumatic stress disorder. **2.** the spontaneous recurrence of the perceptual distortions and disorientation to time and place experienced during a previous period of hallucinogen intoxication. Flashbacks may occur months or even years after the last use of the drug and are associated particularly with LSD.

flashbulb memory a vivid, enduring memory associated with a personally significant and emotional event, often including such details as where the individual was or what he or she was doing at the time of the event. People often believe that such memories have the quality of a photograph taken at the moment they experienced the event, and they believe with high confidence that these memories are accurate. However, recent research has shown that although flashbulb memories are more likely to be retained than the memory of an everyday event, they are not always accurate.

flat affect total or near absence of appropriate emotional responses to situations and events. See also SHALLOW AFFECT.

flexion n. the bending of a joint in a limb (e.g., the elbow joint) so that two parts of the limb (e.g., the forearm and upper arm) are brought toward each other.

flexor n. a muscle whose contraction bends a part of the body, such as the biceps muscle of the upper arm. Compare EXTENSOR.

flicker fusion frequency see CRITICAL FLICKER FREQUENCY.

flight into health in psychotherapy, an abrupt "recuperation" by a prospective client after or during intake interviews and before entry into therapy proper or, more commonly, by a client in ongoing therapy. Psychoanalytic theory interprets the flight into health as an unconscious DEFENSE MECHANISM.

flight into illness in psychotherapy, the sudden development of physical symptoms by a client or prospective client. Psychoanalytic theory interprets this as an unconscious DEFENSE MECHANISM that is used to avoid examination of a deeper underlying conflict.

flooding *n.* a technique in BEHAVIOR THERAPY in which the individual is exposed directly to a maximum-intensity anxiety-producing situation or stimulus, either described or real, without any attempt made to lessen or avoid anxiety or fear during the exposure. An individual with claustrophobia, for example, might be asked to spend extended periods of time in a small room. Flooding techniques aim to diminish or extinguish the undesired response to a feared situation or stimulus and are used primarily in the treatment of individuals with phobias and similar disorders. It is distinct from SYSTEMATIC DESENSITIZATION, which involves a gradual, step-by-step approach to encountering the feared situation or stimulus while attempting throughout to maintain a nonanxious state. See also IMPLOSIVE THERAPY.

floor effect the situation in which a large proportion of participants perform very poorly on a task or other evaluative measure, thus skewing the distribution of scores and making it impossible to differentiate among the many individuals at that low level. For example, a test whose items are too difficult for those taking it would show a floor effect because most people would obtain or be close to the lowest possible score of 0. Compare CEILING EFFECT.

flow *n.* a state of optimal experience arising from intense involvement in an activity that is enjoyable, such as playing a sport, performing a musical passage, or writing a creative piece. Flow arises when one's skills are fully utilized yet equal to the demands of the task, intrinsic motivation is at a peak,

one loses self-consciousness and temporal awareness, and one has a sense of total control, effortlessness, and complete concentration on the immediate situation (the here and now).

fluent aphasia see APHASIA.

fluid intelligence (**fluid ability**) see CATTELL–HORN THEORY OF INTELLIGENCE.

fluoxetine *n.* an antidepressant that is the prototype of the SSRIs (selective serotonin reuptake inhibitors). Fluoxetine differs from other SSRIs in that it and its biologically active metabolic product, norfluoxetine, have a prolonged HALF-LIFE of 5 to 7 days after a single dose. U.S. trade name: **Prozac**.

Flynn effect the gradual cross-cultural rise in raw scores obtained on measures of general intelligence. These increases have been roughly 9 points per generation (i.e., 30 years). [James **Flynn** (1934–), New Zealand philosopher who first documented its occurrence]

focal psychotherapy a form of BRIEF PSYCHOTHERAPY in which a single problem (e.g., excessive anxiety) is made the target of the entire course of treatment. The therapist continually redirects the process to avoid deviations from this specifically identified aim.

focal seizure see PARTIAL SEIZURE.

focus group a small set of people, typically 8 to 12 in number, who share characteristics (e.g., working parents with 5- to 8-year-old children) and are selected to discuss a topic of which they have personal experience (e.g., their children's reading abilities and school performance). Originally used in marketing to determine consumer response to particular products, focus groups are now used for determining typical reactions, adaptations, and solutions to any number of issues, events, or topics and are associated particularly with QUALITATIVE RESEARCH.

folie à deux see SHARED PSYCHOTIC DISORDER. [French, "double" madness]

follicle *n.* a cluster of cells enclosing, protecting, and nourishing a cell or structure within, such as a hair follicle. —**follicular** *adj.*

follicle-stimulating hormone (**FSH**) a GONADOTROPIN released by the anterior pituitary gland that, in females, stimulates the development in the ovary of a graafian follicle, a pouchlike cavity where an ovum (egg cell) is produced during the MENSTRUAL CYCLE. The same hormone in males stimulates Sertoli cells in the testis to produce spermatozoa. Also called **follitropin**.

follow-up study a long-term research project designed to examine the degree to which effects seen shortly after the imposition of an intervention persist over time.

foot-in-the-door technique a two-step procedure for enhancing compliance in which a minor initial request is presented immediately before a more substantial target request. Agreement to the initial request makes people more likely to agree to the target request than would have been the case if the latter had been presented on its own. See also DOOR-IN-THE-FACE TECHNIQUE; LOW-BALL TECHNIQUE; THAT'S-NOT-ALL TECHNIQUE.

forced-choice question see FIXED-ALTERNATIVE QUESTION.

forced compliance effect the tendency of a person who has behaved in a way that contradicts his or her attitude to subsequently alter the attitude to be consistent with the behavior. It is one way of reducing COGNITIVE DISSONANCE. Also called **induced compliance effect**.

forebrain *n.* the part of the brain that develops from the anterior section of the NEURAL TUBE in the embryo, containing the CEREBRUM and the DIENCEPHALON. The former comprises the cerebral hemispheres with their various regions (e.g., BASAL GANGLIA, AMYGDALA, HIPPOCAMPUS); the lat-

ter comprises the THALAMUS and HYPOTHALAMUS. Also called **prosencephalon**.

foreclosure *n.* see IDENTITY FORECLOSURE.

forensic neuroscience an emerging field in which the regulation of certain behaviors, including criminal, antisocial, sociopathic, and psychopathic, is viewed in light of their neural mechanisms. Theoretically, these behaviors are seen as arising not from an individual's failure to know right from wrong but from neural mechanisms that may be functioning improperly.

forensic psychology the application of psychological principles and techniques to situations involving the civil and criminal legal systems. Its functions include assessment and treatment services, provision of advocacy and expert testimony, policy analysis, and research on such topics as eyewitness accounts, offender behavior, interrogations, and investigative practices.

forgetting *n.* the failure to remember material previously learned. Numerous processes and theories have been proposed throughout the long history of study to account for forgetting, including DECAY THEORY and INTERFERENCE THEORY. Forgetting typically is a normal phenomenon, but it may also be pathological, as, for example, in amnesia.

forgiveness *n.* willfully putting aside feelings of resentment toward an individual who has committed a wrong, been unfair or hurtful, or otherwise harmed one in some way. Forgiveness is not equated with reconciliation or excusing another, and it is not merely accepting what happened or ceasing to be angry. Rather, it involves a voluntary transformation of one's feelings, attitudes, and behavior toward the individual, so that one is no longer dominated by resentment and can express compassion, generosity, or the like toward the individual. Forgiveness is sometimes considered an important process in psychotherapy and in counseling.

formal operational stage the fourth and final stage in the PIAGETIAN THEORY of cognitive development, beginning around age 12, during which complex intellectual functions, such as abstract thinking, logical processes, conceptualization, and judgment, develop. See also CONCRETE OPERATIONAL STAGE; PREOPERATIONAL STAGE; SENSORIMOTOR STAGE.

formal thought disorder disruptions in the form or structure of thinking. Examples include derailment, frequent interruptions and jumps from one idea to another, and tangentiality (constant digressions to irrelevant topics). It is distinct from THOUGHT DISORDER, in which the disturbance relates to thought content.

formants *pl. n.* the frequency bands of speech sounds produced by the vocal cords and other physical features of the head and throat. A simple sound, such as the vowel /a/, may span several kilohertz of frequencies.

fornix *n.* (*pl.* **fornices**) any arch-shaped structure, especially the long tract of white matter in the brain arching between the HIPPOCAMPUS and the HYPOTHALAMUS.

forward conditioning in CLASSICAL CONDITIONING, the pairing of two stimuli such that the conditioned stimulus is presented before the unconditioned stimulus. Also called **forward pairing**. Compare BACKWARD CONDITIONING.

forward selection a technique used in creating MULTIPLE REGRESSION models in which independent variables from a large set of such variables are added to the REGRESSION EQUATION in the order of their predictive power (i.e., largest to smallest increase in the COEFFICIENT OF MULTIPLE DETERMINATION) until a preset criterion is reached and there is no further significant change in

the model's predictive power. Also called **stepup selection**.

foster care temporary care provided to children in settings outside their family of origin by individuals other than their natural or adoptive parents. Foster care is intended to protect children whose parents are unavailable, abusive, or incapable of providing proper care, with the ultimate goal being to find a secure and permanent home. Typically, a child is placed with a family approved for foster care, and the family is paid a fee by a public child welfare agency. Although these **foster home** arrangements are more common, children may also be placed in group homes or institutions.

four-card problem see WASON SELECTION TASK.

Fourier analysis the mathematical analysis of complex waveforms using the fact that they can be expressed as an infinite sum of sine and cosine functions (a **Fourier series**). It is accomplished via a **Fourier transform**, a mathematical operation that analyzes any waveform into a set of simple waveforms with different frequencies and amplitudes. Fourier analysis is particularly important in the study of sound and the theoretical understanding of visual analysis. [Jean Baptiste Joseph **Fourier** (1768–1830), French mathematician and physicist]

fourth ventricle see VENTRICLE.

fovea centralis a small depression in the central portion of the retina in which RETINAL CONE cells are most concentrated and an image is focused most clearly. Also called **fovea**. —**foveal** *adj.*

fractionation *n.* a psychophysical procedure to scale the magnitude of sensations in which an observer adjusts a variable stimulus to be half that of a standard stimulus.

fragile X syndrome a genetic condition that causes a range of developmental problems, including learning disabilities, social anxiety, and cognitive impairment. The disorder is so named because of alterations in the *FMR1* gene, on the arm of the X chromosome, that abnormally expand and destabilize it. Males with fragile X syndrome also have characteristic physical features (e.g., large ears, prominent jaw and forehead) that become more apparent with age.

frame *n.* in cognitive psychology, a set of parameters defining a particular mental SCHEMA by which an individual perceives and evaluates the world. See also PERCEPTUAL SET.

frame of reference in social psychology, the set of assumptions or criteria by which a person or group judges ideas, actions, and experiences. A frame of reference can often limit or distort perception, as in the case of prejudice and stereotypes.

framing *n.* the process of defining the context or issues surrounding a question, problem, or event in a way that serves to influence how the context or issues are perceived and evaluated. See also REFRAMING.

fraternal twins see DIZYGOTIC TWINS.

F ratio (symbol: *F*) in an ANALYSIS OF VARIANCE or a MULTIVARIATE ANALYSIS OF VARIANCE, the amount of explained variance divided by the amount of ERROR VARIANCE; that is, the ratio of between-groups variance to within-group variance. Its value determines whether to accept the NULL HYPOTHESIS stating that there is no difference between the treatment and control conditions, with a large value indicating the presence of a significant effect. Also called *F* **statistic**; *F* **value**.

free association a basic process in psychoanalysis and other forms of psychodynamic psychotherapy, in which the patient is encouraged to verbalize without censorship or selection whatever thoughts come to mind, no matter how embarrassing, illogical, or irrelevant. The object is to allow uncon-

scious material, such as inhibited thoughts and emotions, traumatic experiences, or threatening impulses, to come to the surface where they can be interpreted.

freedom from harm one of the basic rights of research participants that is ensured by an INSTITUTIONAL REVIEW BOARD. Freedom from harm states that a research participant should not incur undue risk as a result of taking part in a study. See also PARTICIPANTS' RIGHTS.

freedom to withdraw one of the basic rights of research participants that is ensured by an INSTITUTIONAL REVIEW BOARD. Freedom to withdraw allows a research participant to drop out of a study at any time without penalty. See also PARTICIPANTS' RIGHTS.

free-floating anxiety a diffuse, chronic sense of uneasiness and apprehension not directed toward any specific situation or object. It may be a characteristic of a number of anxiety disorders, in particular GENERALIZED ANXIETY DISORDER.

free nerve ending a highly branched terminal portion of a sensory neuron. Found particularly in the different layers of skin, free nerve endings are the most common type of nerve ending and act as pain and temperature receptors.

free radical an atom or molecule that has at least one "unpaired" electron in its outer shell. This makes it highly reactive and able to engage in rapid chain reactions that destabilize the molecules around it, thus causing the formation of more free radicals. Free radicals can damage cells and have been implicated in aging, inflammation, and the progression of various pathological conditions, including cancer.

free recall a type of memory task in which participants attempt to remember previously studied information in any order. One common finding in free-recall studies is that the first and last items that are presented in a study list are best remembered.

free-response question a test or survey item that allows the respondent to answer entirely as he or she pleases, as opposed to a FIXED-ALTERNATIVE QUESTION, in which the respondent must choose from several provided options.

free-running rhythm a cycle of behavior or physiological activity that occurs if external stimuli do not provide ENTRAINMENT.

free will the power or capacity of a human being for self-direction. The concept of free will thus suggests that inclinations, dispositions, thoughts, and actions are not determined entirely by forces over which people have no independent directing influence. Free will is generally seen as necessary for moral action and responsibility and is implied by much of our everyday experience, in which we are conscious of having the power to do or forbear. However, it has often been dismissed as illusory by advocates of DETERMINISM, who hold that all occurrences, including human actions, are predetermined.

frequency *n.* **1.** (symbol: *f*) the number of occurrences of a phenomenon, particularly a CATEGORICAL VARIABLE such as sex. For example, it is often of interest to find the frequencies or counts of the men and women who are participating in a research study. **2.** the number of repetitions of a periodic waveform in a given unit of time. The standard measure of frequency is the hertz (Hz); this replaces, and is equivalent to, cycles per second (cps).

frequency distribution a tabular representation of the number of times a specific value or datum point occurs. The left column lists the different categories or scores of a CONTINUOUS VARIABLE, and the right column lists the number of occurrences of each. When a frequency distribution is plotted on a graph, it is often called a **frequency curve, frequency diagram,** or **frequency polygon.** When represented mathematically via an equation, it is called a **frequency function.**

frequency modulation see MODULATION.

frequency selectivity the property of a system that enables it to be "tuned" to respond better to certain frequencies than to others. The frequency selectivity of the auditory system is a fundamental aspect of hearing and has been a major research theme for many decades. Also called **bandwidth selectivity.**

frequency theory a late 19th-century theory specifying that pitch is coded by the rate at which ACTION POTENTIALS are generated by auditory neurons within the BASILAR MEMBRANE of the ear. For example, a 100 Hz tone would be signaled by 100 impulses per second in the AUDITORY NERVE. However, frequency theory cannot explain the perception of sounds above 500 Hz because the REFRACTORY PERIOD of a neuron renders it incapable of firing at such high rates. This discrepancy was accounted for by the later VOLLEY THEORY.

Freudian slip in the popular understanding of psychoanalytic theory, an unconscious error or oversight in writing, speech, or action that is held to be caused by unacceptable impulses breaking through the EGO's defenses and exposing the individual's true wishes or feelings. See PARAPRAXIS; SLIP OF THE TONGUE. [Sigmund **Freud,** Austrian neurologist (1856–1939)]

friendship *n.* a voluntary relationship between two or more people that is relatively long-lasting and in which those involved tend to be concerned with meeting the others' needs and interests as well as satisfying their own desires.

frontal cortex the CEREBRAL CORTEX of the frontal lobe. It is associated with decision making, planning, insight, judgment, the ability to concentrate, and impulse control. See also PREFRONTAL CORTEX.

frontal lobe one of the four main lobes of each cerebral hemisphere of the brain, lying in front of the CENTRAL SULCUS. It is concerned with motor and higher order EXECUTIVE FUNCTIONS. See also PREFRONTAL LOBE.

frontal lobe syndrome deterioration in personality and behavior resulting from lesions in the frontal lobe. Typical symptoms include loss of initiative, inability to plan activities, difficulty with abstract thinking, PERSEVERATION, impairments in social judgment and impulse control, and mood disturbances such as apathy or mania.

frotteurism *n.* a PARAPHILIA in which an individual deliberately and persistently seeks sexual excitement by rubbing against other people. This may occur as apparently accidental contact in crowded public settings, such as elevators or lines.

frustration *n.* **1.** the thwarting of impulses or actions that prevents individuals from obtaining something they have been led to expect based on past experience, as when a hungry animal is prevented from obtaining food that it can see or smell or when a child is prevented from playing with a visible toy. **2.** the emotional state an individual experiences when such thwarting occurs. —**frustrate** *vb.*

frustration–aggression hypothesis the theory that (a) frustration always produces an aggressive urge and (b) aggression is always the result of prior frustrations.

frustration tolerance the ability of an individual to delay gratification or to preserve relative equanimity when encountering obstacles. The growth of adequate frustration tolerance generally occurs as part of a child's cognitive and affective develop-

ment but may also be strengthened to more adaptive levels later in life through therapeutic intervention.

***F* test** any of a class of statistical procedures, such as ANALYSIS OF VARIANCE or MULTIPLE REGRESSION, that rely on the assumption that the calculated statistic—the F RATIO—follows the F DISTRIBUTION when the null hypothesis is true.

fugue *n.* see DISSOCIATIVE FUGUE.

fully functioning person in CLIENT-CENTERED THERAPY, a person with a healthy personality, who experiences freedom of choice and action, is creative, and is able to live fully in the present and respond freely and flexibly to new experiences without fear.

function *n.* **1.** in biology, an activity of an organ or an organism that contributes to the organism's FITNESS, such as the secretion of a sex hormone by a gonad to prepare for reproduction or the defensive behavior of a female with young toward an intruder. **2.** (symbol: f) a mathematical procedure that relates or transforms one number, quantity, or entity to another according to a defined rule. For example, if $y = 2x + 1$, y is said to be a function of x. This is often written $y = f(x)$.

functional *adj.* **1.** denoting or referring to a disorder for which there is no known physiological or structural basis. In psychology and psychiatry, functional disorders are improperly considered equivalent to PSYCHOGENIC disorders. **2.** based on or relating to use rather than structure.

functional age an individual's age as determined by measures of functional capability indexed by age-normed standards. Functional age is distinct from CHRONOLOGICAL AGE and represents a combination of physiological, psychological, and social age. The functional age of a child is measured in terms of the developmental level he or she has reached. In adults, it is calculated by measuring a range of variables that correlate closely with chronological age, such as eyesight, hearing, mobility, cardiopulmonary function, concentration, and memory.

functional analysis the detailed analysis of a behavior to identify contingencies that sustain the behavior.

functional autonomy the ability of a person to perform independently the various tasks required in daily life, a core concept in rehabilitation. See ACTIVITIES OF DAILY LIVING; INSTRUMENTAL ACTIVITIES OF DAILY LIVING.

functional fixedness the tendency to perceive an object only in terms of its most common use. For example, people generally perceive cardboard boxes as containers, thus hindering them from potentially flipping the boxes over for use as platforms on which to place objects (e.g., books).

functionalism *n.* a general psychological approach that views mental life and behavior in terms of active adaptation to environmental challenges and opportunities. Functionalism was developed at the beginning of the 20th century as a revolt against the atomistic point of view of STRUCTURALISM, which limited psychology to the dissection of states of consciousness and the study of mental content rather than mental activities. Functionalism emphasizes the causes and consequences of human behavior; the union of the physiological with the psychological; the need for objective testing of theories; and the applications of psychological knowledge to the solution of practical problems, the evolutionary continuity between animals and humans, and the improvement of human life.

functional magnetic resonance imaging (**fMRI; functional MRI**) a form of MAGNETIC RESONANCE IMAGING used to localize areas of cognitive activation, based on the correlation be-

tween brain activity and local changes in blood flow to the brain.

functional neurological symptom disorder see CONVERSION DISORDER.

functional stimulus in stimulus–response experiments, the characteristic of the stimulus that actually produces a particular effect on the organism and governs its behavior. This may be different from the NOMINAL STIMULUS as defined by the experimenter. For example, if an experimenter presents a blue square to a pigeon as a nominal stimulus, the functional stimulus may simply be the color blue. Also called **effective stimulus**.

function word in a language, a word that has little or no meaning of its own but plays an important grammatical role: Examples include the articles (*a, an, the*), prepositions (*in, of*, etc.), and conjunctions (*and, but*, etc.). The distinction between function words and CONTENT WORDS is of great interest to the study of language disorders, language acquisition, and psycholinguistic processing.

fundamental attribution error in ATTRIBUTION THEORY, the tendency to overestimate the degree to which an individual's behavior is determined by his or her abiding personal characteristics, attitudes, or beliefs and, correspondingly, to minimize the influence of the surrounding situation on that behavior (e.g., financial or social pressures). Also called **correspondence bias**. See also ULTIMATE ATTRIBUTION ERROR.

fusiform gyrus a spindle-shaped ridge on the inferior (lower) surface of each TEMPORAL LOBE in the brain. It lies between the inferior temporal gyrus and the PARAHIPPOCAMPAL GYRUS and is involved in high-level visual processing. The **fusiform face area** (**FFA**), for example, is believed to specialize in face recognition. See also OCCIPITAL LOBE.

Gg

GABA$_A$ receptor one of the two main types of receptor protein that bind the neurotransmitter GAMMA-AMINOBUTYRIC ACID (GABA), the other being the GABA$_B$ RECEPTOR. It is located at most synapses of most neurons that use GABA as a neurotransmitter. The predominant inhibitory receptor in the central nervous system, it functions as a chloride channel (see ION CHANNEL).

GABA$_B$ receptor one of the two main types of receptor protein that bind the neurotransmitter GAMMA-AMINOBUTYRIC ACID (GABA), the other being the GABA$_A$ RECEPTOR. GABA$_B$ receptors, which are G PROTEIN-coupled, are less plentiful in the brain than GABA$_A$ receptors, and their activation results in relatively long-lasting neuronal inhibition.

galvanic skin response (GSR) a change in the electrical properties (conductance or resistance) of the skin in reaction to stimuli, owing to the activity of sweat glands located in the fingers and palms. Although strictly an indication of physiological arousal, the galvanic skin response is widely considered a reflection of emotional arousal and stress as well.

gambler's fallacy a failure to recognize the independence of chance events, leading to the mistaken belief that one can predict the outcome of a chance event on the basis of the outcomes of past chance events. For example, a person might think that the more often a tossed coin comes up heads, the more likely it is to come up tails in subsequent tosses, although each coin toss is independent of any other and the true probability of the outcome of any toss is still just .5.

gambling disorder see PATHOLOGICAL GAMBLING.

game *n.* a social interaction, transaction, or other organized activity with formal rules. In psychotherapy, for example, it is a situation in which members of a group take part in some activity designed to elicit emotions or stimulate revealing interactions and interrelationships. In PLAY THERAPY, games are often used as a projective or observational technique. See also ZERO-SUM GAME.

gamete *n.* either of the female or male reproductive cells that take part in fertilization to produce a zygote. In humans and other animals, the female gamete is the OVUM and the male gamete is the SPERMATOZOON. Gametes contain the HAPLOID number of chromosomes rather than the DIPLOID number found in body (somatic) cells. See also GERM CELL.

game theory a branch of mathematics concerned with the analysis of the behavior of decision makers (called players) whose choices affect one another. Game theory is often used in both theoretical modeling and empirical studies of conflict, cooperation, and competition, and it has helped structure interactive decision-making situations in numerous disciplines, including economics, political science, organizational and social psychology, and ethics.

gamma-aminobutyric acid (GABA) a major inhibitory NEUROTRANSMITTER in the mammalian nervous system that is synthesized from the amino acid glutamic acid.

gamma motor neuron see MOTOR NEURON.

gamma movement see APPARENT MOVEMENT.

gamma wave in the brain's electromagnetic field activity, a type of low-amplitude BRAIN WAVE ranging from 25 to 60 Hz (peaking near 40 Hz) that is associated with cognitive activities such as perception and learning. Also called **gamma rhythm**.

ganglion *n.* (*pl.* **ganglia**) a collection of CELL BODIES of neurons that lies outside the central nervous system (the BASAL GANGLIA, however, are an exception). Many invertebrates have only distributed ganglia and no centralized nervous system. Compare NUCLEUS. —**ganglionic** *adj.*

ganglion cell see RETINAL GANGLION CELL.

gap junction a type of intercellular junction consisting of a gap of about 2 to 4 nm between the plasma membranes of two cells, spanned by protein channels that allow passage of electrical signals. See ELECTRICAL SYNAPSE.

garbage in, garbage out (GIGO) an expression indicating that if the data used in analyses are not reliable or coherent, the results will not prove useful. The phrase is used as a reminder to researchers to pay attention to how studies are designed and how data are collected and not to depend on analyses to produce meaningful results when the input data are not themselves meaningful.

gate-control theory the hypothesis that the subjective experience of pain is modulated by large nerve fibers in the spinal cord that act as gates, such that pain is not the product of a simple transmission of stimulation from the skin or some internal organ to the brain. Rather, sensations from noxious stimulation impinging on pain receptors have to pass through these spinal gates to the brain in order to emerge as pain perceptions. The status of the gates, however, is subject to a variety of influences (e.g., drugs, injury, emotions, possibly even instructions coming from the brain itself), which can operate to shut them, thus inhibiting pain transmission, or cause them to be fully open, thus facilitating transmission.

gatekeeper *n.* a health care professional, usually a PRIMARY CARE provider associated with a MANAGED CARE organization, who determines a patient's access to health care services and whose approval is required for referrals to specialists.

gateway drug a substance whose use is thought to promote progression to using more harmful substances. For example, alcohol, tobacco, and cannabis are often considered to be gateways to heroin, cocaine, LSD, or PCP use. Introduced in the 1950s, the concept became the most popular framework for understanding drug use among adolescent populations, guiding prevention efforts and shaping governmental policy. However, research suggests that certain personality traits (e.g., impulsivity), rather than the substances themselves, are more likely to be associated both with early drug use (e.g., of tobacco and alcohol) and with the progression to drugs that have a higher abuse potential.

gating *n.* the automatic inhibition or exclusion from attention of certain sensory stimuli when attention is focused on other stimuli. That is, while one is attending to specific information in the environment, other information does not reach one's awareness.

Gaussian distribution see NORMAL DISTRIBUTION. [Karl Friedrich **Gauss** (1777–1855), German mathematician]

gender *n.* the condition of being male, female, or neuter. In a human context, the distinction between gender and sex reflects the usage of these terms: Sex usually refers to the biological aspects of maleness or femaleness, whereas gender implies the psychological, behavioral, social, and cultural aspects of being male or female (i.e., masculinity or femininity).

gender bias any one of a variety of stereotypical beliefs about individuals on the basis of their sex, particularly as related to the differential treatment of females and males. These biases often are expressed linguistically, as in use of the phrase *physicians and their wives* (instead of *physicians and their spouses*, which avoids the implication that physicians must be male) or of the term *he* when people of both sexes are being discussed.

gender consistency the understanding that one's own and other people's maleness or femaleness is fixed across situations, regardless of superficial changes in appearance or activities.

gender constancy a child's emerging sense of the permanence of being a boy or a girl, an understanding that occurs in a series of stages: GENDER IDENTITY, GENDER STABILITY, and GENDER CONSISTENCY.

gender differences typical differences between men and women that are specific to a particular culture and influenced by its attitudes and practices. Gender differences emerge in a variety of domains, such as careers, communication, and interpersonal relationships. See also SEX DIFFERENCES.

gender dysphoria 1. discontent with the physical or social aspects of one's own sex. **2.** a psychiatric diagnosis that replaces GENDER IDENTITY DISORDER and shifts clinical emphasis from cross-gender identification itself to a focus on the possible distress arising from a sense of mismatch, or incongruence, that one may have about one's experienced gender versus one's assigned gender.

gender identity one's self-identification as male or female. Although the dominant approach in psychology for many years had been to regard gender identity as residing in individuals, the important influence of societal structures, cultural expectations, and personal interactions in its development is now recognized as well. Significant evidence also exists to support the conceptualization of gender identity as influenced by both environmental and biological factors. See

CISGENDER; GENDER CONSTANCY; TRANSGENDER. See also GENDER ROLE.

gender identity discordance a continuing sense that one's anatomical sex is wrong, with a persistent wish to be the other sex. This phrase is sometimes used in place of GENDER IDENTITY DISORDER and TRANSSEXUALISM to avoid connotations of pathology. See also GENDER DYSPHORIA.

gender identity disorder a disorder characterized by clinically significant distress or impairment of functioning due to cross-gender identification (i.e., a desire to be or actual insistence that one is of the other sex) and persistent discomfort arising from the belief that one's sex or gender is inappropriate to one's true self. The disorder is distinguished from simple dissatisfaction or nonconformity with gender roles. See GENDER DYSPHORIA.

gender pay gap the percentage difference between female and male median annual earnings that is thought to result from undervaluing and underpaying work done by women.

gender psychology the exploration of the concepts of masculinity and femininity across cultures and the influence of those concepts on behavior, health, interpersonal relationships, and psychological processes. Although gender psychology originally denoted the analysis of biological sex differences between men and women, the field has grown to encompass the social construction of gender as well. Current topics of study are broad, including within-sex variability, GENDER IDENTITY and GENDER ROLES, sexuality and sexual orientation, gender stereotypes and their origins, and other explorations of men's and women's experiences, attitudes, and attributes.

gender research the study of issues related to the norms and expectations associated with being male or female. Gender research may involve qualitative studies that use focus groups or interviews to understand gendered behavior as well as quantitative analyses that examine potential gender group differences or prediction models. For example, traditional research has assessed whether there are significant group differences between men and women on math and science performance. In recent times, more complex prediction models have been examined to demonstrate that multiple factors (e.g., cultural influences, norms) are needed to understand male and female performance. Gender research also investigates gay, lesbian, and transgender concerns, as well as issues of political equality for women and the LGBTQ community.

gender role the pattern of behavior, personality traits, and attitudes that define masculinity or femininity in a particular culture. It frequently is considered the external manifestation of the internalized GENDER IDENTITY, although the two are not necessarily consistent with one another.

gender schema the organized set of beliefs and expectations that guides one's understanding of maleness and femaleness.

gender stability the understanding that one's own or other people's maleness or femaleness does not change over time. See GENDER CONSTANCY.

gender stereotype a relatively fixed, overly simplified concept of the attitudes and behaviors considered normal and appropriate for a male or female in a particular culture. Gender stereotypes often support the social conditioning of GENDER ROLES.

gender typing expectations about people's behavior that are based on their biological sex, or the process through which individuals acquire and internalize such expectations.

gene *n.* the basic unit of heredity, responsible for storing genetic information and transmitting it to subsequent generations. The observable character-

istics of an organism (i.e., its PHENOTYPE) are determined by numerous genes, which contain the instructions necessary for the functioning of the organism's constituent cells. Each gene consists of a section of DNA, a large and complex molecule that, in higher organisms, is arranged to form the CHROMOSOMES of the cell nucleus. Instructions are contained in the chemical composition of the DNA, according to the GENETIC CODE. In classical genetics, a gene is described in terms of the trait with which it is associated and is investigated largely by virtue of the variations brought about by its different forms, or ALLELES. At the molecular level, most genes encode proteins, which carry out the functions of the cell or act to regulate the expression of other genes.

gene mapping the creation of a schematic representation of the arrangement of genes, genetic markers, or both as they occur in the genetic material of an organism.

general adaptation syndrome (**GAS**) the physiological consequences of severe stress. The syndrome has three stages: alarm, resistance, and exhaustion. The first stage, the **alarm reaction** (or **alarm stage**), comprises two substages: the **shock phase**, marked by a decrease in body temperature, blood pressure, and muscle tone and loss of fluid from body tissues; and the **countershock phase**, during which the sympathetic nervous system is aroused and there is an increase in adrenocortical hormones, triggering a defensive reaction, such as the FIGHT-OR-FLIGHT RESPONSE. The **resistance stage** (or **adaptation stage**) consists of stabilization at the increased physiological levels, possibly resulting in hypertension, cardiovascular disturbance, depleted resources, and permanent organ changes. The **exhaustion stage** is characterized by breakdown of acquired adaptations to a prolonged stressful situation; it is evidenced by such signs as sleep disturbances, irritability, severe loss of concentration, restlessness, trembling that disturbs motor coordination, fatigue, anxiety attacks, and depressed mood.

general factor (symbol: *g*) a hypothetical basic ability that underlies the performance of different varieties of intellectual tasks, in contrast to SPECIFIC FACTORS, which are alleged each to be unique to a single task. The general factor represents individuals' abilities to perceive relationships and to derive conclusions from them.

generalizability *n.* the extent to which results or findings obtained from a sample are applicable to a broader population. For example, a theoretical model of change would be said to have high generalizability if it applied to numerous behaviors (e.g., smoking, diet, substance use, exercise) and varying populations (e.g., young children, teenagers, middle-aged and older adults). A finding that has greater generalizability also is said to have greater EXTERNAL VALIDITY, in that conclusions pertain to situations beyond the original study.

generalization *n.* **1.** the process of deriving a concept, judgment, principle, or theory from a limited number of specific cases and applying it more widely, often to an entire class of objects, events, or people. **2.** in conditioning, see STIMULUS GENERALIZATION. —**generalize** *vb.*

generalized anxiety disorder (**GAD**) excessive anxiety and worry about a range of concerns (e.g., finances, health, work) accompanied by such symptoms as restlessness, fatigue, impaired concentration, irritability, muscle tension, and disturbed sleep.

generalized other in SYMBOLIC INTERACTIONISM, the aggregation of people's viewpoints. It is distinguished from specific other people and their individual views.

generalized seizure a seizure in which abnormal electrical activity involves the entire brain rather than a

specific focal area. The two most common forms are ABSENCE SEIZURES and some TONIC–CLONIC SEIZURES.

general linear model (**GLM**) a large class of statistical techniques, including REGRESSION ANALYSIS, ANALYSIS OF VARIANCE, and CORRELATION ANALYSIS, that describe the relationship between a DEPENDENT VARIABLE and one or more explanatory or INDEPENDENT VARIABLES. Most statistical techniques employed in the behavioral sciences can be subsumed under the general linear model.

General Problem Solver (**GPS**) a computer program so named because its approach to problem solving using MEANS–ENDS ANALYSIS was intended to address many diverse problems and problem types.

general systems theory an interdisciplinary conceptual framework that views an entity or phenomenon holistically as a set of elements interacting with one another (i.e., as a system) and that aims to identify and understand the principles applicable to all systems. According to the theory, the impact of each element in a system depends on the role played by other elements in the system, and order arises from interaction among them. The theory was designed to move beyond the reductionistic and mechanistic tradition in science (see REDUCTIONISM) and to integrate the fragmented approaches and different classes of phenomena studied. Also called **systems theory**.

generation gap the differences in values, morals, attitudes, and behavior apparent between younger and older people in a society. The term was first used with reference to the burgeoning youth culture of the late 1960s.

generative grammar an approach to linguistics in which the goal is to account for the infinite set of possible grammatical sentences in a language using a finite set of generative rules. Unlike earlier inductive approaches that set out to describe and draw inferences about grammar on the basis of a corpus of natural language, the theories of generative grammar that were developed by U.S. linguist Noam Chomsky (1928–) in the 1950s and 1960s took for their basic data the intuitions of native speakers about what is and is not grammatical. In taking this approach, Chomsky revolutionized the whole field of linguistics, effectively redefining it as a branch of COGNITIVE PSYCHOLOGY. Much research in PSYCHOLINGUISTICS has since focused on whether the various models suggested by generative grammar have psychological reality in the production and reception of language. See also PHRASE-STRUCTURE GRAMMAR; TRANSFORMATIONAL GENERATIVE GRAMMAR.

generativity versus stagnation the seventh stage of ERIKSON'S EIGHT STAGES OF PSYCHOSOCIAL DEVELOPMENT. Generativity is the positive goal of middle adulthood, interpreted in terms not only of procreation but also of creativity and fulfilling one's full parental and social responsibilities toward the next generation, in contrast to a narrow interest in the self, or self-absorption. Also called **generativity versus self-absorption**.

gene therapy the insertion of segments of healthy DNA into human body cells to correct defective segments responsible for disease development. A carrier molecule called a vector is used to deliver the therapeutic gene to the patient's target cells, restoring them to a normal state of producing properly functioning proteins. Although experimental, current gene therapy holds significant promise as an effective treatment for a variety of pathological conditions, including neurodegenerative disorders. It is not, however, without its share of challenges and limitations: (a) difficulties integrating therapeutic DNA into the genome and the rapidly dividing nature of many cells have prevented any long-term benefits; (b) if the body's immune system response to foreign objects is triggered, benefits of the therapy may be mitigated; and (c) conditions that arise from mutations in a single gene are the best candidates for gene therapy, yet some of the most commonly occurring disorders (e.g., heart disease, high blood pressure, Alzheimer's disease, arthritis, diabetes) are caused by the combined effects of variations in many genes. There are also ethical, legal, and social concerns associated with the practice. See also GENETIC ENGINEERING.

genetic code the instructions in genes that "tell" the cell how to make specific proteins. The code resides in the sequence of bases occurring as constituents of DNA or RNA. These bases are represented by the letters A, T, G, and C (which stand for adenine, thymine, guanine, and cytosine, respectively). In messenger RNA, uracil (U) replaces thymine. Each unit, or codon, of the code consists of three consecutive bases.

genetic counseling an interactive method of educating a prospective parent about genetic risks, benefits and limitations of genetic testing, reproductive risks, and options for surveillance and screening related to diseases with potentially inherited causes.

genetic determinism the doctrine that human and nonhuman animal behavior and mental activity are largely (or completely) controlled by the genetic constitution of the individual and that responses to environmental influences are for the most part innately determined. See BIOLOGICAL DETERMINISM.

genetic engineering techniques by which the genetic contents of living cells or viruses can be deliberately altered, either by modifying the existing genes or by introducing novel material (e.g., a gene from another species). Genetic engineering is undertaken for many different reasons; for example, there have been attempts to modify defective human body cells in the hope of treating certain genetic diseases. There remains, however, considerable public concern about the risks and limits of genetic engineering.

genetic epistemology a term used by Swiss child psychologist and epistemologist Jean Piaget (1896–1980) to denote his theoretical approach to and experimental study of the development of knowledge.

genetic psychology the study of the development of mental functions in children and their transformation across the lifespan. In the 19th and early 20th centuries, the term was preferred over the synonymous DEVELOPMENTAL PSYCHOLOGY.

genetics *n.* the branch of biology that is concerned with the mechanisms and phenomena of heredity.

genitalia *pl. n.* the reproductive organs of the male or female. The **male genitalia** include the penis, testes and related structures, prostate gland, seminal vesicles, and bulbourethral glands. The **female genitalia** consist of the vulva, vagina, vestibular glands, uterus, ovaries, fallopian tubes, and related structures. The **external genitalia** comprise the vulva (including the clitoris, labia, and vestibule of the vagina) in females and the penis and testicles in males. Also called **genitals**.

genital stage in classical psychoanalytic theory, the final stage of PSYCHOSEXUAL DEVELOPMENT, ideally reached in puberty, when the OEDIPUS COMPLEX has been fully resolved and erotic interest and activity are focused on intercourse with a sexual partner. Also called **genital phase**.

genius *n.* an extreme degree of intellectual or creative ability, or any person who possesses such ability.

genome *n.* all of the genetic material contained in an organism or cell. The HUMAN GENOME PROJECT mapped the estimated 20,000 to 25,000 genes in human DNA.

genotype *n.* the genetic composition of an individual organism as a whole or

at one or more specific positions or loci on a chromosome. Compare PHENOTYPE. **—genotypic** *adj.*

genotype–environment effects the influences of genetic constitution on experience, based on the proposal that an individual's genotype affects which environments he or she encounters and the type of experiences he or she has.

geometric illusion any misinterpretation by the visual system of a figure made of straight or curved lines. Examples of such illusions are the MÜLLER-LYER ILLUSION and the ZÖLLNER ILLUSION.

geon *n.* see RECOGNITION BY COMPONENTS THEORY.

geostatistics *n.* a set of methods for analyzing data related to the physical environment. In psychology, for example, geostatistics could be used to understand which factors in the environment can bring about or exacerbate behavioral conditions, such as substance abuse, or spread diseases, such as AIDS.

geriatric assessment a multidisciplinary evaluation of an older person's medical history as well as current physical and mental health, functional and cognitive abilities, and psychosocial stressors (e.g., loss of spouse) that is used to diagnose and to plan treatment for cognitive, emotional, and social problems that the individual may have.

geriatric neuropsychology an applied subspecialty in neuropsychology addressing the assessment of cognitive dysfunction (e.g., memory loss) in older adults and aimed at improving their functioning and quality of life.

geriatrics *n.* the branch of medicine that deals with the assessment, diagnosis, and treatment of disorders in older adults. **—geriatric** *adj.*

germ cell any of the cells in the gonads that give rise to the GAMETES by a process involving growth and MEIOSIS. See OOGENESIS; SPERMATOGENESIS.

gerontology *n.* the scientific interdisciplinary study of old age and the aging process. —**gerontological** *adj.* —**gerontologist** *n.*

Gerstmann's syndrome a set of four symptoms associated with lesions of a specific area of the (usually left) PARIETAL LOBE. They are inability to recognize one's individual fingers, inability to distinguish between the right and left sides of one's body, inability to perform mathematical calculations, and inability to write. The existence of Gerstmann's syndrome as a true independent entity is subject to debate. [Josef G. **Gerstmann** (1887–1969), Austrian neurologist]

gestalt *n.* an entire perceptual configuration (from German: "shape," "form"), made up of elements that are integrated and interactive in such a way as to confer properties on the whole configuration that are not possessed by the individual elements.

gestalt principles of organization principles of perception, derived by the Gestalt psychologists, that describe the tendency to perceive and interpret certain configurations at the level of the whole rather than in terms of their component features. Some examples include the laws of CLOSURE, GOOD CONTINUATION, and PRÄGNANZ. Also called **gestalt laws of organization**.

Gestalt psychology a psychological approach that focuses on the dynamic organization of experience into patterns or configurations. This view was espoused in the early 20th century as a revolt against STRUCTURALISM, which analyzed experience into static, atomistic sensations, and also against the equally atomistic approach of BEHAVIORISM, which attempted to dissect complex behavior into elementary conditioned reflexes. Gestalt psychology holds instead that experience is an organized whole of which the pieces are

an integral part. Later experiments gave rise to GESTALT PRINCIPLES OF ORGANIZATION, which were then applied to the study of learning, insight, memory, social psychology, and art.

gestalt therapy a form of psychotherapy in which the central focus is on the totality of the client's functioning and relationships in the here and now rather than on investigation of past experiences and developmental history. One of the themes is that growth occurs by assimilation of what is needed from the environment and that psychopathology arises as a disturbance of contact with the environment. Gestalt techniques, which can be applied in either a group or an individual setting, are designed to bring out spontaneous feelings and self-awareness and promote personality growth.

gestation *n.* the development of the embryo and fetus in the uterus until birth. —**gestational** *adj.*

gesture *n.* **1.** a movement, such as the waving of a hand, that communicates a particular meaning or indicates the individual's emotional state or attitude. Gestures can enhance, clarify, or moderate the meaning of verbal communication. **2.** a statement or act, usually symbolic, that is intended to influence the attitudes of others (as in *a gesture of goodwill*). —**gestural** *adj.*

ghrelin *n.* a peptide secreted by endocrine cells in the stomach that binds to growth hormone receptors in the hypothalamus and anterior pituitary, stimulating appetite and the release of growth hormone.

giftedness *n.* the state of possessing a great amount of natural ability, talent, or intelligence, which usually becomes evident at a very young age. Giftedness in intelligence is often categorized as an IQ of two standard deviations above the mean or higher (130 for most IQ tests), obtained on an individually administered IQ test. Many schools and service organizations now use a combination of attributes as the basis for assessing giftedness, including one or more of the following: high intellectual capacity, academic achievement, demonstrable real-world achievement, creativity, task commitment, proven talent, leadership skills, and physical or athletic prowess. —**gifted** *adj.*

gland *n.* an organ that secretes a substance for use by or discharge from the body. EXOCRINE GLANDS release their products through a duct onto internal or external bodily surfaces, whereas ENDOCRINE GLANDS are ductless and secrete their products directly into the bloodstream.

glass ceiling an unofficial, intangible psychological, social, or organizational barrier that prevents able and ambitious individuals, particularly women and members of minority groups, from rising to the highest positions of authority in many organizations.

Glass's *d* an EFFECT SIZE measure that represents the standardized difference between means (i.e., the difference in average values for two samples divided by the STANDARD DEVIATION of the second sample). It is often used in META-ANALYSIS and other research in which it is important to determine whether an effect persists across studies in order to consolidate a result. Also called **Glass's delta**. See also COHEN'S D. [Gene V. **Glass** (1940–), U.S. statistician]

glaucoma *n.* a common eye disease marked by raised intraocular pressure in one or both eyes and, if uncontrolled, severe peripheral visual field loss.

glia *n.* nonneuronal tissue in the nervous system that provides structural, nutritional, and other kinds of support to neurons. It may consist of very small cells (MICROGLIA) or relatively large ones (MACROGLIA). The latter include ASTROCYTES, EPENDYMAL CELLS, and the two types of cells that form the MYELIN SHEATH around axons: OLIGODENDRO-CYTES in the central nervous system and SCHWANN CELLS in the peripheral nervous system. Also called **neuroglia**. —**glial** *adj.*

glioma *n.* a form of brain tumor that develops from support cells (glia) of the central nervous system. There are three main types, grouped according to the form of support cell involved: astrocytoma (from ASTROCYTES), ependymoma (from EPENDYMAL CELLS), and oligodendroglioma (from OLIGODENDROCYTES). Glioma is the most common type of brain cancer and accounts for about a quarter of spinal cord tumors. Also called **neuroglioma**.

globus pallidus one of the BASAL GANGLIA. It is the main output region of the basal ganglia: Its output neurons terminate on thalamic neurons, which in turn project to the cerebral cortex.

glossolalia *n.* utterances that have a phonic similarity to human language but no intelligible semantic content. Glossolalia is found in religious ecstasy ("speaking in tongues") and in hypnotic or mediumistic trances. See also NEOLOGISM; WORD SALAD.

glossopharyngeal nerve the ninth CRANIAL NERVE, which supplies the pharynx, soft palate, and posterior third of the tongue, including the taste buds of that portion. It contains both motor and sensory fibers and is involved in swallowing and conveying taste information.

glucagon *n.* a polypeptide hormone, secreted by the A cells of the ISLETS OF LANGERHANS, that increases the concentration of glucose in the blood. It opposes the effects of INSULIN by promoting the breakdown of glycogen and fat reserves to yield glucose.

glucocorticoid *n.* any CORTICOSTEROID hormone that acts chiefly on carbohydrate metabolism. An example is CORTISOL.

glucoreceptor *n.* any of certain cells in the HYPOTHALAMUS that bind glucose. Glucoreceptors are a putative mechanism for detecting levels of circulating glucose and conveying this information to brain areas.

glucose *n.* a soluble sugar, abundant

in nature, that is a major source of energy for body tissues. The brain relies almost exclusively on glucose for its energy needs. Glucose is derived from the breakdown of carbohydrates, proteins, and—to a much lesser extent—fats. Its concentration in the bloodstream is tightly controlled by the opposing actions of the hormones INSULIN and GLUCAGON.

glucostatic theory the proposition that short-term regulation of food intake is governed by the rate of glucose metabolism (i.e., utilization) rather than by overall blood levels of glucose. See also LIPOSTATIC HYPOTHESIS.

glutamate *n.* a salt or ester of the amino acid glutamic acid that serves as the predominant excitatory NEUROTRANSMITTER in the brain. Glutamate exerts its effects by binding to GLUTAMATE RECEPTORS on neurons and plays a critical role in cognitive, motor, and sensory functions.

glutamate hypothesis the notion that decreased activity of the excitatory neurotransmitter glutamate is responsible for the clinical expression of schizophrenia. The hypothesis developed from observations that administration of NMDA-type glutamate receptor antagonists, such as PCP, produces psychotic symptoms in humans. See also DOPAMINE HYPOTHESIS.

glutamate receptor any of various receptors that bind and respond to the excitatory neurotransmitter glutamate. Glutamate receptors are found on the surface of most neurons. There are two main divisions: IONOTROPIC RECEPTORS and METABOTROPIC RECEPTORS. Ionotropic glutamate receptors are further divided into three classes: **NMDA receptors** (binding the agonist NMDA as well as glutamate), **AMPA receptors** (binding the agonist AMPA as well as glutamate), and **kainate receptors** (binding kainic acid as well as glutamate). Metabotropic glutamate receptors (mGlu or mGluR) are subdivided

into several classes denoted by subscript numbers (i.e., $mGlu_1$, $mGlu_2$, etc.).

glutamatergic *adj.* responding to, releasing, or otherwise involving glutamate. For example, a **glutamatergic neuron** is one that uses glutamate as a neurotransmitter. Also called **glutaminergic**.

glycine *n.* an amino acid that serves as one of the two major inhibitory neurotransmitters in the central nervous system (particularly the spinal cord), the other being GAMMA-AMINOBUTYRIC ACID (GABA). Glycine is also a cotransmitter with glutamate at excitatory NMDA GLUTAMATE RECEPTORS.

gnostic neuron see GRANDMOTHER CELL.

goal setting a process that establishes specific, time-based behavior targets that are measurable, achievable, and realistic. In work-related settings, for example, this practice usually provides employees with both (a) a basis for motivation, in terms of effort expended, and (b) guidelines or cues to behavior that will be required if the goal is to be met.

Golgi apparatus an irregular network of membranes and vesicles within a cell that is responsible for modifying, sorting, and packaging proteins produced within the cell. [Camillo **Golgi** (1843–1926), Italian histologist]

Golgi tendon organ a receptor in muscle tendons that sends impulses to the central nervous system when a muscle contracts. [Camillo **Golgi**]

gonad *n.* either of the primary male and female sex organs—that is, the TESTIS or the OVARY, respectively. —**gonadal** *adj.*

gonadotropin *n.* any of several hormones that stimulate functions of the gonads. Gonadotropins include FOLLICLE-STIMULATING HORMONE and LUTEINIZING HORMONE, which are produced by the anterior pituitary gland, and chorionic gonadotropin, which is produced by the placenta. **—gonado-tropic** *adj.*

gonadotropin-releasing hormone (GnRH) a hormone secreted by neurons of the hypothalamus that controls the release of LUTEINIZING HORMONE and FOLLICLE-STIMULATING HORMONE from the anterior pituitary gland.

good continuation one of the GESTALT PRINCIPLES OF ORGANIZATION. It states that people tend to perceive objects in alignment as forming smooth, unbroken contours. For example, when two lines meet in a figure, the preferred interpretation is of two continuous lines: A cross is interpreted as a vertical line and a horizontal line rather than as two right angles meeting at their vertices. Also called **law** (or **principle**) **of continuity**; **law** (or **principle**) **of good continuation**.

good death an end of life that is in accordance with the dying person's values and is consistent with his or her wishes with regard to medical and surgical interventions; life-support technology (e.g., ventilation, feeding tube); pain management and alleviation of suffering; location where he or she wants to die (e.g., home, hospice, hospital); and emotional, spiritual, religious, or other available support prior to and during the dying process.

goodness of fit the degree to which values predicted by a model agree with empirically observed values. For example, a researcher may wish to assess whether a pattern of frequencies from a study is the same as theoretically expected, whether two CATEGORICAL VARIABLES are independent, or whether a REGRESSION EQUATION correctly predicts obtained data. A small, nonsignificant value from a statistical **goodness-of-fit test** indicates a well-fitting model.

G protein any of a class of proteins that are coupled to the intracellular portion of a type of membrane RECEPTOR (**G-protein-coupled receptor**) and are activated when the receptor binds an appropriate ligand (e.g., a neurotransmitter) on the extracellular surface. G proteins thus have a role in signal transduction, serving to transmit the signal from the receptor to other cell components (e.g., ion channels) in various ways, such as by controlling the synthesis of SECOND MESSENGERS within the cell.

graded potential any change in electric potential of a neuron that is not propagated along the cell (as is an ACTION POTENTIAL) but declines with distance from the source. RECEPTOR POTENTIALS are an example.

gradient *n.* **1.** the slope of a line or surface. **2.** a measure of the change of a physical quantity (e.g., temperature). **3.** a graduated change in the strength of a DRIVE resulting from a change in the environment, such as time interval or distance from a situation.

gradual withdrawal see TAPERING.

graduated and reciprocated initiatives in tension reduction (GRIT) an approach to intergroup conflict reduction that encourages the parties to communicate cooperative intentions, engage in behaviors that are consistent with these intentions, and initiate cooperative responses even in the face of competition. GRIT is usually recommended when disputants have a prolonged history of conflict, misunderstanding, misperception, and hostility.

grammar *n.* in linguistics, an abstract system of rules that describes how a language works. Although it is traditionally held to consist of SYNTAX (rules for arranging words in sentences) and MORPHOLOGY (rules affecting the form taken by individual words), PHONOLOGY and SEMANTICS are also included in some modern systems of grammar. **—grammatical** *adj.*

grand mal seizure see TONIC–CLONIC SEIZURE.

grand mean a numerical average (MEAN) of a group of averages. For example, if an ANALYSIS OF VARIANCE reveals average values of 3, 10, and 20 on a response or DEPENDENT VARIABLE for three groups of study participants, the grand mean of scores—that is, the average of all participants' responses regardless of the condition of the INDE-PENDENT VARIABLES—is $(3 + 10 + 20)/3 = 11$.

grandmother cell any hypothetical neuron in the visual system that is stimulated only by a single highly complex and meaningful stimulus, such as a particular individual (e.g., one's grandmother) or a particular well-known object (e.g., the Sydney Opera House). It is an extension of the FEATURE DETECTOR concept to a degree that has been dismissed by many as overly simplistic and untenable, although recent research has provided support for the concept by revealing a much higher degree of neuronal specificity than previously believed. Also called **gnostic neuron**.

granule cell a type of small, grainlike neuron found in certain layers of the cerebral cortex and cerebellar cortex.

granulocyte *n.* see LEUKOCYTE.

graph *n.* a visual representation of the relationship between numbers or quantities that are plotted on a drawing with reference to axes at right angles (the horizontal x-axis and the vertical y-axis) and linked by lines, dots, or the like. BAR GRAPHS and HISTOGRAMS are commonly used examples.

grapheme *n.* a minimal meaningful unit in the writing system of a particular language. It is usually a letter or fixed combination of letters corresponding to a PHONEME in that language. —**graphemic** *adj.*

graphology *n.* the study of the physical characteristics of handwriting, particularly as a means of inferring the writer's psychological state or personality characteristics. Graphology is based on the premise that writing is a form of

expressive behavior, but there is little empirical evidence for its validity. Also called **handwriting analysis**. —**graphological** *adj.* —**graphologist** *n.*

grasp reflex an involuntary grasping by an individual of anything that touches the palm. This reflex is typical of infants, but in older individuals, it may be a sign of FRONTAL LOBE damage or disease.

gravida *n.* a pregnant woman. The use of a Roman numeral after the term indicates the number of pregnancies a particular woman has undergone (e.g., **gravida IV** indicates a woman in her fourth pregnancy). In contrast, the term **gravid** (*adj.*) is used primarily to describe an egg-laying organism, usually a fish or reptile, when it is carrying eggs.

gray matter any area of neural tissue that is dominated by CELL BODIES and is devoid of myelin, such as the CEREBRAL CORTEX. Compare WHITE MATTER.

great man theory a view of political leadership and historical causation that assumes that history is driven by a small number of exceptional individuals (traditionally presumed to be men) with certain innate characteristics that predispose them for greatness. A ZEITGEIST (spirit of the times) view of history, in contrast, supposes that history is largely determined by economics, technological development, and a broad spectrum of social influences.

grief *n.* the anguish experienced after significant loss, usually the death of a beloved person. Grief is often distinguished from BEREAVEMENT and MOURNING. Not all bereavements result in a strong grief response, and not all grief is given public expression (see DISENFRANCHISED GRIEF). Grief often includes physiological distress, separation anxiety, confusion, yearning, obsessive dwelling on the past, and apprehension about the future.

grief counseling the provision of advice, information, and psychological support to help individuals whose ability to function has been impaired by someone's death, particularly that of a loved one or friend. It includes counseling for the grieving process and practical advice concerning arrangements for the funeral and burial of the loved one. Grief counseling is sometimes offered by staff in specialized agencies (e.g., hospices), or it may be carried out in the context of other counseling.

grief work (griefwork) the theoretical process through which bereaved people gradually reduce or transform their emotional connection to the person who has died and thereby refocus appropriately on their own ongoing lives. Grief work has in recent years revolved around the notion of a "continuing bond." That is, the bereaved does not sever all emotional connections with the deceased but instead transforms the relationship symbolically as an ongoing bond that provides a sense of meaning and value that is conducive to forming new relationships.

grit *n.* a personality trait characterized by perseverance and passion for achieving long-term goals. Grit entails working strenuously to overcome challenges and maintaining effort and interest over time despite failures, adversities, and plateaus in progress.

grooming *n.* **1.** a basic function of self-care that includes maintaining one's body, hair, clothes, and general appearance. Reacquiring grooming skills that have been lost or compromised due to mental or physical impairment is a central aspect of many rehabilitation programs. **2.** behavior in which a nonhuman animal picks through its own or another animal's hair, fur, or feathers. Whereas the main function of self-grooming is hygienic (i.e., to remove dirt and parasites), the grooming of other members of an animal's group may serve both hygienic and social functions. See ALLO-GROOMING.

gross motor describing activities or skills that use large muscles to move the trunk or limbs and control posture to maintain balance. Examples of **gross motor skills** include waving an arm, walking, hopping, and running. Compare FINE MOTOR.

ground *n.* the relatively homogeneous and indistinct background of FIGURE–GROUND perceptions.

grounded theory a set of procedures for the systematic analysis of unstructured QUALITATIVE data so as to derive by INDUCTION a supposition that explains the observed phenomena.

group *n.* any collection or assemblage, particularly of items or individuals. For example, in social psychology the term refers to two or more interdependent individuals who influence one another through social interactions involving roles and norms, a degree of cohesiveness, and shared goals. In research, a group denotes a collection of participants who all experience the same experimental conditions and whose responses are to be compared to the responses of one or more other collections of research participants.

group cohesion the unity or solidarity of a group, including the integration of the group for both social and task-related purposes. Group cohesion is indicated by the strength of the bonds that link members to the group as a whole, the sense of belongingness and community within the group, the feelings of attraction for specific group members and for the group itself, and the degree to which members coordinate their efforts to achieve goals. Group cohesion frequently is considered essential to effective GROUP THERAPY.

group-comparison design a type of research approach that investigates potential differences across sets of individuals who are often randomly assigned to a CONTROL condition or to one or more specific EXPERIMENTAL CONDITIONS. Also called **group-difference design**.

group contagion see SOCIAL CONTAGION.

group dynamics 1. the processes, operations, and changes that occur within social groups, which affect patterns of affiliation, communication, conflict, conformity, decision making, influence, leadership, norm formation, and power. **2.** the field of psychology devoted to the study of groups and group processes.

grouped data information that is grouped into one or more sets in order to analyze, describe, or compare outcomes at a combined level rather than at an individual level. For example, data from a FREQUENCY DISTRIBUTION may be arranged into CLASS INTERVALS. See also GROUP-COMPARISON DESIGN.

group effect a research finding specific to the group of individuals to which a participant belongs. For example, a researcher might be interested in a group effect of a specific reading intervention, or in a group effect of book reading for students in the current decade who may be reading less than previous sets of students owing to the greater use of the computer and television.

group identity 1. the image of a group (e.g., reputation, appraisal, expectations about) held by its members or by those external to the group. **2.** an individual's sense of self as defined by group membership. See SOCIAL IDENTITY.

grouping *n.* in statistics, the process of arranging scores in categories, intervals, classes, or ranks.

group interview an interview in which one or more questioners elicit information from two or more respondents in an experimental or real-life situation. The participation and interaction of a number of people, particu-

larly if they are acquainted with each other as members of a club or similar group, is believed to yield more informative responses than are typically obtained by interviewing individuals separately.

group mind a hypothetical explanation for the apparent uniformity of individuals' emotional, cognitive, and behavioral reactions when in large crowds and collectives; it supposes that a crowd of people can, in certain instances, become a unified entity that acts as if guided by a single consciousness created by the fusion of the individual minds in a collective. This controversial idea assumes that the group mind is greater than the sum of the psychological experiences of the individuals and that it can become so powerful that it can overwhelm the will of the individual.

group norm see SOCIAL NORM.

group polarization the tendency for members of a group discussing an issue to move toward a more extreme version of the positions they held before the discussion began. As a result, the group as a whole tends to respond in more extreme ways than one would expect, given the sentiments of the individual members prior to deliberation.

group process the interpersonal component of a group session, in contrast to the content (such as decisions or information) generated during the session.

group-serving bias any one of a number of cognitive tendencies that contribute to an overvaluing of one's group, particularly the tendency to credit the group for its successes but to blame external factors for its failures. Compare SELF-SERVING BIAS. See also ULTIMATE ATTRIBUTION ERROR.

group socialization theory a theory of personality development proposing that children are primarily socialized by their peers and that the influences of parents and teachers are filtered through children's peer groups. According to this theory, children seek to be like their peers rather than like their parents.

group therapy treatment of psychological problems in which two or more participants interact with each other on both an emotional and a cognitive level in the presence of one or more psychotherapists who serve as catalysts, facilitators, or interpreters. The approaches vary, but in general they aim to provide an environment in which problems and concerns can be shared in an atmosphere of mutual respect and understanding. Group therapy seeks to enhance self-respect, deepen self-understanding, and improve interpersonal relationships. Also called **group psychotherapy**. Compare INDIVIDUAL THERAPY.

groupthink *n.* a strong concurrence-seeking tendency that interferes with effective group decision making. Symptoms include apparent unanimity, illusions of invulnerability and moral correctness, biased perceptions of the OUTGROUP, interpersonal pressure, and self-censorship.

growth spurt any period of accelerated physical development, especially the pubescent growth spurt.

guided imagery a mind–body technique involving the deliberate prompting of mental images to induce a relaxed, focused state with the goal of achieving such varied purposes as managing stress or pain, promoting healing, or enhancing performance.

guided participation a process in which the influences of social partners and sociocultural practices combine in various ways to provide children and other learners with direction and support, while the learners themselves also shape their learning engagements. It occurs not only during explicit instruction but also during routine activities

and communication in everyday life. See SOCIOCULTURAL PERSPECTIVE.

guiding fiction a personal principle that serves as a guideline by which individuals can understand and evaluate their experiences and determine their lifestyle (e.g., hard work equals success). In individuals considered to be in good or reasonable mental health, the guiding fiction is assumed to be realistic and adaptive. In those who are not, it is assumed to be unrealistic and nonadaptive.

guilt *n.* a SELF-CONSCIOUS EMOTION characterized by a painful appraisal of having done (or thought) something that is wrong and often by a readiness to take action designed to undo or mitigate this wrong. It is distinct from SHAME, in which there is the additional strong fear of one's deeds being publicly exposed to judgment or ridicule. —**guilty** *adj.*

guilty but mentally ill (**GBMI**) a court judgment that may be made in some states when defendants plead INSANITY. Defendants found guilty but mentally ill are treated in a mental hospital until their mental health is restored; they then serve the remainder of their sentence in the appropriate correctional facility.

gustation *n.* see TASTE. —**gustatory** *adj.*

gustatory encoding see VISUAL ENCODING.

gustatory system the primary structures and processes involved in an organism's detection of and responses to taste stimuli. The gustatory system includes lingual papillae, TASTE BUDS and TASTE CELLS, taste TRANSDUCTION, neural impulses and pathways, and associated brain areas and their functions (see TASTE CORTEX; SOLITARY NUCLEUS).

gyrus *n.* (*pl.* **gyri**) a ridged or raised portion of the cerebral cortex, bounded on either side by a SULCUS.

Hh

habilitation *n.* the process of enhancing the independence, well-being, and level of functioning of an individual with a disability or disorder by providing appropriate resources, such as treatment or training, to enable that person to develop skills and abilities he or she had not had the opportunity to acquire previously. The term is often used specifically to refer to the functional training of children with congenital disabilities, such as congenital visual impairment. Compare REHABILITATION.

habit *n.* a well-learned behavior or automatic sequence of behaviors that is relatively situation specific and over time has become motorically reflexive and independent of motivational or cognitive influence—that is, it is performed with little or no conscious intent. —**habitual** *adj.*

habituation *n.* **1.** the diminished effectiveness of a stimulus in eliciting a response, following repeated exposure to the stimulus. Compare DISHABITUATION. **2.** the process of becoming psychologically dependent on the use of a particular drug, such as cocaine, but without the increasing tolerance and physiological dependence that are characteristic of addiction; the preferred term is PSYCHOLOGICAL DEPENDENCE.

hair cell 1. any of the sensory receptors for hearing, located in the ORGAN OF CORTI within the cochlea of the inner ear. They respond to vibrations of the BASILAR MEMBRANE via movement of the fine hairlike structures (**stereocilia**) that protrude from them. **2.** any of the sensory receptors for balance, similar in structure to the cochlear hair cells. They are located in the inner ear within the ampullae of the SEMICIRCULAR CANALS (forming part of the CRISTA) and within the SACCULE and UTRICLE (forming part of the MACULA).

half-life (symbol: $t_{1/2}$) *n.* in pharmacokinetics, the time necessary for the concentration of an administered drug in the blood to fall by 50%. Clinically, half-life varies among individuals as a result of age, disease states, or concurrent administration of other drugs.

halfway house a transitional living arrangement for people, such as individuals recovering from alcohol or substance abuse, who have completed treatment at a hospital or rehabilitation center but still require support to assist them in restructuring their lives.

hallucination *n.* a false sensory perception that has a compelling sense of reality despite the absence of an external stimulus. It may affect any of the senses, but AUDITORY HALLUCINATIONS and VISUAL HALLUCINATIONS are most common. Hallucinations are typically a symptom of a PSYCHOTIC DISORDER, particularly schizophrenia, but also may result from substance use, neurological abnormalities, and other conditions. It is important to distinguish hallucinations from ILLUSIONS, which are misinterpretations of real sensory stimuli.

hallucinogen *n.* a substance capable of producing a sensory effect (visual, auditory, olfactory, gustatory, or tactile) in the absence of an actual stimulus. Because they produce alterations in perception, cognition, and mood, hallucinogens are also called **psychedelic drugs** or **psychedelics** (from the Greek, meaning "mind-manifesting"). —**hallucinogenic** *adj.*

hallucinosis *n.* a pathological condition characterized by prominent and persistent hallucinations without alterations of consciousness, particularly when caused by the direct physiological effects of a substance or associated with neurological factors.

halo effect a rating bias in which a general evaluation (usually positive) of a person, or an evaluation of a person on a specific dimension, influences judgments of that person on other specific dimensions. For example, a person who is generally liked might be judged as more intelligent, competent, and honest than he or she actually is.

handedness *n.* the consistent use of one hand rather than the other in performing certain tasks. The preference usually is related to a DOMINANCE effect of the MOTOR CORTEX on the opposite side of the body. See LATERALITY.

handicap *n.* any disadvantage or characteristic that limits or prevents a person from performing various physical, cognitive, or social tasks or from fulfilling particular roles within society. For example, a nonaccessible building entry or exit for a person in a wheelchair would be considered a handicap, as would the person's inability to walk. The term generally is considered pejorative, and its use has fallen into disfavor. See also DISABILITY. —**handicapped** *adj.*

handwriting analysis see GRAPHOLOGY.

haploid *adj.* describing a nucleus, cell, or organism that possesses only one representative of each chromosome, as in a sperm or egg cell. In most organisms, including humans, fusion of the haploid sex cells following fertilization restores the normal DIPLOID condition of body cells, in which the chromosomes occur in pairs. Hence for humans, the **haploid number** is 23 chromosomes, which is half the full complement of 46 chromosomes.

happiness *n.* an emotion of joy, gladness, satisfaction, and well-being. —**happy** *adj.*

haptic *adj.* relating to the sense of touch and the cutaneous sensory system in general. It typically refers to active touch, in which the individual intentionally seeks sensory stimulation, moving the limbs to gain information about an object or surface.

hard determinism the doctrine that human actions and choices are causally determined by forces and influences over which a person exercises no meaningful control. The term can also be applied to nonhuman events, implying that all things must be as they are and could not possibly be otherwise. Compare SOFT DETERMINISM.

hardiness *n.* an ability to adapt easily to unexpected changes combined with a sense of purpose in daily life and of personal control over what occurs in one's life. Hardiness dampens the negative effects of stress and can be a PROTECTIVE FACTOR against illness. —**hardy** *adj.*

harmonic mean a measure of CENTRAL TENDENCY. It is computed for *n* scores by dividing the scores by the sum of their RECIPROCALS; that is, *n* divided by the sum of $1/x_1 + 1/x_2 + 1/x_n$.

harm reduction an approach designed to reduce the adverse effects of risky behaviors (e.g., alcohol use, drug use, indiscriminate sexual activity), rather than to eliminate the behaviors altogether. Programs focused on alcohol use, for example, do not advocate abstinence but attempt instead to teach people to anticipate the hazards of heavy drinking and learn to drink safely.

hashish *n.* the most potent CANNABIS preparation. It contains the highest concentration of delta-9-TETRAHYDRO-CANNABINOL (THC) because it consists largely of pure resin from one of the species of the *Cannabis* plant from which it is derived.

Hawthorne effect the effect on the behavior of individuals of knowing that they are being observed or are taking part in research. The Hawthorne effect is typically positive and is named after the Western Electric Company's Hawthorne Works plant in Cicero, Illinois, where the phenomenon was first observed during a series of studies on worker productivity conducted from 1924 to 1932. These **Hawthorne Studies** evolved into a much wider consideration of the role of worker attitudes, supervisory style, and GROUP DYNAMICS.

hazing *n.* the initiation of new members into a group by subjecting them to rituals that involve mental or physical discomfort, harassment, embarrassment, ridicule, or humiliation.

health *n.* the condition of one's mind, body, and spirit, the ideal being freedom from illness, injury, pain, and distress.

health–belief model a model that identifies the relationships of the following factors to the likelihood of taking preventive health action: (a) individual perceptions about susceptibility to and seriousness of a disease, (b) sociodemographic variables, (c) environmental cues, and (d) perceptions of the benefits and costs.

health care proxy see ADVANCE DIRECTIVE.

health care psychology see HEALTH PSYCHOLOGY.

health maintenance organization see HMO.

health promotion education, wellness programs, public policies, fiscal measures, legislation, or other coordinated actions that aim to give people more control over their physical and mental health, with the goal of improving their overall health and well-being.

health psychology the subfield of psychology that focuses on (a) the examination of the relationships between behavioral, cognitive, psychophysiological, and social and environmental factors and the establishment, maintenance, and detriment of health; (b) the integration of psychological and biological research findings in the design of empirically based interventions for the prevention and treatment of illness; and (c) the evaluation of physical and psychological status before, during, and after medical and psychological treatment. Also called **health care psychology**.

hearing loss the inability to hear a normal range of tone frequencies, a normally perceived level of sound intensity, or both.

Hebbian synapse a junction between neurons that is strengthened when it successfully fires the POSTSYNAPTIC cell. See DUAL TRACE HYPOTHESIS. [Donald O. **Hebb** (1904–1985), Canadian psychobiologist]

hebephrenia *n.* see DISORGANIZED SCHIZOPHRENIA.

hedonics *n.* the branch of psychology concerned with the study of pleasant and unpleasant sensations and thoughts, especially in terms of their role in human motivation.

hedonism *n.* **1.** in philosophy, the doctrine that pleasure is an intrinsic good and the proper goal of all human action. One of the fundamental questions of ethics has been whether pleasure can or should be equated with the good in this way. **2.** in psychology, any theory that suggests that pleasure and the avoidance of pain are the only or the major motivating forces in human behavior. Hedonism is a foundational principle in psychoanalysis, in behaviorism, and in theories that stress self-actualization and need fulfillment. —**hedonistic** *adj.*

helping *n.* a type of PROSOCIAL behavior in which one or more individuals act to improve the status or well-being of one or more others. Although helping behavior is typically in response to a minor request that involves little individual risk, all helping behavior incurs some cost to the individual providing it. See also ALTRUISM.

helplessness theory see LEARNED HELPLESSNESS.

hemianopia (hemianopsia; hemiopia) *n.* loss of vision in half the normal visual field. Hemianopia may result from a lesion in the OPTIC CHIASM or the OPTIC RADIATIONS. —**hemianopic** or **hemianoptic** adj.

hemineglect n. see UNILATERAL NEGLECT.

hemiplegia n. complete paralysis that affects one side of the body, most often as a result of a stroke. —**hemiplegic** adj.

hemispatial neglect see UNILATERAL NEGLECT.

hemisphere n. either of the symmetrical halves of the cerebrum (see CEREBRAL HEMISPHERE) or the CEREBELLUM. —**hemispheric** or **hemispherical** adj.

hemispherectomy n. surgical removal of either one of the cerebral hemispheres of the brain, most often the nondominant hemisphere for treatment of intractable epilepsy.

hemispheric asymmetry the idea that the two cerebral hemispheres of the brain are not identical but differ in size, shape, and function. The functions that display the most pronounced asymmetry are language processing in the left hemisphere and visuospatial processing in the right hemisphere.

hemispheric lateralization the processes whereby some functions, such as manual dexterity or speech production, are controlled or influenced more by one cerebral hemisphere than the other. Researchers now prefer to speak of hemispheric lateralization or **hemispheric specialization** for particular functions, rather than hemispheric or lateral DOMINANCE. Also called **cerebral lateralization**.

hemorrhage n. bleeding: any loss of blood from an artery or vein. A hemorrhage may be external, internal, or within a tissue, such as the skin. Brain hemorrhages may arise from head injuries or ANEURYSMS, causing widespread damage in some cases. —**hemorrhagic** adj.

hereditarianism n. the view that genetic inheritance is the major influence on behavior. Opposed to this view is ENVIRONMENTALISM, the belief that environmental influences and learning account for the major differences between people. See also GENETIC DETERMINISM; NATURE–NURTURE. —**hereditarian** adj.

heredity n. the transmission of traits from parents to their offspring. Study of the mechanisms and laws of heredity is the basis of the science of GENETICS. Heredity depends on the character of the genes contained in the parents' CHROMOSOMES, which in turn depends on the particular GENETIC CODE carried by chromosomal DNA.

Hering theory of color vision a theory of color vision postulating that there are three sets of receptors, one of which is sensitive to white and black, another to red and green, and the third to yellow and blue. The breaking down (catabolism) of the receptors' photopigments is supposed to yield one member of these pairs (white, red, or yellow), whereas the building up (anabolism) of the same pigments yields the other (black, green, or blue). See OPPONENT PROCESS THEORY OF COLOR VISION. [proposed in 1875 by Ewald **Hering** (1834–1918), German physiologist]

heritability n. a statistical estimate of the contribution of inheritance to a given trait or function in a population (but not in particular individuals). Heritabilities can range from 0, indicating no contribution of heritable factors, to 1, indicating total contribution of heritable factors.

heritage n. any cultural tradition, custom, or resource passed from preceding to successive generations.

hermaphroditism n. the condition of possessing both male and female sex organs (in humans, e.g., possessing both ovarian and testicular tissue). Hermaphroditism is very rare and should not be confused with the more common PSEUDOHERMAPHRODITISM, in which the gonads are of one sex but the external genitalia are either ambiguous or of the other sex. See also INTERSEX. —**hermaphrodite** n.

hermeneutics n. the theory or science of interpretation. Hermeneutics is concerned with the ways in which humans derive meaning from language or other symbolic expression. Two main strains of hermeneutic thought have developed. In the first, a key concept is the need to gain insight into the mind of the person or people whose expression is the subject of interpretation. In the second, more radical, strain of hermeneutics, the project of interpretation has been expanded to include the human being itself. This suggests that all human behavior can be understood as meaningful expression, much as one would understand a written text. This shift has given rise to a broad movement within philosophy, psychology, and literary criticism in which richness of interpretation is considered more valuable than consistent methodology or arriving at the "correct" interpretation. This type of hermeneutics has also informed other contemporary movements, notably EXISTENTIALISM, POSTMODERNISM, and POSTSTRUCTURALISM. —**hermeneutic** adj.

heroin n. a highly addictive OPIOID that is a synthetic analog of MORPHINE and three times more potent. In many countries, it is used clinically for pain management, but it is not legally available in the United States because of concerns about its potential for abuse. Its rapid onset of action leads to an intense initial high, followed by a period of euphoria and a sense of well-being.

hertz (symbol: Hz) n. the unit of FREQUENCY equal to one cycle per second. [Heinrich Rudolf **Hertz** (1857–1894), German physicist]

Heschl's gyrus one of several transverse ridges on the upper side of the TEMPORAL LOBE of the brain that are associated with the sense of hearing. [Richard **Heschl** (1824–1881), Austrian pathologist who first traced the auditory pathways of humans to this convolution]

heterogamy n. a marriage between partners from dissimilar ethnic, racial, religious, educational, or socioeconomic backgrounds. Compare HOMOGAMY. —**heterogamous** adj.

heterogeneity of variance the situation in which the variance of a random variable is different at each level or value of another variable; that is, the variance in y is a function of the variable x. Heterogeneity of variance violates one of the basic assumptions of REGRESSION ANALYSIS and other statistical procedures. Also called **heteroscedasticity**. Compare HOMOGENEITY OF VARIANCE.

heterogeneous adj. composed of diverse elements. Compare HOMOGENEOUS. —**heterogeneity** n.

heteronomous stage in the theory of moral development proposed by Swiss child psychologist and epistemologist Jean Piaget (1896–1980), the stage during which the child, at approximately 6 to 10 years of age, equates morality with the rules and principles of his or her parents and other authority figures. That is, the child evaluates the rightness or wrongness of an act only in terms of adult sanctions for or against it and of the consequences or possible punishment it may bring. Also called **heteronomous morality**. Compare AUTONOMOUS STAGE; PREMORAL STAGE.

heteronormativity n. the assumption that heterosexuality is the standard for defining normal sexual behavior and that male–female differences and gender roles are the natural and immutable essentials in normal human relations. According to some social theorists, this assumption is fundamentally embedded in, and legitimizes, social and legal institutions that devalue, marginalize, and discriminate against people who deviate from its normative principle (e.g., gay men, lesbians, bisexuals, transgendered persons, and questioning persons).

heterophily *n.* any tendency to make social connections by individuals who differ from one another in some way. It is less common than HOMOPHILY. Complementarity, which occurs when people with different but complementary characteristics form a relationship, is an example of heterophily.

heteroscedasticity *n.* see HETEROGENEITY OF VARIANCE. —**heteroscedastic** *adj.*

heterosexuality *n.* sexual attraction to or activity between members of the opposite sex. —**heterosexual** *adj.*

heterozygous *adj.* possessing different forms of a gene (i.e., different ALLELES) at a given genetic locus on each of a pair of HOMOLOGOUS chromosomes. Compare HOMOZYGOUS. —**heterozygote** *n.*

heuristic *n.* **1.** in cognition, an experience-based strategy for solving a problem or making a decision that often provides an efficient means of finding an answer but cannot guarantee a correct outcome. By contrast, an ALGORITHM guarantees a solution but may be much less efficient. Some heuristics, such as the AVAILABILITY HEURISTIC or REPRESENTATIVENESS HEURISTIC, involve systematic bias. **2.** in the social sciences, a conceptual device, such as a model or working hypothesis, that is intended to explore or limit the possibilities of a question rather than to provide an explanation of the facts.

heuristic-systematic model (**HSM**) a theory of persuasion postulating that the validity of a persuasive message can be assessed in two different ways. **Systematic processing** involves the careful scrutiny of the merits of attitude-relevant information in the message. **Heuristic processing** involves the use of a subset of information in the message as a basis for implementing a simple decision rule to determine if the message should be ac-

cepted (e.g., judging a message to be valid because its source is highly credible).

hidden observer an intrapsychic entity with awareness of experiences that occur outside of an individual's consciousness, hypothesized to explain the dissociative phenomenon in which a hypnotized person who has been told to block certain stimuli (e.g., pain induced by ice-cold water) still registers the sensation yet denies experiencing it. It is as if a dissociated observer is registering the stimuli that the hypnotized person has successfully blocked. See also NEODISSOCIATION THEORY.

hierarchical linear model (**HLM**) a statistical model that acknowledges different levels in the data, such that individuals or entities within each level have correlated scores. Hierarchical linear models are often used in educational research because they can account for the fact that students within a classroom will behave similarly, as will classrooms within the same school, and so on up the hierarchy of levels. Also called **multilevel model**.

hierarchical model a statistical procedure that takes into account situations in which lower level variables or entities are part of a larger set or sets. For example, a hierarchical FACTOR ANALYSIS model posits that relationships among a subset of lower level primary variables (e.g., verbal, mathematical, and social intelligence) can be explained by a higher order or general factor (e.g., general intelligence). Also called **nested model**.

hierarchy *n.* a clear ordering of individuals or phenomena on some dimension. For example, in neuroscience, there is a hierarchy of organization of control systems such that one area of the brain controls another, which in turn may control a specific type of action. See also MASLOW'S MOTIVATIONAL HIERARCHY.

hierarchy of motives (**hierarchy**

of needs) see MASLOW'S MOTIVATIONAL HIERARCHY.

higher mental process any of the more complex types of cognition, such as analytical thinking, judgment, imagination, memory, and language.

higher order conditioning in CLASSICAL CONDITIONING, a procedure in which the CONDITIONED STIMULUS of one experiment acts as the UNCONDITIONED STIMULUS of another, for the purpose of conditioning a NEUTRAL STIMULUS. For example, after pairing a tone with food, and establishing the tone as a conditioned stimulus that elicits salivation, a light could be paired with the tone. If the light alone comes to elicit salivation, then higher order conditioning has occurred.

higher order correlation see PARTIAL CORRELATION.

higher order interaction in an ANALYSIS OF VARIANCE, the joint effect of three or more independent variables on the dependent variable. For example, a researcher could conduct a study to assess the effect of a particular treatment (e.g., treatment vs. no treatment) as well as the effect of education level and socioeconomic status on cognitive functioning. This design would allow an examination of the MAIN EFFECTS for treatment, education, and socioeconomic status individually; the two-way interactions between treatment and education, education and socioeconomic status, and treatment and socioeconomic status; and the higher order three-way interaction among treatment, education, and socioeconomic status.

higher order processes see EXECUTIVE FUNCTIONS.

high risk significantly heightened vulnerability to a disorder or disease. An individual's risk status is influenced by genetic, physical, and behavioral factors or conditions. For example, children of a parent with bipolar disorder have a much greater risk of developing the disorder than other children, and individuals who engage in unprotected sex are at high risk of contracting HIV and other sexually transmitted diseases.

hindbrain *n.* the posterior of three bulges that appear in the embryonic brain as it develops from the NEURAL TUBE. The bulge eventually becomes the MEDULLA OBLONGATA, PONS, and CEREBELLUM. Also called **rhombencephalon**.

hindsight bias the tendency, after an event has occurred, to overestimate the extent to which the outcome could have been foreseen. Hindsight bias stems from (a) cognitive inputs—people selectively recall information consistent with what they now know to be true; (b) metacognitive inputs—people may misattribute their ease of understanding an outcome to its assumed prior likelihood; and (c) motivational inputs—people have a need to see the world as orderly and predictable.

hinge *n.* either of the scores in a data set that divide the lower 25% of cases (the lower hinge) and the upper 25% of cases (the upper hinge) from the remainder of the cases.

hippocampus *n.* (*pl.* **hippocampi**) a seahorse-shaped part of the forebrain, in the basal medial region of the TEMPORAL LOBE, that is implicated in DECLARATIVE MEMORY and learning. —**hippocampal** *adj.*

histogram *n.* a graphical depiction of continuous data using bars of varying height, similar to a BAR GRAPH but with blocks on the *x*-axis adjoining one another so as to denote their continuous nature. For example, to show the average credit card debt of individuals, bars along the *x*-axis would represent amount of debt and would be connected to one another, while the heights of the bars would represent the number or frequency of individuals with each debt amount.

histology *n.* the scientific study of

the microscopic structure and organization of body tissues. —**histological** *adj.* —**histologist** *n.*

historical analysis research that examines past events to understand current or future events. For example, researchers could perform a historical analysis of an individual's or a family's substance use experiences to understand the present substance use behavior of that person or group.

historical prospective study a research project that examines LONGITUDINAL DATA obtained in the past to track the incidence of a particular disorder over time and its association with various risk factors. For example, a researcher could examine the health records of smokers and nonsmokers to follow the path of an illness from before its manifestation through to its diagnosis and treatment. It is distinct from PROSPECTIVE RESEARCH generally, which begins with individuals who are apparently healthy in the present and moves forward to investigate whether a specific disorder will occur over time.

histrionic personality disorder a personality disorder characterized by a pattern of long-term self-dramatization in which individuals crave activity and excitement, overreact to minor events, experience angry outbursts, and are prone to manipulative suicide threats and gestures.

HIV human immunodeficiency virus: a parasitic agent in blood, semen, and vaginal fluid that destroys a class of LYMPHOCYTES with a crucial role in the immune response. HIV infection can occur by various routes—unprotected sexual intercourse, administration of contaminated blood products, sharing of contaminated needles and syringes by intravenous drug users, or transmission from an infected mother to her child in utero or through breast milk—and is characterized by a gradual deterioration of immune function that can progress to AIDS.

HIV dementia see AIDS DEMENTIA COMPLEX.

HMO health maintenance organization: a health plan that offers a range of services through a specified network of health professionals and facilities to subscribing members for a fixed fee. Members select a primary care provider who coordinates all care and authorizes all services. The HMO is reimbursed through fixed, periodic prepayments (capitated rates) by, or on behalf of, each member for a specified period of time.

holdover effect see CARRYOVER EFFECT.

holism *n.* any approach or theory holding that a system or organism is a coherent, unified whole with emergent properties that cannot be fully explained in terms of individual parts or characteristics. Thus, an analysis or understanding of the parts does not provide an understanding of the whole. —**holistic** *adj.*

holophrase *n.* one of the single-word utterances characteristic of children in the early stages of language acquisition, such as *dada* or *yes*. These are considered to involve a SPEECH ACT going beyond the literal meaning of the single word so that, for example, *cookie* means *I want a cookie now*. —**holophrastic** *adj.*

holophrastic stage see ONE-WORD STAGE.

homelessness *n.* the condition of being without a permanent residence, often due to economic inability or mental or physical incapacity to maintain a residence. Research has shown that homeless people have higher rates of substance abuse, mental disorders (e.g., depression, anxiety, schizophrenia), cognitive deficits, and behavioral difficulties as well as poor self-esteem and poor SELF-EFFICACY. Disabilities and various medical conditions (e.g., cardiorespiratory disease, diabetes, sexually transmitted disease) are common as well. Some of these factors are also among the potential consequences of homelessness.

homeostasis *n.* the regulation by an organism of all aspects of its internal environment, including body temperature, salt–water balance, acid–base balance, and blood sugar level. This involves monitoring changes in the external and internal environments by means of RECEPTORS and adjusting bodily processes accordingly. —**homeostatic** *adj.*

homeostatic principle in social psychology, the principle that individuals have a need to maintain or restore an optimal level of environmental, interpersonal, and psychological stimulation. For example, if an individual experiences excessive solitude, he or she will seek out others to restore the desired amount of companionship. The principle is analogous to the biological concept of HOMEOSTASIS.

home range the entire space through which a nonhuman animal moves during its normal activities. The space may or may not be defended from other members of the same species. The part of the home range in which the greatest activity occurs is known as the core area.

homing *n.* the ability of organisms to return to an original home after traveling or being transported to a point that is a considerable distance from the home and that lacks most visual clues as to its location. See also NAVIGATION.

homogamy *n.* a marriage between partners from similar ethnic, racial, religious, educational, or socioeconomic backgrounds. Compare HETEROGAMY. —**homogamous** *adj.*

homogeneity of variance the statistical assumption of equal variance, meaning that the average squared distance of a score from the mean is the same across all groups sampled in a study. This condition must be fulfilled in many statistical methods, including ANALYSIS OF VARIANCE and REGRESSION ANALYSIS. Also called **homoscedasticity**. Compare HETEROGENEITY OF VARIANCE.

homogeneous *adj.* having the same, or relatively similar, composition throughout. Compare HETEROGENEOUS. —**homogeneity** *n.*

homologous *adj.* describing chromosomes that are identical in terms of their visible structure and location of gene segments, although they may carry different ALLELES. Humans and other DIPLOID organisms possess homologous pairs of chromosomes in the nuclei of their body cells.

homophily *n.* the tendency for individuals who are socially connected in some way to display certain affinities, such as similarities in demographic background, attitudes, values, and so on. Compare HETEROPHILY.

homophobia *n.* dread or fear of gay men and lesbians, associated with prejudice and anger toward them, that leads to discrimination in such areas as employment, housing, and legal rights and sometimes to violence or murder.

homoscedasticity *n.* see HOMOGENEITY OF VARIANCE. —**homoscedastic** *adj.*

homosexuality *n.* sexual attraction or activity between members of the same sex. Although the term can refer to homosexual orientation in both men and women, current practice distinguishes between gay men and lesbians, and homosexuality itself is now commonly referred to as same-sex sexual orientation or activity. —**homosexual** *adj., n.*

homozygous *adj.* possessing identical forms of a gene (i.e., identical ALLELES) at a given genetic locus on each of a pair of HOMOLOGOUS chromosomes. Compare HETEROZYGOUS. —**homozygote** *n.*

homunculus *n.* (*pl.* **homunculi**) **1.** a putative process or entity in the mind or the nervous system whose operations are invoked to explain some aspect of human behavior or experience. The problem with such theories is that the behavior or experience of the homunculus usually requires explanation in exactly the same way as that of the person as a whole. As a result, homunculus theories tend to end in circular reasoning. For example, some information-processing theories invoke a "decision-making process" to explain the making of decisions. **2.** in neuroanatomy, a figurative representation, in distorted human form, of the relative sizes of motor and sensory areas in the brain that correspond to particular parts of the body. For example, the brain area devoted to the tongue is much larger than the area for the forearm, so the homunculus has a correspondingly larger tongue. —**homuncular** *adj.*

honestly significant difference test see TUKEY'S HONESTLY SIGNIFICANT DIFFERENCE TEST.

hope *n.* the expectation that one will have positive experiences or that a potentially threatening or negative situation will not materialize or will ultimately result in a favorable state of affairs. Hope has been characterized in the psychological literature in various ways, including as a CHARACTER STRENGTH, an emotion, a component of motivation, a mechanism that facilitates coping with stress, or a combination of these features. See also OPTIMISM. —**hopeful** *adj.*

hopelessness *n.* the feeling that one will not experience positive emotions or an improvement in one's condition. Hopelessness is common in MAJOR DEPRESSIVE EPISODES and other DEPRESSIVE DISORDERS and is often implicated in suicides and attempted suicides. —**hopeless** *adj.*

horizontal cell see RETINAL HORIZONTAL CELL.

horizontal décalage in PIAGETIAN THEORY, the invariant order in which accomplishments occur within a particular stage of development. For example, an understanding of CONSERVATION of quantity is always achieved before understanding conservation of weight, which is achieved before understanding conservation of volume. Compare VERTICAL DÉCALAGE.

horizontal plane an imaginary flat surface that divides the body or brain into upper and lower parts.

horizontal–vertical illusion the misperception that vertical lines are longer than horizontal lines when both are actually the same length. The vertical element of an uppercase letter *T*, for example, looks longer than the cross bar, even when the lengths are identical.

hormone *n.* a substance secreted into the bloodstream by an ENDOCRINE GLAND or other tissue or organ to regulate processes in distant target organs and tissues. These secretions include those released from the anterior and posterior PITUITARY GLAND; the CORTICOSTEROIDS and EPINEPHRINE from the adrenal glands; and the SEX HORMONES from the reproductive glands. —**hormonal** *adj.*

hormone replacement therapy (HRT) the administration of sex hormones either to relieve menopausal symptoms in women or to increase testosterone levels in men. For women, the use of HRT, usually with an estrogen or a combined estrogen–progestin preparation, is controversial because long-term use may increase the risk of breast cancer, cardiovascular disease, stroke, and other conditions associated with the aging process. For men, HRT with testosterone is used to treat hypogonadism, but there have been controversies with this use as well, particularly in regard to the development of prostate cancer. Some experts believe that further research (in the form of double BLIND, randomized controlled studies) is necessary.

hospice *n.* a place or a form of care for terminally ill individuals. Instead of curing disease and prolonging life, the hospice concept emphasizes patient comfort, psychological well-being, and pain management. See also PALLIATIVE CARE.

hostile aggression see AGGRESSION.

hostility *n.* the overt expression of intense animosity or antagonism in action, feeling, or attitude. —**hostile** *adj.*

H spread see INTERQUARTILE RANGE.

hue *n.* the subjective quality of color, which is determined primarily by wavelength and secondarily by amplitude. It differs from tone (light or dark value of a particular color) and value (the relative lightness or darkness of colors).

human engineering the design of environments and equipment that promote optimum use of human capabilities and optimum safety, efficiency, and comfort. See also ENGINEERING PSYCHOLOGY.

human factors 1. the considerations to be made when designing, evaluating, or optimizing systems for human use, especially with regard to safety, efficiency, and comfort. See also HUMAN SYSTEMS INTEGRATION. **2.** a common synonym of ERGONOMICS.

human factors psychology a branch of psychology that studies the role of HUMAN FACTORS in operating systems, with the aim of redesigning environments, equipment, and processes to fit human abilities and characteristics.

Human Genome Project an international project to map each human gene and determine the complete sequence of base pairs in human DNA. The project began in 1990 and was completed in 2003. It has yielded vast amounts of valuable information about the genes responsible for various diseases, which may lead to the development of effective genetic screening tests and, possibly, treatments.

human immunodeficiency virus see HIV.

humanism *n.* a perspective that begins with a presumption of the inherent dignity and worth of humankind and that focuses attention on the study and representation of human beings and human experiences. Within psychology, humanism refers to theories and perspectives that seek to uphold human values and to resist the reduction of human beings and behaviors to merely natural objects and events. —**humanist** *adj., n.* —**humanistic** *adj.*

humanistic–existential therapy see EXISTENTIAL–HUMANISTIC THERAPY.

humanistic perspective the assumption in psychology that people are essentially good and constructive, that the tendency toward SELF-ACTUALIZATION is inherent, and that, given the proper environment, human beings will develop to their maximum potential.

humanistic psychology an approach to psychology that flourished between the 1940s and the early 1970s and that is most visible today as a family of widely used approaches to psychotherapy and counseling. It derives largely from ideas associated with EXISTENTIALISM and PHENOMENOLOGY and focuses on individuals' capacity to make their own choices, create their own style of life, and actualize themselves in their own way. Its approach is holistic, and its emphasis is on the development of human potential through experiential means rather than the analysis of the unconscious or the modification of behavior.

humanistic therapy any of a variety of psychotherapeutic approaches that reject psychoanalytic and behavioral approaches; seek to foster personal growth through direct experience; and focus on the development of human potential, the here and now, concrete personality change, responsibility for oneself, and trust in natural processes and spontaneous feeling. Some examples of humanistic therapy are CLIENT-

CENTERED THERAPY, GESTALT THERAPY, and EXISTENTIAL PSYCHOTHERAPY.

human systems integration (**HSI**) an area of research that investigates the means by which knowledge about the cognitive and physiological requirements for optimal human task performance (e.g., attention, decision making, biomechanics) can be translated into the effective design of complex technologies used to support that performance. The focus of research is primarily on advanced computer-based systems (e.g., those used in air traffic control) and their effects on the people using them. See ERGONOMICS; HUMAN FACTORS.

humiliation *n.* a feeling of shame as a result of being disgraced or deprecated. The feeling sometimes leads to depression and deterioration of the individual's sense of SELF-ESTEEM.

humor *n.* **1.** the capacity to perceive or express the amusing aspects of a situation. There is little agreement about the essence of humor and the reasons one laughs or smiles at jokes or anecdotes. Some philosophers have theorized that individuals laugh at people and situations that make them feel superior, whereas others have emphasized the element of surprise in humor or its "playful pain" as a mechanism for taking serious things lightly and thereby triumphing over them. **2.** the semifluid substance that occupies the spaces in the eyeball. **3.** in antiquity, one of four bodily fluids (blood, black bile, yellow bile, and phlegm) that were thought to be responsible for a person's physical and psychological characteristics. —**humoral** *adj.* —**humorous** *adj.*

hunger *n.* the sensation caused by a need for food. Traditional conceptualizations viewed hunger as resulting from imbalances in HOMEOSTASIS and food intake as necessary to maintain in the body an optimum balance of nutrients. Contemporary theories, however, largely consider hunger to be initiated by the gradual disappearance of the inhibitory effects generated from the previous meal.

Huntington's disease (**HD**) a progressive hereditary disease associated with degeneration of nerve cells, particularly in the caudate nucleus of the BASAL GANGLIA and in the CEREBRAL CORTEX. It is characterized by abnormalities of gait and posture, motor incoordination, and involuntary jerking motions (CHOREA) as well as DEMENTIA, mood disturbances, and personality and behavioral changes. Also called **Huntington's chorea.** [George **Huntington** (1850–1916), U.S. physician]

hydrocephalus *n.* a condition caused by accumulation of cerebrospinal fluid in the ventricles of the brain, with symptoms such as headache, nausea, poor coordination, slowing or loss of development, lethargy, irritability, or changes in personality or cognition. Hydrocephalus commonly occurs as a congenital anomaly or due to obstruction of cerebrospinal fluid from head injury, brain tumor, or hemorrhage. —**hydrocephalic** *adj.*

hydrophobia *n.* a persistent and irrational fear of water, resulting in avoidance of activities involving water, such as swimming, drinking, or washing one's hands. —**hydrophobic** *adj.*

hydrotherapy *n.* the therapeutic use of water to promote recovery from disease or injury. Hydrotherapy includes such treatments as baths, streams of water (douches), and aquatic sports or exercise.

5-hydroxytryptamine (**5-HT**) *n.* see SEROTONIN.

hygiene factors in the TWO-FACTOR THEORY OF WORK MOTIVATION, certain aspects of the working situation that can produce discontent if they are poor or lacking but that cannot by themselves motivate employees to improve their job performance. These include pay, relations with peers and supervisors, working conditions, and benefits. Compare MOTIVATORS.

hyperactivity *n.* a condition characterized by spontaneous gross motor activity or restlessness that is excessive for the age of the individual. It is a prominent feature of ATTENTION-DEFICIT/HYPERACTIVITY DISORDER. —**hyperactive** *adj.*

hyperaldosteronism *n.* see ALDOSTERONE.

hyperalgesia *n.* an abnormal sensitivity to pain.

hyperarousal *n.* **1.** one of three sets of criteria used to diagnose POSTTRAUMATIC STRESS DISORDER and ACUTE STRESS DISORDER. Symptoms of hyperarousal include exaggerated startle response, disturbed sleep, difficulty in concentrating or remembering, and excessive vigilance. **2.** a physiological response to stress. Also called **acute stress response**. See also FIGHT-OR-FLIGHT RESPONSE.

hypercomplex cell a neuron in the visual cortex for which the optimal stimulus is a moving line of specific length or a moving corner.

hyperkinesis *n.* **1.** excessive involuntary movement. **2.** restlessness or HYPERACTIVITY. Also called **hyperkinesia**. —**hyperkinetic** *adj.*

hyperlexia *n.* the development of extremely good reading skills at a very early age, well ahead of word comprehension or cognitive ability. Children with hyperlexia often start to recognize words without instruction and before any expressive language develops. —**hyperlexic** *adj.*

hypermnesia *n.* **1.** an extreme degree of retentiveness and recall, with unusual clarity of memory images. **2.** in memory testing, a net increase in the total number of items recalled from one test to another. Hypermnesia usually occurs when information is repeatedly tested in close succession.

hyperopia *n.* farsightedness. Hyperopia is due to an abnormally short eyeball, which causes the image of

close objects to be blurred because the focal point of one or both eyes lies behind, rather than on, the retina. Compare MYOPIA.

hyperphagia *n.* pathological overeating, particularly when due to a metabolic disorder or to a brain lesion. Compare HYPOPHAGIA. —**hyperphagic** *adj.*

hyperpolarization *n.* an increase in the electric potential across the plasma membrane of a cell, especially a neuron, such that the inner surface of the membrane becomes more negative in relation to the outer surface. It occurs during the final portion of an ACTION POTENTIAL or in response to inhibitory neural messages. Compare DEPOLARIZATION.

hypersomnia *n.* excessive sleepiness during daytime hours or abnormally prolonged episodes of nighttime sleep. This can be a feature of certain DYSSOMNIAS or other sleep or mental disorders, or it can be associated with neurological dysfunction or damage, a general medical condition, or substance use. Compare HYPOSOMNIA.

hyperspecificity *n.* a behavioral situation in which a learned association between two stimuli fails to generalize when the stimuli are presented in a novel combination. Although hyperspecificity is a common occurrence, it has been observed particularly in such disorders as amnesia and autism.

hypertension *n.* high blood pressure: a circulatory disorder characterized by persistent arterial blood pressure that exceeds a standard, which usually is 140/90 mmHg. Often, there is no obvious cause, but in some people, high blood pressure can be traced to such conditions as tumors of the adrenal gland, chronic kidney disease, or hormone abnormalities. Compare HYPOTENSION. —**hypertensive** *adj.*

hyperthyroidism *n.* overactivity of the thyroid gland, resulting in excessive production of thyroid hormones and a consequent increase in metabolic rate. Manifestations include nervousness, excessive activity, weight loss, and other physical problems. Compare HYPO-THYROIDISM.

hyperventilation *n.* abnormally rapid and deep breathing, usually due to anxiety or emotional stress. It lowers the carbon dioxide level of the blood and produces symptoms such as light-headedness and numbness or tingling in the extremities.

hypesthesia (hypaesthesia) *n.* severely diminished sensitivity in any of the senses, especially the touch sense. Also called **hypoesthesia (hypo-aesthesia)**.

hypnagogic *adj.* describing or relating to the drowsy state that occurs in the transition from wakefulness to sleep.

hypnogenic *adj.* **1.** sleep producing. **2.** hypnosis inducing.

hypnosis *n.* (*pl.* **hypnoses**) the procedure, or the state induced by that procedure, in which suggestion is used to evoke changes in sensation, perception, cognition, emotion, or control over motor behavior. Subjects appear to be receptive, to varying degrees, to suggestions to act, feel, and behave differently than in an ordinary waking state. As a specifically psychotherapeutic intervention, hypnosis is referred to as HYPNOTHERAPY.

hypnotherapy *n.* the use of hypnosis in psychological treatment, either in BRIEF PSYCHOTHERAPY directed toward alleviation of symptoms and modification of behavior patterns or in long-term psychotherapy aimed at personality adaptation or change. Although discussions of its clinical applications engender controversy, there is scientific evidence that hypnotherapy can be applied with some success to a wide range of health problems, such as hypertension, asthma, insomnia, bruxism, chronic and acute pain, habit modification (e.g., overeating, smok-

ing), mood and anxiety disorders (e.g., some phobias), and personality disorders. There is also some evidence demonstrating its effectiveness as an adjunctive therapy, that is, as a secondary intervention used concurrently with a primary intervention. Also called **clinical hypnosis**.

hypnotic 1. *n.* a drug that helps induce and sustain sleep by increasing drowsiness and reducing motor activity. In general, hypnotics differ from SEDATIVES only in terms of the dose administered, with higher doses used to produce sleep or anesthesia and lower doses to produce sedation or relieve anxiety. BENZODIAZEPINES are among the most widely prescribed hypnotics. **2.** *adj.* pertaining to hypnosis or sleep.

hypnotic susceptibility the degree to which an individual is able to enter into hypnosis. Although many individuals can enter at least a light trance, people vary greatly in their ability to achieve a moderate or deep trance. Also called **hypnotizability**.

hypoactive sexual desire disorder persistent and distressing deficiency or absence of sexual interest and desire to engage in sexual activity. This may be global, involving all forms of sexual activity, or situational, limited to one partner or one type of sexual activity.

hypoactivity *n.* abnormally slowed or deficient motor or other activity, as may occur, for example, with depression.

hypochondriasis *n.* a SOMATOFORM DISORDER characterized by a preoccupation with the fear or belief that one has a serious physical disease, based on the incorrect and unrealistic interpretation of bodily symptoms. This fear or belief interferes with social and occupational functioning despite medical reassurance that no physical disorder exists. The diagnosis of hypochondriasis has recently been replaced with two separate diagnoses: SOMATIC SYMPTOM

DISORDER and ILLNESS ANXIETY DIS-
ORDER.

hypoglossal nerve the 12th CRA-
NIAL NERVE, a motor nerve that
originates in the brain and innervates
the muscles of the tongue, lower jaw,
and areas of the neck and chest.

hypokinesis *n.* abnormal slowness in
the initiation of voluntary movement.
Also called **hypokinesia**. Compare
BRADYKINESIA. —**hypokinetic** *adj.*

hypomanic episode a period of elevated, expansive, or irritable mood accompanied by various combinations of
inflated self-esteem, a decreased need
for sleep, increased speech, racing
thoughts, distractibility, increased activity or PSYCHOMOTOR AGITATION, and
increased involvement in risky activities
(e.g., buying sprees, sexual indiscretions). Hypomanic episodes are characteristic of BIPOLAR DISORDER and
CYCLOTHYMIC DISORDER. Also called
hypomania.

hypophagia *n.* pathologically
reduced food intake. Compare
HYPERPHAGIA.

hyposomnia *n.* a reduction in a person's sleep time, often as a result of
insomnia or some other sleep disturbance. Compare HYPERSOMNIA.

hypotension *n.* abnormally low
blood pressure, causing dizziness and
fainting. Compare HYPERTENSION.
—**hypotensive** *adj.*

**hypothalamic–pituitary–
adrenal axis (HPA axis)** a major
mammalian system maintaining body
homeostasis by regulating the neuroendocrine and sympathetic nervous
systems as well as modulating immune
function. Consisting of the HYPOTHALA-
MUS in the center of the brain, the PITU-
ITARY GLAND directly underneath, and
the ADRENAL GLANDS on top of the kidneys, the HPA axis helps regulate such
widely varied processes as food consumption, digestion, energy usage (in
the form of glucose metabolism),
reproduction and sexual behavior,

cardiovascular functioning, memory
acquisition and retrieval, and emotion;
it also forms the core of the physiological response to stress. Dysfunction of
the HPA axis has been implicated in
the pathophysiology of numerous
conditions, such as mood and anxiety
disorders, eating disorders, alcohol dependence, gastrointestinal disorders,
chronic fatigue syndrome, fibromyal-
gia, cancer, and autoimmune diseases.
Also called **hypothalamic–pituitary–
adrenocortical system (HPA system)**. See also SYMPATHETIC–ADRENAL–
MEDULLARY AXIS.

hypothalamus *n.* (*pl.* **hypothalami**)
part of the DIENCEPHALON of the brain,
lying ventral to the THALAMUS, that
contains nuclei with primary control
of the autonomic (involuntary) functions of the body. It also helps integrate
autonomic activity into appropriate
responses to internal and external
stimuli. Additionally, it is involved in
appetite, thirst, sleep, and sexuality.
—**hypothalamic** *adj.*

hypothesis *n.* (*pl.* **hypotheses**) an
empirically testable proposition about
some fact, behavior, relationship, or the
like, usually based on theory, that states
an expected outcome resulting from
specific conditions or assumptions.

hypothesis testing a statistical inference procedure for determining
whether a given proposition about a
population PARAMETER should be rejected on the basis of observed sample
data. See also SIGNIFICANCE TESTING.

hypothetico-deductive method
a method of scientific inquiry in which
the credibility or explanatory power of
a falsifiable hypothesis is tested by making predictions on the basis of this
hypothesis and determining whether
these predictions are consistent with
empirical observations. It is one of the
most widely used SCIENTIFIC METHODS
for disproving hypotheses and building
corroboration for those that remain.

**hypothetico-deductive reason-
ing** the logical reasoning that, accord-

ing to the PIAGETIAN THEORY of cognitive development, emerges in early adolescence and marks the FORMAL OPERATIONAL STAGE. Hypothetico-deductive reasoning is distinguished by the capacity for abstract thinking and hypothesis testing.

hypothyroidism *n.* underactivity of the thyroid gland, resulting in underproduction of thyroid hormones and a consequent decrease in metabolic rate. Manifestations include fatigue, weakness, weight gain, and other physical problems. Dysphoria, depression, and psychosis can be seen in more severe forms. Compare HYPERTHYROIDISM.

hypovolemic thirst thirst caused by depletion of the volume of extracellular fluid, as, for example, by blood loss (i.e., hypovolemia) or vomiting. Also called **volumetric thirst**. Compare OSMOMETRIC THIRST.

hypoxia *n.* reduced oxygen in the body tissues, including the brain. This can result in widespread brain injury depending on the degree of oxygen deficiency and its duration. Signs and symptoms of hypoxia vary according to its cause but generally include shortness of breath, rapid pulse, fainting, and mental disturbances (e.g., delirium, euphoria). See also ANOXIA. —**hypoxic** *adj.*

hysterectomy *n.* the surgical removal of the uterus. It may include excision of the cervix and a part of the vagina as well.

hysteria *n.* the historical name for the condition now largely classified as CONVERSION DISORDER but with symptoms dispersed across other formal diagnoses as well (e.g., HISTRIONIC PERSONALITY DISORDER). Although technically outdated, it is often used as a lay term for any psychogenic disorder characterized by symptoms such as paralysis, blindness, loss of sensation, and hallucinations and is often accompanied by suggestibility, emotional outbursts, and histrionic behavior. —**hysterical** *adj.*

Ii

iatrogenic *adj.* denoting or relating to a pathological condition that is inadvertently induced or aggravated in a patient by a health care provider. For example, an **iatrogenic addiction** is a dependence on a substance, most often a painkiller or sedative, originally prescribed by a physician to treat a physical or psychological disorder.

iconic memory the brief retention of an image of a visual stimulus beyond cessation of the stimulus. This iconic image usually lasts less than a second. In a MULTISTORE MODEL OF MEMORY, iconic memory precedes SHORT-TERM MEMORY.

id *n.* in psychoanalytic theory, the component of the personality that contains the instinctual, biological drives that supply the psyche with its basic energy or LIBIDO. Austrian neurologist Sigmund Freud (1856–1939) conceived of the id as the most primitive component of the personality, located in the deepest level of the unconscious; it has no inner organization and operates in obedience to the PLEASURE PRINCIPLE. Thus, the infant's life is dominated by the desire for immediate gratification of instincts, such as hunger and sex, until the EGO begins to develop and operate in accordance with reality. See also PRIMARY PROCESS; STRUCTURAL MODEL.

idea *n.* in cognitive psychology, a mental image or cognition that is ultimately derived from experience but that may occur without direct reference to perception or sensory processes.

idealism *n.* in philosophy, the position that reality, including the natural world, is not independent of mind. Positions range from strong forms, holding that mind constitutes the things of reality, to weaker forms, holding that reality is correlated with the workings of the mind. There is also a range of po-

sitions as to the nature of mind, from those holding that mind must be conceived of as absolute, universal, and apart from nature itself to those holding that mind may be conceived of as individual minds. See also MIND–BODY PROBLEM. Compare MATERIALISM. **—idealist** *n.* **—idealistic** *adj.*

ideal self in models of self-concept, a mental representation of an exemplary set of psychological attributes that one strives or wishes to possess.

idée fixe a firmly held, irrational idea or belief that is maintained despite evidence to the contrary. It may take the form of a delusion and become an obsession.

identical twins see MONOZYGOTIC TWINS.

identification *n.* **1.** the process of associating the self closely with other individuals and their characteristics or views. This process takes many forms and operates largely on a nonconscious or preconscious level. **2.** in psychoanalytic theory, a DEFENSE MECHANISM in which the individual incorporates aspects of his or her OBJECTS inside the EGO to alleviate the anxiety associated with OBJECT LOSS or to reduce hostility between himself or herself and the object.

identity *n.* **1.** an individual's sense of self, defined by (a) a set of physical, psychological, and interpersonal characteristics that is not wholly shared with any other person and (b) a range of affiliations (e.g., ethnicity) and social roles. Identity involves a sense of continuity, or the feeling that one is the same person today that one was yesterday or last year (despite physical or other changes). Also called **personal identity.** **2.** in cognitive development, awareness that an object is the same even though it may undergo transformations. For example, a coffee cup remains the same object despite differences in distance, size, color, lighting, orientation, and shape. Also called **object identity**.

identity crisis a phase of life marked by experimentation; changing, conflicting, or newly emerging values; and a lack of commitment to one's usual roles in society (especially in work and family relationships).

identity diffusion in the EGO PSYCHOLOGY of German-born U.S. psychologist Erik Erikson (1902–1994), a possible outcome of the IDENTITY VERSUS IDENTITY CONFUSION stage, whereby the individual emerges with an uncertain sense of identity and confusion about his or her wishes, attitudes, and goals.

identity foreclosure premature commitment to an identity: the unquestioning acceptance by individuals (usually adolescents) of the role, values, and goals that others (e.g., parents, close friends, teachers, athletic coaches) have chosen for them.

identity style an adolescent's characteristic mode of approaching problems and decisions that are relevant to his or her personal identity or sense of self. Three basic identity styles are recognized. Information-oriented individuals are skeptical about their self-constructions and willing to test and revise aspects of their self-identity when confronted with discrepant feedback. Normative individuals deal with identity questions and decisional situations by conforming to the prescriptions and expectations of significant others. Diffuse-avoidant-oriented individuals are reluctant to face up to and confront personal problems and decisions.

identity versus identity confusion the fifth of ERIKSON'S EIGHT STAGES OF PSYCHOSOCIAL DEVELOPMENT, marked by an identity crisis that occurs during adolescence. During this stage, the individual may experience a psychosocial MORATORIUM and "try on"

different roles and identify with different groups before forming a cohesive, positive identity that allows him or her to contribute to society; alternatively, the individual may remain confused about his or her sense of identity, a state Erikson calls IDENTITY DIFFUSION.

ideology *n.* a more or less systematic ordering of ideas with associated doctrines, attitudes, beliefs, and symbols that together form a more or less coherent philosophy for a person, group, or sociopolitical movement. —**ideological** *adj.*

idiocentric *adj.* denoting interest in or focus on one's self rather than on other objects or people. Compare ALLOCENTRIC. See also EGOCENTRISM. —**idiocentrism** *n.*

idiographic *adj.* relating to the description and understanding of an individual case, as opposed to the formulation of NOMOTHETIC general laws. An **idiographic approach** involves the thorough, intensive study of a single person or case in order to obtain an in-depth understanding of that person or case. In those areas of psychology in which the individual person is the unit of analysis (e.g., in personality, developmental, or clinical psychology), the idiographic approach has appeal because it emphasizes that individual's characteristic traits and the uniqueness of his or her behavior and adjustment.

idiolect *n.* a DIALECT spoken at the level of an individual. In one sense, all speakers have an idiolect because no two people use their native language in the same way. However, the term is reserved for the most idiosyncratic forms of personal language use, especially those involving eccentricities of construction or vocabulary. —**idiolectal** *adj.*

idiosyncrasy *n.* a habit or quality of body or mind peculiar to an individual. For example, a person's abnormal response to a drug may be considered an idiosyncrasy. —**idiosyncratic** *adj.*

idiosyncrasy-credit model an explanation of the leniency that groups sometimes display when high-status members violate group norms. This model assumes that such individuals, by contributing to the group in significant ways and expressing loyalty to it, build up **idiosyncrasy credits**, which they "spend" whenever they make errors or deviate from the group's norms.

idiot savant (*pl.* **idiots savants** or, less often, **idiot savants**) see SAVANT. [French, "learned idiot"]

id psychology in psychoanalysis, an approach that focuses on the unorganized, instinctual impulses contained in the ID that seek immediate pleasurable gratification of primitive needs. The id is believed to dominate the lives of infants and is frequently described as primitive and irrational until it is disciplined by the other two major components of the personality: the EGO and the SUPEREGO. Compare EGO PSYCHOLOGY.

illness anxiety disorder a disorder characterized by high anxiety about one's health, by excessive preoccupation with having an illness or acquiring it, and by behaviors associated with the presumed or feared condition (e.g., repeatedly checking oneself for possible signs of illness), yet with no significant somatic symptoms that would warrant such concern. It is one of two replacement diagnoses for HYPOCHONDRIASIS. See also SOMATIC SYMPTOM DISORDER.

illusion *n.* a false sensory percept, resulting from the misinterpretation of stimuli. For example, parallel railroad tracks appear to meet in the distance. Other common visual illusions include APPARENT MOVEMENT, the MÜLLER-LYER ILLUSION, the PONZO ILLUSION, and the ZÖLLNER ILLUSION. The distorted percepts that may accompany abnormal conditions, such as delirium and schizophrenia, or that occur in those taking mind-altering drugs are more properly called HALLUCINATIONS. —**illusory** *adj.*

illusory conjunction the attribution of a characteristic of one stimulus to another stimulus when the stimuli are presented only briefly. Illusory conjunctions are most common with visual stimuli when, for example, the color of one form can be attributed to a different form.

illusory correlation an overestimation of the degree of relationship (i.e., correlation) between two variables. For example, if an unusual action occurred at the same time that an adolescent was present in a group of adults, the assumption that the action was carried out by the adolescent would be an illusory correlation.

image *n.* **1.** a likeness or cognitive representation of an earlier sensory experience recalled without external stimulation. For example, remembering the shape of a horse or the sound of a jet airplane brings to mind an image derived from earlier experiences with these stimuli. **2.** a representation of an object produced by an optical system. See also RETINAL IMAGE.

imagery *n.* **1.** cognitive generation of sensory input from the five senses, which is recalled from experience or self-generated in a nonexperiential form. **2.** mental images considered collectively, or the particular type of imagery characteristic of an individual, such as VISUAL IMAGERY.

imaginal exposure a type of EXPOSURE THERAPY used for treating individuals with anxiety disorders (e.g., phobias, obsessive-compulsive disorder, posttraumatic stress disorder). Vivid imagery evoked through speech is used by the therapist to expose the client mentally to an anxiety-evoking stimulus. Compare IN VIVO EXPOSURE.

imaginary audience the belief of an adolescent that others are constantly focusing attention on him or her, scrutinizing behaviors, appearance, and the like. The adolescent feels as though he or she is continually the central topic of interest to a group of spectators (i.e., an audience) when in fact this is not the case. It is an early adolescent construct reflective of acute self-consciousness.

imaging *n*. the process of scanning the brain or other organs or tissues to obtain an optical image that can be used for medical and research purposes, such as locating abnormalities or studying anatomy and function. Techniques used include COMPUTED TOMOGRAPHY, POSITRON EMISSION TOMOGRAPHY (PET), anatomical MAGNETIC RESONANCE IMAGING (aMRI), and FUNCTIONAL MAGNETIC RESONANCE IMAGING (fMRI).

imago *n*. an unconscious mental image of another person, especially the mother or father, that influences the way in which an individual relates to others. The imago is typically formed in infancy and childhood and is generally an idealized or otherwise not completely accurate representation. The term was originally used by Austrian neurologist Sigmund Freud (1856–1939) and the early psychoanalysts, and its meaning has carried over into other schools of psychology and psychotherapy.

imitation *n*. the process of copying the behavior of another person, group, or object, intentionally or unintentionally. It is a basic form of learning that accounts for many human skills, behaviors, and social customs, but it can also take pathological form, as in ECHOLALIA and ECHOPRAXIA. Some theorists propose that true imitation requires that an observer be able to take the perspective of the model. This contrasts with MIMICRY and other forms of SOCIAL LEARNING. —**imitate** *vb*.

immanent justice the belief that rules are fixed and immutable and that punishment automatically follows misdeeds regardless of extenuating circumstances. Children up to the age of 8 equate the morality of an act only with its consequences; not until later do they develop the capacity to judge motive and subjective considerations. Compare DISTRIBUTIVE JUSTICE.

immaterialism *n*. the philosophical position that denies the independent existence of matter as a substance in which qualities might inhere. Sensible objects are held to exist as the sum of the qualities they produce in the perceiving mind, with no material substratum. It is difficult to distinguish such a position from IDEALISM, which holds that mind is essential to all reality and that things and qualities exist only as perceived. Compare MATERIALISM.

immaturity *n*. a state of incomplete growth or development (e.g., neural immaturity). The term, however, is often used to describe childish, maladaptive, or otherwise inappropriate behaviors, particularly when indicative of a lack of age-relevant skills.

immediate memory a type or stage of memory in which an individual recalls information recently presented, such as a street address or telephone number, although this information may be forgotten after its immediate use. See also SHORT-TERM MEMORY.

immune system a complex system in vertebrates that helps protect the body against pathological effects of foreign substances (ANTIGENS), such as viruses and bacteria. The organs involved include the bone marrow and thymus, in which LYMPHOCYTES—the principal agents responsible for specific immune responses—are produced, together with the spleen, lymph nodes, and other lymphoid tissues and various chemicals (e.g., CYTOKINES) that mediate the immune response.

impairment *n*. a decrement in the body's typical physiological or psychological functioning.

Implicit Association Test (IAT) an IMPLICIT ATTITUDE measure in which participants must judge whether a set of target words are members of a specified category (e.g., insects) as well as whether a second set of intermixed words, selected to be highly evaluative in nature, are positive or negative. If attitudes toward the category are positive, judging the target words should be faster when the same response key is used for category membership and positive words than when the same response key is used for category membership and negative words. Negative attitudes produce the opposite pattern.

implicit attitude a relatively enduring and general evaluative response of which a person has little or no conscious awareness. Compare EXPLICIT ATTITUDE.

implicit learning learning of a cognitive or behavioral task that occurs without intention to learn or awareness of what has been learned. Implicit learning is evidenced by improved task performance rather than as a response to an explicit request to remember. See also IMPLICIT MEMORY.

implicit measure a measurement of a psychological construct that is obtained while the individual being assessed is unaware that the measurement is taking place. Implicit measures are often used in social cognition research. For example, a word-stem completion task might be employed to assess emotion implicitly such that *jo_* could be completed to form a positive emotional word (e.g., *joy*) or a neutral word (e.g., *jog*).

implicit memory memory for a previous event that is produced indirectly, without an explicit request to recall the event and without awareness that memory is involved. For instance, after seeing the word *store* in one context, a person would complete the word fragment *st_r_* as *store* rather than *stare*, even without remembering that *store* had been recently encountered. This term is used interchangeably with NON-DECLARATIVE MEMORY. Compare EXPLICIT MEMORY.

implicit personality theories see NAIVE PERSONALITY THEORIES.

implicit self theory the proposal that people hold a self-belief that psychological attributes (e.g., personality,

emotion, intelligence) either are fixed, essential qualities that are impossible to control (**entity theory**) or are more malleable, controllable, and able to be developed gradually (**incremental theory**). These self-beliefs imply certain expectancies, which in turn guide behavior.

implosive therapy a technique in BEHAVIOR THERAPY that is similar to FLOODING but distinct in generally involving imagined stimuli and in attempting to enhance anxiety arousal by adding imaginary exposure cues believed by the therapist to be relevant to the client's fear. Also called **implosion therapy**.

impotence *n.* the inability of a man to complete the sex act due to partial or complete failure to achieve or maintain erection. This condition is called MALE ERECTILE DISORDER in psychiatric contexts and ERECTILE DYSFUNCTION in other clinical contexts. Impotence may also denote premature ejaculation, limited interest in sex, orgasm without pleasure, or coitus without ejaculation. —**impotent** *adj.*

impression formation the process in which an individual develops a SCHEMA of some object, person, or group. Early research on impression formation demonstrated that impressions were often influenced by the PRIMACY EFFECT; more recent studies have focused on the roles played in the process by such factors as the perceiver's cognitive processes (e.g., how readily some types of ideas come to mind) and feelings (e.g., anger can predispose the perceiver to stereotype an individual).

impression management behaviors intended to control how others perceive oneself, especially by guiding them to attribute desirable traits to oneself. Impression management has been offered as an alternative explanation for some phenomena that traditionally have been interpreted in terms of COGNITIVE DISSONANCE THEORY. Some psychologists distinguish impression management from SELF-PRESENTATION by proposing that impression management involves only deliberate, conscious strategies.

imprinting *n.* a simple yet profound and highly effective learning process that occurs during a CRITICAL PERIOD in the life of some animals. A well-known example is that of newly hatched chicks, which tend to follow the first moving object, human or animal, that catches their attention. Some investigators believe that such processes are instinctual; others regard them as a form of PREPAREDNESS.

impulsive *adj.* describing or displaying behavior characterized by little or no forethought, reflection, or consideration of the consequences of an action, particularly one that involves taking risks. Compare REFLECTIVE. **—impulsiveness** or **impulsivity** *n.*

inappropriate affect emotional responses that are not in keeping with the situation or are incompatible with expressed thoughts or wishes, such as smiling when told about the death of a friend.

inattentional blindness a failure to notice unexpected but perceptible stimuli in a visual scene while one's attention is focused on something else in the scene. In two classic experiments, many participants focusing on judging the line lengths of a cross failed to notice a simultaneously presented square, and many focusing on counting the number of passes made by a basketball team failed to notice a person dressed in a gorilla suit walk by. Various factors affect the rate of inattentional blindness, including the visual relationship of the unexpected item to other items, the meaningfulness of the unexpected item, and—most significantly—the observer's attentional SET and COGNITIVE LOAD. See also CHANGE BLINDNESS.

incentive *n.* an external stimulus, such as a condition or an object, that enhances or serves as a motive for behavior.

incentive theory the theory that motivation arousal depends on the interaction between environmental incentives (i.e., stimulus objects)—both positive and negative—and an organism's psychological and physiological states (e.g., drive states).

incest *n.* sexual activity between family members, whether related by blood or not. Some form of **incest taboo**, or prohibition in custom or law against incest between first-degree relatives (e.g., father–daughter, mother–son, brother–sister), is found in nearly every society. **—incestuous** *adj.*

incidence *n.* the rate of occurrence of new cases of a given event or condition (e.g., a disorder, disease, symptom, or injury) in a particular population in a given period. An **incidence rate** is normally expressed as the number of cases per some standard proportion (1,000 or 100,000 are commonly used) of the entire population at risk per year. See also PREVALENCE.

incidental learning learning that is not premeditated, deliberate, or intentional and that is acquired as a result of some other, possibly unrelated, mental activity. Some theorists believe that much learning takes place without any intention to learn, occurring incidentally to other cognitive processing of information. See also LATENT LEARNING.

inclusion *n.* the practice of teaching students with disabilities in the same classroom as other students to the fullest extent possible, via the provision of appropriate supportive services.

inclusive fitness the REPRODUCTIVE SUCCESS not only of an individual but also of all of that individual's relatives in proportion to their degree of genetic relatedness. In calculating estimates of reproductive success, it is assumed that parents, offspring, and siblings have an average of 50% of their genes in common; that grandparents and grand-offspring, as well as uncles or aunts and nieces or nephews, share 25% of genes; and that first cousins share 12.5% of genes.

incompetence *n.* **1.** the inability to carry out a required task or activity adequately. **2.** in law, the inability to make sound judgments regarding one's transactions or personal affairs. In criminal proceedings more specifically, incompetence is the inability of a defendant to participate meaningfully in the process by communicating with attorneys and understanding all elements of the criminal justice system, from initial interrogation to sentencing. Also called **incompetency**. Compare COMPETENCE. —**incompetent** *adj.*

incongruence *n.* **1.** lack of consistency or appropriateness, as in INAPPROPRIATE AFFECT or as when one's subjective evaluation of a situation is at odds with reality. **2.** as defined by U.S. psychologist Carl Rogers (1902–1987), a lack of alignment between the real self and the ideal self. —**incongruent** *adj.*

incremental learning see ALL-OR-NONE LEARNING.

incremental theory see IMPLICIT SELF THEORY.

incus *n.* see OSSICLES.

independence *n.* **1.** freedom from the influence or control of other individuals or groups. **2.** complete lack of relationship between two or more events, sampling units, or variables, such that none is influenced by any other and that changes in one have no implication for changes in any other. For example, a standard assumption in many statistical analyses is **independence of observations**, or the fact that the occurrence of one observation does not influence the occurrence of any others. —**independent** *adj., n.*

independent events the situation in which observing one event does not provide any additional information

about the occurrence or outcome of another event. For example, the outcome of a coin flip and the Dow Jones Industrial Average are independent events, whereas the temperatures of two consecutive days are not necessarily independent. Compare DEPENDENT EVENTS.

independent groups see INDEPENDENT SAMPLES.

independent-groups design see BETWEEN-SUBJECTS DESIGN.

independent living 1. the ability of an individual to perform—without assistance from others—all or most of the daily functions typically required to be self-sufficient, including those tasks essential to personal care (see ACTIVITIES OF DAILY LIVING) and to maintaining a home and job. **2.** a philosophy and civil reform movement promoting the rights of people with disabilities to determine the course of their lives and be full, productive members of society with access to the same social and political freedoms and opportunities as individuals without disabilities.

independent random sampling see SIMPLE RANDOM SAMPLING.

independent random variables RANDOM VARIABLES that exhibit a complete lack of relationship, such that no information about one variable, x, conveys any information about another variable, y.

independent samples groups of individuals or sets of data that are unrelated to one other. For example, experimental groups consisting of different and unrelated participants are independent samples, as are the data sets obtained from these groups. Also called **independent groups**. Compare DEPENDENT SAMPLES.

independent sampling a process for selecting a sample of study participants from a larger potential group of individuals such that the probability of each person being selected for inclusion is not influenced by which people have been chosen already. The resulting samples will be INDEPENDENT SAMPLES.

independent self-construal a view of the self that emphasizes one's separateness and unique traits and accomplishments and that downplays one's embeddedness in a network of social relationships. Compare INTER-DEPENDENT SELF-CONSTRUAL.

independent variable (IV) the variable in an experiment that is specifically manipulated or is observed to occur before the outcome variable in order to assess its effect or influence. Independent variables may or may not be causally related to the DEPENDENT VARIABLE. In statistical analyses, an independent variable is likely to be referred to as a **causal variable**, **explanatory variable**, or PREDICTOR VARIABLE.

indeterminism *n.* the philosophical position that events do not have necessary and sufficient causes. Indeterminism manifests itself in psychology as the doctrine that humans have FREE WILL and are able to act independently of antecedent or current situations, as in making choices. Compare DETERMINISM. **—indeterminist** *adj.*

index case see PROBAND.

indicator variable **1.** see DUMMY VARIABLE. **2.** see MANIFEST VARIABLE.

indirect relationship in STRUCTURAL EQUATION MODELING, a correlation between two variables that involves an intervening variable or MEDIATOR. For example, age may affect rate of pay, which in turn may affect job satisfaction: This being so, the correlation between age and job satisfaction would be an indirect relationship.

individual differences traits or other characteristics by which individuals may be distinguished from one another. This is the focus of DIFFERENTIAL PSYCHOLOGY, for which the term **individual differences psychology** is increasingly used.

individualism *n.* a social or cultural tradition, ideology, or personal outlook

that emphasizes the individual and his or her rights, independence, and relationships with other individuals. Compare COLLECTIVISM. **—individualist** *n.* **—individualistic** *adj.*

individualized education program (IEP) a plan describing the special education and related services specifically designed to meet the unique educational needs of a student with a disability. Each IEP must be documented in writing, tailored to a particular child, and implemented in accordance with the requirements of U.S. federal law.

individual psychology the psychological theory of Austrian psychiatrist Alfred Adler (1870–1937), which is based on the idea that throughout life individuals strive for a sense of mastery, completeness, and belonging and are governed by a conscious drive to overcome their sense of inferiority by developing to their fullest potential, obtaining their life goals, and creating their own styles of life.

individual therapy treatment of psychological problems that is conducted on a one-to-one basis. One therapist sees one client at a time, tailoring the process to his or her unique needs in the exploration of contributory factors and in the alleviation of symptoms. Also called **individual psychotherapy**. Compare GROUP THERAPY.

individuation *n.* **1.** the physiological, psychological, and sociocultural processes by which a person attains status as an individual human being and exerts himself or herself as such in the world. **2.** in the psychoanalytic theory of Swiss psychiatrist Carl Jung (1875–1961), the gradual development of a unified, integrated personality that incorporates greater amounts of the UNCONSCIOUS, both personal and collective, and resolves any conflicts that exist, such as those between introverted and extraverted tendencies.

indoleamine *n.* any of a class of BIO-

GENIC AMINES formed by an indole molecule, which is produced as a breakdown metabolite of tryptophan, and an amine group. Indoleamines include the neurotransmitter serotonin and the hormone melatonin.

induced abortion the deliberate, premature removal of the fetus from the uterus prior to the stage of viability (ability to live outside the uterus) by artificial means, such as drugs or mechanical devices.

induced compliance effect see FORCED COMPLIANCE EFFECT.

induction *n.* **1.** a general conclusion, principle, or explanation derived by reasoning from particular instances or observations. See INDUCTIVE REASONING. Compare DEDUCTION. **2.** the process of inductive reasoning itself. **3.** in conditioning, the phenomenon in which REINFORCEMENT of some forms of behavior results in an increased probability not only of those forms but also of similar but nonreinforced forms. For example, if lever presses with forces between 0.2 and 0.3 N are reinforced, presses with forces less than 0.2 N or greater than 0.3 N will increase in frequency, although they are never explicitly reinforced. Also called **response generalization.** —**inductive** *adj.*

inductive reasoning the form of reasoning in which inferences and general principles are drawn from specific observations and cases. Inductive reasoning is a cornerstone of the scientific method in that it underlies the process of developing hypotheses from particular facts and observations. Compare DEDUCTIVE REASONING.

industrial and organizational psychology (I/O psychology) the branch of psychology that studies human behavior in the work environment and applies general psychological principles to work-related issues and problems, notably in such areas as personnel selection and training, employee evaluation, work conditions, accident prevention, job analysis, job satisfac-

tion, leadership, team effectiveness, and work motivation. Also called **occupational psychology; organizational psychology; work psychology.**

industry versus inferiority the fourth of ERIKSON'S EIGHT STAGES OF PSYCHOSOCIAL DEVELOPMENT, occurring from ages 6 to 11 years, during which the child learns to be productive and to accept evaluation of his or her efforts or becomes discouraged and feels inferior or incompetent.

infancy *n.* the earliest period of postnatal life, in humans generally denoting the time from birth through the first year. —**infant** *n.*

infant-directed speech the specialized style of speech that adults and older children use when talking specifically to infants, which usually includes much inflection and repetition. See also CHILD-DIRECTED SPEECH.

infantile amnesia see CHILDHOOD AMNESIA.

infantile sexuality in psychoanalytic theory, the concept that PSYCHIC ENERGY or LIBIDO concentrated in various organs of the body throughout infancy gives rise to erotic pleasure. This is manifested in sucking the mother's breast during the ORAL STAGE of psychosexual development, in defecating during the ANAL STAGE, and in self-stimulating activities during the early GENITAL STAGE. The term and concept, first enunciated by Austrian neurologist Sigmund Freud (1856–1939), proved highly controversial from the start, and it is more in line with subsequent thought to emphasize the sensual nature of breast-feeding, defecation, and discovery of the body in childhood and the role of the pleasurable feelings so obtained in the origin and development of sexual feelings.

infantilism *n.* behavior, physical characteristics, or mental functioning in older children or adults that is characteristic of that of infants or young children. See REGRESSION.

inferential statistics a broad class of statistical techniques that allow inferences about characteristics of a population to be drawn from a sample of data from that population. These techniques include approaches for testing hypotheses, estimating the value of parameters, and selecting among a set of competing models. Compare DESCRIPTIVE STATISTICS.

inferential test any statistical procedure used to evaluate hypotheses about differences between sample and population distributions. Examples include the CHI-SQUARE TEST, the F TEST, and the T TEST.

inferior *adj.* in anatomy, lower, below, or toward the feet. Compare SUPERIOR.

inferior colliculus see COLLICULUS.

inferior frontal gyrus an anatomically poorly defined region of the frontal lobe that includes BROCA'S AREA and is involved in language production, risk aversion, and empathetic response to facial expressions.

inferiority complex a basic feeling of inadequacy and insecurity, deriving from actual or imagined physical or psychological deficiency, that may result in behavioral expression ranging from the social withdrawal brought by immobilizing timidity to the overcompensation manifested in excessive competition and aggression. Compare SUPERIORITY COMPLEX.

inferior olivary complex (**inferior olivary nucleus; inferior olive**) see OLIVARY NUCLEUS.

inferior temporal gyrus a ridge that extends along the lower surface of the TEMPORAL LOBE of the brain. It has a role in language, semantic memory, visual processing, and sensory integration.

inferotemporal cortex (**IT cortex**) a region of the brain on the inferior (lower) portion of the outer layer (cortex) of the temporal lobe that is involved in the perception of form. This area of visual ASSOCIATION CORTEX contains neurons with very complicated stimulus requirements. See also GRANDMOTHER CELL.

infertility *n.* inability to produce offspring due to low reproductive capacity in the male partner, the female partner, or both. —**infertile** *adj.*

infidelity *n.* the situation in which one partner in a marriage or intimate relationship becomes sexually or emotionally involved with a person other than the partner's spouse or girlfriend or boyfriend. Infidelity has been linked to significant adverse emotional and behavioral consequences, especially for the individual who is cheated on, including decreased self-esteem and increased risk of depression and suicide. It is cited as a common cause of divorce or relationship dissolution.

informatics *n.* the science of using technology to collect, process, analyze, utilize, classify, store, and generally manage data and knowledge. Informatics is used in computer design, databases, and human interface design. See BIOINFORMATICS.

informational influence those interpersonal processes that challenge the correctness of an individual's beliefs or the appropriateness of his or her behavior, thereby promoting change. Such influence may occur directly, as a result of communication and persuasion, or indirectly, through comparison of oneself with others. Compare INTERPERSONAL INFLUENCE; NORMATIVE INFLUENCE.

information overload the state that occurs when the amount or intensity of information exceeds the individual's processing capacity, leading to anxiety, poor decision making, and other undesirable consequences.

information processing (**IP**) in cognitive psychology, the flow of information through the human nervous system, involving the operation of perceptual systems, memory stores, decision processes, and response mechanisms. **Information processing psychology** is the approach that concentrates on understanding these operations.

information-processing model

any conceptualization of memory as involving the progressive transfer of information through a system, much as a computer manipulates information in order to store, retrieve, and generate responses to it. The most popular such model, sometimes referred to as the **three-stage model**, views memory as a system with three distinct components—SENSORY MEMORY, which collects and transforms material; SHORT-TERM MEMORY, which temporarily holds material; and LONG-TERM MEMORY, which more permanently retains material and recalls it as needed— that sequentially process information through the stages of encoding, storage, and retrieval.

information theory the principles relating to the communication or transmission of information, which is defined as any message that reduces uncertainty. These principles deal with such areas as the encoding and decoding of messages, types of channels of communication and their capacity to throughput information, the application of mathematical methods to the process, the problem of noise (distortion), and the relative effectiveness of various kinds of FEEDBACK.

informed consent a person's voluntary agreement to participate in a procedure on the basis of his or her understanding of its nature, its potential benefits and possible risks, and available alternatives. Informed consent is a fundamental requirement of research with humans and typically involves having participants sign documents, prior to the start of a study, that describe specifically what their involvement would entail and noting that they are free to decline participation or to withdraw from the research at any time. In therapeutic contexts, the prin-

ciple of informed consent has provided a foundation for ADVANCE DIRECTIVES.

infradian rhythm any periodic variation in physiological or psychological function recurring in a cycle of less than 24 hours, such as variations in arousal levels. Compare CIRCADIAN RHYTHM; ULTRADIAN RHYTHM.

infrasound *n.* sound whose frequency is too low to be detected by human hearing, generally encompassing the range of 20 Hz to .001 Hz. The scientific study of infrasound is known as **infrasonics**. Able to cover long distances and circumvent or penetrate obstacles without dispersing, infrasonic waves are used by many nonhuman animals to communicate and have a variety of applications in geological monitoring (e.g., prediction of volcanic eruptions, detection of earthquakes). Compare ULTRASOUND.

ingratiation *n.* efforts to win the liking and approval of other people, especially by deliberate IMPRESSION MANAGEMENT. Ingratiation is usually regarded as strategic, insincere, and manipulative. —**ingratiate** *vb.*

ingroup *n.* any group to which one belongs or with which one identifies, but particularly a group judged to be different from other groups (OUT-GROUPS).

ingroup bias the tendency to favor one's own group, its members, its characteristics, and its products, particularly in reference to other groups. The favoring of the ingroup tends to be more pronounced than the rejection of the OUTGROUP, but both tendencies become more pronounced during periods of intergroup contact. At the regional, cultural, or national level, this bias is often termed ETHNOCENTRISM.

inhalant *n.* any of a variety of volatile substances that can be inhaled to produce intoxicating effects. Anesthetic gases (e.g., ether, chloroform, nitrous oxide), industrial solvents (e.g., toluene, gasoline, trichloroethylene, various aerosol propellants), and organic nitrites (e.g., amyl nitrite) are common inhalants. Household products, such as model airplane glue, nail polish remover, spray paint, fabric protector, cooking spray, and correction fluid, are also used as inhalants, especially by adolescents.

inhibition *n.* **1.** the process of restraining one's impulses or behavior, either consciously or unconsciously, due to factors such as lack of confidence, fear of consequences, or moral qualms. **2.** in conditioning, the active blocking or delay of a response to a stimulus. **3.** in psychoanalysis, an unconscious mechanism by which the SUPEREGO controls instinctive impulses that would threaten the EGO if allowed conscious expression or, in some psychoanalytic theories, might jeopardize attachment. For example, inhibited sexual desire may result from unconscious feelings of guilt implanted by parents. —**inhibit** *vb.* —**inhibited** *adj.*

inhibition of return (**IOR**) difficulty in returning attention to a previously attended location. When attention has been directed to a location for a period of time, another period of time follows in which it is more difficult to redirect attention to that location than to direct it elsewhere.

inhibitory neurotransmitter see NEUROTRANSMITTER.

inhibitory postsynaptic potential (**IPSP**) a brief increase in the difference in electrical charge across the membrane of a neuron that is caused by the transmission of a signal from a neighboring neuron across the synapse (specialized junction) separating them. IPSPs decrease the probability that the postsynaptic neuron will initiate an ACTION POTENTIAL and hence fire a nerve impulse. Compare EXCITATORY POSTSYNAPTIC POTENTIAL.

inhibitory synapse a specialized type of junction at which activity from one neuron (in the form of an ACTION POTENTIAL) reduces the probability of activity in an adjacent neuron by initiating an INHIBITORY POSTSYNAPTIC POTENTIAL. Compare EXCITATORY SYNAPSE.

initiative versus guilt the third of ERIKSON'S EIGHT STAGES OF PSYCHOSOCIAL DEVELOPMENT, which occurs during the child's 3rd through 5th years. In planning, launching, and initiating fantasy, play, and other activity, the child learns to believe in his or her ability to pursue goals successfully. However, if these pursuits often fail or are criticized, the child may develop instead a feeling of self-doubt and guilt.

injunctive norm any of various socially determined consensual standards (SOCIAL NORMS) that describe how people should act, feel, and think in a given situation, irrespective of how they typically respond in the setting. Individuals who violate these standards are often judged negatively. Compare DESCRIPTIVE NORM.

inkblot test see RORSCHACH INKBLOT TEST.

innate *adj.* denoting a capability or characteristic existing in an organism from birth, belonging to the original or essential constitution of the body or mind. Innate processes should be distinguished from those that develop later in infancy and childhood under maturational control.

innate releasing mechanism (**IRM**) in ethology, the hypothesized neurological means by which organisms exhibit a FIXED ACTION PATTERN given a particular RELEASER, suggesting that there is a direct correspondence between a specific elicitor and a specific behavioral event.

inner ear the part of the ear that comprises the bony and membranous LABYRINTHS and contains the sense organs responsible for hearing and balance. For hearing, the major structure is the COCHLEA. For the sense of balance, the major structures are the

SEMICIRCULAR CANALS, SACCULE, and UTRICLE.

inner nuclear layer the layer of retinal cell bodies interposed between the photoreceptors and the RETINAL GANGLION CELLS. The inner nuclear layer contains AMACRINE CELLS, RETINAL HORIZONTAL CELLS, RETINAL BIPOLAR CELLS, and MÜLLER CELLS.

inner plexiform layer the synaptic layer in the retina in which contacts are made between the dendrites of RETINAL GANGLION CELLS, BIPOLAR NEURONS, and AMACRINE CELLS.

inner scribe see VISUOSPATIAL SKETCHPAD.

innervation *n.* the supply of nerves to an organ (e.g., muscle or gland) or a body region. —**innervate** *vb.*

inpatient *n.* a person who has been formally admitted to a hospital for at least 24 hours for observation, diagnosis, or treatment, as distinguished from an OUTPATIENT or an emergency-room patient.

insanity *n.* in law, a condition of the mind that renders a person incapable of being responsible for his or her criminal acts. Whether a person is insane, in this legal sense, is determined by judges and juries, not psychologists or psychiatrists. —**insane** *adj.*

insecure attachment in the STRANGE SITUATION, one of several patterns of a generally negative parent–child relationship in which the child fails to display confidence when the parent is present, sometimes shows distress when the parent leaves, and reacts to the returning parent by avoidance (**avoidant attachment**) or with ambivalence (**ambivalent attachment**). Compare SECURE ATTACHMENT.

insight *n.* **1.** the clear and often sudden discernment of a solution to a problem by means that often are not obvious. There are many different theories of how insights are formed and of the kinds of insights that exist. **2.** in psychotherapy, an awareness of underlying sources of emotional, cognitive, or behavioral responses and difficulties in oneself or another person.

insight learning a cognitive form of learning involving the mental rearrangement or restructuring of the elements in a problem to achieve a sudden understanding of the problem and arrive at a solution. Insight learning was described in the 1920s and was offered as an alternative to TRIAL-AND-ERROR LEARNING.

insight therapy any form of psychotherapy based on the theory that a client's problems cannot be resolved without his or her gaining self-understanding and thus becoming aware of their origins. This approach—characteristic, for example, of PSYCHOANALYSIS and PSYCHODYNAMIC PSYCHOTHERAPY—contrasts with therapies directed toward removal of symptoms or behavior modification.

insomnia *n.* difficulty in initiating or maintaining a restorative sleep, which results in fatigue, the severity or persistence of which causes clinically significant distress or impairment in functioning. Such sleeplessness may be caused by a transient or chronic physical condition or psychological disturbance.—**insomniac** *n.*

instinct *n.* **1.** an innate, species-specific biological force that impels an organism to do something, particularly to perform a certain act or respond in a certain manner to specific stimuli. **2.** in classical psychoanalytic theory, a basic biological drive (e.g., hunger, thirst, sex, aggression) that must be fulfilled to maintain physical and psychological equilibrium. Austrian neurologist Sigmund Freud (1856–1939) classified instincts into two types: those derived from the LIFE INSTINCT and those derived from the DEATH INSTINCT. **3.** in popular usage, any inherent or unlearned predisposition (behavioral or otherwise) or motivational force. —**instinctive** or **instinctual** *adj.*

institutionalization *n.* **1.** placement of an individual in an institution for therapeutic or correctional purposes or when he or she is incapable of living independently, often as a result of a physical or mental condition. **2.** an individual's gradual adaptation to institutional life over a long period, especially when this is seen as rendering him or her passive, dependent, and generally unsuited to life outside the institution. **—institutionalize** *vb.*

institutionalized racism differential treatment of individuals on the basis of their racial group by religious organizations, governments, businesses, the media, educational institutions, and other large social entities. Examples include DISCRIMINATION in hiring, promotion, and advancement at work; restrictive housing regulations that promote segregation; unfair portrayal of minority members in newspapers and magazines; and legal statutes that restrict the civil liberties of the members of specific racial categories. A parallel phenomenon exists for SEXISM.

institutional research a study conducted to obtain information about an academic setting. For example, a university may research its faculty, staff, students, finances, technology, campus climate, and other characteristics so as to facilitate better decision making.

institutional review board (IRB) a committee named by an agency or institution to review research proposals originating within that organization for ethical acceptability and compliance with the organization's codes of conduct. IRBs help protect research participants and are mandatory at any U.S. institution receiving federal funds for research.

instrumental activities of daily living (IADLs) activities essential to an individual's ability to function autonomously, including cooking, doing laundry, using the telephone, managing money, shopping, getting to places

beyond walking distance, and the like. See also ACTIVITIES OF DAILY LIVING.

instrumental aggression see AGGRESSION.

instrumental conditioning any form of CONDITIONING in which the correct response is essential for REINFORCEMENT. Instrumental conditioning is similar to OPERANT CONDITIONING and usually involves complex activities in order to reach a goal, such as when a rat is trained to navigate a maze to obtain food. It contrasts with CLASSICAL CONDITIONING, in which reinforcement is given regardless of the response.

instrumentalism *n.* a theory of knowledge that emphasizes the pragmatic value, rather than the truth value, of ideas. In this view, the value of an idea, concept, or judgment lies in its ability to explain, predict, and control one's concrete functional interactions with the experienced world. This view is related to PRAGMATISM. **—instrumentalist** *adj., n.*

insula *n.* (*pl.* **insulae**) a region of the cerebral cortex of primate brains that is buried in a cleft near the lower end of the LATERAL SULCUS. It is thought to play a major role in emotion (particularly negative emotions, such as disgust), taste, self-awareness, and motor control of functions such as swallowing and speech articulation. [from Latin, "island"]

insulin *n.* a hormone, secreted by the B cells of the ISLETS OF LANGERHANS in the pancreas, that facilitates the transfer of glucose molecules through cell membranes. Together with GLUCAGON, it plays a key role in regulating blood sugar and carbohydrate metabolism.

intake interview 1. the initial interview with a client by a therapist or counselor to obtain both information regarding the issues or problems that have brought the client into therapy or counseling and preliminary information regarding personal and family history. **2.** the initial interview with a patient who is being admitted into a psychiatric hospital, day treatment program, or inpatient substance abuse facility. An intake interview may be carried out by a specialist who may not necessarily treat the patient, with the information obtained used to determine the best course of treatment and the appropriate therapist to provide it.

integrated care a consistent, systematic, and coordinated set of health care services that are developed, managed, and delivered to individual patients over a range of organizations and by a variety of associated professionals and other care providers. The approach seeks to reduce fragmented care (i.e., diagnosis and treatment by multiple unconnected and minimally communicating doctors and caregivers); to improve clinical outcomes, quality of life, patient satisfaction, effectiveness, and efficiency (ideally using EVIDENCE-BASED PRACTICE guidelines); and to reduce costs. The efficacy of integrated care is often viewed and measured from two perspectives: that of the patient and that of the organizations and individual service providers. Also called **integrated medicine**.

integration *n.* the coordination or unification of parts into a totality. This general meaning has been incorporated into a wide variety of psychological contexts and topics. For example, the integration of personality denotes the gradual bringing together of constituent traits, behavioral patterns, motives, and so forth to form an organized whole that functions effectively and with minimal effort or without conflict.

integrative behavioral couples therapy a form of BEHAVIORAL COUPLES THERAPY that specifically focuses on helping partners to develop acceptance and greater emotional understanding of one another and to integrate that understanding with an effort to identify, address, and change problematic patterns in their relationship that bother them both.

integrative psychotherapy psychotherapy that selects theoretical models or techniques from various therapeutic schools to suit the client's particular problems. For example, PSYCHODYNAMIC PSYCHOTHERAPY and GESTALT THERAPY may be combined through the practice of INTERPRETATION of material in the here and now.

integrity versus despair the eighth and final stage of ERIKSON'S EIGHT STAGES OF PSYCHOSOCIAL DEVELOPMENT, which occurs during old age. In this stage, the individual reflects on the life he or she has lived and may develop either integrity—a sense of satisfaction in having lived a good life and the ability to approach death with equanimity—or despair—a feeling of bitterness about opportunities missed and time wasted, and a dread of approaching death.

intellectual disability a DEVELOPMENTAL DISABILITY characterized by mild to profound limitations in cognitive function (e.g., learning, problem solving, reasoning, planning) and in adaptive behavior, impairing one's ability to acquire skills typical for one's age group as a child or necessary for one's later independent functioning as an adult. It is now the preferred term for MENTAL RETARDATION.

intelligence *n.* the ability to derive information, learn from experience, adapt to the environment, understand, and correctly utilize thought and reason. See also IQ. —**intelligent** *adj.*

intelligence quotient see IQ.

intelligence test an individually administered test used to determine a person's level of intelligence by measuring his or her ability to solve problems, form concepts, reason, acquire detail, and perform other intellectual tasks. It comprises mental, verbal, and performance tasks of graded difficulty that have been standardized by use on a representative sample of the population.

intensity *n.* **1.** the quantitative value

of a stimulus or sensation. **2.** the strength of any behavior, such as an impulse or emotion. —**intense** *adj.*

intention *n.* a prior conscious decision to perform a behavior. In experiments, intention is often equated with the goals defined by the task instructions. —**intentional** *adj.*

interaction *n.* a relationship between two or more systems, people, or groups that results in mutual or reciprocal influence. See also SOCIAL INTERACTION. —**interact** *vb.*

interaction effect in a FACTORIAL DESIGN, the joint effect of two or more independent variables on a dependent variable above and beyond the sum of their individual effects, such that the value of one variable is contingent on the value of another. For example, if a researcher is studying how gender (female vs. male) and dieting (Diet A vs. Diet B) influence weight loss, an interaction effect would occur if women using Diet A lost more weight than men using Diet A. Interaction effects may obscure MAIN EFFECTS. Compare ADDITIVE EFFECT.

interactionism *n.* **1.** the position that mind and body are distinct, incompatible substances that nevertheless interact, so that each has a causal influence on the other. This position is particularly associated with French philosopher and mathematician René Descartes (1596–1650). See CARTESIAN DUALISM; MIND–BODY PROBLEM. **2.** a set of approaches, particularly in personality psychology, in which behavior is explained not in terms of personality attributes or situational influences but by references to interactions that typify the behavior of a certain type of person in a certain type of setting. —**interactionist** *adj.*

interaction process analysis (**IPA**) a technique used to study the emotional, intellectual, and behavioral interactions among members of a group. It requires observers to classify

every behavior displayed by each group member into one of 12 mutually exclusive categories, such as "asks for information" or "shows tension." See also STRUCTURED OBSERVATION.

intercoder reliability see INTER-RATER RELIABILITY.

intercorrelation *n.* the degree of relationship between each variable and every other variable in a group of variables.

interdependence *n.* a state in which two or more people, situations, variables, or other entities rely on or react with one another such that one cannot change without affecting the other. Also called **interdependency**. —**interdependent** *adj., n.*

interdependence theory an approach to analyzing social interactions and relationships that focuses on how each person's outcomes depend on the actions of others. More specifically, interdependence theory identifies the most important characteristics of social situations and describes their implications for understanding how individuals make choices and take action. A central element of the theory is the proposition that people have standards against which they compare their current outcomes. When people's actual experiences are inconsistent with their standards, they may act to alter the situation.

interdependent self-construal a view of the self that emphasizes one's embeddedness in a network of social relationships and that downplays one's separateness and unique traits or accomplishments. Compare INDEPENDENT SELF-CONSTRUAL.

interdisciplinary approach a manner of dealing with psychological, medical, or other scientific questions in which individuals from different disciplines or professions collaborate to obtain a more thorough, detailed understanding of the nature of the questions and consequently develop more comprehensive answers. Also called **multidisciplinary approach**.

interference *n.* **1.** the blocking of learning or of memory RETRIEVAL by the learning or remembering of other conflicting material. Interference has many sources, including prior learning (**proactive interference**), subsequent learning (**retroactive interference**), competition during recall (**output interference**), and presentation of other material. **2.** the mutual effect on meeting of two or more light, sound, or other waves, the overlap of which produces a new pattern of waves.

interference theory the hypothesis that forgetting is due to competition from other learning or other memories.

intergenerational trauma a phenomenon in which the descendants of a person who has experienced a terrifying event show adverse emotional and behavioral reactions to the event that are similar to those of the person himself or herself. These reactions vary by generation but often include shame, increased anxiety and guilt, a heightened sense of vulnerability and helplessness, low self-esteem, depression, suicidality, substance abuse, DISSOCIATION, hypervigilance, intrusive thoughts, difficulty with relationships and attachment to others, difficulty in regulating aggression, and extreme reactivity to stress. Also called **multigenerational trauma**; **secondary traumatization**.

interjudge reliability see INTER-RATER RELIABILITY.

intermittent explosive disorder an impulse-control disorder consisting of multiple episodes in which the individual fails to resist aggressive impulses and commits assaultive acts or destroys property. These aggressive acts are significantly out of proportion to any precipitating factors, are not caused by any other mental disorder or a general medical condition, and are not substance induced. Compare ISOLATED EXPLOSIVE DISORDER.

intermittent reinforcement in operant or instrumental conditioning, any pattern of REINFORCEMENT in which only some responses are reinforced. Also called **partial reinforcement**.

intermodal matching see CROSS-MODAL MATCHING.

intermodal perception the coordination or integration of information from two or more senses, such as touch and vision.

internal attribution see DISPOSITIONAL ATTRIBUTION.

internal capsule a large band of nerve fibers in the BASAL GANGLIA that extends between the CAUDATE NUCLEUS on its medial side and the GLOBUS PALLIDUS and PUTAMEN on its lateral side. It contains afferent and efferent fibers from all parts of the cerebral cortex as they converge near the brainstem. See also EXTERNAL CAPSULE.

internal consistency the degree of interrelationship or homogeneity among the items on a test, such that they are consistent with one another and measuring the same thing. Internal consistency is an index of the RELIABILITY of a test. Also called **internal reliability**.

internalization *n.* **1.** the nonconscious mental process by which the characteristics, beliefs, feelings, or attitudes of other individuals or groups are assimilated into the self and adopted as one's own. **2.** in psychoanalytic theory, the process of incorporating an OBJECT relationship inside the psyche, which reproduces the external relationship as an intrapsychic phenomenon. For example, through internalization the relationship between father and child is reproduced in the relationship between SUPEREGO and EGO or, in relational theory, between self and other. The term is often mistakenly used as a synonym for INTROJECTION. —**internalize** *vb.*

internal locus of control see LOCUS OF CONTROL.

internal respiration see RESPI-RATION.

internal validity the degree to which a study or experiment is free from flaws in its internal structure and its results can therefore be taken to represent the true nature of the phenomenon under investigation. In other words, internal validity pertains to the soundness of results obtained within the controlled conditions of a particular study, specifically with respect to whether one can draw reasonable conclusions about cause-and-effect relationships among variables. Compare EXTERNAL VALIDITY.

internal working model of attachment a cognitive construction or set of assumptions about the workings of relationships, such as expectations of support or affection. The earliest relationships may form the template for this internal model, which may be positive or negative. See also ATTACHMENT THEORY.

International Classification of Diseases (**ICD**) the global standard for diagnostic classification of all health conditions as compiled by the World Health Organization (WHO) for clinical, health management, and epidemiological purposes. At the national level, WHO's member countries use the *ICD* in morbidity and mortality statistics, whereas individual practitioners—including those in the United States—use its codes for reimbursement for services. Based on a formal classification system originally developed in 1893, the *ICD* has since undergone numerous revisions. The current version, ***ICD–10***, published in 1992 as the *International Statistical Classification of Diseases and Related Health Problems*, uses a four-character alphanumeric coding system to classify diseases and disorders and their subtypes, including those relating to mental and behavioral disorders. Another revision, ***ICD–11***, is expected in 2017. See also DSM–5.

Internet addiction a behavioral pattern characterized by excessive or obsessive online and offline computer use that leads to distress and impairment. The condition, though controversial, has attracted increasing attention in the popular media and among health care professionals. Expanding research has identified various subtypes, including those involving excessive gaming, sexual preoccupations, and e-mail and text messaging.

Internet meme see MEME.

interneuron *n.* any neuron that is neither sensory nor motor but connects other neurons within the central nervous system. Also called **connector neuron**.

interobserver reliability see INTERRATER RELIABILITY.

interoception *n.* sensitivity to stimuli inside the body, resulting from the response of specialized sensory cells called **interoceptors** to occurrences within the body (e.g., from the viscera). Compare EXTEROCEPTION.

interpersonal *adj.* pertaining to actions, events, and feelings between two or more individuals. For example, **interpersonal skill** is an aptitude enabling a person to carry on effective interactions and relationships with others, such as the ability to communicate thought and feeling or to assume appropriate social responsibilities.

interpersonal attraction see ATTRACTION.

interpersonal influence direct SOCIAL PRESSURE exerted on a person or group by another person or group in the form of demands or threats on the one hand or promises of rewards or social approval on the other. Compare INFORMATIONAL INFLUENCE; NORMATIVE INFLUENCE.

interpersonal psychotherapy (**IPT**) a time-limited form of psychotherapy based on the theory that relations with others constitute the primary force motivating human behavior. The therapist helps the client explore current and past experiences in detail, clarifying the client's interpersonal reactions to significant others as well as general environmental influences on personal adaptive and maladaptive thinking and behavior.

interpersonal theory the theory of personality that was developed by U.S. psychiatrist Harry Stack Sullivan (1892–1949), which is based on the belief that people's interactions with other people determine their sense of security, sense of self, and the dynamics that motivate their behavior. For Sullivan, personality is the product of a long series of stages in which the individual gradually develops "good feeling" toward others and a sense of a "good me" toward himself or herself.

interpolation *n.* a strategy for determining an unknown value given knowledge of surrounding data points. For example, if the average score on a test is 70 for a group of beginner students and the average score on the same test is 90 for an advanced group of students, one might use interpolation to estimate an average score of 80 on the test for an intermediate group of students.

interposition *n.* a monocular DEPTH CUE occurring when two objects are in the same line of vision and the closer object, which is fully in view, partly conceals the farther object.

interpretation *n.* in psychotherapy, explanation by the therapist of the client's issues, behaviors, or feelings. Interpretation typically is made along the lines of the conceptual framework or dynamic model of the particular therapy. In psychoanalysis, for example, the analyst uses the constructs of psychoanalytic theory to interpret the patient's early experiences, dreams, character defenses, and resistance. Although interpretation exists to some extent in almost any form of therapy, it is a critical procedural step in psychoanalysis and in other forms of PSYCHODYNAMIC PSYCHOTHERAPY.

interpretivism *n.* in EPISTEMOLOGY, the assertion that knowledge is deeply tied to the act of interpretation; there are multiple apprehendable and equally valid realities as opposed to a single objective reality. Interpretivism thus represents a form of RELATIVISM. See also CONSTRUCTIVISM.

interquartile range (IQR) an index of the dispersion within a data set: the difference between the 75th and 25th PERCENTILE scores (also known as the upper and lower HINGES) within a distribution. Also called **H spread; midspread**.

interrater reliability the extent to which independent evaluators produce similar ratings in judging the same abilities or characteristics in the same target person or object. It often is expressed as a CORRELATION COEFFICIENT. If consistency is high, a researcher can be confident that similarly trained individuals would likely produce similar scores on targets of the same kind. Also called **intercoder reliability; interjudge reliability; interobserver reliability; interscorer reliability**.

interrupted time-series design a QUASI-EXPERIMENTAL DESIGN in which the effects of an intervention are evaluated by comparing outcome measures obtained at several time intervals before and several time intervals after the intervention was introduced. Unlike traditional TIME-SERIES DESIGNS, which make use of a continuous predictor variable, an interrupted time-series design uses a categorical predictor—the absence or presence of an intervention.

interscorer reliability see INTERRATER RELIABILITY.

intersensory perception the coordination of information presented through separate sensory modalities into an integrated experience. Information from one sensory source is transmitted to the ASSOCIATION CORTEX, where it can be integrated with information from another sensory source.

Also called **cross-modal perception**. See SENSORY INTERACTION.

intersex *n.* **1.** a modern and evolving term for HERMAPHRODITISM and PSEUDO-HERMAPHRODITISM, the condition of possessing the sexual characteristics of both sexes. Sometimes called **intersexualism**; **intersexuality**. **2.** an individual who exhibits sexual characteristics of both sexes. However, using phrases such as "an intersex individual" or "a person with intersex conditions" is considered preferable. —**intersex** *adj.*

intersubjectivity *n.* the sharing of subjective experience between two or more people. Intersubjectivity is seen as essential to language and the production of social meaning. The term is often applied to the relationship between a therapist and a client. —**intersubjective** *adj.*

interval data numerical values that indicate magnitude but lack a "natural" zero point. Interval data represent exact quantities of the variables under consideration, and when arranged consecutively they have equal differences among adjacent values (regardless of the specific values selected) that correspond to genuine differences between the physical quantities being measured. Temperature is an example of interval data: The difference between 50 °F and 49 °F is the same as the difference between 40 °F and 39 °F, but a temperature of 0 °F does not indicate that there is no temperature. Compare RATIO DATA. See also INTERVAL SCALE.

interval estimate an estimated range of likely values for a given population PARAMETER. For example, a researcher might use data from a sample to determine that the average score on a particular variable in the larger population falls between 20 and 25. Compare POINT ESTIMATE.

interval reinforcement the REINFORCEMENT of the first response to a stimulus after a predetermined interval has elapsed. Reinforcement may be given at uniform or variable intervals; the number of responses during the interval is irrelevant. Compare RATIO REINFORCEMENT.

interval scale a scale marked in equal intervals so that the difference between any two consecutive values on the scale is equivalent regardless of the two values selected. Interval scales lack a true, meaningful zero point, which is what distinguishes them from RATIO SCALES. For example, Fahrenheit temperature uses an interval scale: The difference between 50 °F and 49 °F is the same as the difference between 40 °F and 39 °F, but a temperature of 0 °F does not indicate that there is no temperature. See also INTERVAL DATA.

interval variable a variable that is measured using an INTERVAL SCALE. Because values on such a scale are equally spaced, the differences between values of an interval variable are meaningful. Compare ORDINAL VARIABLE.

intervening variable see MEDIATOR.

intervention *n.* **1.** Generally, any treatment undertaken to halt, manage, or alter the course of the pathological process of a disease or disorder. **2.** action on the part of a psychotherapist to deal with the issues and problems of a client. The selection of the intervention is guided by the nature of the problem, the orientation of the therapist, the setting, and the willingness and ability of the client to proceed with the treatment. **3.** a technique in addictions counseling in which significant individuals in a client's life meet with him or her, in the presence of a trained counselor, to express their observations and feelings about the client's addiction and related problems. The session, typically a surprise to the client, may last several hours, after which the client has a choice of seeking a recommended treatment immediately (e.g., as an inpatient) or ignoring the intervention. If the client chooses not to seek treatment, participants state the interpersonal consequences; for example, a spouse may request that the client move out. **4.** in research design, an EXPERIMENTAL MANIPULATION. —**intervene** *vb.*

interview *n.* a directed conversation in which a researcher, therapist, clinician, employer, or the like (the **interviewer**) intends to elicit specific information from an individual (the **interviewee**) for purposes of research, diagnosis, treatment, or employment. Conducted face to face, by telephone, or online, interviews may be either standardized, including set questions, or open ended, varying with material introduced in responses by the interviewee.

interviewer effect the influence of the characteristics of an interviewer on the responses provided by an interviewee. The interviewer's age, gender, and level of experience may affect the manner in which the interviewee responds, as may his or her general demeanor and nonverbal cues. For example, a person might discuss sensitive topics, such as sexual or drinking behavior, more openly and truthfully with an interviewer who is of the same gender.

intimacy *n.* an interpersonal state of extreme emotional closeness such that each party's PERSONAL SPACE can be entered by any of the other parties without causing discomfort to that person. Intimacy characterizes close, familiar, and usually affectionate or loving personal relationships and requires the parties to have a detailed knowledge or deep understanding of each other. —**intimate** *adj.*

intimacy versus isolation the sixth of ERIKSON'S EIGHT STAGES OF PSYCHOSOCIAL DEVELOPMENT, which extends from late adolescence through courtship and early family life to early middle age. During this period, individuals must learn to share and care without losing themselves; if they fail, they will feel alone and isolated.

intimate partner violence physi-

cal, psychological, or sexual abuse of one person by another in a close relationship. The couple may be heterosexual or same sex, and they may be (or have been) dating, married, or living together. Apart from violence and threats of abuse, control is a hallmark of the abusive intimate partner relationship, with the aggressor controlling the partner's access to family and friends, taking control of shared finances, and constantly monitoring the partner's activities. Victims of intimate partner violence are at greater risk for developing depression, substance abuse, and other disorders. See also DOMESTIC VIOLENCE.

intoxication *n.* see SUBSTANCE INTOXICATION.

intraclass correlation the degree of homogeneity among unordered members (people, items, etc.) of a group. For example, it may reflect the level of agreement among different judges rating a specific attribute. It is indexed by the **intraclass correlation coefficient (ICC)**, which ranges from 0 to 1 in value. A larger ICC indicates more homogeneity and thus that a correspondingly smaller proportion of the total variance in a dependent variable is attributable to individual differences within the group.

intrapersonal *adj.* describing factors operating or constructs occurring within the person, such as attitudes, decisions, self-concept, self-esteem, or self-regulation.

intrapsychic *adj.* pertaining to impulses, ideas, conflicts, or other psychological phenomena that arise or occur within the psyche or mind. An **intrapsychic conflict**, for example, is the clash of opposing forces within the psyche, such as conflicting drives, wishes, or agencies. Compare EXTRAPSYCHIC.

intrinsic motivation an incentive to engage in a specific activity that derives from pleasure in the activity itself (e.g., a genuine interest in a subject studied) rather than because of any external benefits that might be obtained (e.g., money, course credits). Compare EXTRINSIC MOTIVATION.

introjection *n.* **1.** a process in which an individual unconsciously incorporates aspects of external reality into the self, particularly the attitudes, values, and qualities of another person or a part of another person's personality. Introjection may occur, for example, in the mourning process for a loved one. **2.** in psychoanalytic theory, the process of absorbing the qualities of an external OBJECT into the psyche in the form of an internal object or mental REPRESENTATION (i.e., an **introject**), which then has an influence on behavior. This process is posited to be a normal part of development, as when introjection of parental values and attitudes forms the SUPEREGO, but it may also be used as a DEFENSE MECHANISM in situations that arouse anxiety. —**introject** *vb.* —**introjective** *adj.*

introjective depression intense sadness and DYSPHORIA involving punitive, relentless feelings of self-doubt, self-criticism, and self-loathing. The individual with introjective depression becomes involved in numerous activities in an attempt to compensate for his or her excessively high standards, constant drive to perform and achieve, and feelings of guilt and shame over not having lived up to expectations. Compare ANACLITIC DEPRESSION.

intromission *n.* the act of putting one thing into something else, especially the insertion of the penis into the vagina. —**intromissive** *adj.*

intropunitive *adj.* referring to the punishment of oneself: tending to turn anger, blame, or hostility internally, against the self, in response to frustration. Compare EXTRAPUNITIVE. —**intropunitiveness** *n.*

introspection *n.* the attempt to directly access one's own internal psychological processes, judgments, perceptions, or states. —**introspective** *adj.*

introspectionism *n.* the doctrine that the basic method of psychological investigation is or should be INTROSPECTION. Historically, such an approach is associated with the school of psychological STRUCTURALISM. —**introspectionist** *adj.*

introversion *n.* orientation toward the internal private world of one's self and one's inner thoughts and feelings, rather than toward the outer world of people and things. Introversion is a broad personality trait and, like EXTRAVERSION, exists on a continuum of attitudes and behaviors. Introverts are relatively withdrawn, reserved, quiet, and deliberate; they may tend to mute or guard expression of positive affect, adopt skeptical views or positions, and prefer to work independently. —**introversive** or **introverted** *adj.* —**introvert** *n.*

intrusion error in a memory test, the recall of an item that was not among the material presented for remembering. Intrusion errors can be informative about the nature of forgetting, as when the intrusion is a synonym, rhyme, or associate of a correct item.

intuition *n.* immediate insight or perception, as contrasted with conscious reasoning or reflection. Intuitions have been characterized alternatively as quasi-mystical experiences or as the products of instinct, feeling, minimal sense impressions, or unconscious forces. —**intuit** *vb.* —**intuitive** *adj.*

invariance *n.* **1.** in the theory of ECOLOGICAL PERCEPTION, any property of an object that remains constant despite changes in the point of observation or surrounding conditions. **2.** the property of being unchanged by a statistical TRANSFORMATION. For example, after a constant value has been added to each of a set of scores on a test, the degrees of difference among the scores will demonstrate invariance, being the same for the original and transformed set. —**invariant** *adj.*

invasive *adj.* **1.** denoting procedures or tests that require puncture or incision of the skin or insertion of an instrument or foreign material into the body. **2.** able to spread from one tissue to another, or having the capacity to spread, as in the case of an infection or a malignant tumor. Compare NON-INVASIVE.

inverse agonist see AGONIST.

inverse correlation see NEGATIVE CORRELATION.

inverted-U hypothesis a proposed correlation between motivation (or AROUSAL) and performance such that performance is poorest when motivation or arousal is at very low or very high states. This function is typically referred to as the YERKES–DODSON LAW. Emotional intensity (motivation) increases from a zero point to an optimal point, increasing the quality of performance; increase in intensity after this optimal point leads to performance deterioration and disorganization, forming an inverted U-shaped curve. The optimal point is reached sooner (i.e., at lower intensities) the less well learned or more complex the performance.

investment model a theory developed to explain why people stay in abusive relationships (e.g., with romantic partners or friends). According to the model, commitment is a function of a comparison of the relationship to the individual's expectations as well as the quality of the best available alternative and the magnitude of the individual's investment in the relationship; the investment of resources serves to increase commitment by increasing the costs of leaving the relationship. The investment model has since been extended to other areas, including employment and education.

invincibility fable see PERSONAL FABLE.

in vitro referring to biological conditions or processes that occur or are made to occur outside of a living body, usually in a laboratory test tube; an example is IN VITRO FERTILIZATION. Compare EX VIVO; IN VIVO. [Latin, literally: "in glass"]

in vitro fertilization (IVF) a procedure in which an ovum (egg) is removed from a woman's body, fertilized externally with sperm, and then returned to the uterus. It is used to treat the most difficult cases of infertility, but success rates for the procedure are not high.

in vivo referring to biological conditions or processes that occur or are observed within the living organism. Compare EX VIVO; IN VITRO. [Latin, literally: "in life"]

in vivo desensitization a technique used in BEHAVIOR THERAPY, usually to reduce or eliminate phobias, in which the client is exposed to stimuli that induce anxiety. The therapist, in discussion with the client, produces a hierarchy of anxiety-invoking events or items relating to the anxiety-producing stimulus or phobia. The client is then exposed to the actual stimuli in the hierarchy, rather than asked simply to imagine them. Success depends on the client overcoming anxiety as the events or items are encountered. See also SYSTEMATIC DESENSITIZATION.

in vivo exposure a type of EXPOSURE THERAPY, generally used for treating individuals with phobias, obsessive-compulsive disorder, and other anxiety disorders, in which the client directly experiences anxiety-provoking situations or stimuli in real-world conditions. For example, a client who fears flying could be accompanied by a therapist to the airport to simulate boarding a plane while practicing anxiety-decreasing techniques, such as deep breathing. Compare IMAGINAL EXPOSURE.

involuntary *adj.* describing activity, movement, behavior, or other processes (e.g., reflexes) that occur without intention or volition, as opposed to those that are intentionally initiated. Compare VOLUNTARY.

involuntary hospitalization the confinement of a person with a serious mental illness to a mental hospital by medical authorization and legal direction. Individuals so hospitalized may be considered dangerous to themselves or others, may fail to recognize the severity of their illness and the need for treatment, or may be unable to have their daily living and treatment needs otherwise met in the community or to survive without medical attention. Compare VOLUNTARY ADMISSION.

involutional *adj.* describing the decline of the body or any of its parts from an optimal level of functioning as a result of increasing age. —**involution** *n.*

iodopsin *n.* any one of three PHOTOPIGMENTS found in the RETINAL CONES. Each consists of 11-*cis*-retinal combined with one of three different proteins, each of which confers a different wavelength sensitivity on the iodopsin. See also RHODOPSIN.

ion *n.* an atom or molecule that has acquired an electrical charge by gaining or losing one or more electrons. —**ionic** *adj.*

ion channel a group of proteins forming a channel that spans a cell membrane, allowing the passage of ions between the extracellular environment and the cytoplasm of the cell. Ion channels are selective; allow passage of ions of a particular chemical nature, size, or electrostatic charge; and may be ungated (i.e., always open) or gated, opening and closing in response to chemical, electrical, or mechanical signals. Ion channels are important in the transmission of neural signals between neurons at a SYNAPSE.

ionotropic receptor a receptor protein that includes an ION CHANNEL that is opened when the receptor is activated. See GLUTAMATE RECEPTOR. Compare METABOTROPIC RECEPTOR.

ipsative *adj.* referring back to the self. For example, ipsative analyses of personal characteristics involve assessing multiple psychological attributes and conducting within-person analyses of the degree to which an individual possesses one attribute versus another.

ipsative scale a scale in which the points distributed to the various different items must sum to a specific total. All participants will have the same total score, but the distribution of the points among the various items will differ for each individual. For example, a supervisor using an ipsative scale to indicate an employee's strength in different areas initially might assign 20 points for communication, 30 for timeliness, and 50 for work quality but a few months later assign 30 points for communication, 30 for timeliness, and 40 for quality of work. The total number of points distributed in each case, however, is the same (100). Compare NORMATIVE SCALE.

ipsilateral *adj.* situated on or affecting the same side of the body. Compare CONTRALATERAL. —**ipsilaterally** *adv.*

IQ intelligence quotient: a standard measure of an individual's intelligence level based on psychological tests. In the early years of intelligence testing, IQ was calculated by dividing the MENTAL AGE by the CHRONOLOGICAL AGE and multiplying by 100 to produce a **ratio IQ**. This concept has now mostly been replaced by the DEVIATION IQ, computed as a function of the discrepancy of an individual score from the mean (or average) score. The mean IQ is customarily 100, with slightly more than two thirds of all scores falling within plus or minus 15 points of the mean (usually one standard deviation). Some tests yield more specific IQ scores, such as a verbal IQ and a performance IQ. Discrepancies between the two can be used diagnostically to detect learning disabilities or specific cognitive deficiencies. Additional data are often derived from IQ tests, such as performance speed, freedom from distractibility, verbal comprehension, and PERCEPTUAL ORGANIZA-TION indices. There are critics who consider the concept of IQ (and other intelligence scales) to be flawed. They point out that the IQ test is more a measure of previously learned skills and knowledge than of underlying native ability, and they refer to cases of misrepresentation of facts in the history of IQ research.

iris *n.* a muscular disk that surrounds the pupil of the eye and controls the amount of light entering the eye by contraction or relaxation. The stroma of the iris, which faces the cornea, contains a pigment that gives the eye its coloration; the back of the iris is lined with a dark pigment that restricts light entry to the pupil, regardless of the apparent color of the iris.

irrational *adj.* lacking in reason or sound judgment: illogical or unreasonable.

ischemia *n.* deficiency of blood in an organ or tissue, due to functional constriction or actual obstruction of a blood vessel. **—ischemic** *adj.*

islets of Langerhans clusters of secretory cells within the pancreas. The A (or alpha) cells secrete GLUCA-GON, the B (or beta) cells secrete INSU-LIN, and the D (or delta) cells secrete SOMATOSTATIN. Together these hormones play a key role in regulating blood sugar and carbohydrate metabolism. [Paul **Langerhans** (1847–1888), German anatomist]

isolated explosive disorder an impulse-control disorder characterized by a single, discrete episode in which the individual commits a violent, catastrophic act, such as shooting strangers during a sudden fit of rage. The episode is out of all proportion to any precipitating stress, is not due to any other mental disorder or to a general medical condition, and is not substance induced. Compare INTERMITTENT EXPLOSIVE DISORDER.

isolation *n.* **1.** the condition of being separated, voluntarily or involuntarily, from social contact with others. **2.** in psychoanalytic theory, a DEFENSE MECH-ANISM that relies on keeping unwelcome thoughts and feelings from forming associative links with other thoughts and feelings, with the result that the unwelcome material is rarely activated. **—isolate** *vb.*

isosensitivity function see RE-CEIVER-OPERATING CHARACTERISTIC CURVE.

item analysis a set of procedures used to evaluate the statistical merits of individual items comprising a psychological measure or test. These procedures may be used to select items for a test from a larger pool of initial items or to evaluate items on an established test.

item response theory (**IRT**) a psychometric theory of measurement based on the concept that the probability that an item will be answered correctly is a function of an underlying trait or ability that is not directly observable. Item response theory models differ in terms of the number of parameters included in the model. For example, the RASCH MODEL is based on the single parameter of item difficulty. Compare CLASSICAL TEST THEORY.

iteration *n.* the repetition of a certain computational step until further repetition no longer changes the outcome or until the repetition meets some other predefined criterion.

Jj

James–Lange theory the theory that different feeling states stem from the feedback from the viscera and voluntary musculature to the brain. This theory hypothesizes that there are as many physiological responses as there are different intrapsychic feelings and that each of these responses precedes rather than follows the feeling. [William **James** (1842–1910), U.S. psychologist and philosopher; Carl Georg **Lange** (1834–1900), Danish physiologist]

jargon *n.* specialized words and forms of language used within a particular profession or field of activity. Although jargon is often unavoidable when dealing with technical or specialist subjects, inappropriate or unnecessary use can alienate outsiders, who find it unintelligible.

jealousy *n.* a negative emotion in which an individual resents a third party for appearing to take away (or being likely to take away) the affections of a loved one. Jealousy requires a triangle of social relationships among three individuals: the one who is jealous, the partner with whom the jealous individual has or desires a relationship, and the rival who represents a threat to that relationship. —**jealous** *adj.*

jet lag a maladjustment of CIRCADIAN RHYTHMS that results from traveling through several time zones in a short span of time. Rest, work, eating, body temperature, and adrenocortical-secretion cycles may require several days to adjust to local time.

jigsaw method a team-learning technique initially designed to foster a cooperative learning environment that reduces prejudice and social isolation and improves academic achievement. Students work in groups on a content unit. The teacher assigns specific topics in the unit to each group member and allows students with the same topics to leave their group to study the topic with others who have that same assignment. The students then return to their original groups and teach their topics to the other members. Also called **jigsaw classroom**.

job analysis the collection and analysis of information about a specific job, including the behaviors, tools, working conditions, and skills involved. Data are obtained through interviews with or written questionnaires from those doing or supervising the job, or through observation or audiovisual recordings of the job in action. Job analysis is the first step in developing effective personnel selection, employee evaluation, job evaluation, and personnel training programs.

job satisfaction the attitude of a worker toward his or her job, often expressed as a hedonic response of liking or disliking the work itself, the rewards (pay, promotions, recognition), or the context (working conditions, colleagues).

joint attention attention overtly focused by two or more people on the same object, person, or action at the same time, with each being aware of the other's interest. Joint attention is an important developmental tool: Around 9 months of age, infants can follow their parents' gaze and begin to imitate what their parents do.

joy *n.* a feeling of extreme gladness, delight, or exultation of the spirit arising from a sense of well-being or satisfaction. The feeling of joy may take two forms: passive and active. **Passive joy** involves tranquility and a feeling of contentment with things as they are. **Active joy** involves a desire to share one's feelings with others.

just noticeable difference (JND; **jnd**) see DIFFERENCE THRESHOLD.

just-world hypothesis the idea that the world is a fair and orderly place where what happens to people generally is what they deserve. This view enables an individual to confront his or her physical and social environments as though they were stable and predictable but may, for example, result in the belief that the innocent victim of an accident or attack must somehow be responsible for or deserve it. Also called **belief in a just world**; **just-world bias**.

juvenile delinquency illegal behavior by a minor (usually identified as a person younger than 18 years) that would be considered criminal in an adult. Examples are vandalism, theft, rape, arson, and aggravated assault.

Kk

kainate receptor see GLUTAMATE RECEPTOR.

kappa *n*. see COHEN'S KAPPA.

K complex a brief, high-amplitude spike-and-rebound waveform recorded in the scalp electroencephalograph during sleep onset. K complexes and SLEEP SPINDLES occur normally during Stage 2 NREM sleep (see SLEEP STAGES). They may suppress sleep disruptions and coordinate memory consolidation.

kindness *n*. benevolent and helpful action intentionally directed toward another person. Kindness is often considered to be motivated by the desire to help another, not to gain explicit reward or to avoid explicit punishment. See ALTRUISM. —**kind** *adj.*

kinesics *n*. the study of the part played by body movements, such as hand gestures, eye movements, and so on, in communicating meaning. See BODY LANGUAGE.

kinesthesis *n*. the sense that provides information through receptors in the muscles, tendons, and joints, enabling humans and other animals to control and coordinate their movements, including walking, talking, facial expressions, gestures, and posture. Also called **kinesthesia**. See PROPRIOCEPTION. —**kinesthetic** *adj.*

kin selection a variation of NATURAL SELECTION that favors behavior by individuals that will increase the chances of their relatives surviving and reproducing successfully (see ALTRUISM). Individuals share 50% of their genes with a parent or sibling, so if they risk their own ability to reproduce or survive but help their parents or more than two siblings to reproduce or survive, they will benefit indirectly by gaining INCLUSIVE FITNESS.

Kinsey Scale an index of an individual's relative position on a 7-point continuum of sexual orientation, ranging from 0 (exclusively heterosexual, with no same-sex interest) to 6 (exclusively homosexual, with no heterosexual interest). Points 1 through 5 represent gradations of predominant versus incidental heterosexual–homosexual behaviors and thoughts. [developed in 1948 by U.S. zoologist and sex researcher Alfred **Kinsey** (1894–1956) and colleagues]

kinship network the system of formal and informal relationships that make up an EXTENDED FAMILY in a given culture or society, typically based on blood ties, marriage, or adoption. The analysis of kinship networks in preindustrial societies has been a major concern of cultural anthropology. Also called **kinship system.**

kleptomania *n*. an impulse-control disorder characterized by a repeated failure to resist impulses to steal objects that have no immediate use or intrinsic value to the individual, accompanied by feelings of increased tension before committing the theft and pleasure or relief during the act. —**kleptomaniac** *n*.

Klinefelter's syndrome a disorder in which males are born with an extra X chromosome, resulting in small testes, absence of sperm, enlarged breasts, intellectual disability, and abnormal behavior. Also called **XXY syndrome**. [Harry F. **Klinefelter** Jr. (1912–1990), U.S. physician]

Klüver–Bucy syndrome a condition resulting from damage to both medial TEMPORAL LOBES and marked by hypersexuality and a tendency to examine all objects by touch or by placing them in the mouth. Other symptoms may include an inability to visually recognize objects, decreased emotional responsivity (including loss of normal fear and anger responses), distractibility, and memory loss. [Heinrich **Klüver** (1897–1975), German-born U.S. neurologist; Paul **Bucy** (1904–1992), U.S. neurosurgeon]

knowledge base an individual's general background knowledge, which influences his or her performance on most cognitive tasks.

knowledge function of an attitude the role an attitude can play in helping to interpret ambiguous information or to organize information. For example, a positive attitude toward a friend may assist in attributing that person's negative behavior to situational factors rather than to personal characteristics.

Kohlberg's theory of moral development the concept that the cognitive processes associated with moral judgment develop through three main levels: the PRECONVENTIONAL LEVEL, the CONVENTIONAL LEVEL, and the POSTCONVENTIONAL LEVEL. [Lawrence **Kohlberg** (1927–1987), U.S. psychologist]

Kolmogorov–Smirnov goodness-of-fit test a NONPARAMETRIC method for comparing the distribution from a sample data set to an expected distribution or the known distribution of a given population. If the test yields a discrepancy (D) larger than the CRITICAL VALUE, then the sample data are considered to be significantly different from the reference distribution. Also called **Kolmogorov–Smirnov D test**. [Andrei Nikolaevich **Kolmogorov** (1903–1987) and Nikolai Vasilevich **Smirnov** (1900–1966), Soviet mathematicians]

Korsakoff's syndrome a syndrome occurring primarily in cases of severe, chronic alcoholism. It is caused by thiamine (vitamin B_1) deficiency and damage to the MAMMILLARY BODIES. Patients with Korsakoff's syndrome demonstrate dense amnesia, which is thought to be due to lesions in the thalamus. Other symptoms include CONFABULATION, lack of insight, apathy, and impoverished conversation. The syndrome often follows an episode of WERNICKE'S ENCEPHALOPATHY. Also called **Korsakoff's disease**; **Korsakoff's psychosis**. [first described in 1887 by Sergei **Korsakoff** (1853–1900), Russian neurologist]

Kruskal–Wallis one-way analysis of variance a NONPARAMETRIC TEST for assessing whether the MEDIANS of multiple samples of ranked data are equal. It is an extension of the MANN–WHITNEY U TEST, which is conducted when there are only two independent samples. Also called **Kruskal–Wallis test**. [William Henry **Kruskal** (1919–2005) and Wilson Allen **Wallis** (1912–1998), U.S. statisticians]

kurtosis *n.* the fourth MOMENT of a PROBABILITY DISTRIBUTION. It is a statistical description of the degree of peakedness of that distribution. For example, the ages of a sample of college freshmen would probably show kurtosis, having a high peak at age 18. See LEPTOKURTIC; MESOKURTIC; PLATYKURTIC.

kwashiorkor *n.* malnutrition caused by inadequate intake of protein. The symptoms include fluid accumulation in the tissues, liver disorders, impaired growth, distention of the abdomen, and pigment changes in the skin and hair. Cerebral development also may be impaired. See also MARASMUS.

LI

labeled-line theory of taste coding a theory postulating that each gustatory neuron type comprises a private circuit (labeled line) through which the presence of its associated primary taste quality is signaled. The taste is perceived exclusively as a product of activity in that labeled line; activity in neurons outside the labeled line contributes only noise. Compare PATTERN THEORY OF TASTE CODING.

labeling *n.* **1.** in psychological assessment, classifying a patient according to a certain diagnostic category. Patient labeling may be incomplete or misleading, because not all cases conform to the sharply defined characteristics of standard diagnostic categories. **2.** medication information provided on a drug container or **package insert** (also called **direction circular**) that specifies indications, side effects, dosages, mechanisms of action, and other information necessary for a physician to prescribe the medication correctly. Also called **prescribing information (PI)**; **professional labeling**.

labeling theory the sociological hypothesis that describing an individual in terms of particular behavioral characteristics may have a significant effect on his or her behavior, as a form of SELF-FULFILLING PROPHECY. For example, describing an individual as deviant and then treating him or her as such may result in mental disorder or delinquency.

la belle indifférence inappropriate lack of concern about the implications or seriousness of one's physical symptoms, often seen in CONVERSION DISORDER.

labile *adj.* liable to change, as in labile affect. —**lability** *n.*

laboratory research scientific study conducted in a laboratory or other such workplace, where the investigator has some degree of direct control over the environment and can manipulate the INDEPENDENT VARIABLES. Although laboratory research generally has greater INTERNAL VALIDITY than FIELD RESEARCH does, it tends to be less generalizable to the real world (i.e., has less EXTERNAL VALIDITY). See EXPERIMENTAL RESEARCH.

labyrinth *n.* in anatomy, the complex system of cavities, ducts, and canals within the temporal bone of the skull that makes up the inner ear. The bony (or osseous) labyrinth is a system of bony cavities that houses the membranous labyrinth, a membrane-lined system of ducts containing the receptors for hearing and balance.

laceration *n.* a jagged tear or cut: a wound with rough, irregular edges.

lactation *n.* **1.** the formation and release of milk by the mammary glands. It is a form of NURSING that occurs only in female mammals and is divided into lactogenesis—the initiation of milk production—and galactopoiesis—the subsequent maintenance of milk production and secretion. Lactation is regulated primarily by the hormones prolactin, which facilitates and sustains milk production, and OXYTOCIN, which stimulates the milk letdown reflex to facilitate milk excretion. **2.** the period during which this process occurs.

laddering *n.* a knowledge elicitation technique used in interviews to impose a systematic framework on questioning so as to reveal complex themes across answers. In laddering, a respondent replies to a series of "why?" probes, thus requiring him or her to expose and explain choices or preferences and justify behavior in terms of goals, values, and personal constructs. Laddering provides greater scope for probing salient issues while optimizing the often limited time available with respondents.

lag effect a cognitive phenomenon in which long-term retention of information improves with increased separation (lag) between repeated presentations of the material within a single period of study. For example, a student preparing for a Spanish vocabulary exam would remember more from a study session by reviewing one long list of words multiple times instead of dividing it into three smaller lists because there would be a longer lag between the repeated presentations of each word in the former method. See also PRIMACY EFFECT; RECENCY EFFECT; SPACING EFFECT.

Lamarckism *n.* the theory that changes acquired by an organism during its lifetime—for example, through use, disuse, or injury of particular parts—can be inherited by its offspring. Although extensive research over centuries failed to find proof of such inheritance of acquired characteristics, current evidence suggests that natural or environmentally induced changes to DNA expression that occur during an organism's lifetime can result in acquired characteristics that may be inherited by offspring. [Jean-Baptiste **Lamarck** (1744–1829), French natural historian] —**Lamarckian** *adj.*

lambda (symbol: λ) see EIGENVALUE.

language *n.* **1.** a system for expressing or communicating thoughts and feelings through speech sounds or written symbols. **2.** any comparable nonverbal means of communication, such as SIGN LANGUAGE or the languages used in computer programming.

language acquisition the process by which children learn language. Although often used interchangeably with **language development**, this term is preferred by those who emphasize the active role of the child as a learner with considerable innate linguistic knowledge.

language acquisition device

(**LAD**) a hypothetical faculty used to explain a child's ability to acquire language. In the early model proposed by U.S. linguist Benjamin Lee Whorf (1897–1941), the LAD is an inherited mechanism that enables children to develop a language structure from linguistic data supplied by parents and others. In the reinterpretation of U.S. linguist Noam Chomsky (1928–), however, the LAD contains significant innate knowledge that actively interprets the input: Only this can explain how a highly abstract COMPETENCE in language results from a relatively deprived input.

language acquisition support system (**LASS**) the adults and older children who help a young child to acquire language. Children learn language in and from conversation: Family members talk to them, tailoring their language to the children's level of comprehension and often using higher pitch and exaggerated intonation. The LASS is conceptualized as essential to language learning and may interact with the LANGUAGE ACQUISITION DEVICE of the younger child.

language disorder see SPEECH AND LANGUAGE DISORDER.

language learning disability (**LLD**) see SPECIFIC LANGUAGE IMPAIRMENT.

language therapy see SPEECH THERAPY.

latency stage in classical psychoanalytic theory, the stage of PSYCHOSEXUAL DEVELOPMENT in which overt sexual interest is sublimated and the child's attention is focused on skills and peer activities with members of his or her own sex. This stage is posited to last from the resolution of the OEDIPUS COMPLEX, at about age 6, to the onset of puberty. Also called **latency phase**.

latent construct see LATENT VARIABLE.

latent content 1. the hidden or disguised meanings, wishes, and ideas beneath the MANIFEST CONTENT of any utterance or other form of communication. **2.** in psychoanalytic theory, the unconscious wishes seeking expression in dreams or fantasies. This unconscious material is posited to encounter censorship and to be distorted by the DREAM-WORK into symbolic representations to protect the EGO. Through DREAM ANALYSIS, the latent content may be uncovered.

latent factor see LATENT VARIABLE.

latent learning learning that is acquired without conscious effort, awareness, intention, or reinforcement and is not manifested as a change in performance until a specific need for it arises. For example, a student writing an exam may be able to cite a quotation encountered earlier accurately without having made an effort previously to learn it. See also INCIDENTAL LEARNING.

latent variable a theoretical entity or construct that is used to explain one or more MANIFEST VARIABLES. Latent variables cannot be directly observed or measured but rather are approximated through various measures presumed to assess part of the given construct. For example, a researcher interested in student conscientiousness might develop a survey containing items pertaining to behavior indicative of conscientiousness, such as consistently attending classes and turning in assignments on time. Participants' responses could then be analyzed to identify patterns of interrelationships from which the values of the latent variable of conscientiousness are inferred. Also called **latent construct**; **latent factor**. See also FACTOR ANALYSIS; STRUCTURAL EQUATION MODELING.

lateral *adj.* toward the side of the body or of an organ. Compare MEDIAL. —**laterally** *adv.*

lateral geniculate nucleus
(**LGN**) either of a pair of NUCLEI that protrude slightly from each side of the thalamus to the rear. Each LGN receives the fibers of the retinal ganglion cells and relays information to the VISUAL CORTEX via OPTIC RADIATIONS. Also called **lateral geniculate body**. See MAGNOCELLULAR SYSTEM; PARVOCELLULAR SYSTEM. See also MEDIAL GENICULATE NUCLEUS.

lateral hypothalamic syndrome a four-stage pattern of recovery from lesions of the LATERAL HYPOTHALAMUS induced in nonhuman animals. The first stage is marked by inability to eat and drink (aphagia and adipsia), and without assistance (e.g., forced feeding), the animal is likely to die. The second stage includes a period of continued inability to drink and poor appetite for food (adipsia-anorexia), when only wet, palatable foods are accepted. In the third stage, the animal will eat hydrated dry food but continues to avoid water intake and may suffer dehydration. Recovery is the fourth stage, in which new, altered feeding and drinking habits are established and the animal maintains a stable, albeit lower, body weight. Compare VENTROMEDIAL HYPOTHALAMIC SYNDROME.

lateral hypothalamus (**LH**) the region of the HYPOTHALAMUS that may be involved in the regulation of eating. Lesions of the lateral hypothalamus in animals result in fasting and weight loss. Stimulation of that part of the brain increases food intake.

lateral inhibition in perception, a mechanism for detecting contrast in which a sensory neuron is excited by one particular receptor but inhibited by neighboring (lateral) receptors. In vision, for example, lateral inhibition is seen in neurons that respond to light at one position but are inhibited by light at surrounding positions.

laterality *n.* the preferential use of one side of the body for certain functions, such as eating, writing, and stepping. See also HANDEDNESS.

lateralization *n.* one-sided preferences, such as HANDEDNESS and eye dominance. Observed more frequently in humans than in other primates, lateralization is manifested in the way tasks are performed and can also be inferred from the effects of localized brain damage. See also HEMISPHERIC LATERALIZATION.

lateral lemniscus a bundle of nerve fibers running from auditory nuclei in the brainstem upward through the PONS and terminating in the inferior COLLICULUS and MEDIAL GENICULATE NUCLEUS.

lateral sulcus a prominent groove that runs along the lateral surface of each cerebral hemisphere, separating the TEMPORAL LOBE from the FRONTAL LOBE and PARIETAL LOBE. Also called **lateral fissure; Sylvian fissure**.

lateral thinking creative thinking that deliberately attempts to reexamine basic assumptions and change perspective or direction to provide a fresh approach to solving a problem. This term is often used synonymously with DIVERGENT THINKING.

lateral ventricle a chamber of complex shape that lies within each cerebral hemisphere in the brain and serves as a reservoir of cerebrospinal fluid (see VENTRICLE). Each lateral ventricle communicates with the THIRD VENTRICLE at a point near the thalamus.

late-selection theory any theory of attention proposing that selection occurs after stimulus identification. According to late-selection theory, within sensory limits, all stimuli—both attended and unattended—are processed to the same deep level of analysis until stimulus identification occurs; subsequently, only the most important stimuli are selected for further processing. Compare EARLY-SELECTION THEORY.

Latin square a type of WITHIN-SUBJECTS DESIGN in which treatments, denoted by Latin letters, are administered in sequences that are systematically varied such that each treatment occurs equally often in each position of the sequence (first, second, third, etc.). The

number of treatments administered must be the same as the number of groups or individual participants receiving them. For example, for an experimental design involving four treatments (A, B, C, and D) and four people, one person might receive Treatment A, then B, then C, and then D; a second person might receive them in sequence B, C, D, and A; a third person in sequence C, D, A, and B; and a fourth person in sequence D, A, B, and C. It is important to note that although Latin squares control for ORDER EFFECTS they do not control for CARRYOVER EFFECTS or PRACTICE EFFECTS.

law of closure see CLOSURE.

law of common fate see COMMON FATE.

law of common region see COMMON REGION.

law of continuity see GOOD CONTINUATION.

law of effect broadly, the principle that consequences of behavior act to modify the future probability of occurrence of that behavior. As originally postulated by U.S. psychologist Edward L. Thorndike (1874–1949), the law of effect stated that if a response R produces a satisfying state of affairs (or a positive reinforcer), then an association is formed between R and the stimuli S present at the time R was made. As a result of this S–R association, R occurs whenever the organism encounters S. This part of the law of effect was the foundation of S–R theories of learning.

law of good continuation see GOOD CONTINUATION.

law of parsimony the principle that the simplest explanation of an event or observation is the preferred explanation. Simplicity is understood in various ways, including the requirement that an explanation should (a) make the smallest number of unsupported assumptions, (b) postulate the existence of the fewest entities, and (c) invoke the fewest unobservable constructs. Also called **principle of parsimony**. See OCCAM'S RAZOR.

law of Prägnanz see PRÄGNANZ.

law of proximity see PROXIMITY.

law of similarity 1. a principle of association stating that like produces like: Encountering or thinking about something (e.g., one's birthday month) tends to bring to mind other similar things (e.g., other people one knows with the same birthday month). **2.** see SIMILARITY.

law of symmetry see SYMMETRY.

lazy eye see AMBLYOPIA.

leadership *n.* the processes involved in leading others, including organizing, directing, coordinating, and motivating their efforts toward achieving certain group or organizational goals. Leadership tends to be reciprocal (leaders influence followers, and followers influence leaders) and cooperative rather than coercive. See TRANSACTIONAL LEADERSHIP; TRANSFORMATIONAL LEADERSHIP.

leadership style the stable behavioral tendencies and methods displayed by a particular leader when guiding a group. Common styles include autocratic, in which the leader exercises unrestricted authority; bureaucratic, in which the leader rigidly adheres to prescribed routine; charismatic, in which the leader articulates distal goals and visions; democratic, in which the leader establishes and maintains an egalitarian group climate; and laissez-faire, in which the leader provides little guidance.

learned helplessness a phenomenon in which repeated exposure to uncontrollable stressors results in individuals failing to use any control options that may later become available. Essentially, individuals are said to learn that they lack behavioral control over environmental events, which, in turn, undermines the motivation to make changes or attempt to alter situations. Learned helplessness was first described in 1967 after experiments revealed that nonhuman animals exposed to a series of unavoidable electric shocks later failed to learn to escape these shocks when tested in a different apparatus, whereas animals exposed to shocks that could be terminated by a response did not show interference with escape learning in another apparatus. In the 1970s, the concept was extended to clinical depression in humans. According to **learned helplessness theory**, vulnerability to depression arises when people repeatedly exposed to stressful situations beyond their control develop an inability to make decisions or engage effectively in purposeful behavior. Subsequent research has shown a robust fit between the concept and POSTTRAUMATIC STRESS DISORDER as well.

learned optimism an explanatory style that attributes causes for negative events to factors that are external, unstable, and specific: That is, problems are believed to be caused by other people or situational factors, the causes are seen as fleeting in nature, and they are localized to one or a few situations in one's life. According to LEARNED HELPLESSNESS theory, the manner in which individuals routinely explain the events in their lives can drain or enhance motivation, reduce or increase persistence, and enhance vulnerability to depression or protect against it, making learned optimism a putative mechanism that protects against or ameliorates depression.

learning *n.* the acquisition of novel information, behaviors, or abilities after practice, observation, or other experiences, as evidenced by change in behavior, knowledge, or brain function. Learning involves consciously or nonconsciously attending to relevant aspects of incoming information, mentally organizing the information into a coherent cognitive representation, and integrating it with relevant existing knowledge activated from long-term memory.

learning curve a graphic representation of the course of learning of an individual or a group. A measure of performance (e.g., gains, errors) is plotted along the vertical axis; the horizontal axis shows trials or time. Also called **acquisition curve**.

learning disability (**LD**) any of various conditions with a neurological basis that are marked by substantial deficits in acquiring certain scholastic or academic skills, particularly those associated with written or expressive language. Learning disabilities include learning problems that result from perceptual disabilities, brain injury, and MINIMAL BRAIN DYSFUNCTION but exclude those that result from visual impairment or hearing loss; intellectual disability; emotional disturbance; or environmental, cultural, or economic factors.

learning disorder (**LD**) any neurologically based information-processing disorder characterized by achievement that is substantially below that expected for the age, education, and intelligence of the individual, as measured by standardized tests in reading and mathematics and written material. Major types of learning disorders are DISORDER OF WRITTEN EXPRESSION, MATHEMATICS DISORDER, NONVERBAL LEARNING DISORDER, and READING DISORDER. This term is essentially synonymous with LEARNING DISABILITY.

learning set a phenomenon observed when a participant is given a succession of discrimination problems to learn, such as learning that one object contains a food reward and a different object does not. After a large number of such problems, the participant acquires a rule or MENTAL SET for solving them, and successive discriminations are learned faster.

learning style see COGNITIVE STYLE.

learning theory a body of concepts and principles developed to explain the learning process. Learning theory actually encompasses a number of specific theories whose common interest is the description of the basic laws of learning, usually derived from studies of classical and instrumental conditioning and verbal learning.

least restrictive environment (**LRE**) in the United States, an educational setting that gives a student with disabilities the opportunity to receive instruction within a classroom that meets his or her learning needs and physical requirements. See also MAINSTREAMING.

least significant difference (**LSD**) see FISHER LEAST SIGNIFICANT DIFFERENCE TEST.

left brain the left cerebral hemisphere of the brain. The term is sometimes used to describe functions or aspects of COGNITIVE STYLE supposedly mediated by the left (rather than by the right) hemisphere, such as analytical thinking. Compare RIGHT BRAIN. See also HEMISPHERIC LATERALIZATION.

left hemisphere the left half of the cerebrum, the part of the brain concerned with sensation and perception, motor control, and higher level cognitive processes. The two CEREBRAL HEMISPHERES differ somewhat in function; for example, in most people, the left hemisphere has greater responsibility for speech. See HEMISPHERIC LATERALIZATION. Compare RIGHT HEMISPHERE.

lens *n.* in vision, a transparent, biconvex structure in the anterior portion of the eyeball (just behind the IRIS) that provides the fine, adjustable focus of the optical system. It is composed of tiny hexagonal prism-shaped cells, called **lens fibers**, fitted together in concentric layers.

lenticular nucleus see BASAL GANGLIA.

leptin *n.* a protein, manufactured and secreted by fat cells, that may communicate to the brain the amount of body fat stored and may help to regulate food intake. Leptin receptors have been found in the hypothalamus, and, when they are stimulated, food intake is reduced.

leptokurtic *adj.* describing a frequency distribution that is more peaked than the NORMAL DISTRIBUTION, having more scores in the center and fewer at the two extremes. See also MESOKURTIC; PLATYKURTIC.

lesbianism *n.* female–female sexual orientation or behavior. See also HOMOSEXUALITY. —**lesbian** *adj.*, *n.*

Lesch's alcoholism typology

(**LAT**) a four-part categorization of individuals with ALCOHOL DEPENDENCE. **Type I** individuals do not experience cravings when not drinking but develop strong cravings once they start; they experience withdrawal symptoms much sooner in their drinking experiences than do other alcoholics. **Type II** individuals drink in response to conflict and to self-medicate psychiatric symptoms. **Type III** individuals generally have underlying affective disorders and often sleep disorders; they usually have a family history of alcoholism. **Type IV** individuals have usually experienced either brain trauma or a difficult childhood and have a tendency toward impulsivity. [developed by Austrian psychiatrist Otto-Michael **Lesch**]

lesion *n.* any disruption of or damage to the normal structure or function of an organ or part of an organ due to injury, disease, or a surgical procedure. A lesion may be a wound, ulcer, tumor, cataract, or any other pathological change in tissue.

less-is-more hypothesis the prop-

osition that the cognitive limitations of infants and young children may serve to simplify the body of language they process, thus making it easier for them to learn the complicated syntactical system of any human language. The name is derived from the famous design dictum of German-born U.S. architect Ludwig Mies van der Rohe (1886–1969).

lethality scale a set of criteria used to predict the probability of a suicide or attempted suicide occurring. A variety of such scales exist, most including gender, prior suicide attempts, and psychiatric diagnosis and history.

leukocyte (**leucocyte**) *n.* a type of blood cell that plays a key role in the body's defense against infection. Leukocytes include neutrophils, basophils, and eosinophils (known collectively as **granulocytes** because their cytoplasm contains granules), which ingest foreign particles; and LYMPHOCYTES, which are involved in the production of antibodies and other specific immune responses.

leukotomy (**leucotomy**) *n.* see LOBOTOMY.

level *n.* in an experimental design, the quantity, magnitude, or category of the INDEPENDENT VARIABLE (or variables) being studied. For example, if a researcher is assessing the effect of alcohol on cognition, each specific amount of alcohol included in the study is a level (e.g., 0.0 oz, 0.5 oz, 1.0 oz, 1.5 oz).

level of analysis the area of focus chosen when examining a multilayered phenomenon, such as the individual (micro-) level, the group or organizational (meso-) level, or the societal (macro-) level.

level-of-aspiration theory a conceptual approach to performance in which one's initial goals and ambitions are assumed to influence both particular performances and their emotional, motivational, and behavioral consequences.

level of measurement see MEASUREMENT LEVEL.

level of significance see SIGNIFICANCE LEVEL.

levels-of-processing model of

memory the theory that ENCODING of information into memory and therefore its subsequent RETENTION depend on the depth of cognitive ELABORATION that the information receives and that deeper encoding improves memory.

lexical access in psycholinguistics, the process by which an individual produces a specific word from his or her MENTAL LEXICON or recognizes it when used by others.

lexical decision a task in which the participant is presented with strings of letters, such as HOUSE or HOUPE, and is required to determine whether each string spells a word. The REACTION TIME required to make the decision is usually measured.

lexicon *n.* the vocabulary of a language and, in psychology, the lexical knowledge of an individual. See MENTAL LEXICON.

LGBTQ abbreviation for *l*esbian, *g*ay, *b*isexual, *t*ransgender, and *q*uestioning or *q*ueer: an inclusive term used to refer to the homosexual population in all of its diverse forms, to those with both homosexual and heterosexual preferences, and to those whose GENDER IDENTITY differs from the culturally determined gender roles for their birth sex.

libido *n.* in psychoanalytic theory, either the PSYCHIC ENERGY of the LIFE INSTINCT in general or the energy of the SEXUAL INSTINCT in particular. In his first formulation, Austrian neurologist Sigmund Freud (1856–1939) conceived of this energy as narrowly sexual, but subsequently he broadened the concept to include all expressions of love, pleasure, and self-preservation. See also EROS. —**libidinal** *adj.* —**libidinize** *vb.* —**libidinous** *adj.*

lie detector see POLYGRAPH.

lie scale a set of items within a psychological instrument (particularly a personality assessment) used to indicate whether a respondent has been truthful in answering. For example, an honest participant would respond similarly to the items "I never regret the life decisions I have made" and "I've never

done anything I later wished I could take back," which are different ways of presenting the same concept. Conversely, a respondent trying to present himself or herself as positively as possible might answer such related questions inconsistently.

life crisis a period of distress and major adjustment associated with a significant life event, such as divorce or death of a family member. In studies relating health to life crises, individuals experiencing recent major stress-producing events are more likely than others to show significant alterations in mental and physical health status.

life cycle the sequence of developmental stages through which an organism passes between a specified stage of one generation (e.g., fertilization, birth) and the same stage in the next generation.

life events important occasions throughout the lifespan that are either age-related and thus expected (e.g., marriage, retirement) or unrelated to age and unexpected (e.g., accidents, relocation). Contextual theories of personality often assume that personality is shaped by reactions to stress produced by critical life events.

life expectancy the number of years that a person can, on average, expect to live. Life expectancy is based on statistical probabilities and increases with improvements in medical care and hygiene.

life-history method a STRUCTURED INTERVIEW that attempts to summarize historical data about events that are relevant to evaluating a person's current functioning.

life instinct in psychoanalytic theory, the drive comprising the self-preservation instinct, which is aimed at individual survival, and the SEXUAL INSTINCT, which is aimed at the survival of the species. In the dual instinct theory of Austrian neurologist Sigmund Freud (1856–1939), the life instinct, or EROS, stands opposed to the DEATH INSTINCT, or THANATOS.

life review the process whereby individuals, especially older adults, reflect on and analyze past life experiences. Life review is often used in counseling older adults with mild depression or people of any age with terminal illness, sometimes as an adjunct to psychotherapy.

life satisfaction the extent to which a person finds life rich, meaningful, full, or of high quality. Numerous standardized measures have been developed to provide an index of a person's life satisfaction in comparison to various normative groups. Improved life satisfaction is often a goal of treatment, especially with older people. See also QUALITY OF LIFE.

life space in the FIELD THEORY of German-born U.S. social psychologist Kurt Lewin (1890–1947), the "totality of possible events" for one person at a particular time; a person's possible options together with the environment that contains them. The life space is a representation of the environmental, biological, social, and psychological influences that define one person's unique reality at a given moment in time. Contained within the life space are positive and negative forces, or pressures, on the individual to approach a goal or move away from a perceived danger.

lifespan *n.* **1.** the maximum age that can be obtained by any given individual within a particular species. **2.** the precise length of an individual's life.

lifespan developmental psychology the study of psychological and behavioral change across and within individuals from conception through death. Such an approach assumes that human developmental processes are complex, interactive, and fully understood only in the context of influencing events. It also assumes that there is no end state of maturity and

that not all developmental change is related to chronological age.

lifestyle *n.* the typical way of life or manner of living that is characteristic of an individual or group, as expressed by behaviors, attitudes, interests, and other factors.

light adaptation the process by which the eye adjusts to conditions of high illumination, as occurs when a person exits a dark theater into a sunny parking lot. It takes less than 10 minutes and involves constriction of the pupil and a shift in the sensitivity of the retina so that the RETINAL CONES become active in place of the RETINAL RODS. Compare DARK ADAPTATION.

lightness constancy see BRIGHTNESS CONSTANCY.

light therapy see PHOTOTHERAPY.

likelihood function a formula that yields the probability of obtaining a particular distribution of values in a sample for each known value of an associated population PARAMETER. In other words, it indicates how likely a particular population is to produce the observed sample data under certain conditions.

likelihood ratio (**LR**) the ratio of two probabilities, *a/b*, where *a* is the probability of obtaining the data observed if a particular research hypothesis (A; the NULL HYPOTHESIS) is true and *b* is the probability of obtaining the data observed when a different hypothesis (B; the ALTERNATIVE HYPOTHESIS) is true.

Likert scale a type of direct attitude measure that consists of statements reflecting strong positive or negative evaluations of an object. Five-point scales are common and a neutral middle point may or may not be included. For example, an assessment item might include the following choices: *strongly disagree, disagree, neither disagree nor agree, agree,* and *strongly agree.* The respondent chooses the option most representative of his or her view (e.g., on whether same-sex marriages should be permitted), and these ratings are summed to provide a total attitude score for a topic of interest. [Rensis **Likert** (1903–1981), U.S. psychologist]

limbic lobe a fifth subdivision of each cerebral hemisphere that is often distinguished in addition to the four main lobes (i.e., frontal, occipital, parietal, and temporal). It comprises the CINGULATE CORTEX, PARAHIPPOCAMPAL GYRUS, and hippocampal formation.

limbic system a loosely defined, widespread group of brain nuclei that innervate each other to form a network that is involved in autonomic and visceral processes and mechanisms of emotion, memory, and learning. It includes the LIMBIC LOBE, THALAMUS, and certain cortical and subcortical structures, such as the HIPPOCAMPUS and AMYGDALA.

limen *n.* see THRESHOLD.

limited-capacity system a conceptualization of WORKING MEMORY in which resource constraints restrict the processing of information. When new information is encountered, older information is either relegated to long-term memory or eliminated, providing the resources to retain the newer data. ATTENTION and CONSCIOUSNESS are often similarly conceived of as limited-capacity systems. See also CHUNKING.

linear *adj.* describing any relationship between two variables (*x* and *y*) that can be expressed in the form $y = a + bx$, where *a* and *b* are numerical constants. No COEFFICIENT can be raised to a power greater than 1 or be the denominator of a fraction. When depicted graphically, the relationship is a straight line. Compare NONLINEAR.

linearizing *n.* see LINEAR TRANSFORMATION.

linear model any model for empirical data that attempts to relate the values of an outcome or dependent variable to the explanatory or independent variables through a linear func-

tion, that is, one that simply sums terms and includes no exponents greater than 1. Most commonly used statistical techniques (ANALYSIS OF VARIANCE, REGRESSION ANALYSIS, etc.) can be represented as linear models. Compare NONLINEAR MODEL.

linear perspective one of the monocular DEPTH CUES, arising from the principle that the size of an object's visual image is a function of its distance from the eye. Thus, two objects appear closer together as the distance from them increases, as seen in the tracks of a railroad that appear to converge on the horizon.

linear regression a REGRESSION ANALYSIS in which the predictor or independent variables (*x*s) are assumed to be related to the criterion or dependent variable (*y*) in such a manner that increases in an *x* variable result in consistent increases in the *y* variable. In other words, the direction and rate of change of one variable is constant with respect to changes in the other variable. Compare NONLINEAR REGRESSION.

linear relationship an association between two variables that when subjected to REGRESSION ANALYSIS and plotted on a graph forms a straight line. In linear relationships, the direction and rate of change in one variable are constant with respect to changes in the other variable.

linear transformation the TRANSFORMATION of a set of raw data using an equation that involves addition, subtraction, multiplication, or division with a constant. An example is the transformation of *x* to *y* by means of the equation $y = a + bx$, where *a* and *b* are numerical constants. A plot of such transformed data would form a straight line. Data are often subjected to **linearizing** to determine whether a linear model provides a better fitting or more parsimonious explanation of the variables.

line graph a graph in which data points representing a series of individual measurements are shown to be connected by straight line segments. Line graphs often are used to show trends over time, such as population growth.

linguistic determinism the hypothesis, most commonly associated with the U.S. linguists Edward Sapir (1884–1939) and Benjamin Lee Whorf (1897–1941), that the semantic structure of a particular language determines the structure of mental categories among its speakers. Because languages differ in how they refer to basic categories and dimensions, such as time, space, and duration, native speakers of these languages are assumed to show corresponding differences in their ways of thinking. Also called **Sapir–Whorf hypothesis**. Compare LINGUISTIC RELATIVITY. See also ANTHROPOLOGICAL LINGUISTICS.

linguistic relativity the observation that languages differ in the ways in which semantic space is identified and categorized. For example, the Native American language Hopi uses one word for water in a natural setting and another word for water in a vessel but has only one word for flying objects, which is applied to birds, insects, airplanes, and the like. Linguistic relativity is not to be equated with LINGUISTIC DETERMINISM, which is a theoretical commitment to the idea that these differences have cognitive consequences. See ANTHROPOLOGICAL LINGUISTICS.

linguistics *n.* the scientific study of the physical, structural, functional, psychological, and social characteristics of human language. See also PSYCHOLINGUISTICS; SOCIOLINGUISTICS.

link analysis in ergonomics, the analysis of operational sequences and the movements of workers or objects that these entail to determine the design of tools, equipment, jobs, and facilities that will best serve worker efficiency and safety.

lipostatic hypothesis a hypothesis stating that the long-term regulation of food intake is governed by the concentration in the blood of free fatty acids, which result from the metabolism of fat. High concentrations indicate the breakdown of fat, and food consumption increases accordingly; low concentrations are associated with reduction in consumption. Also called **lipostatic theory**. See also GLUCOSTATIC THEORY.

literacy *n.* the ability to read and write in a language. —**literate** *adj.*

literal replication see REPLICATION.

lithium *n.* an element of the alkali metal group whose salts are used in psychopharmacotherapy as MOOD STABILIZERS. Its primary indication is in managing bipolar disorder, with efficacy in managing acute manic phases and in reducing relapse. Its mechanism of action remains unclear, and toxic doses are no more than two to three times the therapeutic dose so serum monitoring is required. U.S. trade name (among others): **Lithobid**.

Little Albert the name of a boy used by U.S. psychologist John B. Watson (1878–1958) and his graduate student Rosalie Rayner (1899–1935) to demonstrate classical (or Pavlovian) fear conditioning in humans.

Little Hans a landmark case reported in 1909 by Austrian neurologist Sigmund Freud (1856–1939), illustrating the OEDIPUS COMPLEX. Freud traced a child's phobia of horses to CASTRATION ANXIETY stemming from masturbation, to repressed death wishes toward the father, and to fear of retaliation owing to rivalry with the mother, with DISPLACEMENT of these emotions onto horses.

living will see ADVANCE DIRECTIVE.

Lloyd Morgan's canon the principle that the behavior of a nonhuman animal should not be interpreted in complex psychological terms if it can instead be interpreted with simpler concepts. Lloyd Morgan's canon, proposed in 1894, helped eliminate the older concept of ANTHROPOMORPHISM, or the endowment of animals with human traits, although some recent authors have argued that its application over-simplifies the abilities of animals. [Conwy **Lloyd Morgan** (1852–1936), British zoologist and comparative psychologist]

lobe *n.* a subdivision of an organ, such as the brain or the lungs, particularly when rounded and surrounded by distinct structural boundaries, such as fissures. The four main lobes of each cerebral hemisphere of the brain are the FRONTAL LOBE, PARIETAL LOBE, TEMPORAL LOBE, and OCCIPITAL LOBE. —**lobar** *adj.* —**lobate** *adj.*

lobotomy *n.* incision into various nerve tracts in the FRONTAL LOBE of the brain. The surgical procedure, called **prefrontal** (or **frontal**) **lobotomy**, was introduced in 1936: Connections between the frontal lobe and other brain structures—notably the thalamus—were severed by manipulating a narrow blade known as a leukotome inserted into brain tissue through several small holes drilled in the skull. A second procedure, called **transorbital lobotomy**, was devised in 1945 and involved the manipulation of a pointed instrument resembling an ice pick driven with a mallet through the thin bony wall of the eye socket and into the prefrontal brain. Both procedures were widely used to relieve the symptoms of severe mental disorder (including depression and schizophrenia) until the advent of ANTIPSYCHOTIC drugs in the 1950s. These operations did, on occasion, result in improved function for some patients, but others either died as a consequence of the surgery or suffered major personality changes. Such procedures have since been replaced by more sophisticated, stereotactic forms of neurosurgery that are less invasive and whose effects are more certain and less damaging. Also called **leukotomy**.

localization *n.* the ability to determine the physical position or spatial location of a stimulus in any sensory modality.

localization of function the concept that specific parts of the cerebral cortex are relatively specialized for particular types of cognitive and behavioral processes.

location constancy the tendency for a resting object and its setting to appear to have the same position even if the relationship between setting and observer is altered as the observer shifts position. See also OBJECT CONSTANCY.

locomotor play play that involves exaggerated, repetitious movement and is physically vigorous, such as chasing, climbing, and wrestling. It is one of three traditionally identified basic types of play, the others being OBJECT PLAY and SOCIAL PLAY.

locus *n.* (*pl.* **loci**) **1.** the place or position of an anatomical or pathological entity (e.g., a hemorrhage in the brain, a butterfly rash on the skin). **2.** the position of a gene on a chromosome.

locus ceruleus a small bluish-tinted NUCLEUS in the brainstem whose neurons produce NOREPINEPHRINE and modulate large areas of the forebrain. It is involved in arousal and likely has a role in anxiety.

locus of control a construct that is used to categorize people's basic motivational orientations and perceptions of how much control they have over the conditions of their lives. People with an **external locus of control** tend to behave in response to external circumstances and to perceive their life outcomes as arising from factors out of their control. People with an **internal locus of control** tend to behave in response to internal states and intentions and to perceive their life outcomes as arising from the exercise of their own agency and abilities.

logic *n.* **1.** the branch of EPISTEMOLOGY that is concerned with the forms of argument by which a valid conclusion may be drawn from accepted premises. As such, it is also concerned with distinguishing correct from fallacious reasoning. See also DEDUCTIVE REASON-ING. **2.** a particular rule-governed form of symbolic expression used to analyze the relations between propositions. —**logical** *adj.*

logistic regression (**LR**) a form of REGRESSION ANALYSIS used when the outcome or DEPENDENT VARIABLE may assume only one of two categorical values (e.g., pass or fail) and the predictors or INDEPENDENT VARIABLES are either categorical or CONTINUOUS. For example, a researcher could use logistic regression to determine the likelihood of graduating from college (yes or no) given such student information as high school grade point average, college admissions test score, number of advanced placement courses taken in high school, socioeconomic status, and gender. Also called **logistic modeling**.

log-linear analysis a method of examining relationships between two or more CATEGORICAL VARIABLES that involves an analysis of the natural logarithms of frequency counts within a CONTINGENCY TABLE. Log-linear analyses do not distinguish between INDE-PENDENT VARIABLES and DEPENDENT VARIABLES but rather attempt to model all significant associations among all variables, using sets of odds for different category outcomes. Also called **log-linear modeling**.

logogen *n.* a theoretical memory unit, corresponding to a word, letter, or digit, that, when excited, results in the output (recognition) of the unit and recall of characteristics and information associated with that unit. For example, the logogen for *table* is activated by hearing the component sounds or seeing the typographical features of the word, bringing to mind such knowledge as the typical structure and shape of a table and its general function.

loneliness *n.* affective and cognitive uneasiness from being or perceiving oneself to be alone. Psychological theory and research offer multiple perspectives: Social psychologists emphasize the emotional distress that results when inherent needs for intimacy and companionship are not met; cognitive psychologists emphasize the unpleasant and unsettling experience that results from a perceived discrepancy (i.e., deficiency in quantity or quality) between an individual's desired and actual social relationships; and existential or humanistic psychologists may see loneliness as an inevitable, painful aspect of the human condition that nevertheless may contribute to increased self-awareness and renewal.

long axis see AXIS.

longevity *n.* **1.** long life. **2.** the actual length of an individual's life. See also LIFE EXPECTANCY.

longitudinal data information obtained through multiple measurements of the same individuals over a period of time. For example, a researcher investigating the use of coping strategies in college students may evaluate stress levels at the beginning, middle, and end of the fall and spring semesters.

longitudinal design the study of a variable or group of variables in the same cases or participants over a period of time, sometimes several years. An example of a longitudinal design is a multiyear comparative study of the same children in an urban and a suburban school to record their cognitive development in depth. A longitudinal study that evaluates a group of randomly chosen individuals is referred to as a **panel study**, whereas a longitudinal study that evaluates a group of individuals possessing some common characteristic (usually age) is referred to as a **cohort study**. Compare CROSS-SECTIONAL DESIGN.

longitudinal fissure a deep groove that marks the division between the left and right cerebral hemispheres of the brain. At the bottom of the groove, the hemispheres are connected by the COR-PUS CALLOSUM.

long-term care provision of health,

mental health, or other services over a prolonged or extended period to someone with a chronic illness, mental illness, or disability. Care can be provided in an institutional setting or the community (e.g., at home) by health care professionals, family, or friends.

long-term depression (LTD) a long-lasting decrease in the amplitude of neuronal response due to persistent weak synaptic stimulation (in the case of the hippocampus) or strong synaptic stimulation (in the case of the cerebellum). Compare LONG-TERM POTENTIATION.

long-term memory (LTM) a relatively permanent information storage system that enables one to retain, retrieve, and make use of skills and knowledge hours, weeks, or even years after they were originally learned. Various theories have been proposed to explain the biological processes by which this occurs (e.g., the PERSEVERATION–CONSOLIDATION HYPOTHESIS), and a major distinction is made between LTM and WORKING MEMORY. Additionally, LTM is divided into several categories, including DECLARATIVE MEMORY and PROCEDURAL MEMORY.

long-term potentiation (LTP) enhancement of transmission at SYNAPSES, which can last for weeks or more, caused by repeated brief stimulations of one nerve cell that trigger stimulation of a succeeding cell. The capacity for potentiation has been best shown in hippocampal tissue. LTP is studied as a model of the neural changes that underlie memory formation, and it may be a mechanism involved in some kinds of learning. Compare LONG-TERM DEPRESSION.

looking-glass self a SELF-CONCEPT formed by incorporating other people's views of oneself into one's own self-views. The term suggests a self-concept that is, in part, a reflection of other people's impressions, reactions, and opinions. See SYMBOLIC INTERACTIONISM.

loss of consciousness (LOC) a state in which an organism capable of attention and awareness can no longer experience events or exert voluntary control. Examples of conditions associated with loss of consciousness include SLOW-WAVE SLEEP, fainting (syncope), traumatic brain injury, coma, general anesthesia, narcolepsy, and some epileptic seizures.

loudness n. the subjective magnitude of sound. It is determined primarily by intensity but is also affected by other physical properties, such as frequency, spectral configuration, and duration. The unit proposed for loudness is the sone: One sone is defined as the subjective magnitude of a 1 kHz tone presented at 40 dB SPL (decibels sound-pressure level), based on loudness judgments by listeners. Loudness approximately doubles for each 10 dB increase in intensity.

Lou Gehrig's disease see AMYOTROPHIC LATERAL SCLEROSIS. [Henry (**Lou**) **Gehrig** (1903–1941), U.S. baseball player who died of the disease]

love n. a complex emotion involving strong feelings of affection and tenderness for a person, pleasurable sensations in his or her presence, devotion to his or her well-being, and sensitivity to his or her reactions to oneself. Although love takes many forms, the TRIANGULAR THEORY OF LOVE proposes three essential components: passion, intimacy, and commitment. Social psychological research in this area has focused largely on PASSIONATE LOVE, in which sexual desire and excitement predominate, and COMPANIONATE LOVE, in which passion is relatively weak and commitment is strong.

love need in MASLOW'S MOTIVATIONAL HIERARCHY, the third level of the hierarchy of needs, characterized by the striving for affiliation and acceptance. Also called **social need**.

low-ball technique a procedure for enhancing compliance by first obtaining agreement to a request and then revealing the hidden costs of this request. Compliance to the target request is greater than would have been the case if these costs had been made clear at the time of the initial request. See also DOOR-IN-THE-FACE TECHNIQUE; FOOT-IN-THE-DOOR TECHNIQUE; THAT'S-NOT-ALL TECHNIQUE.

low birth weight (**LBW**) infant weight at birth of less than 5.5 pounds (2,500 g) regardless of gestational age. **Very low birth weight** (**VLBW**) refers to weight of less than 3.5 pounds (1,500 g) and **extremely low birth weight** (**ELBW**) is used to describe an infant weight of less than 2.2 pounds (1,000 g) at birth. Children born with VLBW or ELBW are at an increased risk for serious health problems and reduced scores on measures of intelligence. Children born with moderate LBW are at risk for similar, albeit less severe, outcomes.

lower motor neuron see MOTOR NEURON.

LSD lysergic acid diethylamide: a highly potent HALLUCINOGEN that structurally resembles the neurotransmitter serotonin and may act as a PARTIAL AGONIST at serotonin receptors. Originally synthesized in 1938 by Swiss chemist Albert Hoffman, LSD is capable of producing visual distortions or frank hallucinations, together with feelings of euphoria or arousal; it became a widely used and controversial recreational drug during the mid-1960s and early 1970s. The effects of LSD were the subject of research during the 1950s as a possible model for psychosis, and various attempts were made during the 1950s and 1960s to use LSD as an aid to psychotherapy, although they did not prove effective.

lucid dream a dream in which the sleeper is aware that he or she is dreaming and may be able to influence the progress of the dream narrative.

lunacy *n.* **1.** an obsolete name for any mental illness. **2.** in legal contexts, an obsolete name for mental incompetence or INSANITY. —**lunatic** *adj., n.*

luteinizing hormone (**LH**) a GONADOTROPIN secreted by the anterior pituitary gland that, in females, stimulates the rapid growth of a cavity in the ovary until it ruptures and releases an egg cell. In males, it stimulates the interstitial cells of the TESTIS to secrete androgens.

lymphocyte *n.* a type of blood cell that plays a key role in specific immune responses. There are two main classes: **B lymphocytes** (or **B cells**), which mature in the bone marrow and produce circulating antibodies; and **T lymphocytes** (or **T cells**), which mature in the thymus and have particular cell-surface molecules that are capable of ANTIGEN recognition. See also LEUKOCYTE; NATURAL KILLER CELL. —**lymphocytic** *adj.*

lysergic acid diethylamide see LSD.

Mm

macrocephaly *n.* a head circumference that is more than two standard deviations above the mean for age, gender, race, and gestation. Although it can be caused by HYDROCEPHALUS or an unusually large brain, it does not necessarily indicate abnormality. Compare MICROCEPHALY. —**macrocephalic** *adj.*

macroglia *n.* a relatively large type of nonneuronal central nervous system cell. Examples include ASTROCYTES, EPENDYMAL CELLS, and OLIGODENDROCYTES. —**macroglial** *adj.*

macrosystem *n.* in ECOLOGICAL SYSTEMS THEORY, the level of environmental influence that is most distal to the developing individual and that affects all other systems. It includes the values, traditions, and sociocultural characteristics of the larger society. Compare CHRONOSYSTEM; EXOSYSTEM; MESOSYSTEM.

macula *n.* (*pl.* **maculae**) a patch of sensory tissue in the UTRICLE and SACCULE of the inner ear that provides information about the position of the body in relation to gravity. The macula contains sensory HAIR CELLS whose processes (stereocilia) are embedded in a gelatinous matrix containing calcareous particles (OTOLITHS). When the orientation of the head changes, the relatively dense otoliths respond to gravity, causing the gelatinous mass to shift and the stereocilia to flex. This triggers nerve impulses in the hair-cell fibers, which act as signals to the brain.

macula lutea a small spot in the retina that is in direct alignment with the optics of the eye. It contains a yellow pigment and a central depression, the FOVEA CENTRALIS.

macular degeneration dystrophy of the MACULA LUTEA, which affects both eyes and causes progressive loss of central vision. Apart from age, other risk factors for the disease include exposure to ultraviolet light, smoking, hypertension, and possibly zinc deficiency in the diet.

madness *n.* an obsolete name for mental illness or for legal INSANITY.

magical thinking the belief that events or the behavior of others can be influenced by one's thoughts, wishes, or rituals. Magical thinking is typical of children up to 4 or 5 years of age, after which reality thinking begins to predominate.

magnetic resonance imaging (**MRI**) a noninvasive diagnostic technique that uses the responses of hydrogen in tissue molecules to strong magnetic impulses to form a three-dimensional picture of body organs and tissues. See also COMPUTED TOMOGRAPHY; FUNCTIONAL MAGNETIC RESONANCE IMAGING.

magnetoencephalography (**MEG**) *n.* the measurement of the magnetic fields arising from the electrical activity of the brain, using a device called a **magnetoencephalograph** (**MEG**).

magnitude estimation a psychophysical procedure in which participants make subjective judgments of the magnitude of stimuli by assigning them numerical values along a 7- or 10-point scale. The resulting scales often follow a power law (see STEVENS LAW).

magnocellular system the part of the visual system that projects to or originates from large neurons in the two most ventral layers (the **magnocellular layers**) of the LATERAL GENICULATE NUCLEUS. It allows the rapid perception of movement, form, and changes in brightness but is relatively insensitive to stimulus location and color. See also M-CELL. Compare PARVOCELLULAR SYSTEM.

main effect the consistent total effect of a single INDEPENDENT VARIABLE on a DEPENDENT VARIABLE over all other independent variables in an experimental design. It is distinct from, but may be obscured by, an INTERACTION EFFECT between variables.

mainstreaming *n.* the placement of children with disabilities into regular classroom environments on a part-time basis, such that they attend only some regular education classes during the school day and spend the remaining time in special education classes. The aim is to offer each child the opportunity to learn in an environment that has the highest probability of facilitating rehabilitation efforts and supporting academic growth. See also LEAST RESTRICTIVE ENVIRONMENT.

maintenance rehearsal repeating items over and over to maintain them in SHORT-TERM MEMORY, as in repeating a telephone number until it has been dialed. According to the LEVELS-OF-PROCESSING MODEL OF MEMORY, maintenance rehearsal does not effectively promote long-term retention because it involves little ELABORATION of the information to be remembered.

major depressive disorder a mood disorder characterized by persistent sadness and other symptoms of a MAJOR DEPRESSIVE EPISODE but without accompanying episodes of mania or hypomania or mixed episodes of depressive and manic or hypomanic symptoms. Also called **major depression**.

major depressive episode a period in which an individual experiences ANHEDONIA or is persistently sad, pessimistic, or otherwise overly negative. Additional symptoms include appetite changes; insomnia or excessive sleep; PSYCHOMOTOR AGITATION or PSYCHOMOTOR RETARDATION; feelings of worthlessness or guilt; reduced ability to concentrate or make decisions; and recurrent thoughts of death or SUICIDAL IDEATION. One or more major depressive episodes are a characteristic feature of MAJOR DEPRESSIVE DISORDER and BIPOLAR DISORDER.

major tranquilizer see ANTIPSYCHOTIC.

maladaptation *n.* a condition in which biological traits or behavior patterns are detrimental, counterproductive, or otherwise interfere with optimal functioning in various domains, such as successful interaction with the environment and effectual coping with the challenges and stresses of daily life. Compare ADAPTATION. —**maladaptive** *adj.*

maladjustment *n.* inability to maintain effective relationships, function successfully in various domains, or cope with difficulties and stresses. —**maladjusted** *adj.*

malapropism *n.* a linguistic error in which one word is mistakenly used for another having a similar sound, often to ludicrous effect, as in *She was wearing a cream casserole* (for *camisole*).

male climacteric a hypothetical period in some men's lives that has been compared to female menopause (see CLIMACTERIC). Also known as **male menopause**, it occurs some 10 years later than in women and appears to be associated with declines in the levels of various hormones, such as testosterone. Symptoms may include fatigue, problems with memory and concentration, decreased sexual desire, and erectile dysfunction.

male erectile disorder persistent or recurrent inability in a man to achieve or maintain an erection adequate to complete the sex act. The disorder may be situational (occurring only in certain situations or with certain partners) or generalized (occurring in all situations). See also ERECTILE DYSFUNCTION; IMPOTENCE.

male genitalia see GENITALIA.

male menopause see MALE CLIMACTERIC.

male orgasmic disorder persistent or recurrent delay in, or absence of, male orgasm during sexual stimulation that produces arousal.

malignant *adj.* describing a condition that gets progressively worse or is resistant to treatment, particularly a tumor that invades and destroys tissues and that may also spread to other sites. Compare BENIGN.

malingering *n.* the deliberate feigning of an illness or disability to achieve a particular desired outcome. For example, it may take the form of faking mental illness as a defense in a trial or faking an injury to avoid practicing or playing sport. Malingering is distinguished from FACTITIOUS DISORDER in that it involves a specific external factor as the motivating force. —**malingerer** *n.*

malleus *n.* see OSSICLES.

maltreatment *n.* the ABUSE or NEGLECT of another person, which may involve emotional, sexual, or physical action or inaction, the severity or chronicity of which can result in significant harm or injury. Maltreatment also includes such actions as exploitation and denial of basic needs (e.g., food, shelter, medical attention).

mammillary body either of a pair of small, spherical nuclei at the base of the brain, slightly posterior to the infundibulum (pituitary stalk), that are components of the LIMBIC SYSTEM.

mammography *n.* a diagnostic procedure that uses low-dose X-ray photography to detect breast tumors or other abnormalities, either noncancerous (BENIGN) or cancerous (MALIGNANT). The X-ray negative produced is called a **mammogram**.

managed care any system of health care delivery that regulates the use of member benefits to contain expenses. The term is also used to denote the organization of health care services and facilities into groups to increase cost-effectiveness. Such **managed care organizations** (**MCOs**) include HMOs, preferred provider organizations, point-of-service plans, exclusive provider organizations, physician–hospital organizations, integrated delivery systems, and independent practice associations.

mand *n.* in linguistics, a category of UTTERANCES in which the speaker makes demands on the hearer, as in *Listen to me* or *Pass the salt, please.*

mania *n.* **1.** generally, a state of excitement, overactivity, and PSYCHOMOTOR AGITATION, often accompanied by overoptimism, grandiosity, or impaired judgment. **2.** more specifically, a MANIC EPISODE or, sometimes, a HYPOMANIC EPISODE.

manic *adj.* relating to MANIA.

manic-depressive illness see BIPOLAR DISORDER.

manic episode a period characterized by elevated, expansive, or irritable mood, often with several of the following symptoms: an increase in activity or PSYCHOMOTOR AGITATION; talkativeness; racing thoughts; inflated self-esteem or grandiosity; a decreased need for sleep; extreme distractibility; and intense pursuit of activities that are likely to have unfortunate consequences (e.g., buying sprees, sexual indiscretions). One or more manic episodes are characteristic of BIPOLAR DISORDER. See also MIXED EPISODE.

manifest content **1.** the matter that is overtly expressed and consciously intended in any utterance or other form of communication. **2.** in psychoanalytic theory, the images and events of a dream or fantasy as experienced and recalled by the dreamer or fantasist, as opposed to the LATENT CONTENT, which is posited to contain the hidden meaning. See also DREAM ANALYSIS; DREAM-WORK.

manifest variable a variable whose values can be directly observed or measured, as opposed to one whose values must be inferred. In STRUCTURAL EQUA-

TION MODELING and FACTOR ANALYSIS, manifest variables are used to study LATENT VARIABLES. Also called **indicator variable**.

manipulation *n.* **1.** behavior designed to exploit, control, or otherwise influence others to one's advantage. **2.** the adjustment of an independent variable such that one or more groups of participants are exposed to specific treatments while one or more other groups are not. For example, a health researcher could introduce a manipulation so that a portion of the participants in a study randomly receive a new drug, whereas the remaining participants receive a PLACEBO.

manipulation check any means by which an experimenter evaluates the efficacy of an experimental variable, that is, verifies that a particular manipulation affected the participants as intended.

Mann–Whitney *U* test a NONPARAMETRIC TEST of centrality for ranked data that contrasts scores from two independent samples to assess whether there are significant differences between the two sets of rankings. The statistic obtained from this test, *U*, is calculated by summing the number of ranks in one group that are smaller than each of the ranks in the other group. [Henry Berthold **Mann** (1905–2000), Austrian-born U.S. mathematician; Donald Ransom **Whitney** (1915–2001), U.S. statistician]

mantra *n.* any verbal formula used for spiritual, religious, or meditative purposes to help block out extraneous thoughts and induce a state of relaxation that enables the individual to reach a deeper level of consciousness.

manualized therapy interventions that are performed according to specific guidelines for administration, maximizing the probability of therapy being conducted consistently across settings, therapists, and clients.

marasmus *n.* a condition, usually oc-curring in infancy, that is characterized by apathy, withdrawal, and emaciation resulting from severe malnutrition. If left untreated, it can result in delayed physical and cognitive development and, in some cases, death. Marasmus tends to occur mostly in developing countries, often as a result of famine, premature or abrupt weaning, or vitamin insufficiency due to limitations in food variety. See also KWASHIORKOR.

marginalization *n.* a reciprocal process through which an individual or group with distinctive qualities, such as idiosyncratic values or customs, becomes identified as one that is not accepted fully into the larger group. —**marginalize** *vb.*

margin of error (**MOE**) a statistic expressing the CONFIDENCE INTERVAL associated with a given measurement; it is an allowance for a slight miscalculation or an acceptable deviation. The larger the margin of error for the sample data, the less confidence one has that the results obtained are accurate for the entire population of interest.

marijuana (**marihuana**) *n.* see CANNABIS.

marital separation the situation in which a previously cohabiting married couple stops living together and instead maintains individual residences, finances, and so forth. When the couple has children, the term **parental separation** is often used. Separation may be informal via mutual agreement or legally arranged via an official, enforceable document. In both cases, the partners remain married, which distinguishes separation from divorce.

marital therapy see COUPLES THERAPY.

market research research undertaken to understand the size and nature of a particular market, together with any significant trends or challenges. This may involve interviews to assess the relative positions of various suppliers in the minds of consumers. The

masking

term **marketing research** is used more specifically to mean research into the effectiveness of marketing techniques.

masking *n.* **1.** in perception, the partial or complete obscuring of one stimulus (the target) by another (the masker). **Forward masking** occurs when the masker is presented a short time before the target stimulus, **backward masking** occurs when it is presented shortly afterward, and **simultaneous masking** occurs when the two stimuli are presented at the same instant. **2.** in statistics, the obscuring of the effect of one variable by the effect of another variable. For example, a researcher interested in whether risky sexual behavior is related to alcohol use might find that an experience of sexual abuse exerts a stronger influence on sexual behavior, thus masking the effect of alcohol use. —**mask** *vb.*

Maslow's motivational hierarchy the hierarchy of human motives, or needs, as described by U.S. psychologist Abraham Maslow (1908–1970). PHYSIOLOGICAL NEEDS for air, water, food, sleep, and so forth are at the base; followed by safety and security (the SAFETY NEEDS); then love, affection, and gregariousness (the LOVE NEEDS); then prestige, competence, and power (the ESTEEM NEEDS); and—at the highest level—aesthetic needs, the need for knowing, and SELF-ACTUALIZATION (the METANEEDS).

masochism *n.* the derivation of pleasure from experiencing pain and humiliation. The term generally denotes SEXUAL MASOCHISM but is also applied to experiences not involving sex, such as martyrdom, religious self-flagellation, or asceticism. In classical psychoanalytic theory, masochism is interpreted as resulting from the DEATH INSTINCT or from aggression turned inward because of excessive guilt feelings. [Leopold Sacher **Masoch** (1835–1895), Austrian writer] —**masochist** *n.* —**masochistic** *adj.*

mass action the generalization by

U.S. neuropsychologist Karl S. Lashley (1890–1958) that the size of a cortical lesion, rather than its specific location, determines the extent of any resulting performance decrement. Proposed in 1929, the concept reflects Lashley's belief that large areas of the cortex function together in learning and other complex processes. This concept is no longer considered completely valid. See also EQUIPOTENTIALITY.

massed practice a learning procedure in which practice trials occur close together in time, either in a single lengthy session or in sessions separated by short intervals. Massed practice is often found to be less effective than DISTRIBUTED PRACTICE.

mastery orientation an adaptive pattern of achievement behavior in which individuals enjoy and seek challenge, persist in the face of obstacles, and tend to view their failings as due to lack of effort or poor use of strategy rather than to lack of ability.

masturbation *n.* manipulation of one's own genital organs, typically the penis or clitoris, for purposes of sexual gratification. Masturbation may also include the use of mechanical devices (e.g., a vibrator) or self-stimulation of other organs, such as the anus or nipples. —**masturbate** *vb.*

matched-pairs design a study involving two groups of participants in which each member of one group is paired with a similar person in the other group, that is, someone who matches him or her on one or more variables that are not the main focus of the study but nonetheless could influence its outcome. For example, a researcher evaluating the effectiveness of a new drug in treating Alzheimer's disease might identify pairs of individuals of the same age and intelligence and then randomly assign one person from each pair to the treatment condition that will receive the drug and the other to the control condition that will not.

matched-pairs *t* test a statistical

procedure used to test for significant differences between the two sets of data obtained from a MATCHED-PAIRS DESIGN. For example, a researcher could use a matched-pairs *t* test to assess whether relationship satisfaction significantly differs between two sets of individuals who have been matched for age and gender, where one set has been married for 5 years and the other for 10 years. Also called **paired-samples *t* test**.

matching *n.* a procedure for ensuring that participants in different study conditions are comparable at the beginning of the research on one or more key variables that have the potential to influence results. After multiple sets of matched individuals are created, one member of each set is assigned at random to the EXPERIMENTAL GROUP and the other to the CONTROL GROUP. See also MATCHED-PAIRS DESIGN.

matching hypothesis the proposition that people tend to form relationships with individuals who have a similar level of social value, often with an emphasis on equality in physical attractiveness. Research indicates that this similarity tends to be greater for couples having a romantic relationship than for friends.

materialism *n.* **1.** the philosophical position that everything, including mental events, is composed of physical matter and is thus subject to the laws of physics. From this perspective, the mind is considered to exist solely as a set of brain processes (see MIND–BODY PROBLEM). **2.** the position that the causes of behavior are to be found in the material of the body, particularly the nervous system. It is nearly always associated with HARD DETERMINISM. Compare IDEALISM; IMMATERIALISM. —**materialist** *adj., n.* —**materialistic** *adj.*

maternal brain in the mammalian female nervous system, the multilevel changes to neurons and neuronal activity that occur to enhance a mother's cognition and behavior toward her young during the pre- and postnatal period.

maternal deprivation lack of adequate nurturing for a young animal or child due to the absence or premature loss of, or neglect by, its mother or primary caregiver, postulated to affect an individual's early behavioral, physical, social, and emotional development negatively.

maternal environment conditions in the uterus of a pregnant woman that affect fetal development and are hypothesized to have long-term postnatal effects on the health of the child. See FETAL PROGRAMMING.

mate value an overall assessment of a person's desirability as a romantic or reproductive partner. Many factors contribute to a person's mate value, such as youthfulness, physical attractiveness, status, and wealth. The higher a person's mate value, the more selective he or she can be when choosing a partner.

mathematics anxiety apprehensiveness and tension associated with the performance of arithmetic and other mathematical tasks. Mathematics anxiety has been proposed as an important factor undermining the development of mathematical skills: It frequently causes distress, disrupts the use of working memory for maintaining task focus, negatively affects achievement scores, and potentially results in dislike and avoidance of all math-related tasks.

mathematics disorder a LEARNING DISORDER in which mathematical ability is substantially below what is expected given the person's chronological age, education, and measured intelligence. It may involve (among other problems) difficulties in counting, performing mathematical operations, and reading numerical symbols.

matriarchy *n.* **1.** a society in which descent and inheritance is **matrilineal**, that is, traced through the female only.

2. more loosely, a family, group, or society in which women are dominant. Compare PATRIARCHY. —**matriarchal** *adj.*

maturation *n.* **1.** the biological processes involved in an organism's becoming functional or fully developed. **2.** naturally occurring time-related changes in a participant (e.g., growth, fatigue, attention shifts) that pose a threat to the INTERNAL VALIDITY of a study. For example, a researcher may study substance use in a set of individuals from early adolescence to late adulthood. In the study, substance use may naturally decline as a function of the development of the participants rather than because of the influence of an experimental intervention.

maturity *n.* a state of completed growth or development, as in adulthood.

maze *n.* a system of intersecting paths and blind alleys that must be navigated from an entrance to an exit. Various types of mazes are often used in studies of human and animal cognition, such as to investigate spatial learning and memory, the organization of cognitive maps, and the foraging strategies of predators searching for prey.

M-cell *n.* any of various large neurons in the two most ventral layers of the LATERAL GENICULATE NUCLEUS. M-cells are the origin of the MAGNOCELLULAR SYSTEM. See also P-CELL.

MDMA *n.* 3,4-methylenedioxymeth*a*mphetamine: a catecholamine-like stimulant that may produce visual disturbances and hallucinations at high doses. It is among the most commonly used illicit drugs, generally sold under the name **Ecstasy**. Intoxication is characterized by euphoria, feelings of closeness and spirituality, and diverse symptoms of autonomic arousal. When used during periods of intense activity (as often occurs during rave parties), it may be toxic or fatal.

mean *n.* the numerical average of a set of scores, computed as the sum of all scores divided by the number of scores. For example, suppose a health researcher sampled five individuals and found their numbers of hours of exercise per week to be 3, 1, 5, 4, and 7, respectively. The mean number of exercise hours per week thus would be $(3 + 1 + 5 + 4 + 7)/5 = 20/5 = 4$. The mean is the most widely used statistic for describing CENTRAL TENDENCY. Also called **arithmetic mean**. See also HARMONIC MEAN.

mean deviation for a set of numbers, a measure of dispersion or spread equal to the average of the differences between each number and the mean value. It is given by $(\Sigma | x_i - \mu |)/n$, where μ is the mean value and n the number of values.

mean difference a measure of variability in a data set calculated as the average of the distances between each score and each of the other scores, disregarding whether the deviation is positive or negative. For example, consider the following three scores: 1, 3, and 9. The mean difference would be calculated as $(|1-3| + |1-9| + |3-1| + |3-9| + |9-1| + |9-3|)/6 = (2 + 8 + 2 + 6 + 8 + 6)/6 = 32/6 = 5.33$.

mean effect size in a META-ANALYSIS, a measure of the average EFFECT SIZE across multiple studies. For example, an investigator analyzing several studies assessing a new treatment may determine a mean effect size by calculating the average standardized difference between treatment and control groups over all of the studies.

mean length of utterance (MLU) a measure of language development in young children based on the average length of UTTERANCES in their spontaneous speech. It is usually calculated by counting MORPHEMES rather than words and is based on at least 100 successive utterances.

means–ends analysis any problem-solving strategy that assesses the difference between the current state and a desired end state and attempts to discover means to reduce that difference. Such a strategy would not discard means to the end that appear to be "blocked," but it would consider possible ways to overcome any such intermediate problem.

mean square (symbol: *MS*) an estimator of variance calculated as a SUM OF SQUARES divided by its DEGREES OF FREEDOM. It is used primarily in the ANALYSIS OF VARIANCE, in which an F RATIO is obtained by dividing the mean square between groups by the mean square within groups. The mean square also is used to determine the accuracy of REGRESSION ANALYSIS models.

mean square error (symbol: *MSE*) the average amount of ERROR VARIANCE within a data set, given as the typical squared distance of a score from the mean score for the set. Mean square error may be calculated in both ANALYSIS OF VARIANCE and REGRESSION ANALYSIS. A large mean square error indicates that scores are not homogeneous within groups or are not consistent with prediction.

measure *n.* an item or set of items that provides an indication of the quantity or nature of the phenomenon under study. It is sometimes necessary in research to have more than one measure for each of the main variables of interest.

measurement *n.* the act of appraising the extent of some amount, dimension, or criterion—or the resultant descriptive or quantified appraisal itself. A measurement is often, but not always, expressed as a numerical value.

measurement error in CLASSICAL TEST THEORY, any difference between an observed score and the actual or true score. Measurement error may arise from flaws in the assessment instrument, mistakes in using the instrument, or random or chance factors. For example, an investigator may obtain biased results from a survey because of

problems with question wording or response options, question order, variability in administration, and so forth.

measurement invariance the situation in which a scale or construct provides the same results across several different samples or populations. For example, an intelligence test could be said to have measurement invariance if it yields similar results for individuals of varying gender, ethnicity, or age. Compare SELECTION INVARIANCE.

measurement level the degree of specificity, accuracy, and precision in a particular set of observations or scores, as reflected in the MEASUREMENT SCALE used.

measurement model in STRUCTURAL EQUATION MODELING, a model that quantifies the association between observations obtained during research (indicators) and theoretical underlying constructs or factors. When carrying out a CONFIRMATORY FACTOR ANALYSIS, for example, one assesses a hypothesized measurement model that specifies the relationships between observed indicators and the LATENT VARIABLES that support or affect them.

measurement scale any of four common methods for quantifying attributes of variables during the course of research, listed in order of increasing power and complexity: NOMINAL SCALE, ORDINAL SCALE, INTERVAL SCALE, and RATIO SCALE.

measurement theory a field of study that examines the attribution of values to traits, characteristics, or constructs. Measurement theory focuses on assessing the true score of an attribute, such that an obtained value has a close correspondence with the actual quantity.

mechanistic theory the assumption that psychological processes and behaviors ultimately can be understood in the same way that mechanical or physiological processes are understood. Its explanations of human behavior are based on the model or metaphor of a machine, reducing complex psychological phenomena to simpler physical phenomena. See REDUCTIONISM.

mechanoreceptor *n.* a receptor that is sensitive to mechanical forms of stimuli. Examples of mechanoreceptors are the receptors in the ear that translate sound waves into nerve impulses, the touch receptors in the skin, and the receptors in the joints and muscles.

medial *adj.* toward or at the middle of the body or of an organ. Compare LATERAL. —**medially** *adv.*

medial forebrain bundle a collection of nerve fibers passing through the midline of the forebrain to the hypothalamus. It includes tracts originating in the LOCUS CERULEUS, SUBSTANTIA NIGRA, and ventral tegmental area and provides the chief pathway for reciprocal connections between the hypothalamus and the BIOGENIC AMINE systems of the brainstem.

medial geniculate nucleus either of a pair of nuclei in the THALAMUS that process auditory information. Each receives input from the inferior COLLICULUS and sends output to the AUDITORY CORTEX. See also LATERAL GENICULATE NUCLEUS.

medial lemniscus either of a pair of somatosensory tracts in the midbrain carrying fibers from the spinal cord that communicate with the thalamus.

medial temporal gyrus (**median temporal gyrus**) see MIDDLE TEMPORAL GYRUS.

median *n.* the midpoint in a distribution, that is, the score or value that divides it into two equal-sized halves. The median is a measure of CENTRAL TENDENCY that is particularly useful when analyzing data that have SKEWNESS (i.e., lopsidedness), because it is more resistant to the influence of extreme values.

median test a NONPARAMETRIC method that assesses the equality of the midpoints (medians) in two or more samples of data to determine whether they come from the same population. The term generally is used to refer to the WILCOXON–MANN–WHITNEY TEST.

media psychology a subspecialty in psychology that studies the influence of television, film, radio, the Internet, social media, advertising, mobile communications, and various other media on people's thoughts, perceptions, emotions, beliefs, behaviors, and relationships.

mediation *n.* in dispute resolution, use of a neutral outside person to help the contending parties communicate and reach a compromise. Mediation is commonly used for couples involved in separation or divorce proceedings.

mediational deficiency in problem solving, a person's inability to make use of a particular strategy to benefit task performance even if it has been taught to him or her. Compare PRODUCTION DEFICIENCY; UTILIZATION DEFICIENCY.

mediator *n.* **1.** an unseen process, event, or system that exists between a stimulus and a response, between the source and destination of a neural impulse, or between the transmitter and receiver of communications. **2.** in statistical analyses, an **intervening variable** that accounts for an observed relation between two other variables. For example, a researcher may posit a model involving an INDEPENDENT VARIABLE of ability, a mediator of self-efficacy, and a DEPENDENT VARIABLE of achievement. Thus, ability is hypothesized to influence self-efficacy, which in turn is thought to influence achievement.

medical model the concept that mental and emotional problems are analogous to biological problems—that is, they have detectable, specific, physiological causes (e.g., an abnormal gene or damaged cell) and are amenable to cure or improvement by specific treatment.

meditation *n*. profound and extended contemplation or reflection in order to achieve focused attention or an otherwise ALTERED STATE OF CONSCIOUSNESS and to gain insight into oneself and the world. Traditionally associated with spiritual and religious exercises, meditation is now also used to provide relaxation and relief from stress; treat such symptoms as high blood pressure, pain, and insomnia; and promote overall health and well-being.

medulla *n*. the central or innermost region of an organ. For example, the adrenal medulla is the central portion of the ADRENAL GLAND. Compare CORTEX. —**medullary** *adj*.

medulla oblongata the lowest, most tailward part of the HINDBRAIN. It contains many nerve tracts that conduct impulses between the spinal cord and higher brain centers, as well as autonomic nuclei involved in the control of breathing, heartbeat, and blood pressure.

megalomania *n*. a highly inflated conception of one's importance, power, or capabilities.

meiosis *n*. a special type of division of the cell nucleus that occurs during the formation of the sex cells (ova and spermatozoa). During meiosis, a parental cell in the gonad produces four daughter cells that are all HAPLOID, possessing only one of each chromosome. During fertilization, the ova and spermatozoa fuse, which restores the double set of chromosomes within the nucleus of the zygote thus formed. Compare MITOSIS.

melancholia *n*. an archaic name for depression. —**melancholic** *adj*.

melatonin *n*. a hormone, produced mainly by the PINEAL GLAND as a metabolic product of the neurotransmitter serotonin, that helps to regulate seasonal changes in physiology and may also influence puberty. It is implicated in the initiation of sleep and in the regulation of the sleep–wake cycle.

membrane *n*. a thin layer of tissue that covers a surface, lines a cavity, or connects or divides anatomical spaces or organs. In cells, the membrane surrounds the cytoplasm and acts to control the passage of substances in and out of the cell (see ION CHANNEL).

membrane potential a difference in electric potential across a membrane, especially the plasma membrane of a cell. See also RESTING POTENTIAL.

meme *n*. a unit of practice or belief through which a society or culture evolves and that passes from one generation to the next. In this sense, the term is a kind of metaphorical parallel to the term GENE. Relatedly, an **Internet meme** is an idea (e.g., a hashtag, hyperlink, picture, or video) that is widely popularized and distributed on the World Wide Web, for example, via social networks and news sources.

memory *n*. **1.** the ability to retain information or a representation of past experience, based on the mental processes of learning or ENCODING, RETENTION across some interval of time, and RETRIEVAL or reactivation of the memory. **2.** specific information or a specific past experience that is recalled. **3.** the hypothesized part of the brain where traces of information and past experiences are stored. See LONG-TERM MEMORY; SHORT-TERM MEMORY.

memory consolidation see CONSOLIDATION.

memory-enhancing drug see COGNITIVE ENHANCER.

memory span the number of items that can be recalled immediately after one presentation. Usually, the items consist of letters, words, numbers, or syllables that the participant must reproduce in order. A distinction may be drawn between visual memory span and auditory memory span, depending on the nature of the presentation.

memory trace a hypothetical modification of the nervous system that encodes a representation of informa-

M

tion or a learning experience. See ENGRAM.

menarche *n.* the first incidence of MENSTRUATION in a female, marking the onset of puberty. The age at which menarche occurs varies among individuals and cultures. —**menarcheal** *adj.*

Mendelian inheritance a type of inheritance that conforms to the basic principles developed around 1865 by Austrian monk Gregor Mendel (1822–1884), regarded as the founder of genetics. Mendelian inheritance is essentially determined by genes located on chromosomes, which are transmitted from both parents to their offspring. It includes dominant, recessive, and SEX-LINKED inheritance. See DOMINANT ALLELE; RECESSIVE ALLELE.

meninges *pl. n.* (*sing.* **meninx**) the three membranous layers that provide a protective cover for the brain and spinal cord. They consist of a tough outer **dura mater**, a middle **arachnoid mater**, and a thin, transparent **pia mater**, which fits over the various contours and fissures of the cerebral cortex.

meningioma *n.* a benign brain tumor that develops in the arachnoid layer of the MENINGES. Meningiomas are typically slow growing and cause damage mainly by pressure against the brain.

menopause *n.* see CLIMACTERIC. —**menopausal** *adj.*

menstrual cycle a modified ESTROUS CYCLE that occurs in most primates, including humans (in which it averages 28 days), and is regulated by cyclical changes in the concentrations of GONADOTROPINS secreted by the anterior pituitary gland. In the follicular phase of the cycle, FOLLICLE-STIMULATING HORMONE (FSH) and LUTEINIZING HORMONE (LH) stimulate development of an ovum and secretion of estrogen within the ovary, culminating in OVULATION. The luteal phase begins immediately after ovulation, when a yellowish glan-

dular mass called the corpus luteum forms and secretes progesterone, which inhibits further secretion of FSH and LH. If fertilization does not occur, this phase ends with menstruation and a repeat of the follicular phase.

menstruation *n.* a periodic discharge of blood and endometrial tissue from the uterus through the vagina that occurs in women as part of the MENSTRUAL CYCLE.

mental *adj.* **1.** of or referring to the MIND or to processes of the mind, such as thinking, feeling, sensing, and the like. **2.** phenomenal or consciously experienced. In contrast to physiological or physical, which refer to objective events or processes, mental denotes events known only privately and subjectively; it may refer to the COGNITIVE PROCESSES involved in these events, to differentiate them from physiological processes.

mental aberration a pathological deviation from normal thinking, particularly as a symptom of a mental or emotional disorder.

mental age (**MA**) a numerical scale unit derived by dividing an individual's results in an intelligence test by the average score for other people of the same age. Thus, a 4-year-old child who scored 150 on an IQ test would have a mental age of 6 (the age-appropriate average score is 100; therefore, MA = $(150/100) \times 4 = 6$). The MA measure of performance is not effective beyond the age of 14.

mental disorder any condition characterized by cognitive and emotional disturbances, abnormal behaviors, impaired functioning, or any combination of these. Such disorders cannot be accounted for solely by environmental circumstances and may involve physiological, genetic, chemical, social, and other factors. Specific classifications of mental disorders are elaborated in the American Psychiatric Association's *Diagnostic and Statistical Manual of Mental Disorders* (see DSM–5) and the World Health Organization's INTERNATIONAL CLASSIFICATION OF DISEASES. Also called **mental illness**; **psychological disorder**. See also PSYCHOPATHOLOGY.

mental handicap impaired cognitive ability that interferes with independent functioning in the community. Use of the term is now generally discouraged in preference to INTELLECTUAL DISABILITY.

mental health a state of mind characterized by emotional well-being, relative freedom from anxiety and disabling symptoms, and a capacity to establish constructive relationships and cope with the ordinary demands and stresses of life.

mental health care a category of health care services associated with psychological assessment and intervention. This type of care includes but is not limited to psychological screening and testing, psychotherapy and family therapy, and neuropsychological rehabilitation.

mental health parity in U.S. health care law, the mandate that the limits and financial requirements imposed by insurers to benefits for treatment of mental health and substance use disorders not be more restrictive than those applied to medical and surgical benefits.

mental hospital see PSYCHIATRIC HOSPITAL.

mental hygiene a general approach aimed at maintaining mental health and preventing mental disorder through such means as educational programs, promotion of a stable emotional and family life, prophylactic and early treatment services (see PRIMARY PREVENTION), and public health measures. The term itself is no longer widely used.

mental illness see MENTAL DISORDER.

mental imagery see IMAGERY.

mentalism *n.* a position that insists on the reality of explicitly mental phenomena, such as thinking and feeling, as independent entities that cannot be reduced to physical or physiological phenomena. The term is often used as a synonym for IDEALISM, but some forms of mentalism may hold that mental events, although not reducible to physical substances, are nonetheless grounded in physical processes. Most modern cognitive theories are examples of this latter type of mentalism. —**mentalist** *adj.*

mental lexicon the set of words that a person uses regularly (productive vocabulary) or recognizes when used by others (receptive vocabulary). Psycholinguistics has proposed various models for such a lexicon, in which words are mentally organized with respect to such features as meaning, lexical category (e.g., noun, verb), frequency, length, and sound.

mental model any internal representation of the relations between a set of elements, as, for example, between the elements of a mathematics or physics problem, the terms of a syllogism, or the configuration of objects in a space. Such models may contain perceptual qualities and may be abstract in nature. They can be manipulated to provide dynamic simulations of possible scenarios and are thought to be key components in decision making.

mental representation a hypothetical entity that is presumed to stand for a perception, thought, memory, or the like during cognitive operations. For example, when doing mental arithmetic, one presumably operates on mental representations that correspond to digits and numerical operators; when one imagines looking at the reverse side of an object, one presumably operates on a mental representation of that object.

mental retardation (**MR**) intellectual function that is significantly below average, as demonstrated by a measured IQ of 70 or below. The disorder may be the result of brain injury, disease, or genetic causes and is typically characterized by an impairment of educational, social, and vocational abilities. It is now more commonly known as IN-TELLECTUAL DISABILITY.

mental set a temporary readiness to perform certain psychological functions that influences the response to a situation or stimulus, such as the tendency to apply a previously successful technique in solving a new problem. Essentially synonymous with the older term EINSTELLUNG, mental set is often determined by instructions but need not be.

mentoring *n.* the provision of instruction, encouragement, and other support to an individual (e.g., student, youth, colleague) to aid his or her overall growth and development or pursuit of greater learning skills, a career, or other educational or work-related goals. Numerous **mentoring programs** exist within occupational, educational, and other settings; they use a variety of techniques and procedures to develop productive relationships between mentors and their respective protégés.

mere-exposure effect the finding that individuals show an increased preference (or liking) for a stimulus as a consequence of repeated exposure to that stimulus. This effect is most likely to occur when there is no preexisting negative attitude toward the stimulus object, and it tends to be strongest when the person is not consciously aware of the stimulus presentations.

mescaline *n.* a HALLUCINOGEN derived from the peyote cactus. The effects of mescaline often include nausea and vomiting as well as visual hallucinations involving lights and colors; they have a slower onset than those of LSD and usually last 1 to 2 hours. Its likely mechanism of action is via serotonin and dopamine receptors.

mesencephalon *n.* see MIDBRAIN. —**mesencephalic** *adj.*

mesmerism *n.* a therapeutic technique popularized in the late 18th century by German physician Franz Anton Mesmer (1734–1815). The procedure involved the application of magnets to ailing parts of a patient's body and the induction of a trancelike state by gazing into the patient's eyes, making certain "magnetic passes" over him or her with the hands, and so forth. Mesmerism was gradually superseded by HYPNOSIS. —**mesmerist** *n.* —**mesmeric** *adj.* —**mesmerize** *vb.*

mesokurtic *adj.* describing a FRE-QUENCY DISTRIBUTION that is neither flatter nor more peaked than the NOR-MAL DISTRIBUTION. That is, a mesokurtic arrangement of values follows a bell-shaped curve, with the majority of scores clustered around a value at the midpoint and a few extreme scores tapering off on either side. See also PLATYKURTIC; LEPTOKURTIC.

mesosystem *n.* in ECOLOGICAL SYS-TEMS THEORY, the groups and institutions outside the home (e.g., day care, school, a child's peer group) that influence the child's development and interact with aspects of the **microsystem** (e.g., relations in the home). Compare CHRONOSYSTEM; EXOSYSTEM; MACRO-SYSTEM.

messenger RNA (**mRNA**) a type of RNA that carries instructions from a cell's genetic material (usually DNA) to the protein-manufacturing apparatus elsewhere in the cell and directs the assembly of protein components in precise accord with those instructions. The instructions are embodied in the sequence of bases in the mRNA, according to the GENETIC CODE.

meta-analysis *n.* a quantitative technique for synthesizing the results of multiple studies of a phenomenon into a single result by combining the EFFECT SIZE estimates from each study into a single estimate of the combined effect size or into a DISTRIBUTION of effect sizes. For example, a researcher could conduct a meta-analysis of several studies on the association between self-efficacy and achievement, integrating the findings into an overall correlation.

metabolic syndrome a collection of conditions that increases an individual's risk for cardiovascular disease, stroke, and Type 2 diabetes. These include hypertension, elevated insulin levels, nonalcoholic fatty liver disease, and obesity.

metabolism *n.* the physical and chemical processes within a living cell or organism that are necessary to maintain life. It includes **catabolism**, the breaking down of complex molecules into simpler ones, often with the release of energy; and **anabolism**, the synthesis of complex molecules from simple ones. —**metabolic** *adj.*

metabotropic receptor a neurotransmitter receptor that does not itself contain an ION CHANNEL but may use a G PROTEIN to open a nearby ion channel. Compare IONOTROPIC RECEPTOR.

metacognition *n.* awareness of one's own cognitive processes, often involving a conscious attempt to control them. The TIP-OF-THE-TONGUE PHENOMENON, in which one struggles to retrieve something that one knows one knows, provides an interesting and common example of metacognition. —**metacognitive** *adj.*

metalinguistic awareness a conscious awareness of the formal properties of language as well as its functional and semantic properties. It is associated with a mature stage in language and cognitive development and does not usually develop until around age 8.

metamemory *n.* awareness of one's own memory processes, often involving a conscious attempt to direct or control them. It is an aspect of METACOGNITION.

metamotivation *n.* in the humanistic psychology of U.S. psychologist Abraham Maslow (1908–1970), those motives that impel an individual to "character growth, character expression, maturation, and development,"

operating on the level of SELF-ACTUALIZATION and transcendence in the hierarchy of needs (see MASLOW'S MOTIVATIONAL HIERARCHY). Compare DEFICIENCY MOTIVATION.

metaneed *n.* in the humanistic psychology of U.S. psychologist Abraham Maslow (1908–1970), the highest level of need that comes into play primarily after the lower level needs have been met. Metaneeds constitute the goals of self-actualizers and include the needs for knowledge, beauty, and creativity. See also MASLOW'S MOTIVATIONAL HIERARCHY.

metapsychology *n.* **1.** generally, the theoretical or speculative (rather than experimental) investigation of fundamental questions about the human mind and behavior, such as the MIND–BODY PROBLEM. **2.** the term used by Austrian neurologist Sigmund Freud (1856–1939) to denote his own psychological theory, emphasizing its ability to offer comprehensive explanations of psychological phenomena on a fundamental level. —**metapsychological** *adj.*

metatheory *n.* a higher order theory about theories, allowing one to analyze, compare, and evaluate competing bodies of ideas. The concept of a metatheory suggests that theories derive from other theories, so that there are always prior theoretical assumptions and commitments behind any theoretical formulation. —**metatheoretical** *adj.*

methadone *n.* a synthetic OPIOID analgesic that is used for pain relief and as a substitute for heroin and other opioids in METHADONE MAINTENANCE THERAPY. It has a long duration of action, both preventing withdrawal symptoms and blocking the reinforcing effects of these opioids.

methadone maintenance therapy a drug-rehabilitation therapy in which those with dependence on heroin and other opiates are prescribed a daily oral dose of methadone to blunt craving for these drugs and to diminish withdrawal symptoms. A controversial treatment, it is nonetheless widely considered the most effective approach to heroin addiction.

methamphetamine *n.* a stimulant whose chemical structure is similar to that of amphetamine. It is used for treating attention-deficit/hyperactivity disorder in children and as a short-term aid to obesity treatment in adults. Like all AMPHETAMINES, methamphetamine is prone to abuse and dependence.

method of adjustment a psychophysical technique in which the participant adjusts a variable stimulus to match a constant or standard. For example, the observer is shown a standard visual stimulus of a specific intensity and is asked to adjust a comparison stimulus to match the brightness of the standard.

method of constant stimuli a psychophysical procedure for determining the sensory threshold by randomly presenting several stimuli known to be close to the threshold. The threshold is the stimulus value that was detected 50% of the time.

method of limits a psychophysical procedure for determining the sensory threshold by gradually increasing or decreasing the magnitude of the stimulus presented in discrete steps. That is, a stimulus of a given intensity is presented to a participant; if it is perceived, a stimulus of lower intensity is presented on the next trial, until the stimulus can no longer be detected. If it is not perceived, a stimulus of higher intensity is presented, until the stimulus is detected.

method of loci a MNEMONIC technique in which items that are to be remembered are converted into mental images and associated with specific positions or locations. For instance, to remember a shopping list, each product could be imagined at a different location along a familiar street.

method of successive approxi-

mations a method of shaping OPERANT BEHAVIOR by reinforcing responses similar to the desired behavior. Initially, responses roughly approximating the desired behavior are reinforced. Later, only responses closely approximating the desired behavior are reinforced. Also called **successive-approximations method**.

methodological behaviorism a form of BEHAVIORISM that concedes the existence and reality of conscious events but contends that the only suitable means of studying them scientifically is via their expression in behavior. Compare RADICAL BEHAVIORISM. See NEOBEHAVIORISM.

methodology *n.* **1.** the science of method or orderly arrangement; specifically, the branch of logic concerned with the application of the principles of reasoning to scientific and philosophical inquiry. **2.** the system of methods, principles, and rules of procedure used within a particular discipline. For example, in research and experimental design the term refers to the techniques used to collect information, and in statistics it refers to the procedures used to analyze such data.

methylphenidate *n.* a stimulant related to the AMPHETAMINES and with a similar mechanism of action. It blocks the reuptake of CATECHOLAMINES from the synaptic cleft and stimulates presynaptic release of catecholamines. Methylphenidate is used as an adjunct to antidepressant therapy and to increase concentration and alertness in patients with brain injuries, brain cancer, or dementia. It is also used for the treatment of attention-deficit/hyperactivity disorder and narcolepsy. U.S. trade name (among others): **Ritalin**.

metric *n.* a scale or system used to express amount or quantity. For example, the Fahrenheit scale is a metric for assessing temperature, and the system of IQ points is a metric for assessing intelligence.

Meynert's nucleus see BASAL

NUCLEUS OF MEYNERT. [Theodor H. **Meynert** (1833–1892), Austrian neurologist]

microcephaly *n.* a condition in which the circumference of the head is more than two standard deviations below the mean for age, gender, race, and gestation. It may be present at birth or develop in the first few years of life. Depending on the severity of their accompanying syndrome, children with microcephaly may have intellectual disability, delayed motor functions and speech, facial distortions, dwarfism or short stature, hyperactivity, seizures, difficulties with coordination and balance, and other brain or neurological abnormalities. Compare MACROCEPHALY. —**microcephalic** *adj.*

microelectrode *n.* an electrode with a tip no larger than a few micrometers in diameter that can be inserted into a single cell. In studies of neurophysiology and disorders of the nervous system, intracellular microelectrodes with tips less than 1 µm in diameter are able to stimulate and record activity within a single neuron.

microgenetic method a research methodology for studying cognitive developmental change, involving (a) observations of individual children throughout a period of change, (b) a high density of observations relative to the rate of change within that period, and (c) intensive trial-by-trial analyses intended to infer the processes that gave rise to the change.

microglia *n.* an extremely small type of nonneuronal central nervous system cell (GLIA) that removes cellular debris from injured or dead cells. —**microglial** *adj.*

micrographia *n.* a disorder characterized by very small, often unreadable writing and associated most often with PARKINSON'S DISEASE.

microsleep *n.* a momentary loss of awareness when a person is fatigued or sleep-deprived, especially during monotonous tasks, such as driving, looking at a computer, or passively monitoring machinery. Microsleep episodes are more likely to occur in the predawn and midafternoon hours and can be a major risk factor for traffic and industrial accidents.

microsystem *n.* see MESOSYSTEM.

microtubule *n.* a small, hollow, cylindrical structure (typically 20 nm–26 nm in diameter), numbers of which occur in various types of cell. Microtubules are part of the cell's internal scaffolding (cytoskeleton) and form the spindle during cell division. In neurons, microtubules are involved in AXONAL TRANSPORT.

midbrain *n.* a relatively small region of the upper brainstem that connects the FOREBRAIN and HINDBRAIN. It contains the TECTUM (and associated inferior and superior COLLICULI), TEGMENTUM, and SUBSTANTIA NIGRA. Also called **mesencephalon**.

middle ear a membrane-lined cavity in the temporal bone of the skull. It is filled with air and communicates with the nasopharynx through the EUSTACHIAN TUBE. It contains the OSSICLES, which transmit sound vibrations from the outer ear and the tympanic membrane (eardrum) to the OVAL WINDOW of the inner ear.

middle temporal gyrus (**MTG**) a ridge or convolution on the temporal lobe that may have roles in recognizing familiar faces, comprehending language, and visually assessing whether an action is rational. Also called **medial** (or **median**) **temporal gyrus**.

midlife crisis a period of psychological distress thought to occur in some individuals during the middle years of adulthood, roughly from ages 35 to 65. Causes may include significant life events and health or occupational problems and concerns.

midline *n.* a bisecting or median line, especially in reference to an imaginary median line or plane through the body or a part of the body.

midpoint *n.* see MEDIAN.

midrange *n.* the average of the lowest and highest scores in a set of data. The midrange is a measure of CENTRAL TENDENCY more prone to bias than the MEAN, MEDIAN, and MODE because it relies solely on the two most extreme scores, which potentially are OUTLIERS.

midspread *n.* see INTERQUARTILE RANGE.

midwife *n.* a professionally trained and licensed health care provider of primary medical services for women, including perinatal (prenatal, delivery, and postpartum) care for pregnant women and new mothers and most family planning and gynecological services for healthy women of all ages. Midwives work together with obstetrics and gynecology (OB/GYN) doctors. —**midwifery** *n.*

migraine headache a headache that is recurrent, usually severe, usually limited to one side of the head, and likely to be accompanied by nausea, vomiting, and sensitivity to light. Migraine headaches may be preceded by a sensation of flickering or flashing light, blacking out of part of the visual field, or illusions of colors or patterns.

migration *n.* **1.** travel by nonhuman animals over relatively long distances to or from breeding areas. Migration is observed in birds, fish, and some mammals and insects (among others). In some species, it is seasonal, involving movement from a breeding area to an overwintering area; in others, particularly the salmon, it is observed only once in the lifetime of an individual. **2.** in the development of the nervous system, the movement of nerve cells from their origin in the ventricular zone to establish distinctive cell populations, such as brain nuclei and layers of the cerebral cortex.

milieu *n.* (*pl.* **milieux**) the environ-

ment in general or the social environment more specifically.

milieu therapy psychotherapeutic treatment based on modification or manipulation of the client's life circumstances or immediate environment so as to promote healthier, more adaptive cognitions, emotions, and behavior. See also THERAPEUTIC COMMUNITY.

military psychology the application of psychological principles, theories, and methods to the evaluation, selection, assignment, and training of military personnel, as well as to the design of military equipment. This field also includes the application of clinical and counseling techniques to the maintenance of morale and mental health in military settings and covers human functioning in a variety of environments during times of peace and war.

mimicry *n.* **1.** the presence of physical or behavioral traits in one species that so closely resemble those of another species that they confuse observers. This resemblance makes it possible for an organism either to evade predators or to attract prey. **2.** a form of SOCIAL LEARNING in which people, without conscious awareness or intent, automatically copy other people's physical movements (behaviors such as postures, gestures, and mannerisms), facial expressions, speech patterns, and emotions during interpersonal interactions. It is thought that the behavioral form in particular, called **behavioral mimicry**, arises out of the need to affiliate and facilitates an effort to establish rapport with others. See also IMITATION.

mind *n.* **1.** broadly, all intellectual and psychological phenomena of an organism, encompassing motivational, affective, behavioral, perceptual, and cognitive systems; that is, the organized totality of an organism's MENTAL and PSYCHIC processes and the structural and functional cognitive components on which they depend. The term, however, is also used more narrowly to denote only cognitive activities and functions, such as perceiving, attending, thinking, problem solving, language, learning, and memory. The nature of the relationship between the mind and the body, including the brain and its mechanisms or activities, has been, and continues to be, the subject of much debate. See MIND–BODY PROBLEM. **2.** a set of EMERGENT PROPERTIES automatically derived from a brain that has achieved sufficient biological sophistication. In this sense, the mind is considered more the province of humans and of human consciousness than of organisms in general. **3.** human consciousness regarded as an immaterial entity distinct from the brain. See CARTESIAN DUALISM. **4.** the brain itself and its activities. In this view, the mind essentially is both the anatomical organ and what it does.

mind–body problem the problem of accounting for and describing the relationship between mental and physical processes (psyche and soma). Solutions to this problem fall into six broad categories: (a) INTERACTIONISM, in which mind and body are separate processes that nevertheless exert mutual influence; (b) parallelism, in which mind and body are separate processes with a point-to-point correspondence but no causal connection; (c) IDEALISM, in which only mind exists and the soma is a function of the psyche; (d) double-aspect theory, in which body and mind are both functions of a common entity; (e) epiphenomenalism, in which mind is a by-product of bodily processes; and (f) MATERIALISM, in which body is the only reality and the psyche is non-existent.

mindfulness *n.* purposeful awareness of one's internal states and surroundings. The concept has been applied to various therapeutic interventions—for example, mindfulness-based COGNITIVE BEHAVIOR THERAPY, mindfulness-based stress reduction, and mindfulness meditation—to help people avoid destructive or automatic habits and responses by learning to observe their thoughts, emotions, and other present-moment experiences without judging or reacting to them. —**mindful** *adj.*

mineralocorticoid *n.* any CORTICOSTEROID hormone that affects ion concentrations in body tissues and helps to regulate the excretion of salt and water. In humans, the principal mineralocorticoid is ALDOSTERONE.

minimal brain dysfunction (**MBD**) a relatively mild impairment of brain function that is presumed to account for a variety of subtle and non-specific disturbances seen in certain learning or behavioral disabilities. These signs include short attention span, distractibility, impulsivity, hyperactivity, emotional lability, poor motor coordination, visual-perceptual disturbance, and language difficulties.

minimal group a group lacking interdependence, GROUP COHESION, structure, and other characteristics typically found in social groups. An example is a group of people disembarking from a bus.

minimally conscious state (**MCS**) a condition in which a person who has experienced severe brain injury or deterioration retains a limited awareness of self and environment through residual cognitive functions. The individual is awake and occasionally able to communicate and do simple voluntary activities that demonstrate an engagement with surroundings. For example, he or she may produce intelligible verbalizations (e.g., saying *yes* or *no*), follow simple commands (e.g., blinking when asked), gesture, or grasp objects. Formerly called **quasi-vegetative state**.

Minnesota Multiphasic Personality Inventory (**MMPI**) one of the most widely used SELF-REPORT tools for assessing personality, first published in 1940. It has broad applications across a range of mental health, medical, substance abuse, forensic, and personnel screening settings as a measure of psychological maladjustment. The version currently in use, the **MMPI–2** (1989), features 567 true–false questions that assess symptoms, attitudes, and beliefs that relate to emotional and behavioral problems.

minor depression see DYSTHYMIA.

minority group a population subgroup with social, religious, ethnic, racial, or other characteristics that differ from those of the majority of the population. The term is sometimes extended to cover any group that is the subject of oppression and discrimination, whether or not it literally comprises a minority of the population.

minority influence social pressure exerted on the majority of a group by a smaller faction of the group. Studies suggest that minorities who argue consistently prompt the group to reconsider even long-held or previously unquestioned assumptions and procedures.

minority stress the physiological and psychological effects associated with the adverse social conditions experienced by ethnic and racial minorities, lesbians, gay men, bisexual and transgender individuals, and others who are members of stigmatized social groups. The concept frequently is invoked by researchers to explain the increased rates of depression, anxiety, substance abuse, body image problems, eating disorders, cardiovascular disease, and other conditions among members of minority or marginalized groups.

minor tranquilizer see ANXIOLYTIC.

mirror neuron a type of cell in the brains of certain animals (including humans) that responds in the same way to a given action (e.g., grasping an object) whether the animal performs the action itself or sees another animal perform the action.

misandry n. hatred or contempt for

men. Compare MISOGYNY. —**misandrist** n., adj.

misanthropy n. a hatred, aversion, or distrust of human beings and human nature. —**misanthrope** n. —**misanthropic** adj.

misattribution n. an incorrect inference as to the cause of an individual's or group's behavior or of an interpersonal event. **Misattribution of arousal** is an effect in which the physiological stimulation generated by one stimulus is mistakenly ascribed to another source. See also ATTRIBUTION THEORY.

misattunement n. **1.** a lack of rapport between infant and parent or caregiver such that the infant's efforts at communication and expression are not responded to in a way that allows the infant to feel understood. **2.** in psychoanalysis, a lack of empathy by a therapist or analyst toward a patient. Compare ATTUNEMENT; EMPATHIC FAILURE.

miscarriage n. see ABORTION.

misinformation effect a phenomenon in which a person mistakenly recalls misleading information that an experimenter has provided, instead of accurately recalling the correct information that had been presented earlier. The misinformation effect is studied in the context of EYEWITNESS MEMORY.

misogyny n. hatred or contempt for women. Compare MISANDRY. —**misogynist** n. —**misogynistic** adj.

missing at random (**MAR**) the situation in which the absence of certain points from a data set is unrelated to the nature of the particular items but may be explained by other variables. For example, assume a researcher surveyed 100 students on a college campus about their weekly amount of alcohol, drug, and cigarette use but 12 individuals failed to note their use for an item. If all 12 people are male, and if there is no consistency as to which item was left blank by which person, then the pattern of responses on the survey could be related to sex.

misspecification *n.* the situation in which the number of variables, factors, PARAMETERS, or some combination of these was not correctly specified in a statistical model, with the result that the model does not offer a reasonable representation of obtained data. Misspecification is indicated by such things as large RESIDUALS between the data and that predicted by the model, large STANDARD ERRORS for the parameter estimates, or a nonsignificant result from a GOODNESS-OF-FIT test.

mitochondrion *n.* (*pl.* **mitochondria**) a membrane-bound structure that is the main site of energy production in cells. Mitochondria are most numerous in cells with a high level of metabolism. They have their own DNA (mitochondrial DNA). —**mitochondrial** *adj.*

mitosis *n.* (*pl.* **mitoses**) the type of division of a cell nucleus that produces two identical daughter nuclei, each possessing the same number and type of chromosomes as the parent nucleus. It is usually accompanied by division of the cytoplasm, leading to the formation of two identical daughter cells. Compare MEIOSIS. —**mitotic** *adj.*

mixed design a study that combines features of both a BETWEEN-SUBJECTS DESIGN and a WITHIN-SUBJECTS DESIGN. For example, a researcher might use a mixed design to study the influence of different types of music on relaxation. He or she could divide participants into a CONTROL GROUP and two EXPERIMENTAL GROUPS, determine the baseline level of physiological arousal prior to hearing any music, and then introduce the music and test participants while they listen. He or she could then determine what specific reduction in arousal may have occurred throughout the listening period. Here, music type is a between-subjects factor (each participant hears only a single genre of music), and physiological arousal is a

within-subjects factor (each participant is evaluated on this variable on multiple occasions and the assessments are compared).

mixed episode an episode of a mood disorder in which symptoms meeting criteria for both a MAJOR DEPRESSIVE EPISODE and a MANIC EPISODE are prominent over the course of the disturbance. One or more mixed episodes may be a feature of BIPOLAR DISORDER.

mixed-methods research a study that combines aspects of both QUALITATIVE RESEARCH and QUANTITATIVE RESEARCH. For example, a researcher studying a disease could conduct a focus group with a set of individuals who would share their experiences in dealing with the disease, and then supplement those qualitative findings by surveying a different set of individuals to obtain quantitative knowledge of risk factors for the disease.

mixed receptive-expressive language disorder a developmental communication disorder that combines the symptoms of EXPRESSIVE LANGUAGE DISORDER with the symptoms of semantic comprehension problems, leading to difficulty with word associations, categorization, and verbal mediation in general.

mnemonic *n.* any device or technique used to assist memory, usually by forging a link or association between the new information to be remembered and information previously encoded. For instance, one might remember the numbers in a password by associating them with familiar birth dates, addresses, or room numbers. See also METHOD OF LOCI.

mob psychology CROWD PSYCHOLOGY, as applied to disorderly, unruly, and emotionally charged groups of people.

modal *n.* pertaining to a particular MODE, model, technique, or process. In linguistics, modal refers to the mood of a verb; that is, for example, whether it is *indicative* (states a fact), *imperative* (expresses an order or command), or *subjunctive* (expresses a wish or a state of possibility).

modal action pattern (MAP) the typical or most common behavioral pattern expressed in response to a RELEASER. In classical ethology, the term FIXED ACTION PATTERN was used to describe behavioral responses, but this term obscures the variation in behavior typically seen within and between individuals.

modality *n.* **1.** a particular therapeutic technique or process (e.g., psychodynamic). **2.** a medium of sensation, such as vision or hearing. See SENSE.

mode *n.* the most frequently occurring score in a set of data, which is sometimes used as a measure of CENTRAL TENDENCY.

model *n.* a graphic, theoretical, or other type of representation of a concept or of basic behavioral or bodily processes (e.g., a disorder) that can be used for various investigative and demonstrative purposes, such as enhancing understanding of the concept or process, proposing hypotheses, showing relationships, or identifying epidemiological patterns.

modeling *n.* **1.** a technique used in COGNITIVE BEHAVIOR THERAPY and BEHAVIOR THERAPY in which learning occurs through observation and imitation alone, without comment or reinforcement by the therapist. **2.** the process in which one or more individuals or other entities serve as examples (models) that a child will emulate. Models are often parents, other adults, or other children, but they may also be symbolic (e.g., a book or television character). See also SOCIAL LEARNING THEORY.

moderating effect the effect that occurs when a third variable changes the nature of the relationship between a predictor and an outcome. For example, STRUCTURAL EQUATION MODELING can be used to assess whether a predicted association between quantitative skill and performance fits equally well across different teaching style groups (e.g., lecture based vs. hands-on learning). If the prediction is different across the two groups, then teaching style is said to have produced a moderating effect.

moderator *n.* an INDEPENDENT VARIABLE that changes the nature of the relationship between other variables. For example, if a researcher examined the relationship between gender and math performance, a significant difference might emerge. However, if teaching style were taken into account, such that those who learned math by applied, hands-on methods performed better than those who learned with traditional lecture styles, regardless of gender, one could say that teaching style was a moderator of the relationship between gender and math performance.

modernism *n.* in philosophy, a set of general characteristics marking the whole period from the 17th century to the present day. These include a sense that religious dogma and classical metaphysics can no longer provide a sure foundation in intellectual matters and a quest for certain knowledge from other sources. Traditional psychology can be seen to be the product of modernism to the extent that it is characterized by faith in scientific method, pursuit of control and prediction of behavior, explanation in terms of laws and principles, and the assumption that human behavior is ultimately rational as opposed to irrational. See also POSTMODERNISM. —**modernist** *adj., n.*

modernization *n.* the complex set of processes by which a largely rural and traditional society becomes a developed industrial society. Modernized societies are typically conceived as those societies that tend toward the secular and urbanized and that place a high value on science and technology, education, social mobility, acquired wealth, democratic government, and the rule of law. **—modernize** *vb.*

modern racism a contemporary form of PREJUDICE against members of other racial groups that is expressed indirectly and covertly. A modern racist, for example, expresses prejudice by condemning another group's cultural values or by avoiding any contact with members of that group. See also AVERSIVE RACISM.

modified replication see REPLICATION.

modularity *n.* a theory of the human mind in which the various components of cognition are characterized as independent modules, each with its own specific domain and particular properties.

modulation *n.* changes in some parameter of a waveform (e.g., amplitude, frequency, phase) so that the information contained by the variations of this parameter can be transmitted by the wave, which is known as the **carrier wave. Amplitude modulation** (AM) refers to changes in amplitude that are relatively slow compared to the usually sinusoidal variations in the carrier. In **frequency modulation** (FM), the frequency of the carrier is varied, but its amplitude remains constant. In **phase modulation**, the relative phase of the carrier wave is varied in accordance with the amplitude of the signal variations.

modulus *n.* see ABSOLUTE VALUE.

molar *adj.* characterized by or pertaining to units, masses, and systems in their entirety. **Molar analysis** in psychology is a way of examining behavioral processes as holistic units, extended through time. This approach stresses comprehensive concepts or overall frameworks or structures. Compare MOLECULAR.

molecular *adj.* characterized by or pertaining to the component parts of a phenomenon, process, or system. **Molecular analysis** in psychology is a way of examining behavioral processes in terms of elemental units, sometimes analyzing them in a moment-by-moment or phase-by-phase manner. Compare MOLAR.

molecular genetics the branch of biology that is concerned with the structure and processes of genetic material at the molecular level.

moment *n.* the power to which the expected value of a RANDOM VARIABLE is raised. Thus, $E(x^k)$ is the kth moment of x. The first moment is usually the MEAN of a variable, the second moment refers to VARIANCE, the third moment relates to SKEWNESS, and the fourth moment concerns KURTOSIS. Having each of these moments for a set of scores, a researcher knows the center point of the data, how spread out the values are, whether they are lopsided, and whether they are peaked or flat.

monism *n.* the position that reality consists of a single substance, whether this is identified as mind, matter, or God. In the context of the MIND–BODY PROBLEM, monism is any position that avoids DUALISM. **—monist** *adj., n.* **—monistic** *adj.*

monoamine *n.* a chemical compound that contains only one amine group, $-NH_2$. Monoamines include neurotransmitters such as the CATECHOLAMINES norepinephrine and dopamine and the INDOLEAMINE serotonin.

monoamine hypothesis the theory that depression is caused by a deficit in the production or uptake of the compounds serotonin, norepinephrine, and dopamine. This theory has been used to explain the effects of MONOAMINE OXIDASE INHIBITORS but is now regarded as too simplistic.

monoamine oxidase inhibitor (**MAOI; MAO inhibitor**) a group of antidepressant drugs that function by inhibiting the activity of the enzyme **monoamine oxidase** in presynaptic neurons, thereby increasing the amounts of monoamine neurotransmitters (serotonin, norepinephrine, and dopamine) available for release at the presynaptic terminal. There are two categories of MAOIs: irreversible and reversible inhibitors. Irreversible MAOIs bind tightly to the enzyme and permanently inhibit its ability to metabolize any monoamine. This may lead to dangerous interactions with foods and beverages containing the amino acid tryptophan or tyramine, particularly those produced by enzymatic action or by aging (e.g., cheeses, preserved meats and fish). In contrast, reversible MAOIs do not bind permanently to the enzyme, thereby allowing it to take part in the metabolism of amino acids and other amines. The availability of other effective antidepressants lacking the drug–food interactions of the MAOIs has led to a precipitous decline in their use, particularly of the irreversible agents.

monochromatism (**monochromatopsia**) *n.* a partial color blindness in which the eye contains only one type of cone PHOTOPIGMENT instead of the typical three: Everything appears in various shades of a single color. See also ACHROMATISM; DICHROMATISM; TRICHROMATISM.

monocular cue see DEPTH CUE.

monogamy *n.* **1.** a mating system in which two individuals mate exclusively with each other. Many species, including human beings, display serial monogamy, in which there is an exclusive social bond with each of a series of sexual partners at different times during the individual's life. Compare POLYANDRY; POLYGYNANDRY; POLYGYNY. **2.** traditionally, marriage to only one spouse at a time. Compare POLYGAMY. —**monogamous** *adj.*

monopolar neuron see UNIPOLAR NEURON.

monotonic *adj.* denoting a variable that either increases or decreases as a second variable either increases or decreases, respectively: The relationship is not necessarily LINEAR, but there are no changes in direction. A **monotonically increasing** variable is one that rises consistently as a second variable increases, for example, level of performance in relation to amount of practice if this were observed to be the case. In contrast, depression would be a **monotonically decreasing** variable if its severity were found to fall consistently as a person's level of perseveration declined.

monozygotic twins (**MZ twins**) twins, always of the same sex, that develop from a single fertilized ovum (zygote) that splits in the early stages of MITOSIS to produce two individuals who carry the same complement of genes; that is, they are clones, with identical DNA. Also called **identical twins**. Compare DIZYGOTIC TWINS.

mood *n.* **1.** any short-lived emotional state, usually of low intensity (e.g., a cheerful mood, an irritable mood). **2.** a disposition to respond emotionally in a particular way that may last for hours, days, or even weeks, perhaps at a low level and without the person knowing what prompted the state. Moods differ from EMOTIONS in lacking an object; for example, the emotion of anger can be aroused by an insult, but an angry mood may arise when one does not know what one is angry about or what elicited the anger. Disturbances in mood are characteristic of MOOD DISORDERS.

mood congruent relating to a consistency or agreement between a particular expressed feeling and the general emotional context within which it occurs. In psychiatric diagnosis, for example, the term relates to a consistency between the expression of a particular symptom or behavior with those characteristics or patterns of ideation or action used to classify a particular mental disorder. Inconsistencies are described as **mood incongruent**.

mood-congruent memory consistency between one's mood state and the emotional context of memories recalled. During positive mood states, individuals will tend to retrieve pleasant memories, whereas during negative mood states, negative thoughts and associations will more likely come to mind.

mood-dependent memory the finding that memory for an event can be recalled more readily when one is in the same emotional mood (e.g., happy or sad) as when the memory was initially formed. See also STATE-DEPENDENT MEMORY.

mood disorder a psychiatric condition in which the principal feature is a prolonged, pervasive emotional disturbance, such as a DEPRESSIVE DISORDER, BIPOLAR DISORDER, or substance-induced mood disorder. Also called **affective disorder**.

mood incongruent see MOOD CONGRUENT.

mood stabilizer any of various drugs used in the treatment of BIPOLAR DISORDERS and CYCLOTHYMIC DISORDER. Because they reduce the symptoms of mania or manic episodes, mood stabilizers are sometimes known as **antimanic drugs**. Mood stabilizers are also occasionally used in the management of severe affective lability found in some personality disorders (e.g., borderline personality disorder).

moon illusion see SIZE–DISTANCE PARADOX.

moral *adj.* **1.** relating to the distinction between right and wrong behavior. **2.** describing a behavior that is considered ethical or proper.

moral absolutism the belief that the morality or immorality of an action can be judged according to fixed standards of right and wrong. According to Swiss child psychologist and epistemologist Jean Piaget (1896–1980), moral absolutism is characteristic of young children in the HETERONOMOUS STAGE of moral development, who interpret laws

and rules as absolute. See MORAL REALISM. Compare MORAL RELATIVISM.

moral development the gradual formation of an individual's concepts of right and wrong, conscience, ethical and religious values, social attitudes, and ethical behavior. Some of the major theorists in the area of moral development are Austrian neurologist Sigmund Freud (1856–1939), Swiss child psychologist and epistemologist Jean Piaget (1896–1980), German-born U.S. psychologist Erik Erikson (1902–1994), and U.S. psychologist Lawrence Kohlberg (1927–1987).

morality *n.* a system of beliefs or set of values relating to right conduct, against which behavior is judged to be acceptable or unacceptable.

moral realism the type of thinking characteristic of younger children, who equate good behavior with obedience just as they equate the morality of an act only with its consequences. For example, 15 cups broken accidentally would be judged to be a far worse transgression than 1 cup broken mischievously, because more cups are broken. Moral realism shapes the child's thinking until the age of about 8, when the concepts of intention, motive, and extenuating circumstances begin to modify the child's early MORAL ABSOLUTISM. Compare MORAL RELATIVISM.

moral relativism the belief that the morality or immorality of an action is determined by social custom rather than by universal or fixed standards of right and wrong. According to Swiss child psychologist and epistemologist Jean Piaget (1896–1980), moral relativism is characteristic of children in the AUTONOMOUS STAGE of moral development, who consider the intention behind an act along with possible extenuating circumstances when judging its rightness or wrongness. Compare MORAL ABSOLUTISM; MORAL REALISM.

moral therapy a form of psychotherapy from the 19th century based on the belief that a person with a men-

moratorium

tal disorder could be helped by being treated with compassion, kindness, and dignity in a clean, comfortable environment that provided freedom of movement, opportunities for occupational and social activity, and reassuring talks with physicians and attendants. This approach advocating humane and ethical treatment was a radical departure from the prevailing practice at that time of viewing the "insane" with suspicion and hostility, confining them in unsanitary conditions, and routinely abusing them through the use of such practices as mechanical restraint, physical punishment, and bloodletting. The THERAPEUTIC COMMUNITY of today has its roots in this movement. Also called **moral treatment**.

moratorium *n.* in ERIKSON'S EIGHT STAGES OF PSYCHOSOCIAL DEVELOPMENT, the experimental period of adolescence in which, during the task of discovering who one is as an individual separate from family of origin and as part of the broader social context, young people try out alternative roles before making permanent commitments to an IDENTITY. See IDENTITY VERSUS IDENTITY CONFUSION.

morbid *adj.* unhealthy, diseased, or otherwise abnormal.

morbidity *n.* a pathological (diseased) condition or state, either biological or functional, or the relative incidence of such a condition or state in a given population.

Moro reflex a reflex in which a newborn infant, when startled, throws out the arms, extends the fingers, and often quickly brings the arms back together as if clutching or embracing. In normal, healthy babies, the Moro reflex disappears during the 1st year. See also STARTLE RESPONSE. [Ernst **Moro** (1874–1951), German physician]

morpheme *n.* in linguistic analysis, a unit of meaning that cannot be analyzed into smaller such units. For example, the word *books* is composed of two morphemes, *book* and the suffix *-s*

signifying a plural noun. —**morphemic** *adj.*

morphine *n.* the primary active ingredient in OPIUM, first synthesized in 1806 and widely used as an analgesic and sedative. It interacts predominantly with the mu OPIOID RECEPTOR. Prolonged administration or abuse can lead to dependence and to withdrawal symptoms on cessation.

morphology *n.* **1.** the branch of biology concerned with the forms and structures of organisms. **2.** the branch of linguistics that investigates the form and structure of words. It is particularly concerned with the regular patterns of inflection (modification of word form; e.g., by the addition of a suffix) and word formation in a language. With SYNTAX, morphology is one of the two traditional subdivisions of GRAMMAR. —**morphological** *adj.*

Morris water maze a device used to test spatial learning in nonhuman animals, consisting of a water-filled tank with a platform hidden underwater. An animal is placed in the water and can escape only by finding and climbing on the hidden platform. Typically, a variety of external cues are provided for spatial reference. [devised in 1981 by Richard G. M. **Morris**, British neuroscientist]

mortality *n.* **1.** the state or condition of being subject to illness, decline, and death. **2.** the frequency of death in a population.

mortality effect the degree to which circumstances or behavior increase or decrease the incidence of death. For example, the mortality effect of a fatty diet and lack of exercise could be early death from heart disease.

mortality rate a measure of how often death occurs, usually with respect to a specific illness, characteristic, behavior, or population. For example, a researcher could estimate the mortality rate for individuals who have been diagnosed with cancer.

motherese *n.* the distinctive form of speech used by parents and other caregivers with infants and young children. It is characterized by grammatically simple and phonologically clear utterances, often delivered in a high-pitched sing-song intonation.

mother surrogate a substitute for an individual's biological mother (e.g., a sister, grandmother, stepmother, adoptive mother), who assumes the responsibilities of that person and may function as a role model and significant attachment figure.

motion aftereffect (**MAE**) the perception that a stationary object or scene moves following prolonged fixation of a moving stimulus. The illusory movement is in the opposite direction to the movement of the stimulus that induced the effect. The best known example is the **waterfall illusion**, produced by watching a waterfall for a period and then shifting one's gaze to the stationary surrounding scenery; the stationary objects appear to move upward.

motion parallax the interrelated movements of elements in a scene that can occur when the observer moves relative to the scene. Motion parallax is a DEPTH CUE.

motivated forgetting a memory lapse motivated by a desire to avoid a disagreeable recollection. It is one of the cognitive mechanisms that have been suggested as a cause of delayed memories of childhood trauma.

motivation *n.* the impetus that gives purpose or direction to behavior and operates in humans at a conscious or unconscious level. Motives are frequently divided into (a) physiological, primary, or organic motives, such as hunger, thirst, and need for sleep; and (b) personal, social, or secondary motives, such as affiliation, competition, and individual interests and goals. An important distinction must also be drawn between internal motivating forces and external factors that can encourage or discourage certain behaviors. See EXTRINSIC MOTIVATION; INTRINSIC MOTIVATION. —**motivate** *vb.* —**motivated** *adj.* —**motivational** *adj.*

motivators *pl. n.* in the TWO-FACTOR THEORY OF WORK MOTIVATION, those aspects of the working situation that can increase satisfaction and motivation itself. Motivators involve the actual work rather than the work context and are increased by means of job ENRICHMENT and expansion of responsibilities. Compare HYGIENE FACTORS.

motive *n.* **1.** a specific physiological or psychological state of arousal that directs an organism's energies toward a goal. See MOTIVATION. **2.** a reason offered as an explanation for or cause of an individual's behavior.

motor *adj.* involving, producing, or referring to muscular movements.

motor aphasia a form of nonfluent APHASIA characterized by difficulty in producing articulate speech. An example is BROCA'S APHASIA, for which motor aphasia is often used as a synonym.

motor cortex the region of the frontal lobe of the brain responsible for the control of voluntary movement. It is divided into two parts. The **primary motor cortex** is the main source of neurons in the corticospinal tract (see VENTROMEDIAL PATHWAY). The **secondary motor cortex**, made up of the PREMOTOR AREA and the SUPPLEMENTARY MOTOR AREA, is specialized for planning upcoming movements and learning new movements. Also called **motor strip**.

motor development the changes in motor skills that occur over an entire lifespan, which reflect the development and deterioration of muscular coordination and control and are also affected by personal characteristics, the environment, and interactions of these two factors.

motor neuron a neuron whose axon connects directly to muscle fibers.

There are two types: **lower motor neurons** (or **alpha motor neurons**), found in the cranial nerves and the spinal cord and that are responsible for muscle contraction; and **upper motor neurons** (or **gamma motor neurons**), found in the corticospinal tract (see VENTROMEDIAL PATHWAY) and that modulate the sensitivity of MUSCLE SPINDLES, thus influencing activity of the lower motor neurons. Also called **motoneuron**.

motor program a stored representation, resulting from motor planning and refined through practice, that is used to produce a coordinated movement. Motor programs store the accumulated experience underlying skill at a task.

motor strip see MOTOR CORTEX.

motor system the complex of skeletal muscles, neural connections with muscle tissues, and structures of the central nervous system associated with motor functions.

motor unit a group of muscle fibers that respond collectively and simultaneously because they are connected by nerve endings to a single motor neuron.

mourning *n.* the process of feeling or expressing grief following the death of a loved one, or the period during which this occurs. It typically involves apathy and dejection, loss of interest in the outside world, and diminution in activity and initiative. These reactions are similar to depression but are less persistent and are not considered pathological. See also BEREAVEMENT.

Mozart effect a temporary increase in the affect or performance of research participants on tasks involving spatial–temporal reasoning after listening to the music of Austrian composer Wolfgang Amadeus Mozart (1756–1791). More generally, the term refers to the possibility that listening to certain types of music enhances inherent cognitive functioning. Some experts propose an AROUSAL THEORY perspective, such that listening to music heightens emotional levels that correspond to better performance.

Müller cell an elongated cell that traverses and supports all the layers of the retina, collecting light and directing it toward the PHOTORECEPTORS. A component of the INNER NUCLEAR LAYER, these cells were originally called **Müller fibers** because of their thin, stretched shape. [Heinrich **Müller** (1820–1864), German anatomist]

Müllerian duct either of a pair of ducts that occur in a mammalian embryo and develop into female reproductive structures (fallopian tubes, uterus, and upper vagina) if testes are not present in the embryo. Compare WOLFFIAN DUCT. [Johannes **Müller** (1801–1858), German anatomist and physiologist]

Müller-Lyer illusion a GEOMETRIC ILLUSION in which a difference is perceived in the length of a line depending on whether arrowheads at either end are pointing toward each other or away from each other. [first described in 1889 by Franz **Müller-Lyer** (1857–1916), German psychiatrist and sociologist]

multicollinearity *n.* in MULTIPLE REGRESSION, the state that occurs when several INDEPENDENT VARIABLES are extremely highly interrelated, making it difficult to determine separate effects on the DEPENDENT VARIABLE. For example, if a researcher includes predictors of self-esteem, self-efficacy, and self-concept in an analysis with a dependent variable of achievement, multicollinearity most likely will be present.

multicultural psychology an extension of general psychology that recognizes that multiple aspects of identity influence a person's worldview, including race, ethnicity, language, sexual orientation, gender, age, disability, class status, education, religious or spiritual orientation, and other cultural dimensions, and that both universal and culture-specific phenomena should be taken into consideration when psychologists are helping clients, training students, advocating for social change and justice, and conducting research.

multicultural therapy 1. any form of psychotherapy that takes into account not only the racial and ethnic diversity of clients but also their diversity in spirituality, sexual orientation, ability and disability, and social class and socioeconomic status; the potential cultural bias (e.g., racism, sexism) of the practitioner; the history of oppressed and marginalized groups; acculturation issues for immigrant clients; and the politics of power as they affect clients. **2.** any form of therapy that assesses, understands, and evaluates a client's behavior in the multiplicity of cultural contexts (e.g., ethnic, national, demographic, social, economic) in which that behavior was learned and is displayed.

multidimensionality *n.* the quality of a scale, test, or so forth that is capable of measuring more than one dimension of a construct. For example, a psychometrician may be interested in investigating the multidimensionality of a new scale to measure cognitive functioning. Compare UNIDIMENSIONALITY. —**multidimensional** *adj.*

multidimensional scaling (MDS) an analytic method that represents perceived similarities among stimuli by arranging similar stimuli in spatial proximity to one another, while disparate stimuli are represented far apart from one another. Multidimensional scaling is an alternative to FACTOR ANALYSIS for dealing with large matrices of data or stimuli.

multidisciplinary approach see INTERDISCIPLINARY APPROACH.

multifactorial *adj.* consisting or arising out of several factors, variables, or causes.

multifactorial inheritance inheritance of a trait, such as height or predisposition to a certain disease, that is determined not by a single gene but

by many different genes acting cumulatively. Such traits show continuous, rather than discrete, variation among the members of a given population and are often significantly influenced by environmental factors, such as nutritional status. Also called **polygenic inheritance**.

multigenerational trauma see INTERGENERATIONAL TRAUMA.

multi-infarct dementia see VASCULAR DEMENTIA.

multilevel model see HIERARCHICAL LINEAR MODEL.

multimethod approach a design that uses more than one procedure for measuring the main characteristic or construct of interest. For example, a researcher could use a multimethod approach to understanding relationship satisfaction by simultaneously collecting data from a survey, asking one or both of the partners to give their own self-report, and systematically observing the degree of relationship satisfaction.

multinomial *adj.* describing a measurement that can have more than two categories or outcomes. For example, a professor assigning grades of A, B, C, D, or F to students in his or her course is making a multinomial decision, whereas assigning grades of pass or fail would be a binomial decision.

multinomial distribution a probability distribution that describes the theoretical distribution of *n* objects sampled at random from a population of *k* kinds of things with regard to the number of each of the kinds that appears in the sample. By contrast, a BINOMIAL DISTRIBUTION involves just two variables, categories, or objects.

multiple baseline design an experimental approach in which two or more behaviors are assessed to determine their initial, stable expression (i.e., baseline) and then an intervention or manipulation is applied to one of the behaviors while the others are unaffected. After a period, the manipulation is then applied to the next behavior while the remaining behaviors are unaltered, and so forth until the experimental manipulation has been applied in sequential fashion to all of the behaviors in the design. In successively administering a manipulation to different behaviors after initial behaviors have been recorded, a multiple baseline design allows for inferences about the effect of the intervention.

multiple comparison test any of various statistical procedures used to follow up on a significant result from an ANALYSIS OF VARIANCE by determining which groups in particular differ in their mean values. Examples include the FISHER LEAST SIGNIFICANT DIFFERENCE TEST, the SCHEFFÉ TEST, and TUKEY'S HONESTLY SIGNIFICANT DIFFERENCE TEST. See also POST HOC COMPARISON.

multiple correlation coefficient (symbol: R) a numerical index of the degree of relationship between a particular variable and two or more other variables. Its value ranges from -1 to $+1$, with the former indicating a strong negative relationship and the latter a strong positive relationship. Also called **multiple R**.

multiple determination see OVERDETERMINATION.

multiple-intelligences theory the idea that intelligence is made up of eight distinct categories: linguistic, musical, bodily-kinesthetic, logical-mathematical, spatial, naturalist, intrapersonal, and interpersonal.

multiple personality disorder see DISSOCIATIVE IDENTITY DISORDER.

multiple R see MULTIPLE CORRELATION COEFFICIENT.

multiple regression a statistical technique for examining the linear relationship between a continuous DEPENDENT VARIABLE and a set of two or more INDEPENDENT VARIABLES. It is often used to predict a single outcome variable from a set of predictor variables. For example, an educational psychology researcher could use multiple regression to predict college achievement (e.g., grade point average) from the variables of high school grade point average, Scholastic Assessment Test (SAT) reading score, SAT mathematics score, and SAT writing score.

multiple sclerosis (MS) a disease characterized by inflammation and multifocal scarring of the protective MYELIN SHEATH of nerves, which damages and destroys the sheath and the underlying nerve, disrupting neural transmission. Symptoms include visual disturbances, fatigue, weakness in the hands and feet, numbness, stiffness or muscular spasms, muscle and back pain, difficulties with coordination and balance, loss of bladder or bowel control, and depression. Some individuals also experience cognitive impairments, such as difficulties with concentration, attention, memory, and judgment. The cause of MS is unknown but may be related to AUTOIMMUNITY.

multiplication rule a rule stating that the joint probability of two independent events occurring together or in succession is equal to the probability of the first event times the probability of the second event. For example, the multiplication rule would indicate that the probability of drawing a heart followed by the probability of drawing a spade is equal to $13/52 \times 13/52 = .25 \times .25 = .0625$. Also called **multiplication law**. Compare ADDITION RULE.

multipolar neuron a neuron that has many dendrites and a single axon extending from the CELL BODY. Also called **multipolar cell**. Compare BIPOLAR NEURON; UNIPOLAR NEURON.

multistore model of memory any theory hypothesizing that information can move through and be retained in any of several memory storage systems, usually of a short-term and a long-term variety.

multivariate *adj.* consisting of or otherwise involving a number of distinct variables. For example, a multivariate study of ability could involve multiple measures of intelligence and achievement. Compare UNIVARIATE. See also BIVARIATE.

multivariate analysis a set of statistical procedures for studying the relationships between one or more predictors and several outcome or DEPENDENT VARIABLES. Examples include FACTOR ANALYSIS for assessing the relationships among a large set of measures and a small set of underlying factors; MULTIVARIATE ANALYSIS OF VARIANCE for assessing potential group differences on several dependent variables; and STRUCTURAL EQUATION MODELING, which examines a theoretically based pattern of relationships among multiple independent, dependent, and even mediating variables. Also called **multivariate statistics**. Compare UNIVARIATE ANALYSIS.

multivariate analysis of variance (**MANOVA**) a statistical procedure for assessing possible group differences on a set of outcome or DEPENDENT VARIABLES. For example, a researcher could conduct a multivariate analysis of variance to assess whether a group of participants who receive a new educational method differ significantly from another group of participants who are taught with a traditional method on a set of achievement variables, such as quiz scores, homework scores, exam scores, and project scores. It is an extension of the univariate ANALYSIS OF VARIANCE, which examines a single dependent variable.

multivariate distribution the arrangement of scores obtained on several variables. For example, a health researcher may want to examine the multivariate distribution of scores on level of exercise, cholesterol level, and blood pressure in a sample of individuals at risk for heart disease. Compare UNIVARIATE DISTRIBUTION.

Münchausen syndrome a severe and chronic form of FACTITIOUS DISOR-

DER characterized by repeated and elaborate fabrication of clinically convincing physical symptoms and a false medical and social history. Other features include excessive traveling from place to place, recurrent hospitalization, and scars from previous (unnecessary) investigative surgery. [Baron Karl Friedrich Hieronymus von **Münchhausen** (1720–1797), German soldier-adventurer famous for his tall tales but not for having the disorder itself]

Münchausen syndrome by proxy (**MSP**) a psychological disorder in which caregivers fabricate or intentionally cause symptoms in those they are caring for in order to seek and obtain medical investigation or treatment. Typically, the caregiver is the mother, who behaves as if distressed about her child's illness and denies knowing what caused it. Also called **factitious disorder by proxy**.

mundane realism the extent to which an experimental situation resembles a real-life situation or event. See also EXPERIMENTAL REALISM.

muscarinic receptor (**mAChR**) a type of ACETYLCHOLINE RECEPTOR that responds to the alkaloid muscarine as well as to acetylcholine. Muscarinic receptors are found in smooth muscle, cardiac muscle, endocrine glands, and the central nervous system and chiefly mediate the inhibitory activities of acetylcholine. Compare NICOTINIC RECEPTOR.

muscle fiber a microscopic strand of muscle tissue that functions as a molecular machine converting chemical energy into force. Thousands of muscle fibers are linked by connective tissue into a muscle. Each fiber is, in turn, composed of millions of longitudinally aligned protein filaments. It is the interaction of **actin** and **myosin** protein molecules (sometimes together referred to as **actomyosin**) in these filaments that creates muscle contraction.

muscle spindle a receptor that lies within skeletal muscle, parallel to the main contractile MUSCLE FIBERS, that sends impulses to the central nervous system when the muscle is stretched.

music therapy the use of music (e.g., singing, performing, listening) as an adjunct to the treatment or rehabilitation of individuals to enhance their psychological, physical, cognitive, or social functioning.

mutation *n.* a permanent change in the genetic material of an organism. It may consist of an alteration to the number or arrangement of chromosomes (a chromosomal mutation) or a change in the composition of DNA, generally affecting only one or a few bases in a particular gene (a point mutation). Mutations can occur spontaneously, but many are due to exposure to agents (mutagens) that significantly increase the rate of mutation; these include X-rays and other forms of radiation and certain chemicals. A mutation occurring in a body cell cannot be inherited, whereas a mutation in a reproductive cell producing ova or spermatozoa can be transmitted to an individual's offspring.

mutism *n.* lack or absence of speaking. The condition may result from a structural defect in the organs necessary for speech, congenital or early deafness in which an individual's inability to hear spoken words inhibits the development of speech, neurological damage or disorder, psychological disorders (e.g., CONVERSION DISORDER, CATATONIC SCHIZOPHRENIA), or severe emotional disturbance (e.g., extreme anger). See also SELECTIVE MUTISM.

mutualism *n.* an interaction in which two species live together in close association, to the mutual benefit of both. See also SYMBIOSIS.

mutual reward theory see REWARD THEORY.

myasthenia gravis a disorder in which the body produces antibodies against ACETYLCHOLINE RECEPTORS, causing faulty transmission of nerve impulses at neuromuscular junctions. Affected muscles—initially those of the face and neck—are easily fatigued and may become paralyzed temporarily (e.g., speech may become slurred after a period of talking). The disease is progressive, eventually affecting muscles throughout the body.

myelin sheath the insulating layer around many axons that increases the speed of conduction of nerve impulses and accounts for the color of WHITE MATTER. It consists mainly of phospholipids and is laid down by GLIA, which wrap themselves around adjacent axons. The myelin sheath is interrupted by small gaps, called NODES OF RANVIER, which are spaced about every millimeter along the axon.

Myers–Briggs Type Indicator (**MBTI**) a personality test designed to classify individuals according to their expressed choices between contrasting alternatives in certain categories of traits. The categories are (a) Extraversion–Introversion, (b) Sensing–Intuition, (c) Thinking–Feeling, and (d) Judging–Perceiving. The participant is assigned a type (e.g., INTJ, ESFP) according to the pattern of choices made. The test has little credibility among research psychologists but is widely used in educational counseling and human resource management to help improve work and personal relationships, increase productivity, and identify interpersonal communication preferences and skills. [Isabel Briggs **Myers** (1897–1980), U.S. personologist, and her mother Katharine Cook **Briggs** (1875–1968)]

myopia *n.* nearsightedness: a refractive error due to an abnormally long eye. The retinal image is blurred because the focal point of one or both eyes lies in front of, rather than on, the retina. Compare HYPEROPIA.

myosin *n.* see MUSCLE FIBER.

myotonia *n.* increased tone and contractility of a muscle, with slow or delayed relaxation. —**myotonic** *adj.*

Nn

naive participant a participant who has not previously taken part in a particular research study and has not been made aware of the experimenter's hypothesis.

naive personality theories a set of ideas that laypeople tend to hold about how specific personality traits cluster together within a person. Such theories, which are often held implicitly rather than explicitly, are a major concern of ATTRIBUTION THEORY. Also called **implicit personality theories**.

naming explosion a stage in language development, usually occurring during a child's 2nd year, when a marked increase occurs in the rate at which new words are acquired. This stage marks a change in the cognitive and linguistic underpinnings of children's language use: It indicates their increased understanding that words are symbols that refer to actual things in the world. Also called **vocabulary spurt**.

narcissism *n.* excessive self-love or egocentrism. —**narcissist** *n.* —**narcissistic** *adj.*

narcissistic personality disorder a personality disorder with the following characteristics: (a) an exaggerated sense of importance, talent, and achievements; (b) fantasies of unlimited sex, power, brilliance, or beauty; (c) an exhibitionistic need for attention and admiration; (d) either cool indifference or feelings of rage or humiliation as a response to criticism or defeat; and (e) various interpersonal disturbances, such as feeling entitled to special favors or taking advantage of others.

narcolepsy *n.* a disorder consisting of excessive daytime sleepiness accompanied by brief "attacks" of sleep during waking hours. These sleep attacks may occur at any time or during any activity, including in potentially dangerous situations such as while driving an automobile. The attacks are marked by immediate entry into REM SLEEP without going through the usual initial stages of sleep. —**narcoleptic** *adj.*

narcotic 1. *n.* originally, any drug that induces a state of stupor or insensibility (narcosis). More recently, the term referred to strong OPIOIDS used clinically for pain relief, but this usage is now considered imprecise and pejorative; the term is still sometimes used in legal contexts to refer to a wide variety of abused substances. **2.** *adj.* of or relating to narcotics or narcosis.

narrative analysis a type of QUALITATIVE ANALYSIS in which a researcher collects and examines stories from individuals about a variety of concrete life situations. The goal is to understand how individuals experience certain events, structure them into coherent sequences, and give them subjective meaning.

narrative psychology a field in psychology that investigates the value of stories and storytelling in giving meaning to individuals' experiences—shaping their memory of past events, their understanding of the present, and their projections of future events—and in defining themselves and their lives.

narrative therapy treatment for individuals, couples, or families that helps them reinterpret and rewrite their life events into true but more life-enhancing narratives or stories. Narrative therapy posits that individuals are primarily meaning-making beings who can reauthor their life stories by reconstruing problems or events in a more helpful light. See also CONSTRUCTIVISM.

nativism *n.* **1.** the doctrine that the mind has certain innate structures and that experience plays a limited role in the creation of knowledge. See also CONSTRUCTIVISM; EMPIRICISM. **2.** the tenet that mental and behavioral traits are largely determined by hereditary, rather than environmental, factors. See NATURE–NURTURE. **—nativist** *adj., n.* **—nativistic** *adj.*

natural category see BASIC-LEVEL CATEGORY.

natural childbirth an approach to labor and child delivery that does not include (or is designed to eliminate) the need for medical interventions, such as anesthetics. The mother receives preparatory education in areas such as breathing and relaxation, exercise of the muscles involved in labor and delivery, and postural positions that make labor more comfortable.

natural experiment the study of a naturally occurring situation as it unfolds in the real world. For example, an investigator might evaluate the influence of a new community policing program by observing neighborhood activities after it has been implemented and comparing the outcome to that for neighborhoods in which the policy has not been implemented. Since such real-life events cannot be manipulated or prearranged, natural experiments are QUASI-EXPERIMENTAL DESIGNS rather than true experiments.

naturalism *n.* in philosophy, the doctrine that reality consists solely of natural objects and that therefore the methods of natural science offer the only reliable means to knowledge and understanding of reality. Naturalism is closely related to MATERIALISM and opposes any form of supernaturalism that posits the existence of realities beyond the natural and material world. See also POSITIVISM. **—naturalistic** *adj.*

naturalistic observation data collection in a field setting, without laboratory controls or manipulation of variables. These procedures are usually carried out by a trained observer, who watches and records the everyday behavior of participants in their natural environments. Examples of naturalistic observation include an ethologist's study of the behavior of chimpanzees and a developmental psychologist's observation of playing children. Compare STRUCTURED OBSERVATION.

natural killer cell (**NK cell**) a type of LYMPHOCYTE that destroys infected or cancerous cells. Unlike the B and T lymphocytes, natural killer cells do not require the target cells to display on their surface foreign ANTIGENS combined with host histocompatibility proteins.

natural reinforcer a stimulus or circumstance, such as food or water, that does not depend on learning to become desirable. Natural reinforcers are more precisely known as **unconditioned** or **primary reinforcers**, in contrast to **conditioned** or **secondary reinforcers**, which are initially neutral stimuli (e.g., tones, lights) that become desirable through training.

natural selection the process by which such forces as competition, disease, and climate tend to eliminate individuals who are less well adapted to a particular environment and favor the survival and reproduction of better adapted individuals, thereby changing the nature of the population over successive generations. This is the fundamental mechanism driving the evolution of living organisms and the emergence of new species, as proposed independently by British naturalists Charles Darwin (1809–1882) and Alfred Russel Wallace (1823–1913). Compare ARTIFICIAL SELECTION.

nature *n.* **1.** the phenomena of the natural world, including plants, non-human animals, and physical features, as opposed to human beings and their creations. **2.** the innate, presumably genetically determined, characteristics and behaviors of an individual. In psychology, the characteristics most often and traditionally associated with nature are temperament, body type, and personality. —**natural** *adj.*

nature–nurture the dispute over the relative contributions of hereditary and constitutional factors (NATURE) and environmental factors (NURTURE) to the development of an individual. Nativists emphasize the role of heredity, whereas environmentalists emphasize sociocultural and ecological factors, including family attitudes, child-rearing practices, and economic status. Most scientists now accept that there is a close interaction between hereditary and environmental factors in the ontogeny of behavior (see EPIGENESIS).

navigation *n.* the mechanisms used by an organism to find its way through the environment, such as to a MIGRATION site or its home site. Some navigational cues used by nonhuman animals include the sun or stars as a compass, olfactory cues, visual cues (e.g., rivers or coastlines), and wind-shear effects from air masses crossing mountain ranges.

nay-saying *n.* answering questions negatively regardless of their content, which can distort the results of surveys, questionnaires, and similar instruments. Compare YEA-SAYING.

near-death experience (NDE) an image, perception, event, interaction, or feeling (or a combination of any of these) reported by some people after a life-threatening episode. Typical features include a sense of separation from the body, often accompanied by the ability to look down on the situation; a peaceful and pleasant state of mind; and an entering into light. Frightening NDEs have been reported as well. There is continuing controversy regarding the existence, cause, and nature of NDEs.

nearsightedness *n.* see MYOPIA.

Necker cube a line drawing of a cube in which all angles and sides can be seen, as if it were transparent. It is an AMBIGUOUS FIGURE whose three-dimensionality fluctuates when viewed

for a prolonged period of time. [Louis Albert **Necker** (1730–1804), Swiss geologist and crystallographer]

necrophilia *n.* sexual interest in or sexual contact with dead bodies. It is a rare PARAPHILIA seen almost exclusively in men. In some cases, they kill the victim themselves, but most frequently they gain access to corpses via mortuaries, morgues, or graves. —**necrophile** *n.* —**necrophilic** *adj.*

need *n.* a condition of tension in an organism resulting from deprivation of something required for survival, well-being, or personal fulfillment.

need for achievement (n-Ach) a strong desire to accomplish goals and attain a high standard of performance and personal fulfillment. People with a high need for achievement often undertake tasks in which there is a high probability of success and avoid tasks that are either too easy (because of lack of challenge) or too difficult (because of fear of failure).

need for affiliation (n-Aff) the desire to have personal relationships with other individuals, which manifests itself in the urge to form friendships and other attachments and to join organizations and enjoy social gatherings. People with a high need for affiliation often seek the approval and acceptance of others.

need for cognition a personality trait reflecting a person's tendency to enjoy engaging in extensive cognitive activity. This trait primarily reflects a person's motivation to engage in cognitive activity rather than his or her actual ability to do so. Individuals high in need for cognition tend to develop attitudes or take action based on thoughtful evaluation of information.

need to belong the motivation, rooted in both biology and social norms, to be part of relationships, to belong to groups, and to be accepted by others. See also LOVE NEED.

negative affect the internal feeling

state (AFFECT) that occurs when one has failed to achieve a goal or to avoid a threat or when one is not satisfied with the current state of affairs. The tendency to experience such states is known as **negative affectivity**.

negative correlation a relationship between two variables in which the value of one variable increases as the value of the other decreases. For example, the discovery that infants who are held more tend to cry less is a negative correlation. Also called **inverse correlation**. Compare POSITIVE CORRELATION.

negative feedback 1. an arrangement whereby some of the output of a system, whether mechanical or biological, is fed back to reduce the effect of input signals. Such systems, which measure the deviation from a desired state and apply a correction, are important in achieving HOMEOSTASIS, whereas systems employing POSITIVE FEEDBACK tend to amplify small deviations and become highly unstable. **2.** criticism, disapproval, and other negative information received by a person in response to his or her performance.

negative priming the ability of a preceding stimulus to inhibit the response to a subsequent stimulus. This is measured by the detectability of the second stimulus or the time taken to make a response to the second stimulus.

negative punishment punishment that results because some stimulus or circumstance is removed as a consequence of a response. For example, if a response results in a subtraction of money from an accumulating account, and the response becomes less likely as a result of this experience, then negative punishment has occurred. Compare POSITIVE PUNISHMENT.

negative reinforcement the removal, prevention, or postponement of an unpleasant stimulus as a consequence of a response, which, in turn, increases the probability of that response. Compare POSITIVE REINFORCEMENT.

negative schizophrenia a form of schizophrenia characterized by a predominance of NEGATIVE SYMPTOMS, suggesting deficiency or absence of behavior normally present in a person's repertoire, as shown in apathy, blunted affect, emotional withdrawal, poor rapport, and lack of spontaneity. Compare POSITIVE SCHIZOPHRENIA.

negative skew see SKEWNESS.

negative-state-relief model the hypothesis that helping behavior is used by some people in stressful situations and periods of boredom and inactivity to avoid or escape negative moods.

negative symptom a deficit in the ability to perform the normal functions of living—for example, logical thinking, self-care, and social interaction—as shown in apathy, blunted affect, emotional withdrawal, poor rapport, and lack of spontaneity. In schizophrenia, a predominance of negative symptoms is often associated with a poor prognosis. Compare POSITIVE SYMPTOM.

negative transfer a process in which previous learning obstructs or interferes with present learning. For instance, tennis players who learn racquetball must often unlearn their tendency to take huge, muscular swings with the shoulder and upper arm. See also TRANSFER OF TRAINING. Compare POSITIVE TRANSFER.

negative triad see COGNITIVE TRIAD.

negativism *n.* an attitude characterized by persistent resistance to the suggestions of others or the tendency to act in ways that are contrary to the expectations, requests, or commands of others, typically without any identifiable reason for opposition. Although such reactions may be considered a healthy expression of self-assertion in young children and adolescents, persistent or extreme negativism at any age may be associated with a number of disorders. **—negativistic** *adj.*

neglect *n.* **1.** failure to provide for the basic needs of a person in one's care. The neglect may be emotional (e.g., rejection or apathy), material (e.g., withholding food or clothing), or service-oriented (e.g., depriving of education or medical attention). See also MALTREATMENT. **2.** a neurological syndrome characterized by lack of awareness of a specific area of the visual field or side of the body. This is most often associated with an injury to the right cerebral hemisphere with corresponding left-sided neglect. Neglect has also been found in auditory, tactile, and proprioceptive tasks.

neobehaviorism *n.* an approach to psychology that emphasized the development of comprehensive theories and frameworks of behavior, such as those of U.S. psychologists Clark L. Hull (1884–1952) and Edward C. Tolman (1886–1959), through empirical observation of behavior and the use of consciousness and mental events as explanatory devices. It thus contrasted with classical BEHAVIORISM, which was concerned with freeing psychology of mentalistic concepts and explanations. See also RADICAL BEHAVIORISM. **—neobehaviorist** *adj.*, *n.*

neocortex *n.* regions of the CEREBRAL CORTEX that are the most recently evolved and contain six main layers of cells. Neocortex, which comprises the majority of human cerebral cortex, includes the primary sensory and motor cortex and association cortex. Also called **neopallium**. Compare ALLOCORTEX. **—neocortical** *adj.*

neodissociation theory a theory that explains the dissociative phenomena of hypnosis as a result of divided consciousness. For example, hypnotic analgesia can produce subjective relief from pain while physiological measures indicate that some pain response is still being registered. See also HIDDEN OBSERVER.

neo-Freudian 1. *adj.* denoting an approach that derives from the CLASSICAL PSYCHOANALYSIS of Austrian neurologist Sigmund Freud (1856–1939) but with modifications and revisions that typically emphasize social and interpersonal elements over biological instincts. The term is not usually applied to the approaches of Freud's contemporaries, who broke away from his school quite early. German-born U.S. psychologist Erik Erikson (1902–1994), German-born U.S. psychoanalysts Erich Fromm (1900–1980) and Karen D. Horney (1885–1952), and U.S. psychiatrist Harry Stack Sullivan (1892–1949) are considered to be among the most influential neo-Freudian theorists and practitioners. **2.** *n.* an analyst or theoretician who adopts such an approach.

neologism *n.* a newly coined word or expression, often one whose origin is nonsensical (e.g., *klipno* for watch). In a neurological or psychopathological context, neologisms typically are associated with aphasia or schizophrenia. **—neologistic** *adj.*

neonate *n.* a newborn human or nonhuman animal. Human infants born after the normal gestational period of 36 weeks are known as full-term neonates; infants born before the end of this period are known as preterm neonates.

neonativism *n.* the belief that much cognitive knowledge, such as OBJECT PERMANENCE and certain aspects of language, is innate, requiring little in the way of specific experience to be expressed. Neonativists hold that cognitive development is influenced by biological constraints and that individuals are predisposed to process certain types of information. **—neonativist** *adj.*, *n.*

neopallium *n.* see NEOCORTEX.

neoplasm *n.* a new, abnormal growth; that is, a benign or malignant tumor, although the term is generally used to specify a malignancy (see CAN-

CER). A neoplasm usually grows rapidly by cellular proliferation but generally lacks structural organization. —**neoplastic** *adj.*

nerve *n.* a bundle of AXONS outside the central nervous system (CNS), enclosed in a sheath of connective tissue to form a cordlike structure. Nerves connect the CNS with the tissues and organs of the body. They may be motor, sensory, or mixed. Compare TRACT.

nerve cell see NEURON.

nerve growth factor (**NGF**) an endogenous polypeptide that stimulates the growth and development of neurons in SPINAL GANGLIA and in the ganglia of the SYMPATHETIC NERVOUS SYSTEM.

nervous breakdown a lay term for an emotional illness or other mental disorder that has a sudden onset, produces acute distress, and significantly interferes with one's functioning.

nervous system the system of NEURONS, NERVES, TRACTS, and associated tissues that, together with the endocrine system, coordinates activities of the organism in response to signals received from the internal and external environments. The nervous system of higher vertebrates is often considered in terms of its divisions, principally the CENTRAL NERVOUS SYSTEM and the PERIPHERAL NERVOUS SYSTEM.

nested model see HIERARCHICAL MODEL.

nesting *n.* in an experimental design, the appearance of the levels of one factor (the **nested factor**) only within a single level of another factor. For example, classrooms are nested within a school because each specific classroom is found only within a single school; similarly, schools are nested within school districts.

neural correlate an association between a physical occurrence in the nervous system and a mental state or event. In the cerebellum, for example, the neural correlate of fear memory is

provided by a LONG-TERM POTENTIATION of the excitatory synapses between the PARALLEL FIBERS and the PURKINJE CELLS.

neural Darwinism a neurobiological theory that uses Darwinian NATURAL SELECTION to account for brain development and functioning in terms of selectionist amplification, pruning, and strengthening of neurons, synapses, and dynamic signaling.

neural network 1. a technique for modeling the neural changes in the brain that underlie cognition and perception in which a large number of simple hypothetical neural units are connected to one another. **2.** an ARTIFICIAL INTELLIGENCE system used for learning and classifying data and applied in research on pattern recognition, speech recognition, machine translation of languages, and financial prediction, among other areas. Neural networks are usually abstract structures modeled on a computer and consist of a number of interconnected processing elements, each with a finite number of inputs and outputs. The elements in a network can have a "weight" determining how they process data, which can be adjusted according to experience. The analogy is with the supposed action of neurons in the brain.

neural pathway any route followed by a nerve impulse through central or peripheral fibers of the nervous system. A neural pathway may consist of a simple REFLEX ARC or a complex but specific route, such as that followed by impulses transmitting a specific wavelength of sound from the COCHLEA to the AUDITORY CORTEX.

neural plasticity the ability of the nervous system to change in response to experience or environmental stimulation. For example, following an injury, remaining neurons may adopt certain functions previously performed by those that were damaged. Also called **neuroplasticity**.

neural quantum theory a theory to explain linear psychophysical functions, which are sometimes obtained instead of the ogival (S-shaped) form, whereby changes in sensation are assumed to occur in discrete steps. In this context, *quantum* refers to a functionally distinct unit in the neural mechanisms that mediate sensory experience—that is, a perceptual rather than a physical unit. Also called **quantal hypothesis**; **quantal theory**.

neural synchrony the simultaneous firing or activation of neurons in multiple areas of the brain, particularly in response to the same stimulus. Many motor processes and EXECUTIVE FUNCTIONS appear to be based on neural synchrony within and across different specialized brain areas. Additionally, recent research suggests dysfunctions in neural synchrony may be associated with several psychological disorders, including AUTISM SPECTRUM DISORDERS.

neural tube a structure formed during early development of an embryo, when folds of the neural plate curl over and fuse. Cells of the neural tube differentiate along its length to form swellings that correspond to the future FOREBRAIN, MIDBRAIN, and HINDBRAIN; the posterior part of the tube develops into the spinal cord. The cavity of the tube ultimately becomes the interconnected cerebral VENTRICLES and the central canal of the spinal cord. **Neural tube defects**, caused by faulty development of the neural tube from the neural plate, give rise to neurological disorders, intellectual disability, or physical disability of varying severity. See also NEURULATION.

neurite *n.* a projection from the neuronal cell body: an AXON or a DENDRITE. This general term is used especially in relation to developing neurons whose axons and dendrites often are difficult to distinguish from one another.

neuritic plaque see AMYLOID PLAQUE.

neuroanatomy *n.* the study of the structures and relationships among the various parts of the nervous system. —**neuroanatomist** *n.*

neuroblast *n.* an undifferentiated cell that is capable of developing into a neuron.

neurochemistry *n.* the branch of NEUROSCIENCE that deals with the roles of atoms, molecules, and ions in the functioning of nervous systems.

neurocognition *n.* see COGNITIVE NEUROSCIENCE. —**neurocognitive** *adj.*

neurodegenerative disease any disease characterized by progressive nervous system dysfunction and loss of neural tissue. Alzheimer's disease and Parkinson's disease are examples of neurodegenerative diseases.

neurodevelopmental hypothesis a prominent theory stating that schizophrenia results from an early brain lesion, either fetal or neonatal, that disrupts normal neurological development and leads to abnormalities and later psychotic symptoms. Consequences of this early disruption appear in childhood and adolescence, prior to the actual onset of schizophrenic symptoms, as subtle differences in motor coordination, cognitive and social functioning, and temperament. There is evidence that supports this hypothesis, and risk factors operating in early life (e.g., obstetric complications) have been shown to be associated with the later development of schizophrenia.

neuroeconomics *n.* a rapidly emerging field that focuses on understanding how the brain assesses the costs and benefits of the possible outcomes of specific economic actions and then uses this information to make choices. Neuroeconomics challenges the assumption that economic decision making is a logical, analytical process, suggesting instead that it often involves emotion and other psychological variables. For example, individuals making buying decisions tend to show overactivation in the "wanting" or reward area of the brain.

neuroeducation *n.* the study of the activities that occur in the brain when individuals learn and the application of this knowledge to improve classroom instructional practices and optimize curriculum design. This emerging field represents the intersection of neuroscience, psychology, and education, integrating research on neuronal functioning with educational improvement to understand how the brain enables learning, working memory, intelligence, and creative thinking. Also called **brain-based learning; educational neuroscience**.

neuroethics *n.* a rapidly growing subdiscipline of medical ethics that focuses on the moral, social, and public policy implications of conducting neuroscience research and of translating the findings into clinical practice.

neurofeedback *n.* a type of BIOFEED-BACK training intended to enable people to alter their brain waves by using information from a video display or auditory signal of electroencephalograph (EEG) recordings of their brain-wave characteristics. Neurofeedback has been used with mixed results in the treatment of attention-deficit/hyperactivity disorder and epilepsy. Also called **EEG biofeedback**.

neurofibrillary tangles twisted strands of abnormal filaments within neurons that are associated with Alzheimer's disease. The filaments form microscopically visible knots or tangles consisting of tau protein, which normally is associated with MICROTUBULES. If the structure of tau is rendered abnormal, the microtubule structure collapses, and the tau protein collects in neurofibrillary tangles.

neurogenesis *n.* the production of new neurons during early nervous system development and throughout the lifespan. The failure or interruption of neurogenesis is implicated in Alzhei-

mer's, Parkinson's, depression, bipolar disorder, and schizophrenia.

neuroglia *n.* see GLIA. —**neuroglial** *adj.*

neuroglioma *n.* see GLIOMA.

neurohormone *n.* a hormone produced by neural tissue and released into the general circulation.

neuroimaging *n.* the use of various technologies to noninvasively study the structures and functions of the brain. These technologies include MAGNETIC RESONANCE IMAGING, FUNCTIONAL MAGNETIC RESONANCE IMAGING, COMPUTED TOMOGRAPHY, and POSITRON EMISSION TOMOGRAPHY.

neuroleptic *n.* see ANTIPSYCHOTIC.

neurological evaluation analysis of the data gathered by an examining physician of an individual's mental status and sensory and motor functioning. The examination typically includes assessment of cognition, speech, orientation and level of alertness, muscular strength and tone, muscle coordination and movement, tendon reflexes, cranial nerve function, pain and temperature sensitivity, and discriminative senses.

neurology *n.* a branch of medicine that deals with the nervous system in both healthy and diseased states. **Neurologists** diagnose and treat patients with stroke, dementia, headaches, and back pain, among other disorders of the nervous system. —**neurological** *adj.*

neuromarketing *n.* a subdiscipline of MARKET RESEARCH that examines changes in brain activity as they relate to product liking and purchasing and other consumer behavior. For example, while monitoring volunteers as they watch television advertisements or shop in supermarkets, researchers may analyze blood flow to different regions of the brain or record the brain's electrical activity to help determine why those individuals prefer certain brands or how they make decisions to buy specific items. Also called **consumer neuroscience**.

neuromodulator *n.* a substance that modulates the effectiveness of a neurotransmitter by influencing its release or RECEPTOR response to it.

neuromuscular junction the junction between a motor neuron and the END PLATE of the muscle cell it innervates. When impulses arrive at the AXON terminus of the neuron, a neurotransmitter diffuses across the gap separating the axon and end plate, triggering muscle contraction.

neuron (neurone) *n.* the basic cellular unit of the nervous system. Each neuron is composed of a CELL BODY; fine, branching extensions (DENDRITES) that receive incoming nerve signals; and at least one long extension (AXON) that conducts nerve impulses to its branching terminal. The axon terminal transmits impulses to other neurons or to effector organs (e.g., muscles and glands) via junctions called SYNAPSES or NEUROMUSCULAR JUNCTIONS. Neurons can be classified according to their function as MOTOR NEURONS, SENSORY NEURONS, or INTERNEURONS. There are various structural types, including UNIPOLAR NEURONS, BIPOLAR NEURONS, and MULTIPOLAR NEURONS. The axons of vertebrate neurons are often surrounded by a MYELIN SHEATH. Also called **nerve cell**. —**neuronal** *adj.*

neuropeptide *n.* any of several chains of amino acids that are released by neurons as NEUROTRANSMITTERS or NEUROHORMONES. They include the ENDOGENOUS OPIOIDS, hypothalamic RELEASING HORMONES, pituitary hormones, and others.

neuropharmacology *n.* the scientific study of the effects of drugs on the nervous system. —**neuropharmacological** *adj.* —**neuropharmacologist** *n.*

neurophysiology *n.* a branch of NEUROSCIENCE that is concerned with the normal and abnormal functioning

of the nervous system, including the chemical and electrical activities of individual neurons. —**neurophysiological** *adj.* —**neurophysiologist** *n.*

neuroplasticity *n.* see NEURAL PLASTICITY.

neuropsychological assessment an evaluation of the presence, nature, and extent of brain damage or dysfunction. The evaluation is derived from the results of various NEUROPSYCHOLOGICAL TESTS.

Neuropsychological Assessment Battery (NAB) an integrated battery consisting of 33 tests for assessing cognitive skills in adults (ages 18–97) with a variety of neurological disorders. The tests are organized in six modules, including five domain-specific modules (comprised of tests for attention, language, memory, spatial ability, and executive functions) and a screening module.

neuropsychological test any of various clinical instruments for assessing cognitive impairment, including those measuring memory, language, learning, attention, and visuospatial and visuoconstructive functioning. The STROOP COLOR–WORD INTERFERENCE TEST is an example.

neuropsychology *n.* the branch of science that studies the physiological processes of the nervous system and relates them to behavior and cognition, in terms both of their normal function and of the dysfunctional processes associated with brain damage. —**neuropsychological** *adj.* —**neuropsychologist** *n.*

neuroreceptor *n.* a molecule located in a neuron cell membrane that binds molecules of a particular neurotransmitter, hormone, drug, or the like and initiates a particular response within the neuron.

neuroscience *n.* the scientific study of the nervous system—including its anatomy, chemistry, and physiology—and the applications of this knowledge in such fields as psychology, psychiatry, and pharmacology.

neurosis *n.* any one of a variety of mental disorders characterized by significant anxiety or other distressing emotional symptoms, such as persistent and irrational fears, obsessive thoughts, compulsive acts, dissociative states, and somatic and depressive reactions. The symptoms do not involve gross personality disorganization or loss of contact with reality. Most of the disorders that used to be called neuroses are now classified as ANXIETY DISORDERS. —**neurotic** *adj., n.*

neurosurgery *n.* surgical procedures performed on the brain, spinal cord, or peripheral nerves for the purpose of restoring functioning or preventing further impairment. See also PSYCHO-SURGERY. —**neurosurgeon** *n.* —**neurosurgical** *adj.*

neurotic anxiety in psychoanalytic theory, anxiety that originates in unconscious conflict and is maladaptive in nature: It has a disturbing effect on emotion and behavior and also intensifies resistance to treatment. Neurotic anxiety contrasts with realistic anxiety about an external danger or threat and with moral anxiety, which is guilt posited to originate in the superego.

neuroticism *n.* one of the dimensions of the FIVE-FACTOR PERSONALITY MODEL and the BIG FIVE PERSONALITY MODEL, characterized by a chronic level of emotional instability and proneness to psychological distress.

neurotic need in psychoanalytic theory, an excessive drive or demand that may arise out of the strategies individuals use to defend themselves against BASIC ANXIETY. Ten neurotic needs have been enumerated: for affection and approval, for a partner to take over one's life, for restriction of one's life, for power, for exploitation of others, for prestige, for admiration, for achievement, for self-sufficiency and independence, and for perfection.

neurotransmission *n.* the process by which a signal or other activity in a neuron is transferred to an adjacent neuron, effector organ or gland, or other cell. **Synaptic transmission**, which occurs between two neurons via a SYNAPSE, is largely chemical, involving the release and binding of NEUROTRANSMITTER, but it may also be electrical (see ELECTRICAL SYNAPSE).

neurotransmitter *n.* any of various chemicals that mediate transmission of signals across the junctions (SYNAPSES) between neurons. When triggered by a nerve impulse, the neurotransmitter is released from the terminal button of an AXON, travels across the SYNAPTIC CLEFT, and binds to and reacts with RE-CEPTOR molecules in the postsynaptic membrane. Neurotransmitters include amines (e.g., NOREPINEPHRINE, SEROTO-NIN) and amino acids (e.g., GLUTAMATE, GLYCINE). **Excitatory neurotransmitters** depolarize the postsynaptic neurons, resulting in a greater likelihood of an ACTION POTENTIAL. **Inhibitory neurotransmitters** hyperpolarize the postsynaptic neurons, resulting in a smaller likelihood of an action potential. Some neurotransmitters (e.g., ACETYLCHO-LINE, DOPAMINE) have both excitatory and inhibitory functions.

neurotrophin *n.* any of various proteins that promote the development and survival of specific populations of neurons. Some neurotrophins play a crucial role in cognition, learning, and memory formation by modulating synaptic PLASTICITY. Also called **neurotrophic factor**.

neurulation *n.* the process of development of the rudimentary nervous system in early embryonic life, including formation of the NEURAL TUBE.

neutral stimulus in CLASSICAL CON-DITIONING, a stimulus that does not elicit a response of the sort to be measured as an index of conditioning. For example, the sound of a bell has no effect on salivation, therefore it is a neutral stimulus with respect to salivation and a good candidate for conditioning of that response.

Newman–Keuls multiple comparison test a statistical procedure in which sets of means are compared following a significant result from an ANALYSIS OF VARIANCE. The mean values of all experimental groups are arranged in order of size and formed into pairs, and the differences between members of each pair are evaluated against a critical value. [D. **Newman**, British statistician; M. **Keuls**, Dutch horticulturalist]

nicotine *n.* an alkaloid obtained primarily from the tobacco plant (*Nicotiana tabacum*). One of the most widely used psychoactive drugs, nicotine produces multiple pharmacological effects on the central nervous system by activating NICOTINIC RECEPTORS, thus facilitating the release of several neurotransmitters, particularly dopamine. —**nicotinic** *adj.*

nicotinic receptor (nAchR) a type of ACETYLCHOLINE RECEPTOR that responds to nicotine as well as to acetylcholine. Nicotinic receptors mediate chiefly the excitatory activities of acetylcholine, including those at NEUROMUSCULAR JUNCTIONS. There are several nicotinic receptor subtypes, some of which have roles in memory and other cognitive functions. Compare MUSCARINIC RECEPTOR.

night blindness a visual impairment marked by partial or complete inability to see objects in a dimly lighted environment. Night blindness can be inherited or due to defective DARK ADAPTATION or a dietary deficiency of vitamin A.

nightmare *n.* a frightening or otherwise disturbing dream in which fear, sadness, despair, disgust, or some combination thereof forms the emotional content. Nightmares contain visual imagery and some degree of narrative structure and typically occur during REM SLEEP. See SLEEP TERROR DISORDER. —**nightmarish** *adj.*

night terror see SLEEP TERROR DISORDER.

nitric oxide a compound present in numerous body tissues, where it has a variety of functions. In the brain and other parts of the central nervous system, it functions as a neurotransmitter, or as an agent that influences neurotransmitters. In peripheral tissues, it is involved in the relaxation of smooth muscle.

NMDA receptor see GLUTAMATE RECEPTOR.

nociceptor *n.* a sensory RECEPTOR that responds to stimuli that are generally painful or detrimental to the organism.

nocturnal *adj.* active or occurring during darkness. Compare DIURNAL.

node *n.* in an associative model of memory, a point or unit representing a single concept or feature. Nodes are connected to other nodes (usually representing semantically related concepts and features) by links in an associative network, and they may be activated or inhibited to varying degrees depending on the conditions. —**nodal** *adj.*

node of Ranvier any of successive regularly spaced gaps in the MYELIN SHEATH surrounding an axon, which permit the exchange of ions across the plasma membrane at those points and allow the nerve impulse to leap from one node to the next. [Louis A. **Ranvier** (1835–1922), French pathologist]

noise *n.* any unwanted sound or, more generally, any unwanted disturbance (e.g., electrical noise), particularly if it interferes with, obscures, reduces, or otherwise adversely affects the clarity or precision of an ongoing process, such as the communication of a message or signal.

nominal data numerical values that represent membership in specific categories. For example, the category male could be labeled 0 and the category female labeled 1, with each person in the population of interest (e.g., a particular town) assigned the number corresponding to his or her sex. Nominal data are similar to CATEGORICAL DATA, and the two terms are often used interchangeably.

nominal scale a sequence of numbers that do not indicate order, magnitude, or a true zero point but rather identify items as belonging to mutually exclusive categories. For example, a nominal scale for the performance of a specific group of people on a particular test might arbitrarily use the number 1 to denote pass and the number 2 to denote fail. A nominal scale is one of four types of measurement scales, the others being an ORDINAL SCALE, an INTERVAL SCALE, and a RATIO SCALE. See also CATEGORICAL SCALE.

nominal stimulus in stimulus–response experiments, the stimulus as defined and presented by the experimenter. This may be different from the FUNCTIONAL STIMULUS experienced by the organism.

nominal variable a variable whose possible values are unordered categories or labels. For example, choice of college major is a nominal variable.

nomothetic *adj.* relating to the formulation of general laws as opposed to the study of an individual case. A **nomothetic approach** involves the study of groups of people or cases for the purpose of discovering universally valid laws or principles that characterize the average person. Compare IDIOGRAPHIC.

nonadherence *n.* failure of an individual to follow a prescribed therapeutic regimen, likely due to inadequate communication between the practitioner and the individual, physical or cognitive limitations of the patient, or adverse effects that are not being adequately addressed. A primary aspect of health psychology involves methods of reducing nonadherence. Also called **noncompliance**.

nonassociative learning a fre-

quency-based process in which an organism's behavior toward a specific stimulus changes over time in the absence of any evident consequences that would induce such change. There are two major forms of nonassociative learning: HABITUATION and SENSITIZATION.

noncentrality parameter in many PROBABILITY DISTRIBUTIONS used in statistical hypothesis testing, a population characteristic that has a value different from zero when the NULL HYPOTHESIS under test is false. This parameter is important in determining the POWER of a statistical procedure.

nonconscious *adj.* **1.** describing that which is not explicitly in the contents of current awareness or experience. **2.** a synonym for UNCONSCIOUS. Compare PRECONSCIOUS; SUBCONSCIOUS.

noncontingent reinforcement the process or circumstances in which a stimulus known to be effective as a REINFORCER is presented independently of any particular behavior.

nondeclarative memory a collection of various forms of memory that operate automatically and accumulate information that is not accessible to conscious recollection. For instance, one can do something faster if one has done it before, even if one cannot recall the earlier performance. Nondeclarative memory includes PROCEDURAL MEMORY and PRIMING. Compare DECLARATIVE MEMORY.

nondirectional hypothesis a hypothesis that one experimental group will differ from another without specification of the expected direction of the difference. For example, a researcher might hypothesize that college students will perform differently from elementary school students on a memory task without predicting which group of students will perform better. Also called **two-tailed hypothesis**. Compare DIRECTIONAL HYPOTHESIS.

nondirectional test a statistical

test of an experimental hypothesis that does not specify the expected direction of an effect or a relationship. Also called **two-tailed test**. Compare DIRECTIONAL TEST.

nondirective interview see UNSTRUCTURED INTERVIEW.

nondirective therapy see CLIENT-CENTERED THERAPY.

nonexperimental *adj.* denoting a research project that is lacking manipulation of INDEPENDENT VARIABLES by a researcher or RANDOM ASSIGNMENT of participants to treatment conditions, as in OBSERVATIONAL STUDIES and QUASI-EXPERIMENTAL DESIGNS.

nonfluent aphasia see APHASIA.

noninvasive *adj.* **1.** denoting procedures or tests that do not require puncture or incision of the skin or insertion of an instrument or device into the body for diagnosis or treatment. **2.** not capable of spreading from one tissue to another, as in the case of a benign tumor. Compare INVASIVE.

nonlinear *adj.* describing any relationship between two variables (x and y) that cannot be expressed in the form $y = a + bx$, where a and b are numerical constants. The relationship therefore does not appear as a straight line when depicted graphically. Compare LINEAR.

nonlinear model any model that attempts to relate the values of an outcome or dependent variable to the explanatory or independent variables by using an equation that involves exponents. Compare LINEAR MODEL.

nonlinear regression a procedure for analyzing the relationship between an independent or predictor variable (x) and a dependent or outcome variable (y) wherein the REGRESSION EQUATION involves exponential forms of x. That is, the changes in y are not consistent for unit changes in the x variable but are a function of the particular values of x. Compare LINEAR REGRESSION. See REGRESSION ANALYSIS.

nonmetric *adj.* describing data that are nominal or ordinal, such that they cannot be precisely quantified. Examples include *yes/no* answers or a list ranking individuals on some attribute.

nonnormative *adj.* deviating from a specific standard of comparison for a person or group of people, particularly a standard determined by cultural ideals of how things ought to be. This general term is used in a variety of contexts, referring, for example, to socially deviant behavior, ordinary life events happening at unusual times (e.g., a 78-year-old man earning his bachelor's degree), or statistical results that are well above or below the mean or other measure of CENTRAL TENDENCY. Compare NORMATIVE.

nonparametric *adj.* describing any analytic method that does not involve making ASSUMPTIONS about the data of interest. Compare PARAMETRIC.

nonparametric statistics statistical procedures in which the nature of the data being analyzed is such that certain common assumptions about the distribution of the attribute(s) in the population being tested (e.g., normality, homogeneity of variance) are not necessary or applicable. Compare PARAMETRIC STATISTICS.

nonparametric test a type of HYPOTHESIS TEST that does not make any assumptions (e.g., of normality or homogeneity of variance) about the population of interest. Nonparametric tests generally are used in situations involving NOMINAL DATA or ORDINAL DATA. Also called **distribution-free test**; **nonparametric hypothesis test**. Compare PARAMETRIC TEST.

nonrandomized design any of a large number of research designs in which participants or cases are not assigned to experimental conditions via a chance process. For example, FIELD EXPERIMENTS often are nonrandomized. Compare RANDOMIZED DESIGN.

nonreactive measure see UNOB-TRUSIVE MEASURE.

nonregulatory drive any generalized state of arousal or motivation that serves functions that are not related to preserving physiological HOMEOSTASIS and thus are not necessary for the survival of the individual organism (e.g., sex, achievement). Compare REGULA-TORY DRIVE.

non-REM sleep see NREM SLEEP.

nonresponse *n.* a participant's failure to answer one or more survey, questionnaire, or test items or to provide a measurement on some study variable. In many research situations, participants who do not answer questions differ in some important, systematic way from those who do answer. The basic method for compensating for such **non-response** (or **nonresponder**) **bias** involves estimating the probability that each sample case will become a respondent.

nonsense syllable any three-letter combination used to study learning of items that do not already have meaning or associations with other information in memory.

nonshared environment in behavior genetic analyses, aspects of an environment that individuals living together (e.g., in a family household) do not share and that therefore cause them to become dissimilar to each other. Examples of nonshared environmental factors include different friends or teachers that siblings in the same household might have at school or elsewhere outside of the home. Compare SHARED ENVIRONMENT.

nonsignificant *adj.* see NOT SIGNIFICANT.

nonverbal auditory agnosia see AUDITORY AGNOSIA.

nonverbal communication (NVC) the act of conveying information without the use of words. Nonverbal communication occurs through facial expressions, gestures, body language, tone of voice, and other physical indications of mood, attitude, approbation, and so forth, some of which may require knowledge of the culture or subculture to understand.

nonverbal learning disorder (NLD) a LEARNING DISORDER that is characterized by limited skills in critical thinking and deficits in processing nonverbal information. This affects a child's academic progress as well as other areas of functioning, which may include social competencies, visual-spatial abilities, motor coordination, and emotional functioning.

non-zero-sum game in GAME THE-ORY, a situation in which the rewards and costs experienced by all players do not balance (i.e., they add up to less than or more than zero). In such a situation, unlike a ZERO-SUM GAME, one player's gain is not necessarily another player's loss.

nootropic *n.* an obsolete name for COGNITIVE ENHANCER.

noradrenergic *adj.* responding to, releasing, or otherwise involving norepinephrine (noradrenaline). For example, a **noradrenergic neuron** is one that employs norepinephrine as a neurotransmitter.

norepinephrine (NE) *n.* a catecholamine neurotransmitter and hormone produced mainly by brainstem nuclei and in the adrenal medulla. Also called **noradrenaline**.

norm *n.* **1.** a standard or range of values that represents the typical performance of a group or of an individual (e.g., of a certain age) against which comparisons can be made. **2.** a conversion of a raw score into a scaled score that is more easily interpretable, such as a percentile or an IQ score. —**normative** *adj.*

normal *adj.* relating to what is considered standard, average, or typical, used particularly as an indication that a person is mentally healthy and does not have a psychological disorder.

normal distribution a THEORETICAL DISTRIBUTION in which values pile up in the center at the mean and fall off into tails at either end. When plotted, it gives the familiar bell-shaped curve expected when variation about the mean value is random. Many statistical models are based on the assumption that data follow a normal distribution. For example, it is reasonable to expect that human height follows a normal distribution with a mean of 5 feet and several inches, such that very few adults are less than 3 feet or greater than 7 feet tall. Also called **Gaussian distribution**.

normality *n.* **1.** a broad concept that is roughly the equivalent of MENTAL HEALTH. **2.** in statistics, the condition in which a data set presents a NORMAL DISTRIBUTION of values.

normal random variable any variable whose values are theoretically infinite but follow a NORMAL DISTRIBUTION that is centered around the mean for the population and that has a STANDARD DEVIATION matching that of the population.

normal science a science at the stage of development when it is characterized by a PARADIGM consisting of universal agreement about the nature of the science; its practices, assumptions, and methods; and satisfaction with its empirical progress.

normal score see STANDARDIZED SCORE.

normal variable see NORMAL RANDOM VARIABLE.

normative *adj.* pertaining to a particular standard of comparison for a person or group of people, often as determined by cultural ideals regarding behavior, achievements, and other concerns. For example, a **normative life event** such as marriage is expected to occur during a similar period within the lifespans of many individuals, and

normative data reflect group averages with regard to particular variables or factors, such as the language skills of 10-year-olds. Compare NONNORMATIVE.

normative influence the personal and interpersonal processes that cause individuals to feel, think, and act in ways that are consistent with SOCIAL NORMS, standards, and conventions. Those who consistently violate the group's norms are often subjected to negative interpersonal consequences (e.g., ostracism, ridicule, punishment), whereas those who conform are typically rewarded. Compare INFORMATIONAL INFLUENCE; INTERPERSONAL INFLUENCE.

normative scale any evaluative instrument on which the respondent provides ratings for a series of items or chooses scores to indicate his or her agreement with a series of statements. Unlike an IPSATIVE SCALE, there is no requirement for these scores to sum to a particular total (e.g., 100%). For example, a supervisor using a normative scale to assess an employee's job performance might be asked to choose a number from 1 to 5 to indicate how well the employee performed in each of several areas, such as communication, timekeeping, and quality of work. The scores given in any area would not be affected by those given in any of the others.

normative science a scientific approach concerned with establishing NORMS or typical or desirable values for behavior, education, health, or other cultural or societal factors. In contrast to **descriptive science**, which attempts to characterize behavior and other phenomena as they actually exist, normative science attempts to determine what they should be in order to satisfy various criteria.

norm-referenced test any assessment in which scores are interpreted by comparison with a standard of typical performance, generally the average score obtained by members of a specified group. For example, if a student obtains a score of 70% on a norm-referenced reading test, but the standard test score (norm) for those of the same age is 90%, then the student has done relatively poorly. See also CRITERION-REFERENCED TEST.

not significant (**NS**) denoting a result from a statistical hypothesis-testing procedure that does not allow the researcher to conclude that differences in the data obtained for different samples are meaningful and legitimate. In other words, a result that is not significant does not permit the rejection of the NULL HYPOTHESIS; any observed differences are considered to be due to chance or random factors. Also called **nonsignificant**.

novelty *n.* the quality of being new and unusual. It is one of the major determining factors directing attention. The attraction to novelty has been shown to begin as early as 1 year of age; for example, when infants are shown pictures of visual patterns, they will stare longer at a new pattern than at a pattern they have already seen. As people age, the attraction to novelty is manifested as a desire for a change, even in the absence of dissatisfaction with the present situation.

novelty seeking a personality trait characterized by a strong interest in having new experiences; it is often associated with risk-taking behavior, and hence the term may be used synonymously with SENSATION SEEKING.

NREM sleep *non*rapid-*e*ye-*m*ovement sleep: four SLEEP STAGES in which dreams are relatively uncommon and the eyes remain still behind their closed lids. The increasing appearance of DELTA WAVES is another prominent index of NREM sleep. Also called **non-REM sleep**. Compare REM SLEEP.

nuclear family a family unit consisting of two parents and their dependent children (whether biological or adopted). Compare EXTENDED FAMILY.

nucleus *n.* (*pl.* **nuclei**) **1.** a large membrane-bound compartment, found in the cells of nonbacterial organisms, that contains the bulk of the cell's genetic material in the form of chromosomes. **2.** in the central nervous system, a mass of CELL BODIES belonging to neurons with the same or related functions. Compare GANGLION.

nucleus accumbens a large mass of cell bodies in the forebrain that forms part of the LIMBIC SYSTEM. Dopamine release in this region may mediate the reinforcing qualities of many activities, including drug abuse.

nucleus of the solitary tract (**NST**) see SOLITARY NUCLEUS.

null finding the situation in which the outcome of a statistical hypothesis-testing procedure indicates that there is no relationship, or no significant relationship, between experimental variables. Also called **null result**.

null hypothesis (**NH**; symbol: H_0) a statement that a study will find no meaningful differences between the groups or conditions under investigation, such that there is no relationship among the variables of interest and that any variation in observed data is the result of chance or random processes. For example, if a researcher is investigating a new technique to improve the skills of children who have difficulty reading, the null hypothesis would predict no difference between the average reading performances of those children who receive the intervention and those who do not. Compare ALTERNATIVE HYPOTHESIS.

null hypothesis significance testing see SIGNIFICANCE TESTING.

numbsense *n.* the ability of some people who have lost feeling in part or all of their body to respond to tactile stimuli in the insensible area. Such individuals insist that they are not aware of any tactile sensations. See also BLINDSIGHT; DEAF HEARING.

nursing *n.* **1.** a health care profession

that focuses on the protection and promotion of health through the alleviation and treatment of illness, injury, disease, and physical suffering. **2.** the provision of nourishment by a female for her young offspring until they are capable of obtaining their own food. Nursing in mammals primarily involves the secretion of milk from the mammary glands, as stimulated by the hormones prolactin and OXYTOCIN. Other vertebrates exhibit different forms of nursing behavior. For example, some birds produce a milklike substance (crop milk) within their digestive system that is regurgitated to feed young chicks.

nurture *n.* the totality of environmental factors that influence the development and behavior of a person, particularly sociocultural and ecological factors such as family attributes, child-rearing practices, and economic status. See also NATURE–NURTURE.

nystagmus *n.* involuntary, rapid movement of the eyeballs. The eyeball motion may be rotational, horizontal, vertical, or a mixture.

Oo

obedience *n.* behavior in compliance with a direct command, often one issued by a person in a position of authority. Examples include a child who cleans his or her room when told to do so by a parent and a soldier who follows the orders of a superior officer. Obedience has the potential to be highly destructive and ethically questionable, however, as demonstrated in the BEHAVIORAL STUDY OF OBEDIENCE. —**obedient** *adj.*

obesity *n.* the condition of having excess body fat resulting in overweight, variously defined in terms of absolute weight, weight–height ratio (see BODY MASS INDEX), distribution of subcutaneous fat, and societal and aesthetic norms. The basic causes are genetic, environmental, behavioral, or some interaction of these. Obesity predisposes one to heart disease, diabetes, and other serious medical conditions, and obese individuals may develop emotional and psychological problems relating to BODY IMAGE. —**obese** *adj.*

object *n.* **1.** an entity in the environment (i.e., a thing, person, or condition) that acts as a stimulus and elicits a response from an organism; that is, a **stimulus object. 2.** the "other"; that is, any person or symbolic representation of a person that is not the self and toward whom behavior, cognitions, or affects are directed. **3.** in psychoanalytic theory, the person, thing, or part of the body through which an INSTINCT can achieve its aim of gratification.

object constancy 1. in OBJECT RELATIONS THEORY, the ability of an infant to maintain an attachment that is relatively independent of gratification or frustration, based on a cognitive capacity to conceive of a mother who exists when she is out of sight and who has positive attributes when she is unsatis-

fying. Thus, an infant becomes attached to the mother herself rather than to her tension-reducing ministrations. **2.** see PERCEPTUAL CONSTANCY.

object identity see IDENTITY.

objectification *n.* see REIFICATION.

objective *adj.* **1.** having verifiable existence in the external world, independently of any opinion or judgment. **2.** impartial or uninfluenced by personal feelings, interpretations, or prejudices. Compare SUBJECTIVE.

objective self-awareness a reflective state of self-focused attention in which a person evaluates himself or herself and attempts to attain correctness and consistency in beliefs and behaviors. This state involves the viewing of oneself as a separate object, acknowledging limitations and the existing disparity between the ideal self and the actual self. Objective self-awareness is often a necessary part of SELF-REGULATION.

objective test a type of assessment instrument consisting of a set of items or questions that have specific correct answers (e.g., *How much is 2 + 2?*), such that no interpretation, judgment, or personal impressions are involved in scoring. Compare SUBJECTIVE TEST.

objectivity *n.* a quality of a research study such that its hypotheses, choices of variables studied, measurements, techniques of control, and observations are as free from bias as possible. Compare SUBJECTIVITY.

objectivity illusion the tendency of people to see themselves as more impartial, more insightful, and less biased than others. For example, someone who likes a particular song might think that his or her opinion is based on objective reasoning and assume that the opinion of someone who dislikes the song is subjective and biased.

object learning the process of making a connection or association between one aspect of an object (e.g., the color of dark chocolate) and another (e.g., the taste of dark chocolate).

object loss in psychoanalytic theory, the actual loss of a person who has served as a good OBJECT, which precedes INTROJECTION and is involved in separation anxiety. In this perspective, adult grief and mourning are related to object loss and separation anxiety in infancy and childhood, which often intensifies and complicates the grief reaction.

object permanence knowledge of the continued existence of objects even when they are not directly perceived. Milestones that indicate the acquisition of object permanence include reaching for and retrieving a covered object (about 8 months), retrieving an object at Location B even though it was previously hidden several times at Location A (about 12 months), and removing a series of covers to retrieve an object, even though the infant only witnessed the object being hidden under the outermost cover (about 18 months).

object play play that involves the manipulation of items in the environment, such as banging toys together, throwing them around, or arranging them in specific configurations. It is one of three traditionally identified basic types of play (the others being LOCOMOTOR PLAY and SOCIAL PLAY).

object relations theory any psychoanalytically based theory that views the need to relate to OBJECTS as more central to personality organization and motivation than the vicissitudes of the INSTINCTS. These theories developed from and in reaction to classic Freudian theories of psychodynamics.

oblique rotation a transformational system used in FACTOR ANALYSIS when two or more factors (i.e., LATENT VARIABLES) are correlated. Oblique rotation reorients the factors so that they fall closer to clusters of vectors representing MANIFEST VARIABLES, thereby simplifying the mathematical description of the manifest variables. See also ORTHOGONAL ROTATION.

observation *n.* the careful, close examination of an object, process, or other phenomenon for the purpose of collecting data about it or drawing conclusions. —**observational** *adj.*

observational learning the acquisition of information, skills, or behavior through watching the performance of others, either directly or via such media as films and videos.

observational study research in which the experimenter passively observes the behavior of the participants without any attempt at intervention or manipulation of the behaviors being observed. Such studies typically involve observation of cases under naturalistic conditions rather than the random assignment of cases to experimental conditions.

observer bias any expectations, beliefs, or personal preferences of a researcher that unintentionally influence his or her recordings during an OBSERVATIONAL STUDY. See EXPERIMENTER EFFECT.

obsession *n.* a persistent thought, idea, image, or impulse that is experienced as intrusive and inappropriate and results in marked anxiety, distress, or discomfort. Common obsessions include repeated thoughts about contamination, a need to have things in a particular order or sequence, repeated doubts, aggressive or horrific impulses, and sexual imagery. The response to an obsession is often an effort to ignore or suppress the thought or impulse or to neutralize it by a COMPULSION. —**obsessional** *adj.* —**obsessive** *adj.*

obsessive-compulsive disorder (**OCD**) a disorder characterized by recurrent intrusive thoughts (obsessions)

obsessive-compulsive personality disorder

that prompt the performance of neutralizing rituals (COMPULSIONS). Typical obsessions involve themes of contamination, dirt, or illness (fearing that one will contract or transmit a disease) and doubts about the performance of certain actions (e.g., preoccupation that one has neglected to turn off a home appliance). Common compulsive behaviors include repetitive cleaning or washing, checking, ordering, repeating, and hoarding. The obsessions and compulsions are recognized by affected individuals as excessive or unreasonable and cause significant distress that interferes with functioning. Although OCD has traditionally been considered an ANXIETY DISORDER, it is increasingly thought to be in a separate diagnostic category.

obsessive-compulsive personality disorder a personality disorder characterized by an extreme need for perfection, an excessive orderliness, an inability to compromise, and an exaggerated sense of moral responsibility (see SCRUPULOSITY).

Occam's razor the maxim that, given a choice between two hypotheses, the one involving the fewer assumptions should be preferred. In other words, one should apply the LAW OF PARSIMONY and choose simpler explanations over more complicated ones. [William of **Occam** or **Ockham** (c. 1285–1347), English Franciscan monk and Scholastic philosopher]

occipital lobe the most rearward subdivision of each cerebral hemisphere, roughly shaped like a pyramid and lying under the skull's occipital bone. It is involved in basic visual functions (e.g., acuity; contrast sensitivity) as well as higher level ones (e.g., figure-ground segregation based on textural cues). A specific region of the occipital lobe, the **occipital face area** (**OFA**), has been identified as crucial to face recognition. See also FUSIFORM GYRUS.

occlusion *n.* an obstruction or closure. Occlusion of a cerebral artery, for

example, may cause a thrombotic or embolic STROKE. —**occlusive** *adj.*

occupational psychology see INDUSTRIAL AND ORGANIZATIONAL PSYCHOLOGY.

occupational therapy (**OT**) for individuals who have been injured or who have an illness, impairment, or other mental or physical disability or disorder, a therapeutic, rehabilitative process that uses purposeful tasks and activities to improve health; prevent further injury or disability; enhance quality of life; and develop, sustain, or restore the highest possible level of independence. It typically includes assessment of an individual's ability to function independently, the development and implementation of a customized treatment program, and recommendations for adaptive modifications in both home and work environments as well as training in the use of appropriate assistive devices.

ocular dominance column a vertical slab of STRIATE CORTEX in which the neurons are preferentially responsive to stimulation through one of the two eyes. It is important for binocular vision. Ocular dominance columns for each eye alternate in a regular pattern, so that an electrode inserted tangentially to the cortical surface encounters neurons that are responsive to stimulation through first the IPSILATERAL eye, then the CONTRALATERAL eye, then back to the ipsilateral eye. Compare ORIENTATION COLUMN.

oculomotor nerve the third CRANIAL NERVE, which innervates most of the muscles associated with movement and accommodation of the eye and constriction of the pupil.

Oedipus complex in classical psychoanalytic theory, the erotic feelings of the son toward the mother, accompanied by rivalry and hostility toward the father, during the PHALLIC STAGE of psychosexual development. Austrian neurologist Sigmund Freud (1856–1939) saw the Oedipus complex as the basis for NEUROSIS when it is not adequately resolved by the boy's fear of castration and gradual IDENTIFICATION with the father. The corresponding relationship involving the erotic feelings of the daughter toward the father, and rivalry toward the mother, is referred to as the **female Oedipus complex**, which is posited to be resolved by the threat of losing the mother's love and by finding fulfillment in the feminine role. Contemporary psychoanalytic thought has decentralized the importance of the Oedipus complex and has largely modified the classical theory by emphasizing the earlier, primal relationship between child and mother. See also CASTRATION COMPLEX.

off-label *adj.* denoting or relating to the clinical use of a drug for a purpose that has not been approved by the U.S. Food and Drug Administration.

off response (**OFF response**) the depolarization of a neuron in the visual system that occurs in response to light decrement. Neurons with off responses in the center of their receptive fields are often called **off cells**. Compare ON RESPONSE.

ogive *n.* the somewhat flattened S-shaped curve typically obtained by graphing a cumulative FREQUENCY DISTRIBUTION. Consider the example of test results from students in a classroom. Cumulative frequency values would be given along the vertical *y*-axis and obtained test scores along the horizontal *x*-axis. The plot would increase slightly at either end, indicating that few students received very low or very high scores, but rise much more steeply in the center, indicating that the majority of students received average scores.

oldest old see ADULTHOOD.

old-old *adj.* see ADULTHOOD.

olfaction *n.* the sense of smell, involving stimulation of receptor cells in the nasal passages by airborne volatile substances called odorants. Molecules of odorants are absorbed into nasal

mucus and carried to the OLFACTORY EPITHELIUM, where they stimulate the OLFACTORY RECEPTORS. In turn, the receptors carry impulses in axonal bundles through tiny holes in the cribriform plate, a bony layer separating the base of the skull from the nasal cavity. On the top surface of the cribriform plate rests the OLFACTORY BULB, which receives the impulses and sends them on to a region of the brain called the periamygdaloid cortex. —**olfactory** *adj.*

olfactory bulb a bulblike ending on the olfactory nerve in the anterior region of each cerebral hemisphere. This first synapse in the olfactory system picks up excitation from the nose, specifically from the cilia in the OLFACTORY EPITHELIUM.

olfactory cortex a three-layered area of CEREBRAL CORTEX at the base of the TEMPORAL LOBE that is attached to the OLFACTORY BULB and devoted to the sense of smell. The olfactory cortex receives and interprets information from OLFACTORY RECEPTORS in the nasal cavity and is involved in the identification of odors.

olfactory encoding see VISUAL ENCODING.

olfactory epithelium an area of OLFACTORY RECEPTORS in the lining of the upper part of the nose. The epithelium is separated from the OLFACTORY BULB by a sievelike layer called the cribriform plate, through which the receptor cells synapse with cells in the olfactory bulb.

olfactory hallucination a false perception of odors, which are usually unpleasant or repulsive, such as poison gas or decaying flesh.

olfactory nerve the first CRANIAL NERVE, which carries sensory fibers concerned with the sense of smell. It originates in the olfactory lobe and is distributed to OLFACTORY RECEPTORS in the nasal mucous membrane.

olfactory receptor a spindle-shaped receptor cell in the OLFACTORY EPITHELIUM of the nasal cavity that is sensitive to airborne volatile substances called odorants. Cilia at the base of the olfactory receptors contain receptor sites for odorants. The receptors themselves collectively form the OLFACTORY NERVE, which synapses with cells in the OLFACTORY BULB.

olfactory system the primary structures and processes involved in an organism's detection of and responses to airborne volatile substances. The olfactory system includes several million OLFACTORY RECEPTORS in the nasal cavity, the OLFACTORY EPITHELIUM and VOMERONASAL SYSTEM, and the various associated neural pathways and brain areas.

oligodendrocyte *n.* a type of non-neuronal central nervous system cell (GLIA) that forms MYELIN SHEATHS around axons. Also called **oligodendroglia**.

olivary nucleus an olive-shaped mass of gray matter in the medulla oblongata. It consists of two sets of nuclei: the **inferior olivary complex** (or **inferior olivary nucleus** or **inferior olive**), which is believed to be involved in motor control; and the **superior olivary complex** (or **superior olivary nucleus** or **superior olive**), which plays a significant role in the perception and localization of sound. Also called **olivary complex**.

omega squared (symbol: ω^2) a measure of the strength of association based on the proportion of variance in one measure predictable from variance in other measures. In ANALYSIS OF VARIANCE, it indicates how much variation in a DEPENDENT VARIABLE can be explained by variation in one or more INDEPENDENT VARIABLES.

one-parameter model see RASCH MODEL.

one-tailed hypothesis see DIRECTIONAL HYPOTHESIS.

one-tailed test see DIRECTIONAL TEST.

one-trial learning the mastery of a skill after the first training trial.

one-way analysis of variance a type of ANALYSIS OF VARIANCE used to evaluate the influence of different levels or conditions of a single INDEPENDENT VARIABLE on a single DEPENDENT VARIABLE. The mean values of two or more samples are examined in order to determine the probability that they have been drawn from the same population.

one-word stage the developmental period, between approximately 10 and 18 months, when children use one word at a time when speaking. Complex ideas are sometimes expressed with a single word, accompanied by gestures and emphasis. For example, depending on the context and how the word is spoken, *milk* may mean *That is milk, I want more milk,* or *I spilled the milk.* Also called **holophrastic stage**. See HOLOPHRASE.

online social network a set of interconnected individuals who interact using computer-based technologies rather than through face-to-face interactions. An example is a community of Internet video gamers, the members of which each have defined roles and relationships.

on response (**ON response**) the depolarization of a neuron in the visual system that occurs in response to light increment. Neurons with on responses in the center of their receptive fields are often called **on cells**. Compare OFF RESPONSE.

ontogeny *n.* the biological origin and development of an individual organism from fertilization of the egg cell until death. Compare PHYLOGENY. **—ontogenetic** *adj.*

oogenesis *n.* the process by which germ cells divide and differentiate to produce female gametes (ova). In humans, primary oocytes are formed in the ovary during embryonic development and then enter MEIOSIS, remaining suspended at this stage until puberty. Each month thereafter, one primary oocyte resumes meiosis to produce two unequally sized daughter cells: The larger one is the secondary oocyte, and the smaller is a polar body, which contains little cytoplasm. Following OVULATION, the secondary oocyte undergoes meiosis again to produce an ovum and another polar body. The first and second polar bodies eventually degenerate.

open-ended interview an interview in which the interviewee is asked questions that cannot be answered with a simple *yes* or *no*. For example, a human resources staff member interviewing a candidate for employment might ask, "What were the major responsibilities of your most recent job?" Open-ended interviews encourage interviewees to talk freely and extensively, thus providing information that might not be obtained otherwise.

open-field test an experimental technique for quantifying behaviors and physiological reactions (e.g., those indicative of anxiety) in rats and other small animals. The animal is placed in a space divided into squares so that the researcher may observe the number of squares the animal traverses in a specified time period.

open question a test or survey item that does not include any multiple-choice response options. Compare FIXED-ALTERNATIVE QUESTION.

operant *n.* a class of responses that produces a common effect on the environment. An operant is defined by its effect rather than by the particular type of behavior producing that effect. For example, all of a rat's actions that result in a lever being moved 4 mm downward, regardless of whether these actions are two-handed or one-handed, constitute an operant. Compare RESPONDENT.

operant behavior behavior that produces an effect on the environment

and whose likelihood of recurrence is influenced by consequences. Operant behavior is nearly always voluntary behavior.

operant conditioning the process in which behavioral change (i.e., learning) occurs as a function of the consequences of behavior. Examples are teaching a dog to do tricks and rewarding a child who dislikes studying when he or she completes homework assignments on time. The term is essentially equivalent to INSTRUMENTAL CONDITIONING.

operant conditioning chamber an apparatus used to study behavior, consisting of a relatively small and austere environment with devices that can present stimuli (e.g., reinforcers) and measure responses. For example, the apparatus for a rat might consist of a 25 cm³ space containing a food tray, which can be filled by an automatic feeder located outside the space, and a small lever that the rat may press to release food from the feeder. The apparatus was initially developed in the 1930s by U.S. psychologist B. F. Skinner (1904–1990) and later became known colloquially as the **Skinner box**.

operant response a single instance from an OPERANT class. For example, if lever pressing has been conditioned, each single lever press is an operant response.

operation *n.* a type of cognitive SCHEME that is mental (i.e., requires symbols), derives from action, exists in an organized system in which it is integrated with all other operations, and follows a set of logical rules, most importantly that of REVERSIBILITY.

operational definition a description of something in terms of the operations (procedures, actions, or processes) by which it could be observed and measured. For example, the operational definition of anxiety could be in terms of a test score, withdrawal from a situation, or activation of the sympathetic nervous system. The process of creating an operational definition is known as **operationalization**.

operationalism *n.* the position that the meaning of a scientific concept depends on the procedures used to establish it, so that each concept can be defined by a single observable and measurable operation. An example is defining an emotional disorder as a particular score on a diagnostic test. Also called **operationism**.

opiate *n.* any of a variety of natural and semisynthetic compounds derived from OPIUM. They include the alkaloids MORPHINE and CODEINE and their derivatives (e.g., HEROIN [diacetylmorphine]). Opiates, together with synthetic compounds having the pharmacological properties of opiates, are known as OPIOIDS.

opinionnaire *n.* a type of measure for assessing the attitudes or beliefs of an individual about particular topics. It comprises a list of various statements that the respondent is asked to endorse or reject.

opinion survey a technique in which a large number of people are polled to determine their collective views, beliefs, or attitudes about a particular topic (e.g., preferences for U.S. presidential candidates). Information so obtained often is extrapolated to a broader population with a given MARGIN OF ERROR.

opioid *n.* any of a group of compounds that include the naturally occurring OPIATES (e.g., morphine), their synthetic and semisynthetic derivatives (e.g., heroin), and the ENDOGENOUS OPIOIDS. Opioids are used clinically as pain relievers, anesthetics, cough suppressants, and antidiarrheal drugs, and many are subject to abuse and dependence.

opioid receptor a type of cell that binds opioids (including ENDOGENOUS OPIOIDS) and mediates their effects via G PROTEINS. It is generally agreed that

there are at least three classes: mu (μ), kappa (κ), and delta (δ) opioid receptors. Opioid receptors are widely distributed in the brain, spinal cord, and periphery, and each type of receptor is differentially distributed. The more recently discovered nociceptin/orphanin FQ receptor generally is included in the opioid receptor family as well.

opium *n.* the dried resin of the unripe seed pods of the opium poppy, *Papaver somniferum*. Opium contains more than 20 alkaloids, the principal one being MORPHINE, which accounts for most of its pharmacological (including addictive) properties. Natural and synthetic derivatives of opium (see OPIATE; OPIOID) induce analgesia and euphoria and produce a deep, dreamless sleep.

opponent process theory of color vision any one of a class of theories describing color vision on the basis of the activity of mechanisms that respond to red–green, blue–yellow, or black–white. The HERING THEORY OF COLOR VISION, the most highly developed opponent process theory, contrasted with the YOUNG–HELMHOLTZ THEORY OF COLOR VISION, which relied on receptors sensitive to specific regions of the spectrum. In the 1950s, researchers suggested that both theories were correct, the Young–Helmholtz model describing a first stage of processing in the visual system whose outputs were then fed into an opponent process. This combined theory is known as the **dual process theory of color vision**.

opportunity sampling see CONVENIENCE SAMPLING.

oppositional defiant disorder a behavior disorder of childhood characterized by recurrent disobedient, negativistic, or hostile behavior toward authority figures that is more pronounced than usually seen in children of similar age. The defiant behaviors typically do not involve aggression, destruction, theft, or deceit, which distinguishes this disorder from CONDUCT DISORDER.

optical flow pattern see OPTIC FLOW.

optic ataxia inability to direct the hand to an object under visual guidance, typically caused by damage to the cortex of the PARIETAL LOBE. It is a feature of BÁLINT'S SYNDROME.

optic chiasm the location at the base of the brain at which the optic nerves from the two eyes meet. In humans, the nerve fibers from each retina cross, so that each hemisphere of the brain receives input from both eyes. This partial crossing is called a *partial decussation.*

optic disk the area of the retina at which the axons of the RETINAL GANGLION CELLS gather before leaving the retina to form the optic nerve. Because this region contains no photoreceptors, it creates a BLIND SPOT in the visual field.

optic flow in the retinal image of the eye, the pattern and velocity of observed visual information about the motion of objects in an external scene relative to the motion of the observer. Optical flow patterns play an important role in locomotion, coordination and balance, and the perception of movement.

optic nerve the second CRANIAL NERVE, which carries the axons of RETINAL GANGLION CELLS and extends from the retina to the OPTIC CHIASM.

optic radiations nerve fibers that project from the LATERAL GENICULATE NUCLEUS to the VISUAL CORTEX in the occipital lobe and to the pretectum, a structure in the midbrain important for the reflexive contraction of the pupils in the presence of light.

optics *n.* the study of the physics of light, including its relations to the mechanisms of vision.

optic tract the bundle of optic nerve fibers after the partial crossing of the optic nerves at the OPTIC CHIASM. The major targets of the optic tract are the LATERAL GENICULATE NUCLEUS in the thalamus and the superior colliculus in the midbrain.

optimal foraging theory a theory of foraging behavior arguing that NATURAL SELECTION has created optimal strategies for food selection (based on nutritional value and costs of locating, capturing, and processing food) and for deciding when to leave a particular patch to seek resources elsewhere.

optimism *n.* hopefulness: the attitude that good things will happen and that people's wishes or aims will ultimately be fulfilled. Most individuals lie somewhere on the spectrum between the two polar opposites of pure optimism and pure PESSIMISM but tend to demonstrate relatively stable situational tendencies in one direction or the other. **—optimistic** *adj.*

optokinetic reflex (OKR) the involuntary compensatory eye movements that allow the eyes to maintain fixation on a visual target as it moves. The optokinetic reflex is driven by signals from neurons in the retina. Compare VESTIBULO-OCULAR REFLEX.

oral history personal background information provided by an individual during an interview, such as his or her thoughts, experiences of important events, and family relationships. They can be collected, transcribed, and analyzed as part of research studies.

oral stage in the classical psychoanalytic theory of Austrian neurologist Sigmund Freud (1856–1939), the first stage of PSYCHOSEXUAL DEVELOPMENT, occupying the 1st year of life, in which the LIBIDO is concentrated on the mouth as the principal erotic zone. The stage is divided into the early **oral-sucking phase**, during which gratification is achieved by sucking the nipple during feeding, and the later **oral-biting phase**, when gratification is also achieved by biting. Fixation during each of these phases is posited to cause a particular type of oral personality. Also called **oral phase**.

orbitofrontal cortex the CEREBRAL CORTEX of the ventral part of each FRONTAL LOBE, having strong connections to the HYPOTHALAMUS. Lesions of the orbitofrontal cortex can result in loss of inhibitions, forgetfulness, and apathy broken by bouts of euphoria.

orchidectomy *n.* the surgical removal of a testis. An orchidectomy may be performed when a testis is injured or diseased, as when the male reproductive system has been affected by cancer. Also called **orchiectomy**.

order effect 1. in WITHIN-SUBJECTS DESIGNS, the influence of the order in which treatments are administered. As individuals participate in first one and then another treatment condition, they may experience increased fatigue, boredom, and familiarity with or practice with reacting to the independent variable. Any of these conditions could affect the participants' responses and CONFOUND the results of the study. Researchers often use COUNTERBALANCING to control for order effects. See also CARRYOVER EFFECT; SEQUENCE EFFECT. **2.** the influence of the order in which items or statements are listed on surveys and questionnaires. Order effects make it difficult to know whether change over time reflects legitimate respondent differences or question effects.

ordinal data numerical values that represent rankings along a continuum, as in a judge's assignment of a 2 to denote that a particular performance was fair and a 3 to denote that a subsequent performance was better. Ordinal data may be counted and arranged in sequence but may not be manipulated arithmetically because the difference between adjacent values is unspecified and may vary.

ordinal scale a sequence of numbers that do not indicate magnitude or a true zero point but rather reflect a rank ordering on the attribute being measured. For example, an ordinal

scale for the performance of a specific group of people on a particular test might use the number 1 to indicate the person who obtained the highest score, the number 2 to indicate the person who obtained the next highest score, and so on. It is important to note that an ordinal scale does not provide any information about the degree of difference between adjacent ranks (e.g., it is not clear what the actual point difference is between the rank 1 and 2 scores). Compare INTERVAL SCALE; NOMINAL SCALE; RATIO SCALE.

ordinal variable a variable whose possible values have a clear rank order. For example, attitude is an ordinal variable as it may be denoted with ordered points indicating increasing or decreasing values, such as 1 = *strongly disagree*, 2 = *disagree*, 3 = *agree*, and 4 = *strongly agree*. Compare INTERVAL VARIABLE.

ordinate *n.* the vertical coordinate in a graph or data plot; that is, the *y*-axis. See also ABSCISSA.

organic *adj.* denoting a condition or disorder that results from structural alterations of an organ or tissue. In psychology and psychiatry, the term is equivalent to *somatic* or *physical*, as contrasted with FUNCTIONAL or PSYCHOGENIC.

organism *n.* an individual living entity, such as an animal, plant, or bacterium, that is capable of reproduction and growth.

organization *n.* **1.** a structured entity consisting of various components that interact to perform one or more functions, as in a business or industry. **2.** in GESTALT PSYCHOLOGY, an integrated perception composed of various components that appear together as a single whole, such as a face. See GESTALT PRINCIPLES OF ORGANIZATION. **3.** in PIAGETIAN THEORY, the coordinated biological activities of the organism as determined by genetic factors, interactions with the environment, and level of maturation. Inherent in this theory is the concept that mental processes become increasingly structured, initially developing through reflex behavior and responses to immediate stimulation and gradually becoming capable of reflecting the child's own thoughts. —**organizational** *adj.*

organizational behavior management (**OBM**) the application of BEHAVIOR ANALYSIS to individuals and groups in business, industry, government, and human service settings. OBM focuses on organizational problems such as lack of knowledge and skills, occupational injuries, and productivity improvement. Interventions are antecedent-based (e.g., task clarification, equipment modification) and consequence-based (e.g., praise, monetary and nonmonetary rewards).

organizational culture a distinctive pattern of thought and behavior shared by members of the same organization and reflected in their language, values, attitudes, beliefs, and customs. The culture of an organization is in many ways analogous to the personality of an individual.

organizational effect a long-term effect of hormonal action typically occurring in fetal development or the early postnatal period that leads to permanent changes in behavior and neural functioning. For example, the presence of testosterone in young male rats leads to long-term male-typical behavior, and female rats can be masculinized by neonatal exposure to testosterone. Compare ACTIVATIONAL EFFECT.

organizational psychology see INDUSTRIAL AND ORGANIZATIONAL PSYCHOLOGY.

organ of Corti a specialized structure that sits on the BASILAR MEMBRANE within the cochlea in the inner ear. It contains the HAIR CELLS (the sensory receptors for hearing), their nerve endings, and supporting cells. See also TECTORIAL MEMBRANE. [Alfonso **Corti** (1822–1876), Italian anatomist]

orgasm *n.* the climax of sexual stimulation or activity, when the peak of pleasure is achieved, marked by the release of tension and rhythmic contractions of the perineal muscles, anal sphincter, and pelvic reproductive organs. In men, orgasm is also accompanied by the emission of semen (EJACULATION); in women, it is accompanied by contractions in the lower part of the vagina, in the uterus, and in the pelvic floor. See also SEXUAL-RESPONSE CYCLE. —**orgasmic** or **orgastic** *adj.*

orientation *n.* **1.** awareness of the self and of outer reality; that is, the ability to identify one's self and to know the time, the place, and the person one is talking to. **2.** the act of directing the body or of moving toward an external stimulus, such as light, gravity, or some other aspect of the environment. **3.** in vision, the degree of tilt of the long axis of a visual stimulus. For example, a vertical bar is oriented at 0°; a horizontal bar is oriented at 90°. Many neurons in the visual system respond most vigorously to a stimulus of a certain orientation: They are said to be **orientation selective**. —**orient** *vb.*

orientation column a vertical slab of STRIATE CORTEX in which all the neurons are maximally responsive to stimuli of the same orientation. Adjacent columns have slightly different orientation preferences. Compare OCULAR DOMINANCE COLUMN.

orienting response a behavioral response to an altered, novel, or sudden stimulus, such as turning one's head toward an unexpected noise. Physiological components of the orienting response have been identified as well, including dilation of pupils and blood vessels and changes in heart rate and electrical resistance of the skin.

orthogonal rotation a transformational system used in FACTOR ANALYSIS in which the different underlying or LATENT VARIABLES are required to remain separated from or uncorrelated

with one another. See also OBLIQUE RO-
TATION.

orthomolecular medicine a form
of COMPLEMENTARY AND ALTERNATIVE
MEDICINE that uses nutritional approaches to prevent or treat disorders.
Proponents of this approach believe
that biochemical imbalances in the
body are a contributing factor to disease and that using vitamins, minerals,
and other substances natural to the
body corrects these imbalances.

osmometric thirst thirst resulting
from a loss of cellular fluids and a relative increase in OSMOTIC PRESSURE. Also
called **osmotic thirst**. Compare HYPO-
VOLEMIC THIRST.

osmoreceptor *n.* a hypothetical receptor in the HYPOTHALAMUS that
responds to changes in the concentrations of various substances in the
body's extracellular fluid and to cellular
dehydration. It also regulates the secretion of VASOPRESSIN and contributes to
thirst.

osmosis *n.* the passive movement of
solvent molecules through a differentially permeable membrane (e.g., a cell
membrane) separating two solutions of
different concentrations. The solvent
tends to flow from the weaker solution
to the stronger solution. —**osmotic** *adj.*

osmotic pressure the pressure required to prevent the passage of water
(or other solvents) through a semipermeable membrane (e.g., a cell
membrane) from an area of low concentration of solute to an area of
higher concentration.

ossicles *pl. n.* the chain of three tiny
bones in the middle ear that transmit
sound vibrations from the tympanic
membrane (eardrum) to the OVAL WIN-
DOW of the inner ear. They are the
malleus (or hammer), which is attached to the tympanic membrane; the
incus (or anvil); and the **stapes** (or stir-
rup), whose footplate nearly fills the
oval window. The ossicles allow efficient

transmission of airborne sound waves
into the fluid-filled cochlea.

osteoporosis *n.* a disorder in which
the bones become brittle and break easily, due to loss of calcified bone as a
result of disease or aging.

ostracism *n.* an extreme form of rejection in which one is excluded and
ignored in the presence of others. Ostracism has powerful negative effects
on psychological well-being and is
detrimental to multiple domains of self-
functioning. Research suggests that
ostracism activates the ANTERIOR CIN-
GULATE CORTEX, the area of the brain
involved in experiencing physical pain.

otolith *n.* any of numerous tiny calcium particles embedded in the
gelatinous matrix of the VESTIBULAR
SACS of the inner ear. See MACULA.

ought self in analyses of self-concept,
a mental representation of a set of attributes that one is obligated to possess
according to social norms or one's personal responsibilities.

outcome research a systematic investigation of the effectiveness of a type
or technique of intervention (e.g., a
new form of psychotherapy for treating
depression) or of the comparative effectiveness of different intervention types
or techniques (e.g., cognitive behavior
therapy vs. drug therapy for depression). Compare PROCESS RESEARCH.

outcome variable see DEPENDENT
VARIABLE.

outer ear see EXTERNAL EAR.

outer nuclear layer the layer of
cell bodies of the rods and cones in the
retina.

outer plexiform layer the synaptic
layer in the retina in which contacts are
made between PHOTORECEPTORS, RETI-
NAL BIPOLAR CELLS, and RETINAL
HORIZONTAL CELLS.

outgroup *n.* any group to which one
does not belong or with which one does
not identify. Compare INGROUP.

outgroup homogeneity bias the tendency to assume that the members of other groups are very similar to each other, particularly in contrast to the assumed diversity of the membership of one's own group.

outlier *n.* an extreme observation or measurement, that is, a score that significantly differs from all others obtained. For instance, assume a researcher administered an intelligence test to a group of people. If most individuals obtained scores near the average IQ of 100 yet one person had an IQ of 150, the latter score would be an outlier. Outliers can significantly influence SUMMARY STATISTICS and estimates of PARAMETER values, and they may distort research findings if they are the result of error.

out-of-body experience a dissociative experience during which the individual imagines or feels that his or her mind, soul, or spirit has left the body and is acting or perceiving independently. Such experiences are sometimes reported by those who have recovered from a NEAR-DEATH EXPERIENCE; they have also been reported by those using hallucinogens or undergoing hypnosis.

outpatient *n.* a person who obtains a diagnosis, treatment, or other service at a hospital, clinic, physician's office, or other health care facility without overnight admission. Compare INPATIENT.

output interference see INTERFERENCE.

outreach *n.* activity that brings clinical, educational, or practical services (e.g., transportation to clinics or schools) to a community or population that may not otherwise have easy or any access to the services.

oval window a membrane-covered opening within the SCALA VESTIBULI of the inner ear. Vibration of the stapes (see OSSICLES) is transmitted to the oval window and into the fluid-filled COCHLEA.

ovariectomy *n.* the surgical removal of an ovary. This procedure may be performed when the ovaries are diseased or injured. Under some circumstances, as when a woman is at very high risk for ovarian cancer, it may be performed as a preventive measure.

ovary *n.* the female reproductive organ, which produces ova (egg cells) and sex hormones (estrogens and progesterone). In humans, the two ovaries are almond-shaped organs normally located in the lower abdomen on either side of the upper end of the uterus, to which they are linked by the FALLOPIAN TUBES. See also MENSTRUAL CYCLE; OOGENESIS. **—ovarian** *adj.*

overcompensation *n.* see COMPENSATION. **—overcompensate** *vb.*

overconfidence *n.* a cognitive bias characterized by an overestimation of one's actual ability to perform a task successfully, by a belief that one's performance is better than that of others, or by excessive certainty in the accuracy of one's beliefs. Compare UNDERCONFIDENCE. **—overconfident** *adj.*

overdetermination *n.* in psychoanalytic theory, the concept that several unconscious factors may combine to produce one symptom, disorder, or aspect of behavior. Because drives and defenses operate simultaneously and derive from different layers of the personality, a single symptom may serve more than one purpose or fulfill more than one unconscious wish. Also called **multiple determination. —overdetermined** *adj.*

overextension *n.* the tendency of very young children to extend the use of a word beyond the scope of its specific meaning, such as by referring to all animals as "doggie." Compare UNDEREXTENSION.

overgeneralization *n.* the process of extending something beyond the circumstances to which it actually applies. It is a common linguistic tendency of young children to generalize standard grammatical rules to apply to irregular words (e.g., pluralizing *foot* as *foots*). See OVEREXTENSION; OVERREGULARIZATION.

overjustification effect a paradoxical effect in which rewarding a person for his or her performance can lead to lower interest in the activity. The introduction of the reward weakens the strong INTRINSIC MOTIVATION that was the key to the person's original high performance.

overlearning *n.* practice that is continued beyond the point at which the individual knows or performs the task as well as can be expected. The benefits of overlearning may be seen in increased persistence of the learning over time or better retention and memory. —**overlearned** *adj.*

overload *n.* a psychological condition in which situations and experiences are so cognitively, perceptually, and emotionally stimulating that they tax or even exceed the individual's capacity to process incoming information. See COGNITIVE OVERLOAD; INFORMATION OVERLOAD; SENSORY OVERLOAD; STIMULUS OVERLOAD.

overprotection *n.* the process of sheltering a child to such an extent that he or she fails to become independent and may experience later adjustment and other difficulties. —**overprotected** *adj.*

overregularization *n.* a transient error in linguistic development in which the child attempts to make language more regular than it actually is. An example is saying *breaked* instead of *broken*. See also OVEREXTENSION; OVERGENERALIZATION.

overt *adj.* denoting anything that is not hidden or that is directly observable, open to view, or publicly known. Compare COVERT.

overweight *adj.* the condition of having more body fat than is considered normal or healthy for an individual of a particular age, body type, or build. One of the most frequently used standards for assessing the percentage of body fat is the BODY MASS INDEX. See also OBESITY.

ovulation *n.* in OOGENESIS, the production of a mature secondary oocyte and its release from the ovary into a fallopian tube. See also OVUM.

ovum *n.* (*pl.* **ova**) an egg cell: a single female GAMETE that develops from a secondary oocyte following its release from the ovary at OVULATION. See also OOGENESIS.

oxytocin *n.* a PEPTIDE produced in the hypothalamus and released by the posterior PITUITARY GLAND into the blood, where it acts as a hormone, or into the central nervous system, where it acts as a neurotransmitter. Although perhaps best known for its role in stimulating labor and the expression of breast milk, oxytocin is present and serves important functions in both sexes. It facilitates social affiliation, and it has been shown to influence sexual pleasure, reproductive functions, and parental behavior. Additionally, research with nonhuman animals suggests that oxytocin—and the structurally similar compound VASOPRESSIN—is important for pair-bond formation, mate guarding, and recognition of social stimuli.

Pp

Pacinian corpuscle a type of receptor that is sensitive to contact and vibration. It consists of a nerve-fiber ending surrounded by concentric layers of connective tissue. Pacinian corpuscles are found in the fingers, the hairy skin, the tendons, and the abdominal membrane. [Filippo **Pacini** (1812–1883), Italian anatomist]

package insert see LABELING.

pain *n.* an unpleasant sensation elicited by stimulation of NOCICEPTORS, which occur in groups throughout the body but particularly in surface tissues. Pain may also be a feeling of severe distress and suffering resulting from acute anxiety, grief (e.g., at the loss of a loved one), or other nonphysical factors. Psychologists have made important contributions to understanding pain by demonstrating the psychosocial and behavioral factors involved in the etiology, severity, exacerbation, maintenance, and treatment of both physical and psychic pain. See also GATE-CONTROL THEORY.

pain disorder a SOMATOFORM DISORDER characterized by severe, prolonged pain that significantly interferes with a person's ability to function. The pain cannot be accounted for solely by a medical condition, and it is not feigned or produced intentionally (compare FACTITIOUS DISORDER; MALINGERING).

paired-associates learning a technique used in studying learning in which participants learn syllables, words, or other items in pairs and are later presented with one half of each pair to which they must respond with the matching half.

paired sample any research sample in which each participant is matched on a particular variable to a participant in a second sample. This helps ensure that any differences on an outcome variable are not due to differences between participants on the matching variables. Frequently, paired samples are achieved by matching individuals on personal characteristics, such as age and gender. See MATCHED-PAIRS DESIGN.

paired-samples *t* test see MATCHED-PAIRS T TEST.

pairing *n.* in behavioral studies, the juxtaposing of two events in time. For example, if a tone is presented immediately before a puff of air to the eye, the tone and the puff have been paired.

pairwise comparison a procedure in which the data obtained from each level of a variable in a FACTORIAL DESIGN are compared separately to the data from every other level. For example, if a researcher is assessing the differences in student achievement resulting from three different types of content presentation, statistical tests would be used to evaluate the different outcomes of each pair of content methods (i.e., Method 1 and Method 2, 1 and 3, and 2 and 3). DUNNETT'S MULTIPLE COMPARISON TEST and TUKEY'S HONESTLY SIGNIFICANT DIFFERENCE TEST involve pairwise comparisons.

pairwise deletion a method in which data for a variable pertinent to a specific assessment are included, even if values for the same individual on other variables are missing. For example, consider a researcher studying the influence of age, education level, and current salary on the socioeconomic status of a sample of employees. If assessing specifically how education and salary influence socioeconomic status, he or she could include all participants for whom that data had been recorded even if they were missing information on age, as the latter variable is not of interest in the current analysis. Also called **available-case analysis**.

paleocortex *n.* see ALLOCORTEX.

paleopallium *n.* see ALLOCORTEX.

paleopsychology (palaeopsychology) *n.* the study of certain psychological processes in contemporary humans that are believed to have originated in earlier stages of human and, perhaps, nonhuman animal evolution. —**paleopsychological** *adj.*

palliative care terminal care that focuses on symptom control and comfort instead of aggressive, cure-oriented intervention. This is the basis of the HOSPICE approach. Emphasis is on careful assessment of the dying patient's condition throughout the end phase of life in order to provide the most effective medications to relieve pain and manage other symptoms (e.g., respiratory distress, nausea).

palsy *n.* an obsolete name for paralysis, although still used in such compound names as CEREBRAL PALSY.

panel data observations on multiple phenomena collected over multiple time periods for the same group of individuals or other units. Repeated observations permit the researcher to study the dynamics of change using techniques such as TIME-SERIES ANALYSIS. For example, the values of the gross annual income for each of 500 randomly chosen households in New York City collected for each of 10 years would be panel data.

panel study see LONGITUDINAL DESIGN.

panic *n.* a sudden, uncontrollable fear reaction that may involve terror, confusion, and irrational behavior and that is precipitated by a perceived threat (e.g., earthquake, fire, being caught in an elevator).

panic attack a sudden onset of intense apprehension and fearfulness in the absence of actual danger, accompanied by the presence of such physical symptoms as heart palpitations, difficulty breathing, chest pain or discomfort, choking or smothering sensations, sweating, and dizziness. The attack occurs in a discrete period of time and often involves fears of losing control or dying.

panic disorder (PD) an ANXIETY DISORDER characterized by recurrent, unexpected PANIC ATTACKS that are associated with (a) persistent concern about having another attack, (b) worry about the possible consequences of the attacks, (c) significant change in behavior related to the attacks (e.g., avoiding situations, not going out alone), or (d) a combination of any or all of these.

Papez circuit a circular network of nerve centers and fibers in the brain that is associated with emotion and memory. It includes the hippocampus, FORNIX, MAMMILLARY BODY, anterior thalamus, CINGULATE CORTEX, and PARAHIPPOCAMPAL GYRUS. Damage to any component of this system leads to amnesia. Also called **Papez circle**. [first described in 1937 by James W. **Papez** (1883–1958), U.S. neuroanatomist]

paradigm *n.* **1.** a model, pattern, or representative example, as of the functions and interrelationships of a process, a behavior under study, or the like. **2.** a set of assumptions, attitudes, concepts, values, procedures, and techniques that constitutes a generally accepted theoretical framework within, or a general perspective of, a discipline.

paradoxical sleep see REM SLEEP.

parahippocampal gyrus a ridge (gyrus) on the medial (inner) surface of the TEMPORAL LOBE of cerebral cortex, lying over the HIPPOCAMPUS. It is a component of the LIMBIC SYSTEM thought to be involved in spatial or topographic memory.

parakinesis *n.* in parapsychology, the purported movement of objects at a rate and trajectory disproportionate to the contact made with them. The phenomenon is closely related to that of

PSYCHOKINESIS, which involves the purported manipulation of objects by thought alone.

paralanguage *n.* the vocal but non-verbal elements of communication by speech, such as tone, stress, volume and speed of delivery, voice quality, hesitations, and nonlinguistic sounds, such as sighs, whistles, or groans. These **paralinguistic cues** can help shape the total meaning of an utterance; they can, for example, convey the fact that a speaker is angry or sarcastic when this would not be apparent from the same words written down. In some uses, the term is extended to include gestures, facial expressions, and other aspects of BODY LANGUAGE.

parallax *n.* an illusion of movement of objects in the visual field when the head is moved from side to side. Objects beyond a point of visual fixation appear to move in the same direction as the head movement; those closer seem to move in the opposite direction. Parallax provides a monocular cue for DEPTH PERCEPTION.

parallel distributed processing (**PDP**) any model of cognition based on the idea that the representation of information is distributed as patterns of activation over a richly connected set of hypothetical neural units that function interactively and in parallel with one another. See PARALLEL PROCESSING.

parallel fiber any of the axons of the GRANULE CELLS that form the outermost layer of the cerebellar cortex.

parallel processing INFORMATION PROCESSING in which two or more sequences of operations are carried out simultaneously by independent processors. A capacity for parallel processing in the human brain would account for people's apparent ability to carry on different cognitive functions at the same time, such as driving a car while also listening to music and having a conversation. The term is usually reserved for processing at a higher, symbolic level, as opposed to the level of individual

neural units described in models of PARALLEL DISTRIBUTED PROCESSING. Compare SERIAL PROCESSING.

parameter *n.* **1.** a characteristic of a POPULATION that is described or estimated by a STATISTIC obtained from sample data. For example, the mean score on a national exam for a sample of colleges provides an estimate of this parameter in the population of colleges. **2.** any of the variables in a statistical model that is studied or used to explain an outcome or relationship.

parameter space the set of experimental variables that are used as input into a model and serve as the basis for estimation of PARAMETERS in a population.

parametric *adj.* describing any analytic method that makes ASSUMPTIONS about the data of interest. Compare NONPARAMETRIC.

parametric statistics statistical procedures that are based on ASSUMPTIONS about the distribution of the attributes in the population being tested (e.g., that there is a NORMAL DISTRIBUTION of values). Compare NONPARAMETRIC STATISTICS.

parametric test a form of HYPOTHESIS TESTING that involves one or more assumptions about the underlying arrangement of values in the population from which the sample is drawn. Common parametric tests include ANALYSIS OF VARIANCE, REGRESSION ANALYSIS, CHI-SQUARE TESTS, T TESTS, and Z TESTS. Also called **parametric hypothesis test**. Compare NONPARAMETRIC TEST.

paramnesia *n.* see FALSE MEMORY.

paranoia *n.* a persistent, well-systematized, and logically constructed set of persecutory delusions, such as being conspired against, poisoned, or maligned. —**paranoiac** *n., adj.*

paranoid personality disorder a personality disorder characterized by (a) pervasive, unwarranted suspiciousness and distrust (e.g., expectation of trickery or harm, overconcern with hidden motives and meanings); (b) hypersensitivity (e.g., being easily slighted or offended, readiness to counterattack); and (c) restricted affectivity (e.g., emotional coldness, no true sense of humor).

paranoid schizophrenia a subtype of schizophrenia characterized by prominent delusions or auditory hallucinations. Delusions are typically persecutory, grandiose, or both; hallucinations are typically related to the content of the delusional theme. Cognitive functioning and mood are affected to a much lesser degree than in other types of schizophrenia.

paranormal *adj.* denoting any purported phenomenon involving the transfer of information or energy that cannot be explained by existing scientific knowledge. See also EXTRASENSORY PERCEPTION; PARAPSYCHOLOGY.

paraphilia *n.* any of a group of disorders in which unusual or bizarre fantasies or behavior are necessary for sexual excitement, including preference for a nonhuman object (e.g., animals), repetitive sexual activity involving real or simulated suffering or humiliation (e.g., whipping, bondage), or repetitive sexual activity with nonconsenting partners. Paraphilias include such specific types as FETISHISM, PEDOPHILIA, EXHIBITIONISM, VOYEURISM, SEXUAL MASOCHISM, and SEXUAL SADISM. —**paraphiliac** *adj.*

parapraxis *n.* a minor error that is thought (especially in CLASSICAL PSYCHOANALYSIS) to express unconscious wishes, attitudes, or impulses. Examples include SLIPS OF THE TONGUE, forgetting significant events, mislaying objects, unintentional puns, and motivated accidents. Also called **parapraxia**. See also FREUDIAN SLIP.

paraprofessional *n.* a trained but not professionally credentialed worker who assists in the treatment of patients in both hospital and community settings.

parapsychology *n.* the systematic study of alleged psychological phenomena involving the transfer of information or energy that cannot be explained in terms of presently known scientific data or laws. Such study has focused largely on the various forms of EXTRASENSORY PERCEPTION, such as TELEPATHY and CLAIRVOYANCE, but also encompasses such phenomena as alleged poltergeist activity and the claims of mediums. Although **parapsychologists** are committed to scientific methods and procedures, the field is still regarded with suspicion by most scientists, including most psychologists. —**parapsychological** *adj.* —**parapsychologist** *n.*

parasomnia *n.* any disorder characterized by abnormal behavior or physiological events during sleep or during the transitional state between sleep and waking. Examples include SLEEP TERROR DISORDER and SLEEPWALKING DISORDER. The parasomnias form one of two broad groups of primary sleep disorders, the other being DYSSOMNIAS.

parasuicide *n.* a range of behaviors involving deliberate self-harm that may or may not be intended to result in death.

parasympathetic nervous system one of two branches of the AUTONOMIC NERVOUS SYSTEM, the other being the SYMPATHETIC NERVOUS SYSTEM. It is the system that controls rest, repair, enjoyment, eating, sleeping, sexual activity, and social dominance, among other functions. It stimulates salivary secretions and digestive secretions in the stomach and produces pupillary constriction, decreases in heart rate, and increased blood flow to the genitalia during sexual excitement. Also called **parasympathetic division**.

paraventricular nucleus (**PVN**) a particular collection of neurons in the HYPOTHALAMUS that synthesize numerous hormones, among them OXYTOCIN and VASOPRESSIN.

parental alliance see COPARENTING.

parental investment theory the proposition that many sex differences in sexually reproducing species (including humans) can be understood in terms of the amount of time, energy, and risk to their own survival that males and females put into parenting versus mating (including the seeking, attaining, and maintaining of a mate).

parental separation see MARITAL SEPARATION.

parenting *n.* all actions related to the raising of offspring. Researchers have described different human **parenting styles**—ways in which parents interact with their children—with most classifications varying on the dimensions of emotional warmth and control. One of the most influential of these classifications is that of U.S. developmental psychologist Diana Baumrind (1927–), involving four types of styles: **authoritarian parenting**, in which the parent or caregiver stresses obedience and employs strong forms of punishment; **authoritative parenting**, in which the parent or caregiver encourages a child's autonomy yet still places certain limitations on behavior; **permissive parenting**, in which the parent or caregiver makes few demands and avoids exercising control; and **rejecting–neglecting parenting**, in which the parent or caregiver is more attentive to his or her needs than those of the child.

paresis *n.* partial or incomplete paralysis.

paresthesia *n.* an abnormal skin sensation, such as tingling, tickling, burning, itching, or pricking, in the absence of external stimulation. Paresthesia may be temporary, as in the "pins and needles" feeling experienced after having sat with one's legs crossed too long, or chronic and due to such factors as neurological disorder or drug side effects. —**paresthetic** *adj.*

parietal lobe one of the four main subdivisions of each cerebral hemisphere. It occupies the upper central area of each hemisphere, behind the FRONTAL LOBE, ahead of the OCCIPITAL LOBE, and above the TEMPORAL LOBE. Parts of the parietal lobe participate in somatosensory activities, such as the discrimination of size, shape, and texture of objects; visual activities, such as visually guided actions; and auditory activities, such as speech perception.

Parkinson's disease (PD) a progressive neurodegenerative disease caused by the death of dopamine-producing neurons in the SUBSTANTIA NIGRA of the brain, which controls balance and coordinates muscle movement. Symptoms typically begin late in life with mild tremors, increasing rigidity of the limbs, and slowness of voluntary movements. Later symptoms include postural instability, impaired balance, and difficulty walking. Dementia occurs in some 20% to 60% of patients, usually in older patients in whom the disease is far advanced, and depression and anxiety are often observed as well. [first described in 1817 by James **Parkinson** (1755–1824), British physician]

parsimony *n.* see LAW OF PARSIMONY.

part correlation the association between two variables, *x* and *y*, with the influence of a third variable, *z*, removed from one (but only one) of the two variables. This can help a researcher to get a clearer understanding of the relationship between *x* and *y*. Compare PARTIAL CORRELATION.

partial agonist a substance that binds to a receptor but fails to produce the same degree of response as a full AGONIST at the same receptor site or exerts only part of the action exerted by the endogenous neurotransmitter that it mimics. Minor variations in the chemical structure of either the receptor or the binding substance may dictate whether the substance acts as a full or partial agonist at any particular receptor site.

partial correlation the association between two variables, x and y, with the influence of one or more other variables (z_1, z_2) statistically removed, controlled, or held constant; the effect of the z variable is removed from both x and y. For example, the partial correlation between salary and education level can be examined after the effects of age on each are removed. It is often of interest to learn whether a correlation is significantly reduced in magnitude once a third variable is removed. Also called **higher order correlation**. Compare PART CORRELATION.

partialing *n.* a statistical approach used to control the influence of certain variables on other variables of interest and thus clarify a specific relationship being examined. In a MULTIPLE REGRESSION model, for example, a researcher may want to remove the effects of a set of COVARIATES before examining the final coefficients of interest in the REGRESSION EQUATION.

partial reinforcement see INTERMITTENT REINFORCEMENT.

partial reinforcement effect (**PRE**) increased RESISTANCE TO EXTINCTION after intermittent reinforcement rather than after continuous reinforcement.

partial seizure a seizure that occurs in a localized area of the brain, often the temporal lobe. Simple partial seizures produce no alteration of consciousness despite clinical manifestations, which may include sensory, motor, or autonomic activity. Complex partial seizures may produce similar sensory, motor, or autonomic symptoms but are also characterized by some impairment or alteration of consciousness during the event. Also called **focal seizure**.

participant *n.* a person who takes part in an investigation, study, or experiment, such as by performing tasks set by the experimenter or by answering questions posed by a researcher. Participants may also be referred to as SUBJECTS, particularly by those who wish to avoid the implication that experimentees are involved in the construction, design, conduct, and analysis of the experiment.

participant modeling a procedure for changing behavior in which effective styles of behavior are demonstrated step-by-step and analyzed by a therapist for an individual, who then practices the modeled behavior. Various aids are introduced to help, such as videotaped enactments of effective and ineffective behavioral responses to prototypical situations in a variety of social contexts. By contrast, **symbolic modeling** is a procedure in which the individual only observes, but does not also practice, a modeled behavior as enacted in film, videotape, or other media.

participant observation an observational method in which a trained investigator studies a preexisting group by joining it as a member, while avoiding a conspicuous role that would alter the group processes and bias the data. The researcher's role may be known or unknown to the other members of the group. For example, cultural anthropologists become **participant observers** when they enter the life of a given culture to study its structure and processes.

participants' rights in a study approved by an INSTITUTIONAL REVIEW BOARD, a set of conditions relating to participants in the study and their role in the research. Participants normally should be informed about the purpose of the study, its procedures, and the associated costs and benefits; that their data from the study will be kept confidential; whom they can contact if they have any concerns about the study; and that they can leave the study at any time without penalty. See also INFORMED CONSENT.

part method of learning a learning technique in which the material is divided into sections, each to be mastered separately in a successive order. Compare WHOLE METHOD OF LEARNING.

paruresis *n.* a fear of urinating, resulting in an inability to urinate where others may be present (e.g., in public restrooms). It is considered a SOCIAL PHOBIA.

parvocellular system the part of the visual system that projects to or originates from small neurons in the four dorsal layers (the **parvocellular layers**) of the LATERAL GENICULATE NUCLEUS. It allows the perception of fine details, colors, and large changes in brightness, but it conducts information relatively slowly because of its small cells and slender axons. See also P-CELL. Compare MAGNOCELLULAR SYSTEM.

passion *n.* an intense, driving, or overwhelming feeling or conviction, particularly a strong sexual desire. Passion is often contrasted with emotion, in that passion affects a person unwillingly. —**passionate** *adj.*

passionate love a type of love in which emotional arousal and usually sexual passion are prominent features; along with COMPANIONATE LOVE, it is one of the two main types of love identified by social psychologists. Passionate lovers tend to be preoccupied with each other. See also ROMANTIC LOVE; TRIANGULAR THEORY OF LOVE.

passive-aggressive *adj.* characteristic of behavior that is seemingly innocuous, accidental, or neutral but that indirectly displays an unconscious aggressive motive. For example, a child who appears to be compliant but is routinely late for school, misses the bus, or forgets his or her homework may be expressing unconscious resentment at having to attend school.

passive-aggressive personality disorder a personality disorder of long standing in which AMBIVALENCE and NEGATIVISM toward the self and others is expressed by such means as

procrastination, dawdling, stubbornness, intentional inefficiency, "forgetting" appointments, or misplacing important materials. The pattern persists even when more adaptive behavior is clearly possible; it frequently interferes with occupational, social, and academic success.

passive euthanasia the intentional withholding of treatment that might prolong the life of a person who is approaching death. It is distinguished from ACTIVE EUTHANASIA, in which direct action (e.g., a lethal injection) is taken to end the life. Courts have ruled that physicians do not have to try every possible intervention to prolong life, but opinions differ on where the line should be drawn. There is also controversy regarding the significance of the passive–active distinction, since both approaches result in shortening the life.

passive joy see JOY.

past-life regression a highly controversial hypnotic technique in which a person is encouraged to move back in time to reexperience a supposed previous existence. Therapists who conduct past-life regression believe that individuals' current psychological and physical problems (e.g., phobias, insomnia) can be understood and resolved by discovering their origins in the experiences (e.g., traumas, unresolved conflicts, mistakes) of previous lives. Most hypnotherapists are skeptical of the practice, however, and do not recognize it as a legitimate therapeutic tool. See also AGE REGRESSION.

patch-clamp technique the use of very fine-bore pipette MICROELECTRODES, clamped by suction onto tiny patches of the plasma membrane of a neuron, to record the electrical activity of a single square micrometer of the membrane, including single ION CHANNELS.

paternalism *n.* a policy or attitude in which those having authority over others extend this authority into areas usually left to individual choice or conscience (e.g., smoking, sexual behavior), usually on the grounds that this is necessary for the welfare or protection of the individuals concerned. —**paternalist** *n.* —**paternalistic** *adj.*

path analysis a type of STRUCTURAL EQUATION MODELING used to examine a set of relationships between variables. Results are displayed using a figure in which boxes denote measured variables, bidirectional arrows show correlations, directional arrows show causal or predictive relations, and arrows coming from nowhere show error associated with the prediction model. GOODNESS OF FIT is tested by comparing models with more pathways to models with fewer pathways. Also called **path modeling**. See PATH DIAGRAM.

path diagram in PATH ANALYSIS, a figure describing the causal relationships or logical ordering hypothesized among variables. Each measured variable is designated by a box, and latent variables are represented by ovals. COVARIANCES are represented by curved lines with arrowheads at both ends. Paths are represented by straight lines with an arrowhead pointing from the INDEPENDENT VARIABLE toward the DEPENDENT VARIABLE. Associated with each path is either an asterisk or a number. The asterisks indicate free PARAMETERS, whose values will be estimated from the data, whereas the numbers indicate fixed parameters, whose values do not change as a function of the data.

pathogen *n.* any agent (e.g., bacterium, virus) that contributes to disease or otherwise induces unhealthy structural or functional changes. —**pathogenicity** *n.*

pathological aggression aggression that is violent, explicitly directed against individuals or property, and either part of a long-standing repertoire of destructive or hurtful behavior or a sudden, paroxysmal reaction to a real or perceived provocation. It may be a manifestation of psychiatric disorder, neurological disease or injury, sub-

stance abuse (e.g., of alcohol), and some sexual behaviors (e.g., sexual sadism).

pathological gambling an addiction disorder characterized by chronic, maladaptive wagering, leading to significant interpersonal, professional, or financial difficulties. Also called **gambling disorder**.

pathology *n.* **1.** the scientific study of functional and structural changes involved in physical and mental disorders and diseases. **2.** more broadly, any departure from what is considered healthy or adaptive. —**pathological** *adj.* —**pathologist** *n.*

patient *n.* a person receiving health care from a licensed health professional. See INPATIENT; OUTPATIENT. See also PATIENT–CLIENT ISSUE.

patient abuse harm caused by treatment providers to those in their care by exploiting their patients' vulnerability and their own position of influence and trust to engage in inappropriate, unprofessional behavior. Such abuse, which sometimes takes the form of sexual involvement with a patient, is usually grounds for legal and professional action against the practitioner. Also called **client abuse**.

patient–client issue the dilemma of how to identify the recipient of psychological services or intervention (i.e., the nomenclature used for the recipient). Psychiatrists, many clinical psychologists, and some other mental health providers tend to follow the traditional language of the medical model and refer to the people seeking their services as **patients**. Counseling psychologists, some clinical psychologists, social workers, and counselors tend to avoid the word *patient*, which is associated with illness and dysfunction, and instead use the word **client** to refer to the person seeking their services.

patient history in therapy and counseling, a systematic account of an individual's development from birth to the present, including meaningful aspects of his or her emotional, social, and intellectual development. The account is taken by the therapist or counselor directly from the individual and may additionally be derived from autobiographical material or reports from family members. See also CASE HISTORY.

patients' rights any statement, listing, summary, or the like that articulates the rights that health care providers (e.g., physicians, medical facilities) ethically ought to provide to those receiving their services. These rights include (a) the provision of adequate information regarding treatment benefits, risks, costs, and alternatives; (b) fair treatment (e.g., respect, responsiveness, timely attention to health issues); (c) autonomy over medical decisions (e.g., obtaining full consent for medical interventions); and (d) CONFIDENTIALITY.

patient variable any characteristic of an individual in treatment, such as gender, age, personality, attitude, race, ethnicity, socioeconomic status, religious background, and cognitive status (e.g., intellectual disability), that may influence the process and outcome of treatment.

patriarchy *n.* **1.** a society in which descent and inheritance is **patrilineal**, that is, traced through the male only. **2.** more loosely, a family, group, or society in which men are dominant. Compare MATRIARCHY. —**patriarchal** *adj.*

pattern recognition the ability to recognize and identify a complex whole composed of, or embedded in, many separate elements. Pattern recognition is not only a visual ability; in audition, it refers to (a) the recognition of temporal patterns of sounds or (b) the recognition of patterns of excitation of the BASILAR MEMBRANE, such as that which occurs during the perception of vowels in speech.

pattern theory of taste coding a theory postulating that each taste stim-

ulus evokes a unique pattern of neural activity from the TASTE-CELL population and that this pattern serves as the neural representation of the evoking stimulus. Taste quality is coded in the shape of the evoked pattern, whereas intensity is represented by the total discharge rate. Compare LABELED-LINE THEORY OF TASTE CODING.

Pavlovian conditioning see CLASSICAL CONDITIONING. [Ivan **Pavlov** (1849–1936), Russian physiologist]

P-cell *n.* any of various small neurons in the four dorsal layers of the six-layered LATERAL GENICULATE NUCLEUS. P-cells are the origin of the PARVOCELLULAR SYSTEM. The RETINAL GANGLION CELLS that provide input to the P-cells of the lateral geniculate nucleus are called **P-ganglion cells**. See also M-CELL.

PCP *n.* 1-(1-*p*henyl*c*yclohexyl)*p*iperidine (phencyclidine): a hallucinogenic drug, sometimes referred to as a "psychedelic anesthetic" because it was originally developed as an amnestic analgesic for use in surgical contexts and was later found to produce a psychedelic or dissociative reaction. Its medical use was discontinued because of its powerfully adverse reactions, from agitation and delirium to coma. Because intoxication with PCP can produce symptoms resembling both the positive and negative symptoms of schizophrenia, some consider it to be a useful drug model of that disorder. PCP became common as an illicit drug in the 1970s and has remained popular, despite speculation on its potential to damage nerve tissue. It can be smoked, inhaled nasally, or taken orally or intravenously.

peak experience a moment of awe, ecstasy, or sudden insight into life as a powerful unity that transcends space, time, and the self. Peak experiences may at times occur for individuals in their pursuit of SELF-ACTUALIZATION. See also HUMANISTIC PSYCHOLOGY; TRANSPERSONAL PSYCHOLOGY.

Pearson product-moment correlation coefficient see PRODUCT-MOMENT CORRELATION COEFFICIENT. [Karl **Pearson** (1857–1936), British statistician and biometrician]

Pearson's r see PRODUCT-MOMENT CORRELATION COEFFICIENT. [Karl **Pearson**]

pecking order regular patterns of dominance (pecking, threatening, chasing, fighting, avoiding, crouching, and vocalizing) in chickens and other animals. This term has been extended to denote any (usually linear) sequence of authority, status, and privilege that prevails in some organizations and social groups. See also DOMINANCE HIERARCHY.

pediatric adj. pertaining to the health and medical care of children or to child development. **Pediatrics** is the medical specialty dealing with wellness care and treatment of disease in infants, children, and adolescents.

pediatric neuropsychology a specialty that studies the behavior and cognitive abilities of children in terms of the neural mechanisms that underlie brain activity, especially in cases of brain damage or other neurological disorder. See also SCHOOL NEUROPSYCHOLOGY.

pediatric psychology an interdisciplinary field of research and practice that addresses physical, behavioral, and emotional development as it interacts with health and illness in children, adolescents, and families. Related to the larger field of HEALTH PSYCHOLOGY, pediatric psychology focuses on the child in the contexts of the family, school, and health care settings.

pedophilia n. a PARAPHILIA in which sexual acts or fantasies involving prepubertal children are the persistently preferred or exclusive method of achieving sexual excitement. The children are usually many years younger than the **pedophile**. Sexual activity may consist of looking and touching but may include intercourse. —**pedophilic** adj.

peer n. an individual who shares a feature or function (e.g., age, sex, occupation, social group membership) with one or more other individuals. In developmental psychology, a peer is typically an age mate with whom a child or adolescent interacts.

peer facilitation the use of a peer counseling model, generally within a group setting, to pursue educational or problem-solving goals. For example, peer facilitation has been used with elementary school children to mediate conflict and in college-level distance learning (e.g., correspondence coursework, computerized software learning programs) to increase student participation in online discussions.

peer group a group of individuals who share one or more characteristics, such as age, social status, economic status, occupation, or education. Members of a peer group typically interact with each other on a level of equality and exert influence on each other's attitudes, emotions, and behavior (see PEER PRESSURE).

peer pressure the influence exerted by a peer group on its individual members to fit in with or conform to the group's norms and expectations. Peer pressure may have positive SOCIALIZATION value but may also have negative consequences for mental or physical health. Also called **peer-group pressure**.

penis n. the male organ for urination and for INTROMISSION, during which it enters the female's vagina to deliver semen. The urethra runs through the penis, which is composed largely of erectile tissue and has a mushroom-shaped cap (glans penis). —**penile** adj.

penis envy in the classical psychoanalytic theory of Austrian neurologist Sigmund Freud (1856–1939), the hypothesized desire of girls and women to possess the male genital organ. German-born U.S. psychoanalyst Karen D. Horney (1885–1952), among others, later argued that penis envy is not an envy of the biological organ itself but represents women's envy of men's superior social status. In any sense, the concept has been actively disputed from the beginning and is rarely considered seriously in current psychology. See also CASTRATION COMPLEX.

penology *n*. the scientific study of the management of correctional facilities and the rehabilitation of criminals.

peptide *n*. a short chain of AMINO ACIDS linked by **peptide bonds**. Peptides are usually identified by the number of amino acids in the chain: dipeptides have two amino acids, tripeptides three, tetrapeptides four, and so on. See also POLYPEPTIDE; PROTEIN.

peptide hormone any hormone that is classed chemically as a peptide. Peptide hormones include CORTICOTROPIN, OXYTOCIN, and VASOPRESSIN.

percentile *n*. the location of a score in a distribution expressed as the percentage of cases in the data set with scores equal to or below the score in question. Thus, if a score is said to be in the 90th percentile, this means that 90% of the scores in the distribution are equal to or lower than that score.

percept *n*. the product of PERCEPTION: the stimulus object or event as experienced by the individual.

perception *n*. the process or result of becoming aware of objects, relationships, and events by means of the senses, which includes such activities as recognizing, observing, and discriminating. These activities enable organisms to organize and interpret the stimuli received into meaningful knowledge.

perceptual constancy the phenomenon in which an object or its properties (e.g., size, shape, color) appear unchanged despite variations in the stimulus itself or in the external conditions of observation, such as ob-

ject orientation or level of illumination. Examples of perceptual constancy include BRIGHTNESS CONSTANCY, COLOR CONSTANCY, SHAPE CONSTANCY, and SIZE CONSTANCY.

perceptual defense in psychoanalytic theory, a misperception that occurs when anxiety-arousing stimuli are unconsciously distorted. For example, if the stimulus word *anal* is presented, individuals may report seeing the innocuous *canal*.

perceptual filtering the process of focusing attention on a selected subset of the large number of sensory stimuli that are present at any one time. This filtering is necessary because the cognitive and physical capacity of an individual to process and respond to multiple sources of information is limited.

perceptual organization the process enabling such properties as structure, pattern, and form to be imposed on the senses to provide conceptual organization. Recent research has more precisely defined the properties that enable such organized tasks.

perceptual set 1. a temporary readiness to perceive certain objects or events rather than others. For example, a person driving a car has a perceptual set to identify anything in the car or on the road that might affect his or her safety. **2.** a SCHEMA or FRAME that influences the way in which a person perceives objects, events, or people. For example, an on-duty police officer and a painter might regard a crowded street scene with very different perceptual sets.

perfect correlation a relationship between two variables, *x* and *y*, in which the change in value of one variable is exactly proportional to the change in value of the other. That is, knowing the value of one variable exactly predicts the value of the other variable (i.e., $r_{xy} = 1.0$). When graphed, a perfect correlation forms a perfectly straight line. It is uncommon to observe this type of relationship in actual data. See also CORRELATION COEFFICIENT.

perfectionism *n.* the tendency to demand of others or of oneself an extremely high or even flawless level of performance, in excess of what is required by the situation. It is associated with depression, anxiety, eating disorders, and other mental health problems. —**perfectionist** *adj., n.*

performance *n.* **1.** any activity or collection of responses that leads to a result or has an effect on the environment. **2.** in linguistics, see COMPETENCE.

performance anxiety apprehension and fear of the consequences of being unable to perform a task or of performing it at a level that will lead to expectations of higher levels of performance achievement. Fear of taking a test, public speaking, participating in classes or meetings, playing a musical instrument in public, and eating in public are common examples. If the fear associated with performance anxiety is focused on negative evaluation by others, embarrassment, or humiliation, the anxiety may be classified as a SOCIAL PHOBIA.

performance enhancing drug a substance taken inappropriately or illegally (i.e., without a prescription) to build muscle, boost stamina, and increase speed for the purpose of achieving a heightened level of performance in competitive sports or to improve concentration for the purpose of achieving better performance in activities requiring sustained attention (e.g., studying, taking tests, conducting research, long-haul truck driving). The substances most often identified as performance enhancing drugs are anabolic-androgenic steroids (for enhanced physical functioning) and stimulant medications such as Adderall and Ritalin (for enhanced mental functioning), the latter used off-label from their prescribed purpose in treating at-

tention-deficit/hyperactivity disorder and narcolepsy.

performance management a system for improving individual, work team, and organizational results. It relies on a continuous process that provides formal goal setting, timely and structured feedback, regular performance review, and opportunities for employee development and training.

performance test any test of ability requiring primarily motor, rather than verbal, responses, such as a test requiring manipulation of a variety of different objects.

periaqueductal gray (**PAG**) a region of the brainstem, rich in nerve cell bodies (i.e., gray matter), that surrounds the CEREBRAL AQUEDUCT. A component of the LIMBIC SYSTEM, it plays an important role in organizing defensive behaviors (e.g., freezing). Also called **central gray**.

perilymph *n.* the fluid that fills the space between the membranous LABYRINTH and the walls of the bony labyrinth in the inner ear. —**perilymphatic** *adj.*

perimenopause *n.* see CLIMACTERIC. —**perimenopausal** *adj.*

period effect any outcome associated with living during a particular time period or era, regardless of how old one was at the time. Period effects may be difficult to distinguish from AGE EFFECTS and COHORT EFFECTS in research.

peripheral dyslexia see VISUAL WORD-FORM DYSLEXIA.

peripheral nervous system (**PNS**) the portion of the nervous system that lies outside the brain and spinal cord—that is, all parts outside the CENTRAL NERVOUS SYSTEM. Afferent fibers of the PNS bring messages from the sense organs to the central nervous system; efferent fibers transmit messages from the central nervous system to the muscles and glands. The PNS includes the CRANIAL NERVES, SPINAL

NERVES, and parts of the AUTONOMIC NERVOUS SYSTEM.

peripheral route to persuasion the process by which attitudes are formed or changed as a result of using peripheral cues (factors external to the merits of the argument) rather than carefully scrutinizing and thinking about the central merits of attitude-relevant information. See also ELABORATION-LIKELIHOOD MODEL. Compare CENTRAL ROUTE TO PERSUASION.

perirhinal cortex a structure in the medial TEMPORAL LOBE adjacent to the hippocampus that plays an important role as an interface between visual perception and memory.

permanent vegetative state see VEGETATIVE STATE.

permastore n. long-term or permanent memory that develops after extensive learning, training, or experience. Details of foreign languages or algebra learned years ago in school, and even the names of classmates, are said to be retained in permastore.

permissiveness n. an interpersonal style or approach that involves giving a wide range of freedom and autonomy to those with whom one has dealings or over whom one has authority. For example, it refers to a particular parenting style in which the child is given wide latitude in expressing his or her feelings and opinions and in which artificial restrictions and punishment are avoided as much as possible. —**permissive** adj.

permissive parenting see PARENTING.

permutation n. an ordered arrangement of elements from a set. A permutation is similar to a COMBINATION but distinguished by its emphasis on order. For example, if there are three colored objects—red (R), white (W), and blue (B)—there are six possible permutations of these objects: RWB, RBW, WBR, WRB, BRW, and BWR.

perseverance effect the phenomenon in which people's beliefs about themselves and others persist despite a lack of supporting evidence or even a contradiction of supporting evidence.

perseveration n. **1.** an inability to interrupt a task or to shift from one strategy or procedure to another. Perseveration may be observed, for example, in workers under extreme task demands or environmental conditions; in the abnormal or inappropriate repetition of a sound, word, or phrase, as occurs in stuttering; or in the inappropriate repetition of behavior in individuals with frontal lobe damage. **2.** according to the PERSEVERATION–CONSOLIDATION HYPOTHESIS, the repetition, after a learning experience, of neural processes that are responsible for memory formation, which is necessary for the consolidation of LONG-TERM MEMORY. —**perseverate** vb.

perseveration–consolidation hypothesis the hypothesis that information passes through two stages in memory formation. During the first stage, the memory is held by perseveration (repetition) of neural activity and is easily disrupted. During the second stage, the memory becomes fixed, or consolidated, and is no longer easily disrupted. The perseveration–consolidation hypothesis guides much contemporary research on the biological basis of long-term learning and memory. See also DUAL TRACE HYPOTHESIS.

persistence n. **1.** continuance or repetition of a particular behavior, process, or activity despite cessation of the initiating stimulus. **2.** the quality or state of maintaining a course of action or keeping at a task and finishing it despite the obstacles (such as opposition or discouragement) or the effort involved. —**persistent** adj.

persistent depressive disorder see DYSTHYMIC DISORDER.

persistent noncognitive state see VEGETATIVE STATE.

persistent vegetative state (PVS)
see VEGETATIVE STATE.

persona *n.* in the approach of Swiss psychiatrist Carl Jung (1875–1961), the public face an individual presents to the outside world, in contrast to more deeply rooted and authentic personality characteristics. This sense has now passed into popular usage.

personal attribution see DISPOSITIONAL ATTRIBUTION.

personal construct one of the concepts by which an individual perceives, understands, predicts, and attempts to control the world. In some psychotherapeutic approaches, understanding a client's personal constructs is a central way for a therapist to help that person begin to change rigid or negative beliefs. See REPERTORY GRID.

personal disposition in the personality theory of U.S. psychologist Gordon W. Allport (1897–1967), any of a number of enduring characteristics that describe or determine an individual's behavior across a variety of situations and that are peculiar to and uniquely expressed by that individual. Personal dispositions are divided into three categories: Cardinal dispositions, such as a thirst for power, are the most pervasive and influence virtually every behavior of that person; central dispositions, such as friendliness, are less pervasive but nonetheless generally influential and easy to identify; and secondary dispositions, such as a tendency to keep a neat desk, are much more narrowly expressed and situation specific.

personal fable a belief in one's uniqueness and invulnerability, which is an expression of adolescent EGOCENTRISM and may extend further into the lifespan. Also called **invincibility fable**.

personal identity see IDENTITY.

personalism *n.* **1.** the philosophical position that human personality is the sole means through which reality can be understood or interpreted. The human being is seen as a unique living whole, irreducible in value or worth, who is striving toward goals and is at once self-contained yet open to the surrounding world. Personalism reorients the material of psychology around an experiencing individual as a systematic focal point. Thus, the findings of psychology can be organized only by reference to such a unique, living individual as the originator, carrier, and regulator of all psychological states and processes. This is a core position of the school of **personalistic psychology**. **2.** a tendency to believe that another person's actions are directed at oneself rather than being an expression of that individual's characteristics.

personality *n.* the enduring configuration of characteristics and behavior that comprises an individual's unique adjustment to life, including major traits, interests, drives, values, self-concept, abilities, and emotional patterns. Personality is generally viewed as a complex, dynamic integration or totality shaped by many forces, including hereditary and constitutional tendencies; physical maturation; early training; identification with significant individuals and groups; culturally conditioned values and roles; and critical experiences and relationships. Various theories explain the structure and development of personality in different ways, but all agree that personality helps determine behavior.

personality assessment the evaluation of such factors as intelligence, skills, interests, aptitudes, creative abilities, attitudes, and facets of psychological development by a variety of methods and techniques. These include (a) observational methods that use behavior sampling, interviews, and rating scales; (b) personality inventories, such as the MINNESOTA MULTIPHASIC PERSONALITY INVENTORY; and (c) projective techniques, such as the THEMATIC APPERCEPTION TEST. The uses of personality assessment are numerous, including in the clinical evaluation of children and adults; in educational and vocational counseling; in industry and other organizational settings; and in rehabilitation.

personality disorder (PD) any in a group of disorders involving pervasive patterns of perceiving, relating to, and thinking about the environment and the self that interfere with long-term functioning of the individual and are not limited to isolated episodes. Among the specific types are paranoid, schizoid, schizotypal, antisocial, borderline, histrionic, narcissistic, avoidant, dependent, and obsessive-compulsive. Each type has its own entry in the dictionary.

personality inventory a personality assessment device that usually consists of a series of statements covering various characteristics and behavioral patterns to which the participant responds by choosing among fixed answers, such as *true, false, always, often, seldom,* or *never,* as applied to himself or herself. The scoring of such tests is objective, and the results are interpreted according to standardized norms. An example is the MINNESOTA MULTIPHASIC PERSONALITY INVENTORY.

personality profile 1. a graphic presentation of results from psychological testing that provides a summary of a person's traits or other unique attributes and tendencies. For example, a profile of an individual's test results from the MINNESOTA MULTIPHASIC PERSONALITY INVENTORY would display his or her scores on measures of depression, hysteria, masculinity/femininity, paranoia, social introversion, and other attributes. **2.** a summary of traits and behavioral tendencies that are believed to be typical of a particular group or category of individuals (e.g., people employed in a particular profession).

personality psychology the branch of psychology that systematically investigates the nature and definition of personality as well as its

development, structure, trait constructs, dynamic processes, variations, and maladaptive forms (i.e., personality disorders). The field rests on a long history of theoretical formulation (e.g., trait theories, psychoanalytic theories, role theories, learning theories, type theories) that has aimed to synthesize cognitive, emotional, motivational, developmental, and social elements of human individuality into integrative frameworks for making sense of the individual human life. It has also developed numerous tests and assessments to measure and understand aspects of personality.

personality study the study of the dynamic structure of major trait constructs, of how traits affect actions and selection of social settings, and of the stability of traits throughout the lifespan. For example, a researcher might be interested in understanding how conscientiousness manifests itself from adolescence to late adulthood.

personality test any instrument used to help evaluate personality or measure personality traits. Personality tests may collect self-report data, in which participants answer questions about their personality or select items that describe themselves, or they may take the form of projective tests (see PROJECTIVE TECHNIQUE) to measure both the conscious and unconscious aspects of a participant's personality.

personality trait a relatively stable, consistent, and enduring internal characteristic that is inferred from a pattern of behaviors, attitudes, feelings, and habits in the individual. The study of personality traits can be useful in summarizing, predicting, and explaining an individual's conduct, and a variety of personality trait theories exist.

personal space an area of defended space around an individual. Personal space differs from other types of defended space (e.g., territory) by being a surrounding "bubble" that moves with the individual. Because human use of personal space varies among cultures, it must at least in part be a learned behavior.

personal unconscious in the ANALYTIC PSYCHOLOGY of Swiss psychiatrist Carl Jung (1875–1961), the portion of each individual's unconscious that contains the elements of his or her own experience as opposed to the COLLECTIVE UNCONSCIOUS, which contains the ARCHETYPES universal to humankind. The personal unconscious consists of everything subliminal, forgotten, and repressed in an individual's life.

person-centered therapy see CLIENT-CENTERED THERAPY.

personnel psychology the branch of INDUSTRIAL AND ORGANIZATIONAL PSYCHOLOGY that deals with the selection, placement, training, promotion, evaluation, and counseling of employees.

person perception the processes by which people think about, appraise, and evaluate other people. An important aspect of person perception is the attribution of motives for action (see ATTRIBUTION THEORY).

persuasion *n.* an active attempt by one person to change another person's attitudes, beliefs, or emotions associated with some issue, person, concept, or object. —**persuasive** *adj.*

pervasive developmental disorder any one of a class of disorders characterized by severe and widespread impairment in social interaction and verbal or nonverbal communication or by the presence of stereotyped behavior, interests, and activities. These disorders are frequently apparent from an early age; they include ASPERGER'S DISORDER, AUTISM, CHILDHOOD DISINTEGRATIVE DISORDER, and RETT SYNDROME. See AUTISM SPECTRUM DISORDER.

pessimism *n.* the attitude that things will go wrong and that people's wishes or aims are unlikely to be fulfilled. Most individuals lie somewhere on the spectrum between the two polar opposites

of pure OPTIMISM and pure pessimism but tend to demonstrate relatively stable situational tendencies in one direction or the other. —**pessimistic** *adj.*

petit mal seizure see ABSENCE SEIZURE.

phallic stage in the classical psychoanalytic theory of Austrian neurologist Sigmund Freud (1856–1939), the third stage of PSYCHOSEXUAL DEVELOPMENT beginning around age 3, when the LIBIDO is focused on the genital area (penis or clitoris) and discovery and manipulation of the body become a major source of pleasure. During this period, boys are posited to experience CASTRATION ANXIETY, girls to experience PENIS ENVY, and both to experience the OEDIPUS COMPLEX. Also called **phallic phase**.

phallus *n.* (*pl.* **phalli**) the penis or an object that resembles the form of the penis. As a symbolic object, the phallus often represents fertility or potency.

phantasy *n.* in the OBJECT RELATIONS THEORY of Austrian-born British psychoanalyst Melanie Klein (1882–1960), one of the unconscious constructions, wishes, or impulses that are presumed to underlie all thought and feeling. The *ph* spelling is used to distinguish this from the everyday form of FANTASY, which can include conscious daydreaming.

phantom limb the feeling that an amputated limb is still present, often manifested as tingling or pain in the area of the missing limb (**phantom limb pain**). It is thought that the brain's cortical representation of the limb remains intact and, in the absence of normal somesthetic stimulation, becomes active spontaneously or as a result of stimulation from other brain tissue.

pharmacological antagonism see ANTAGONIST.

pharmacology *n.* the branch of science that involves the study of substances that interact with living organisms to alter some biological process affecting the HOMEOSTASIS of an organism. Therapeutic (or medical) pharmacology deals with the administration of substances to correct a state of disease or to enhance well-being. —**pharmacological** or **pharmacologic** *adj.*

pharmacotherapy *n.* the treatment of a disorder by the administration of drugs, as opposed to such means as surgery, psychotherapy, or complementary and alternative methods. Also called **drug therapy**. See PSYCHOPHARMACO-THERAPY.

phase locking the tendency for a neural ACTION POTENTIAL to occur at a certain phase of a pure-tone (single-frequency) auditory stimulus. Phase locking underlies the ability to localize sounds based on interaural phase differences or interaural time differences (see BINAURAL CUE). Its role in monaural hearing is uncertain, but it has been proposed as a mechanism for the coding of pitch.

phase modulation see MODULA-TION.

phencyclidine *n.* see PCP.

phenomenal self the SELF as experienced by the individual at a given time. Only a small portion of self-knowledge is active in working memory or consciousness at any time. The same person might have a very different phenomenal self at different times, without any change in self-knowledge, simply because different views are brought into awareness by events.

phenomenal space the environment as experienced by an individual at a given time. The term refers not to objective reality but to personal and subjective reality, including everything within one's field of awareness. In the phenomenological personality theory of U.S. psychologist Carl Rogers (1902–1987), it is also known as the

phenomenological field. Also called **phenomenal field**.

phenomenology *n.* a movement in European philosophy initiated by German philosopher Edmund Husserl (1859–1938). In his writings of the 1910s and 1920s, Husserl argued for a new approach to human knowledge in which mental events should be studied and described in their own terms, rather than in terms of their relationship to events in the body or in the external world. However, phenomenology should be distinguished from introspection as it is concerned with the relationship between acts of consciousness and the objects of such acts. Husserl's approach proved widely influential in psychology, especially GESTALT PSYCHOLOGY and EXISTENTIAL PSYCHOLOGY. —**phenomenological** *adj.* —**phenomenologist** *n.*

phenomenon *n.* (*pl.* **phenomena**) an observable event or physical occurrence. In Greek philosophy, most notably that of Plato (c. 427–c. 347 BCE), phenomena are the sensible things that constitute the world of experience, as contrasted with the transcendent realities that are known only through reason. German philosopher Immanuel Kant (1724–1804) used the term *phenomena* to refer to things as they appear to the senses and are interpreted by the categories of human understanding. For Kant, knowledge of phenomena is the kind of knowledge available to human beings; in contrast, knowledge of *noumena*, or things in themselves, remains beyond human experience or reason. —**phenomenal** *adj.*

phenothiazine *n.* any of a group of chemically related compounds that are mostly used as ANTIPSYCHOTIC drugs, having been originally developed as such in the 1950s. It is commonly assumed that their therapeutic effects are produced by blockade of a particular type of dopamine receptor. They also block acetylcholine, histamine, and norepinephrine receptors. A variety of adverse side effects is associated with their use, including EXTRAPYRAMIDAL SYMPTOMS, TARDIVE DYSKINESIA, and sedation.

phenotype *n.* the observable characteristics of an individual, such as morphological or biochemical features and the presence or absence of a particular disease or condition. Phenotype is determined by the expression of the individual's GENOTYPE coupled with the effects of environmental factors (e.g., nutritional status, climate). —**phenotypic** *adj.*

phenylketonuria (**PKU**) *n.* an inherited metabolic disease marked by a deficiency of an enzyme (phenylalanine hydroxylase) needed to utilize the amino acid phenylalanine. Unless it is diagnosed in early infancy and treated by a restricted dietary intake of phenylalanine, phenylketonuria leads to severe intellectual disability and other nervous-system disorders.

pheromone *n.* a chemical signal that is released outside the body by members of a species and that influences the behavior of other members of the same species. For example, it may serve to attract a mate or to act as an alarm. The existence of true pheromones in humans is controversial, although scents (e.g., perfumes, body odors) may play a role in sexual attraction and arousal. Compare ALLOMONE.

phi coefficient (symbol: φ) a measure of association for two DICHOTOMOUS VARIABLES. For example, the phi coefficient could be used to examine the relationship between gender (male [0] and female [1]) and left- (0) or right-handedness (1). A table could be constructed to record the frequency of people with a 0 on both variables (i.e., left-handed males), a 1 on both variables (i.e., right-handed females), a 0 on the first variable and a 1 on the other (i.e., right-handed males), and vice versa (i.e., left-handed females). The pairs of responses on the variables could then be analyzed and a phi coeffi-

cient calculated to determine whether any relationship exists.

philosophy *n.* the intellectual discipline that uses careful reasoned argument to elucidate fundamental questions, notably those concerning the nature of reality (metaphysics), the nature of knowledge (EPISTEMOLOGY), and the nature of moral judgments (ETHICS). Psychology as a scientific discipline has its roots in the epistemological preoccupations of 18th- and 19th-century philosophy and continues to be influenced by philosophical ideas. —**philosopher** *n.* —**philosophical** *adj.*

phi phenomenon an illusion of APPARENT MOVEMENT seen when two lights flash on and off about 150 m apart. The light appears to move from one location to the other. The phi phenomenon is a form of beta movement.

phobia *n.* a persistent and irrational fear of a specific situation, object, or activity (e.g., heights, dogs, water, blood, driving, flying), which is consequently either strenuously avoided or endured with marked distress. See SPECIFIC PHOBIA. See also SOCIAL PHOBIA. —**phobic** *adj.*

phoneme *n.* a speech sound that plays a meaningful role in a language and cannot be analyzed into smaller meaningful sounds, conventionally indicated by slash symbols: /b/. In English, for example, /p/ and /b/ are phonemes because they distinguish between [pan] and [ban] and other such pairs. —**phonemic** *adj.*

phonemics *n.* the branch of linguistics concerned with the classification and analysis of the PHONEMES in a language. Whereas PHONETICS tries to characterize all possible sounds represented in human language, phonemics identifies which of the phonetic distinctions are considered meaningful within a given language.

phonetics *n.* the branch of linguistics that studies the physical properties of

P

speech sounds and the physiological means by which these are produced and perceived (placing the tongue or lip in contact with the teeth, directing the airstream against the hard palate, etc.).

phonological buffer see PHONO-LOGICAL LOOP.

phonological disorder a disorder characterized by failure to develop and consistently use speech sounds that are appropriate for the child's age. It most commonly involves misarticulation of the later acquired speech sounds, such as [l], [r], [s], [z], [ch], [sh], or [th], but it may also include substitution of sounds (e.g., [t] for [k]) or omission of sounds (e.g., final consonants).

phonological dyslexia a form of acquired DYSLEXIA characterized primarily by difficulties in reading pronounceable nonwords. Semantic errors are not seen in this type of dyslexia, a feature that distinguishes it from DEEP DYSLEXIA. See also SURFACE DYSLEXIA.

phonological loop a component in WORKING MEMORY that holds and manipulates auditory information over short intervals of time. For example, the effort of trying to remember a telephone number by repeating it over and over in the few moments before dialing would take place in the phonological loop. It comprises a **phonological store** or **phonological buffer** (or **acoustic** or **articulatory store**) within which memory traces fade after 2 seconds unless an **articulatory control process** (or **articulatory rehearsal system**) refreshes them by subvocal REHEARSAL. The phonological store thus "remembers" speech sounds in their temporal order, whereas the articulatory control process "repeats" the series of words on a loop to prevent them from decay. It has also been suggested that the phonological loop is important to reading comprehension and may function primarily as a language learning device, rather than as a mechanism for the memorization of familiar words. Also called **articulatory loop**.

phonology *n.* the branch of linguistics that studies the system of speech sounds in a language or in language generally. The term is less specific than either PHONEMICS or PHONETICS. —**phonological** *adj.*

phosphene *n.* a sensation of a light flash (as in "seeing stars") in the absence of actual light stimulation to the eye. It may occur with the eyes closed and can be caused by mechanical stimulation of the retina, by rubbing the eyes, or by direct stimulation of the visual cortex.

photographic memory exceptionally detailed and highly accurate recollection of information or visual experiences. Photographic memory is widely but mistakenly considered synonymous with an EIDETIC IMAGE.

photopigment *n.* a substance in a RETINAL ROD or RETINAL CONE that interacts with light to initiate a chemical cascade resulting in the conversion of light energy into an electrical signal. All rods contain the photopigment RHODOPSIN, whereas cones have one of three different photopigments (IO-DOPSINS), each with a different wavelength sensitivity.

photoreceptor *n.* a visual receptor: a RETINAL ROD or a RETINAL CONE.

phototherapy *n.* therapy that involves exposure to ultraviolet or infrared light. It is used for treating not only certain medical conditions (e.g., jaundice, psoriasis) but also depression and SEASONAL AFFECTIVE DISORDER.

phrase-structure grammar (**PSG**) a type of GENERATIVE GRAMMAR in which a system of **phrase-structure rules** is used to describe a sentence in terms of the grammatical structures that generate its form and define it as grammatical. The phrase-structure rules are usually set out in the form X→ Y + Z, in which the arrow is an instruction to reformulate ("rewrite") X

P

in terms of its immediate constituents (Y + Z). Formal phrase-structure analysis of this kind was developed by U.S. linguist Noam Chomsky (1928–), whose TRANSFORMATIONAL GENERATIVE GRAMMAR added an important new dimension by proposing that sentences have a DEEP STRUCTURE as well as the linear SURFACE STRUCTURE described in phrase-structure grammar and that the relationship between the two levels can be described through a system of transformational rules.

phrenology *n.* a theory of personality formulated in the 18th and 19th centuries by German physician Franz Josef Gall (1757–1828) and Austrian philosopher and anatomist Johann Kaspar Spurzheim (1776–1832). It stated that specific abilities or personality traits are represented by specific areas of the brain: The size of these brain areas determines the degree of the corresponding skill or trait. Proponents of the theory argued that the size of such locations could be indicated by bumps and hollows on the skull surface. See also PHYSIOGNOMY. —**phrenological** *adj.* —**phrenologist** *n.*

phylogeny *n.* **1.** the evolutionary origin and development of a particular group of organisms. Also called **phylogenesis**. Compare ONTOGENY. **2.** a diagram that shows genetic linkages between ancestors and descendants. Also called **phylogenetic tree**. —**phylogenetic** *adj.*

physical abuse deliberately aggressive or violent behavior by one person toward another that results in bodily injury. Physical abuse may involve such actions as punching, kicking, biting, choking, burning, shaking, and beating, which may at times be severe enough to result in permanent damage (e.g., TRAUMATIC BRAIN INJURY) or death. It is most frequently observed in relationships of trust, particularly between parents and children or between intimate partners. Individuals who experience physical abuse often feel helpless and isolated and are prone to

the subsequent development of numerous pathological conditions, including depression, eating disorders, posttraumatic stress disorder, anxiety disorders, and substance use problems. See also BATTERED-CHILD SYNDROME; BATTERED-WOMAN SYNDROME.

physical dependence the state of an individual who has repeatedly taken a drug and experiences unpleasant physiological symptoms (see SUBSTANCE WITHDRAWAL) if he or she discontinues its use. Also called **physiological dependence**. Compare PSYCHOLOGICAL DEPENDENCE.

physical therapy (PT) 1. the treatment of pain, injury, or disease using physical or mechanical methods, such as exercise, heat, water, massage, or electric current. The treatment is administered by a trained **physical therapist. 2.** a branch of medicine and health care that identifies, corrects, alleviates, and prevents temporary, prolonged, or permanent movement dysfunction or physical disability.

physician-assisted suicide see ASSISTED DEATH.

physiognomy *n.* **1.** the form of a person's physical features, especially the face. **2.** the attempt to read personality from facial features and expression, assuming, for example, that a person with a receding chin is weak or one with a high forehead is bright. The idea dates back to Greek philosopher Aristotle (383–322 BCE) and was later developed into a pseudoscientific system by Swiss pastor Johann Lavater (1741–1801) and by Italian criminologist and psychiatrist Cesare Lombroso (1835–1909). See also PHRENOLOGY.

physiological antagonism see ANTAGONIST.

physiological arousal aspects of AROUSAL shown by physiological responses, such as increases in blood pressure and rate of respiration and decreased activity of the gastrointestinal system. Such primary arousal responses are largely governed by the SYMPATHETIC NERVOUS SYSTEM, but responses of the PARASYMPATHETIC NERVOUS SYSTEM may compensate or even overcompensate for the sympathetic activity. See also AUTONOMIC NERVOUS SYSTEM.

physiological correlate an association between a physiological measure and a behavioral measure. The existence of a physiological correlate may suggest a causal relation, but it does not establish a cause.

physiological dependence see PHYSICAL DEPENDENCE.

physiological need any of the requirements for survival, such as food, water, oxygen, and sleep. Physiological needs make up the lowest level of MASLOW'S MOTIVATIONAL HIERARCHY. Also called **basic need**. Compare PSYCHOLOGICAL NEED.

physiological psychology a term used interchangeably with BIOLOGICAL PSYCHOLOGY or PSYCHOPHYSIOLOGY.

physiology *n.* **1.** the science of the functions of organisms, including the chemical and physical processes involved and the activities of the cells, tissues, and organs, as opposed to static anatomical or structural factors. **2.** the processes and functions characteristic of or identifiable in a particular organism. —**physiological** *adj.* —**physiologist** *n.*

Piagetian theory the proposal by Swiss child psychologist and epistemologist Jean Piaget (1896–1980) that cognitive development occurs in four major stages: (a) the SENSORIMOTOR STAGE (roughly 0–2 years of age), (b) the PREOPERATIONAL STAGE (roughly 2–7 years), (c) the CONCRETE OPERATIONAL STAGE (roughly 7–12 years), and (d) the FORMAL OPERATIONAL STAGE (roughly 12 years and beyond). Each stage builds on the preceding one, and passage through the stages is facilitated by a balance of two processes: **assimilation**, in which new informa-

tion is incorporated into already existing cognitive structures, and **accommodation**, in which already existing structures are changed to accommodate new information.

pia mater see MENINGES.

pica *n.* a rare eating disorder marked by a persistent craving for unnatural, nonnutritive substances, such as plaster, paint, hair, starch, or dirt. Although it can affect individuals at any age, onset of the disorder most commonly occurs in children, and it can have serious consequences, depending on the substance ingested. For example, lead pica, often found in children living in older housing with lead paint, can result in irreversible mental impairment.

Pick's disease a type of dementia marked by progressive degeneration of the frontal and temporal areas of the brain and by the presence of particles called **Pick bodies** in the cytoplasm of the neurons. The disease is characterized by personality changes and deterioration of social skills and complex thinking; symptoms include problems with new situations and abstractions, difficulty in concentrating, loss of memory, lack of spontaneity, gradual emotional dullness, loss of moral judgment, and disturbances of language. [described in 1892 by Arnold **Pick** (1851–1924), Czech psychiatrist and neuroanatomist]

pidgin *n.* an improvised contact language incorporating elements of two or more languages, often devised for purposes of basic commerce, such as trading. Pidgins are characterized by simple rules and limited vocabulary. Compare CREOLE.

pie chart a graphic display in which a circle is cut into wedges, with the area of each wedge being proportional to the percentage of cases in the category represented by that wedge. For example, a researcher might use a pie chart to present the results of a survey on the sources of psychology-related literature used by the general public, with each wedge representing the percentage of respondents citing a particular source, such as an advice column, the Internet, a self-help book, a popular magazine, and academic literature.

Pike's Peak model a competencies-based approach to training professionals in the delivery of psychological services to older adults. The model provides nonmandatory guidelines that allow individuals from the doctoral to the postlicensure level of training to obtain professional development in this domain.

piloerection *n.* a temporary raising of the hairs covering the surface of the skin caused by contraction of the pilo-erector muscles, which are attached to the individual FOLLICLES from which each hair arises. Piloerection is involuntary, being directed by the SYMPA-THETIC NERVOUS SYSTEM, and elicited by cold, fear, or a startling stimulus. In mammals with a thick, visible covering of hair (e.g., cats), piloerection serves a protective function, making an animal seem larger and deterring attack. In humans, whose skin has only a sparse covering of hair, piloerection creates a temporary roughness as the muscles pucker the surrounding skin, giving rise to such colloquial names for the effect as *goose bumps*, *goose flesh*, and *goose pimples*. Also called **pilomotor response**.

pilot study a small, preliminary study designed to evaluate procedures and measurements in preparation for a subsequent, more detailed research project. Although pilot studies are conducted to reveal information about the viability of a proposed project and to implement necessary modifications, they may also provide useful initial data on the topic of study and suggest avenues or offer implications for future research.

pineal gland a small, cone-shaped gland attached by a stalk to the posterior wall of the THIRD VENTRICLE of the brain; it is part of the EPITHALAMUS. In amphibians and reptiles, the gland appears to function as a part of the visual system. In mammals, it secretes the hormone MELATONIN and is an important component of the circadian system regulating BIOLOGICAL RHYTHMS. Also called **pineal body**.

pinna *n.* (*pl.* **pinnae**) the funnel-shaped part of the external ear that projects beyond the head. Consisting of cartilage, it collects and focuses sounds toward the EXTERNAL AUDITORY MEATUS (auditory canal). Also called **auricle**.

piriform area see PYRIFORM AREA.

pitch *n.* the subjective attribute that permits sounds to be ordered on a musical scale. One of the primary theories concerning the basis for pitch perception is the PLACE THEORY.

pituitary gland a gland, pea-sized in humans, that lies at the base of the brain and is connected by a stalk (the infundibulum) to the HYPOTHALAMUS. The anterior lobe produces and secretes seven hormones—thyroid-stimulating hormone, follicle-stimulating hormone, corticotropin, luteinizing hormone, growth hormone, prolactin, and mel-anocyte-stimulating hormone—in response to RELEASING HORMONES from the hypothalamus. The posterior lobe secretes two hormones, vasopressin and oxytocin, which are synthesized in the hypothalamus and transported down axons in the infundibulum. The pituitary's role in secreting such hormones, which regulate the production of other hormones, has resulted in its designation as the "master gland of the endocrine system."

placebo *n.* (*pl.* **placebos**) a pharmacologically inert substance, such as a sugar pill, that is often administered as a control in testing new drugs. Placebos used in double-BLIND trials may be dummies (which appear to be identical in all respects to the active drug under investigation) or active placebos (inert agents that may produce side effects characteristic of the drug under investigation). Formerly, placebos were occasionally used as diagnostic or psychotherapeutic agents, for example, in relieving pain or inducing sleep by suggestion, but the ethical implications of deceiving patients in this fashion makes the practice problematic. See PLACEBO EFFECT.

placebo control group a group of participants in a study who receive an inert substance (placebo) instead of the active drug under investigation, thus functioning as a CONTROL GROUP against which to make comparisons regarding the effects of the active drug.

placebo effect a clinically significant response to a therapeutically inert substance or nonspecific treatment (placebo), deriving from the recipient's expectations or beliefs regarding the intervention. It is now recognized that placebo effects accompany the administration of any drug (active or inert) and contribute to the therapeutic effectiveness of a specific treatment. For example, patients given a placebo to relieve headaches may report statistically significant reductions in headaches in studies that compare them with patients who receive no treatment at all.

place cell a neuron in the HIPPOCAMPUS that fires selectively when an animal is in a particular spatial location or moving toward that location.

placenta *n.* the specialized organ produced by the mammalian embryo that attaches to the wall of the uterus to permit removal of waste products and to provide nutrients, energy, and gas exchange for the fetus via the maternal circulation. —**placental** *adj.*

place theory the theory that (a) sounds of different frequencies stimulate different places along the BASILAR MEMBRANE and (b) pitch is coded by the place of maximal stimulation. The first proposition is strongly supported by experimental evidence and stems from the fact that the mammalian auditory system shows TONOTOPIC ORGANIZATION. The second hypothesis remains controversial.

planned comparison see A PRIORI COMPARISON.

planning fallacy the tendency to underestimate the amount of time needed to complete a future task, due in part to the reliance on overly optimistic performance scenarios.

plantar reflex the involuntary flexing of the toes of a healthy child when the sole of the foot is stroked. The plantar reflex appears around age 2 and replaces the earlier BABINSKI REFLEX.

planum temporale a region of the superior temporal cortex of the brain, adjacent to the primary AUDITORY CORTEX, that includes part of WERNICKE'S AREA. In most people, it is larger in the left cerebral hemisphere than in the right hemisphere.

plaque *n.* a small patch of abnormal tissue on or within a bodily structure, formed as the result of an accumulation of substances or as the result of localized damage. Examples of the former type include the AMYLOID PLAQUES of Alzheimer's disease, arising from clumps of beta-amyloid protein, and the atheromatous plaques of ATHEROSCLEROSIS, consisting of lipid deposits on the lining of arterial walls. Examples of the latter type include the demyelination plaques on the protective nerve sheaths of individuals with MULTIPLE SCLEROSIS.

plasticity *n.* flexibility and adaptability. Plasticity of the nervous or hormonal systems makes it possible to learn and register new experiences. Early experiences can also modify and shape gene expression to induce long-lasting changes in neurons or endocrine organs.

platykurtic *adj.* describing a distribution of scores that is flatter than a NORMAL DISTRIBUTION, having more scores at the extremes and fewer in the center. See also MESOKURTIC; LEPTOKURTIC.

play *n.* activities that appear to be freely sought and pursued solely for the sake of individual or group enjoyment. Play is a cultural universal and is typically regarded as an important mechanism in children's cognitive, social, and emotional development. Various types of play have been described—with LO-COMOTOR PLAY, OBJECT PLAY, and SO-CIAL PLAY generally considered to be the three basic forms—and numerous theories about the specific functions of play have been proposed, including that play prepares children for activities or roles they will encounter as adults; that it assists in establishing social relations among peers; or, simply, that it provides exercise and uses up excess energy. Other theories claim that play is a means for children to deal with anxiety-producing events; promotes cognitive competence by helping children incorporate new information into existing cognitive structures; and provides children with opportunities to establish meaning through symbolic action. Although the preponderance of research on play focuses on the activities of children, the play behavior of nonhuman animals is also actively studied; this likewise appears to serve several important developmental functions, such as enhancing confidence and strengthening sensorimotor systems.

play therapy the use of play activities and materials (e.g., clay, water, blocks, dolls, puppets, finger paint) in child psychotherapy. Play-therapy techniques are based on the theory that such activities mirror the child's emotional life and fantasies, enabling the child to "play out" feelings and problems and to test out new approaches and understand relationships in actions rather than words.

pleasure center any of various areas of the brain (including areas of the hypothalamus and limbic system) that, on intracranial self-stimulation (through direct application of electric current through implanted electrodes), have been implicated in producing pleasure. The existence of pure pleasure centers has not been definitively estab-

lished, particularly because the self-stimulation response rate varies according to such factors as the duration and strength of the electrical stimulation. Also called **reward center**.

pleasure principle the view that human beings are governed by the desire for gratification, or pleasure, and for the discharge of tension that builds up as pain or "unpleasure" when gratification is lacking. In classical psychoanalytic theory, it is the psychic force that motivates people to seek immediate gratification of instinctual, or libidinal, impulses, such as sex, hunger, thirst, and elimination. It dominates the ID and operates most strongly during childhood. Later, in adulthood, it is opposed by the REALITY PRINCIPLE of the EGO.

plethysmography n. the process of recording and measuring volume or volume changes in organs or body tissues, such as the blood supply flowing through an organ.

pluralistic ignorance the situation in which virtually every member of a group privately disagrees with what are considered to be the prevailing attitudes and beliefs of the group as a whole.

point biserial correlation coefficient (symbol: r_{pb}; r_{pbis}) a numerical index reflecting the degree of relationship between two random variables, one CONTINUOUS and one dichotomous (binary). An example is the association between the propensity to experience an emotion (measured using a scale) and gender (male or female). Also called **point biserial r**. Compare RANK BISERIAL CORRELATION COEFFICIENT.

point estimate a single estimated numerical value, determined from a sample, of a given population PARAMETER. Point estimates can often be tested for STATISTICAL SIGNIFICANCE if their STANDARD ERRORS are also known. Compare INTERVAL ESTIMATE.

point of subjective equality (PSE) the value of a comparison stimulus that, for a given observer, is equally likely to be judged as higher or lower than that of a standard stimulus.

Poisson regression an analytic model that has as its dependent variable a count variable and any of a number of predictor variables. For example, a researcher may hypothesize that dyadic adjustment, number of years as a couple, and personality characteristics predict the number of times that one member of a couple interrupts the other during a problem-solving task. [Siméon D. **Poisson** (1781–1840), French mathematician]

polarization *n.* a difference in electric potential between two surfaces or two sides of one surface because of chemical activity. Polarization occurs normally in living cells, such as neurons and muscle cells, which maintain a positive charge on one side of the plasma membrane and a negative charge on the other.

polyandry *n.* **1.** an animal mating system in which a female mates with more than one male but a male mates with only one female. Compare POLYGYNANDRY; POLYGYNY. **2.** marriage of a woman to more than one husband at the same time, which is an accepted custom in certain cultures. Compare MONOGAMY. See also POLYGAMY. —**polyandrous** *adj.*

polygamy *n.* marriage to more than one spouse at the same time, which is an accepted custom in certain cultures. See also BIGAMY. Compare MONOGAMY. —**polygamous** *adj.* —**polygamist** *n.*

polygenic *adj.* relating to two or more genes.

polygenic inheritance see MULTIFACTORIAL INHERITANCE.

polygenic trait an attribute that is determined by numerous genes rather than a single gene. An example is a person's height. Also called **polygenetic trait**. See MULTIFACTORIAL INHERITANCE.

polygraph *n.* a device that measures

and records several physiological indicators of stress, such as heart rate, blood pressure, and GALVANIC SKIN RESPONSE. The instrument has been widely used in the interrogation of criminal suspects and in employee screening to measure marked physiological reactions to questions about such issues as theft, sexual deviation, or untruthfulness. It has been colloquially referred to as a **lie detector**, although no one has ever documented a close relation between physiological patterns and deceptive behavior. The accuracy of polygraph examinations is controversial, and the results are not accepted as evidence in many U.S. courts of law.

polygynandry *n.* an animal mating system in which females mate with multiple males and males mate with multiple females. Compare MONOGAMY; POLYANDRY; POLYGYNY.

polygyny *n.* **1.** an animal mating system in which a male mates with more than one female but a female mates with only one male. Compare POLYANDRY; POLYGYNANDRY. **2.** marriage of a man to more than one wife at the same time, which is an accepted custom in certain cultures. Compare MONOGAMY. See also POLYGAMY. —**polygynous** *adj.*

polymorphism *n.* **1.** in biology, the condition of having multiple behavioral or physical types within a species or population. In some fish species, for example, there are two distinct sizes of males: Larger males defend territory and attract females to mate with them; smaller males, often with the physical appearance of females, stay close to the large male and inseminate some of the eggs. **2.** in genetics, the presence in a population of two or more variants of a gene (i.e., ALLELES) at a given genetic locus. For example, the variety of human blood groups is due to polymorphism of particular genes governing the characteristics of red blood cells. —**polymorphic** *adj.*

polymorphous perversity in the classical psychoanalytic theory of Austrian neurologist Sigmund Freud (1856–1939), the response of the human infant to many kinds of normal, everyday activities posited to provide sexual excitation, such as touching, smelling, sucking, rocking, defecating, and urinating.

polynomial regression a type of REGRESSION ANALYSIS in which the relationship between an explanatory or independent variable and an outcome or dependent variable is modeled as a polynomial, that is, as a mathematical expression consisting of multiple terms, each of which is the product of a constant (a) and a variable (x) raised to a whole number exponent. Polynomial regression is appropriate for expressing higher order NONLINEAR effects among variables while retaining all other aspects of linear approaches.

polypeptide *n.* a molecule consisting of numerous (usually more than 10–20) AMINO ACIDS linked by PEPTIDE bonds. Polypeptides are assembled by the cell into PROTEINS.

polysomnography *n.* the recording of various physiological processes (e.g., eye movements, brain waves, heart rate, respiration) throughout the night for the diagnosis of sleep-related disorders. —**polysomnograph** *n.*

pons *n.* a swelling on the ventral surface of the brainstem, between the MIDBRAIN and the MEDULLA OBLONGATA. It serves primarily as a bridge or transmission structure between different areas of the nervous system. It also works with the CEREBELLUM in controlling equilibrium and with the CEREBRAL CORTEX in smoothing and coordinating voluntary movements. —**pontine** *adj.*

Ponzo illusion a visual illusion in which the upper of two parallel horizontal lines of equal length appears to be longer than the bottom of the two lines when they are flanked by oblique lines that are closer together at the top than they are at the bottom. [Mario **Ponzo** (1882–1960), Italian psychologist]

pooled estimate a single estimated value for a population PARAMETER (e.g., a mean) obtained by averaging several independent estimates of that parameter.

pop-out *n.* in visual search tasks, a target that is different from the distractors (stimuli, or some aspect of them, that are irrelevant to the preformed task itself). One or more basic features will mark the pop-out as distinct from the other stimuli, hence allowing the target to be easily detected and identified regardless of the number of distractors.

population *n.* in statistics, a theoretically defined, complete group of objects (people, nonhuman animals, institutions) from which a SAMPLE is drawn to obtain empirical observations and to which results can be generalized.

population correlation coefficient (symbol: ρ) an index expressing the degree of association between two continuously measured variables for a complete POPULATION of interest. For example, a researcher could obtain income and education information for all families in a town and calculate a population correlation coefficient for the entire town. In contrast, the SAMPLE CORRELATION COEFFICIENT indexes the association for a specific subset of those cases (e.g., every fourth family from a list of all those in the town).

population mean (symbol: μ) the average (MEAN) value on a variable for a complete POPULATION of interest. In many research settings, this value is estimated using the SAMPLE MEAN, but in situations when information is known for all the units of interest, it can be calculated directly. For example, the mean household income for an entire town may be determined by averaging the responses from a survey returned by all of the households in the town.

population psychology a subfield of psychology that studies the relationships between the characteristics and dynamics of human populations and the attitudes and behavior of individuals and groups. Population psychology is particularly concerned with family planning and fertility regulation (i.e., reproductive behavior), high population density, and public policy development. Additional research topics include family formation and structure, migration, urbanization, mortality, and population education.

population variance (symbol: σ²) the square of the population STANDARD DEVIATION. It is a measure reflecting the spread (DISPERSION) of scores in a complete population of interest (e.g., the test scores of all students at a school). See also SAMPLE VARIANCE.

population vector the mechanism used in the MOTOR CORTEX to encode the direction of an intended movement. The activity in each neuron increases when the intended movement is close to its preferred direction. The direction of the intended movement is derived from the activity across the population of neurons.

positive affect the internal feeling state (AFFECT) that occurs when a goal has been attained, a source of threat has been avoided, or the individual is satisfied with the present state of affairs. The tendency to experience such states is called **positive affectivity**.

positive correlation a relationship between two variables in which both rise and fall together. For example, one would expect to find a positive correlation between study hours and test performance. Also called **direct correlation**. Compare NEGATIVE CORRELATION.

positive discrimination see REVERSE DISCRIMINATION.

positive feedback 1. an arrangement whereby some of the output of a system, whether mechanical or biological, is fed back to increase the effect of input signals. Positive feedback is rare in biological systems. **2.** acceptance, approval, affirmation, or praise received by a person in response to his or her performance. Compare NEGATIVE FEEDBACK.

positive–negative asymmetry the tendency of people to give disproportionate weight and consideration to negative information and events in decision making and perception. For example, voters are more inclined to reject a candidate on the basis of the negative information they receive about that person than they are inclined to accept a candidate on the basis of the positive information they receive.

positive psychology a field of psychological theory and research that focuses on the psychological states (e.g., contentment, joy), individual traits or CHARACTER STRENGTHS (e.g., integrity, altruism), and social institutions that enhance SUBJECTIVE WELL-BEING and make life most worth living. A manual, *Character Strengths and Virtues: A Handbook and Classification*, serves this perspective in a manner parallel to the *Diagnostic and Statistical Manual of Mental Disorders* for the categorization of mental illness.

positive punishment punishment that results because some stimulus or circumstance is presented as a consequence of a response. For example, if a response results in presentation of a loud noise and the response becomes less likely as a result of this experience, then positive punishment has occurred. Compare NEGATIVE PUNISHMENT.

positive regard feelings of warmth, caring, acceptance, and importance expressed by someone toward another. Positive regard is considered necessary for psychological health and the development of a consistent sense of self-worth and is also a cornerstone of certain therapeutic approaches, particularly that of U.S. psychologist Carl Rogers (1902–1987). See also CONDITIONAL POSITIVE REGARD; UNCONDITIONAL POSITIVE REGARD.

positive reinforcement an increase in the probability of occurrence of some activity because that activity results in the presentation of a stimulus or of some desired circumstance. Compare NEGATIVE REINFORCEMENT.

positive reward theory see REWARD THEORY.

positive schizophrenia a form of schizophrenia in which POSITIVE SYMPTOMS predominate, as evidenced in bizarre behavior, illogical speech or writing, or expression of hallucinations and delusions. Although more dramatically evident than NEGATIVE SCHIZOPHRENIA, the positive aspect is usually less challenging to treat.

positive skew see SKEWNESS.

positive symptom a symptom of schizophrenia that represents an excess or distortion of normal function, as distinct from a deficiency in or lack of normal function (compare NEGATIVE SYMPTOM). Positive symptoms include delusions or hallucinations, disorganized behavior, and manifest conceptual disorganization. They are more dramatic and less distinctive of schizophrenia than are negative symptoms.

positive transfer the improvement or enhancement of present learning by previous learning. For instance, learning to drive a car could facilitate learning to drive a truck. See also TRANSFER OF TRAINING. Compare NEGATIVE TRANSFER.

positivism n. a family of philosophical positions holding that all meaningful propositions must be reducible to sensory experience and observation and thus that all genuine knowledge is to be built on strict adherence to empirical methods. Its effect is to establish science as the model for all forms of valid inquiry and to dismiss the truth claims of religion, metaphysics, and speculative philosophy. Positivism was extremely influential in the early development of psychology and continues to be a major force in contemporary psychology. —**positivist** adj.

positivity effect an increasing tendency for older adults, compared to younger people, to attend to, recall, and process positive information to a greater degree than they do negative information.

positron emission tomography (**PET**) an imaging technique using radiolabeled tracers—such as 2-deoxyglucose labeled with fluorine-18—that emit positively charged particles (**positrons**) as they are metabolized. This technique enables documentation of functional changes that occur during the performance of mental activities. It is also used to detect damage or disease (e.g., cancer) in other organs of the body.

possible self a mental representation of what one could become. Possible selves are cognitive manifestations of enduring goals, aspirations, fears, and threats that provide plans and strategies for the future. They may be positive, providing an image of something to strive for, or negative, providing an image of something to be avoided.

postcentral gyrus a ridge in the PARIETAL LOBE of the brain, just behind the CENTRAL SULCUS, that is the site of the PRIMARY SOMATOSENSORY AREA.

postcolonialism n. the multidisciplinary (e.g., historical, linguistic, political, philosophical) study or analysis of the experience and the local and global effects of colonization. Whereas historical **colonialism** emphasized the differences between the colonizers and the colonized, usually marginalizing the latter, postcolonialism represents an attempt to bring the two cultures together, such as when indigenous writers of previously colonized lands explain aspects and values of their traditional cultural identity in the language of the colonizers.

postconventional level in KOHLBERG'S THEORY OF MORAL DEVELOPMENT, the third and highest level of moral reasoning, characterized by an individual's commitment to moral principles sustained independently of any identification with family, group, or country. Also called **postconventional morality**. See also CONVENTIONAL LEVEL; PRECONVENTIONAL LEVEL.

posterior *adj.* in back of or toward the back. In reference to two-legged upright animals, this term sometimes is used interchangeably with DORSAL to mean toward the back surface of the body. Compare ANTERIOR.

posterior cingulate cortex (PCC) the back, more flattened part of the CINGULATE CORTEX, a structure in the forebrain that forms a collar around the CORPUS CALLOSUM. Like the ANTERIOR CINGULATE CORTEX, the PCC also is divided into two sections, referred to as the **dorsal posterior cingulate cortex** and the **ventral posterior cingulate cortex**, respectively. The PCC has been shown to play a role in numerous processes, including EPISODIC MEMORY, SPATIAL ATTENTION, PREATTENTIVE PROCESSING, sensory integration, motor intention, emotional responses, and self-reflection and other self-referential processing. Additionally, it is a key component of the LIMBIC SYSTEM. Structural and functional alterations of the PCC appear to underlie several disorders, including Alzheimer's disease, autism, depression, dyslexia, and schizophrenia.

posterior commissure see COMMISSURE.

postformal thought adult cognition that includes an understanding of the relative, nonabsolute nature of knowledge; an acceptance of contradiction as a basic aspect of reality; the ability to synthesize contradictory thoughts, feelings, and experiences into more coherent, all-encompassing wholes; and the ability to resolve both ill- and well-defined problems.

post hoc comparison any examination in which two or more quantities are compared after data have been collected and without prior plans to carry out the particular comparison. For example, after obtaining a significant F RATIO for a data set, a researcher may perform post hoc comparisons to follow up on and help explain the initial findings. Different statistical tests are required for post hoc comparisons than for A PRIORI COMPARISONS. Also called **a posteriori comparison**; **unplanned comparison** (or **contrast**).

post hoc test a statistical procedure conducted on the basis of the findings obtained from previous analyses. Most commonly, the phrase refers to comparisons of the mean values obtained on a variable by different study groups, with these comparisons made only after an overall ANALYSIS OF VARIANCE has revealed a significant F RATIO, indicating that there is some effect or difference across the groups that should be examined further.

posthypnotic amnesia an individual's inability to remember what transpired during a period of hypnosis. Typically, this is induced by instruction of the hypnotist.

posthypnotic suggestion a suggestion made to a person during hypnosis that he or she acts out after the hypnotic trance. The suggested act may be carried out in response to a prearranged cue, and the person may not know why he or she is performing the action.

postmodernism *n.* a number of related philosophical tendencies that developed in reaction to classical MODERNISM during the late 20th century. They see the ideal of objective truth that has been a guiding principle in the sciences and most other disciplines since the 17th century as basically flawed: There can be no such truth, only a plurality of "narratives" and "perspectives." Postmodernism emphasizes the construction of knowledge and truth through discourse and lived experience, the similar construction of the self, and RELATIVISM in all questions of value. See also POSTSTRUCTURALISM. **—postmodern** *adj.*

postpartum depression a MAJOR DEPRESSIVE EPISODE or, less commonly, a similar but less serious mood disorder, that affects some women within 4 weeks to 6 months after childbirth.

poststructuralism *n.* a broad intellectual movement that developed from French STRUCTURALISM in the late 1960s and 1970s. It is rooted in the structuralist account of language given by Swiss linguist Ferdinand de Saussure (1857–1913), which holds that linguistic SIGNS acquire meaning only through structural relationships with other signs in the same language system. Poststructuralism endorses the arbitrariness of the sign but proceeds to question the whole idea of fixed and determinate meaning, and ultimately the idea of personal identity itself. In psychology, poststructuralism is mainly significant because of its influence on the radical psychoanalytical theories of the 1960s and 1970s. For example, Jacques Lacan (1901–1981), who trained and practiced as a psychiatrist and psychoanalyst, rejected the idea of a stable autonomous EGO and reinterpreted the Freudian UNCONSCIOUS in terms of Saussure's structural linguistics. —**poststructuralist** *adj.*

postsynaptic potential (**PSP**) the electric potential at a dendrite or other surface of a neuron after an impulse has reached it across a SYNAPSE. Postsynaptic potentials may be either EXCITATORY POSTSYNAPTIC POTENTIALS or INHIBITORY POSTSYNAPTIC POTENTIALS.

posttest an assessment carried out after the application of some intervention, treatment, or other condition to measure any changes that have occurred. Posttests often are used in research contexts, in conjunction with PRETESTS, to isolate the effects of a variable of interest. For example, in a study examining whether a new therapy helps to alleviate depression, participants might receive the therapy and then complete a short symptom inventory, the results of which would be compared to those from an inventory taken prior to the treatment.

posttraumatic amnesia (**PTA**) a disturbance of memory following a physical injury (e.g., a concussion) or a psychologically upsetting experience (e.g., combat, sexual abuse). The traumatic event itself, or events following the trauma, may be forgotten. The period of forgetting may be continuous, or the person may experience vague, incomplete recollections of the traumatic event.

posttraumatic growth the positive psychological, and sometimes physiological, improvements that can accompany or result from direct engagement with profoundly challenging situations and life crises.

posttraumatic stress disorder (**PTSD**) a disorder that may result when an individual lives through or witnesses an event in which there is a threat to life or physical integrity and safety and experiences fear, terror, or helplessness. The symptoms are characterized by (a) reexperiencing the trauma in painful recollections, flashbacks, or recurrent dreams or nightmares; (b) avoidance of activities or places that recall the traumatic event, as well as diminished responsiveness (emotional numbing), with disinterest in significant activities and with feelings of detachment and estrangement from others; and (c) chronic physiological arousal, leading to such symptoms as an exaggerated startle response, disturbed sleep, difficulty in concentrating or remembering, and guilt about surviving the trauma when others did not (see SURVIVOR GUILT). More recently, it has been posited that exposure to the traumatic event may be secondhand if the event happens to a loved one or if there is repeated exposure to aversive details (e.g., as with first responders performing their work in the case of a disaster).

posture *n.* the position or bearing of

the body. Types of posture include *erect* (upright), *recumbent* (reclining), *prone* (lying face down), and *supine* (lying face up). Movement typically involves coordinated changes in posture (e.g., to maintain balance or distribute forces). —**postural** *adj.*

potency *n.* **1.** the ability of a male to perform sexual intercourse, that is, to maintain an erection and achieve ejaculation. Compare IMPOTENCE. **2.** in pharmacology, see DOSE–RESPONSE RELATIONSHIP. —**potent** *adj.*

potential *n.* **1.** the capacity to develop or come into existence. **2.** a property of an electric field equal to the energy needed to bring one unit of electric charge from infinity to a given point. Because messages in the nervous system are conveyed by electrochemical potentials, many kinds of potential are of importance in neuroscience and biological psychology, including the ACTION POTENTIAL, GRADED POTENTIAL, MEMBRANE POTENTIAL, POSTSYNAPTIC POTENTIAL, and RESTING POTENTIAL.

power *n.* **1.** the capacity to influence others, even when they try to resist this influence. Social power derives from a number of sources: control over rewards and punishments; a right to require and demand obedience; respect for the powerholder; others' belief that the powerholder possesses superior skills and abilities; and the powerholder's access to and use of informational resources. **2.** a measure of how effective a statistical procedure is at identifying real differences between populations: It is the probability that use of the procedure will lead to the NULL HYPOTHESIS of no effect being rejected when the ALTERNATIVE HYPOTHESIS is true. For example, if a given statistical test has a power of .70, then there is a 70% probability that its use will result in the null hypothesis correctly being rejected as false, with a corresponding 30% chance that its use will lead to a TYPE II ERROR.

power law see STEVENS LAW.

power of the situation a basic premise of social psychology that assumes people's thoughts, actions, and emotions are influenced substantially by the social setting. For example, the responses of participants in the BEHAVIORAL STUDY OF OBEDIENCE are attributed to the power of the social situation created by the researcher rather than to the dispositional characteristics of the participants. See also STANFORD PRISON STUDY.

power test a type of test intended to calculate the participant's level of mastery of a particular topic under conditions of little or no time pressure. Test items become progressively more difficult. Compare SPEED TEST.

practical intelligence the ability to apply one's intelligence in practical, everyday situations. In the TRIARCHIC THEORY OF INTELLIGENCE, it is the aspect of intelligence that requires adaptation to, shaping of, and selection of new environments. Compare ANALYTICAL INTELLIGENCE; CREATIVE INTELLIGENCE.

practical significance the extent to which a study result has meaningful applications in real-world settings. An experimental result may lack STATISTICAL SIGNIFICANCE or show a small EFFECT SIZE yet potentially be important. For example, consider a study showing that the consumption of baby aspirin helps prevent heart attacks: Even if the effect is small, the finding may be of practical significance if it saves lives over time. Also called **substantive significance**. See also CLINICAL SIGNIFICANCE.

practice effect any change or improvement that results from practice or repetition of task items or activities. The practice effect is of particular concern in experimentation involving WITHIN-SUBJECTS DESIGNS, because participants' performance on the variable of interest may improve simply from repeating the activity rather than from any study manipulation imposed by the researcher.

practicum *n.* supervised clinical experience offered as part of a course of study for the purpose of on-site, in-person professional training. Practicums may occur in inpatient, correctional, or residential settings or in outpatient settings such as private practices, mental health centers, and social service agencies.

pragmatics *n.* in linguistics, the analysis of language in terms of its functional communicative properties (rather than its formal and structural properties, as in PHONOLOGY, SEMANTICS, and GRAMMAR) and in terms of the intentions and perspectives of its users.

pragmatism *n.* a philosophical position holding that the truth value of a proposition or a theory is to be found in its practical consequences: If, for example, the hypothesis of God makes people virtuous and happy, then it may be considered true. Although some forms of pragmatism emphasize only the material consequences of an idea, more sophisticated positions recognize conceptual and moral consequences. Arguably, all forms of pragmatism tend toward RELATIVISM, because they can provide no absolute grounds—only empirical grounds—for determining truth, and no basis for judging whether the consequences in question are to be considered good or bad. See also INSTRUMENTALISM. **—pragmatist** *adj., n.*

Prägnanz *n.* one of the GESTALT PRINCIPLES OF ORGANIZATION. It states that people tend to perceive forms as the simplest and most meaningful, stable, and complete structures that conditions permit. Also called **law** (or **principle**) **of Prägnanz**. [German: "terseness"]

praxis *n.* **1.** a medical name for motor planning, or the brain's ability to conceive, organize, and carry out a sequence of actions. Inadequate praxis is APRAXIA. **2.** practice, as opposed to theory. The term is sometimes used to denote knowledge derived from and expressed chiefly in practical or productive activity, as opposed to theoretical or conceptual knowledge.

preafference *n.* a central brain process in which the SOMATOSENSORY AREA is primed to expect the particular sensory inputs (sights, sounds, etc.) that are predicted as the consequence of an intended motor action. It is the means by which, for example, a person turning his or her head understands immediately that the motion perceived is in the body and not in the external world. Preafference has also been proposed as a neural basis for what is experienced subjectively as ATTENTION.

preattentive processing cognitive processing of a stimulus that occurs nonconsciously before attention has focused on this particular stimulus from among the array of those present in a given environment. An example of this is the disambiguation of a particular word from among an array of printed words before conscious understanding of the word's meaning. See also PARALLEL PROCESSING.

precentral gyrus a ridge in the FRONTAL LOBE of the brain, just in front of the CENTRAL SULCUS, that is crucial for motor control, being part of the MOTOR CORTEX.

precipitating cause the particular factor, sometimes a traumatic or stressful experience, that is the immediate cause of a mental or physical disorder. Compare PREDISPOSING CAUSE.

precision *n.* a measure of accuracy. In statistics, an estimate with a small STANDARD ERROR is regarded as having a high degree of precision. **—precise** *adj.*

precognition *n.* in parapsychology, the purported ability to see or experience future events through some form of EXTRASENSORY PERCEPTION. In a test of precognition, the participant would be asked to predict the outcome of a future set of trials involving ZENER CARDS or similar stimulus materials. **—pre-cognitive** *adj.*

preconscious (**Pcs**) **1.** *adj.* denoting or relating to unattended mental contents that can be readily accessed and brought to awareness. **2.** *n.* in the classical psychoanalytic theory of Austrian neurologist Sigmund Freud (1856–1939), the level of the psyche that contains thoughts, feelings, and impulses not presently in awareness but that can be more or less readily called into consciousness. Examples are the face of a friend, a verbal cliché, or the memory of a recent event. Compare CONSCIOUS; SUBCONSCIOUS; UNCONSCIOUS.

preconventional level in KOHL-BERG'S THEORY OF MORAL DEVELOPMENT, the first level of moral reasoning, characterized by the child's evaluation of actions in terms of material consequences. Also called **preconventional morality**. See also CONVENTIONAL LEVEL; POSTCONVENTIONAL LEVEL.

prediction *n.* an attempt to foretell what will happen in a particular case, generally on the basis of past instances or accepted principles. In science, the use of prediction and observation to test hypotheses is a cornerstone of the empirical method (see FALSIFIABILITY). By their very nature, however, the theories, constructs, and explanatory models current in psychology are not always open to direct validation or falsification in this way. **—predict** *vb.* **—predictable** *adj.* **—predictive** *adj.*

predictive research the assessment of variables at one point in time so as to predict a phenomenon assessed at a later point in time. For example, a researcher might collect high school data, such as grades, extracurricular activities, teacher evaluations, advanced courses taken, and standardized test scores, in order to predict such college success measures as grade point average at graduation, awards received, and likelihood of pursuing further education.

predictive validity evidence that a test score or other measurement correlates with a variable that can only be assessed at some point after the test has been administered or the measurement made. For example, the predictive validity of a test designed to predict the onset of a disease would be strong if high test scores were associated with individuals who later developed that disease. It is one of three types of CRITERION VALIDITY. Also called **prospective validity**.

predictor variable a variable used to estimate, forecast, or project future events or circumstances. In personnel selection, for example, predictors such as qualifications, relevant work experience, and job-specific skills may be used to estimate an applicant's future job performance. In REGRESSION ANALYSIS and other models, predictor variables are investigated to assess the strength and direction of their association with an outcome or DEPENDENT VARIABLE. This term sometimes is used interchangeably with INDEPENDENT VARIABLE.

predisposing cause a factor that increases the probability that a mental or physical disorder or hereditary characteristic will develop but that is not the immediate cause of it. Compare PRECIPITATING CAUSE.

predisposition *n.* a susceptibility to developing a disorder or disease, the actual development of which may be initiated by the interaction of certain biological (e.g., genetic), psychological, or environmental factors.

preferential looking technique a method for assessing the perceptual capabilities of human infants and nonhuman animals. Infants will preferentially fixate a "more interesting" stimulus when it is presented at the same time with a "less interesting" stimulus, but only if the stimuli can be distinguished from one another. To minimize bias, on each trial the investigator is positioned so that he or she can observe the infant and make a judgment about which stimulus the infant fixates, but the stimuli themselves are visible only to the infant.

prefrontal cortex the most anterior (forward) part of the cerebral cortex of each frontal lobe in the brain. It functions in attention, planning, working memory, and the expression of emotions and appropriate social behaviors; its development in humans parallels improvement in cognitive control and behavioral inhibition as an individual grows into adulthood. Damage to the prefrontal cortex leads to emotional, motor, and cognitive impairments.

prefrontal lobe the furthest forward area of each CEREBRAL HEMISPHERE of the brain, which is concerned with such functions as memory and learning, emotion, and social behavior. See also FRONTAL LOBE.

prefrontal lobotomy see LOBOTOMY.

prejudice *n*. **1.** a negative attitude toward another person or group formed in advance of any experience with that person or group. Prejudices include an emotional component (ranging from mild nervousness to hatred), a cognitive component (assumptions and beliefs about groups, including STEREOTYPES), and a behavioral component (negative behaviors, including DISCRIMINATION and violence). They tend to be resistant to change because they distort the individual's perception of information pertaining to the group. Prejudice based on racial grouping is RACISM; prejudice based on sex is SEXISM; prejudice based on chronological age is AGEISM; and prejudice based on disability is ABLEISM. **2.** any preconceived attitude or view, whether favorable or unfavorable.

prelinguistic *adj*. denoting or relating to the period of an infant's life before he or she has acquired the power of speech. The **prelinguistic period** includes the earliest infant vocalizations as well as the babbling stage typical of

the second half of the first year. HOLO-PHRASES usually emerge around the time of the child's first birthday.

Premack's principle the view that the opportunity to engage in behavior with a relatively high baseline probability will reinforce behavior of lower baseline probability. For example, a hungry rat may have a high probability of eating but a lower probability of pressing a lever. Making the opportunity to eat depend on pressing the lever will result in reinforcement of lever pressing. Also called **Premack's rule**. [David **Premack** (1925–2015), U.S. psychologist]

premature ejaculation a sexual dysfunction in which male ORGASM occurs with minimal sexual stimulation, before, on, or shortly after penetration or simply earlier than desired. The diagnosis takes into account such factors as age, novelty of the sexual partner, and the frequency and duration of intercourse.

prematurity *n*. a state of underdevelopment, particularly in an infant born before it has completed the full gestational period of a normal pregnancy.

premenstrual dysphoric disorder a MOOD DISORDER in women that begins in the week prior to the onset of menstruation and subsides within the first few days of menstruation. Women experience markedly depressed mood, anxiety, feelings of helplessness, and decreased interest in activities. In contrast to PREMENSTRUAL SYNDROME, the symptoms must be severe enough to impair functioning in social activities, work, and relationships.

premenstrual syndrome (PMS) a collection of psychological and physical symptoms experienced by women during the week prior to the onset of menstruation and subsiding within the first few days of menstruation. Symptoms can include mood swings, irritability, fatigue, headache, bloating, abdominal discomfort, and breast tenderness. In contrast to the more severe PREMENSTRUAL DYSPHORIC DISORDER, premenstrual syndrome has a less distinctive pattern of symptoms and does not involve major impairment in social and occupational functioning.

premise *n.* a proposition forming part of a larger argument: a statement from which a further statement is to be deduced, especially as one of a series of such steps leading to a conclusion.

premoral stage 1. in the theory of moral development proposed by Swiss child psychologist and epistemologist Jean Piaget (1896–1980), the stage at which children under the age of 5 are unaware of rules as cooperative agreements; that is, they are unable to distinguish right from wrong. Compare AUTONOMOUS STAGE; HETERONOMOUS STAGE. **2.** the stage that precedes the PRECONVENTIONAL LEVEL in KOHLBERG'S THEORY OF MORAL DEVELOPMENT and corresponds to infancy (birth to roughly 18 months).

premorbid *adj.* characterizing an individual's condition before the onset of some disease or disorder. —**premorbidity** *n.*

premorbid functioning an individual's cognitive functioning prior to a neurological trauma or disease, as estimated to determine the degree of loss or impairment caused by the damage. This estimate is based on testing and assessments conducted after the damage has occurred; it may include consideration of such factors as educational level, occupational history, and individual and family reports. Also called **baseline functioning**.

premotor area an area of the MOTOR CORTEX concerned with motor planning, or the ability to conceive, organize, and carry out a sequence of actions. In contrast to the SUPPLEMENTARY MOTOR AREA, input to the premotor area is primarily visual, and its activity is usually triggered by external events. Also called **premotor cortex**.

prenatal *adj.* prior to birth: pertaining to that which exists or occurs between conception and birth.

preoccupation *n.* a state of being self-absorbed and "lost in thought," which ranges from transient absentmindedness to a symptom of mental disorder, as when an individual with schizophrenia withdraws from external reality and turns inward on the self.

preoccupied attachment an adult attachment style that combines a negative INTERNAL WORKING MODEL OF ATTACHMENT of oneself, characterized by doubt in one's own competence and efficacy, and a positive internal working model of attachment of others, characterized by one's trust in the ability and dependability of others. Compare DISMISSIVE ATTACHMENT; FEARFUL ATTACHMENT; SECURE ATTACHMENT.

preoperational stage the second major period in the PIAGETIAN THEORY of cognitive development, approximately between the ages of 2 and 7, when the child becomes able to record experience in a symbolic fashion and to represent an object, event, or feeling in speech, movement, drawing, and the like. The child's thought processes tend to be intuitive and prelogical, and egocentrism diminishes noticeably with the emerging ability to adopt the point of view of others. See also CONCRETE OPERATIONAL STAGE; FORMAL OPERATIONAL STAGE; SENSORIMOTOR STAGE.

preoptic area a region of the HYPOTHALAMUS lying above and slightly anterior to the OPTIC CHIASM. Nuclei here are involved in temperature regulation and in the release of hypothalamic hormones.

preparedness *n.* the biological predisposition to learn associations between certain stimuli, responses, and reinforcers quickly because of their fit with genetic traits that evolved to enhance the chances of a species' survival. For example, it has been suggested that humans readily learn certain phobias (e.g., fear of snakes) because of a predisposition to fear anything that could pose a threat to their survival. Preparedness (or **prepared learning**) also has been proposed as an explanation for why both human and nonhuman animals readily learn to associate certain foods with gastric illness and are more likely to avoid such foods in the future (see CONDITIONED TASTE AVERSION).

pre–post design see PRETEST–POST-TEST DESIGN.

presbycusis *n.* the gradual diminution of hearing acuity associated with aging.

presbyopia *n.* a normal, age-related change in vision due to decreased lens elasticity and accommodative ability, resulting in reduced ability to focus vision on near tasks (e.g., reading).

prescribing information (**PI**) see LABELING.

prescribing psychology an area of clinical psychology in which licensed, appropriately trained practitioners are legally authorized to prescribe medications for the treatment of emotional and mental disorders. In addition to fulfilling all other requirements required for professional licensure as a practicing clinician, **prescribing psychologists** must complete a postdoctoral psychopharmacology training program and pass a national certification exam. In the United States, only New Mexico, Louisiana, and Illinois permit this specialty practice.

prescription drug a medication that can be legally acquired only from a pharmacy and only on the basis of a written, faxed, telephoned, or electronically submitted order (the **prescription**, **scrip**, or **script**) from a physician.

presenile dementia see DEMENTIA.

presenteeism *n.* coming to work when one is ill, injured, or otherwise unable to function at full capacity on the job. The resulting reduction in productivity is a growing financial and

safety concern for employers, particularly since research suggests presenteeism is more prevalent and damaging than ABSENTEEISM. Factors that drive presenteeism include a large workload, fear of missing deadlines, fear of disciplinary action or job loss, missed pay, the desire to conserve leave for future use, loyalty to coworkers or company, and JOB SATISFACTION.

presenting symptom a problem that is offered by a client or a patient as the reason for seeking treatment. In psychotherapy, for example, a client may present with such issues as depression, anxiety, anger, or family or marital problems, and these may become the focus of treatment or may represent a different, underlying problem that is not recognized or regarded by the client as requiring help.

pressure *n.* excessive or stressful demands, imagined or real, made on an individual to think, feel, or act in particular ways. The experience of pressure is often the source of cognitive and affective discomfort or disorder, as well as of maladaptive coping strategies, the correction of which may be a mediate or end goal in psychotherapy.

prestriate cortex visually responsive regions in the cerebral cortex outside the STRIATE CORTEX. On the basis of function and connectivity, the prestriate cortex has been divided into multiple VISUAL AREAS. Also called **extrastriate cortex**; **prestriate area**.

pretest *n.* **1.** an initial assessment designed to measure existing characteristics (e.g., knowledge, ability) before some intervention, condition, or treatment is introduced. Pretests often are given to research participants before they take part in a study. For example, in a study examining whether training helps math performance, participants might be administered a short math test to assess their knowledge prior to undergoing the training. See also POST-TEST. **2.** a test administered before the main study to ensure that participants understand the instructions and procedures.

pretest–posttest design a research design in which the same assessment measures are given to participants before and after they have received a treatment or been exposed to a condition, in order to determine if there are any changes that could be attributed to the treatment or condition. Also called **before–after design**; **pre-post design**.

pretraumatic stress disorder a condition characterized by prolonged, significant anxiety about a potential threatening or otherwise devastating event, such as a terrorist attack or wartime violence. The individual remains in a constant state of worry and heightened stress at his or her perceived helplessness to prevent the expected future trauma and often mentally experiences the dreaded event again and again. The resulting symptoms (e.g., uncertainty, irritability, concentration difficulties, insomnia, appetite disturbances) are so intense as to affect daily functioning negatively.

prevalence *n.* the total number or percentage of cases (e.g., of a disease or disorder) existing in a population, either at a given point in time (point prevalence) or during a specified period (period prevalence). For example, health researchers may want to investigate the prevalence of a new disease in an area, whereas education researchers may be interested in the prevalence of bullying or cheating among students of a certain age group. See also INCIDENCE.

prevention *n.* behavioral, biological, or social interventions intended to reduce the risk of disorders, diseases, or social problems for both individuals and entire populations. See PRIMARY PREVENTION; SECONDARY PREVENTION; TERTIARY PREVENTION.

preventive coping a stress-management strategy in which one prepares for possible events in the long term by building up resources to help minimize the severity of their impact. Examples of such events that may or may not occur in the distant future include job loss, forced retirement, crime, illness, or poverty. Preventive coping is not born out of an acute stress situation but rather from reasonable concern about the inherent hazards of daily living. See also PROACTIVE COPING.

pride *n.* a SELF-CONSCIOUS EMOTION that occurs when a goal has been attained and one's achievement has been recognized and approved by others. It differs from JOY and HAPPINESS in that these emotions do not require the approval of others to be experienced. Pride can also become antisocial if the sense of accomplishment is not deserved or the reaction is excessive. —**proud** *adj.*

primacy effect the tendency for facts, impressions, or items that are presented first to be learned or remembered better than material presented later in the sequence. This can occur in both formal learning situations and social contexts. For example, it can result in a **first-impression bias**, in which the first information gained about a person has an inordinate influence on later impressions and evaluations of that person. Compare RECENCY EFFECT.

primal scene in classical psychoanalytic theory, the child's first observation, in reality or fantasy, of parental intercourse or seduction, which is interpreted by the child as an act of violence.

primary ability any of the seven unitary factors proposed in the early 20th century to be essential components of intelligence: verbal ability, word fluency, numerical ability, spatial intelligence, memory, perceptual speed, and reasoning. Also called **primary mental ability**.

primary aging changes associated with normal aging that are inevitable and caused by intrinsic biological or genetic factors. Examples include the appearance of gray hair and decreased skin elasticity. However, some age-related processes are accelerated by environmental influences, making the distinction between primary aging and SECONDARY AGING imprecise.

primary auditory cortex (A1) see AUDITORY CORTEX.

primary care the basic or general health care a patient receives when he or she first seeks assistance from a health care system. General practitioners, family practitioners, internists, obstetricians, gynecologists, and pediatricians are known as **primary care providers (PCPs)**. Compare SECONDARY CARE; TERTIARY CARE.

primary caregiver see CAREGIVER.

primary circular reaction in PIAGETIAN THEORY, a type of repetitive action that represents the earliest nonreflexive infantile behavior. For example, in the first months of life, a hungry baby may repeatedly attempt to put a hand in the mouth. Primary circular reactions develop in the SENSORIMOTOR STAGE, following the activation of such basic reflexes as sucking, swallowing, crying, and moving the arms and legs. See also SECONDARY CIRCULAR REACTION; TERTIARY CIRCULAR REACTION.

primary cortex any of the regions of the CEREBRAL CORTEX that receive the main input from sensory receptors or send the main output to muscles. Examples are the STRIATE CORTEX and PRIMARY SOMATOSENSORY AREA. Most neurons in primary sensory regions have more direct sensory input than do neurons in adjacent sensory cortical regions.

primary drive an innate drive, which may be universal or species-specific, that is created by deprivation of a needed substance (e.g., food) or by the need to engage in a specific activity (e.g., nest building in birds). Compare SECONDARY DRIVE.

primary gain in psychoanalytic theory, the basic psychological benefit derived from possessing neurotic symptoms, essentially relief from anxiety generated by conflicting or unexpressed impulses. Compare SECONDARY GAIN.

primary group any of the small, long-term groups characterized by face-to-face interaction and high levels of GROUP COHESION, solidarity, and group identification. These groups are primary in the sense that they are the initial socializers of the individual members, providing them with the foundation for attitudes, values, and a social orientation. Families, partnerships, and long-term psychotherapy groups are examples of such groups. Compare SECONDARY GROUP.

primary gustatory cortex see TASTE CORTEX.

primary mental ability see PRIMARY ABILITY.

primary motor cortex see MOTOR CORTEX.

primary prevention research and programs, designed for and directed to nonclinical populations or populations at risk, that seek to promote and lay a firm foundation for mental, behavioral, or physical health so that psychological disorders, illness, or disease will not develop. Compare SECONDARY PREVENTION; TERTIARY PREVENTION.

primary process in psychoanalytic theory, unconscious mental activity in which there is free, uninhibited flow of psychic energy from one idea to another. This mental process operates without regard for logic or reality, is dominated by the PLEASURE PRINCIPLE, and provides hallucinatory fulfillment of wishes. Examples are the dreams, fantasies, and magical thinking of young children. These processes are posited to predominate in the ID. Compare SECONDARY PROCESS.

primary reinforcement 1. in OPERANT CONDITIONING, the process in which presentation of a stimulus or circumstance following a response increases the future probability of that response, without the need for special experience with the stimulus or circumstance. That is, the stimulus or circumstance, known as an **unconditioned** or **primary reinforcer**, functions as effective reinforcement without any special experience or training. **2.** the contingent occurrence of such a stimulus or circumstance after a response. Also called **unconditioned reinforcement**. Compare SECONDARY REINFORCEMENT.

primary reinforcer see NATURAL REINFORCER; PRIMARY REINFORCEMENT.

primary sensory area any area within the NEOCORTEX of the brain that acts to receive sensory input—for most senses, from the thalamus. The primary sensory area for hearing is in the temporal lobe, for vision in the occipital lobe (see STRIATE CORTEX), and for touch and taste in the parietal lobe (see PRIMARY SOMATOSENSORY AREA; TASTE CORTEX). See also SECONDARY SENSORY AREA.

primary sex characteristic see SEX CHARACTERISTIC.

primary somatosensory area (**S1**) an area of the cerebral cortex, located in a ridge of the anterior PARIETAL LOBE just posterior to the CENTRAL SULCUS, where the first stage of cortical processing of tactile information takes place. It receives input from the ventroposterior nuclear complex of the thalamus and projects to other areas of the parietal cortex. See also SECONDARY SOMATOSENSORY AREA.

primary taste cortex see TASTE CORTEX.

primary visual cortex (**V1**) see STRIATE CORTEX.

primate *n.* a member of the Primates, an order of mammals that includes the lemurs, monkeys, apes, and humans. Characteristics of the order include an opposable thumb (i.e., a thumb capable of touching the other digits), a relatively large brain, and binocular vision.

The young are usually born singly and mature over an extended period.

priming *n.* the effect in which recent experience of a stimulus facilitates or inhibits later processing of the same or a similar stimulus. In REPETITION PRIMING, presentation of a particular sensory stimulus increases the likelihood that participants will identify the same or a similar stimulus later in the test. In SEMANTIC PRIMING, presentation of a word or sign influences the way in which participants interpret a subsequent word or sign. —**prime** *vb.*

principal components analysis (**PCA**) a data reduction approach in which a number of independent linear combinations of underlying explanatory variables are identified for a larger set of original observed variables. The result of PCA is a new set of variables (called **principal components**) that are uncorrelated with each other and ordered in terms of the percentage of the total variance for which they account. The technique is similar in its aims to FACTOR ANALYSIS but has different technical features.

principal factor analysis an approach to identifying the dimensions underlying associations among a set of variables by using a COVARIANCE MATRIX as input. Principal factor analysis requires that dimensions be extracted in a particular way. Specifically, the first dimension extracted must account for the maximum possible variance, having the highest squared correlation with the variables it underlies; the second dimension must account for the next maximal amount of variance and be uncorrelated with the previously extracted dimension; and so forth.

principle of beneficence in research ethics, the requirement of INSTITUTIONAL REVIEW BOARDS that studies "do good" with respect to the work being conducted, the benefits to society at large, and the treatment of participants. Thus, the researcher should maximize the possible benefits

P

of each study and consider its potential impact in the broadest sense. For example, in a study of implicit attitudes, a researcher might note that understanding more about the measurement of attitudes toward sensitive topics may lead to reduced societal prejudice. See also PRINCIPLE OF NONMALEFICENCE.

principle of closure see CLOSURE.

principle of common fate see COMMON FATE.

principle of common region see COMMON REGION.

principle of continuity see GOOD CONTINUATION.

principle of good continuation see GOOD CONTINUATION.

principle of nonmaleficence in research ethics, the requirement of INSTITUTIONAL REVIEW BOARDS that studies "do no harm" to participants. When a person considers taking part in a study, there is an expectation that he or she will leave the study in a state that is no worse than when the study began. Where negative consequences are not entirely avoidable—as in an experiment in which a participant is required to recall painful memories, for example—researchers have a duty to minimize the impact of such consequences. See also PRINCIPLE OF BENEFICENCE.

principle of parsimony see LAW OF PARSIMONY.

principle of Prägnanz see PRÄGNANZ.

principle of proximity see PROXIMITY.

principle of similarity see SIMILARITY.

principle of symmetry see SYMMETRY.

prisoner abuse physical or psychological harm perpetrated on an incarcerated individual by those in authority over him or her. Such abuse may include sleep deprivation; refusal of health care; threatened harm to family members; beatings, torture, and other forms of violent coercion; sexual abuse and humiliation; and "enhanced" interrogation techniques utilizing coercive means to extract information from a prisoner or detainee.

prisoner's dilemma a situation in which each participant must choose between a self-beneficial course of action that could be costly for the other players and an action that would bring a smaller individual payoff but would lead to some benefits for all the players. The name derives from a police tactic, used when incriminating evidence is lacking, in which two suspects are separated and told that the one who confesses will go free whereas the other will receive a heavy sentence. If both confess, both will receive a moderate sentence; if neither confesses, lack of evidence means that they will both escape with a light sentence. The prisoner's dilemma is used in investigations of competition and cooperation and has implications for SOCIAL EXCHANGE THEORY and the study of SOCIAL DILEMMAS.

privacy *n.* **1.** the state in which an individual's or a group's desired level of social interaction is not exceeded. **2.** the right to control (psychologically and physically) others' access to one's personal world, such as by regulating others' input through use of physical or other barriers (e.g., doors, partitions) and by regulating one's own output in communication with others. **3.** the right of patients and others (e.g., consumers) to control the amount and disposition of the information they divulge about themselves. See PRIVILEGED COMMUNICATION. **—private** *adj.*

private acceptance see CONVERSION.

private adoption see ADOPTION.

private speech spontaneous self-directed talk in which a person "thinks aloud," particularly as a means of regulating cognitive processes and guiding behavior.

privation *n.* absence of something needed or desired, particularly something required to satisfy essential physiological needs, such as those for food and sleep. Privation is distinct from DEPRIVATION, which involves the initial presence and then removal of such requirements.

privileged communication confidential information, especially as provided by an individual to a professional in the course of their relationship, that may not be divulged to a third party without the knowledge and consent of that individual. This protection applies to communications not only between patients and physicians, clinical psychologists, psychiatrists, or other health care professionals but also between clients and attorneys, confessors and priests, and, in most instances, spouses.

proactive aggression see AGGRESSION.

proactive coping a stress-management strategy that reflects efforts to build up resources that facilitate promotion toward challenging goals and personal growth. Proactive individuals are motivated to meet challenges, and they see demands and opportunities in the distant future and initiate a constructive path of action toward meeting them. Proactive coping does not arise from any negative appraisals, such as harm, loss, or threat. See also PREVENTIVE COPING.

proactive interference see INTERFERENCE.

probability (symbol: *p*) *n.* the degree to which an event is likely to occur. See also CONDITIONAL PROBABILITY; PROBABILITY LEVEL. —**probabilistic** *adj.*

probability distribution a type of THEORETICAL DISTRIBUTION describing the probability that a random variable will take certain values. The best known example is the bell-shaped NORMAL DISTRIBUTION; others include the

CHI-SQUARE DISTRIBUTION, Student's T DISTRIBUTION, and the F DISTRIBUTION.

probability level (*p* value) in statistical SIGNIFICANCE TESTING, the likelihood that the observed result would have been obtained if the NULL HYPOTHESIS of no real effect were true. Small *p* values (conventionally, those less than .05 or .01) suggest that the chance of experimental results mistakenly being attributed to the independent variables present in the study (rather than to the random factors actually responsible) is small. Traditionally, the null hypothesis is rejected if the value of *p* is no larger than the SIGNIFICANCE LEVEL set for the test. Also called **probability value**.

probability sampling any process in which a sample of participants or cases is chosen from a larger group in such a way that each one has a known (or calculable) likelihood of being included. This requires a well-defined POPULATION and an objective selection procedure, as in RANDOM SAMPLING. Additionally, all members of the population must have some (i.e., nonzero) chance of being selected.

probability value see PROBABILITY LEVEL.

proband *n.* the family member whose possible genetic disease or disorder forms the center of the investigation into the extent of the illness in the family. Also called **index case**.

probit analysis a type of REGRESSION ANALYSIS in which a dichotomous outcome variable is related to any of a number of different predictor or independent variables. The technique assumes that a latent process generated the observed binary data and often produces very similar results to LOGISTIC REGRESSION. Also called **probit regression**.

problem checklist a type of self-report scale listing various personal, social, educational, or vocational problems. The participant indicates the items that apply to his or her situation.

problem drinking an informal and broad term referring to alcohol use with negative consequences, ranging from occasional drunkenness leading to missed days of work to a full ALCOHOL USE DISORDER.

problem-focused coping a stress-management strategy in which a person directly confronts a stressor in an attempt to decrease or eliminate it. For example, a student who is anxious about an upcoming examination might cope by studying more, attending every class, and attending special review sessions to ensure he or she fully understands the course material. Problem-focused coping may be used primarily when a person appraises a stressor as within his or her capacity to change. Compare EMOTION-FOCUSED COPING.

problem solving the process by which individuals attempt to overcome difficulties, achieve plans that move them from a starting situation to a desired goal, or reach conclusions through the use of higher mental functions, such as reasoning and creative thinking. In laboratory studies, many animals display problem-solving strategies, such as the *win–stay, lose–shift strategy*, which allows an animal to solve a new problem quickly based on whether the first response was successful or unsuccessful.

problem space the mental representation of a problem and of all the possible paths to solving it.

procedural memory long-term memory for the skills involved in particular tasks. It is demonstrated by skilled performance and is often separate from the ability to verbalize this knowledge (see DECLARATIVE MEMORY). Knowing how to type or skate, for example, requires procedural memory.

proceptivity *n.* the period during mating behavior when females actively solicit males for copulation. Proceptivity is distinguished from the more passive RECEPTIVITY to indicate the female's active role in mating.

process loss in the social psychology of groups, any action, operation, or dynamic that prevents the group from reaching its full potential, such as reduced effort (SOCIAL LOAFING), inadequate coordination of effort, poor communication, or ineffective leadership.

process research the study of various mechanisms or processes of psychotherapy as they influence the success of treatment or the reactions that the therapist or client may have. A basic goal of process research is to identify therapeutic elements that are most effective in bringing about positive change. Compare OUTCOME RESEARCH.

process schizophrenia a form of schizophrenia that begins early in life, develops gradually, is believed to be due to endogenous (biological or physiological) rather than environmental factors, and has a poor prognosis. Psychosocial development before the onset of the disorder is poor; individuals are withdrawn, are socially inadequate, and indulge in excessive fantasies. Compare REACTIVE SCHIZOPHRENIA.

Procrustes analysis in statistical analysis, an approach in which empirical data are superimposed onto some fixed target matrix or other structure of theoretical interest. The name derives from the robber in Greek mythology who forced his victims to fit his bed by stretching them or cutting off their limbs.

prodigy *n.* an individual, typically a child, who displays unusual or exceptional talent or intelligence, often in a discrete area of expertise, such as mathematics, music, or chess. Prodigies do not always develop into accomplished adults: There appears to be an important transition between the two stages, and only a proportion of prodigies successfully negotiate this transition. See also GIFTEDNESS.

prodrome *n.* an early symptom or symptoms of a mental or physical disorder. A prodrome frequently serves as a warning or premonitory sign that may, in some cases, enable preventive measures to be taken. Examples are the auras that often precede epileptic seizures or migraine headaches and the headache, fatigue, dizziness, and insidious impairment of ability that often precede a stroke. —**prodromic** *adj.* —**prodromal** *adj.*

production deficiency in problem solving, failure to find the right or best strategy for completing a task (sometimes even after successful instruction), as opposed to failure in implementing it. Compare MEDIATIONAL DEFICIENCY; UTILIZATION DEFICIENCY.

production task 1. a cognitive test in which the participant is required to generate as many items as possible that adhere to specified criteria. For example, in a word-production task, individuals may be asked to list as many exemplars from a given subject category (e.g., flower names) as possible. **2.** any test of linguistic development in which the participant is required to speak or write rather than to demonstrate understanding of material spoken or written by others. For example, in an experiment assessing foreign-language acquisition, native-English speakers studying German might be asked to read aloud a series of German sentences.

productivity *n.* **1.** the capacity to produce goods and services having exchange value. Vocational REHABILITATION programs often use the productivity of people with disabilities as a major measure of the effectiveness of the programs. **2.** one of the formal properties of all language, consisting of the ability to combine individual words to produce an unlimited number of sentences.

product-moment correlation

coefficient (symbol: *r*) an index of the degree of linear relationship between two variables. Devised by British statistician and biometrician Karl Pearson (1857–1936), it is often known as the **Pearson product-moment correlation coefficient (Pearson's *r*)** and is one of the most commonly used SAMPLE CORRELATION COEFFICIENTS.

professional labeling see LABELING.

progesterone *n.* a hormone that stimulates the proliferation of the endometrium (lining) of the uterus required for implantation of an embryo. If implantation occurs, progesterone continues to be secreted, maintaining the pregnant uterus and preventing further release of egg cells from the ovary. It also stimulates development of milk-secreting cells in the breasts.

prognosis *n.* a prediction of the course, duration, severity, and outcome of a condition, disease, or disorder. Prognosis may be given before any treatment is undertaken, so that the patient or client can weigh the benefits of different treatment options. —**prognostic** *adj.*

programmed cell death the orderly death and disposal of surplus tissue cells, which occurs as part of tissue remodeling during development, or of worn-out and infected cells, which occurs throughout life. Also called **apoptosis**.

programmed instruction a learning technique, used for self-instruction and in academic and some applied settings, in which the material is presented in a series of sequential, graduated steps, or frames. The learner is required to make a response at each step: If the response is correct, it leads to the next step; if it is incorrect, it leads to further review of the material presented in the prior step. Also called **programmed learning**.

progressive relaxation a technique in which the individual is trained to relax the entire body by becoming aware of tensions in various muscle groups and then relaxing one muscle group at a time. In some cases, the individual consciously tenses specific muscles or muscle groups and then releases tension to achieve relaxation throughout the body.

projection *n.* in psychoanalytic and psychodynamic theories, the process by which one attributes one's own individual positive or negative characteristics, affects, and impulses to another person or group. This is often a DEFENSE MECHANISM in which unpleasant or unacceptable impulses, stressors, ideas, affects, or responsibilities are attributed to others. For example, the defense mechanism of projection enables a person conflicted over expressing anger to change "I hate him" to "He hates me." Such defensive patterns are often used to justify prejudice or evade responsibility. —**project** *vb.*

projective technique any assessment procedure that consists of a series of relatively ambiguous stimuli designed to elicit unique, sometimes highly idiosyncratic, responses that reflect the personality, cognitive style, and other psychological characteristics of the respondent. Examples of this type of procedure are the RORSCHACH INKBLOT TEST and the THEMATIC APPERCEPTION TEST, as well as sentence-completion, word-association, and drawing tests. Projective techniques are quite controversial, with opinions ranging from the expressed belief that personality assessment is incomplete without data from at least one or more of these procedures to the assertion that such techniques lack important psychometric features such as RELIABILITY and VALIDITY.

proliferation *n.* rapid reproduction or multiplication, particularly of new or diseased cells. Both benign and malignant tumors, for instance, experience a high rate of cell division and growth.

promiscuity *n.* transient, casual sexual relations with a variety of partners. In humans, this type of behavior is often regarded unfavorably; however, in many other animal species, females appear to display promiscuity to prevent certainty of paternity but often mate with the most dominant or successful male at the time when conception is most likely. —**promiscuous** *adj.*

prompt *n.* see RETRIEVAL CUE.

propinquity *n.* the physical and sometimes psychological nearness of two or more people to each other, an element in the formation of close relationships. See also PROXEMICS.

propinquity effect the tendency of individuals to form close relationships with people they repeatedly encounter. That is, the more often one comes into contact with another person, the more likely it is that one will form a friendship or romantic relationship with that person. For example, next-door neighbors often are friends with one another, as are classmates and coworkers.

proportional *adj.* having a constant ratio between quantities, such that the overall relationship does not change. For example, consider a researcher who is examining the differences between two treatments among males and females as follows: 10 males in Treatment A and 20 males in Treatment B; 20 females in Treatment A and 40 females in Treatment B. Although there are unequal numbers of people in each treatment condition, the ratio or proportion between them remains the same—twice as many females as males.

proportional sampling a form of STRATIFIED SAMPLING in which one draws cases for study from certain groups (e.g., gender, race/ethnicity) in the proportions that are observed in the larger population. For example, if a university has 60% female students and 40% male students, a researcher would obtain a sample comprising the same percentages or proportions, such as 120 females and 80 males in a

200-student subset. Also called **proportionate sampling**.

proprioception *n.* the sense of body movement and position, resulting from stimulation of **proprioceptors** located in the muscles, tendons, and joints and of various specialized receptors in the VESTIBULAR SYSTEM. Proprioception enables the body to determine its spatial orientation without visual clues and to maintain postural stability. —**proprioceptive** *adj.*

prosencephalon *n.* see FOREBRAIN.

prosocial *adj.* denoting or exhibiting behavior that benefits one or more other people, such as providing assistance to an older adult crossing the street. Compare ANTISOCIAL.

prosody *n.* the pattern of stress, intonation, intensity, or duration of speech.

prosopagnosia *n.* a form of VISUAL AGNOSIA in which the ability to perceive and recognize faces is impaired, whereas the ability to recognize other objects may be relatively unaffected. Prosopagnosia can be distinguished from **prosopamnesia**, which is an abnormal difficulty in remembering faces, even though they are perceived normally.

prospective memory remembering to do something in the future, such as taking one's medicine later. Prospective memory contrasts with **retrospective memory**, or remembering past events.

prospective research research that starts with the present and follows participants forward in time to examine trends, predictions, and outcomes. Examples include randomized experiments and LONGITUDINAL DESIGNS. Compare RETROSPECTIVE RESEARCH.

prospective sampling a sampling method in which cases are selected for inclusion in experiments or other research on the basis of their exposure to a risk factor. Participants are then followed to see if the condition of interest develops. For example, young children who were exposed to lead in their drinking water and those who were not exposed to this risk factor could be included in a study and then followed through time to assess health problems that emerge when they are adolescents. Compare RETROSPECTIVE SAMPLING.

prospective validity see PREDICTIVE VALIDITY.

protected class under U.S. antidiscrimination law, groups that cannot be unfairly excluded from some process or opportunity (e.g., in job hiring, education, housing) on the basis of sex, age, familial status, race, ethnicity, religion, national origin, physical or mental handicap, or prior military service.

protected *t* test see FISHER LEAST SIGNIFICANT DIFFERENCE TEST.

protective factor a clearly defined behavior or constitutional (e.g., genetic), psychological, environmental, or other characteristic that is associated with a decreased probability that a particular disease or disorder will develop in an individual, that reduces the severity of an existing pathological condition, or that mitigates the effects of stress generally. For example, exercising regularly can serve as a protective factor by decreasing the likelihood or severity of coronary heart disease, hypertension, and depression. Compare RISK FACTOR.

protein *n.* a molecule that consists of a long-chain polymer of AMINO ACIDS. Proteins are involved in virtually every function performed by a cell; they are the principal building blocks of living organisms and, in the form of ENZYMES, the basic tools for construction, repair, and maintenance. See also PEPTIDE.

protein hormone any of a class of substances secreted into the bloodstream that regulate processes in distant target organs and tissues and that consist of a long-chain polymer of AMINO ACIDS. Examples are growth hormone and insulin.

protocol *n.* **1.** the original notes of a

P

study or experiment recorded during or immediately after a session or trial, particularly as recorded from participant's verbalizations during the process. **2.** a treatment plan, especially at the level of its steps and their order.

protocol analysis a methodology in which people are encouraged to think out loud as they perform some task. Transcripts of these sessions are then analyzed to investigate the cognitive processes underlying performance of the task.

prototype *n.* in concept formation, the best or average exemplar of a category. For example, the prototypical bird is some kind of mental average of all the different kinds of birds of which a person has knowledge or with which a person has had experience. —**prototypal, prototypical,** or **prototypic** *adj.*

proxemics *n.* the study of interpersonal spatial behavior. Proxemics is concerned with territoriality, interpersonal distance, spatial arrangements, crowding, and other aspects of the physical environment that affect behavior.

proximal *adj.* **1.** situated near or directed toward the trunk or center of an organism. **2.** near or mostly closely related to the point of reference or origin. Compare DISTAL. —**proximally** *adv.*

proximal stimulus the physical energy from a stimulus as it directly stimulates a sense organ or receptor, in contrast to the DISTAL STIMULUS in the actual environment. In reading, for example, the distal stimulus is the printed page of a book, whereas the proximal stimulus is the light energy reflected by the page that stimulates the photoreceptors of the retina.

proximate cause the most direct or immediate cause of an event. In a sequence of occurrences, it is the one that directly produces the effect. For example, the proximate cause of Smith's aggression may be an insult, but the

REMOTE CAUSE may be Smith's early childhood experiences. In law, proximate cause is important in liability cases where it must be determined whether the actions of the defendant are sufficiently related to the outcome to be considered causal, or if the actions set in motion a chain of events that led to an outcome that could have been reasonably foreseen.

proximate explanation an explanation for behavior in terms of physiological mechanisms or developmental experiences.

proximity *n.* one of the GESTALT PRINCIPLES OF ORGANIZATION. It states that people tend to organize objects close to each other into a perceptual group and interpret them as a single entity. Also called **law** (or **principle**) **of proximity**.

proximodistal *adj.* from the central to the peripheral. The term typically is used in the context of maturation to refer to the tendency to acquire motor skills from the center outward, as when children learn to move their heads, trunks, arms, and legs before learning to move their hands and feet. Compare CEPHALOCAUDAL.

Prozac *n.* a trade name for FLUOXETINE.

pseudocholinesterase (PChE) *n.* a synonym of butyrylcholinesterase. See CHOLINESTERASE.

pseudodementia *n.* deterioration or impairment of cognitive functions in the absence of neurological disorder or disease. The condition may occur, reversibly, in a MAJOR DEPRESSIVE EPISODE—particularly among older adults, in which case the preferred term is **dementia syndrome of depression**—or as a psychological symptom of FACTITIOUS DISORDER.

pseudohermaphroditism *n.* a congenital abnormality in which the gonads (ovaries or testicles) are of one sex, but one or more contradictions exist in the morphological criteria of sex. In female pseudohermaphroditism, the individual is a genetic and gonadal female with partial masculinization, such as an enlarged clitoris resembling a penis and labia majora resembling a scrotum. In male pseudohermaphroditism, the individual is a genetic and gonadal male with incomplete masculinization, including a small penis and a scrotum that lacks testes. See INTERSEX. —**pseudohermaphrodite** *n.*

pseudopsychology *n.* an approach to understanding or analyzing the mind or behavior that uses unscientific or fraudulent methods. Examples include PHRENOLOGY and PHYSIOGNOMY. See also PARAPSYCHOLOGY. —**pseudopsychological** *adj.*

psi *n.* **1.** the Greek letter ψ, often used to symbolize psychology. **2.** the phenomena or alleged phenomena studied in PARAPSYCHOLOGY, including EXTRASENSORY PERCEPTION, PRECOGNITION, and PSYCHOKINESIS.

psilocin *n.* an indolealkylamine HALLUCINOGEN that is the principal psychoactive compound in "magic mushrooms" of the genus *Psilocybe*, which were used by the Aztecs for religious and ceremonial purposes. **Psilocybin**, first isolated in 1958, differs from psilocin only in having an additional phosphate group; it is rapidly metabolized in the body and converted to psilocin.

psyche *n.* in psychology, the mind in its totality, as distinguished from the physical organism. The term, which historically had come to refer to the soul or the very essence of life, derives from the character of Psyche in Greek mythology, a beautiful princess who, at the behest of her divine lover, Eros, son of Aphrodite, is made immortal by Zeus.

psychedelic drug see HALLUCINOGEN.

psychiatric evaluation 1. an assessment, based on present problems and symptoms, of an individual's bio-logical, mental, and social functioning, which may or may not result in a diagnosis of a mental illness. **2.** an assessment to determine legal competency or the need for involuntary commitment (as in the case of an individual threatening suicide).

psychiatric hospital a public or private institution providing inpatient treatment to individuals with mental disorders. Also called **mental hospital**.

psychiatric nursing a nursing specialty that provides holistic care to individuals with mental disorders or behavioral problems so as to promote their physical and psychosocial well-being. It emphasizes the use of interpersonal relationships as a therapeutic agent and considers the environmental factors that influence mental health. Among other functions, **psychiatric nurses** assist patients with ACTIVITIES OF DAILY LIVING, administer psychotropic medication and manage side effects, participate in recreational activities with patients, educate patients and their families about mental health issues and lifestyle choices, and conduct group therapy.

psychiatrist *n.* a physician who specializes in the diagnosis, treatment, prevention, and study of mental, behavioral, and personality disorders. In the United States, education for this profession consists of 4 years of premedical training in college; a 4-year course in medical school, the final 2 years of which are spent in clerkships studying with physicians in at least five specialty areas; and a 4-year residency in a hospital or agency approved by the American Medical Association. After completing residency, most psychiatrists take a voluntary examination for certification by the American Board of Psychiatry and Neurology.

psychiatry *n.* the medical specialty concerned with the study, diagnosis, treatment, and prevention of mental, behavioral, and personality disorders.

As a medical specialty, psychiatry is based on the premise that biological causes are at the root of mental and emotional problems, although some psychiatrists do not adhere exclusively to the biological model and additionally treat problems as social and behavioral ills. Training for psychiatry includes the study of psychopathology, biochemistry, genetics, psychopharmacology, neurology, neuropathology, psychology, psychoanalysis, social science, and community mental health, as well as the many theories and approaches advanced in the field itself. —**psychiatric** *adj.*

psychic 1. *adj.* denoting phenomena associated with the mind. **2.** *adj.* denoting a class of phenomena, such as TELEPATHY and CLAIRVOYANCE, that appear to defy scientific explanation. The term is also applied to any putative powers, forces, or faculties associated with such phenomena. See PSI. **3.** *n.* a medium, sensitive, or other person with alleged paranormal abilities.

psychic determinism the position, associated particularly with Austrian neurologist Sigmund Freud (1856–1939), that mental (psychic) events do not occur by chance but always have an underlying cause that can be uncovered by analysis.

psychic energy in classical psychoanalytic theory, the dynamic force behind all mental processes. According to Austrian neurologist Sigmund Freud (1856–1939), the basic sources of this energy are the INSTINCTS or drives that are located in the ID and seek immediate gratification according to the PLEASURE PRINCIPLE. Swiss psychiatrist Carl Jung (1875–1961) also believed that there is a reservoir of psychic energy, but he objected to Freud's emphasis on the pleasurable gratification of biological instincts and emphasized the means by which this energy is channeled into the development of the personality and the expression of cultural and spiritual values. See also LIBIDO.

psychoactive drug any drug that has significant effects on psychological processes, such as thinking, perception, and emotion. Psychoactive drugs include those taken recreationally to produce an altered state of consciousness (e.g., HALLUCINOGENS) and therapeutic agents designed to ameliorate a mental condition (e.g., ANTIDEPRESSANTS, SEDATIVES, ANTIPSYCHOTICS). Psychoactive drugs are often referred to as **psychotropic drugs** (or **psychotropics**) in clinical contexts.

psychoanalysis *n.* an approach to the mind, personality, psychological disorders, and psychological treatment originally developed by Austrian neurologist Sigmund Freud (1856–1939) at the beginning of the 20th century. The hallmark of psychoanalysis is the assumption that much mental activity is unconscious and, consequently, that understanding people requires interpreting the unconscious meaning underlying their overt, or manifest, behavior. Psychoanalysis (often shortened to **analysis**) focuses primarily on the influence of such unconscious forces as repressed impulses, internal conflicts, and childhood traumas on the mental life and adjustment of the individual. The foundations on which CLASSICAL PSYCHOANALYSIS rests are (a) the concept of INFANTILE SEXUALITY; (b) the OEDIPUS COMPLEX; (c) the theory of INSTINCTS or drives; (d) the PLEASURE PRINCIPLE and the REALITY PRINCIPLE; (e) the threefold structure of the psyche into ID, EGO, and SUPEREGO; and (f) the central importance of anxiety and DEFENSE MECHANISMS in neurotic reactions. The goal of psychoanalytic therapy is to bring about basic modifications in an individual's personality, which is accomplished by establishing a constructive relationship through which the analyst can elicit and interpret the unconscious conflicts that have produced the individual's neurosis. The specific methods used to achieve this goal are FREE ASSOCIATION, DREAM ANALYSIS, analysis of RESISTANCES and defenses, and working through the feelings revealed in the TRANSFERENCE and COUNTERTRANSFERENCE process. **—psychoanalytic** *adj.*

psychoanalyst *n.* a therapist who has undergone special training in psychoanalytic theory and practice and who applies to the treatment of mental disorders the techniques developed by Austrian neurologist Sigmund Freud (1856–1939). In the United States, psychoanalysts are usually trained first as psychiatrists, clinical psychologists, or other mental health professionals and then undergo extensive training at a psychoanalytic institute. All recognized training centers require a thorough study of the works of Freud and others in the field, supervised clinical training, a TRAINING ANALYSIS, and a personal program of psychoanalysis.

psychoanalytic theory the diverse complex of assumptions and constructs underlying the approach known as PSYCHOANALYSIS. Classically, the term refers specifically to the formulations of Austrian neurologist Sigmund Freud (1856–1939), but it now also applies to such offshoots and counterapproaches as ANALYTIC PSYCHOLOGY, INDIVIDUAL PSYCHOLOGY, and OBJECT RELATIONS THEORY.

psychobiology *n.* **1.** a school of thought in the mental health professions in which the individual is viewed as a holistic unit and both normal and abnormal behavior is explained in terms of the interaction of biological, sociological, and psychological determinants. **2.** see BIOLOGICAL PSYCHOLOGY. **—psychobiological** *adj.*

psychocardiology *n.* see CARDIAC PSYCHOLOGY.

psychodrama *n.* a method of psychotherapy in which clients enact their concerns to achieve new insight about themselves and others. Its central premise is that spontaneity and creativity are crucial for the balanced, integrated personality and that humans are all improvising actors on the stage of life. Clients may ROLE PLAY in a variety of scenes either lived or imagined. The process involves (a) a *protagonist*, the client or central figure in the drama; (b) a *director*, or therapist, who guides this process and assists the client with alternative enactments and interpretations; and (c) *auxiliary egos*, therapeutic actors who assist the protagonist in completing his or her interaction with significant others in the drama.

***Psychodynamic Diagnostic Manual* (PDM)** a handbook for the diagnosis and treatment of mental health disorders that attempts to characterize an individual's personality and emotional, social, and interpersonal functioning in both healthy and maladaptive forms. Published in 2006 by a task force of various major psychoanalytical and psychological organizations, the *PDM* is meant to serve as a complement to the *Diagnostic and Statistical Manual of Mental Disorders* (see DSM–5) and the INTERNATIONAL CLASSIFICATION OF DISEASES. Although based on current neuroscience and treatment OUTCOME RESEARCH, the classification adapts many concepts from PSYCHODYNAMIC THEORY.

psychodynamic psychotherapy those forms of psychotherapy, falling within or deriving from the psychoanalytic tradition, that view individuals as reacting to unconscious forces (e.g., motivation, drive), that focus on processes of change and development, and that place a premium on self-understanding and making meaning of what is unconscious. Most psychodynamic therapies share certain features, such as emphasis on dealing with the unconscious in treatment and on analyzing TRANSFERENCE. Also called **dynamic psychotherapy**.

psychodynamic theory a constellation of theories of human functioning that are based on the interplay of drives and other forces within the person, especially (and originating in) the psychoanalytic theories developed by

Austrian neurologist Sigmund Freud (1856–1939) and his colleagues and successors, such as Anna Freud (1895–1982), Carl Jung (1875–1961), and Melanie Klein (1882–1960). Later psychodynamic theories, although retaining concepts of the interworking of drives and motives to some degree, emphasize the process of change and incorporate interpersonal and transactional perspectives of personality development.

psychogenic *adj.* resulting from mental factors. The term is used particularly to denote or refer to a disorder that cannot be accounted for by any identifiable physical dysfunction and is believed to be due to psychological factors (e.g., a conversion disorder). In psychology and psychiatry, psychogenic disorders are improperly considered equivalent to FUNCTIONAL disorders.

psychohistory *n.* the application of psychoanalytic theory to the study of historical figures, events, and movements.

psychokinesis (**PK**) *n.* in parapsychology, the alleged ability to control external events and move or change the shape of objects through the power of thought. Examples include the supposed ability of certain psychics to influence a roll of dice or to bend a piece of metal by exerting "mind over matter." See also TELEKINESIS. **—psychokinetic** *adj.*

psycholinguistics *n.* a branch of psychology that employs formal linguistic models to investigate language use and the cognitive processes that accompany it. In particular, various models of GENERATIVE GRAMMAR have been used to explain and predict LANGUAGE ACQUISITION in children and the production and comprehension of speech by adults. To this extent, psycholinguistics is a specific discipline, distinguishable from the more general area of psychology of language, which encompasses many other fields and approaches. **—psycholinguistic** *adj.*

psychological abuse see EMOTIONAL ABUSE.

psychological acculturation see ACCULTURATION.

psychological assessment the gathering and integration of data to evaluate a person's behavior, abilities, and other characteristics, particularly for the purposes of making a diagnosis or treatment recommendation. Psychologists assess diverse psychiatric problems (e.g., anxiety, substance abuse) and nonpsychiatric concerns (e.g., intelligence, career interests) in a range of clinical, educational, organizational, forensic, and other settings. Assessment data may be gathered through interviews, observation, standardized tests, self-report measures, physiological or psychophysiological measurement devices, or other specialized procedures and apparatuses.

psychological autopsy an analysis that is conducted following a person's death to reconstruct his or her mental state prior to dying. It is often performed when a death occurs in a complex, ambiguous, or equivocal (unexplained) manner to determine if the death was the result of natural causes, accident, homicide, or suicide.

psychological debriefing (**PD**) an intervention immediately following a traumatic event (e.g., a disaster) that aims to mitigate long-term distress and prevent the emergence of posttraumatic stress disorder in those exposed to the event. It relies predominantly on the affected individual's full and free expression of feeling, the normalization of distress, and psychoeducation about presumed symptoms.

psychological dependence 1. reliance on a psychoactive substance for its pleasurable effects. The dependence is signaled by a high rate of drug use, a craving for the drug, and the tendency to relapse after cessation of use. Stimulation of PLEASURE CENTERS has been suggested as the driving force behind drug addiction, with TOLERANCE and

PHYSICAL DEPENDENCE co-occurring but not essential related phenomena. **2.** reliance on others for emotional support, often characterized as an excessive need for their guidance, reassurance, and validation.

psychological determinism see DETERMINISM.

psychological disorder see MENTAL DISORDER.

psychological field in the thought of German-born U.S. social psychologist Kurt Lewin (1890–1947), the individual's LIFE SPACE or environment as he or she perceives it at any given moment. See also FIELD THEORY.

psychological model 1. a theory, usually including a mechanism for predicting psychological outcomes, intended to explain specific psychological processes. **2.** a representation of human cognitive and response characteristics used to approximate and evaluate the performance of an actual individual in a complex situation, such as a novel aircraft cockpit.

psychological need any need that is essential to mental health or that is otherwise not a biological necessity. It may be generated entirely internally, as in the need for pleasure, or it may be generated by interactions between the individual and the environment, as in the need for social approval, justice, or job satisfaction. Psychological needs comprise the four higher levels of MASLOW'S MOTIVATIONAL HIERARCHY. Compare PHYSIOLOGICAL NEED.

psychological test any standardized instrument, including scales and self-report inventories, used to measure behavior, emotional functioning, intelligence and cognitive abilities (e.g., reasoning, comprehension), aptitudes, values, interests, and personality characteristics. For example, a researcher might use a psychological test of emotional intelligence to examine whether some managers make better decisions

in conflict situations than do others. Also called **psychometric test**.

psychological warfare a broad class of tactics designed to influence the attitudes, beliefs, and behavior of soldiers and civilians with regard to military operations. These include attempts to bolster the attitudes and morale of one's own people as well as to change or undermine the attitudes and morale of an opposing army or civilian population.

psychologist *n.* an individual who is professionally trained in one or more branches or subfields of PSYCHOLOGY. Training is obtained at a university or a school of professional psychology, leading to a doctoral degree in philosophy (PhD), psychology (PsyD), or education (EdD). Psychologists work in a variety of settings, including laboratories, schools, social agencies, hospitals, clinics, the military, industry and business, prisons, the government, and private practice. The professional activities of psychologists are also varied but can include psychological counseling, involvement in other mental health care services, educational testing and assessment, research, teaching, and business and organizational consulting. Formal certification or professional licensing is required to practice independently in many of these settings and activities.

psychology *n.* **1.** the study of the mind and behavior. Historically, psychology was an area within philosophy and emerged from it (see EPISTEMOLOGY). It is now a diverse scientific discipline comprising several major branches of research (e.g., experimental, biological, cognitive, lifespan developmental, personality, social), as well as several subareas of research and applied psychology (e.g., clinical, industrial/organizational, school and educational, human factors, health, neuropsychology, cross-cultural). Research in psychology involves observation, experimentation, testing, and analysis to explore the biological,

P

cognitive, emotional, personal, and social processes or stimuli underlying human and animal behavior. The practice of psychology involves the use of psychological knowledge for any of several purposes: to understand and treat mental, emotional, physical, and social dysfunction; to understand and enhance behavior in various settings of human activity (e.g., school, workplace, courtroom, sports arena, battlefield); and to improve machine and building design for human use. **2.** the supposed collection of behaviors, traits, attitudes, and so forth that characterize an individual or a group (e.g., the psychology of women). **—psychological** *adj.*

psychometric *adj.* **1.** of or relating to PSYCHOMETRICS. **2.** of or relating to PSYCHOPHYSICS.

psychometric function see PSYCHOPHYSICAL FUNCTION.

psychometric research studies in the field of psychological measurement, including the development of new measures and appropriate methods for their scoring, the establishment of RELIABILITY and VALIDITY evidence for measures, and the examination of item and scale properties and their dimensions.

psychometrics *n.* the branch of psychology concerned with the quantification and measurement of mental attributes, behavior, performance, and the like, as well as with the design, analysis, and improvement of the tests, questionnaires, and other instruments used in such measurement. Also called **psychometric psychology**; **psychometry**.

psychometric scaling the creation of an instrument to measure a psychological concept through a process of analyzing responses to a set of test items or other stimuli. It involves identifying item properties, noting whether responses match theoretical formats, reducing the larger set of items into a smaller number (e.g., through EXPLORATORY FACTOR ANALYSIS), and

determining appropriate scoring methods.

psychometric test see PSYCHOLOGICAL TEST.

psychomotor *adj.* relating to movements or motor effects that result from mental activity.

psychomotor agitation restless physical activity arising from mental tension or disturbance. It includes pacing, hand wringing, and pulling or rubbing clothing and other objects and is a common symptom of both MAJOR DEPRESSIVE EPISODES and MANIC EPISODES. Also called **psychomotor excitement**.

psychomotor retardation a slowing down or inhibition of mental and physical activity, manifest as slow speech with long pauses before answers, slowness in thinking, and slow body movements. Psychomotor retardation is a common symptom of MAJOR DEPRESSIVE EPISODES.

psychoneuroimmunology *n.* the study of how the brain and behavior affect immune responses. **—psychoneuroimmunological** *adj.*

psychonomic *adj.* denoting an approach to psychology that emphasizes quantitative measurement, experimental control, and OPERATIONAL DEFINITIONS.

psychopathic personality see ANTISOCIAL PERSONALITY DISORDER.

psychopathology *n.* **1.** the scientific study of mental disorders, including their theoretical underpinnings, etiology, progression, symptomatology, diagnosis, and treatment. The term in this sense is sometimes used synonymously with ABNORMAL PSYCHOLOGY. **2.** the behavioral or cognitive manifestations of such disorders. The term in this sense is sometimes considered synonymous with MENTAL DISORDER itself. **—psychopathological** *adj.* **—psychopathologist** *n.*

psychopathy *n.* **1.** a synonym for

ANTISOCIAL PERSONALITY DISORDER. **2.** formerly, any psychological disorder or mental disease. —**psychopathic** *adj.*

psychopharmacology *n.* the study of the influence of drugs on mental, emotional, and behavioral processes. Psychopharmacology is concerned primarily with the mode of action of various substances that affect different areas of the brain and nervous system, including drugs of abuse. —**psychopharmacological** *adj.* —**psychopharmacologist** *n.*

psychopharmacotherapy *n.* the use of pharmacological agents in the treatment of mental disorders. For example, acute or chronic schizophrenia is treated by administration of antipsychotic drugs or other agents. Although such drugs do not cure mental disorders, they may—when used appropriately—produce significant relief from symptoms.

psychophysical *adj.* of or relating to the relationship between physical stimuli and mental events.

psychophysical function a psychometric relationship between a stimulus and judgments about the stimulus, as expressed in a mathematical formula. In the METHOD OF CONSTANT STIMULI, it is the proportion of *yes* responses (i.e., that the stimuli were perceived) as a function of physical magnitude of the stimuli. Also called **psychometric function**.

psychophysical method any of the standard techniques used in investigating psychophysical problems, such as the METHOD OF ADJUSTMENT and the METHOD OF LIMITS.

psychophysical research empirical studies, often conducted in a laboratory setting, linking properties of a physical stimulus to a sensory response. For example, in a study of hearing, a participant might be requested to distinguish a number of different sounds by their loudness.

psychophysical scaling any of the techniques used to construct scales relating physical stimulus properties to perceived magnitude. For example, a respondent in a study may have to indicate the roughness of several different materials that vary in texture. Methods are often classified as direct or indirect, based on how the observer judges magnitude.

psychophysics *n.* a branch of psychology that studies the relationship between the objective physical characteristics of a stimulus (e.g., its measured intensity) and the subjective perception of that stimulus (e.g., its apparent brightness).

psychophysiological research empirical studies that link an individual's bodily responses (e.g., change in heart rate, palmar sweat, eye blink) and mental processes (e.g., memory, cognitive processing, brain function). For example, in addition to collecting data on several performance measures, a psychophysiological researcher might examine cortisol levels in adolescents with a diagnosis of conduct disorder and compare them to levels in those without the disorder.

psychophysiology *n.* the study of the relation between the chemical and physical functions of organisms (physiology) and cognitive processes, emotions, and behavior (psychology). Also called **physiological psychology**. —**psychophysiological** *adj.* —**psychophysiologist** *n.*

psychosexual development in the classical psychoanalytic theory of Austrian neurologist Sigmund Freud (1856–1939), the step-by-step growth of sexual life as it affects personality development. Freud posited that the impetus for psychosexual development stems from a single energy source, the LIBIDO, which is concentrated in different organs throughout infancy and helps produce the various **psychosexual stages**: the ORAL STAGE, ANAL STAGE, PHALLIC STAGE, LATENCY STAGE, and GENITAL STAGE. Each stage gives rise to its own characteristic erotic activities (e.g., sucking and biting in the oral stage), which may persist in characteristic tendencies in later life, especially if sexual development is arrested in a FIXATION at one particular stage.

psychosis *n.* **1.** an abnormal mental state involving significant problems with REALITY TESTING. It is characterized by serious impairments or disruptions in the most fundamental higher brain functions—perception, cognition and cognitive processing, and emotions or affect—as manifested in behavioral phenomena, such as delusions, hallucinations, and significantly disorganized speech. See PSYCHOTIC DISORDER. **2.** historically, any severe mental disorder that significantly interferes with functioning and ability to perform activities essential to daily living.

psychosocial *adj.* describing the intersection and interaction of social and cultural influences on mind, personality, and behavior.

psychosocial development **1.** according to the theory of German-born U.S. psychologist Erik Erikson (1902–1994), personality development as a process influenced by social and cultural factors throughout the lifespan. See ERIKSON'S EIGHT STAGES OF PSYCHOSOCIAL DEVELOPMENT. **2.** the development of both prosocial behavior (e.g., cooperation) and antisocial behavior (e.g., aggression). Psychosocial development involves changes not only in children's overt behavior but also in their SOCIAL COGNITION. For example, they become able to take the perspective of others and to understand that other people's behavior is based on their knowledge and desires.

psychosocial support various services offered by mental health professionals to those in pressing need. Whether designed to help individuals cope with a serious illness or to alleviate distress in whole communities

following a disaster, such services may range from mental health counseling, psychoeducation, and group support to spiritual support and other assistance. See also SOCIAL SUPPORT.

psychosomatic *adj.* **1.** of or relating to the role of the mind (psyche) in diseases or disorders affecting the body (soma); specifically, the role of psychological factors (e.g., anxiety, depression) in the etiology and course of pathology in bodily systems. **2.** of or referring to any interaction between mind and body.

psychosomatic disorder a type of disorder in which psychological factors are believed to play an important role in the origin or course (or both) of the disorder.

psychosurgery *n.* the treatment of a mental disorder by surgical removal or destruction of selective brain areas. The most well-known example of psychosurgery is prefrontal LOBOTOMY, used primarily from 1935 to 1960 and among the most controversial of psychiatric treatments ever introduced. Contemporary psychosurgery approaches are far more precisely targeted and confined in extent than the early techniques, employing high-tech imaging and a variety of highly controllable methods of producing minute lesions. Additionally, they are used only as a last resort and only for a handful of specific psychiatric disorders—major depressive disorder, bipolar disorder, obsessive-compulsive disorder, and generalized anxiety disorder—that have been resistant to other available therapies.

psychotherapy *n.* any psychological service provided by a trained professional that primarily uses forms of communication and interaction to assess, diagnose, and treat dysfunctional emotional reactions, ways of thinking, and behavior patterns of an individual, couple, family, or group. There are many types of psychotherapy, but generally they fall into four major

categories: PSYCHODYNAMIC PSYCHO-
THERAPY, COGNITIVE THERAPY or
BEHAVIOR THERAPY, HUMANISTIC THER-
APY, and INTEGRATIVE PSYCHOTHERAPY.
The **psychotherapist** is an individual
who has been professionally trained
and licensed (in the United States by a
state board) to treat mental, emotional,
and behavioral disorders by psychological means. **—psychotherapeutic** *adj.*

psychotic *adj.* of, relating to, or affected by PSYCHOSIS or a PSYCHOTIC
DISORDER.

psychotic disorder any of a number of severe mental disorders,
regardless of etiology, characterized by
gross impairment in REALITY TESTING.
The accuracy of perceptions and
thoughts is incorrectly evaluated, and
incorrect inferences are made about external reality, even in the face of
contrary evidence. Specific symptoms
indicative of psychotic disorders are delusions, hallucinations, and markedly
disorganized speech, thought, or behavior; individuals may have little or no
insight into their symptoms.

psychoticism *n.* in the classification
developed by German-born British psychologist Hans Eysenck (1916–1997),
a dimension of personality characterized by aggression, impulsivity,
aloofness, and antisocial behavior and
indicating a susceptibility to psychosis
and psychopathic disorders (see ANTI-
SOCIAL PERSONALITY DISORDER).

psychotropic drug see PSYCHOAC-
TIVE DRUG.

puberty *n.* the stage of development
when the genital organs reach maturity
and secondary SEX CHARACTERISTICS
begin to appear, signaling the start of
ADOLESCENCE. It is marked by ejaculation of sperm in the male, onset of
menstruation and development of
breasts in the female, and, in both
males and females, growth of pubic
hair and increasing sexual interest.
—pubertal *adj.*

pubescence *n.* the period or process
of reaching puberty. **—pubescent** *adj.*

public adoption see ADOPTION.

**Publication Manual of the
American Psychological Association** a reference book offering
guidelines on how to present written
material in the behavioral and social
sciences clearly and effectively. Based
on the special requirements of psychology but applicable to sociology,
business, economics, nursing, social
work, criminology, and other disciplines, the *Publication Manual* describes
the editorial style established by the
American Psychological Association
(APA) and used in all of the books and
journals that it publishes (i.e., APA
STYLE). Besides guidance on the content
and organization of a manuscript, the
Publication Manual offers direction on
such points as grammar and the me-
chanics of writing, the uniform use of
punctuation and abbreviations, the
construction of tables and figures, the
selection of headings, the citation and
formatting of references, and the presentation of statistics. The sixth edition
was published in 2010, and the first
electronic version was made available
in 2013.

punctuated equilibrium a theory
of EVOLUTION proposing that periods of
rapid change, resulting in the development of new species, are separated by
longer periods of little or no change.

punishment *n.* **1.** a physically or
psychologically painful, unwanted, or
undesirable event or circumstance imposed as a penalty on an actual or
perceived wrongdoer. **2.** in OPERANT
CONDITIONING, the process in which the
relationship between a response and
some stimulus or circumstance results
in the response becoming less probable.
For example, a pigeon's pecks on a key
may at first be followed by presentation
of food; this will establish some probability of pecking. Next, each peck
produces a brief electric shock (while
the other conditions remain as before).

If pecking declines as a result, then punishment is said to have occurred, and the shock is called a **punisher**. —**punish** vb.

punitive parenting a parent's habitual use of punishment to teach or control a child, often involving harsh or coercive practices such as yelling at, threatening, pushing, grabbing, hitting, or verbally disparaging the child.

pupil n. the aperture through which light passes on entering the eye. It is located in front of the LENS. The size of the opening is controlled by a circle of muscle (the IRIS) innervated by fibers of the autonomic nervous system.

pupillary reflex the automatic change in size of the pupil in response to light changes. The pupil constricts in response to bright light and dilates in dim light. See also ACCOMMODATION.

pure alexia see ALEXIA.

pure science see BASIC SCIENCE.

pure word deafness a type of AUDITORY AGNOSIA in which an individual is unable to understand spoken language but can comprehend nonverbal sounds and read, write, and speak in a relatively normal manner.

purging n. the activity of expelling food that has just been ingested, usually by vomiting or the use of laxatives. Purging often occurs after an eating binge in ANOREXIA NERVOSA or BULIMIA NERVOSA; its purpose is to eliminate or reduce weight gain.

purging disorder a disturbance in which individuals feel a loss of control after eating only a small amount of food and recurrently vomit up or otherwise expel their meals. It is differentiated from BULIMIA NERVOSA by the absence of binging.

Purkinje cell a type of large, highly branched cell in the CEREBELLAR CORTEX of the brain that receives incoming signals about the position of the body and transmits signals to spinal nerves for coordinated muscle actions. [Jan Evan-

gelista **Purkinje** (1787–1869), Czech physiologist and physician]

putamen n. a part of the lenticular nucleus in the BASAL GANGLIA. It receives input from the motor cortex and is involved in control of movements.

p value n. see PROBABILITY LEVEL.

Pygmalion effect a consequence or reaction in which the expectations of a leader or superior lead to behavior on the part of followers or subordinates that is consistent with these expectations: a form of SELF-FULFILLING PROPHECY. For example, raising manager expectations of the performance of subordinate employees has been found to enhance the performance of those employees.

pyramidal cell a large neuron that has a pyramid-shaped CELL BODY and is found in the cerebral cortex.

pyramidal tract the primary pathway followed by motor neurons that originate in the motor area of the cortex, the premotor area, the somatosensory area, and the frontal and parietal lobes of the brain. Fibers of the pyramidal tract cross in the pyramid of the medulla oblongata and communicate with fibers supplying the peripheral muscles. The pyramidal tract includes the corticospinal tract (see VENTROMEDIAL PATHWAY), and the two terms are occasionally used synonymously.

pyriform area (**piriform area**) a pear-shaped region of the RHINENCEPHALON, at the base of the medial temporal lobe of the brain, that forms part of the OLFACTORY CORTEX.

pyromania n. an impulse-control disorder characterized by (a) repeated failure to resist impulses to set fires and watch them burn, without monetary, social, political, or other motivations; (b) an extreme interest in fire and things associated with fire; and (c) a sense of increased tension before starting the fire and intense pleasure, gratification, or release while committing the act.

Qq

Q sort a data-collection procedure, often used in personality measurement, in which a rater sorts a broad set of stimuli into categories using a specific instruction set. The stimuli are often short descriptive statements (e.g., of personal traits) printed on cards. Examples of the instruction set are "describe yourself," "describe this child," and "describe your friend." In the classic or **structured Q sort**, raters are constrained to place a predetermined number of stimuli in each category.

quadrant *n.* **1.** one of four divisions of a graph of data for two different variables. The quadrants correspond to positive scores on both dimensions (upper right corner of plot), negative scores on both dimensions (lower left corner of plot), and positive scores on one dimension and negative scores on the other dimension (upper left corner and lower right corner, respectively, of the plot). **2.** one of four divisions of the visual field.

quadrantanopia *n.* loss of vision in one fourth, or one quadrant, of the visual field.

quadrant sampling a method for selecting units of analysis (e.g., participants, organizations) from different areas of a space. The space is divided into four sections, and units are drawn from each. Units may be drawn from psychological space as well, such as personality variables that are thought of as arrayed in two-dimensional space.

qualitative *adj.* referring to a variable, study, or analysis that relies on descriptive information without the use of numbers. Compare QUANTITATIVE.

qualitative analysis the investigation of open-ended narratives and other material by researchers or raters who describe dominant themes that emerge. In many cases, specialized computer programs identify these themes using researcher-provided search terms. A major component of the process is the effort to understand the reasons behind the observed themes. Compare QUANTITATIVE ANALYSIS.

qualitative research a method of research that produces descriptive (non-numerical) data, such as observations of behavior or personal accounts of experiences. The goal of gathering this **qualitative data** is to examine how individuals can perceive the world from different vantage points. A variety of techniques are subsumed under qualitative research, including CONTENT ANALYSES of narratives, in-depth interviews, FOCUS GROUPS, PARTICIPANT OBSERVATION, and CASE STUDIES, often conducted in naturalistic settings. Compare QUANTITATIVE RESEARCH.

quality adjusted life years (**QALYs**) a measure that combines the quantity of life, expressed in terms of survival or life expectancy, with the quality of life. The value of a year of perfect health is taken as 1; a year of ill health is worth less than 1; death is taken as 0. The measure provides a method to assess the benefits to be gained from medical procedures and interventions.

quality of life the extent to which a person obtains satisfaction from life. The following are important for a good quality of life: emotional, material, and physical well-being; engagement in interpersonal relations; opportunities for personal (e.g., skill) development; exercising rights and making self-determining lifestyle choices; and participation in society. Enhancing quality of life is a particular concern for those with chronic disease or developmental and other disabilities, for those undergoing medical or psychological treatment, and for older adults.

quantal hypothesis (**quantal theory**) see NEURAL QUANTUM THEORY.

quantification *n.* the process of expressing a concept or variable in numerical form, which may aid in analysis and understanding.

quantile *n.* a value in a series of values in ascending order below which a given percentage of values lies; for example, a 50% quantile (also called a MEDIAN) is the point at which 50% of the values fall below that value (and 50% above). Other types of quantile are quartiles, dividing the series into four equal-sized groups; deciles, dividing it into 10 groups; and percentiles (or centiles), dividing it into 100 groups.

quantitative *adj.* involving the use of a numerical measurement system to gather or analyze data. Compare QUALITATIVE.

quantitative analysis the investigation of data empirically using numerically based techniques. Quantitative analysis includes both DESCRIPTIVE STATISTICS—such as summaries of means and standard deviations of variables—and INFERENTIAL STATISTICS—such as analysis of variance, regression analysis, factor analysis, and hierarchical linear models. Compare QUALITATIVE ANALYSIS.

quantitative psychology the study of methods and techniques for the measurement of human attributes, the statistical and mathematical modeling of psychological processes, the design of research studies, and the analysis of psychological data. Researchers in this area develop new methodologies and evaluate existing methodologies under particular conditions (e.g., with small samples).

quantitative research a method of research that relies on measuring variables using a numerical system, analyzing these measurements using any of a variety of statistical models, and

reporting relationships and associations among the studied variables. For example, these variables may be test scores or measurements of reaction time. The goal of gathering this **quantitative data** is to understand, describe, and predict the nature of phenomena, particularly through the development of models and theories. Quantitative research techniques include experiments and surveys. Compare QUALITATIVE RESEARCH.

quartile *n.* one of the three values in a series of values that divide it into equal-sized fourths. For example, the first (or lower) quartile of a distribution is the data value below which are the lowest 25% of scores, the second quartile is the data value below which are 50% of scores, and the third (or upper) quartile is the data value below which are 75% of scores (or, conversely, above which are 25% of scores). These values provide information to researchers about the relative spread of the distribution.

quartile deviation a measure of DISPERSION that is defined as the value halfway between the first and third quartiles (i.e., half the INTERQUARTILE RANGE). Also called **semi-interquartile range**.

quasi-experimental design a method of research in which assignment of participants to an EXPERIMENTAL GROUP or to a CONTROL GROUP cannot be made at random for either practical or ethical reasons; this is usually the case in FIELD RESEARCH. Examples include studies that investigate the responses of large groups to natural disasters or widespread changes in social policy. Assignment of participants to conditions is usually based on self-selection (e.g., employees who have chosen to work at a particular plant) or selection by an administrator (e.g., children are assigned to particular classrooms by a superintendent of schools). Such designs introduce a set of assumptions or threats to INTERNAL VALIDITY that must be acknowledged by the researcher when interpreting findings. A study using this design is called a **quasi-experiment**.

quasi-independent variable in experimental design, any of the personal attributes, traits, or behaviors that are inseparable from an individual and cannot reasonably be manipulated. These include gender, age, and ethnicity. Such attributes may be modeled and treated as statistically independent but are not subject to RANDOM ASSIGNMENT, as are INDEPENDENT VARIABLES.

quasi-interval scale a rating scale that classifies responses by using ordered options but that lacks equal distances between all scale points. For example, some response items could show equal distances between scale points, whereas for other items respondents could have a difficult time differentiating among options, leading to compression or stretching between scale points. See INTERVAL SCALE.

quasi-observation *n.* **1.** the process of collecting data about a person from a close source, rather than directly from the subject. An example is asking an individual to report on his or her partner's job satisfaction. **2.** the use of mechanical means, such as video surveillance or audiotaping, to record behaviors as a substitute for real-time observation and questioning by a researcher. In marketing research, an example would be the use of surveillance cameras to monitor shopper behavior in stores.

quasirandom sampling see SYSTEMATIC SAMPLING.

quasi-vegetative state see MINIMALLY CONSCIOUS STATE.

questionnaire *n.* a set of questions or other prompts used to obtain information from a respondent about a topic of interest, such as background characteristics, attitudes, behaviors, personality, ability, or other attributes. A questionnaire may be administered with pen and paper, in a face-to-face interview, or via interaction between the respondent and a computer or website.

quota control in survey methodology, an approach that imposes a limit on the number of respondents that are obtained, either in the total sample or in substantively meaningful subgroups (e.g., those defined by gender or ethnicity). The approach allows a researcher to obtain a desired balance of sample sizes across groups for statistical testing. Most computerized surveys include an automatic quota control function.

quota sampling a method of forming a sample in which a prespecified number of individuals with certain background characteristics, such as a particular age, race, ethnicity, gender, or education level, are selected for inclusion. A researcher who uses this approach can obtain a final study sample that has the same proportional characteristics as the target population, enabling statistical testing to be performed on a subset of cases that is appropriately representative of the larger group of interest. See also QUOTA CONTROL.

Rr

race *n.* a socially defined concept sometimes used to designate a portion or subset of the human population with common physical characteristics, ancestry, or language. The term is also loosely applied to geographic, cultural, religious, or national groups. The significance often accorded to racial categories might suggest that such groups are objectively defined and homogeneous; however, there is much heterogeneity within categories, and the categories themselves differ across cultures. Moreover, self-reported race frequently varies, owing to changing social contexts and an individual's possible identification with more than one race. **—racial** *adj.*

racial and ethnic minority psychology see ETHNIC PSYCHOLOGY.

racial socialization the transmission by parents, caregivers, and other influential people of information, values, and perspectives about their race to children of that race, with the goals of instilling pride in their racial heritage and providing strategies for coping with racism, discrimination, and other barriers to success in mainstream society. This term is usually used in research with African Americans. See also ETHNIC SOCIALIZATION.

racism *n.* a form of PREJUDICE that assumes that the members of racial categories have distinctive characteristics and that these differences result in some racial groups being inferior to others. Racism generally includes negative emotional reactions to members of the group, acceptance of negative STEREOTYPES, and DISCRIMINATION against individuals; in some cases it leads to violence. **—racist** *adj., n.*

radial glia a type of nonneuronal cell (GLIA) that forms early in development, spanning the width of the emerging cerebral hemispheres to guide migrating neurons.

radial maze a type of maze that has a central starting point with several arms (typically six to eight) extending from the center. A nonhuman animal might be required to learn to find food only in particular arms or to search systematically through each arm without entering the same arm twice. Radial mazes have been used extensively to study spatial memory and learning.

radical behaviorism the view that behavior, rather than consciousness and its contents, should be the proper topic for study in psychological science. This term is often used to distinguish classical BEHAVIORISM, as originally formulated in 1913 by U.S. psychologist John B. Watson (1878–1958), from more moderate forms of NEOBEHAVIORISM. However, it has evolved to denote as well the form of descriptive behaviorism later proposed by U.S. psychologist B. F. Skinner (1904–1990), which emphasizes the importance of reinforcement and its relationship to behavior (i.e., the environmental determinants of behavior).

rage *n.* intense, typically uncontrolled anger. It is usually differentiated from hostility in that it is not necessarily accompanied by destructive actions but rather by excessive expressions.

random *adj.* **1.** without order or predictability. **2.** determined by chance alone, as in RANDOM SAMPLING.

random assignment in experimental design, the assignment of participants or units to the different conditions of an experiment entirely at random, so that each participant or unit has an equal likelihood of being assigned to any particular condition. This decreases the CONFOUNDING of the treatment under study with other factors by making the different participant groups approximately comparable in all respects except for the treatment. Also called **randomization**. See also RANDOMIZED DESIGN.

random effect an effect arising from an INDEPENDENT VARIABLE in an experimental design whose values or levels are drawn randomly from some larger (conceptual) population of levels that could (in principle) have been selected. For example, a health researcher investigating the relationship between exercise and weight may select a few levels of daily exercise for study (e.g., 0 hours, between 0 and 1 hour, between 1 and 2 hours, between 2 and 3 hours) from a wide range of possible options. Results involving a random effect can be generalized to values beyond those examined in the study. Also called **random factor**. Compare FIXED EFFECT.

random-interval schedule (RI schedule) in conditioning, an arrangement in which the first response after an interval has elapsed is reinforced, the duration of the interval varies randomly from reinforcement to reinforcement, and a fixed probability of reinforcement over time is used to reinforce a response. For example, if every second the probability that reinforcement would be arranged for the next response was .1, then the random-interval schedule value would be 10 seconds (i.e., RI 10 seconds).

randomization *n.* see RANDOM ASSIGNMENT.

randomized block design (RBD) an approach to assigning participants to treatment conditions in which meaningful discrete strata within the sample (e.g., gender, experience) are used to identify homogeneous subsamples; individuals from each subsample or "block" are then assigned randomly to the different conditions. In this way, participants are initially matched on a "blocking variable" that the researcher wishes to control.

randomized clinical trial (RCT) an experimental design in which patients are randomly assigned to a group that will receive an experimental treatment, such as a new drug, or to one that will receive a comparison treatment, a standard-of-care treatment, or a PLACEBO. The RANDOM ASSIGNMENT occurs after recruitment and assessment of eligibility but before the intervention. Also called **randomized controlled trial**.

randomized design any of various experimental designs in which individual participants are assigned to different conditions (groups) using a purely chance process, such as rolling a die. A crucial assumption underlying randomized designs is that any systematic differences between treatment groups will be due to the experimental conditions themselves and not to any other unmeasured factors. Compare NONRANDOMIZED DESIGN.

random mating mating behavior without mate selection. Many early behavioral ECOLOGY theories were based on the idea of random mating, but it is now recognized that most animals select specific mates and often show ASSORTATIVE MATING.

random-ratio schedule (RR schedule) in conditioning, an arrangement in which the number of responses required for each reinforcement varies randomly from reinforcement to reinforcement. It is usually arranged by having the same probability of reinforcement for each response regardless of the history of reinforcement for prior responses. For example, a random-ratio 100 schedule would result from a reinforcement probability of .01 for any given response.

random sampling a process for selecting a sample of study participants from a larger potential group of eligible individuals, such that each person has the same fixed probability of being included in the sample and some chance procedure is used to determine who specifically is chosen. A group formed in this way is known as a **random sample**. The main value of this form of PROBABILITY SAMPLING is its positive impact on GENERALIZABILITY and EXTERNAL VALIDITY.

random selection a procedure for RANDOM SAMPLING of a set of participants or units from a larger set that relies on the use of a chance process to minimize risk of researcher bias, either conscious or nonconscious.

random variable a variable that takes on different values according to a chance process. These values cannot be predicted with certainty and are assumed to vary across studies; however, their frequency can be described in terms of probability. Compare FIXED VARIABLE.

range *n.* a measure of DISPERSION obtained by subtracting the lowest score in a distribution from the highest score. For example, if the highest score on a test is 100 and the lowest score is 10, then the range is $(100 - 10) = 90$ points. Because it describes a raw discrepancy between the low and high scores, range is generally perceived as less informative than other measures of dispersion, such as the STANDARD DEVIATION.

rank biserial correlation coefficient an index of association between a DICHOTOMOUS VARIABLE and an ORDINAL VARIABLE. For example, a researcher might relate experimental condition (experimental vs. control group) to a rank-based measure of task performance. Compare POINT BISERIAL CORRELATION COEFFICIENT.

rank correlation coefficient a numerical index reflecting the degree of relationship between two variables that have each been arranged in ascending or descending order of magnitude (i.e., ranked). It does not reflect the association between the actual values of the variables but rather that between their relative positions in the distribution. For example, placement in a mara-

thon race could be correlated with the runners' heights, but in this case the two variables—race outcome and height—would take the form *first place, second place,* and so on, and *tallest, next tallest,* and so on, respectively (rather than actual times run in the race and specific heights in feet and inches). One of the most commonly used such indexes is the SPEARMAN CORRELATION COEFFICIENT. Also called **rank-order correlation coefficient**.

rank order the arrangement of a series of items (e.g., scores, individuals) in order of magnitude on a particular criterion.

rank-order statistic test any NONPARAMETRIC TEST that allows researchers to evaluate hypotheses related to group differences or associations between ranked variables. Such tests make use of a RANK CORRELATION COEFFICIENT, such as the SPEARMAN CORRELATION COEFFICIENT.

rank-sum test any NONPARAMETRIC TEST that involves combining the data points from two or more samples in a single data set and ranking these values in ascending order. See MANN–WHITNEY U TEST; WILCOXON–MANN–WHITNEY TEST; WILCOXON RANK-SUM TEST.

rape *n.* the nonconsensual oral, anal, or vaginal penetration of an individual by another person with a part of the body or an object, using force or threats of bodily harm or by taking advantage of the individual's inability to deny consent.

raphe nucleus any of multiple groups of SEROTONERGIC neurons in the midline of the brainstem that project widely to the spinal cord, thalamus, basal ganglia, and cerebral cortex. Raphe nuclei are involved in alertness and sleep–wake cycles.

rapid cycling repeated mood disturbances that occur over a short period, most commonly between manic and depressive symptoms. The term is a specifier applied to BIPOLAR DISORDER characterized by four or more mood fluctuations over a 12-month period.

rapid eye movement (**REM**) the large, sweeping eye movements behind closed lids that occur during REM SLEEP.

rapport *n.* a warm, relaxed relationship of mutual understanding, acceptance, and sympathetic compatibility between or among individuals. The establishment of rapport with a client in psychotherapy is frequently a significant mediate goal for the therapist, to facilitate and deepen the therapeutic experience and promote optimal progress and improvement.

Rasch model in ITEM RESPONSE THEORY, a model in which only one parameter, item difficulty, is specified. This is thought to be a parsimonious way to describe the relation between an item response and an underlying dimension and is thus preferred in some cases. Also called **one-parameter model**. [proposed in 1960 by Danish statistician Georg **Rasch** (1901–1980)]

rate coding a type of neural plotting of the frequency at which ACTION POTENTIALS occur. Compare TEMPORAL CODING.

rating scale an instrument that is used to assign scores to people or items along some numerical dimension, such as agreement with an attitude statement or frequency of occurrence. Rating scales can be classified according to the number of points along the dimension that is being assessed (e.g., a 5-point scale, 7-point scale) and the way in which the response labels are ordered along the dimension. See LIKERT SCALE; SEMANTIC DIFFERENTIAL.

ratio data numerical values that indicate magnitude and have a true, meaningful zero point. Ratio data represent exact quantities of the variables under consideration, and when arranged consecutively they have equal differences among adjacent values (regardless of the specific values selected) that correspond to genuine differences

between the physical quantities being measured. Income provides an example: The difference between an income of $40,000 and $50,000 is the same as the difference between $110,000 and $120,000, and an income of $0 indicates a complete and genuine absence of earnings. Ratio data are continuous in nature (i.e., able to take on any of an infinite variety of amounts) and of the highest MEASUREMENT LEVEL, surpassing INTERVAL DATA, ORDINAL DATA, and NOMINAL DATA in precision and complexity.

ratio IQ see IQ.

rational *adj.* pertaining to REASONING or, more broadly, to higher thought processes: influenced by reasoning rather than by emotion. —**rationally** *adv.*

rational emotive behavior therapy (**REBT**) a form of COGNITIVE BEHAVIOR THERAPY based on the concept that an individual's self-defeating beliefs cause negative feelings and lead to undesirable behaviors. REBT uses a variety of cognitive, emotional, and behavioral techniques to interrupt clients' irrational beliefs and encourage them to think and act in more effective, self-enhancing (i.e., rational) ways.

rationalism *n.* **1.** any philosophical position holding that (a) it is possible to obtain knowledge of reality by reason alone, unsupported by experience, and (b) all human knowledge can be brought into a single deductive system. This confidence in reason is central to classical Greek philosophy, but the term *rationalist* is chiefly applied to thinkers in the Continental philosophical tradition initiated by French philosopher and mathematician René Descartes (1596–1650). Rationalism is usually contrasted with EMPIRICISM, which holds that knowledge comes from or must be validated by sensory experience. Psychoanalytical approaches, humanistic psychology, and some strains of cognitive theory are heavily influenced by rationalism. **2.** in general, any position that relies on reason and evidence rather than on faith, intuition, custom, prejudice, or other sources of conviction. —**rationalist** *adj., n.*

rationalization *n.* an EGO DEFENSE in which apparently logical reasons are given to justify unacceptable behavior. In psychoanalytic theory, such behavior is considered to be a DEFENSE MECHANISM used to defend against feelings of guilt, maintain self-respect, and protect oneself from criticism. In psychotherapy, rationalization is considered counterproductive to deep exploration and confrontation of the client's thoughts and feelings and their effect on behavior. —**rationalize** *vb.*

ratio reinforcement in OPERANT CONDITIONING, reinforcement presented after a prearranged number of responses, in contrast to reinforcement delivered on the basis of a time schedule only. In such schedules, the rate of reinforcement is a direct function of the rate of responding. Compare INTERVAL REINFORCEMENT.

ratio scale a measurement scale having a true zero (i.e., zero on the scale indicates an absence of the measured attribute) and a constant ratio of values. Thus, on a ratio scale an increase from 3 to 4 (for example) is the same as an increase from 7 to 8. The existence of a true zero point is what distinguishes a ratio scale from an INTERVAL SCALE.

ratio variable a variable that is measured with a RATIO SCALE (e.g., height, weight).

Raven's Progressive Matrices a nonverbal test of mental ability consisting of abstract designs, each of which is missing one part. The participant chooses the missing component from several alternatives to complete each design. The test comprises 60 designs arranged in five groups of 12; the items within each group become progressively more difficult. The test, published in 1938, is often viewed as the prototypical measure of general intelligence.

[John C. **Raven** (1902–1970), British psychologist]

raw score a participant's score on a test before it is converted to other units or another form or subjected to quantitative or qualitative analysis. For example, a score may be transformed into a percentage (e.g., 45 correct answers out of 50 = 90%) or into a standardized metric such as a Z SCORE (mean of 0; standard deviation of 1) or a T SCORE (mean of 50; standard deviation of 10). Also called **unstandardized score**.

reactance theory a model stating that in response to a perceived threat to—or loss of—a behavioral freedom, a person will experience psychological reactance (or, more simply, reactance), a motivational state characterized by distress, anxiety, resistance, and the desire to restore that freedom. According to this model, when people feel coerced into a certain behavior, they will react against the coercion, often by demonstrating an increased preference for the behavior that is restrained, and may perform the behavior opposite to that desired.

reaction formation in psychoanalytic theory, a DEFENSE MECHANISM in which unacceptable or threatening unconscious impulses are denied and are replaced in consciousness with their opposite. For example, to conceal an unconscious prejudice, an individual may preach tolerance; to deny feelings of rejection, a mother may be overindulgent toward her child. Through the symbolic relationship between the unconscious wish and its opposite, the outward behavior provides a disguised outlet for the tendencies it seems to oppose.

reaction time (**RT**) the time that elapses between the onset or presentation of a stimulus and the occurrence of a specific response to that stimulus. There are several types, including SIMPLE REACTION TIME and CHOICE REACTION TIME. Reaction time can be used to assess various psychological constructs. To assess negative affect, for example, a researcher might measure the time between presentation of various words with emotional connotations and a participant's indication that each word is either "positive" or "negative."

reactive *adj.* associated with or originating in response to a given stimulus or situation. For example, a psychotic episode that is secondary to a traumatic or otherwise stressful event in the life of the individual would be considered reactive and generally associated with a more favorable prognosis than an ENDOGENOUS episode unrelated to a specific trigger.

reactive aggression see AGGRESSION.

reactive depression a MAJOR DEPRESSIVE EPISODE that is precipitated by a distressing event or situation, such as a career setback or relationship dissolution. Also called **exogenous depression**. Compare ENDOGENOUS DEPRESSION.

reactive measure a measure that alters the response under investigation. For example, if participants are aware of being observed, their reactions may be influenced more by the observer and the fact of being observed than by the stimulus object or situation to which they are ostensibly responding. Compare UNOBTRUSIVE MEASURE.

reactive schizophrenia an acute form of schizophrenia that develops in response to precipitating environmental factors, such as extreme stress. The prognosis is generally more favorable than for PROCESS SCHIZOPHRENIA.

readiness potential (RP) an electrical brain potential that precedes volitional muscular movement. It is detectable some 500 to 600 ms before motion occurs. Also called ***Bereitschaftspotential*** (BP).

reading disorder a LEARNING DISORDER that is characterized by a level of reading ability substantially below that expected for a child of a given age, in-

tellectual ability, and educational experience. The reading difficulty involves faulty oral reading, slow oral and silent reading, and often reduced comprehension.

realism *n.* the philosophical doctrine that objects have an existence independent of the observer. —**realist** *adj., n.*

realistic anxiety anxiety in response to an identifiable threat or danger. This type of anxiety is considered a normal response to danger in the real world and serves to mobilize resources to protect the individual from harm.

realistic group conflict theory a conceptual framework predicated on the assumption that intergroup tensions will occur whenever social groups must compete for scarce resources (e.g., food, territory, jobs, wealth, power, natural resources) and that this competition fuels prejudice and other antagonistic attitudes that lead to conflicts such as rivalries and warfare. Also called **realistic conflict theory**.

reality monitoring a specific aspect of SOURCE MONITORING that refers to the process of discriminating between external (real) and internal (imagined) events. A failure or impairment in this process is said to account for such phenomena as FALSE MEMORY and hallucinations.

reality principle in classical psychoanalytic theory, the regulatory mechanism that represents the demands of the external world and requires the individual to forgo or modify instinctual gratification or to postpone it to a more appropriate time. In contrast to the PLEASURE PRINCIPLE, which is posited to dominate the life of the infant and child and govern the ID, or instinctual impulses, the reality principle is posited to govern the EGO, which controls impulses and enables people to deal rationally and effectively with the situations of life.

reality testing any means by which

an individual determines and assesses his or her limitations in the face of biological, physiological, social, or environmental actualities or exigencies. It enables the individual to distinguish between self and nonself and between fantasy and real life. Defective reality testing is the major feature of psychosis.

real self an individual's true wishes and feelings and his or her potential for further growth and development.

reasonable accommodations adjustments made within an employment or educational setting that allow an individual with a physical, cognitive, or psychiatric disability to perform essential functions. These adjustments might include installing ramps in an office cafeteria for wheelchair accessibility, altering the format of a test for a person with learning disabilities, or providing a sign language interpreter for a person with hearing loss.

reasoning *n.* thinking in which logical processes of an inductive or deductive character are used to draw conclusions from facts or premises. —**reason** *vb.*

recall 1. *vb.* to transfer prior learning or past experience to current consciousness: that is, to retrieve and reproduce information; to remember. **2.** *n.* the process by which this occurs.

recall bias the type of BIAS that often occurs when an individual reports a past behavior or event. Although such retrospective reporting may have accurate features, it also tends to include inaccurate aspects, such as a systematic undercount or overcount of the frequency with which a certain behavior occurred. This type of distortion has ramifications in survey methodology and eyewitness testimony.

receiver-operating characteristic curve (**ROC curve**) in a detection, discrimination, or recognition task, the relationship between the proportion of correct *yes* responses (hit rate) and the

proportion of incorrect *yes* responses (false-alarm rate). This is plotted on a graph to show an individual's sensitivity on the particular task: The axes are hit and false-alarm rates, points are marked to denote the different rates obtained under different conditions, and the points are connected to form a smooth arc. For example, a ROC curve may be used to indicate how well a person detects a specific tone in the presence of noise. Also called **isosensitivity function**.

recency effect a memory phenomenon in which the most recently presented facts, impressions, or items are learned or remembered better than material presented earlier. This effect can occur in both formal learning situations and social contexts. For example, it can result in inaccurate ratings of a person's abilities due to the inordinate influence of the most recent information received about that person. Compare PRIMACY EFFECT.

receptive field the discrete region surrounding a sensory cell that can be stimulated to cause the maximal response of the cell. In vision, for example, the receptive field of a retinal ganglion cell comprises the specific set of photoreceptors along the retina that connect with the cell, such that activation of those receptors in turn evokes activation of the ganglion cell.

receptivity *n.* the period of time when a female is responsive to sexual overtures from a male, typically (but not exclusively) around the time of ovulation. Receptivity has a connotation of passive female acceptance or tolerance of male sexual overtures. In contrast, PROCEPTIVITY conveys active solicitation of males by females. —**receptive** *adj.*

receptor *n.* the cell in a sensory system that is responsible for stimulus TRANSDUCTION. Receptor cells are specialized to detect and respond to specific stimuli in the external or internal environment. Examples include the RETINAL

RODS and RETINAL CONES in the eye and the HAIR CELLS in the cochlea of the ear. See also NEURORECEPTOR.

receptor potential the electric potential produced by stimulation of a receptor cell, which is roughly proportional to the intensity of the sensory stimulus and may be sufficient to trigger an ACTION POTENTIAL in a neuron that is connected to the receptor.

receptor site a region of specialized membrane on the surface of a cell (e.g., a neuron) that contains receptor molecules that receive and react with particular messenger molecules (e.g., neurotransmitters).

recessive allele the version of a gene (see ALLELE) whose effects are manifest only if it is carried on both members of a HOMOLOGOUS pair of chromosomes. Hence, the trait determined by a recessive allele (the **recessive trait**) is apparent only in the absence of another version of that same gene (the DOMINANT ALLELE).

recidivism *n.* relapse. The term typically denotes the repetition of delinquent or criminal behavior. —**recidivist** *n., adj.* —**recidivistic** *adj.*

reciprocal *n.* the number that when multiplied by another number gives a result of 1. The reciprocal of *x* is therefore $1/x$ and that of $1/x$ is *x*. So, for example, $1/4$ is the reciprocal of 4.

reciprocal determinism a concept that opposes exclusive emphasis on environmental determination of responses and instead maintains that the environment influences behavior, behavior influences the environment, and both influence the individual, who also influences them. This concept is associated with SOCIAL LEARNING THEORY.

reciprocal inhibition a technique in BEHAVIOR THERAPY that aims to replace an undesired response (e.g., anxiety) with a desired one by COUNTER-CONDITIONING. Reciprocal inhibition relies on the gradual substitution of a response that is incompatible with the original one and is potent enough to neutralize the influence (e.g., anxiety-evoking power) of the original. See also SYSTEMATIC DESENSITIZATION.

reciprocal relationship 1. a correlation between two variables such that the value of one variable is the RECIPROCAL of the value of the other. For example, if a researcher is studying the average time taken to complete a task, then tasks completed per unit time (e.g., 2 per hour) have a reciprocal relationship with unit time taken per task (0.5 hours). **2.** the situation in which two variables can mutually influence one another; that is, each can be both a cause and an effect.

reciprocity *n.* **1.** the quality of an act, process, or relationship in which one person receives benefits from another and, in return, provides an equivalent benefit. **2.** see COMPENSATION. —**reciprocal** *adj.*

reciprocity norm the social standard that people who help others will receive equivalent benefits from them in return. The expectation of reciprocity is common in many interpersonal encounters and relationships. Compare SOCIAL JUSTICE NORM; SOCIAL RESPONSIBILITY NORM.

recognition *n.* a sense of awareness and familiarity experienced when one encounters people, events, or objects that have been encountered before or when one comes on material that has been learned in the past.

recognition by components theory (**RBC theory**) the theory that perception of objects entails their decomposition into a set of simple three-dimensional elements called **geons**, together with the skeletal structure connecting them.

recollection *n.* remembrance, particularly vivid and detailed memory of past events or information pertaining to a specific time or place.

recombination *n.* the exchange of genetic material between paired chromosomes during the formation of sperm and egg cells. It involves the breaking and rejoining of chromatids (filament-like subunits) of homologous chromosomes in a process called **crossing over**. It results in offspring having combinations of genes that are different from those of either parent.

reconstruction *n.* **1.** in psychoanalysis, the revival and interpretation of past experiences that have been instrumental in producing emotional disturbance. **2.** more generally, re-creation or rebuilding. See RECONSTRUCTIVE MEMORY. —**reconstruct** *vb.*

reconstructive memory a form of remembering marked by the re-creation of an experience or event that has been only partially stored in memory. It draws on general knowledge and SCHEMAS for what typically happens in order to reconstruct the experience or event. See CONSTRUCTIVE MEMORY; REPEATED REPRODUCTION.

recovered memory the subjective experience of recalling a prior traumatic event, such as sexual or physical abuse, that had previously been unavailable to conscious recollection. Before recovering the memory, the person may be unaware that the traumatic event occurred. Because such recoveries may occur while the person is undergoing therapy, there is debate about the role that the therapist may have in suggesting or otherwise arousing them. Also called **repressed memory**. See also FALSE MEMORY.

recovery *n.* **1.** consistent progress in the measurable return of abilities, skills, and functions following illness or injury. **2.** a state of ongoing sobriety following long-term substance abuse.

recreational drug any substance that is used in a nontherapeutic manner for its effects on motor, sensory, or cognitive activities or on emotional state.

recurrent *adj.* occurring repeatedly or reappearing after an interval of time

or a period of remission. It is often applied to disorders marked by chronicity, relapse, or repeated episodes (e.g., recurrent depressive symptoms).

redintegration *n.* restoration to completeness, particularly the process of recollecting memories from partial cues or reminders, as in recalling an entire song when a few notes are played. —**redintegrative** *adj.*

red nucleus a NUCLEUS in the brainstem that receives input from the cerebellum and gives rise to the RUBROSPINAL TRACT. In lower vertebrates, it is important in the control of limb movement. In humans, it has a role in crawling in infancy.

reductionism *n.* the strategy of explaining or accounting for some phenomenon or construct by claiming that, when properly understood, it can be shown to be some other phenomenon or construct, where the latter is seen to be simpler, more basic, or more fundamental. The term is mainly applied to positions that attempt to explain human culture, society, or psychology in terms of animal behavior or physical laws. In psychology, a common form of reductionism is that in which psychological phenomena are reduced to biological phenomena, so that mental life is presented as merely a function of biological processes. See also EPIPHENOMENON; MATERIALISM.

redundancy *n.* **1.** the property of having more structure than is minimally necessary. Biological systems or structures often have redundancy so that impairment or failure of a unit will not prevent adequate functioning of the whole. **2.** in linguistics and information theory, the condition of those parts of a communication that could be deleted without loss of essential content. Redundancy includes not only repetitions, tautologies, and polite formulas, but also the multiple markings of a given meaning that are required by conventions of grammar and syntax. For example, in the sentence *All three* *men were running*, the plurality of the subject is signaled four times: by *all*, *three*, and the plural forms *men* and *were*. —**redundant** *adj*.

reeducation *n.* a form of psychological treatment in which the client learns effective ways of handling and coping with problems and relationships through a form of nonreconstructive therapy, such as RELATIONSHIP THERAPY or BEHAVIOR THERAPY. Also called **reeducative therapy**.

reference distribution see THEORETICAL DISTRIBUTION.

reference group a group or social aggregate that individuals use as a standard or frame of reference when selecting and appraising their own abilities, attitudes, or beliefs. Reference groups include formal and informal groups that the individual identifies with and admires, statistical aggregations of noninteracting individuals, imaginary groups, and even groups that deny the individual membership. See also SOCIAL COMPARISON THEORY.

referral *n.* the act of directing a patient to a therapist, physician, agency, or institution for evaluation, consultation, or treatment. —**refer** *vb*.

referred sensation a sensation (e.g., pain, cold) that is localized (i.e., experienced) at a point different from the area stimulated. For example, when a person bumps his or her elbow, the mechanical stimulation of the nerve may cause tingling of the fingers.

reflection of feeling a statement made by a therapist or counselor that is intended to highlight the feelings or attitudes implicitly expressed in a client's communication and to draw them out so that they can be clarified.

reflective *adj.* describing or displaying behavior that is characterized by significant forethought and slow, deliberate examination of available options. Compare IMPULSIVE. —**reflectivity** *n*.

reflex *n.* any of a number of automatic, unlearned, relatively fixed responses to stimuli that do not require conscious effort and that often involve a faster response than might be possible if a conscious evaluation of the input were required. An example is the PUPILLARY REFLEX.

reflex arc a specific arrangement of neurons involved in a reflex. In its simplest form, it consists of an afferent, or sensory, neuron that conducts nerve impulses from a receptor to the spinal cord, where it connects directly or via an INTERNEURON to an efferent motor neuron that carries the impulses to a muscle or gland.

reflexive behavior responses to stimuli that are involuntary or free from conscious control (e.g., the salivation that occurs with the presentation of food) and therefore serve as the basis for CLASSICAL CONDITIONING.

reflexivity *n.* **1.** a bidirectional relationship of cause and effect. **2.** the quality of a relationship among elements such that they are continuously referential to one another. For example, in the context of an arbitrary matching-to-sample procedure, if a stimulus is chosen when it also appears as the sample, reflexivity has been shown.

refraction *n.* the bending of light as it passes through the cornea and lens of the eye so that it is focused on the retina.

refractory period a period of inactivity after a neuron or muscle cell has undergone excitation. As the cell is being repolarized, it will not respond to any stimulus during the early part of the refractory period, called the **absolute refractory period**. In the subsequent **relative refractory period**, it will respond only to a stronger than normal stimulus.

reframing *n.* a process of reconceptualizing a problem by seeing it from a different perspective. Altering the conceptual or emotional context of a problem often serves to alter perceptions of the problem's difficulty and to open up possibilities for solving it. In psychotherapy, for example, the manner in which a client initially frames a problem may be self-defeating. Part of the therapist's response might be to reframe the problem and the thoughts or feelings that the client associates with it, so as to provide alternative ways to evaluate it. Compare RESTATEMENT.

register *n.* a form of a language associated with specific social functions and situations or with particular subject matter. Examples include the different types of language considered appropriate for a scientific meeting, a kindergarten class, or a barroom story. Register differs from DIALECT in that it varies with social context rather than with the sociological characteristics of the user. See ELABORATED CODE.

regression *n.* **1.** a return to a prior, lower state of cognitive, emotional, or behavioral functioning. This term is associated particularly with the psychoanalytic concept of DEFENSE MECHANISMS and denotes a situation in which the individual reverts to immature behavior or to an earlier stage of PSYCHOSEXUAL DEVELOPMENT when threatened with overwhelming external problems or internal conflicts. **2.** shorthand for REGRESSION ANALYSIS generally or any of its specific associated concepts and procedures. —**regress** *vb.* —**regressive** *adj.*

regression analysis any of several statistical techniques that are used to describe, explain, or predict the variance in an outcome or DEPENDENT VARIABLE using scores on one or more predictor or INDEPENDENT VARIABLES. Regression analysis yields a REGRESSION EQUATION as well as an index of the relationship between the dependent and independent variables. For example, a regression analysis could show the extent to which 1st-year grades in college (outcome) are predicted by such factors as standardized test scores, courses taken in high school, letters of recommendation, and particular extracurricular activities.

regression equation the mathematical expression of the relationship between a dependent (outcome or response) variable and one or more independent (predictor) variables that results from conducting a REGRESSION ANALYSIS. It often takes the form $y = a + bx + e$, in which y is the dependent variable, x is the independent variable, a is the intercept, b is the **regression coefficient** (a specific WEIGHT associated with a change in x on y), and e is the ERROR TERM. Also called **regression model**.

regression line a straight or curved line fitting a set of data points. A graphic representation of the REGRESSION EQUATION expressing the hypothesized relationship between an outcome or DEPENDENT VARIABLE and one or more predictors or INDEPENDENT VARIABLES, it summarizes how well the proposed model actually fits the sample data obtained. Data points that do not fall exactly on the line indicate deviations in model fit.

regression toward the mean the tendency for extremely high or extremely low scores to become more moderate (i.e., closer to the MEAN) on retesting over time. In experimental studies, this tendency threatens INTERNAL VALIDITY in that shifts of scores may occur for reasons unrelated to study manipulations or treatments. For example, regardless of the interventions a researcher is investigating to improve mathematics performance (e.g., extra study sessions), low scoring students will tend to perform slightly better on the next math exam, whereas high scoring students will tend to perform slightly worse.

regulatory drive any generalized state of arousal or motivation that helps preserve physiological HOMEOSTASIS and thus is necessary for the survival of the individual organism, such as hunger and thirst. Compare NONREGULATORY DRIVE.

regulatory focus theory a motivational theory that considers people's goal-pursuit processes to be either promotion oriented (i.e., focused on accomplishment needs; sensitive to positive outcomes and to relative pleasure from gains) or prevention oriented (i.e., focused on security needs; sensitive to negative outcomes and to relative pain from losses). One's disposition toward either obtaining gains or avoiding losses influences one's dominant motivations, which in turn affect one's behavioral choices. For example, the theory suggests that a smoker may be motivated either to approach desired end states (e.g., improved lung capacity) or to avoid undesired end states (e.g., illness). Thus, antismoking messages framed to match the smoker's particular regulatory focus should be more effective in convincing him or her to quit smoking than those that do not match. In addition to its implications for designing persuasive messages, regulatory focus theory has been applied to communication more generally, administration and organizational management, and athletic performance.

rehabilitation *n.* the process of bringing an individual to a condition of health or useful and constructive activity, restoring to the fullest possible degree his or her independence, well-being, and level of functioning following injury, disability, or disorder. It involves providing appropriate resources, such as treatment or training, to enable such a person (e.g., one who has had a stroke) to redevelop skills and abilities he or she had acquired previously or to compensate for their loss. Compare HABILITATION.

rehabilitation neuropsychology a specialty area that studies and treats cognitive, behavioral, emotional, and social disturbances in individuals following stroke, traumatic brain injury, spinal cord injury, and other conditions involving neurological damage. The goal of **rehabilitation neuropsychologists** is to optimize the health, independence, and quality of

life of their clients primarily by (a) evaluating their EXECUTIVE FUNCTIONS and other abilities through observation of their behavior and administration of assessment instruments (e.g., NEUROPSYCHOLOGICAL TESTS); and (b) providing cognitive retraining and other clinical interventions to facilitate skill reacquisition or substitution. The field is cross-disciplinary in nature, having relevance to such areas as community psychology, clinical psychology, counseling psychology, family medicine, health psychology, neurology, and psychiatry.

rehearsal *n.* **1.** preparation for a forthcoming event or confrontation that is anticipated with some level of discomfort or anxiety. By practicing what is to be said or done in a future event, the individual may lessen the stress of the event itself. Rehearsal may be carried out in psychotherapy with the therapist coaching or role-playing to help the individual practice for the event. **2.** the repetition of information in an attempt to maintain it longer in memory. According to the DUAL-STORE MODEL OF MEMORY, rehearsal occurs in SHORT-TERM MEMORY and may allow a stronger trace to then be stored in LONG-TERM MEMORY. Although rehearsal implies a verbal process, it is hypothesized to occur in other modalities as well.

reification *n.* treating an abstraction, concept, or formulation as though it were a real object or material thing. The statement *You can't fool Mother Nature* would be an example of reification if taken literally. Also called **objectification**.

reinforcement *n.* **1.** in OPERANT CONDITIONING, a process in which the frequency or probability of a response is increased by a dependent relationship, or contingency, with a stimulus or circumstance (the REINFORCER). **2.** in CLASSICAL CONDITIONING, the presentation of an unconditioned stimulus after a conditioned stimulus.

reinforcement contingency the contingency (relationship) between a response and a REINFORCER. The contingency may be positive (if the occurrence of the reinforcer is more probable after the response) or negative (if it is less probable after the response). Reinforcement contingencies can be arranged by establishing dependencies between a particular type of response and a reinforcer (as when a rat's lever presses are followed by presentation of food), or they can occur as natural consequences of a response (as when a door opens when pushed) or by accident.

reinforcement schedule see SCHEDULE OF REINFORCEMENT.

reinforcement sensitivity theory (RST) as originally described in 1970 by British psychologist Jeffrey Alan Gray (1934–2004), a model in which personality reflects the functioning of three major biological systems that operate independently of one another: the BEHAVIORAL APPROACH SYSTEM (BAS), which responds to conditioned positive (reinforcing) stimuli by initiating approach behavior; the BEHAVIORAL INHIBITION SYSTEM (BIS), which responds to conditioned negative (aversive) stimuli by initiating avoidance behavior; and the fight–flight system (FFS), or fight–flight–freeze system (FFFS), which responds to unconditioned unpleasant or painful stimuli. Individual differences, especially in the reactivity of the BAS and BIS systems to their characteristic inputs, determine one's sensitivity to rewards and to punishments, respectively, which in turn underlie the personality traits of impulsivity and anxiety. RST has had a major effect on motivation and emotion research and has been applied in clinical psychology to understand the mechanisms underlying some psychopathology (e.g., depressive disorders, anxiety disorders, substance abuse).

reinforcer *n.* a stimulus or circumstance that produces REINFORCEMENT when it occurs in a dependent relationship, or contingency, with a response.

reinforcer effect a situation in which one variable strengthens the relationship between two other variables. For example, if performance on a free recall task is enhanced when participants studying words for the memory task are in a positive mood, positive mood has demonstrated a reinforcer effect on study recall. Compare SUPPRESSOR EFFECT.

Reissner's membrane a thin layer of tissue within the auditory LABYRINTH that separates the SCALA VESTIBULI from the SCALA MEDIA inside the cochlea. [Ernst **Reissner** (1824–1878), German anatomist]

rejecting–neglecting parenting see PARENTING.

rejection *n.* denial of love, attention, interest, or approval.

rejection method a technique that uses an algorithm to generate and select random values for a study. Values are automatically included in or excluded from the study sample depending on whether they fall within a particular range. Also called **rejection sampling**.

relapse *n.* the recurrence of a disorder or disease after a period of improvement or apparent cure. The term also refers to recurrence of substance abuse after a period of ABSTINENCE.

relapse prevention use of various procedures to reduce the risk of relapse of a condition, disease, or disorder. For example, clients or patients might be taught cognitive and behavioral skills before the termination of therapy. Relapse prevention has a particular role in disorders, such as addiction and depression, with high relapse rates. See also TERTIARY PREVENTION.

related samples see DEPENDENT SAMPLES.

relational aggression behavior

that manipulates or damages relationships between individuals or groups, such as bullying, gossiping, and humiliation.

relationship *n.* **1.** an association or connection between objects, events, variables, or other phenomena. See also CORRELATION. **2.** a continuing and often committed association between two or more people, as in a family, friendship, marriage, partnership, or other interpersonal link in which the participants have some degree of influence on each other's thoughts, feelings, and actions. In psychotherapy, the therapist–patient relationship is thought to be essential for patient improvement.

relationship therapy 1. any form of psychotherapy that emphasizes the nature of the relationship between client and therapist and views it as the primary therapeutic tool and agent of positive change. Relationship therapy is based on providing emotional support and creating an accepting atmosphere that fosters personality growth and elicits attitudes and past experiences for examination and analysis during sessions. **2.** any form of psychotherapy focused on improving the relationship between individuals by helping them resolve interpersonal issues and modify maladaptive patterns of interactions, thereby fostering the healthy psychosocial growth of all parties. It is an umbrella term encompassing COUPLES THERAPY and FAMILY THERAPY.

relative deprivation the perception by an individual that the amount of a desired resource (e.g., money, social status) he or she has is less than some comparison standard. This standard can be the amount that was expected or the amount possessed by others with whom the person compares himself or herself. According to some research, social unrest tends to be greatest in areas with high levels of relative deprivation.

relative efficiency 1. for two tests (A and B) of the same hypothesis operating at the same SIGNIFICANCE LEVEL, the ratio of the number of cases needed by Test A to the number needed by Test B for each to have the same statistical POWER. The relative efficiency value enables a researcher to determine whether there is a preferred statistical approach for evaluating a particular phenomenon. **2.** for two parameter estimates (A and B), a value reflecting the ratio of the STANDARD ERROR of Estimate A to the standard error of Estimate B.

relative refractory period see REFRACTORY PERIOD.

relativism *n.* in EPISTEMOLOGY, the assertion that there are no absolute grounds for truth or knowledge claims. Thus, what is considered true will depend on individual judgments and local conditions of culture, reflecting individual and collective experience. Such relativism challenges the validity of science except as a catalog of experience and a basis for ad hoc empirical prediction. —**relativist** *adj.*

relaxation *n.* **1.** abatement of intensity, vigor, energy, or tension, resulting in calmness of mind, body, or both. **2.** the return of a muscle to its resting condition after a period of contraction. —**relax** *vb.*

relaxation technique any therapeutic technique to induce relaxation and reduce stress. Also called **relaxation training**.

relearning method see SAVINGS METHOD.

releaser *n.* in ethology, a stimulus that, when presented under the proper conditions, initiates a FIXED ACTION PATTERN. For example, a red belly on a male stickleback fish elicits aggressive behavior from other male sticklebacks but is attractive to gravid female sticklebacks. Also called **sign stimulus**. See also INNATE RELEASING MECHANISM.

releasing hormone any of a class of hormones secreted by the hypothalamus that control the release of hormones by the anterior pituitary gland. GONADOTROPIN-RELEASING HOR-MONE is an example.

reliability *n.* the trustworthiness or consistency of a measure: the degree to which a test or other measurement instrument is free of random error, yielding the same results across multiple applications to the same sample. See ALTERNATE-FORMS RELIABILITY; INTERNAL CONSISTENCY; RETEST RELIABILITY.

REM behavior disorder (RBD) a disorder involving motor activity during REM SLEEP, which typically includes a physical enactment of dream sequences. Because the dreams that are acted out are generally unpleasant or combative, this behavior is usually disruptive and can result in violence.

remedial education a learning process that occurs after the initial, primary instruction of a subject or skill. Remedial education is intended to improve skills that appear deficient in a particular subject or area. For example, **remedial reading** is specialized instruction for individuals whose reading ability is significantly below average or who have faulty reading patterns.

remembering *n.* the process of consciously reviving or bringing to awareness previous events, experiences, or information, or the process of retaining such material.

remission *n.* a reduction or significant abatement in symptoms of a disease or disorder, or the period during which this occurs. Remission of symptoms does not necessarily indicate that a disease or disorder is cured. See also SPONTANEOUS REMISSION.

remote cause a cause that is removed from its effect in time or space but is nevertheless the ultimate or overriding cause. In a sequence of occurrences, it may be considered to be the precipitating event without which the sequence would not have begun (the original cause). For example, the PROXIMATE CAUSE of Smith's aggression may be a trivial snub, but the remote cause

may be Smith's early childhood experiences.

REM rebound the increased occurrence of REM SLEEP following REM-sleep deprivation. It is an example of a rebound phenomenon, in which a previously suppressed activity increases once the restrictions imposed on it are removed.

REM sleep rapid-*eye-mo*vement sleep: the stage of sleep in which most dreaming tends to occur and during which electroencephalograms show activity that resembles wakefulness (hence, it is also known as **paradoxical sleep**) except for inhibition of most skeletal and cranial muscles. REM sleep accounts for one quarter to one fifth of total sleep time. Compare NREM SLEEP.

repeatability *n.* the degree to which specific research studies obtain similar results when they are conducted again. Study and measurement conditions (e.g., instructions, assessments, setting) must be identical on all occasions. See REPLICATION; REPRODUCIBILITY.

repeated measures design see WITHIN-SUBJECTS DESIGN.

repeated reproduction a method for studying memory in which participants repeatedly retrieve the same memory over time. The method often shows that repeated retrieval leads to changes in a memory. Such studies provide evidence to support the theory that memory should be viewed as constructive and reconstructive (see CONSTRUCTIVE MEMORY; RECONSTRUCTIVE MEMORY), rather than being simply reproductive. See also SERIAL REPRODUCTION.

repertory grid a technique used to analyze an individual's PERSONAL CONSTRUCTS. A number of significant concepts are selected, each of which is rated by the participant on a number of dimensions using a numerical scale. The findings are displayed in matrix form and can be subjected to statistical analysis to reveal correlations.

repetition compulsion in psycho-analytic theory, an unconscious need to reenact early traumas in the attempt to overcome or master them. Such traumas are repeated in a new situation symbolic of the repressed prototype. Repetition compulsion acts as a RESISTANCE to therapeutic change since the goal of therapy is not to repeat but to remember the trauma and to see its relation to present behavior.

repetition priming cuing a response to a stimulus through prior exposure to the same or a related stimulus. The effects of repetition priming (e.g., changed speed of response, number of response errors) can occur without explicit memory of the first stimulus.

repetitive transcranial magnetic stimulation (**rTMS**) see TRANSCRANIAL MAGNETIC STIMULATION.

replication *n.* the repetition of an original experiment or research study to verify or bolster confidence in its results. In **exact replication** (or **literal replication**), a researcher uses procedures that are identical to the original experiment or duplicated as closely as possible. In **modified replication**, a researcher incorporates alternative procedures and additional conditions. In **conceptual replication**, a researcher introduces different techniques and manipulations to gain theoretical information.

representation *n.* that which stands for or signifies something else. For example, in cognitive psychology the term denotes a MENTAL REPRESENTATION, whereas in psychoanalytic theory it refers to an **introject** (see INTROJECTION) of a significant figure or to a SYMBOL for a repressed impulse. —**represent** *vb.* —**representational** *adj.* —**representative** *adj.*

representativeness heuristic a strategy for making categorical judgments about a given person or target based on how closely the exemplar matches the typical or average member of the category. For example, given a choice of the two categories *poet* and *accountant*, people are likely to assign a person in unconventional clothes reading a poetry book to the former category; however, the much greater frequency of accountants in the population means that such a person is more likely to be an accountant. The representativeness heuristic is thus a form of the BASE-RATE FALLACY. Compare AVAILABILITY HEURISTIC.

representative sampling the selection of study units (e.g., participants, homes, schools) from a larger group (population) in an unbiased way, such that the sample obtained accurately reflects the total population. For example, a researcher conducting a study of university admissions would need to ensure he or she used a **representative random sample** of schools—in other words, each school would have an equal probability of being chosen for inclusion, and the group as a whole would provide an appropriate mix of different school characteristics (e.g., private or public, student body size, cost, proportion of students admitted, geographic location).

repressed memory see RECOVERED MEMORY.

repression *n.* **1.** in classical psycho-analytic theory and other forms of DEPTH PSYCHOLOGY, the basic DEFENSE MECHANISM that excludes painful experiences and unacceptable impulses from consciousness. Repression operates on an unconscious level as a protection against anxiety produced by objectionable sexual wishes, feelings of hostility, and ego-threatening experiences and memories of all kinds. **2.** the oppression or exclusion of individuals or groups through limitations on their personal rights and liberties. Compare SUPPRESSION. —**repress** *vb.*

reproducibility *n.* the extent to which a study produces the same findings when it is conducted by a different independent researcher. A given research finding is thought to be stronger when it can be both repeated and reproduced. See REPEATABILITY; REPLICATION.

reproduction *n.* **1.** in biology, the production of new individuals from parent organisms, which perpetuates the species. Sexual reproduction involves the fusion of male and female GAMETES in the process of FERTILIZATION; asexual reproduction does not. **2.** the process of replicating information from memory. It potentially is subject to numerous errors or changes, as demonstrated via REPEATED REPRODUCTION and other techniques.

reproductive success the degree to which an individual is successful in producing progeny that in turn are able to produce progeny of their own. Individuals vary in their success in finding mates and reproducing successfully. NATURAL SELECTION is based on this differential reproductive success. The genetic and behavioral traits that lead to greatest reproductive success survive in a population over generations, whereas traits producing low reproductive success eventually become extinct. See also INCLUSIVE FITNESS.

research *n.* the systematic effort to discover or confirm facts, to investigate a new problem or topic, or to describe events and understand relationships among variables, most often by scientific methods of observation and experimentation. Research is essential to science in contributing to the accumulation of generalizable knowledge.

research design a strategic plan of the procedures to be followed during a study in order to reach valid conclusions, with particular consideration given to participant selection and assignment to conditions, data collection, and data analysis. Research designs may take a variety of forms, including not only experiments but also QUASI-EXPERIMENTAL DESIGNS, OBSERVATIONAL STUDIES, LONGITUDINAL DESIGNS, surveys, focus groups, and other nonexperimental methods.

researcher bias any unintended errors in the research process or the interpretation of its results that are attributable to an investigator's expectancies or preconceived beliefs. The term essentially is synonymous with EXPERIMENTER BIAS, but it applies to all types of investigative projects rather than to experimental designs only.

research hypothesis a statement describing the investigator's expectation about the pattern of data that may result from a given study. By stating specific expectations before the data are collected, the investigator makes a commitment about the direction (e.g., Method A will yield higher final exam scores than Method B) and magnitude (e.g., participants' income will increase with more education) of potential relationships based on the study's theoretical framework and related prior studies. See also ALTERNATIVE HYPOTHESIS; NULL HYPOTHESIS.

research method a procedure for the formulation and evaluation of hypotheses that is intended to reveal relationships between variables and provide an understanding of the phenomenon under investigation. In psychology, this generally involves empirical testing and takes the form of the SCIENTIFIC METHOD. See also QUALITATIVE RESEARCH; QUANTITATIVE RESEARCH.

research protocol the complete description of one's outline or plan for conducting a study. It should be as detailed as possible, including elements such as the RESEARCH HYPOTHESIS to be addressed and the rationale for doing so; the materials and resources that will be required; the timeline or duration; the precise sampling, measurement, and analysis procedures that will be used; a discussion of any ethical considerations; and a description of strengths and limitations.

reserve capacity the difference between performance on a psychological task and an individual's maximum capability to perform that task. Training, intervention, and practice can be used to minimize reserve capacity on a given task.

residual 1. *n.* in REGRESSION ANALYSIS, the difference between the value of an empirical observation and the value predicted by a model. Analysis of residuals allows a researcher to judge the fit or appropriateness of the model for the data. **2.** *adj.* denoting remaining ability (e.g., residual hearing) or a remaining disability (e.g., residual loss of vision) after a trauma or surgery.

residual schizophrenia a subtype of schizophrenia diagnosed when there has been at least one schizophrenic episode but positive symptoms (e.g., delusions, hallucinations, disorganized speech or behavior) are no longer present, and only negative symptoms (e.g., flat affect, poverty of speech, avolition) or mild behavioral and cognitive disturbances (e.g., eccentricities, odd beliefs) remain.

residual variance see ERROR VARIANCE.

resilience *n.* the process and outcome of successfully adapting to difficult or challenging life experiences, especially through mental, emotional, and behavioral flexibility and adjustment to external and internal demands. A number of factors contribute to how well people adapt to adversities, predominant among them (a) the ways in which individuals view and engage with the world, (b) the availability and quality of social resources, and (c) specific COPING STRATEGIES. **—resilient** *adj.*

resistance *n.* in psychotherapy and analysis, obstruction—through the client's words or behavior—of the therapist's or analyst's methods of eliciting or interpreting psychic material brought forth in therapy. **—resist** *vb.* **—resistant** *adj.*

resistance stage see GENERAL ADAPTATION SYNDROME.

resistance to extinction the endurance or persistence of a conditioned response in the absence of reinforcement.

resistant attachment another name for ambivalent attachment (see INSECURE ATTACHMENT).

resolution *n.* **1.** a measure of the ability of the eye to detect two distinct objects when these are close together. **2.** a conclusion or ending, as in the resolution of an interpersonal problem or the resolution phase of the SEXUAL-RESPONSE CYCLE.

respect *n.* an attitude of, or behavior demonstrating esteem, honor, regard, concern, and other such positive qualities toward an individual or entity. Respect can serve an important purpose in interpersonal and intergroup relations by aiding in communication, for example. According to many theorists and practitioners, it is considered to play a crucial role as a bidirectional process in psychotherapy.

respiration *n.* **1.** the series of chemical reactions that enables organisms to convert the chemical energy stored in food into energy that can be used by cells. Also called **cellular respiration**; **internal respiration**. **2.** the process by which an animal takes up oxygen from its environment and discharges carbon dioxide. Also called **external respiration**.

respite care assistance, supervision, and recreational or social activities provided for a limited period to a child, older adult, or person with a disability or chronic illness to temporarily relieve family members from caregiving responsibilities.

respondent *n.* **1.** a study participant who is interviewed as part of a research design or who completes a survey or questionnaire. **2.** any REFLEX that can be conditioned by CLASSICAL CONDITIONING procedures. Compare OPERANT.

respondent behavior behavior that is evoked by a specific stimulus and that will consistently and predictably occur if the stimulus is presented. Compare EMITTED BEHAVIOR.

respondent conditioning see CLASSICAL CONDITIONING.

response *n.* any glandular, muscular, neural, or other reaction to a stimulus. A response is a clearly defined, measurable unit of behavior discussed in terms of its result (e.g., pressing a lever, indicating *yes* vs. *no* on a survey item) or its physical characteristics (e.g., raising an arm).

response acquiescence see YEA-SAYING.

response bias 1. the tendency for a study participant to give one answer or type of answer more than others, regardless of the stimulus condition. There are several different types of response bias, including the HALO EFFECT, NAY-SAYING, and YEA-SAYING. See also RESPONSE SET. **2.** in SIGNAL DETECTION THEORY more specifically, the overall willingness to say *yes* (signal present) or *no* (signal not present), regardless of the actual presence or absence of the signal.

response effect the influence of some attribute of the MEASUREMENT SCALE or administration context on a participant's answers to survey or interview items. For example, the order in which response options are presented may affect how a participant will answer, as might the inclusion of a middle or neutral point on an agreement scale or the means by which a survey is conducted (e.g., in person, via the Internet, or by telephone).

response generalization see INDUCTION.

response rate 1. the number of responses that occur within a specified time interval. **2.** the number of individuals who complete an interview, answer a survey, or join a research study compared to the number who were invited to participate, often expressed as a percentage.

response scale any of various types of instruments provided to a respondent to express an answer to an item. Examples of different response scales include FIXED-ALTERNATIVE QUESTIONS, LIKERT SCALES, and SEMANTIC DIFFER-ENTIALS.

response selection an intermediate stage of human information processing in which a response to an identified stimulus is chosen. Response selection is typically studied by varying relationships between the stimuli and their assigned responses.

response set a tendency to answer questions in a systematic manner that is unrelated to their content. An example is the SOCIAL DESIRABILITY response set. See also RESPONSE BIAS.

response variable see DEPENDENT VARIABLE.

restatement *n.* in psychotherapy and counseling, the verbatim repetition or rephrasing by the therapist or counselor of a client's statement. The purpose is not only to confirm that the client's remarks have been understood but also to provide a "mirror" in which the client can perceive his or her feelings and ideas more clearly. Compare REFRAMING.

resting potential the electric potential across the plasma membrane of a neuron when it is in the nonexcited, or resting, state. It is usually in the range of −50 to −100 mV for vertebrate neurons, representing an excess of negatively charged ions on the inside of the membrane. See also ACTION POTENTIAL.

restraint *n.* the ability to control or prevent behaviors that are harmful or otherwise undesirable. See SELF-REGULATION.

restricted code see ELABORATED CODE.

restriction of range the limitation—via sampling, measurement procedures, or other aspects of experimental design—of the full range of total possible scores that may be obtained to only a narrow portion of that total. For example, in a study of the grade point averages of university students, restriction of range occurs if only students from the dean's list are included. Range restriction on a particular variable may lead to such negative effects as failing to observe or improperly characterizing a relationship between the variables of interest.

retardation *n.* a slowing down or delay of an activity or process, as in PSYCHOMOTOR RETARDATION or MENTAL RETARDATION.

retention *n.* the storage and maintenance of a memory. Retention is the second stage of memory, after ENCODING and before RETRIEVAL. —**retentive** *adj.*

retest reliability a measure of the consistency of results on a test or other assessment instrument over time, given as the correlation of scores between the first and second administrations. It provides an estimate of the stability of the construct being evaluated. Also called **test–retest reliability**.

reticular activating system (**RAS**) a part of the RETICULAR FORMATION thought to be particularly involved in the regulation of arousal, alertness, and sleep–wake cycles.

reticular formation an extensive network of nerve cell bodies and fibers within the brainstem, extending from the medulla oblongata to the upper part of the midbrain, that is widely connected to the spinal cord, cerebellum, thalamus, and cerebral cortex. It is most prominently involved in arousal, alertness, and sleep–wake cycles but also controls some aspects of action and posture.

reticulospinal tract see VENTROMEDIAL PATHWAY.

retina *n.* the light-sensitive inner surface of the eye. A layer of neurons lines the inner surface of the back of the eye and provides the sensory signals re-

quired for vision. The retina contains the photoreceptors—that is, the RETINAL RODS and RETINAL CONES—as well as additional neurons that process the signals of the photoreceptors and convey an output signal to the brain by way of the OPTIC NERVE.

retinal bipolar cell any of various neurons in the INNER NUCLEAR LAYER of the retina that receive input from the photoreceptors (RETINAL RODS and RETINAL CONES) and transmit signals to RETINAL GANGLION CELLS and AMACRINE CELLS. Rods and cones are served by different populations of retinal bipolar cells, called rod bipolars and cone bipolars, respectively.

retinal cone any of various photoreceptors in the retina that require moderate to bright light for activation, as opposed to RETINAL RODS, which require very little light for activation. In primates, retinal cones are concentrated in the FOVEA CENTRALIS of the retina, where their high spatial density and the pattern of connections within their pathways are critical for high-acuity vision. The cone pathways also provide information about the color of stimuli. This is achieved by the presence of three different populations of cones, each having their maximum sensitivity to light in the short, middle, or long wavelengths of the spectrum, respectively. Other animals have additional populations of cones; for example, some fish have cones that are sensitive to ultraviolet wavelengths. See also PHOTOPIGMENT.

retinal disparity see BINOCULAR DISPARITY.

retinal ganglion cell the only type of neuron in the retina that sends signals to the brain resulting from visual stimulation. Retinal ganglion cells receive input from RETINAL BIPOLAR CELLS and AMACRINE CELLS. The axons of retinal ganglion cells form the OPTIC NERVE.

retinal horizontal cell any of various neurons in the retina that make lateral connections between photoreceptors, RETINAL BIPOLAR CELLS, and one another. Their cell bodies are located in the INNER NUCLEAR LAYER of the retina.

retinal image the inverted picture of an external object formed on the retina of the eye.

retinal rod any of various photoreceptors in the retina that respond to low light levels, as opposed to RETINAL CONES, which require moderate to bright light for activation. In primates, which have both rods and cones, the rods are excluded from the center of the retina, the FOVEA CENTRALIS. All rods contain the same PHOTOPIGMENT, rhodopsin; therefore, the rod pathways do not provide color information. The connections of the rod pathways enhance retinal sensitivity to light, but acuity is relatively poor.

retinex theory a theory based on the idea that color registration is carried out in the brain. It developed from demonstrations suggesting that wavelengths register on the color-sensitive components of the retina as color-separated "photos" and that the visual mechanisms in the brain then compare the average of the long-wave photos with the average of the shorter-wave photos, assigning different colors according to the ratios between them.

retrieval *n.* the process of recovering or locating information stored in memory. Retrieval is the final stage of memory, after ENCODING and RETENTION.

retrieval cue a prompt or stimulus used to guide memory recall.

retroactive interference see INTERFERENCE.

retrograde amnesia see AMNESIA.

retrograde memory the ability to recall events that occurred or information that was acquired prior to a particular point in time, often the onset of illness or physical damage such as brain injury. For example, an individual with deficits of retrograde memory (i.e., retrograde AMNESIA) might not remem-ber the name of a close childhood friend but would remember the name of a person just introduced to him or her. Compare ANTEROGRADE MEMORY.

retrospection *n.* the process of reviewing or reflecting on an experience from the past, either directed (as in learning and memory research) or spontaneous (as in evaluating one's behavior in a given situation).

retrospective memory see PROSPECTIVE MEMORY.

retrospective research observational, nonexperimental research that tries to explain the present in terms of past events; that is, research that starts with the present and follows participants backward in time. For example, an investigator may select a group of individuals who exhibit a particular depressive symptom and then study them to determine if they had been exposed to a risk factor of interest. Compare PROSPECTIVE RESEARCH.

retrospective sampling a technique in which participants or cases from the general population are selected for inclusion in experiments or other research based on their previous exposure to a risk factor or the completion of some particular process. Participants are then examined in the present to see if a particular condition or state exists, often in comparison to others who were not exposed to the risk or did not complete the particular process. Compare PROSPECTIVE SAMPLING.

Rett syndrome a genetic disorder that occurs almost exclusively in female children who develop normally in early infancy but then, between 6 and 18 months of age, undergo rapid regression in motor, cognitive, and social skills; these skills subsequently stabilize at a level that leaves the child with intellectual disability. Symptoms generally include loss of language skills, hand motion abnormalities (e.g., hand wringing, other repetitive, purposeless movements), learning difficulties, gait disturbances, breathing problems, seizures, and pronounced deceleration of head growth. [first described in 1966 by Andreas **Rett** (1924–1997), Austrian pediatrician]

reuptake *n.* the process by which neurotransmitter molecules that have been released at a SYNAPSE are reabsorbed by the presynaptic neuron that released them. Reuptake is performed by TRANSPORTER proteins in the presynaptic membrane.

reuptake inhibitor a substance that interferes with the reabsorption of neurotransmitters by the presynaptic neurons that released them. For example, selective serotonin reuptake inhibitors (see SSRI) are thought to block the reabsorption of serotonin, thereby increasing the amount of serotonin available to bind to postsynaptic receptors.

reversal design an experimental design, generally used when only a single group is being studied, that attempts to counteract the confounding effects (see CONFOUND) of sequence and treatment by alternating baseline conditions with treatment conditions. See also ALTERNATING TREATMENTS DESIGN.

reversal learning in DISCRIMINATIONS involving two alternatives, the effect of reversing the contingencies associated with the two alternatives. For example, a monkey could be trained under conditions in which lever presses when a red light is on result in food presentation and lever presses when a green light is on are without effect. The contingencies are then reversed, so that presses when the red light is on are ineffective and presses when the green light is on result in food presentation. If the monkey's behavior adapts to the new contingencies (i.e., it presses the lever only when the green light is on), reversal learning has occurred.

reverse discrimination a term sometimes used to denote advantageous or preferential treatment of a historically disfavored or minority group over a generally favored or majority group, as when twice as many women as men are promoted to management positions. The concept of reverse discrimination is controversial, especially in the context of affirmative action and similar policies. Also called **positive discrimination**.

reversibility *n.* in PIAGETIAN THEORY, a mental operation that reverses a sequence of events or restores a changed state of affairs to the original condition. It is exemplified by the ability to realize that a glass of milk poured into a bottle can be poured back into the glass and remain unchanged. See also CONSERVATION.

reversible figure an AMBIGUOUS FIGURE in which the perspective easily shifts, so that at certain times specific elements appear to make up a distinct figure while at other times those same elements appear as an indistinct background (see FIGURE–GROUND). Examples include the NECKER CUBE and RUBIN'S FIGURE.

revolving-door phenomenon the repeated readmission of patients to hospitals or other institutions, often because they were discharged before they had adequately recovered.

reward *n.* a lay word that is nearly synonymous with REINFORCEMENT. Sometimes it is used to describe the intent of someone providing a consequence for behavior, rather than the effectiveness of the consequence (as is required in the definition of reinforcement) in influencing the frequency or probability of occurrence of that behavior.

reward center see PLEASURE CENTER.

reward theory any of a group of hypotheses that focus on the function of satisfying or pleasurable stimuli (rewards) in learning, approach behavior, and decision making. For example, the **reward theory of attraction** states that people develop strong relationships with those with whom they have positive, fulfilling interactions, particularly when the benefits gained do not require much in return. Similarly, the **positive reward theory** states that addiction stems from the perception of substances as pleasant and gratifying, and the **mutual reward theory** of business states that managers and employees work together more productively when each provides the other with something positive in compensation for good performance.

Rhine cards see ZENER CARDS. [Joseph B. **Rhine** (1895–1980), U.S. parapsychologist]

rhinencephalon *n.* the portion of the brain that includes the limbic system; olfactory nerves, bulbs, and tracts; and related structures. The term literally means "smell brain," because early anatomists assumed it was an olfactory organ itself.

rhodopsin *n.* a PHOTOPIGMENT associated mainly with function of the RETINAL ROD cells. Rhodopsin consists of the vitamin A aldehyde 11-*cis* retinal bound to the protein opsin. When activated by light (photons), 11-*cis* retinal is transformed into all-*trans* retinal, which detaches from the opsin. This initiates a cascade of events that results in visual TRANSDUCTION.

rhombencephalon *n.* see HIND-BRAIN.

ribonucleic acid see RNA.

ribosome *n.* an organelle, consisting of RNA and proteins, found in large numbers in all cells and responsible for the translation of genetic information (in the form of messenger RNA) and the assembly of proteins. —**ribosomal** *adj.*

right brain the right cerebral hemisphere of the brain. The term is sometimes used to designate functions or aspects of COGNITIVE STYLE supposedly mediated by the right (rather than by the left) hemisphere, such as creative thinking. Compare LEFT BRAIN. See also HEMISPHERIC LATERALIZATION.

right hemisphere the right half of the cerebrum, the part of the brain concerned with sensation and perception, motor control, and higher level cognitive processes. The two CEREBRAL HEMISPHERES differ somewhat in function; for example, in most people, the right hemisphere has greater responsibility for spatial attention. See HEMISPHERIC LATERALIZATION. Compare LEFT HEMISPHERE.

right to refuse treatment 1. the right of patients to refuse treatment that may be potentially hazardous or intrusive. In the United States, various state laws and court rulings support the right of patients to receive or reject certain treatments, but there is a lack of uniformity in such applications. **2.** the right of terminally ill patients (e.g., those on life-support systems) to refuse treatment intended to prolong their lives.

right to treatment a statutory right, established at varying governmental levels, stipulating that people with disabilities or disorders, usually persistent or chronic in nature, have the right to receive care and treatment suited to their needs. Such statutory rights may apply nationally or to certain state or provincial areas, and they may be limited to certain conditions and disabilities.

rigidity *n.* stiffness or inflexibility, as in muscular rigidity. The term also refers to a personality trait characterized by strong resistance to changing one's behavior, opinions, or attitudes or by the inability to adapt to changing circumstances. —**rigid** *adj.*

risk *n.* **1.** the probability or likelihood that a negative event will occur, such as the risk that a disease or disorder will develop. **2.** the probability of experiencing loss or harm that is associated with an action or behavior. See also AT RISK; RISK FACTOR. —**risky** *adj.*

risk-as-feelings theory a model stating that decision making in situations involving a degree of risk is often driven by emotional reactions, such as worry, fear, or anxiety, rather than by a rational assessment of the desirability and the likelihood of the various possible outcomes.

risk assessment the process of determining the danger an individual who has been confined because of mental illness or criminal acts would be likely to pose if released. The determination may be a clinician-based prediction of dangerous or violent behavior (clinical risk assessment), or it may be based on a specific formula or weighting system using empirically derived predictors (actuarial risk assessment).

risk aversion the tendency, when choosing between alternatives, to avoid options that entail a risk of loss, even if that risk is relatively small. Compare RISK PRONENESS.

risk factor a clearly defined behavior or constitutional (e.g., genetic), psychological, environmental, or other characteristic that is associated with an increased possibility or likelihood that a disease or disorder will subsequently develop in an individual. Compare PROTECTIVE FACTOR.

risk proneness the propensity to be attracted to, or the willingness to tolerate, options that entail a potentially high risk of loss. Compare RISK AVERSION.

risk taking a pattern of engaging in activities or behaviors that are highly subject to chance, particularly those that are physically dangerous (e.g., river rafting, driving while intoxicated) or that simultaneously involve potential for failure as well as for accomplishment or personal benefit (e.g., starting a business, gambling). In some settings (e.g., the workplace, educational institutions), risk taking tends to be associated with a degree of creativity necessary for success and thus viewed positively, whereas in other contexts it is often seen as unnecessary or the result of poor decision making and thus evaluated negatively.

risky shift a tendency for the decisions of individuals to be more risky following group discussion. Research has revealed that group discussion does not make decisions more risky per se but simply serves to polarize group members in the direction of their initial views. Compare CAUTIOUS SHIFT.

Ritalin *n.* a trade name for METHYLPHENIDATE.

rite of passage a ritual that marks a specific life transition, such as birth, menarche, marriage, or death, or the attainment of a milestone, such as a bar mitzvah, graduation, or admission to a profession. In many societies, such rites are considered essential if the individual is to make a successful transition from one status to another.

ritual *n.* **1.** a form of COMPULSION involving a rigid or stereotyped act that is carried out repeatedly and is based on idiosyncratic rules that do not have a rational basis (e.g., having to perform a task in a certain way). Rituals may be performed to reduce distress and anxiety caused by an OBSESSION. **2.** a ceremonial act or rite, usually involving a fixed order of actions or gestures and the saying of certain prescribed words. Anthropologists distinguish between several major categories of ritual: magic rituals, which involve an attempt to manipulate natural forces; calendrical rituals, which mark the passing of time; liturgical rituals, which involve the reenactment of a sacred story or myth; RITES OF PASSAGE; and formal procedures that have the effect of emphasizing both the importance and the impersonal quality of certain social behaviors, as in a court of law. **—ritualism** *n.* **—ritualistic** *adj.*

ritualization *n.* the process by which a normal behavior becomes a communication signal representing the behavior or its physiological consequence. For example, among nonhuman animals, THREAT DISPLAYS may be a ritualization of impending attack, as when dogs pull back their lips in a snarl in response to a threat. This lip-pulling began as a way for dogs to avoid biting themselves in an attack, but as other animals recognized this behavior as a precursor to biting, it became ritualized into a warning communication. Animals learn that ritualized behavior can be an effective form of avoiding a fight.

RNA *ribo*nucleic *a*cid: a nucleic acid that directs the synthesis of protein molecules in living cells. There are three main types of RNA. MESSENGER RNA carries the GENETIC CODE from the cell nucleus to the cytoplasm. Ribosomal RNA is found in ribosomes, small particles where proteins are assembled from amino acids. Transfer RNA carries specific amino acids for protein synthesis. RNA is similar to DNA in structure except that it consists of a single strand of nucleotides (compared with the double strands of DNA), the base uracil occurs instead of thymine, and the sugar unit is ribose, rather than deoxyribose.

robustness *n.* the ability of a statistical procedure to produce valid estimated values for a population characteristic (PARAMETER) despite violations of the ASSUMPTIONS on which the procedure is based.

rod *n.* see RETINAL ROD.

role *n.* a coherent set of behaviors expected of an individual in a specific position within a group or social setting. Since the term is derived from the dramaturgical concept of role (the dialogue and actions assigned to each performer in a play), there is a suggestion that individuals' actions are regulated by the part they play in the social setting rather than by their personal predilections or inclinations.

role confusion a state of uncertainty about a given social or group role.

role play a technique used in human relations training and psychotherapy in which participants act out various social roles in dramatic situations. Origi-

nally developed in PSYCHODRAMA, role play is now widely used in industrial, educational, and clinical settings for purposes such as teaching employees to handle customer complaints, helping change attitudes and relationships among couples or family members, and rehearsing different ways of coping with stresses and conflicts.

role taking looking at a situation from the viewpoint of another person, typically for the purpose of understanding his or her thoughts and actions. Development of role-taking skills is considered an important step in the development of social cognition.

romantic love a type of love in which intimacy and passion are prominent features. In some taxonomies of love, romantic love is identified with PASSIONATE LOVE and distinguished from COMPANIONATE LOVE; in others, it is seen as involving elements of both. See also TRIANGULAR THEORY OF LOVE.

rooting reflex an automatic, unlearned response of a newborn to a gentle stimulus (e.g., the touch of a finger) applied to the corner of the mouth or to the cheek, in which the infant turns his or her head and makes sucking motions.

root mean square (RMS) the square root of the sum of the squares of a set of values divided by the number of values. For a set of values $x_1, x_2, \ldots x_n$, the root mean square value is

$$\sqrt{[(x_1^2 + x_2^2 + \ldots x_n^2)/n]}$$

and describes the average size of the values in the set. In the physical sciences, the term is used as a synonym for STANDARD DEVIATION under certain circumstances.

Rorschach Inkblot Test a PROJECTIVE TECHNIQUE in which the participant is presented with 10 unstructured inkblots (half in black and gray and half including color) and is asked "What might this be?" The examiner classifies the responses according to various structural and thematic (content) factors and attempts to interpret the participant's personality in terms of characteristics such as emotionality, cognitive style, creativity, impulse control, and various defensive patterns. Perhaps the best known—and certainly one of the most controversial—assessment instruments in all of psychology, the Rorschach is widely used and has been extensively researched, with results ranging from those that claim strong support for its clinical utility (e.g., for selecting treatment modalities or monitoring patient change or improvement over time) to those that demonstrate little evidence of validity. [developed in 1921 by Hermann **Rorschach** (1884–1922), Swiss psychiatrist]

Rosenthal effect the situation in which an investigator's expectations about the outcome of a given study unwittingly affect the actual study outcome. A researcher may use BLINDS to prevent the Rosenthal effect from occurring and biasing study results. See also DEMAND CHARACTERISTICS. [Robert **Rosenthal** (1933–), German-born U.S. psychologist]

rostral *adj.* **1.** pertaining to a beak or snout. **2.** situated or occurring toward the nose or beak of an organism, or toward the front or anterior portion of an organism. Compare CAUDAL. **—rostrally** *adv.*

rote learning memorization by repetition without any ELABORATION or other DEEP PROCESSING of the material. For example, a student may prepare to recite a poem before the class by rehearsing it many times in front of a mirror. Rote learning uses strict memorization without comprehension, which tends to result in poorer retention than occurs with strategies that rely on

higher level cognitive mechanisms (e.g., conceptualization, generalization, interpretation); it is factual recall without understanding the reasoning or relationships involved in the material. Also called **rote memory**.

round window a membrane-covered opening in the cochlea where it borders the middle ear (see SCALA TYMPANI). Pressure changes in the cochlea produced by vibration of the OVAL WINDOW are ultimately transmitted to the round window. This permits displacement of the BASILAR MEMBRANE and stimulation of the sensory receptors.

r to z transformation see FISHER'S R TO Z TRANSFORMATION.

Rubin's figure an AMBIGUOUS FIGURE that may be perceived either as one goblet or as two facing profiles. [Edgar **Rubin** (1886–1951), Danish philosopher]

rubrospinal tract a motor pathway that arises from the RED NUCLEUS in the brainstem and descends laterally in the spinal cord, where it stimulates flexor motor neurons and inhibits extensor motor neurons.

rumination *n.* **1.** obsessional thinking involving excessive, repetitive thoughts or themes that interfere with other forms of mental activity. **2.** the voluntary regurgitation of food from the stomach to the mouth, where it is masticated and tasted a second time or ejected. It generally occurs during infancy but may be observed in individuals of any age, particularly those with severe intellectual disability. If it lasts longer than a month following a period of normal feeding, it is diagnosed as **rumination disorder**; individuals may develop potentially fatal weight loss and malnutrition. **—ruminate** *vb.*

Ss

saccade *n.* a rapid eye movement that allows visual fixation to jump from one location to another in the visual field. Once initiated, a saccade cannot change course. Compare SMOOTH-PURSUIT EYE MOVEMENT. —**saccadic** *adj.*

saccule *n.* the smaller of the two VESTIBULAR SACS of the inner ear, the other being the UTRICLE. Like the utricle, it contains a sensory structure called a MACULA. Movements of the head relative to gravity exert a momentum pressure on hair cells within the macula, which then fire nerve impulses indicating a change in body position. —**saccular** *adj.*

sadism *n.* the derivation of pleasure through cruelty and inflicting pain, humiliation, and other forms of suffering on individuals. The term generally denotes SEXUAL SADISM. [Donatien Alphonse François, Comte (Marquis) de **Sade** (1740–1814), French soldier and writer] —**sadist** *n.* —**sadistic** *adj.*

sadness *n.* an emotional state of unhappiness, ranging in intensity from mild to extreme and usually aroused by the loss of something that is highly valued (e.g., by the rupture of a relationship). Persistent sadness is one of the two defining symptoms of a MAJOR DEPRESSIVE EPISODE, the other being ANHEDONIA. —**sad** *adj.*

sadomasochism *n.* sexual activity between consenting partners in which one partner enjoys inflicting pain and the other enjoys experiencing pain. —**sadomasochist** *n.* —**sadomasochistic** *adj.*

safety need a desire for freedom from illness or danger and for a secure, familiar, and predictable environment. Safety needs comprise the second level of MASLOW'S MOTIVATIONAL HIERARCHY, after basic PHYSIOLOGICAL NEEDS.

sagittal *adj.* describing or relating to a plane that divides the body or an organ into left and right portions. A midsagittal plane divides the body centrally into halves, whereas a parasagittal plane lies parallel but to one side of the center. —**sagittally** *adv.*

salient *adj.* distinctive or prominent. A salient stimulus in a multielement array will tend to be easily detected and identified. The noun form, **salience** (or **saliency**), denotes a parameter of a stimulus that indexes its effectiveness in attracting attention. See POP-OUT.

saltation *n.* **1.** a type of conduction of nerve impulses that occurs in nerve fibers that have a MYELIN SHEATH, in which the impulses skip from one NODE OF RANVIER to the next. This permits much faster conduction velocities compared with those of fibers without a sheath. Also called **saltatory conduction. 2.** the phenomenon in which a sensation is felt at a site other than that where it was evoked. For example, auditory saltation is an illusion in which a train of clicks, the first half of which is presented at one location and the other half of which is presented at a second location, is perceived as originating not only from the anchor points but also from locations between them. [from Latin *saltatio*, "dance"]

sample *n.* a subset of a POPULATION of interest that is selected for study with the aim of making inferences to the population. Characteristics that describe observations in this subset, such as the mean, median, or STANDARD DEVIATION, are called STATISTICS.

sample correlation coefficient (symbol: *r*) an index of the degree of association between two variables based on the data in a studied subset (sample) of cases from a larger group of interest. It is a variant of the PRODUCT-MOMENT

402

CORRELATION COEFFICIENT, and the same symbol is used for both statistics. See also POPULATION CORRELATION COEFFICIENT.

sample mean (symbol: $\bar{X}$; M) the arithmetic average (MEAN) of a set of scores obtained from cases in a subset drawn from a larger population. Because each score contributes equally to this index of CENTRAL TENDENCY, it can be affected greatly by OUTLIERS. Many widely used STATISTICAL TESTS are based on the comparison of sample means.

sample reliability the degree to which a subset of items (sample) is representative of the POPULATION from which it is drawn. It is typically indexed by the STANDARD ERROR OF THE MEAN.

sample size the number of observations (cases, individuals, units) included in a selection of items to be studied. This is usually denoted N (for the study as a whole) or n (for subgroups from the study).

sample variance (symbol: s^2) the dispersion of scores within a group selected for study, as opposed to the POPULATION VARIANCE. It is calculated by determining each score's difference from the average for the set, squaring and summing these differences, and then dividing by the total number of scores minus one.

sampling *n*. the process of selecting for study a limited number of units from a larger set. There are various different selection methods, including SIMPLE RANDOM SAMPLING, STRATIFIED SAMPLING, CONVENIENCE SAMPLING, and QUOTA SAMPLING. Each approach has a different potential of obtaining a sample appropriately representative of the POPULATION under study.

sampling bias a systematic and directional error involved in the choice of units, cases, or participants from a larger group for study. Sampling bias can threaten both the INTERNAL VALIDITY and EXTERNAL VALIDITY of the study.

It is associated with a lack of RANDOM SAMPLING and with nonrandom assignment to conditions. Also called **selection bias**.

sampling design the specific approach, method, or strategy that a researcher decides to use for selecting a sample from the larger population. Formulating a design involves determining the nature of the target population, a suitable SAMPLING FRAME for drawing the cases, the desired sample size, whether random or nonrandom selection will be used, and whether there are any important variables on which to stratify selection. Also called **sampling plan**.

sampling error the predictable MARGIN OF ERROR that occurs in studies of samples of cases or observations from a larger POPULATION: It indicates the possible variance between the true value of a parameter in the population and the estimate of that value made from the sample data. For example, a sampling error of 3% in a large national survey finding that 65% of citizens prefer a particular policy means that the true figure could be anywhere between 62% and 68%.

sampling frame the specific source used in drawing a subset of cases or individuals from a larger POPULATION. Any sampling frame should be representative of the target population as a whole. In a study of college students' aspirations for life after graduation, for example, the researchers might decide to use a listing of students obtained from the institution's office of admissions as their sampling frame and randomly select from this list every fifth student.

sampling without replacement a technique for compiling a sample to be used in research that involves selecting an item from the larger set and removing it from the general pool; thus, this particular case cannot be redrawn.

sampling with replacement a technique for compiling a sample to be used in research in which each item selected from the larger set is returned to the general pool. This means that a particular case may be drawn more than once for a given sample.

sanction *n.* a punishment or other coercive measure, usually administered by a recognized authority, that is used to penalize and deter inappropriate or unauthorized actions.

Sapir–Whorf hypothesis see LINGUISTIC DETERMINISM. [Edward **Sapir** (1884–1939) and Benjamin Lee **Whorf** (1897–1941), U.S. linguists]

satiation *n.* **1.** the satisfaction of a desire or need, such as hunger or thirst. **2.** the temporary loss of effectiveness of a REINFORCER due to its repeated presentation. —**satiate** *vb.*

satiety center see VENTROMEDIAL NUCLEUS.

saturation *n.* the purity of a color and the degree to which it departs from white. Colors with high saturation are intense and brilliant (e.g., fuchsia), whereas colors of low saturation are diluted and dull (e.g., pastel pink).

savant *n.* a person with an intellectual disability or an AUTISM SPECTRUM DISORDER who demonstrates exceptional, usually isolated, cognitive abilities, such as rapid calculation, identifying the day of the week for any given date, or musical talent. The term **idiot savant** initially was used to denote such a person but has been discarded as pejorative.

savings method a way of measuring quantitatively, without relying on an individual's conscious memory, how much learned material is retained. In an initial learning session, the number of trials or the amount of time until the individual can achieve a goal, such as one perfect recitation of a list of nonsense syllables, is recorded. At a later time, he or she is retaught the same material. The difference in number of trials or time taken to achieve the goal is compared between the first and second sessions; this is the **savings value** (or **savings score**). Also called **relearning method**.

scaffolding *n.* a teaching style that supports and facilitates the student as he or she learns a new skill or concept, with the ultimate goal of the student becoming self-reliant. It involves teaching material just beyond the level at which the student could learn alone. Technologies (e.g., computer software) that may be used to assist in this process are known as **scaffolded tools**.

scala media one of the three canals that run the length of the COCHLEA in the inner ear. Located between the scala vestibuli and scala tympani, it is filled with fluid and is delimited by REISSNER'S MEMBRANE and the BASILAR MEMBRANE, which supports the ORGAN OF CORTI.

scalar 1. *n.* a quantity having only magnitude and not direction. Compare VECTOR. **2.** *adj.* describing a variable that can be represented by positions on a scale.

scala tympani one of the three canals within the COCHLEA in the inner ear. It is located below the scala media, from which it is separated by the BASILAR MEMBRANE, and contains PERILYMPH. At its basal end is the ROUND WINDOW.

scala vestibuli one of the three canals within the COCHLEA in the inner ear. It is located above the scala media, from which it is separated by REISSNER'S MEMBRANE, and contains PERILYMPH. At its basal end is the OVAL WINDOW.

scale *n.* **1.** a system for ordering test responses in a progressive series, so as to measure a trait, ability, attitude, or the like. For example, an agreement scale used on an attitude survey might have seven response options ranging from *strongly disagree* (1) to *strongly agree* (7). **2.** a sequence of ordered values used as a reference in measuring a physical property (e.g., weight, temperature). **3.** more generally, any test or other assessment instrument as a whole.

scaling *n.* the process of constructing an instrument to measure, assess, and order some quantity or characteristic (e.g., height, weight, happiness, empathy).

scapegoating *n.* blaming: the process of directing one's anger, frustration, and aggression onto others and targeting them as the source of one's problems and misfortunes. —**scapegoat** *n., vb.*

scapegoat theory 1. an analysis of violence and aggression in which individuals undergoing negative experiences (such as workplace layoffs) are assumed to blame an innocent individual or group for causing the experience. Subsequent mistreatment of this scapegoat then serves as an outlet for individuals' frustrations and hostilities. **2.** an analysis of PREJUDICE in which intergroup conflict is assumed to be caused, in part, by the tendency of individuals to blame their negative experiences on other groups.

scatterplot *n.* a graphical representation of the relationship between two continuously measured variables in which one variable is aarrayed on each axis and a dot or other symbol is placed at each point where the values of the variables intersect. The overall pattern of dots provides an indication of the extent to which there is a LINEAR RELATIONSHIP between variables. OUTLIER points are also clearly visible. Also called **dot plot**; **scattergram**.

Schachter–Singer theory the theory that experiencing and identifying emotional states are functions of both physiological arousal and cognitive interpretations of the physical state. Also called **two-factor theory of emotion**. [Stanley **Schachter** (1922–1997) and Jerome E. **Singer** (1924–2010), U.S. psychologists]

Schaie's stages of cognitive development a theory in which human cognitive processes are posited to develop within up to five periods during the lifespan. In the initial acquisitive stage, an individual acquires knowledge and intellectual skills. The achieving stage occurs next, in young adulthood, during which an individual's primary cognitive task is to achieve personal goals (e.g., establishing a career) by applying the intellectual skills learned. The individual then uses those skills in middle adulthood, during the responsible stage, to manage increasingly complex situations arising from family, community, and career responsibilities. This stage may by followed by the executive stage, during which some adults may achieve a high level of intellectual functioning focused on societal rather than on exclusively personal concerns. Finally, in the reintegrative stage, individuals in late adulthood apply their intellectual skills to reexamine their life experiences and priorities. [proposed in the 1970s by K. Warner **Schaie** (1928–   ), Polish-born U.S. psychologist]

schedule of reinforcement in conditioning, a rule that determines which instances of a response will be reinforced. There are numerous types of schedules of reinforcement, such as INTERVAL REINFORCEMENT and RATIO REINFORCEMENT. Also called **reinforcement schedule**.

Scheffé test a POST HOC TEST used after a researcher obtains a significant F RATIO in an ANALYSIS OF VARIANCE that has more than two conditions of an independent variable that are being examined for differences among their mean values. The Scheffé test is considered to be one of the most stringent MULTIPLE COMPARISON TESTS because it is conservative in its identification of statistically significant mean differences between groups. [Henry **Scheffé** (1907–1977), U.S. mathematician]

schema *n.* (*pl.* **schemata**) **1.** a collection of basic knowledge about a concept or entity that serves as a guide to perception, interpretation, imagination, or problem solving. For example, the schema "dorm room" suggests that a bed and a desk are probably part of the scene, that a microwave oven might or might not be, and that expensive Persian rugs probably will not be. **2.** an outlook or assumption that an individual has of the self, others, or the world that endures despite objective reality. For example, "I am a damaged person" and "Anyone I trust will eventually hurt me" are negative schemas that may result from negative experiences in early childhood. A goal of treatment, particularly stressed in COGNITIVE THERAPY, is to help the client to develop more realistic, present-oriented schemas. **—schematic** *adj.*

scheme *n.* a cognitive structure that contains an organized plan for an activity, thus representing generalized knowledge about an entity and serving to guide behavior. For example, there is a simple sucking scheme of infancy, applied first to a nipple and later to a thumb, soft toy, and so forth. This term is often used as a synonym of SCHEMA.

schizoaffective disorder an uninterrupted illness featuring at some time a MAJOR DEPRESSIVE EPISODE or MANIC EPISODE concurrently with characteristic symptoms of schizophrenia (e.g., delusions, hallucinations, disorganized speech, catatonic behavior).

schizoid *adj.* denoting characteristics resembling schizophrenia but in a milder form, involving lack of affect, social passivity, and minimal introspection.

schizoid personality disorder a personality disorder characterized by long-term emotional coldness, absence of tender feelings for others, lack of desire for and enjoyment of close relationships, and indifference to praise or criticism and to the feelings of others. The eccentricities of speech, behavior, or thought that are characteristic of SCHIZOTYPAL PERSONALITY DISORDER are absent in those with schizoid personality disorder.

schizophrenia *n.* a psychotic disorder characterized by disturbances in thinking (cognition), emotional responsiveness, and behavior. Schizophrenia was first formally described in the late 19th century and named DEMENTIA PRAECOX. In addition to delusions, hallucinations, and disorganized speech, symptoms may include abnormal associations in thinking, autistic behavior and thinking, abnormal affect, and ambivalence. These symptoms are associated with marked social or occupational dysfunction. Five distinct subtypes of schizophrenia have been described: CATATONIC SCHIZOPHRENIA, DISORGANIZED SCHIZOPHRENIA, PARANOID SCHIZOPHRENIA, RESIDUAL SCHIZOPHRENIA, and UNDIFFERENTIATED SCHIZOPHRENIA. **—schizophrenic** *adj.*

schizophreniform disorder a disorder whose essential features are identical to those of schizophrenia except that the total duration is between 1 and 6 months (i.e., intermediate between BRIEF PSYCHOTIC DISORDER and schizophrenia) and social or occupational functioning need not be impaired.

schizophrenogenic *adj.* denoting a factor or influence viewed as causing or contributing to the onset or development of schizophrenia.

schizotypal personality disorder a personality disorder characterized by various oddities of thought, perception, speech, and behavior that are not severe enough to warrant a diagnosis of schizophrenia. Symptoms may include perceptual distortions, MAGICAL THINKING, social isolation, vague speech without incoherence, and inadequate rapport with others due to aloofness or lack of feeling.

Scholastic Assessment Test (**SAT**) a test used in selecting candidates for admission to American colleges. Formerly called the **Scholastic Aptitude Test**, it measures critical reading abilities, mathematical reasoning abilities, and writing abilities developed over time through work done in school and independently.

school neuropsychology an emerging specialty whose practitioners seek to provide teachers, educational administrators, and others with a better understanding of their students' cognitive processing strengths and weaknesses, with the ultimate goal of informing their development of educational practices that will most benefit each individual learner. **School neuropsychologists** observe student behavior and administer and interpret NEUROPSYCHOLOGICAL TESTS, among other responsibilities. See also PEDIATRIC NEUROPSYCHOLOGY.

school psychology a field of psychology concerned with psychoeducational problems and other issues arising in primary and secondary schools. **School psychologists** are involved in curriculum assessment and planning, administration of psychoeducational tests, interviews with parents concerning their child's progress and problems, counseling of teachers and students, and research on educational questions and issues.

school refusal persistent reluctance to go to school, which usually occurs during the primary school years and is often a symptom of an educational, social, or emotional problem. School refusal may be a feature of SEPARATION ANXIETY DISORDER and is often associated with physical symptoms (e.g., upset stomach, nausea, dizziness, headache) and anxiety at the start of the day. Also called **school phobia**.

Schwann cell a type of peripheral nervous system cell (GLIA) that forms the MYELIN SHEATH around axons. Extensions of a single Schwann cell wind tightly and many times around several neighboring axons. [Theodor **Schwann** (1810–1882), German physiologist]

science *n.* the systematic study of structure and behavior in the physical, natural, and social worlds, involving the generation, investigation, and test-

ing of HYPOTHESES; the accumulation of data; and the formulation of general laws and theories. There are several major branches, including the natural sciences (e.g., biology, physics) and the social sciences. The subdisciplines of psychology are themselves divided among the different branches.

scientific method a set of procedures, guidelines, assumptions, and attitudes required for the organized and systematic collection, interpretation, and verification of data and the discovery of reproducible evidence, enabling laws and principles to be stated or modified.

sclera *n.* the tough, white outer coat of the eyeball, which is continuous with the cornea at the front and the sheath of the optic nerve at the back of the eyeball.

score *n.* a quantitative value assigned to test results or other measurable responses.

scotoma *n.* an area of partial or complete loss of vision. Scotomas can occur either in the central visual field (central scotoma) or in the periphery (paracentral scotoma).

screening *n.* **1.** a procedure or program to detect early signs of a disease in an individual or population. **2.** the initial evaluation of a patient to determine his or her suitability for psychological or medical treatment generally, a specific treatment approach, or referral to a treatment facility. This evaluation is made on the basis of medical or psychological history, mental status examination, diagnostic formulation, or some combination of these.

script *n.* **1.** a cognitive schematic structure—a mental road map—containing the basic actions (and their temporal and causal relations) that comprise a complex action. **2.** see PRESCRIPTION DRUG.

script theory 1. the proposition that discrete affects, such as joy and fear, are prime motivators of behavior and that personality structure and function can be understood in terms of self-defining affective scenes and scripts. **2.** in TRANSACTIONAL ANALYSIS, the theory that an individual's approach to social situations follows a sequence that was learned and established early in life.

scrupulosity *n.* overconscientiousness with respect to matters of right and wrong, often manifested as an obsession with moral or religious issues (e.g., preoccupation about committing a sin and going to hell) that results in compulsive moral or religious observance and that is highly distressing. It is typically associated with OBSESSIVE-COMPULSIVE PERSONALITY DISORDER.

seasonal affective disorder (**SAD**) a mood disorder in which there is a predictable occurrence of MAJOR DEPRESSIVE EPISODES, MANIC EPISODES, or both at particular times of the year. The typical pattern is the occurrence of major depressive episodes during the fall or winter months.

secondary aging changes due to biological aging but accelerated by disabilities resulting from disease or produced by extrinsic factors, such as stress, trauma, lifestyle, and the environment. Secondary aging is often distinguished from PRIMARY AGING, which is governed by inborn and age-related processes, but the distinction is not a precise one.

secondary auditory cortex (A2) see AUDITORY CORTEX.

secondary care health care services provided by medical specialists (e.g., cardiologists, urologists, dermatologists) to whom, typically, patients are referred by another provider. Compare PRIMARY CARE; TERTIARY CARE.

secondary circular reaction in PIAGETIAN THEORY, a repetitive action emerging around 4 to 5 months of age that signifies the infant's aim of making things happen. This step occurs during the SENSORIMOTOR STAGE. The infant repeats actions, such as rattling the crib,

that have yielded results in the past but is not able to coordinate them so as to meet the requirements of a new situation. See PRIMARY CIRCULAR REACTION; TERTIARY CIRCULAR REACTION.

secondary drive a learned drive; that is, a drive that is developed through association with or generalization from a PRIMARY DRIVE. For example, in an AVOIDANCE CONDITIONING experiment in which a rat must go from one compartment into another to escape an electric shock, the secondary drive is fear of the shock and the primary drive with which it is associated is avoidance of pain.

secondary gain in psychoanalytic theory, the advantage derived from a NEUROSIS in addition to the PRIMARY GAIN of relief from anxiety or internal conflict. Advantages may include extra attention, sympathy, avoidance of work, and manipulation of others. They often prolong the neurosis and create resistance to therapy.

secondary group compared to a PRIMARY GROUP, a larger, less intimate, and more goal-focused group typical of more complex societies. Whereas primary groups, such as families and children's play groups, are the initial socializing agents, secondary groups, such as work groups, clubs, congregations, associations, and so on, become increasingly influential during adolescence and adulthood.

secondary gustatory cortex see TASTE CORTEX.

secondary motor cortex see MOTOR CORTEX.

secondary prevention intervention for individuals or groups that demonstrate early psychological or physical symptoms, difficulties, or conditions (i.e., subclinical problems), which is intended to prevent the development of more serious dysfunction or illness. Compare PRIMARY PREVENTION; TERTIARY PREVENTION.

secondary process in psychoanalytic theory, conscious, rational mental activities under the control of the EGO and the REALITY PRINCIPLE. The secondary process, which includes problem solving, judgment, planning, and systematic thinking, enables individuals to meet both the external demands of the environment and the internal demands of their instincts in rational, effective ways. Compare PRIMARY PROCESS.

secondary reinforcement 1. in OPERANT CONDITIONING, the process in which a neutral stimulus acquires the ability to influence the future probability of a particular response by virtue of being paired with another stimulus that naturally enhances such probability. That is, the initially neutral stimulus or circumstance functions as effective reinforcement only after special experience or training. For example, a person teaching a dog to understand the command "sit" might provide a treat and a simultaneous popping noise from a clicker tool each time the dog successfully performs the behavior. Eventually, the clicker noise itself (the **conditioned** or **secondary reinforcer**) can be used alone to maintain the desired behavior, with no treat reward being necessary. **2.** the contingent occurrence of such a stimulus or circumstance after a response. Also called **conditioned reinforcement**. Compare PRIMARY REINFORCEMENT.

secondary reinforcer see NATURAL REINFORCER; SECONDARY REINFORCEMENT.

secondary sensory area any of the regions of the cerebral cortex that receive direct projections from the PRIMARY SENSORY AREA for any sense modality. An example is the SECONDARY SOMATOSENSORY AREA.

secondary sex characteristic see SEX CHARACTERISTIC.

secondary somatosensory area (**S2**) an area of the cerebral cortex, located in the PARIETAL LOBE on the upper bank of the LATERAL SULCUS, that receives direct projections from the PRIMARY SOMATOSENSORY AREA and other regions of the anterior parietal cortex. It has outputs to other parts of the lateral parietal cortex and to motor and premotor areas.

secondary taste cortex see TASTE CORTEX.

secondary traumatization 1. see INTERGENERATIONAL TRAUMA. **2.** see VICARIOUS TRAUMATIZATION.

secondary visual cortex (V2) the area immediately surrounding the STRIATE CORTEX in the OCCIPITAL LOBES, receiving signals from it secondarily for analysis and further discrimination of visual input in terms of motion, shape (particularly complex shapes), and position.

second-generation antipsychotic see ANTIPSYCHOTIC.

second messenger an ion or molecule inside a cell whose concentration increases or decreases in response to stimulation of a cell RECEPTOR by an agonist (e.g., a neurotransmitter, hormone, or drug). The second messenger acts to relay and amplify the signal from the agonist (the first messenger) by triggering a range of cellular activities. Second messengers include CYCLIC AMP, CYCLIC GMP, and calcium ions.

second-order conditioning in CLASSICAL CONDITIONING, the establishment of a conditioned response as a result of pairing a neutral stimulus with a conditioned stimulus that gained its effectiveness by being paired with an unconditioned stimulus. See HIGHER ORDER CONDITIONING.

second-order schedule a SCHEDULE OF REINFORCEMENT in which the units counted are not single responses but completions of a particular reinforcement schedule. For example, in a second-order fixed-ratio 5 of fixed-interval 30-second schedule [FR 5 (FI 30 seconds)], reinforcement is delivered only after five successive FI 30-second schedules have been completed. Often, a brief stimulus of some sort is presented on completion of each unit schedule.

secure attachment 1. in the STRANGE SITUATION, the positive parent–child relationship, in which the child displays confidence when the parent is present, shows mild distress when the parent leaves, and quickly reestablishes contact when the parent returns. Compare INSECURE ATTACHMENT. **2.** an adult attachment style that combines a view of oneself as worthy of love and the view that others are generally accepting and responsive. Compare DISMISSIVE ATTACHMENT; FEARFUL ATTACHMENT; PREOCCUPIED ATTACHMENT.

secure base a place of safety, represented by an attachment figure (e.g., a parent), that an infant uses as a base from which to explore a novel environment. The infant often returns or looks back to the parent before continuing to explore.

sedative *n.* a drug that has a calming effect and therefore relieves anxiety, agitation, or behavioral excitement by depressing the central nervous system. For example, BENZODIAZEPINES are commonly used as sedatives. A drug that sedates in small doses may induce sleep in larger doses and may be used as a HYPNOTIC; such drugs are commonly known as **sedative–hypnotics**.

segregation *n.* the separation or isolation of people (e.g., ethnic groups) or other entities (e.g., mental processes) so that there is a minimum of interaction between them.

seizure *n.* a discrete episode of uncontrolled, excessive electrical discharge of neurons in the brain. The resulting clinical symptoms vary based on the type and location of the seizure. See EPILEPSY.

selection *n.* the differential survival of some individuals and their offspring compared with others, causing certain physical or behavioral traits to be favored in subsequent generations. The

general process is known as NATURAL SELECTION.

selection bias see SAMPLING BIAS.

selection invariance in choosing among applicants for employment, admission to college, or other purposes, the property of a selection procedure such that it is equally efficient (i.e., has a similar numbers of errors) for all subgroups of applicants (e.g., ethnic or income groups). Compare MEASUREMENT INVARIANCE.

selective adaptation the observation that perceptual adaptation can occur in response to certain stimulus qualities while being unaffected by others. For example, color adaptation can take place independently of motion adaptation.

selective attention concentration on certain stimuli in the environment and not on others, enabling important stimuli to be distinguished from peripheral or incidental ones. Selective attention is typically measured by instructing participants to attend to some sources of information but to ignore others at the same time and then determining their effectiveness in doing this.

selective mutism a rare disorder, most commonly but not exclusively found in young children, characterized by a persistent failure to speak in certain social situations (e.g., at school) despite the ability to speak and to understand spoken language. Currently, selective mutism is thought to be related to severe anxiety and SOCIAL PHOBIA, but the exact cause is unknown.

selective optimization with compensation a process used to adapt to biological and psychological deficits associated with aging. It involves emphasizing and enhancing those capacities affected only minimally by aging (selective optimization) and developing new means of maintaining functioning in those areas that are significantly affected (compensation).

selective serotonin reuptake inhibitor see SSRI.

self *n.* the totality of the individual, consisting of all characteristic attributes, conscious and unconscious, mental and physical. Apart from its basic reference to personal IDENTITY, being, and experience, the term's use in psychology is wide-ranging. According to U.S. psychologist and philosopher William James (1842–1910), for example, self can refer either to the person as the target of appraisal or to the person as the source of one's regulation of perception, thought, and behavior. Swiss psychiatrist Carl Jung (1875–1961) maintained that the self gradually develops by a process of INDIVIDUATION, whereas Austrian psychiatrist Alfred Adler (1870–1937) identified the self with the individual's lifestyle. German-born U.S. psychoanalyst Karen D. Horney (1885–1952) held that one's REAL SELF, as opposed to one's idealized self-image, consists of one's unique capacities for growth and development. And U.S. psychologist Gordon W. Allport (1897–1967) conceived of self as the essence of the individual, consisting of a gradually developing identity and set of personal values, attitudes, and intentions.

self-acceptance *n.* a relatively objective sense or recognition of one's abilities and achievements, together with acknowledgment and acceptance of one's limitations. Self-acceptance is often viewed as a major component of mental health.

self-actualization *n.* the complete realization of that of which one is capable, involving maximum development of abilities and full involvement in and appreciation for life, particularly as manifest in PEAK EXPERIENCES. The term is associated especially with U.S. psychologist Abraham Maslow (1908–1970), who viewed the process of striving toward full potential as fundamental yet obtainable only after the basic needs of physical survival, safety, love and belongingness, and esteem are fulfilled.

self-affirmation *n.* **1.** any behavior that confirms the moral and adaptive adequacy of the self. **2.** in psychotherapy, a positive statement or set of such statements about the self that a person is required to repeat on a regular basis, often as part of a treatment for depression, negative thinking, or low self-esteem.

self-assessment motive the desire to gain accurate information about the self. It leads people to reject flattery or other bias. Also called **accuracy motive**; **appraisal motive**. Compare CONSISTENCY MOTIVE; SELF-ENHANCE-MENT MOTIVE.

self-awareness *n.* self-focused attention or knowledge. There has been a continuing controversy over whether nonhuman animals have self-awareness. Evidence of this in animals most often is determined by whether an individual can use a mirror to groom an otherwise unseen spot on its own forehead.

self-awareness theory any theory of the consequences of focusing attention on the self. Distinctions are sometimes made between subjective self-awareness, arising directly from the observation and experience of oneself as the source of perception and behavior, and objective self-awareness, arising from comparison between the self and (a) the behaviors, attitudes, and traits of others or (b) some perceived standard for social correctness in any one of these areas.

self-complexity *n.* the number of separate, unrelated aspects of the SELF-CONCEPT. For instance, a woman might think of herself in terms of her various social roles (lawyer, friend, mother), her relationships (colleague, competitor, nurturer), her activities (running, playing tennis, writing), her superordinate traits (hardworking, creative), her goals (career success), and so forth. People low in self-complexity have few distinct

411

facets of the self-concept, so they react more extremely to positive and negative events relevant to one of those aspects.

self-concept *n.* one's description and evaluation of oneself, including psychological and physical characteristics, qualities, skills, roles, and so forth. Self-concepts contribute to the individual's sense of identity over time. Although self-concepts are usually available to some degree to the consciousness, they may be inhibited from representation yet still influence judgment, mood, and behavioral patterns. See SELF-IMAGE.

self-conscious emotion an emotion generated when events reflect on the worth or value of the self in one's own or others' eyes. Self-conscious emotions include SHAME, PRIDE, GUILT, and EMBARRASSMENT. Also called **self-evaluative emotion**.

self-consciousness *n.* **1.** a personality trait associated with the tendency to reflect on or think about oneself. Some researchers have distinguished between two varieties of self-consciousness: (a) private self-consciousness, or the degree to which people think about private, internal aspects of themselves (e.g., their thoughts, motives, and feelings) that are not directly open to observation by others; and (b) public self-consciousness, or the degree to which people think about public, external aspects of themselves (e.g., their physical appearance, mannerisms, and overt behavior) that can be observed by others. **2.** extreme sensitivity about one's behavior, appearance, or other attributes and excessive concern about the impression one makes on others, which may lead to embarrassment or awkwardness in the presence of others. —**self-conscious** *adj.*

self-criticism *n.* the evaluation of one's own behavior and attributes, with recognition of one's weaknesses, errors, and shortcomings. Although self-criticism can have a positive effect in fostering personal growth, a tendency toward harsh self-criticism has

been proposed by researchers as a risk factor for depression. —**self-critical** *adj.*

self-deception *n.* the process or result of convincing oneself of the truth of something that is false or invalid, particularly the overestimation of one's abilities and concurrent failure to recognize one's limitations.

self-defeating behavior repetitive actions by an individual that invite failure or misfortune and thus prevent him or her from attaining goals or fulfilling desires.

self-determination *n.* the process or result of engaging in behaviors without interference or undue influence from other people or external demands. Self-determination refers particularly to behaviors that improve one's circumstances, including effective decision making, problem solving, self-management, self-instruction, and self-advocacy.

self-disclosure *n.* the act of revealing personal or private information about one's self to other people. In relationships research, self-disclosure has been shown to foster feelings of closeness and intimacy. In psychotherapy, the revelation and expression by the client of personal, innermost feelings, fantasies, experiences, and aspirations is believed by many practitioners to be a requisite for therapeutic change and personal growth.

self-discrepancy *n.* an incongruity between different aspects of one's self-concept, particularly between one's actual self and either the IDEAL SELF or the OUGHT SELF.

self-efficacy *n.* an individual's subjective perception of his or her capability to perform in a given setting or to attain desired results, proposed by Canadian-born U.S. psychologist Albert Bandura (1925–) as a primary determinant of emotional and motivational states and behavioral change.

self-enhancement *n.* any strategic

behavior designed to increase either SELF-ESTEEM or the esteem of others. Self-enhancement can take the form of pursuing success or merely distorting events to make them seem to reflect better on the self. Compare SELF-PROTECTION.

self-enhancement motive the desire to think well of oneself and to be well regarded by others. This motive causes people to prefer favorable, flattering feedback rather than accurate but possibly unfavorable information about themselves. Compare SELF-ASSESSMENT MOTIVE; CONSISTENCY MOTIVE.

self-esteem *n.* the degree to which the qualities and characteristics contained in one's SELF-CONCEPT are perceived to be positive. It reflects a person's physical self-image, view of his or her accomplishments and capabilities, and values and perceived success in living up to them, as well as the ways in which others view and respond to that person. A reasonably high degree of self-esteem is considered an important ingredient of mental health, whereas low self-esteem and feelings of worthlessness are common depressive symptoms.

self-evaluation maintenance model a conceptual analysis in which an individual is assumed to maintain a positive self-evaluation by (a) associating with high-achieving individuals who excel in areas with low relevance to his or her sense of self-worth and (b) avoiding association with high-achieving individuals who excel in areas that are personally important to him or her.

self-evaluative emotion see SELF-CONSCIOUS EMOTION.

self-fulfilling prophecy a belief or expectation that helps to bring about its own fulfillment, as when a person expects nervousness to impair his or her performance in a job interview or when a teacher's preconceptions about a student's ability influence the child's achievement for better or worse. See PYGMALION EFFECT.

self-handicapping *n.* a strategy of creating obstacles to one's performance, so that future anticipated failure can be blamed on the obstacle rather than on one's lack of ability. If one succeeds despite the handicap, it brings extra credit or glory to the self. —**self-handicap** *vb.*

self-help group a group composed of individuals who meet on a regular basis to help one another cope with a life problem. Unlike therapy groups, self-help groups are not led by professionals, do not charge a fee for service, and do not place a limit on the number of members. They provide many benefits that professionals cannot provide, including friendship, mutual support, experiential knowledge, identity, and a sense of belonging. Each group also develops its own ideology or set of beliefs about the cause of and best means to address the problem that brings members together. For instance, the ideology of Alcoholics Anonymous includes the belief that alcoholism is a lifelong problem and that the first step in addressing it is for group members to admit that they do not have control over their drinking.

self-hypnosis *n.* the process of putting oneself into a trance or trancelike state, typically through AUTOSUGGESTION. Also called **autohypnosis**.

self-ideal *n.* see EGO-IDEAL.

self-identity *n.* see IDENTITY.

self-image *n.* one's view or concept of oneself. Self-image is a crucial aspect of an individual's personality that can determine the success of relationships and a sense of general well-being. A negative self-image is often a cause of dysfunctions and of self-abusive, self-defeating, or self-destructive behavior.

self-injurious behavior see DELIBERATE SELF-HARM.

self-instructional training a form of COGNITIVE BEHAVIOR THERAPY used to modify maladaptive beliefs and cognitions and develop new skills in an individual. The therapist identifies the client's maladaptive thoughts (e.g., "Everybody hates me") and models appropriate behavior while giving spoken constructive **self-instructions** (or **self-statements**). The client then copies the behavior while repeating these instructions aloud.

self-management *n.* **1.** an individual's control of his or her behavior, particularly regarding the pursuit of a specific objective (e.g., weight loss). **2.** a BEHAVIOR THERAPY program in which clients are trained to apply techniques that will help them modify an undesirable behavior, such as smoking, excessive eating, or aggressive outbursts. Clients learn to pinpoint the problem, set realistic goals for changing it, use various contingencies to establish and maintain a desired behavior, and monitor progress.

self-monitoring *n.* **1.** a method used in behavioral management in which individuals keep a record of their behavior (e.g., time spent, form and place of occurrence, feelings during performance), especially in connection with efforts to change or control the self. For example, a therapist may assign a client self-monitoring as homework to encourage better SELF-REGULATION by that person. **2.** a personality trait reflecting an ability to modify one's behavior in response to situational pressures, opportunities, and norms. High self-monitors are typically more apt to conform their behavior to the demands of the situation, whereas low self-monitors tend to behave in accord with their internal feelings.

self-perception theory the hypothesis that people often have only limited access to their attitudes, beliefs, traits, or psychological states. In such cases, they must attempt to infer the nature of these internal cues in a manner similar to the inference processes they use when making judgments about other people. For example, a person may infer what his or her attitude is by considering past behaviors related to

the attitude object: Approach behaviors imply a positive attitude; avoidance behaviors imply a negative attitude.

self-presentation *n.* any behaviors intended to convey a particular image of, or particular information about, the self to other people. Self-presentational motives explain why an individual's behavior often changes as soon as anyone else is thought to be present or watching. Some common strategies of self-presentation include self-promotion and supplication. See also IMPRESSION MANAGEMENT. —**self-presentational** *adj.*

self-protection *n.* any strategic behavior designed to avoid losing either SELF-ESTEEM or the esteem of others. Self-protection fosters a risk-avoidant orientation and is often contrasted with SELF-ENHANCEMENT.

self-reference effect the widespread tendency for individuals to have a superior or enhanced memory for stimuli that relate to the self or SELF-CONCEPT.

self-regulation *n.* the control of one's behavior through the use of such techniques as monitoring (keeping a record of) that behavior, assessing the information obtained during monitoring, and rewarding oneself for appropriate behavior or for attaining a goal. Self-regulatory processes are stressed in BEHAVIOR THERAPY.

self-reinforcement *n.* the rewarding of oneself for appropriate behavior or the achievement of a desired goal. The self-reward may be, for example, buying a treat for oneself after studying for an exam.

self-report *n.* a statement or series of answers to questions that an individual provides about his or her state, feelings, thoughts, beliefs, past behaviors, and so forth. Self-report methods rely on the honesty and self-awareness of the participant and are used especially to measure behaviors or traits that cannot easily be directly observed by others.

self-schema *n.* a cognitive framework comprising organized information and beliefs about the self that guides a person's perception of the world, influencing what information draws the individual's attention as well as how that information is evaluated and retained. Compare SOCIAL SCHEMA.

self-serving bias the tendency to interpret events in a way that assigns credit for success to oneself but denies one's responsibility for failure, which is blamed on external factors. The self-serving bias is regarded as a form of self-deception designed to maintain high self-esteem. Compare GROUP-SERVING BIAS.

self-suggestion *n.* see AUTOSUGGESTION.

self-understanding *n.* the attainment of knowledge about and insight into one's characteristics, including attitudes, motives, behavioral tendencies, strengths, and weaknesses. The achievement of self-understanding is one of the major goals of certain forms of psychotherapy.

self-worth *n.* an individual's evaluation of himself or herself as a valuable, capable human being deserving of respect and consideration. Positive feelings of self-worth tend to be associated with a high degree of SELF-ACCEPTANCE and SELF-ESTEEM.

semantic dementia a selective, progressive impairment in SEMANTIC MEMORY, leading to difficulties in object naming, comprehension of words and their appropriate use in conversation, and appreciation and use of objects. Nonsemantic aspects of language, as well as perceptual and spatial skills, are preserved.

semantic differential a type of scale that researchers use to assess a respondent's views on a certain topic. Participants are asked to rate the topic on a scale that has pairs of opposites, such as *bad–good, unpleasant–pleasant,* or *competitive–cooperative,* as anchors or reference points. Responses to word pairs assessing the evaluative dimension are scaled in some way (e.g., according to theory, by EXPLORATORY FACTOR ANALYSIS) so that items can be averaged or summed to arrive at an index of attitudes. This procedure is one of the most widely used methods of assessing attitudes.

semantic encoding cognitive ENCODING of new information that focuses on its meaningful aspects as opposed to its perceptual characteristics. This will usually involve some form of ELABORATION. See also DEEP PROCESSING.

semanticity *n.* the property of language that allows it to represent events, ideas, actions, and objects symbolically, thereby endowing it with the capacity to communicate meaning.

semantic memory memory for general factual knowledge and concepts, of the kind that endows information with meaning and ultimately allows people to engage in such complex cognitive processes as recognizing objects and using language. Impairments of semantic memory may be seen following brain injury as well as in certain neurological disorders, particularly dementia. Semantic memory is considered by many theorists to be one of the two forms of DECLARATIVE MEMORY, the other being EPISODIC MEMORY.

semantic network a graph used to capture conceptual relationships. This system has been used to model human information storage (particularly the means by which words are connected to meanings and associations in long-term memory), with latencies in retrieval times supposedly reflecting the length of the path of the network searched for the required response.

semantic priming an effect in which the processing of a stimulus is more efficient after the earlier processing of a meaningfully related stimulus, as opposed to an unrelated or perceptually related stimulus. For example, responses to the word *nurse* would be faster following presentation of the word *doctor* than of the word *purse*.

semantics *n.* **1.** in linguistics, the study of meaning in language, as opposed to the study of formal relationships (GRAMMAR) or sound systems (PHONOLOGY). **2.** aspects of language that have to do with meaning, as distinguished from SYNTACTICS or SEMIOTICS.

semenarche *n.* see SPERMARCHE.

semicircular canals a set of three fluid-filled, looped tubular channels in the inner ear that detect movements of the head and provide the sense of dynamic equilibrium that is essential for maintaining balance. They form part of the VESTIBULAR SYSTEM. Each canal has an enlarged portion, inside which is a sensory structure called a CRISTA. This consists of HAIR CELLS whose fine extensions are embedded in a gelatinous cap. When the head moves in a certain plane, fluid flows through the corresponding canal, causing the hairs to bend. This triggers the hair cells to fire nerve impulses, thus sending messages to the brain about the direction and rate of movement.

semi-interquartile range see QUARTILE DEVIATION.

semiotic function see SYMBOLIC FUNCTION.

semiotics *n.* the study of verbal and nonverbal signs and of the ways in which they communicate meaning within particular sign systems. Unlike SEMANTICS, which restricts itself to the meanings expressed in language, semiotics is concerned with human symbolic activity generally and premised on the view that signs can only generate meanings within a pattern of relationships to other signs. Also called **semiology**.

senescence *n.* the biological process of growing old or the period during which this process occurs. —**senescent** *adj.*

senile *adj.* associated with advanced age, referring particularly to cognitive or behavioral deterioration relating to old age.

senile dementia see DEMENTIA.

senile plaque see AMYLOID PLAQUE.

sensate focus an approach in which people with sexual dysfunction are trained to focus attention on their own natural sensual cues and gradually achieve the freedom to enjoy sensory stimuli. The procedures use prescribed body-massage exercises designed to give and receive pleasure, initially involving body parts other than the breasts and genitals and then moving to these areas. This approach allows the partners to relax and enjoy the sensual experience of body caressing without the need to achieve erection or orgasm.

sensation *n.* an irreducible unit of experience produced by stimulation of a sensory RECEPTOR and the resultant activation of the central nervous system, producing basic awareness of a sound, odor, color, shape, or taste or of temperature, pressure, pain, muscular tension, position of the body, or change in the internal organs associated with such processes as hunger, thirst, nausea, and sexual excitement. —**sensational** *adj.*

sensation seeking the tendency to search out and engage in thrilling activities as a method of increasing stimulation and arousal. It typically takes the form of engaging in highly stimulating activities that have an element of danger, such as skydiving or race-car driving. See also NOVELTY SEEKING.

sense *n.* any of the media through which one gathers information about the external environment or about the state of one's body in relation to the environment. They include the five primary senses—vision, hearing, taste, touch, and smell—as well as the senses of pressure, pain, temperature, kinesthesis, and equilibrium. Each sense has its own receptors, responds to characteristic stimuli, and has its own pathways to specific regions in the brain.

sensitive period a stage in development when an organism can most rapidly acquire a particular skill or characteristic. For example, in humans, the 1st year of life is considered significant for the development of a secure attachment bond. Lack of appropriate growth-dependent experiences during a sensitive period does not permanently and irreversibly affect development, as it would during a CRITICAL PERIOD, but rather makes the acquisition process outside the period more difficult.

sensitivity *n.* **1.** the capacity to detect and discriminate. In SIGNAL DETECTION THEORY, sensitivity is measured by D PRIME. **2.** the probability that results from a test will indicate a positive diagnosis given that the individual actually has the condition for which he or she is being tested. Compare SPECIFICITY. **3.** the ability of a cell, tissue, or organism to respond to changes in its external or internal environment. **4.** awareness of and responsiveness to the feelings of others. **5.** susceptibility to being easily hurt or offended.

sensitivity analysis an evaluation of the extent to which the overall outcome of a model or system will be affected by potential changes to the input. In research, sensitivity analysis enables investigators to understand the boundaries of their statistical models and design updated models that can account for the data at hand.

sensitivity training a group process focused on the development of self-awareness, productive interpersonal relations, and responsiveness to the feelings, attitudes, and needs of others. The primary method used in sensitivity training is open, unstructured discussion with a leader functioning as an observer and facilitator, although other techniques, such as ROLE PLAY, may be used. See also T-GROUP.

sensitization *n.* the increased effectiveness of an eliciting stimulus as a

function of its repeated presentation. Water torture, in which water is dripped incessantly onto a person's forehead, is a good example.

sensorimotor stage in PIAGETIAN THEORY, the first major stage of cognitive development, extending from birth through 2 years of age. It is characterized by the development of sensory and motor processes and by the infant's acquisition of rudimentary awareness of the reality of time, space, and cause and effect. See also CONCRETE OPERATIONAL STAGE; FORMAL OPERATIONAL STAGE; PREOPERATIONAL STAGE.

sensorineural deafness see DEAFNESS.

sensory *adj.* relating to the SENSES, to SENSATION, or to a part or all of the neural apparatus and its supporting structures that are involved in any of these.

sensory adaptation see ADAPTATION.

sensory area any area of the cerebral cortex that receives input from sensory neurons, usually via the thalamus. There are specific areas for the different senses, and they are functionally differentiated into PRIMARY SENSORY AREAS and SECONDARY SENSORY AREAS. Also called **sensory cortex**.

sensory ataxia lack of muscular coordination due to the loss of the sense of limb movements.

sensory deprivation the reduction of sensory stimulation to a minimum in the absence of normal contact with the environment. Sensory deprivation may be induced for experimental or clinical purposes, or it may occur in a real-life situation (e.g., in deep-sea diving). Although short periods of sensory deprivation can be beneficial, extended periods have detrimental effects, including hallucinations, delusions, hypersuggestibility, or panic.

sensory interaction the integration of sensory processes when performing a task, as in maintaining balance using sensory input from both vision and PROPRIOCEPTION. See also INTERSENSORY PERCEPTION.

sensory memory brief storage of information from each of the senses, in a relatively unprocessed form beyond the duration of a stimulus, for recoding into SHORT-TERM MEMORY or for comprehension. For instance, sensory memory for visual stimuli, called ICONIC MEMORY, holds a visual image for less than a second, whereas that for auditory stimuli, called ECHOIC MEMORY, retains sounds for a little longer. Also called **sensory-information store (SIS)**.

sensory neuron a neuron that receives information from the environment, via specialized RECEPTOR cells, and transmits this information—in the form of nerve impulses—through SYNAPSES with other neurons to the central nervous system.

sensory overload a state in which one's senses are overwhelmed with stimuli, to the point that one is unable to process or respond to all of them.

sensory system the total structure involved in SENSATION, including the sense organs and their RECEPTORS, afferent sensory neurons, and SENSORY AREAS in the cerebral cortex at which these tracts terminate. There are separate systems for each of the senses. See AUDITORY SYSTEM; GUSTATORY SYSTEM; OLFACTORY SYSTEM; SOMATOSENSORY SYSTEM; VESTIBULAR SYSTEM; VISUAL SYSTEM.

sentence-completion test a test in which the participant must complete a series of unfinished statements (e.g., "Today I am in a __ mood") by filling in the specific missing word or phrase. The test is typically used to evaluate personality in that responses are free and believed to contain psychologically meaningful material.

separation anxiety disorder an anxiety disorder characterized by inap-

propriate, persistent, and excessive anxiety about separation from the home or from major attachment figures. Other features may include worry about harm coming to attachment figures or about major events that might lead to separation from them (e.g., getting lost) and repeated complaints of physical symptoms (e.g., vomiting, nausea, headaches, stomachaches) associated with anticipated separation. These symptoms cause clinically significant distress or impairment in functioning.

separation–individuation *n.* a developmental phase in which the infant gradually differentiates himself or herself from the mother, develops awareness of his or her separate identity, and attains relatively autonomous status.

sequela *n.* (*pl.* **sequelae**) a residual effect of a disease, injury, or mental condition, often in the form of persistent or permanent impairment. For example, flashbacks may be the sequelae of traumatic stress.

sequence effect in WITHIN-SUBJECTS DESIGNS, a difference in scores that emerges because of a particular arrangement of treatments—that is, the presentation of one level of the independent variable has an effect on responses to another level of that variable. A researcher can test for a sequence effect by administering the treatments in various different arrangements (e.g., the arrangement ABC vs. ACB, vs. BCA, and so forth). The sequence effect is distinct from the ORDER EFFECT.

sequential analysis a class of statistical procedures in which decisions about sample size and the type of data to be collected are made or modified as the study proceeds, based on the cumulative findings. This approach contrasts with one in which the sample size is determined in advance and data are not analyzed until the entire sample is collected.

sequential design a research design that allows for termination of the study at various points of data collection if the results do not conform to a desired pattern or if there is danger or cost to participants.

sequential processing see SERIAL PROCESSING.

serial learning the learning of a sequence of items or responses in a precise order. For example, actors must learn their lines in sequence.

serial position curve a graphic representation of the number of items that can be remembered as a function of the order in which they were presented in a list. Items at the beginning and end of the list are usually remembered best, thus producing a U-shaped memory curve.

serial position effect the effect of an item's position in a list of items to be learned on how well it is remembered. The classic serial position effect shows best recall of the first items from a list (see PRIMACY EFFECT) and good recall of the last items (see RECENCY EFFECT), whereas the middle items are less well recalled.

serial processing INFORMATION PROCESSING in which only one sequence of processing operations is carried on at a time. Those who hold that the human information-processing system operates in this way argue that the mind's apparent ability to carry on different cognitive functions simultaneously is explained by rapid shifts between different information sources. Also called **sequential processing**. Compare PARALLEL PROCESSING.

serial reproduction a method for studying memory in which one person reads a set of information before reproducing it for another person, who then reproduces it for a third person, who does the same for a fourth, and so on. Serial reproduction is widely regarded as a model for the social communication of retained information, and as

such it is an important experimental tool in the analysis of rumor and gossip transmission, stereotype formation, and similar phenomena. See also REPEATED REPRODUCTION.

seriation *n.* the process of arranging a collection of items in a specific order (series) on the basis of a particular dimension (e.g., size). According to PIAGETIAN THEORY, this ability is necessary for understanding the concepts of number, time, and measurement and is acquired by children during the CONCRETE OPERATIONAL STAGE.

serotonergic *adj.* responding to, releasing, or otherwise involving serotonin. In the brain, for example, most **serotonergic pathways** originate in the RAPHE NUCLEUS and project diffusely to other sites in the brain and to the spinal cord.

serotonin *n.* a common monoamine neurotransmitter in the central nervous system; it also is found in the gastrointestinal tract, in smooth muscles of the cardiovascular and bronchial systems, and in blood platelets. Serotonin has roles in emotional processing, mood, appetite, sexual desire and performance, sleep, pain processing, hallucinations, and reflex regulation. It is implicated in many psychological conditions, including depressive disorders, anxiety disorders, sleep disorders, aggression, and psychosis; many common psychotropic drugs affect neurotransmission mediated by serotonin. Also called **5-hydroxytryptamine (5-HT)**.

serotonin reuptake inhibitor (SRI) see SSRI.

set *n.* a temporary readiness to respond in a certain way to a specific situation or stimulus. For example, a parent is set to hear his or her baby cry from the next room (a PERCEPTUAL SET), and a poker player is set to use a tactic that has been successful in other games (a MENTAL SET).

set point the preferred level of functioning of an organism or of a system within an organism. When a set point is exceeded (i.e., when physiological responses become higher than the set point), compensatory events take place to reduce functioning; when a set point is not reached, compensatory processes take place to help the organism or system reach the set point. According to the **set-point theory of happiness**, for example, individuals each have a particular baseline of SUBJECTIVE WELL-BEING that is generally stable throughout life and that they are likely to return to despite life-changing events, whether positive or negative.

sex *n.* **1.** the traits that distinguish between males and females. Sex refers especially to physical and biological traits, whereas GENDER refers especially to social or cultural traits, although the distinction between the two terms is not regularly observed. **2.** the physiological and psychological processes related to procreation and erotic pleasure.

sex characteristic any of the traits associated with sex identity. **Primary sex characteristics** (e.g., testes in males, ovaries in females) are directly involved in reproduction of the species. **Secondary sex characteristics** are features not directly concerned with reproduction, such as voice quality, facial hair, and breast size.

sex chromosome a chromosome that determines whether an individual is female or male. Humans and other mammals have two sex chromosomes: the X CHROMOSOME, which carries genes for certain sexual traits and occurs in both females and males; and the smaller Y CHROMOSOME, which is normally found only in males. Diseases coded by genes that are carried only on a sex chromosome (usually the X chromosome) are called SEX-LINKED conditions.

sex differences 1. the differences in physical features between males and females. These include differences in brain structures and in primary and

secondary SEX CHARACTERISTICS. **2.** the differences between males and females in the way they behave and think, with such differences often viewed as driven by actual biological disparity (nature) rather than by differing environmental factors (nurture). See also GENDER DIFFERENCES.

sex hormone any of the hormones that stimulate various reproductive functions. Primary sources of sex hormones are the male and female gonads (i.e., testis and ovary), which are stimulated to produce sex hormones by the pituitary gland. The principal male sex hormones (ANDROGENS) include testosterone; female sex hormones include the ESTROGENS and PROGESTERONE.

sexism *n.* discriminatory and prejudicial beliefs and practices directed against one of the two sexes, usually women. Sexism may be overt, involving the open endorsement of sexist beliefs or attitudes; covert, involving the tendency to hide sexist beliefs or attitudes and reveal them only when it is believed that one will not suffer publicly for them; or subtle, involving unequal treatment that may not be noticed because it is part of everyday behavior or perceived to be unimportant. See also PREJUDICE. —**sexist** *adj.*

sex-linked *adj.* describing either a gene that is located on one of the sex chromosomes, typically the X chromosome (**X-linked**), or a trait determined by such a gene. The process whereby a sex-linked gene or trait is passed on from parent to offspring is called **sex-linked inheritance**. Sex-linked inherited diseases from a defective gene on the X chromosome include hemophilia and are called **X-linked recessive** because the defective gene is usually a RECESSIVE ALLELE. It is carried by females and expressed mostly in their male offspring. Disorders that are **X-linked dominant**, in which only one copy of an allele of a defective gene on the X chromosome is sufficient to cause inherited disorder, may occur in either male or female offspring depending on which parent is affected. There is also a rare form of sex-linked inheritance in which a recessive trait is inherited from father to son by way of a single gene on the Y chromosome (**Y-linked**).

sex role the behavior and attitudinal patterns characteristically associated with being male or female as defined in a given society. Sex roles thus reflect the interaction between biological heritage and the pressures of socialization, and individuals differ greatly in the extent to which they manifest typical sex-role behavior.

sexual abuse violation or exploitation by sexual means. Although the term typically is used with reference to any sexual contact between adults and children, sexual abuse can also occur in any relationship of trust.

sexual aversion disorder negative emotional reactions (e.g., anxiety, fear, disgust) to sexual activity, leading to active avoidance of it and causing distress in the individual or his or her partner.

sexual dimorphism the existence of males and females within a species that differ distinctly from each other in form. See SEX DIFFERENCES.

sexual disorder any impairment of sexual function or behavior. Sexual disorders include SEXUAL DYSFUNCTION and PARAPHILIAS.

sexual dysfunction any sexual disorder characterized by problems in one or more phases of the SEXUAL-RESPONSE CYCLE. The particular dysfunction may be primary, occurring in all sexual situations, or secondary, occurring only with some partners or in some situations. Some examples of sexual dysfunction include ERECTILE DYSFUNCTION, FEMALE ORGASMIC DISORDER, PREMATURE EJACULATION, and DYSPAREUNIA.

sexual harassment conduct of a sexual nature that is unwelcome or considered offensive, particularly in the workplace. According to the U.S. Equal Employment Opportunity Commission, there are two forms of sexual harass-ment: behavior that makes for a hostile work environment and behavior that makes positive employment consequences contingent on compliance with sexual demands.

sexual identity an individual's SEXUAL ORIENTATION.

sexual instinct in classical psychoanalytic theory, the instinct comprising all the erotic drives and sublimations of such drives. It includes not only genital sex but also anal and oral manifestations and the channeling of erotic energy into artistic, scientific, and other pursuits. In his later formulations, Austrian neurologist Sigmund Freud (1856–1939) saw the sexual instinct as part of a wider LIFE INSTINCT that also included the self-preservative impulses of hunger, thirst, and elimination. See also LIBIDO.

sexuality *n.* **1.** the capacity to derive pleasure from various forms of sexual activity and behavior, particularly from sexual intercourse. **2.** an individual's gender identity and sexual orientation, attitudes, and activity. **3.** in classical psychoanalytic theory, the "organ pleasure" derived from all EROGENOUS ZONES and processes of the body.

sexually dimorphic nucleus a mass of cell bodies in the central nervous system that differs in size between males and females. In humans, for example, a nucleus in the hypothalamus that synthesizes GONADOTROPIN-RELEASING HORMONE tends to be larger and more active in males because gonadotropin release is continuous, whereas it is cyclical in females.

sexually transmitted disease (**STD**) an infection transmitted by sexual activity. Numerous STDs have been identified, including those caused by viruses (e.g., hepatitis B, herpes, HIV) and those caused by bacteria (e.g., chlamydia, gonorrhea, syphilis). Also called **sexually transmitted infection** (**STI**).

sexual masochism a PARAPHILIA in

which sexual interest and arousal is repeatedly or exclusively achieved through being humiliated, bound, beaten, or otherwise made to suffer physical harm or threat to life.

sexual orientation one's enduring sexual attraction to male partners, female partners, or both. Sexual orientation may be heterosexual, same sex (gay or lesbian), or bisexual.

sexual-response cycle a conceptualization of a four-stage cycle of sexual response exhibited by both men and women, differing only in aspects determined by male or female anatomy. The stages include the arousal (or excitement) phase; the plateau phase, marked by penile erection in men and vaginal lubrication in women; the orgasmic phase, marked by EJACULATION in men and ORGASM in women; and the resolution phase, wherein further sexual activity immediately after orgasm is not possible. This conceptualization has been criticized for the way that it equates the male and female pattern: The resolution phase, for example, applies only to men, whereas women can experience immediate further arousal and multiple orgasms.

sexual sadism a PARAPHILIA in which sexual excitement is achieved by intentional infliction of physical or psychological suffering on another person. The harm often involves mild bodily injury or humiliation but may escalate to extensive, permanent, or possibly fatal bodily injury over time.

sexual selection a theoretical mechanism for the evolution of anatomical and behavioral differences between males and females, based on mate selection.

shadowing *n.* in cognitive testing, a task in which a participant repeats aloud a message word for word at the same time that the message is being presented, often while other stimuli are presented in the background. It is mainly used in studies of ATTENTION.

shaken baby syndrome (SBS) the neurological consequences of a form of child abuse in which a small child or infant is repeatedly shaken. The shaking causes diffuse, widespread damage to the brain; in severe cases, it may cause death.

shallow affect significant reduction in appropriate emotional responses to situations and events. See also FLAT AFFECT.

shallow processing cognitive processing of a stimulus that focuses on its superficial, perceptual characteristics rather than its meaning. It is considered that processing at this shallow level produces weaker, shorter-lasting memories than DEEP PROCESSING. See also BOTTOM-UP PROCESSING.

shame *n.* a highly unpleasant SELF-CONSCIOUS EMOTION arising from the sense of there being something dishonorable, immodest, or indecorous in one's own conduct or circumstances. It is typically characterized by social withdrawal but may also manifest as defensive, retaliative anger. A proneness to shame is related to depression, anxiety, eating disorders, and low self-esteem. Shame appears to have adaptive functions as well, such as by regulating experiences of excessive and inappropriate interest and excitement. Compare GUILT. —**shameful** *adj.*

sham rage sudden aggressive behavior and motor activity occurring disproportionally in response to a weak or relatively innocuous stimulus. Sham rage initially was observed by researchers in the 1920s: Following surgical DECORTICATION, cats responded to the touch of a hand by growling, spitting, lashing the tail, protracting the claws, and attempting to bite. It subsequently has been demonstrated to occur with damage to or direct electrical stimulation of the LIMBIC SYSTEM as well.

sham surgery in research on the value or usefulness of experimental surgical interventions, the controversial practice of performing surgery that functions as a CONTROL because it mimics the features of the experimental surgery but does not result in the alteration or removal of any bodily structures.

shape constancy a type of PERCEPTUAL CONSTANCY in which an object is perceived as having the same shape when viewed at different angles. For example, a plate is still perceived as circular despite appearing as an oval when viewed from the side.

shaping *n.* the production of new forms of voluntary behavior by reinforcement of successive approximations to the behavior (see METHOD OF SUCCESSIVE APPROXIMATIONS). Also called **behavior shaping**.

shared environment in behavior genetics analyses, those aspects of an environment that individuals living together (e.g., in a family household) share and that therefore cause them to become more similar to each other than would be expected on the basis of genetic influences alone. Examples of shared environmental factors include parental child-rearing style, divorce, or family income. Compare NONSHARED ENVIRONMENT.

shared psychotic disorder a disorder in which the essential feature is an identical or similar delusion that develops in an individual who is involved with another individual who already has a psychotic disorder with prominent delusions. Shared psychotic disorder can involve many people (e.g., an entire family) but is most commonly seen in relationships of only two, in which case it is known as **folie à deux**.

sheltered workshop a rehabilitation facility that provides a controlled, noncompetitive, supportive working environment and individually designed work settings for people with disabilities. Work experience and related services are provided to assist individuals in achieving specific vocational goals.

shock phase see GENERAL ADAPTATION SYNDROME.

shock therapy the treatment of severe mental disorders by administering a drug or an electric current that shocks the central nervous system to induce loss of consciousness or convulsions. See ELECTROCONVULSIVE THERAPY.

short-term memory (**STM**) the reproduction, recognition, or recall of a limited amount of material after a period of about 10 to 30 seconds. STM is often theorized to be separate from LONG-TERM MEMORY, and the two are the components of the DUAL-STORE MODEL OF MEMORY. See also WORKING MEMORY.

short-term psychodynamic psychotherapy see BRIEF PSYCHODYNAMIC PSYCHOTHERAPY.

short-term psychotherapy see BRIEF PSYCHOTHERAPY.

shrinkage *n.* the situation in which the strength of a CORRELATION COEFFICIENT or REGRESSION EQUATION decreases when it is applied to a new data set. Such shrinkage occurs when the initial estimate of the correlation reflects unique characteristics of the initial sample, which are not replicated in subsequent samples.

sibling rivalry competition among siblings for the attention, approval, or affection of one or both parents or for other recognition or rewards, such as in sports or academics.

sick role the behavior expected of a person who is physically ill, mentally ill, or injured. Such expectations can be the individual's own or those of the family, the community, or society in general. They influence both how the person behaves and how others react to him or her. For instance, people in a sick role are expected to cooperate with caregivers and to want to get well but are also provided with an exemption from normal obligations. See also FACTITIOUS DISORDER.

side effect any reaction secondary to the intended therapeutic effect that may occur following administration of a drug or other treatment. Often, these are undesirable but tolerable (e.g., headache, fatigue), although more serious effects (e.g., liver failure, seizures) may also occur.

sign *n.* **1.** an objective, observable indication of a disorder or disease. **2.** in linguistics and SEMIOTICS, anything that conveys meaning; a sign may be either verbal (e.g., a spoken or written word) or nonverbal (e.g., a hairstyle).

signal detection theory (SDT) a body of concepts and techniques from communication theory, electrical engineering, and decision theory that were applied to auditory and visual psychophysics in the late 1950s and are now widely used in many areas of psychology. SDT has provided a valuable theoretical framework for describing perceptual and other aspects of cognition and for quantitatively relating psychophysical phenomena to findings from sensory physiology. A key notion of SDT is that human performance in many tasks is limited by variability in the internal representation of stimuli due to internal or external NOISE. See D PRIME; RECEIVER-OPERATING CHARACTERISTIC CURVE.

signal-to-noise ratio (S/N) the ratio of signal power (intensity) to noise power, usually expressed in DECIBELS. When the signal is speech, it is called the **speech-to-noise ratio**.

significance *n.* the extent to which something is meaningful or of consequence. In statistics and related fields, the term usually denotes STATISTICAL SIGNIFICANCE.

significance level (symbol: α) in SIGNIFICANCE TESTING, a fixed probability of rejecting the NULL HYPOTHESIS of no effect when it is in fact true. It is set at some value, usually .001, .01, or .05, depending on the consequences associated with making a TYPE I ERROR. When a particular effect is obtained experimentally, the PROBABILITY LEVEL (*p*) associated with this effect is compared to the significance level. If the *p* value is less than the α level, the null hypothesis is rejected. Also called **alpha level**.

significance testing in HYPOTHESIS TESTING, a set of procedures used to determine whether the differences between two groups or models are statistically significant (i.e., unlikely to arise solely from chance). In its most common form, significance testing is used to decide whether the NULL HYPOTHESIS of no effect should be rejected. A comparison of the probability statistic obtained from the test to the chosen SIGNIFICANCE LEVEL determines whether an observed effect may be due to chance variance and hence whether the null hypothesis is or is not likely to be correct.

significant difference the situation in which a SIGNIFICANCE TESTING procedure indicates the statistical differences observed between two groups (e.g., a treatment group and a control group) are unlikely to reflect chance variation.

significant other any individual who has a profound influence on another person, particularly on his or her self-image and SOCIALIZATION. Although the term most often denotes a spouse or other person with whom one has a committed romantic relationship, it is also used in psychology and sociology to refer to parents, peers, and others.

sign language any system of communication in which signs formed by hand configuration and movement are used instead of spoken language. The term refers particularly to the system used by people who are deaf or have severe hearing loss, which has its own syntax and methods of conveying nuances of feeling and emotion and is now accepted by most linguists as exhibiting the full set of defining characteristics of human oral–aural language.

sign stimulus see RELEASER.

sign test a NONPARAMETRIC procedure used to determine whether a sample has the same MEDIAN value as another sample or a reference population. Consider a farmer who wants to grow a crop that requires soil with a median acidity level (pH) of 8. The farmer measures the soil in several different areas on his or her property and then compares the pH value of each measurement to the required median value. Each acidity reading above 8 is marked positive using a + sign and each reading below 8 is marked negative with a − sign. If the proportion of positive signs for the group of measurements is significantly different from the proportion of negative signs, then the farmer's sample soil data have a different median than the one required and the desired crop cannot be planted.

similarity n. one of the GESTALT PRINCIPLES OF ORGANIZATION. It states that people tend to organize objects with similar qualities into a perceptual group and interpret them as a whole. Also called **law of similarity**; **principle of similarity**.

simple cell a neuron, most commonly found in the STRIATE CORTEX, that has a receptive field consisting of an elongated center region and two elongated flanking regions. The response of a simple cell to stimulation in the center of the receptive field is the opposite of its response to stimulation in the flanking zones. This means that a simple cell responds best to an edge or a bar of a particular width and with a particular direction and location in the visual field. Compare COMPLEX CELL.

simple correlation the linear association of one variable with one other variable, as quantified by a CORRELATION COEFFICIENT.

simple effect in an experimental design involving multiple independent variables, the consistent total effect on a dependent variable of a particular level (quantity, magnitude, or category) of one independent variable at a particular level of another independent variable.

simple-effects analysis following the identification of an INTERACTION EFFECT among two independent variables, an examination of the effect of one variable at one level of the other variable. For example, if there were two levels of a particular variable, a_1 and a_2, and two levels of a second variable, b_1 and b_2, the comparison of a_1 versus a_2 at b_1 would represent one simple-effects analysis; another would be a comparison of a_1 versus a_2 at b_2.

simple emotion see COMPLEX EMOTION.

simple phobia see SPECIFIC PHOBIA.

simple random sampling the most basic approach to drawing a RANDOM SAMPLE of cases, observations, or individuals from a population, in which the cases are selected individually using a fair process, such as the toss of a coin or a table of random digits. Also called **independent random sampling**.

simple reaction time (SRT) the total time that elapses between the presentation of a stimulus and the occurrence of a response in a task that requires a participant to perform an elementary behavior (e.g., pressing a key) whenever a stimulus (e.g., a light or tone) is presented. The individual makes just a single response whenever the only possible stimulus is presented. Compare CHOICE REACTION TIME.

simple regression a type of REGRESSION ANALYSIS that has only one predictor or independent variable and one outcome or dependent variable. See also MULTIPLE REGRESSION.

simulation n. **1.** an experimental method used to investigate the behavior and psychological processes and functioning of individuals in social and other environments—often those which investigators cannot easily access—by reproducing those environments in a realistic way. For example, simulations are often used in personnel selection to tap job-related dimensions or behaviors. **2.** the artificial creation of experimental data through the use of a mathematical or computer model. The purpose is usually to test the behavior of a statistic or model under controlled conditions.

simultanagnosia *n.* see VISUAL AGNOSIA.

simultaneous conditioning a CLASSICAL CONDITIONING technique in which the conditioned stimulus and the unconditioned stimulus are presented at the same time. Compare DELAY CONDITIONING.

simultaneous regression a type of REGRESSION ANALYSIS in which all predictors or INDEPENDENT VARIABLES are entered into the equation at the same time. Each independent variable's coefficient or WEIGHT is interpreted in the context of all of the other independent variables in the model at that time, some of which may be correlated. Compare STEPWISE REGRESSION.

single blind see BLIND.

single-case design an approach to the empirical study of a process that tracks a single unit (e.g., person, family, class, school, company) in depth over time. For example, a researcher may use a single-case design for a small group of patients with a tic. After observing the patients and establishing the number of tics per hour, the researcher would then conduct an intervention and watch what happens over time, thus revealing the richness of any change. Also called **single-subject (case) design**.

situation *n.* one or more circumstances, conditions, states, or entities in the environment that have the potential to exert causal influences on an individual's behavior. To social psychologists, the term commonly refers to the real or imagined presence of other persons, but it can also refer to the physical environment. A central belief among social psychologists is that situations affect behavior, often powerfully so and often without the person's awareness of such influence.

situational attribution the ascription of one's own or another's behavior, an event, or an outcome to causes outside the person concerned, such as luck, pressure from other people, or external circumstances. Also called **external attribution**. Compare DISPOSITIONAL ATTRIBUTION.

situational differences any distinction arising from environmental characteristics. For example, in a study of men and women in social settings versus business settings, the amount of positive emotion displayed by the participants may be explained by the fact that more positive emotions tend to occur in a social setting regardless of whether the participant is male or female.

situationism *n.* the view that an organism's interaction with the environment and situational factors, rather than personal characteristics and other internal factors, are the primary determinants of behavior. Also called **situationalism**.

situation test a test that places an individual in a natural setting, or in an experimental setting that approximates a natural one, to assess either the individual's ability to solve a problem that requires adaptive behavior under stressful conditions or the individual's reactions to what is believed to be a stressful experience.

size constancy the ability to perceive an object as being the same size despite the fact that the size of its retinal image changes depending on its distance from the observer. It is a type of PERCEPTUAL CONSTANCY.

size–distance paradox an illusion that an object is bigger or smaller than it actually is, caused by a false perception of its distance from the viewer. For example, in the so-called **moon illu-**

sion, the moon appears to be larger on the horizon, where DEPTH CUES make it appear to be farther away, than at its zenith, where there are no depth cues.

skeletal muscle a muscle that provides the force to move a part of the skeleton. Skeletal muscles are attached to the bones by tendons and usually span a joint, so that one end of the muscle is attached via a tendon to one bone and the other end is attached to another bone. Skeletal muscle is composed of numerous slender, tapering MUSCLE FIBERS, the contractile fibrils of which are organized into arrays that give a striped appearance when viewed microscopically. Contraction of skeletal muscle is typically under voluntary control of the central nervous system. Also called **striated muscle**.

skewness *n.* the degree to which a set of scores, measurements, or other numbers are asymmetrically distributed around a central point. When a distribution has a few extreme scores toward the high end relative to the low end (e.g., when a test is difficult and few test takers do well), it has a **positive skew** (or is **positively skewed**), such that the MEAN is greater than the MODE. When a distribution has a few extreme scores toward the low end relative to the high end (e.g., when a test is easy and most test takers do well), it has a **negative skew** (or is **negatively skewed**).

skill *n.* an ability or proficiency acquired through training and practice. Motor skills, for example, are characterized by the ability to perform a complex movement or behavioral sequence quickly, smoothly, and precisely.

skin *n.* the external covering of the body, consisting of an outer layer (epidermis) and a deeper layer (dermis) resting on a layer of fatty subcutaneous tissue. The skin forms a barrier that prevents the entry of foreign substances and pathogens into the body. It defends against injury to underlying tissues, reduces water loss from the body, and forms part of the body's temperature-regulation mechanism through the evaporation of sweat secreted from sweat glands. Various types of sensory nerve endings provide the skin with touch and pressure sensitivity, as well as sensations of pain and temperature.

skin conductance the degree to which the skin transmits a small electric current between two electrodes, changes in which are typically used to measure a person's level of arousal or energy mobilization. Compare SKIN RESISTANCE. See also GALVANIC SKIN RESPONSE.

Skinner box see OPERANT CONDITIONING CHAMBER. [initially developed by B. F. **Skinner** (1904–1990), U.S. psychologist]

skin-picking disorder see EXCORIATION (SKIN-PICKING) DISORDER.

skin resistance the opposition of the skin to the passage of an electric current. Sometimes used in research as a physiological marker of arousal, and more controversially in POLYGRAPH examinations as a manifestation of deception and various emotional states, skin resistance is the reciprocal of SKIN CONDUCTANCE. See also GALVANIC SKIN RESPONSE.

sleep *n.* a circadian state characterized by partial or total suspension of consciousness, voluntary muscle inhibition, and relative insensitivity to stimulation. Other characteristics include unique sleep-related electroencephalogram and brain-imaging patterns (see SLEEP STAGES). These characteristics help distinguish normal sleep from a loss of consciousness due to brain injury, disease, or drugs. See also NREM SLEEP; REM SLEEP.

sleep apnea the temporary cessation of breathing while asleep, which occurs when the upper airway briefly becomes blocked or when the respiratory centers in the brain fail to stimulate respiration.

Severe sleep apnea may be associated with high blood pressure and risk for stroke and heart attack.

sleep cycle a recurring pattern of SLEEP STAGES in which a period of SLOW-WAVE SLEEP is followed by a period of REM SLEEP. In humans, a sleep cycle lasts approximately 90 minutes.

sleep deprivation the condition of getting insufficient sleep. The loss of one night's sleep has a substantial effect on physical and mental functioning: Participants score significantly lower on tests of judgment and SIMPLE REACTION TIME and show impairments in daytime alertness and memory. Sleep loss also may be detrimental to the immune and endocrine systems.

sleep disorder a persistent disturbance of typical sleep patterns (including the amount, quality, and timing of sleep) or the chronic occurrence of abnormal events or behavior during sleep.

sleeper effect the increased impact of a persuasive message over time. This effect is most likely to occur when a person scrutinizes a message with relatively strong arguments and then subsequently receives a cue suggesting the message should be disregarded. The cue may gradually be forgotten, but the impact of the arguments is not.

sleep paralysis brief inability to move or speak just before falling asleep or on awakening, often accompanied by terrifying hallucinations.

sleep psychology a synonym of BEHAVIORAL SLEEP MEDICINE used when the practitioner is a professionally licensed psychologist.

sleep spindles regular electroencephalographic oscillations that rise and fall in amplitude in the shape of symmetrical hairpins or spindles during Stage 2 NREM sleep (see SLEEP STAGES). Spindles are believed to indicate a state of light sleep and are often seen with K COMPLEXES.

sleep stages the stages of nocturnal sleep as distinguished by physiological measures, mainly electroencephalography. Typically, a regular pattern of occipital ALPHA WAVES characteristic of a relaxed state becomes intermittent in Stage 1 sleep, which is marked by drowsiness with upward-rolling eye movements. This progresses to Stage 2, a light sleep characterized by SLEEP SPINDLES and K COMPLEXES. In the deep sleep of Stages 3 and 4, DELTA WAVES predominate. These four stages comprise NREM SLEEP and are interspersed with periods of REM SLEEP, when most dreaming occurs.

sleep terror disorder a SLEEP DISORDER characterized by repeated episodes of abrupt awakening from NREM SLEEP accompanied by signs of disorientation, panic, and intense anxiety. More intense than NIGHTMARES and occurring during the first few hours of sleep, these episodes typically last between 1 and 10 minutes and involve screaming and symptoms of autonomic arousal, such as profuse perspiration, dilated pupils, rapid breathing, and a rapidly beating heart. Also called **night terror**.

sleepwalking disorder a SLEEP DISORDER characterized by persistent incidents of complex motor activity during slow-wave NREM SLEEP. These episodes typically occur during the first hours of sleep and involve getting out of bed and walking or performing more complicated tasks. While in this state, the individual stares blankly and is unresponsive. Also called **somnambulism**.

slip of the tongue a minor error in speech, such as a SPOONERISM, that is not related to a speech disorder or language acquisition. Psychoanalysts refer to such errors as FREUDIAN SLIPS and believe them to reveal unconscious wishes. See also PARAPRAXIS.

slope *n.* the steepness or slant of a line on a graph, measured as the change of value on the Y-AXIS associated with a change of one unit of value on the X-AXIS. See also ACCELERATION.

slow-wave sleep deep sleep that is characterized by increasing percentages of particular types of DELTA WAVES on the electroencephalogram, corresponding to Stages 3 and 4 of NREM SLEEP. See also SLEEP STAGES.

smoothing *n.* a collection of techniques used to reduce the random variation in a data set or in a plot of that data, particularly in TIME-SERIES ANALYSES, so as to more clearly see the underlying trends.

smooth muscle any muscle that is not under the control of the AUTONOMIC NERVOUS SYSTEM (i.e., it is not under voluntary control). Smooth muscles are able to remain in a contracted state for long periods of time or maintain a pattern of rhythmic contractions indefinitely without fatigue. Smooth muscle is found, for example, in the digestive organs, blood vessels, and the muscles of the eyes.

smooth-pursuit eye movement a slow, continuous eye movement that is responsive to feedback provided by brain regions involved in processing visual information, thus enabling continuous fixation on a moving object. Compare SACCADE.

sociability *n.* the tendency and accompanying skills to seek out companionship, engage in interpersonal relations, and participate in social activities. —**sociable** *adj.*

social *adj.* relating to the interactions between individuals, particularly as members of a group or a community.

social adaptation see ADAPTATION.

social age (SA) a numerical scale unit expressing how mature a person is in terms of his or her interpersonal skills and ability to fulfill the norms and expectations associated with particular SOCIAL ROLES, as compared to others of the same CHRONOLOGICAL AGE. SA is similar to MENTAL AGE and is derived

from ratings gathered from the individual.

social anxiety fear of social situations in which embarrassment may occur (e.g., making conversation, meeting strangers, dating) or there is a risk of being negatively evaluated by others. When the anxiety causes an individual significant distress or impairment in functioning, a diagnosis of SOCIAL PHOBIA may be warranted.

social anxiety disorder see SOCIAL PHOBIA.

social class a major group or division of society having a common level of power and prestige on the basis of a common SOCIOECONOMIC STATUS. Often, the members of a particular social class share values and have similar cultural interests and social patterns. A popularly used classification divides individuals into an upper class, a middle class, a working class, the working poor, and an underclass.

social clock in a given culture, the set of norms governing the ages at which particular life events—such as beginning school, leaving home, getting married, having children, and retiring—are expected to occur.

social cognition cognition in which people perceive, think about, interpret, categorize, and judge their own social behaviors and those of others. Major areas of interest include ATTRIBUTION THEORY, PERSON PERCEPTION, SOCIAL INFLUENCE, and the cognitive processes involved in moral judgments.

social-cognitive theory an extension of SOCIAL LEARNING THEORY to include the effects of cognitive processes, such as conceptions, judgment, and motivation, on an individual's behavior and on the environment that influences him or her. Rather than passively absorbing knowledge from environmental inputs, individuals actively influence their learning by interpreting the outcomes of their actions, which then affects their environments and their personal factors, which in turn inform and alter subsequent behavior. Despite the distinction between social-cognitive theory and social learning theory, many individuals use the terms synonymously. Also called **cognitive-social learning theory**.

social communication disorder see SOCIAL (PRAGMATIC) COMMUNICATION DISORDER.

social comparison theory the proposition that people evaluate their abilities and attitudes in relation to those of others in a process that plays a significant role in self-image and subjective well-being. Three types of social comparison are proposed in the theory: (a) upward, or comparing oneself with someone judged to be better than oneself (e.g., by having more wealth or material goods, higher social standing, greater physical attractiveness); (b) downward, or comparing oneself with someone judged to be not as good as oneself; and (c) lateral, or comparing oneself with another who is considered to be more or less equal.

social competence effectiveness or skill in interpersonal relations and social situations, increasingly considered an important component of mental health. Social competence involves the ability to evaluate social situations and determine what is expected or required; to recognize the feelings and intentions of others; and to select social behaviors that are most appropriate for that given context.

social constructivism the school of thought that recognizes knowledge as embedded in social context and sees human thoughts, feelings, language, and behavior as the result of interchanges with the external world. Social constructivism argues that there is no separation between subjectivity and objectivity and that the dichotomy between the person and the situation is false: The person is intimately and intricately bound within social, cultural,

and historical forces and cannot be understood fully without consideration of these forces.

social contagion the spread of behaviors, attitudes, and affect through crowds and other types of social aggregates from one member to another. Social contagion appears to be sustained by relatively mundane interpersonal processes, such as IMITATION, CONFORMITY, UNIVERSALITY, and MIMICRY. Also called **group contagion**.

social decision scheme a strategy or rule used in a group to select a single alternative from among various alternatives proposed and discussed during the group's deliberations. These schemes are sometimes explicitly acknowledged by the group, as when a formal tally of those favoring the alternative is taken and the proposal is accepted only when a certain proportion approve of it, but are sometimes implicit and informal, as when a group accepts the alternative that its most powerful members seem to favor.

social deprivation 1. limited access to society's resources due to poverty, discrimination, or other disadvantage. **2.** lack of adequate opportunity for social experience.

social desirability the bias or tendency of individuals to present themselves in a manner that will be viewed favorably by others. In an experiment, for example, it manifests as the **social desirability response set**, which is the tendency of participants to give answers that are in accordance with social norms or the perceived desires of the researcher rather than genuinely representative of their views.

social determinism the theory or doctrine that individual behaviors are determined by societal events and other interpersonal experiences. See also CULTURAL DETERMINISM.

social development the gradual acquisition of certain skills (e.g., language, interpersonal skills), attitudes, relationships, and behavior that enable the individual to interact with others and to function as a member of society.

social dilemma a situation that creates a conflict between the individual's interests and the collective's interests, such that the individual obtains better outcomes following strategies that over time will lead to suboptimal outcomes for the collective. Although such situations have reward structures that favor individuals who act selfishly, if a substantial number of individuals seek maximum personal gain, their results will be lower than if they had sought collective outcomes. See also SOCIAL TRAP.

social distance the degree to which, psychologically speaking, a person or group wants to remain separate from members of different social groups. This reflects the extent to which individuals or groups accept people of a different ethnicity, race, nationality, or other social background.

social distance scale a measure of intergroup attitudes that asks respondents to indicate their willingness to accept members of other ethnic, national, or social groups in situations that range from relatively distant ("would allow to live in my country") to relatively close ("would admit to kinship by marriage").

social dominance theory (SDT) a general model of the development and maintenance of social dominance and oppression that assumes societies minimize group conflict by creating consensus on ideologies that promote the superiority of one group over others. To work smoothly, these ideologies must be widely accepted within a society despite the group inequality and discrimination they legitimize.

social emotion any emotion that depends on one's appraisal or consideration of another person's thoughts, feelings, or actions. For example, pride arises when one feels favorably evaluated by others and perceives concurrent gains in one's status and rank relative to those others, whereas shame arises from one's feeling poorly evaluated by others and perceiving losses in status and rank. Other commonly studied social emotions include admiration, embarrassment, envy, guilt, and jealousy.

social entrepreneurship see ENTREPRENEURSHIP.

social exchange theory a theory envisioning social interactions as an exchange in which the participants seek to maximize their benefits within the limits of what is regarded as fair or just. Intrinsic to this hypothesis is the RECIPROCITY NORM: People are expected to reciprocate for the benefits they have received.

social facilitation the improvement in an individual's performance of a task that often occurs when others are present. This effect tends to occur with tasks that are uncomplicated or have been previously mastered through practice. See also AUDIENCE EFFECT.

social identity 1. the personal qualities that one claims and displays to others so consistently that they are considered to be part of one's essential, stable self. This public persona may be an accurate indicator of the private, personal self, but it may also be a deliberately contrived image. **2.** in social psychology, the part of SELF-CONCEPT that is derived from memberships in social groups or categories, ranging from family to nationality or race.

social identity theory a conceptual perspective on group processes and intergroup relations that assumes that groups influence their members' self-concepts and self-esteem, particularly when individuals categorize themselves as group members and identify strongly with the group. According to this theory, people tend to favor their INGROUP over an OUTGROUP because the former is part of their self-identity.

social impact theory a theory of

social influence postulating that the amount of influence exerted by a source on a target depends on (a) the strength of the source compared to that of the target (e.g., the social status of the source versus that of the target); (b) the immediacy of the source to the target (e.g., the physical or psychological distance between them); and (c) the number of sources and targets (e.g., several sources influencing a single target).

social influence any change in an individual's thoughts, feelings, or behaviors caused by other people. See also SOCIAL PRESSURE.

social inhibition the restraint placed on an individual's expression of her or his feelings, attitudes, motives, and so forth by the belief that others could learn of this behavior and disapprove of it. See also AUDIENCE EFFECT.

social intelligence the ability to understand people and effectively relate to them.

social interaction any process that involves reciprocal stimulation or response between two or more individuals. Social interaction includes the development of cooperation and competition, the influence of status and social roles, and the dynamics of group behavior, leadership, and conformity. Persistent social interaction between specific individuals leads to the formation of social relationships.

sociality *n.* the tendency to live as part of a group with clear organization of social interactions and the ability to cooperate with and adapt to the demands of the group.

socialization *n.* the process by which individuals acquire social skills, beliefs, values, and behaviors necessary to function effectively in society or in a particular group. —**socialize** *vb.*

social justice norm the socially determined standard that people should be helped by others only if they deserve

to be helped. Compare RECIPROCITY NORM; SOCIAL RESPONSIBILITY NORM.

social learning learning that is facilitated through social interactions with other individuals. Several forms of social learning have been identified, including IMITATION and MIMICRY.

social learning theory the general view that learning is largely or wholly due to modeling, imitation, and other social interactions. More specifically, behavior is assumed to be developed and regulated by external stimulus events, such as the influence of other individuals, and by external reinforcement, such as praise, blame, and reward. For example, if a student receives extra credit for arriving early to class and another student in the classroom observes this, the latter student may model the behavior by arriving a few minutes early each day as well.

social loafing the reduction of individual effort that occurs when people work in groups compared to when they work alone.

social memory 1. memory for socially relevant information. Examples include the ability to recognize other individuals with whom one has had previous contact, as well as the capacity to retain and recall specific details about people and various interactions with them. Social memory also is seen in nonhuman animals—for example, rodents are able to identify other members of their species and to distinguish kin from strangers. Studies suggest that the formation of social memories is linked to the pituitary hormones OXYTOCIN and VASOPRESSIN. **2.** see COLLECTIVE MEMORY.

social need see LOVE NEED.

social network the relatively organized set of relationships that an individual or group has with others, including types and methods of communication, patterns of liking and disliking, and strength of interpersonal connections. See also ONLINE SOCIAL NETWORK.

social neuroscience a discipline whose practitioners aim to elucidate the brain structures that regulate social behavior as well as to understand the reciprocal interactions of the brain's biological mechanisms (especially the nervous, immune, and endocrine systems) with the social and cultural contexts in which human beings operate. See also CULTURAL NEUROSCIENCE.

social norm any of the socially determined consensual standards that indicate (a) what behaviors are considered typical in a given context (DESCRIPTIVE NORMS) and (b) what behaviors are considered proper in the context (INJUNCTIVE NORMS). Whether implicitly or explicitly, these norms not only prescribe the socially appropriate way to respond in the situation (the "normal" course of action) but also proscribe actions that should be avoided if at all possible. Social norms apply across groups and social settings, whereas **group norms** are specific to a particular group.

social penetration theory a model stating that relationships grow closer with increasingly intimate SELF-DISCLOSURES.

social perception the processes by which a person uses the behavior of others to form opinions or make inferences about those individuals, particularly regarding their motives, attitudes, or values.

social phobia an anxiety disorder that is characterized by extreme and persistent SOCIAL ANXIETY or PERFORMANCE ANXIETY and that causes significant distress or prevents participation in social activities. The feared situation is most often avoided altogether or else it is endured with marked discomfort or dread. Also called **social anxiety disorder**.

social play interacting with others for fun or sport, sometimes with vigorous physical contact. It is one of three basic types of play traditionally identified, the others being OBJECT PLAY and LOCOMOTOR PLAY. Social play also occurs among many nonhuman animals, including fish, reptiles, amphibians, insects, nonhuman mammals, and others.

social (pragmatic) communication disorder a developmental disorder characterized by a child's difficulties in the social use of language, including impaired ability to use appropriate language in varying situations, to follow conversational rules such as turn taking, and to understand implied or ambiguous meanings, as in metaphors and humor.

social pressure the exertion of influence on a person or group by another person or group. Social pressure includes rational argument and persuasion (INFORMATIONAL INFLUENCE), calls for conformity (NORMATIVE INFLUENCE), and direct INTERPERSONAL INFLUENCE. See also SOCIAL INFLUENCE.

social psychology as defined by U.S. psychologist Gordon W. Allport (1897–1967), the study of how an individual's thoughts, feelings, and actions are affected by the actual, imagined, or symbolically represented presence of other people.

social reality the consensus of attitudes, opinions, and beliefs held by members of a group or society.

social referencing evaluating one's own modes of thinking, expression, or behavior by comparing them with those of other people so as to understand how to react in a particular situation and to adapt one's actions and reactions in ways that are perceived to be appropriate. See SOCIAL COMPARISON THEORY.

social representation a system, model, or code for unambiguously naming and organizing values, ideas, and conduct, which enables communication and social exchange (i.e., at the levels of language and behavior) among members of a particular group or community.

social responsibility norm the socially determined standard that one should assist those in need when possible. Compare RECIPROCITY NORM; SOCIAL JUSTICE NORM.

social role the set of attitudes and characteristic behaviors expected of an individual who occupies a specific position or performs a particular function in a social context, such as being a spouse or acting as a caregiver for an aging parent.

social role theory a model contending that behavioral differences between men and women can be attributed to cultural standards and expectations about gender rather than to biological factors.

social schema a cognitive structure of organized information, or representations, about social norms and collective patterns of behavior within society. Whereas a SELF-SCHEMA involves a person's conception of herself or himself as an individual and in terms of a particular personal role (or roles) in life, social schemata often underlie the behavior of the person within group contexts—particularly larger group or societal contexts.

social science any of a number of disciplines concerned with the common elements and collective dimensions of human experience. These disciplines traditionally have included anthropology, economics, geography, history, linguistics, political science, psychiatry, psychology, and sociology, as well as associated areas of mathematics and biology. The general goal is to understand social interactions and to propose solutions to social problems.

social self those aspects of one's identity or SELF-CONCEPT that are important to or influenced by interpersonal relationships and the reactions of other people. See also SOCIAL IDENTITY.

social skills a set of learned abilities that enable an individual to interact competently and appropriately in a given social context. The most commonly identified social skills in Western cultures include assertiveness, coping, communication and friendship-making skills, interpersonal problem solving, and the ability to regulate one's cognitions, feelings, and behavior. See also SOCIAL COMPETENCE.

social skills training (SST) a form of individual or group therapy for those who need to overcome social inhibition or ineffectiveness. It uses many techniques for teaching effective social interaction in specific situations (e.g., job interviews, dating), including ASSERTIVENESS TRAINING and behavioral and cognitive REHEARSAL.

social status the relative prestige, authority, and privilege of an individual or group. Social status can be determined by any number of factors—including occupation, level of education, ethnicity, religion, age, achievements, wealth, reputation, authority, and ancestry—with different groups and societies stressing some qualities more than others when allocating status to members.

social stratification the existence or emergence of separate classes or strata in a society. See SOCIAL CLASS; SOCIOECONOMIC STATUS.

social support the provision of assistance or comfort to others, typically to help them cope with biological, psychological, and social stressors. Support may arise from any interpersonal relationship in an individual's social network, involving family members, friends, neighbors, religious institutions, colleagues, caregivers, or self-help groups. It may take the form of practical help (e.g., doing chores), tangible support that involves giving money or other direct material assistance, and emotional support that allows the individual to feel valued, accepted, and understood.

social trap a SOCIAL DILEMMA in which individuals, groups, organizations, or whole societies initiate a course of action or establish a set of relationships that lead to negative or even lethal outcomes in the long term, but that once initiated are difficult to withdraw from or alter. It often arises because of immediate positive reinforcements that support initial behavior that in the long run is harmful.

social work a profession devoted to helping individuals, families, and other groups deal with personal and practical problems within the larger community context of which they are a part. **Social workers** address a variety of problems, including those related to mental or physical disorder, poverty, living arrangements, child care, occupational stress, and unemployment.

society *n.* **1.** an enduring social group living in a particular place whose members are mutually interdependent and share political and other institutions, laws and mores, and a common culture. **2.** any well-established group of individuals (humans or other animals) that typically obtains new members at least in part through sexual reproduction and has relatively self-sufficient systems of action. —**societal** *adj.*

sociobiology *n.* the systematic study of the biological basis for social behavior. **Sociobiologists** believe that populations tend to maintain an optimal level of density by controls—such as aggression, stress, fertility, emigration, predation, and disease—that operate through the Darwinian principle of NATURAL SELECTION. See also EVOLUTIONARY PSYCHOLOGY. —**sociobiological** *adj.*

sociocentrism *n.* **1.** the tendency to put the needs, concerns, and perspective of the social unit or group before one's individual, egocentric concerns. See also ALLOCENTRIC. **2.** the tendency to judge one's own group as superior to other groups across a variety of domains. Whereas ETHNOCENTRISM refers to the selective favoring of one's ethnic, religious, racial, or national groups, sociocentrism usually means the favoring

of smaller groups characterized by face-to-face interaction among members. Compare EGOCENTRISM. —**sociocentric** *adj.*

sociocultural perspective **1.** any viewpoint or approach to health, mental health, history, politics, economics, or any other area of human experience that emphasizes the environmental factors of society, culture, and social interaction. **2.** in developmental psychology more specifically, the view that cognitive development is guided by adults interacting with children, with the cultural context determining to a large extent how, where, and when these interactions take place. See also GUIDED PARTICIPATION; ZONE OF PROXIMAL DEVELOPMENT.

socioeconomic status (**SES**) the position of an individual or group on the socioeconomic scale, which is determined by a combination of social and economic factors such as income, amount and kind of education, type and prestige of occupation, place of residence, and—in some societies or parts of society—ethnic origin or religious background. See SOCIAL CLASS.

sociogenic *adj.* resulting from social factors. For example, a **sociogenic hypothesis** of schizophrenia posits that stressful social conditions, such as living in impoverished circumstances, are major contributors to and causal agents of the disorder.

sociolinguistics *n.* the study of the relationship between language and society and of the social circumstances of language usage, especially as related to characteristics such as gender, social class, and ethnicity.

sociology *n.* the scientific study of the origin, development, organization, forms, and functioning of human society, including the analysis of the relationships between individuals and groups, institutions, and society itself. —**sociological** *adj.* —**sociologist** *n.*

sociometry *n.* a field of research in

which various techniques are used to analyze the patterns of intermember relations within groups and to summarize these findings in mathematical and graphic form. In most cases, each member is represented by a numbered or lettered symbol and relationships are identified by lines between them with arrows indicating the direction of relationships. The method also yields various indices of group structure and GROUP COHESION. —**sociometric** *adj.*

sociopathic personality see ANTI-SOCIAL PERSONALITY DISORDER.

sociopathy *n.* a former name for AN-TISOCIAL PERSONALITY DISORDER.

sodium pump a membrane protein that uses energy from ATP to actively transport sodium ions out of a cell against their concentration gradient. The main sodium pump responsible for maintaining the RESTING POTENTIAL of animal cells, and hence the excitability of neurons and muscle cells, is called **Na+/K+ ATPase**.

soft determinism the position that all events, including human actions and choices, have causes, but that free will and responsibility are compatible with such a view. Compare HARD DETERMINISM.

solipsism *n.* the philosophical position that one can be sure of the existence of nothing outside the self, as other people and things may be mere figments of one's own consciousness. The question posed by solipsism has been put in various ways, but all arise from the fact that one's experience of one's own consciousness and identity is direct and unique, so that one is cut off from the same kind of experience of other minds and the things of the world. —**solipsist** *n.* —**solipsistic** *adj.*

solitary nucleus a collection of neural cell bodies in the medulla oblongata of the brainstem that relays information from the intermediate nerve, glossopharyngeal nerve, and vagus nerve. Gustatory (taste) neurons project from the solitary nucleus to control reflexes of acceptance or rejection, to anticipate digestive processes, and to activate higher levels of the taste system. Also called **nucleus of the solitary tract** (**NST**).

soma *n.* **1.** the physical body (Greek, "body"), as distinguished from the mind or spirit. See MIND–BODY PROBLEM. **2.** in neuroscience, see CELL BODY.

somatic *adj.* **1.** describing, relating to, or arising in the body rather than from the mind. **2.** describing, relating to, or arising in cells of the body other than the sex cells or their precursors (i.e., germ-line cells). Somatic MUTATIONS cannot be transmitted to the offspring of the affected individual.

somatic hallucination the false perception of a physical occurrence within the body, such as feeling electric currents.

somatic nervous system the part of the nervous system comprising the sensory and motor neurons that innervate the sense organs and the skeletal muscles, as opposed to the AUTONOMIC NERVOUS SYSTEM.

somatic symptom disorder a disorder characterized by one or more significant bodily symptoms (e.g., pain) that cause distress or impair daily function and by excessive, maladaptive thoughts or worry about the symptoms, with or without the presence of a medical condition to account for the symptoms. It is one of two replacement diagnoses for HYPOCHONDRIASIS, the other being ILLNESS ANXIETY DISORDER.

somatic therapy the treatment of mental disorders by physical methods that directly influence the body, such as the administration of drugs (PHARMA-COTHERAPY) or the application of a controlled, low-dose electric current (ELECTROCONVULSIVE THERAPY). Also called **somatotherapy**.

somatization *n.* the expression of psychological disturbance in physical (bodily) symptoms. The first use of the word has controversially been attributed to Viennese psychoanalyst Wilhelm Stekel (1868–1940) to describe what is now called CONVERSION.

somatization disorder a SOMATOFORM DISORDER involving a history of multiple physical symptoms for which medical attention has been sought but which are apparently not due to any physical disorder or to the effects of a substance such as a medication. Among the common complaints are difficulty in swallowing or walking, blurred vision, abdominal pain, nausea, diarrhea, painful intercourse, pain in the back or joints, shortness of breath, palpitations, and chest pain.

somatoform disorder any of a group of disorders marked by physical symptoms suggesting a specific medical condition for which there is no demonstrable biological evidence and for which there is positive evidence or a strong probability that they are linked to psychological factors. The group includes SOMATIZATION DISORDER, CONVERSION DISORDER, PAIN DISORDER, HYPOCHONDRIASIS, and BODY DYSMORPHIC DISORDER.

somatosense *n.* any of the senses related to touch and position, including KINESTHESIS, the CUTANEOUS senses, and the senses associated with the joints and VISCERA. Also called **somatic sense**.

somatosensory area either of two main areas of the CEREBRAL CORTEX that can be mapped with EVOKED POTENTIALS to reveal points that respond to stimulation of the various SOMATOSENSES. The somatosensory areas vary somewhat among different species; in humans, the PRIMARY SOMATOSENSORY AREA is located in the anterior parietal lobe, and the SECONDARY SOMATOSENSORY AREA is in the parietal lobe. Also called **somatosensory cortex**.

somatosensory disorder any disorder of sensory information received

from the skin and deep tissue of the body. Associated with impaired or abnormal somatic sensation, such disorders may affect PROPRIOCEPTION and the perception of pain, touch, or temperature.

somatosensory system the parts of the nervous system that serve perception of touch, vibration, pain, temperature, and position (see SOMATOSENSE). Nerve fibers from receptors for these senses enter the spinal cord and ascend to the thalamus, from which they are relayed (directly or indirectly) to the SOMATOSENSORY AREAS of the parietal cortex.

somatostatin *n.* a hormone secreted by the hypothalamus that inhibits the release of growth hormone (somatotropin) by the anterior pituitary gland. It is also secreted by cells in the ISLETS OF LANGERHANS in the pancreas, where it inhibits the secretion of insulin and glucagon.

somatotopic organization the topographic distribution of areas of the MOTOR CORTEX relating to specific activities of skeletal muscles, as mapped by electrically stimulating a point in the cortex and observing associated movement of a skeletal muscle in the face, the trunk, or a limb.

somatotype *n.* the body build or physique of a person, particularly as it relates to his or her temperament or behavioral characteristics. Numerous categories of somatotypes have been proposed by various investigators since ancient times. The classification of individuals in this way is called **somatotypology**.

somnambulism *n.* see SLEEPWALKING DISORDER.

S–O–R psychology stimulus–organism–response psychology: an extension of the S–R PSYCHOLOGY of behaviorists incorporating the notion that factors within the organism help determine what stimuli the organism is sensitive to and which responses may occur.

The O factors could be biological or psychological.

sound *n.* variations in pressure that occur over time in an elastic medium, such as air or water. Sound does not necessarily elicit an auditory sensation—infrasound and ultrasound are respectively below and above the audible range of humans—but in psychology sound usually denotes a stimulus capable of being heard by an organism.

sound localization see AUDITORY LOCALIZATION.

source amnesia impaired memory for how, when, or where information was learned despite good memory for the information itself. Source amnesia is often linked to frontal lobe pathology.

source memory memory for the origin of a memory or of knowledge; that is, memory for where or how one came to know what one now remembers. This construct has been expanded to encompass any aspects of context associated with an event, including spatial-temporal, perceptual, or affective attributes. Although the PREFRONTAL CORTEX is known to be involved in source memory, its exact contribution remains uncertain.

source monitoring the process of determining the origins of one's memories, knowledge, or beliefs, such as whether an event was personally experienced, witnessed on television, or overheard.

spaced practice see DISTRIBUTED PRACTICE.

spacing effect a cognitive phenomenon in which distributing to-be-learned information across time in short, interrupted study sessions leads to better long-term retention than continuous, massed sessions. In other words, DISTRIBUTED PRACTICE is more beneficial than MASSED PRACTICE. For example, a student preparing for a Spanish vocabulary exam on Thursday would remember more by studying the Span-ish–English word pairs during brief sessions (e.g., 1 hour each) on consecutive prior days (e.g., Monday, Tuesday, and Wednesday) than by cramming study into a single session in one day. Also called **distributed-practice effect**. See also LAG EFFECT; PRIMACY EFFECT; RECENCY EFFECT.

spasm *n.* a sudden, involuntary muscle contraction. It may be continuous or sustained (TONIC) or it may alternate between contraction and relaxation (CLONIC). A spasm may be restricted to a particular body part; for example, a vasospasm involves a blood vessel, and a bronchial spasm involves the bronchi. —**spasmodic** *adj.*

spastic *adj.* **1.** relating to SPASM. **2.** relating to increased muscle tension (see SPASTICITY).

spasticity *n.* a state of increased tension of resting muscles resulting in resistance to passive stretching. It is caused by damage to upper MOTOR NEURONS and is marked by muscular stiffness or inflexibility.

spatial attention the manner in which an individual distributes attention over a visual scene. Spatial attention is usually directed at the part of the scene on which a person fixates.

spatial cognition the collection, organization, use, and revision of information about one's environment. Spatial cognition enables people to manage a multitude of everyday tasks, such as getting to the breakfast table, taking the subway to work, or using a joystick to move a character in a virtual game.

spatial learning the acquisition of knowledge about the locations of environmental objects and their relative relationships to one another. For example, many nonhuman animals are able to orient within their home range, and they can remember visual or other cues associated with landmarks in order to locate important resources. Although the hippocampus is essential to spatial learning, the cortex of the PARIETAL

LOBE and other brain structures are selectively involved in the process as well.

spatial memory the capacity to remember the position and location of objects or places, which may include orientation, direction, and distance. Spatial memory is essential for route learning and navigation.

spatial neglect see UNILATERAL NEGLECT.

spatial summation a neural mechanism in which an impulse is propagated by two or more POSTSYNAPTIC POTENTIALS occurring simultaneously at different synapses on the same neuron, when the discharge of a single synapse would not be sufficient to activate the neuron. Compare TEMPORAL SUMMATION.

spatial-temporal reasoning the ability to conceptualize the three-dimensional relationships of objects in space and to mentally manipulate them as a succession of transformations over a period of time. Spatial-temporal reasoning plays an important role in basic tasks such as everyday movement of the body through space.

speaking in tongues see GLOSSOLALIA.

Spearman correlation coefficient (symbol: ρ; r_s) a measure of the degree of relationship between two variables that were scored on an ORDINAL SCALE; that is, the individual observations (cases) can be ranked into two ordered series. The Spearman correlation coefficient ranges in value from $+1$ to -1, with values closer to 1 indicating a stronger relationship and a value of 0 indicating no relationship. Also called **Spearman's rho**. [Charles **Spearman** (1863–1945), British psychologist and psychometrician]

special education specially designed programs, services, and instruction provided to children with learning, behavioral, or physical disabilities (e.g., visual impairment, hearing loss, neurological disorders) to assist them in becoming independent, productive, and valued members of their communities.

special needs the requirements of individuals with physical, mental, or emotional disabilities or with financial, community-related, or resource disadvantages. Special needs may warrant SPECIAL EDUCATION, training, or therapy.

species *n.* the basic unit of biological classification, consisting of a group of organisms that can interbreed to produce fertile offspring.

speciesism *n.* discriminatory, prejudicial, or exploitative practices against nonhuman animals, often on the basis of an assumption of human superiority. —**speciesist** *n., adj.*

species-specific behavior behavior that is common to nearly all members of a particular species and expressed in essentially the same way. Human language is a prominent example.

specific factor 1. (symbol: s) a specialized ability that is postulated to come into play in particular kinds of cognitive tasks. Specific factors, such as mathematical ability, are contrasted with the GENERAL FACTOR (g), which underlies every cognitive performance. Also called **special factor**. 2. in FACTOR ANALYSIS, a LATENT VARIABLE that is significant only to a single MANIFEST VARIABLE. In contrast, a **common factor** pertains to multiple manifest variables.

specificity *n.* 1. the quality of being unique, of a particular kind, or limited to a single phenomenon. For example, a stimulus that elicits a particular response is said to have specificity. 2. the probability that a test yields a negative diagnosis given that the individual does not have the condition for which he or she is being tested. Compare SENSITIVITY.

specific language impairment (**SLI**) a condition characterized by impaired acquisition and use of oral linguistic abilities in the absence of any neurological damage, sensory deficits, intellectual disability, alterations in physiological mechanisms of speech, or environmental factors to account for the disturbance. Children with SLI acquire spoken language skills significantly later than is typical and have varying degrees of difficulty with word sounds, meaning, arrangement, and function. For example, they tend to have limited vocabularies; to make case errors on pronouns (e.g., *him go there* instead of *he goes there*); and to omit the verb *to be* when functioning as auxiliary or copula (e.g., *He running* rather than *he is running* or *John big* rather than *John is big*). Formerly called **language learning disability** (LLD).

specific learning disability (SLD) a substantial deficit in scholastic or academic skills that does not pervade all areas of learning but rather is limited to a particular aspect, such as reading or arithmetic difficulty.

specific phobia an ANXIETY DISORDER, formerly called **simple phobia**, characterized by a marked and persistent fear of a specific object, activity, or situation (e.g., dogs, blood, flying, heights). The fear is out of proportion to the actual danger posed by the feared object or situation or to its context, and it is invariably triggered by the presence or anticipation of that object or situation, which is either avoided or endured with marked anxiety or distress.

spectrogram *n.* a quasi–three-dimensional representation of sound produced by analyzing the variations in frequency and intensity of an auditory stimulus (e.g., human speech) over time.

spectrum *n.* (*pl.* **spectra**) **1.** a distribution of electromagnetic energy displayed by decreasing wavelength. In the case of the **visible spectrum**, it is the series of visible colors (with wavelengths in the range 400–700 nm) produced when white light is refracted

through a prism. **2.** a wide range of associated elements, qualities, actions, or occurrences. **—spectral** *adj.*

speech *n.* the product of oral–motor movement resulting in articulation of language: the utterance of sounds and words.

speech act an instance of the use of speech considered as an action, especially with regard to the speaker's intentions and the effect on a listener. A single utterance usually involves several simultaneous speech acts. The study of speech acts is part of the general field of PRAGMATICS.

speech and language disorder any disorder that affects oral or written communication. A **speech disorder** is one that affects the production of speech, potentially including such problems as poor audibility or intelligibility; unpleasant tonal quality; unusual, distorted, or abnormally effortful sound production; lack of conventional rhythm and stress; and inappropriateness in terms of age or physical or mental development. A **language disorder** is one that affects the expression or comprehension of ideas and feelings, potentially including such problems as reduced vocabulary, omissions of articles and modifiers, understanding of nouns but not verbs, difficulties following oral instructions, and syntactical errors. Although speech disorders and language disorders are two distinct entities, they often occur together and thus generally are referred to together.

speech and language therapy see SPEECH THERAPY.

speech area any of the areas of the cerebral cortex that are associated with language perception and production, either oral or written. The speech production (output) areas tend to be located in the left hemisphere in BROCA'S AREA. Speech perception and comprehension tend to be more bilateral, involving WERNICKE'S AREA in the temporal lobe.

speech perception the process in which a listener decodes, combines, and converts an incoming sound stream into a meaningful sequence and phonological representation.

speech therapy the application of remedies, treatment, and counseling for the improvement of speech production and language comprehension. Also called **speech and language therapy**.

speed test a type of test used to calculate the number of problems or tasks the participant can solve or perform in a predesignated block of time. Compare POWER TEST.

spelling dyslexia a type of VISUAL WORD-FORM DYSLEXIA manifested by letter-by-letter reading. For example, an affected individual reading the word *dog* would say, "D-O-G spells *dog*." Such individuals may have normal spelling and writing ability but cannot read back what they have written down.

spermarche *n.* a male's first ejaculation of semen. Also called **semenarche**.

spermatogenesis *n.* the production of spermatozoa in the seminiferous tubules of the TESTIS. Male germ cells lining the tubules develop into primary spermatocytes, which undergo MEIOSIS to eventually result in mature spermatozoa (four per spermatocyte). In the first meiotic division, each primary spermatocyte gives rise to two HAPLOID secondary spermatocytes, each of which then undergoes a further division to form two spermatids that eventually mature into spermatozoa. The process is controlled by pituitary GONADOTROPINS. —**spermatogenetic** *adj.*

spermatozoon *n.* (*pl.* **spermatozoa**) a single male GAMETE, formed in the seminiferous tubules of the TESTIS, that fuses with a female gamete (see OVUM) in the process of fertilization. Also called **sperm**. See also SPERMATOGENESIS.

spherical aberration see ABERRATION.

sphericity *n.* an assumption, encountered in an ANALYSIS OF VARIANCE of data obtained from the same individuals on multiple occasions, requiring the variations among each individual's set of scores to be equal or the correlations among all time points to be constant. Results from analyses of variance that violate sphericity require adjustments to compensate for an increased propensity of the researcher to draw invalid conclusions by making a TYPE II ERROR.

spider phobia see ARACHNOPHOBIA.

spike potential see ACTION POTENTIAL.

spinal column the backbone, consisting of a series of bones (vertebrae) connected by disks of cartilage (intervertebral disks) and held together by muscles and tendons. It extends from the cranium to the coccyx, encloses the spinal cord, and forms the main axis of the body. Also called **spine**.

spinal cord the part of the central nervous system that extends from the lower end of the MEDULLA OBLONGATA, at the base of the brain, through a canal in the center of the spine as far as the lumbar region. The cord consists of an H-shaped core of gray matter surrounded by white matter tracts of long ascending and descending nerve fibers. The spinal cord is enveloped by the MENINGES and is the origin of the 31 pairs of SPINAL NERVES. See also SPINAL ROOT.

spinal nerve any of the 31 pairs of nerves that originate in the gray matter of the SPINAL CORD and emerge through openings between the vertebrae of the spine to extend into the body's dermatomes (skin areas) and skeletal muscles. The spinal nerves comprise 8 cervical nerves, 12 thoracic nerves, 5 lumbar nerves, 5 sacral nerves, and 1 coccygeal nerve. Each attaches to the spinal cord via two short branches, a DORSAL ROOT and a VENTRAL ROOT. See also SPINAL ROOT.

spinal root the junction of a SPINAL NERVE and the SPINAL CORD. Near the cord, each spinal nerve divides into a DORSAL ROOT carrying sensory fibers and a VENTRAL ROOT carrying motor fibers, as stated by the BELL–MAGENDIE LAW.

spiral ganglion the mass of cell bodies on the inner wall of the COCHLEA, near the organ of Corti, whose axons form the AUDITORY NERVE.

splanchnic nerve any of certain nerves that serve the abdominal VISCERA. They originate in the ganglia of the SYMPATHETIC CHAIN.

split brain a brain in which the two cerebral hemispheres have been separated by partial or complete destruction of the corpus callosum (see COMMISSUROTOMY), thereby blocking direct communication between them. Split-brain surgery is used to treat otherwise intractable epilepsy, because it prevents cortical seizure activity from spreading between the hemispheres.

split-half reliability a measure of the internal consistency of surveys, questionnaires, and other instruments used to assess participant responses on particular constructs. Split-half reliability is determined by dividing the total set of items (e.g., questions) relating to a construct of interest into halves (e.g., odd-numbered and even-numbered questions) and comparing the results obtained from the two subsets of items thus created.

split personality a lay term for an individual with DISSOCIATIVE IDENTITY DISORDER. It is sometimes confused with SCHIZOPHRENIA, which literally means "splitting of the mind" but does not involve the formation of a second personality.

split-plot design a variation of a full FACTORIAL DESIGN in which one of the INDEPENDENT VARIABLES is held constant while all other combinations of conditions are examined. For example, consider a researcher examining the influence on crop yield of four different types of corn seed, three different types of fertilizer, and two different types of planting technique. He or she could have half of the participating farmers plant all of the seed types using one technique and the other half plant all of the seed types using the second technique.

split-span test a test in which brief auditory messages in the form of two different lists of digits or words are presented rapidly and simultaneously, one list to each ear. Participants are required to report as many digits or words as possible in any order. Typically, participants report first the stimuli presented to one ear, then those presented to the other.

spontaneous abortion see ABORTION.

spontaneous recovery the reappearance of a conditioned response, following either operant or classical conditioning, after it has been experimentally extinguished (see EXTINCTION).

spontaneous remission a temporary or permanent reduction or disappearance of symptoms without any therapeutic intervention. It most commonly refers to medical, rather than psychological, conditions.

spoonerism *n*. a SLIP OF THE TONGUE in which two sound elements (usually initial consonants) are unintentionally transposed, resulting in an utterance with a different and often amusing sense. For example, a person might say *sons of toil* instead of *tons of soil*. [W. A. **Spooner** (1844–1930), British academic noted for slips of this kind]

sport and exercise psychology a discipline focused on the development and application of psychological theory for the understanding and modification or enhancement of human behavior in the sport and physical exercise environment. This discipline evolved from an exclusive focus on sport performance and historically has been called **sport psychology**. However, health and well-being through regular participation in vigorous physical activity programs have become of increasing interest to researchers and practitioners to such an extent that the field is progressively becoming two separate disciplines as **exercise psychology** merges with HEALTH PSYCHOLOGY.

spotlight model of attention a model of visual attention that likens the focus of attention to a spotlight. Information outside of the spotlight is presumed not to receive conscious processing. Compare ZOOM-LENS MODEL OF ATTENTION.

spread *n.* see DISPERSION.

spreading activation 1. in neuroscience, a hypothetical process in which the activation of one neuron is presumed to spread to connected neurons, making it more likely that they will fire. **2.** in cognitive psychology, an analogous model for the association of ideas, memories, and the like, based on the notion that activation of one item stored in memory travels through associated links to activate another item. Spreading activation is a feature of some models of SEMANTIC MEMORY.

SQ3R *n.* one of a variety of study methods developed on the basis of research in cognitive psychology. The formula represents a method for enhanced learning of reading material. It consists of five steps: survey, question, read, recite, and review.

squared correlation coefficient see COEFFICIENT OF DETERMINATION.

S–R psychology an approach to psychology in which behavior is conceptualized in terms of stimulus and response. The fundamental goal of adherents is therefore describing functional relationships between stimulus and response—that is, manipulating a stimulus and observing the response.

S–R theories are sometimes contrasted with cognitive theories of learning. See also S–O–R PSYCHOLOGY.

SSRI selective serotonin reuptake inhibitor: any of a class of antidepressants that are thought to act by blocking the reuptake of serotonin into presynaptic neurons in the central nervous system. SSRIs also block the activity of certain subtypes of serotonin AUTORECEPTORS, and this may also be associated with their therapeutic effects. SSRIs have fewer adverse effects than the TRICYCLIC ANTIDEPRESSANTS and the MONOAMINE OXIDASE INHIBITORS, but common side effects include nausea, headache, anxiety, and tremor. Also called **SRI** (**serotonin reuptake inhibitor**).

stability *n.* **1.** the absence of variation or motion, as applied, for example, to genetics (invariance in characteristics), personality (few emotional or mood changes), or body position (absence of body sway). **2.** the property of a system, either open or closed, that regulates its internal environment and tends to maintain a constant condition.

stabilized image an image on the retina that does not move when the eye is moved. A stabilized image will fade rapidly since neurons in the visual system are sensitive to change rather than to sustained stimulation.

stage *n.* a relatively discrete period of time in which functioning is qualitatively different from functioning during other periods.

stages of change the five steps involved in changing health behavior according to the TRANSTHEORETICAL MODEL: (a) precontemplation (not thinking about changing behavior), (b) contemplation (considering changing behavior), (c) preparation (occasionally changing behavior), (d) action (participating in the healthful behavior on a regular basis, resulting in major benefits), and (e) maintenance (continuing the behavior after 6 months of regular use).

stages of grief a hypothetical model, originally described by Swiss-born U.S. psychiatrist and thanatologist Elisabeth Kübler-Ross (1926–2004), depicting psychological states, moods, or coping strategies that occur during the dying process or during periods of BEREAVEMENT, great loss, or TRAUMA. These begin with the **denial stage**, followed by the **anger stage**, **bargaining stage**, **depression stage**, and **acceptance stage**. The stages do not necessarily occur for a set period of time; moreover, they can recur and overlap before some degree of psychological and emotional resolution occurs.

stage theory any hypothetical construct used to describe phases or steps in a process that occurs over time, such as the STAGES OF GRIEF or the PIAGETIAN THEORY of stages of cognitive development.

staircase method a variation of the METHOD OF LIMITS in which stimuli are presented in ascending and descending order. When the observer's response changes, the direction of the stimulus sequence is reversed. This method is efficient because it does not present stimuli that are well above or below threshold.

stalking *n.* a pattern of following or observing a person in an obsessional, intrusive, or harassing manner. The pursued individual is typically a partner from a failed intimate relationship but may be a mental health care provider, a public figure, or other person of interest to the stalker. —**stalk** *vb.* —**stalker** *n.*

standard deviation (symbol: *SD*) a measure of the variability of a set of scores or values within a group, indicating how narrowly or broadly they deviate from the MEAN. A small standard deviation indicates data points that cluster around the mean, whereas a large standard deviation indicates data points that are dispersed across many different values. The standard deviation is expressed in the same units as the original values in the sample or population studied, so that the standard deviation of a series of measurements of weight would be in pounds, for example.

standard error (symbol: *SE*) a quantification of the inherent inaccuracy of a calculated population value that is attributable to random fluctuations within the sample data on which it is based. For example, the SAMPLE MEAN is the usual estimator of a POPULATION MEAN, yet different samples drawn from that same population will yield different values for the mean. Thus, to determine how much sample variability exists, the STANDARD ERROR OF THE MEAN may be obtained by taking the standard deviation of all of the means over all of the samples taken.

standard error of estimate (symbol: *SEE*) for a relationship between two variables (x and y) given by a REGRESSION EQUATION, an index of how closely the predicted value of y for a specific value of x matches its actual value. The smaller the standard error of estimate, the more confident one can be in the accuracy of the estimated (predicted) y value.

standard error of measurement (symbol: *SEM*) an index of the RELIABILITY of an assessment instrument, representing the variation of an individual's scores across multiple administrations of the same test. In essence, the standard error of measurement provides an indication of how confident one may be that an individual's obtained score on any given measurement opportunity represents his or her true score.

standard error of the mean (symbol: *SEM*; σ_M) a statistic that indicates how much the average value (MEAN) for a particular SAMPLE is likely to differ from the average value for the larger POPULATION from which it is drawn. It is equal to $\sigma/\sqrt{n}$, where σ is the standard deviation of the original distribution and n is the sample size.

standardization *n.* **1.** the process of establishing NORMS for a test. **2.** the use of uniform procedures in test administration to ensure that all participants take the same test under the same conditions and are scored by the same criteria, which in turn ensures that results can be compared to each other. **3.** the transformation of data into a distribution of STANDARDIZED SCORES, which allows for comparison of raw scores from different distributions. The Z-SCORE TRANSFORMATION is an example of a standardization.

standardized distribution a NORMAL DISTRIBUTION whose values have undergone transformation so as to have a mean of 0 and a STANDARD DEVIATION of 1. Also called **standard normal distribution**.

standardized interview see STRUCTURED INTERVIEW.

standardized score a value derived from a raw score by subtracting the mean value of all scores in the set and dividing by the STANDARD DEVIATION of the set. The advantage of standardized scores is that they are not reflective of the units of the measuring device from which they were obtained and thus can be compared to one another regardless of the device's scale values. Several types of standardized score exist, including T SCORES and Z SCORES. Also called **normal score; standard score**.

standardized test 1. an assessment instrument whose VALIDITY and RELIABILITY have been established by thorough empirical investigation and analysis. It has clearly defined norms, such that a person's score is an indication of how well he or she did in comparison to a large group of individuals representative of the population for which the test is intended. **2.** an assessment instrument administered in a predetermined manner, such that the questions, conditions of administration, scoring, and interpretation of responses are consistent from one occasion to another.

standard normal distribution see STANDARDIZED DISTRIBUTION.

standard normal variable any random variable whose probable value follows a NORMAL DISTRIBUTION with a mean of 0 and a STANDARD DEVIATION of 1.

standard stimulus an item used as the basis of comparison in the quantitative investigation of physical stimuli and the sensations and perceptions they produce. For example, in the METHOD OF ADJUSTMENT, a participant may be presented with a sound of a particular intensity (the standard stimulus) and then asked to change the intensity of another sound to match.

Stanford–Binet Intelligence Scale (**SB**) a standardized assessment of intelligence and cognitive abilities that includes five verbal subtests. The Stanford–Binet test was so named because it was brought to the United States in 1916 by U.S. psychologist Lewis M. Terman (1877–1956), a professor at Stanford University, as a revision and extension of the original **Binet–Simon Scale** developed to assess the intellectual ability of French children. The present Stanford–Binet Intelligence Scale (**SB5**) is the fourth revision of the test.

Stanford prison study a controversial 1971 study of the psychological effects of coercive situations, conducted by a research team under the direction of U.S. psychologist Philip G. Zimbardo (1933–). The male participants were randomly assigned to the roles of either prisoner or guard in a simulated prison at Stanford University. A variety of methods and situations were used to depersonalize participants, diminish their sense of identity, and increase a sense of power on the one hand (guards) and powerlessness on the other (prisoners). The experiment was terminated after only 6 days of the originally scheduled 14, when several participants showed physical manifestations of stress and psychological trauma. The study is often cited as an example of the POWER OF THE SITUATION.

stapes *n.* (*pl.* **stapedes**) see OSSICLES.

startle response an unlearned, rapid response to sudden, unexpected, and intense stimuli (e.g., loud noises, flashing lights). This response includes behaviors that serve a protective function, such as closing the eyes, lowering the head, and hunching the shoulders.

state *n.* the condition or status of an entity or system at a particular time that is characterized by relative stability of its basic components or elements.

state-dependent learning learning that occurs in a particular biological or psychological state and is better recalled when the individual is subsequently in the same state. For example, a rat trained to run a maze while under the influence of a psychoactive drug (e.g., pentobarbital) may not run it as successfully without the drug.

state-dependent memory a condition in which memory for an event is improved when the person is in the same biological or psychological state as when the memory was initially formed. For example, alcohol may improve one's recall of events experienced when one was previously under the influence of alcohol (although this level of recall is lower than recall under conditions in which both ENCODING and RETRIEVAL occur in sober states). See MOOD-DEPENDENT MEMORY.

statistic *n.* **1.** a number that represents a measurement of some characteristic, construct, variable, or other item of interest. **2.** any function of the observations in a sample that may be used to estimate the unknown but corresponding value in the population. Examples include measures of CENTRAL TENDENCY, such as the MEAN, MEDIAN, and MODE. Statistics often are assigned Roman letters (e.g., *M*, *s*), whereas the equivalent values in the population (called PARAMETERS) are assigned Greek letters (e.g., μ, σ). —**statistical** *adj.*

statistical analysis any of a wide range of techniques used to describe, explore, understand, explain, predict, and test hypotheses about data. It involves the examination of data collected from samples within populations as well as the use of probabilistic models to make inferences and draw conclusions.

statistical model a formal description of the relationships between two or more variables in the form of a mathematical equation. Many STATISTICAL TESTS involve comparing a particular model with the observed data.

statistical significance the degree to which a research outcome cannot reasonably be attributed to the operation of chance or random factors. It is determined during SIGNIFICANCE TESTING and given by a critical *p* value, which is the probability of obtaining the observed data if the NULL HYPOTHESIS (i.e., of no significant relationship between variables) were true. See also CLINICAL SIGNIFICANCE; PRACTICAL SIGNIFICANCE.

statistical test any mathematical technique or procedure used to evaluate the correctness of an empirical hypothesis by determining the likelihood of the sample results occurring by chance. Statistical testing will reveal the probability of committing a TYPE I ERROR if the NULL HYPOTHESIS is rejected. See HYPOTHESIS TESTING.

statistics *n.* the branch of mathematics in which data are used descriptively or inferentially to find or support answers for scientific and other quantifiable questions. —**statistical** *adj.* —**statistician** *n.*

status *n.* **1.** the reputation or position of an individual or group relative to others, such as an individual's standing in a social group. See SOCIAL STATUS. **2.** a persistent condition. For example, **status epilepticus** is a continuous series of seizures.

steady state a condition of stability

or equilibrium. For example, in behavioral studies, it is a state in which behavior is practically the same over repeated observations in a particular context. In pharmacology, it refers to a consistent, effective plasma (or other fluid) concentration of a medication in the body as a result of regular, often daily, doses to replace the amount of the drug that is excreted.

stem-and-leaf plot a graphical method of presenting data that have been measured on an INTERVAL SCALE. A basic stem-and-leaf plot comprises two columns separated by a vertical line; the right column lists the last digit of each data point (the "leaves") and the left column lists all of the other digits from each data point (the "stems"). Each stem is listed only once and no numbers are skipped, even if that means some stems have no leaves. The leaves are listed in increasing order of magnitude in a row to the right of each stem. Also called **stemplot**.

stem cell a cell that is itself undifferentiated but can divide to produce one or more types of specialized tissue cells (e.g., blood cells, nerve cells). Stem cells found in embryos (**embryonic stem cells**) are produced in humans during the BLASTOCYST stage of development and are capable of forming any type of tissue cell; stem cells that occur in adults (**adult stem cells**) are more limited in the range of cell types they can produce. The use of adult stem cells to treat some diseases (e.g., leukemia and lymphoma) has been common since the 1960s, and research continues on the potential use of both types of stem cells as renewable sources of replacement cells and tissues to treat a range of other conditions. There are ethical concerns about human embryonic stem cell research, mainly because harvesting such cells involves destroying the embryo and thus raises questions about the rights of the unborn.

stenosis *n.* the abnormal narrowing of a body conduit or passage. For example, spinal stenosis is a narrowing of

the opening in the spinal column, thereby restricting the spinal cord and resulting in numbness and pain in the lower back and legs. —**stenotic** *adj.*

stepdown selection see BACKWARD ELIMINATION.

stepfamily *n.* a family unit formed by the union of parents one or both of whom brings a child or children from a previous union into the new household. Also called **blended family**.

stepup selection see FORWARD SELECTION.

stepwise regression a group of REGRESSION ANALYSIS techniques that enter predictor (independent) variables into (or delete them from) the REGRESSION EQUATION one variable (or block of variables) at a time according to some predefined criterion. It is contrasted with SIMULTANEOUS REGRESSION, which enters all variables at the same time.

stereocilia *pl. n.* see HAIR CELL.

stereogram *n.* a picture perceived to have depth because it is produced by the binocular summation of two separate images of the same scene, each image slightly offset from the other in the horizontal plane. Although a **stereoscope** is commonly used to view the images, some observers can fuse the two images by simply crossing or uncrossing their eyes.

stereopsis *n.* DEPTH PERCEPTION provided by means of the BINOCULAR DISPARITY of the images from the two eyes.

stereotaxy *n.* determination of the exact location of a specific area within the body by means of three-dimensional measurements. Stereotaxy is used for positioning MICROELECTRODES or other devices in the brain for experimental, diagnostic, or therapeutic purposes and for locating an area of the brain prior to surgery. —**stereotactic** or **stereotaxic** *adj.*

stereotype *n.* a set of cognitive generalizations (e.g., beliefs, expectations) about the qualities and characteristics of the members of a group or social category. Stereotypes simplify and expedite perceptions and judgments, but they are often exaggerated, negative rather than positive, and resistant to revision even when perceivers encounter individuals with qualities that are not congruent with the stereotype. See also PREJUDICE. —**stereotypic** *adj.*

stereotype threat an individual's expectation that negative stereotypes about his or her member group will adversely influence others' judgments of his or her performance and that a poor performance will reflect badly on the member group. This expectation may undermine the individual's actual ability to perform well.

stereotypy *n.* persistent repetition of the same words, movements, or other behavior, particularly as a symptom of disorder (e.g., autism, obsessive-compulsive disorder, schizophrenia).

steroid hormone any of a class of hormones whose molecular structure is based on the steroid nucleus of four interconnected rings of carbon atoms. Examples include the SEX HORMONES and CORTICOSTEROIDS.

Stevens law a psychophysical relationship stating that the psychological magnitude of a sensation is proportional to a power of the stimulus producing it. This can be expressed as $\Psi = ks^n$, where Ψ is the sensation, k is a constant of proportionality, s is the stimulus magnitude, and n is a function of the particular stimulus. Also called **Stevens power law**. See also FECHNER'S LAW; WEBER'S LAW. [Stanley Smith **Stevens** (1906–1973), U.S. psychologist]

stigma *n.* the negative social attitude attached to a characteristic of an individual that may be regarded as a mental, physical, or social deficiency. A stigma implies social disapproval and can lead unfairly to discrimination against and exclusion of the individual.

stimulant *n.* any of various agents that excite functional activity in an organism or in a part of an organism. Stimulants are usually classified according to the body system or function excited (e.g., cardiac stimulants, respiratory stimulants).

stimulation *n.* the act or process of increasing the level of activity of an organism, particularly that of evoking heightened activity in (eliciting a response from) a sensory receptor, neuron, or other bodily tissue.

stimulus *n.* (*pl.* **stimuli**) **1.** any agent, event, or situation—internal or external—that elicits a response from an organism. See CONDITIONED STIMULUS; UNCONDITIONED STIMULUS. **2.** any change in physical energy that activates a sensory receptor. See DISTAL STIMULUS; PROXIMAL STIMULUS.

stimulus control the extent to which behavior is influenced by different stimulus conditions. It can refer to different responses occurring in the presence of different stimuli or to differences in the rate, temporal organization, or physical characteristics of a single response in the presence of different stimuli.

stimulus discrimination the ability to distinguish among different stimuli (e.g., to distinguish a circle from an ellipse) and to respond differently to them.

stimulus generalization the spread of effects of conditioning (either operant or classical) to stimuli that differ in certain aspects from the stimulus present during original conditioning. If responding is indistinguishable from that seen in the presence of the original stimulus, generalization is said to be complete.

stimulus object see OBJECT.

stimulus onset asynchrony (SOA) the time between the onset of one stimulus and the onset of the following stimulus. The term is used mainly in experiments with MASKING.

stimulus overload the condition in which the environment presents too many stimuli to be comfortably processed by an individual, resulting in stress and behavior designed to restore equilibrium.

stochastic model a model in which one or more of the inputs allow for random variation, thus generating a range of potential outcome values. Stochastic models are used to estimate the probabilities of various outcomes occurring under varying conditions. They are widely used in the social and behavioral sciences and also in the financial world. Compare DETERMINISTIC MODEL.

stochastic process a random process: a sequence of events with a random probability pattern such that the occurrence of any event in the sequence is independent of past events. For example, the number of people in a doctor's office who have colds during a 1-month period could be said to follow a stochastic process. In contrast to **deterministic processes**, stochastic processes involve some indeterminacy, and their development over time may only be described by probability distributions.

stop-signal task a procedure used in choice-reaction tasks in which a signal instructing the participant to withhold the response is presented on some trials at varying intervals after presentation of the stimulus. This is done to determine at what point in processing a response can no longer be inhibited.

storage *n.* the state of an item that is retained in memory, after ENCODING and before RETRIEVAL. See also RETENTION.

storytelling *n.* **1.** the recounting by a client of the events, concerns, and problems that led him or her to seek treatment. **2.** the use of symbolic talk and allegorical stories by the therapist to aid the client's understanding of issues.

strabismus *n.* any chronic abnormal alignment of the eyes, making normal binocular fixation and thus binocular vision impossible. Because strabismic eyes look in different directions, they give the brain conflicting messages, which may result in double vision. Alternatively, the brain may simply ignore, or suppress, one eye's view altogether. —**strabismic** *adj.*

stranger anxiety the distress and apprehension experienced by young children when they are around individuals who are unfamiliar to them. Stranger anxiety is a normal part of cognitive development: It usually begins around 8 or 9 months of age and typically lasts into the 2nd year.

Strange Situation an experimental technique used to assess quality of ATTACHMENT in infants and young children (up to the age of 2 years). The procedure subjects the child to increasing amounts of stress induced by a strange setting, the entrance of an unfamiliar person, and two brief separations from the parent. The reaction of the child to each of these situations is used to evaluate the security or insecurity of his or her attachment to the parent.

stratification *n.* arrangement into a layered configuration, as in SOCIAL STRATIFICATION. —**stratify** *vb.*

stratified sampling the process of selecting a sample from a population comprised of various subgroups (strata) in such a way that each subgroup is represented. For example, in a study of college students, a researcher might wish to examine people from different majors (e.g., social sciences, physical sciences, humanities). The selection procedure within each of these strata may be random or systematic.

stream of consciousness the notion that the contents of subjective consciousness are a continuous, dynamic flow of ideas, images, feelings, sensations, intuitions, and so forth, rather than a series of discrete, static components.

strength of association in statistics, the degree of relationship between two or more variables, as measured by such indices as a CORRELATION COEFFICIENT, COEFFICIENT OF DETERMINATION, or OMEGA SQUARED.

stress *n.* the physiological or psychological response to internal or external stressors. Stress involves changes affecting nearly every system of the body, influencing how people feel and behave. For example, it may be manifested by palpitations, sweating, dry mouth, shortness of breath, fidgeting, accelerated speech, augmentation of negative emotions (if already being experienced), and longer duration of stress fatigue. Severe stress is manifested by the GENERAL ADAPTATION SYNDROME. By causing these mind–body changes, stress contributes directly to psychological and physiological disorder and disease and affects mental and physical health, reducing quality of life.

stress hormone a chemical that is part of the body's response to threats and other stressors. The primary stress hormone is CORTISOL. Others include EPINEPHRINE, NOREPINEPHRINE, and CORTICOTROPIN. Together they put the body into a state of alertness (see FIGHT-OR-FLIGHT RESPONSE), accompanied by increased heart rate and respiration, dilated pupils, sweating, diminished sensitivity to pain, and redirection of blood from the gastrointestinal tract to muscles.

stress-inoculation training (SIT) a four-phase training program for stress management often used in COGNITIVE BEHAVIOR THERAPY. Phase 1 entails the identification of one's reactions to stress and their effects on functioning and psychological well-being; Phase 2 involves learning relaxation and self-regulation techniques; Phase 3 consists of learning coping self-statements; and Phase 4 involves assisted progression through a series of increasingly stressful situations using imagery, video, role playing, and real-life situations until

the individual is eventually able to cope with the original stress-inducing situation or event.

stress management the use of specific techniques, strategies, or programs—such as relaxation training, anticipation of stress reactions, and breathing techniques—for dealing with stress-inducing situations and the state of being stressed.

stressor *n.* any event, force, or condition that results in physical or emotional stress. Stressors may be internal or external forces that require adjustment or the use of COPING STRATEGIES on the part of the affected individual.

stretch reflex the contraction of a muscle in response to stretching of that muscle. Stretch reflexes support the body against the pull of gravity.

striate cortex the first region of the cerebral cortex that receives visual input from the thalamus, particularly from the LATERAL GENICULATE NUCLEUS. The striate cortex is located in the occipital lobe and contains a dense band of myelinated fibers that appears as a white stripe. Neurons in the striate cortex project to visual areas in the PRESTRIATE CORTEX and to subcortical visual nuclei. Also called **primary visual cortex (V1)**.

striated muscle see SKELETAL MUSCLE.

striatum *n.* see BASAL GANGLIA.

stroboscopic illusion 1. the apparent motion of a series of separate stimuli occurring in close consecutive order, as in motion pictures. **2.** the apparent motionlessness or reverse motion of a moving object, such as a rotating fan, produced by illuminating it with a series of intermittent light flashes. Also called **stroboscopic effect.**

stroke *n.* disruption of blood flow to the brain, which deprives the tissue of oxygen and nutrients, causing tissue damage and loss of normal function and, potentially, tissue death. A stroke may result from a hemorrhage of a blood vessel in the brain or an embolism or thrombus blocking an artery in the brain. This term is often used interchangeably with CEREBROVASCULAR ACCIDENT. See also TRANSIENT ISCHEMIC ATTACK.

Stroop Color–Word Interference Test a three-part test in which (a) color names are read as fast as possible; (b) the colors of bars or other shapes are rapidly named; and, most importantly, (c) color hues are named quickly when used to print the names of other colors (e.g., the word *green* printed in the color red). The degree to which the participants are subject to interference by the printed words is a measure of their cognitive flexibility, selective attention, and response inhibition (or disinhibition). In clinical neuropsychology, this test is commonly used to assess dysfunction of the frontal lobes of the brain. Also called **Stroop test**. [J. Ridley **Stroop** (1897–1973), U.S. psychologist]

Stroop effect the finding that the time it takes a participant to name the color of ink in which a word is printed is longer for words that denote incongruent color names than for neutral words or for words that denote a congruent color. For example, if the word *blue* is written in red ink (incongruent), participants take longer to say "red" than if the word *glue* is written in red ink (neutral) or if the word *red* is written in red ink (congruent). See STROOP COLOR–WORD INTERFERENCE TEST. [J. Ridley **Stroop**]

structural coefficient in STRUCTURAL EQUATION MODELING, a measure of the amount of change expected in an outcome or DEPENDENT VARIABLE given a one-unit change in the causal or INDEPENDENT VARIABLE and no change in any other variable.

structural equation modeling (**SEM**) any of a broad range of multivariate analysis methods, including FACTOR ANALYSIS and PATH ANALYSIS,

that examine interrelationships among LATENT VARIABLES. For example, assume a researcher hypothesizes that job satisfaction leads to happiness. Both are latent variables that are not directly observable but are defined in terms of other measurable variables, such as judgments of job performance from supervisors and peers; self-reports about attitudes toward job characteristics; and so forth. The researcher could use the measurable data to generate an equation representing the strength and nature of the links among the latent variables.

structural family therapy a type of FAMILY THERAPY that assesses the subsystems, boundaries, hierarchies, and coalitions within a family (its structure) and focuses on direct interactions between the family members as the primary method of inducing positive change. Structural family therapy stresses that when appropriately induced to do so, families with problems will discover their own alternatives to their ineffective patterns of relating to one another.

structuralism *n.* **1.** a movement considered to be the first school of psychology as a science, independent of philosophy. Usually attributed to German psychologist and physiologist Wilhelm Wundt (1832–1920), but probably more strongly and directly influenced by British-born U.S. psychologist Edward Bradford Titchener (1867–1927), structuralism defined psychology as the study of mental experience and sought to investigate the structure of such experience through a systematic program of experiments based on trained INTROSPECTION. **2.** a movement in various disciplines that study human behavior and culture that enjoyed particular currency in the 1960s and 1970s. The movement took its impetus from the approach to linguistic analysis pioneered by Swiss linguist Ferdinand de Saussure (1857–1913), who maintained that a language is a closed system and that written or spoken words acquire meaning through their structural relationships to other signs in the same system. The structuralist model of language was extended to cover essentially all social and cultural phenomena, including human thought and action, in the work of French anthropologist Claude Lévi-Strauss (1908–2009). See also POST-STRUCTURALISM.

structural model 1. in classical psychoanalytic theory, the view that the personality comprises three divisions or functions: (a) the ID, which represents instinctual drives; (b) the EGO, which controls id drives and mediates between them and external reality; and (c) the SUPEREGO, which comprises moral precepts and ideals. **2.** in statistics, any theoretical representation of the relationships among a dependent or outcome variable and multiple independent or predictor variables, whether CONTINUOUS or DISCRETE.

structured interview a method for gathering information in which questions, their wordings, and their order of administration are determined in advance. With structured interviews, comparisons can be made across different samples or interview periods; interviewees can be assessed consistently (e.g., using a common rating scale); and ORDER EFFECTS are minimized. Also called **standardized interview**. Compare UNSTRUCTURED INTERVIEW.

structured observation a systematic method of collecting behavioral data within a controlled environment. In structured observation, researchers (a) select which behaviors are of interest, (b) clearly define the characteristics of each behavior so that observers all agree on the classification, and (c) note the occurrence and frequency of these targeted behaviors in the situation under analysis. Structured observation differs from NATURALISTIC OBSERVATION, which involves observing individuals in their own environments outside of the laboratory.

structured Q sort see Q SORT.

Studentized residual in REGRESSION ANALYSIS, a standardized statistic describing the variation between obtained and predicted values. It is used to identify REGRESSION EQUATIONS that are a poor fit for the observed data. [**Student**, pseudonym of William S. Gosset (1876–1937), British statistician]

Student's *t* distribution see T DISTRIBUTION. [**Student**, pseudonym of William S. Gosset]

Student's *t* test see T TEST. [**Student**, pseudonym of William S. Gosset]

study *n.* **1.** a research investigation conducted for the purpose of understanding, explaining, describing, or predicting some phenomenon of interest. It may be conducted in the laboratory or natural environment, and it may yield quantitative or qualitative data. **2.** any attempt to acquire and remember information.

stupor *n.* a state of lethargy and impaired consciousness, in which an individual is disoriented, unresponsive, and immobile.

stuttering *n.* a disturbance in the normal fluency and sequence of speech. It is characterized by frequent repetition or prolongation of sounds, syllables, or words, with hesitations and pauses that disrupt speech. The disorder interferes with one's ability to communicate with others, especially during stressful situations (e.g., public speaking), and it can be exacerbated by one's awareness of and anxiety over one's dysfluency. **—stutter** *vb., n.*

subconscious *n.* a lay term that is widely used to denote the UNCONSCIOUS or PRECONSCIOUS mind as described by Austrian neurologist Sigmund Freud (1856–1939). It is also popularly associated with AUTOSUGGESTION and HYPNOSIS. **—subconscious** *adj.*

subcortical *adj.* relating to structures or processes in the brain that are located or take place beneath the CEREBRAL CORTEX.

subculture *n.* a group that maintains a characteristic set of customs, behaviors, interests, or beliefs that serves to distinguish it from the larger culture in which the members live. See also COUNTERCULTURE. —**subcultural** *adj.*

subfornical organ a structure in the brain that is responsive to ANGIOTENSIN II and contributes to thirst and drinking behavior. It is located below the FORNIX.

subgranular zone see DENTATE GYRUS.

subitize *vb.* to perceive how many objects are presented, without counting. [from Latin *subito*, "at once"]

subject *n.* the individual human or nonhuman animal that takes part in an experiment or research study and whose responses or performance are reported or evaluated; less frequently, the subject may also be an institution, group, or other entity. Many now recommend that the term PARTICIPANT be used for humans, considering the word *subject* to be depersonalizing and to imply passivity and submissiveness on the part of the experimentee.

subjective *adj.* **1.** taking place or existing only within the mind. **2.** particular to a specific person and thus intrinsically inaccessible to the experience or observation of others. **3.** based on or influenced by personal feelings, interpretations, or prejudices. Compare OBJECTIVE.

subjective contour an edge or border perceived in an image as a result of the inference of the observer. For example, a common form of a Kanizsa figure contains a triangle with sides that consist of subjective contours.

subjective test an assessment tool that is scored according to personal judgment or to standards that are less systematic than those used in OBJECTIVE TESTS. An essay examination is an example of a subjective test. Although

there are no necessarily right or wrong answers, responses are scored based on appraisals of their appropriateness or quality.

subjective well-being (**SWB**) one's appraisal of one's own level of happiness and LIFE SATISFACTION. In self-report measures of subjective well-being, two components are examined: one's **affective well-being**, which refers to the presence of pleasant affect (e.g., feelings of happiness) versus the absence of unpleasant affect (e.g., depressed mood), and one's **cognitive well-being**, which refers to one's evaluation of life overall (i.e., global life satisfaction) and of specific life experiences (e.g., job satisfaction). These components differ in their stability and variability over time and in their relations with other variables.

subjectivity *n.* in empirical research, the failure to attain proper standards of OBJECTIVITY, such as by allowing one's personal feelings or expectations to influence variable measurement, data collection, or other aspects of a study.

subjects-to-variables ratio the number of research participants compared to the number of research variables in a study. The subjects-to-variables ratio provides a guideline for determining what size sample to use to ensure the greatest POWER when conducting a statistical analysis.

subject variable an experience or characteristic of a research participant that is not of primary interest but nonetheless may influence study results and thus must be accounted for during experimentation or data analysis. Examples include age, marital status, religious affiliation, and intelligence. Also called **background variable**.

sublimation *n.* in classical psychoanalytic theory, a DEFENSE MECHANISM in which unacceptable sexual or aggressive drives are unconsciously channeled into socially acceptable modes of expression and redirected into new, learned behaviors, which indirectly provide some satisfaction for the original drives. For example, an exhibitionistic impulse may gain a new outlet in choreography. —**sublimate** *vb.*

subliminal *adj.* denoting or relating to stimuli that are below the DIFFERENCE THRESHOLD or ABSOLUTE THRESHOLD. —**subliminally** *adv.*

subliminal perception the registration of stimuli below the level of awareness, particularly stimuli that are too weak (or too rapid) for an individual to consciously perceive them. There has been much debate about whether responses to subliminal stimuli actually occur and whether it is possible for subliminal commands or advertising messages to influence behavior.

subscale *n.* a SCALE that taps some specific constituent or otherwise differentiated category of information as part of a larger, overall scheme. For example, a test of intelligence might consist of several subscales (or subtests) assessing verbal and performance aspects or dimensions of intelligence, which in combination yield a verbal intelligence score, a performance intelligence score, and an overall intelligence score.

substance *n.* **1.** a drug of abuse (e.g., alcohol, cannabis, cocaine), a medication, or a toxin that is capable of producing harmful effects when ingested or otherwise taken into the body. See SUBSTANCE-RELATED DISORDER. **2.** in philosophy, that which has an independent, self-sufficient existence and remains unalterably itself even though its attributes or properties may change. Philosophers have differed over what qualifies as a substance and whether reality consists of a single substance (see MONISM) or more (see DUALISM).

substance abuse a pattern of compulsive substance use marked by recurrent significant social, occupational, legal, or interpersonal adverse consequences, such as repeated absences from work or school, arrests, and marital difficulties. This diagnosis is

preempted by the diagnosis of SUBSTANCE DEPENDENCE: If the criteria for abuse and dependence are both met, only the latter diagnosis is given.

substance dependence a cluster of cognitive, behavioral, and physiological symptoms indicating continued use of a substance despite significant substance-related problems. There is a pattern of repeated substance ingestion resulting in tolerance, withdrawal symptoms if use is suspended, and an uncontrollable drive to continue use. Substance dependence is often used synonymously with the term ADDICTION.

substance intoxication a reversible syndrome due to the recent ingestion of a specific substance, including clinically significant behavioral or psychological changes as well as one or more signs of physiological involvement. Although symptoms vary by substance, there are some common manifestations, including perceptual disturbances; mood changes; impairments of judgment, attention, and memory; alterations of heartbeat and vision; and speech and coordination difficulties.

substance P a NEUROPEPTIDE that functions as a neurotransmitter in both peripheral and central nervous systems. High concentrations of neurons containing substance P are localized in the DORSAL HORN of the spinal cord, where they play a role in the modulation of pain. In peripheral tissues, substance P acts as a vasodilator.

substance-related disorder any of various disorders caused by the effects of a drug or a toxin. The term also broadly includes mental disorders (e.g., delirium, depression, psychosis) that may be induced by intoxication or withdrawal from various substances, including some medications.

substance use disorder a catchall diagnostic categorization encompassing varying degrees of excessive use of a substance; it combines and replaces

SUBSTANCE ABUSE and SUBSTANCE DEPENDENCE as distinct classifications.

substance withdrawal a syndrome that develops after cessation of prolonged, heavy consumption of a substance. Symptoms vary by substance, but withdrawal generally includes physiological, behavioral, and cognitive manifestations, such as nausea and vomiting, insomnia, mood alterations, and anxiety.

substantia gelatinosa a gelatinous-appearing mass of extensively interconnected small neurons at the tip of the DORSAL HORN of the spinal cord. Some cells in the substantia gelatinosa contain ENDORPHINS and are involved in regulation of pain.

substantia nigra a region of gray matter in the midbrain, named for its dark pigmentation, that sends DOPAMINERGIC neurons to the BASAL GANGLIA. Depletion of dopaminergic neurons in this region is implicated in Parkinson's disease.

substantive significance see PRACTICAL SIGNIFICANCE.

substitution *n.* in psychoanalytic theory, the replacement of unacceptable emotions or unattainable goals with alternative feelings or achievable aims. Substitution may be viewed as a positive adaptation or solution (e.g., adoption when one cannot have a child of one's own) or as a negative, maladaptive response (e.g., emotional eating after a frustrating day at the office). See also DEFENSE MECHANISM.

subthalamic nucleus a component of the subthalamus that receives fibers from the GLOBUS PALLIDUS as a part of the descending pathway from the BASAL GANGLIA.

subthalamus *n.* a part of the brain wedged between the THALAMUS and the HYPOTHALAMUS. It contains the subthalamic nucleus and functions in the regulation of movements controlled by skeletal muscles, together with the

BASAL GANGLIA and the SUBSTANTIA NIGRA. —**subthalamic** *adj.*

subventricular zone an area of the lateral ventricles. It is the largest zone in which NEUROGENESIS occurs in the adult brain and one of the two main such areas, the other being the subgranular zone of the DENTATE GYRUS.

successive-approximations method see METHOD OF SUCCESSIVE APPROXIMATIONS.

sudden infant death syndrome (**SIDS**) the sudden and unexpected death of a seemingly healthy infant during sleep for no apparent reason. The risk of SIDS is greatest between 2 and 6 months of age and is a common cause of death in babies less than 1 year old.

suffering *n.* the experience of pain or acute distress, either physical or psychological, in response to a physical trauma or a significant event, particularly one that is threatening or involves loss (e.g., the death of a loved one).

suggestibility *n.* **1.** an inclination to readily and uncritically adopt the ideas, beliefs, attitudes, or actions of others. **2.** an occasional synonym for HYPNOTIC SUSCEPTIBILITY.

suicidal ideation thoughts about or a preoccupation with killing oneself, often as a symptom of a MAJOR DEPRESSIVE EPISODE.

suicide *n.* the act of killing oneself. Frequently, suicide occurs in the context of a MAJOR DEPRESSIVE EPISODE, but it may also occur as a result of a substance use or other disorder. It sometimes occurs in the absence of any psychiatric disorder, especially in untenable situations, such as extreme or prolonged bereavement or declining health. —**suicidal** *adj.*

suicidology *n.* a multiprofessional discipline devoted to the study of suicidal phenomena and their prevention.

sulcus *n.* (*pl.* **sulci**) a groove, especially one on the surface of the cerebral cortex. The term is often used synonymously with FISSURE. —**sulcal** *adj.*

summary statistics a set of numbers used to communicate succinctly the most important descriptive information about a collection of raw data. For example, the VARIANCE, CENTRAL TENDENCY, SKEWNESS, and KURTOSIS may be used to summarize a sample data set.

summation *n.* **1.** the process in which a neural impulse is propagated by the cumulative effects of two or more stimuli that alone would not be sufficient to activate the neuron. See SPATIAL SUMMATION; TEMPORAL SUMMATION. **2.** (symbol: Σ) a mathematical operation involving the addition of numbers, quantities, or the like.

sum of products the value obtained by multiplying each pair of numbers in a set and then adding the individual totals. For example, for the set of number pairs

2, 4

3, 5

6, 6

1, 4

the sum of cross-products is $(2 \times 4) + (3 \times 5) + (6 \times 6) + (1 \times 4) = 8 + 15 + 36 + 4 = 63$.

sum of squares (symbol: SS) the number obtained by determining the deviation of each point in a data set from some value (such as a mean or predicted value), multiplying each deviation by itself, and adding the resulting products. For example, if an analysis yields a mean score of 5 but a person's actual score is 7, the squared deviation for that individual is $(7 - 5)^2 = 2^2 = 4$: This would be added to the squared deviations of all other individuals in the sample. Various types of sums of squares are calculated in ANALYSIS OF VARIANCE, REGRESSION ANALYSIS, and other statistical procedures.

superego *n.* in psychoanalytic theory, the moral component of the personality that represents parental and societal standards and determines personal standards of right and wrong, or conscience, as well as aims and aspirations (see EGO-IDEAL). In the classic Freudian tripartite structure of the psyche, the EGO, which controls personal impulses and directs actions, operates by the rules and principles of the superego, which stem from parental demands and prohibitions.

superior *adj.* in anatomy, higher, above, or toward the head. Compare INFERIOR.

superior colliculus see COLLICULUS.

superiority complex an exaggerated opinion of one's abilities and accomplishments that derives from an overcompensation for feelings of inferiority. Compare INFERIORITY COMPLEX.

superior olivary complex (**superior olivary nucleus**; **superior olive**) see OLIVARY NUCLEUS.

superordinate goal a goal that can be attained only if the members of two or more groups work together by pooling their skills, efforts, and resources. For example, in the 1954 Robbers Cave experiment studying deliberately induced conflict among two groups of young campers, researchers introduced superordinate goals by creating emergencies and problems that could be resolved only through the joint efforts of both groups.

supervision *n.* oversight: critical evaluation and guidance provided by a qualified and experienced person (the supervisor) to another individual (the trainee) during the learning of a task or process. In psychotherapy and counseling, supervision by a senior therapist or counselor is required while the trainee learns therapeutic techniques. In rural and other remote settings, **telesupervision** has been used to provide feedback to a trainee via technology such as e-mail, telephone, or videoconferencing.

supplementary motor area

(**SMA**) an area of the MOTOR CORTEX involved in planning and learning new movements that have coordinated sequences. In contrast to the PREMOTOR AREA, neuronal input to the supplementary motor area is triggered more by internal representations than by external events.

suppression *n.* a conscious effort to put disturbing thoughts and experiences out of mind, or to control and inhibit the expression of unacceptable impulses and feelings. It is distinct from the unconscious defense mechanism of REPRESSION in psychoanalytic theory. —**suppress** *vb.*

suppressor effect a reduction in the correlation between two variables due to the influence of a third variable. Compare REINFORCER EFFECT.

suprachiasmatic nucleus (SCN) a small region of the HYPOTHALAMUS in the brain, above the OPTIC CHIASM, that is the location of the circadian oscillator, which controls circadian rhythms. It receives direct input from the retina. See also BIOLOGICAL CLOCK.

supraliminal *adj.* describing stimulation that is above the DIFFERENCE THRESHOLD or ABSOLUTE THRESHOLD.

supraoptic nucleus a particular collection of neurons in the HYPOTHALAMUS that lies above the OPTIC CHIASM. Neurons in this nucleus project to the posterior lobe of the PITUITARY GLAND and secrete the hormones OXYTOCIN and VASOPRESSIN.

suprasegmental *adj.* in linguistics, denoting the phonological features of speech that extend over a series of PHONEMES. In English, suprasegmental features include tone (pitch) and stress.

surface dyslexia a form of acquired DYSLEXIA in which a person is overly reliant on spelling-to-sound correspondence and therefore has difficulty reading irregularly spelled words. See also DEEP DYSLEXIA.

surface structure (s-structure) in TRANSFORMATIONAL GENERATIVE GRAM-MAR, the structure of a grammatical sentence as it actually occurs in speech or writing, as opposed to its underlying DEEP STRUCTURE or abstract logical form. The surface structure of a sentence is believed to be generated from the deep structure by a series of transformational rules involving the addition, deletion, or reordering of sentence elements. Psycholinguists have investigated whether and to what extent this may serve as a model for the cognitive processes involved in forming and interpreting sentences.

surface therapy psychotherapy directed toward relieving the client's symptoms and emotional stress through such measures as reassurance, suggestion, and direct attempts to modify attitudes and behavior patterns, rather than through exploration and analysis of unconscious motivation and underlying dynamics. Compare DEPTH THERAPY.

surrogate *n.* a person or object that substitutes for the role of an individual who has a significant position in a family or group. See FATHER SURROGATE; MOTHER SURROGATE.

survey *n.* a study in which a group of participants is selected from a population and data about or opinions from those participants are collected, measured, and analyzed. Information typically is gathered by interview or self-report questionnaire, and the results thus obtained may then be extrapolated to the whole population.

survival analysis a family of statistical methods used to model a variety of time-related outcomes. The simplest application of survival analysis involves estimating the amount of time until the occurrence of an event (e.g., death, illness, graduation, marriage) for a group of individuals.

survival value the degree to which a behavioral, physiological, or physical trait will contribute to REPRODUCTIVE SUCCESS. A trait that can be shown to increase the probability of reproductive success in a given environment has high survival value.

survivor guilt remorse or guilt for having survived a catastrophic event when others did not or for not suffering the ills that others had to endure. It is a common reaction stemming in part from a feeling of having failed to do enough to prevent the event or to save those who did not survive.

susceptibility *n.* vulnerability: readily affected by or at increased risk of acquiring a particular condition, such as an infection, injury, or disorder.

sustained attention attentional focus on a task for an extended length of time.

Sylvian fissure see LATERAL SULCUS.

symbiosis *n.* **1.** any relationship in which two species live together in close association, especially one in which both species benefit. For example, in tropical Amazonia, a species of ant lives on a particular tree species that it uses for food and shelter, at the same time removing lichen and other parasites that might harm the tree. **2.** a mutually reinforcing relationship in which one individual is overdependent on another to satisfy needs. Such a relationship hampers the development or independence of both individuals and usually results in dysfunction when the dominant individual is unwilling to provide for the dependent individual. **—symbiotic** *adj.*

symbol *n.* **1.** any object, figure, or image that represents something else. For example, a rose may suggest ideas of beauty, love, femininity, and transience without being limited to any of these meanings in particular. See also SIGN. **2.** in classical psychoanalytic theory, a disguised representation of a repressed idea, impulse, or wish. See also SYMBOLIZATION. **—symbolic** *adj.*

symbolic function in PIAGETIAN THEORY, the cognitive ability to mentally represent objects that are not in sight. For example, a child playing with a toy can mentally picture and experience the toy even after it has been taken away and he or she can no longer see it. Symbolic function emerges early in the PREOPERATIONAL STAGE. Also called **semiotic function**.

symbolic interactionism a sociological theory that assumes that self-concept is created through interpretation of symbolic gestures, words, actions, and appearances exhibited by others during social interaction. In contrast to Freudian and other approaches that postulate extensive inner dispositions and regard social interaction as resulting from them, symbolic interactionists believe that inner structures result from social interactions. See GENERALIZED OTHER; LOOKING-GLASS SELF.

symbolic modeling see PARTICIPANT MODELING.

symbolization *n.* in classical psychoanalytic theory, the substitution of a symbol for a repressed impulse, affect, or idea in order to avoid censorship by the superego (e.g., dreaming of a steeple instead of a penis). **—symbolize** *vb.*

symmetry *n.* **1.** the mirrorlike correspondence of parts on opposite sides of a center, providing balance and harmony in the proportions of objects. This is considered an aesthetically pleasing quality. **2.** one of the GESTALT PRINCIPLES OF ORGANIZATION. It states that people tend to perceive objects as coherent wholes organized around a center point; this is particularly evident when the objects involve unconnected regions bounded by borders. Also called **law** (or **principle**) **of symmetry**. **3.** in mathematics and statistics, a condition in which values are arranged identically above and below the middle of a data set. Many standard statistical techniques are appropriate only for symmetrical data, such that nonsymmetrical data often are transformed into a roughly symmetrical form prior to analysis. Compare ASYMMETRY. **—symmetrical** *adj.*

sympathetic–adrenal–medul-

lary axis (**SAM**) a neuroendocrine stress-response system that interacts with the HYPOTHALAMIC–PITUITARY–ADRENAL AXIS. A stressor is perceived via the sympathetic nervous system, triggering in humans the production and release of hormones such as epinephrine and norepinephrine by the adrenal gland (in particular, the medulla). Also called **sympathetic adrenomedullary system**.

sympathetic chain either of two beadlike chains of GANGLIA of the sympathetic nervous system, one chain lying on each side of the spinal column.

sympathetic nervous system one of the two divisions of the AUTONOMIC NERVOUS SYSTEM, the other being the PARASYMPATHETIC NERVOUS SYSTEM. It acts as an integrated whole in affecting a large number of smooth muscle systems simultaneously, usually in the service of enhancing the FIGHT-OR-FLIGHT RESPONSE. Typical sympathetic changes include dilation of the pupils to facilitate vision, constriction of the peripheral arteries to supply more blood to the muscles and to the brain, secretion of epinephrine to raise the blood-sugar level and increase metabolism, and reduction of stomach and intestinal activities so that energy can be directed elsewhere. Also called **sympathetic division**.

sympathy *n.* **1.** feelings of concern or compassion resulting from an awareness of the suffering or sorrow of another. **2.** more generally, a capacity to share in and respond to the concerns or feelings of others. **—sympathetic** *adj.* **—sympathize** *vb.*

symptom *n.* any deviation from normal functioning that is considered indicative of physical or mental pathology. **—symptomatic** *adj.*

symptom substitution in the classical psychoanalytic theory of Austrian neurologist Sigmund Freud (1856–1939), the development of a symptom to replace one that has cleared up as a result of treatment. It is said to occur if the unconscious impulses and conflicts responsible for the original symptom are not dealt with effectively.

synapse *n.* the specialized junction through which signals are transmitted from one neuron (the presynaptic neuron) to another (the postsynaptic neuron). In most synapses, the knoblike ending (terminal button) of the axon of a presynaptic neuron faces the dendrite or cell body of the postsynaptic neuron across a narrow gap, the synaptic cleft. The arrival of a neural signal triggers the release of NEUROTRANSMITTER from SYNAPTIC VESICLES in the terminal button into the synaptic cleft. Here the molecules of neurotransmitter activate receptors in the postsynaptic membrane and cause the opening of ION CHANNELS in the postsynaptic cell. **—synaptic** *adj.*

synaptic cleft the gap within a synapse between the knoblike ending of the axon of one neuron and the dendrite or cell body of a neighboring neuron. The synaptic cleft is typically 20 to 30 nm wide.

synaptic transmission see NEUROTRANSMISSION.

synaptic vesicle any of numerous small spherical sacs in the cytoplasm of the knoblike ending of the axon of a presynaptic neuron that contain molecules of NEUROTRANSMITTER. The transmitter is released into the SYNAPTIC CLEFT when a nerve impulse arrives at the axon ending.

synaptogenesis *n.* the formation of synapses between neurons as axons and dendrites grow.

synchronicity *n.* in ANALYTIC PSYCHOLOGY, the simultaneous occurrence of events that appear to have a meaningful connection when there is no explicable causal relationship between these events, as in extraordinary coincidences or purported examples of telepathy.

syncope *n.* fainting: a transient loss of consciousness resulting from sudden reduction in the blood supply to the brain. The most common type is **vasovagal syncope**, in which the drop in blood supply is caused by heightened VAGUS NERVE activity in response to certain triggers, such as standing up too quickly or experiencing unpleasant stimuli. —**syncopal** *adj.*

syndrome *n.* a set of symptoms and signs that are usually due to a single cause (or set of related causes) and together indicate a particular physical or mental disease or disorder.

synergism *n.* the joint action of different elements such that their combined effect is greater than the sum of their individual effects, such as in drug synergism. —**synergistic** *adj.*

synesthesia (synaesthesia) *n.* a condition in which stimulation of one sense generates a simultaneous sensation in another (e.g., seeing colors when viewing letters, numbers, or words on a printed page). These concomitant sensations are automatic, vivid, and consistent over time. There are more than 50 different types of synesthesia. Estimates vary, but nearly 5% of people may have some form of this neurological blending of the senses.

syntactics *n.* the structural and grammatical aspects of language, as distinguished from SEMANTICS.

syntax *n.* the set of rules that describes how words and phrases in a language are arranged into grammatical sentences, or the branch of linguistics that studies such rules. With MORPHOLOGY, syntax is one of the two traditional subdivisions of grammar. —**syntactic** or **syntactical** *adj.*

synthesis *n.* **1.** the bringing together of disparate parts or elements—be they physical or conceptual—into a whole. For example, biosynthesis is the process by which chemical or biochemical compounds are formed from their constituents, and mental synthesis involves combining ideas and images into meaningful objects of thought. **2.** in philoso-

phy, the final stage of a dialectical process: a third proposition that resolves the opposition between THESIS and ANTITHESIS. The synthesis then serves as the thesis in the next phase of the ongoing dialectic. —**synthetic** *adj.*

system *n.* **1.** any collective entity consisting of a set of interrelated or interacting elements that have been organized together to perform a function. For example, a living organism or one of its major bodily structures constitutes a system. **2.** a structured set of facts, concepts, and hypotheses that provide a framework of thought or belief, as in a philosophical system. —**systematic** *adj.*

systematic desensitization a form of BEHAVIOR THERAPY in which COUNTERCONDITIONING is used to reduce anxiety associated with a particular stimulus. It involves the following stages: (a) The client is trained in deep-muscle relaxation; (b) various anxiety-provoking situations related to a particular problem, such as fear of death or of spiders, are listed in order from weakest to strongest; and (c) each of these situations is presented in imagination or in reality, beginning with the weakest, while the client practices muscle relaxation. Since the muscle relaxation is incompatible with the anxiety, the client gradually responds less to the anxiety-provoking situations. See also IN VIVO DESENSITIZATION; RECIPROCAL INHIBITION.

systematic error error in which the data values obtained from a sample deviate by a fixed amount from the true values within the population. For example, a scale that repeatedly provides readings 0.5 g lower than the true weight would be demonstrating systematic error. Systematic errors tend to be consistently positive or negative and may occur as a result of SAMPLING BIAS or MEASUREMENT ERROR.

systematic observation an objective, well-ordered method for close examination of some phenomenon or aspect of behavior so as to obtain reliable data unbiased by observer interpretation. Systematic observation typically involves specification of the exact actions, attributes, or other variables that are to be recorded and precisely how they are to be recorded. The intent is to ensure that, under the same or similar circumstances, all observers will obtain the same results.

systematic processing see HEURISTIC-SYSTEMATIC MODEL.

systematic replication the process of conducting a study again but with certain consistent differences, often in an attempt to extend the original research to different settings or participants. For example, a systematic replication could refine the design (e.g., by using more participants) or the methodology (e.g., by using more standardized procedures or objective measures). Compare DIRECT REPLICATION.

systematic sampling a type of sampling process in which all the members of a population are listed and then some objective, orderly procedure is applied to randomly choose specific cases. For example, the population might be listed alphabetically and every seventh case selected. Also called **quasirandom sampling; systematic random sampling**.

systematic variance see UNSYSTEMATIC VARIANCE.

systems analysis the process—and the specialty area itself—of studying any system (e.g., the circulatory system, an organization, a family) so as to comprehend or clarify its internal workings and its purposes, often with a view to improving interrelations among constituent elements or to achieving a desired end more effectively. —**systems analyst** *n.*

systems theory see GENERAL SYSTEMS THEORY.

Tt

table *n.* a presentation of data in an ordered arrangement of overlaid vertical columns and horizontal rows. As with a GRAPH, the purpose of a table is to communicate information (either in words or numerical values) in a concise, space-efficient manner that can be assessed at a glance and interpreted easily. The intersection of a column and a row is called a CELL. —**tabular** *adj.*

taboo (**tabu**) *n.* a religious, moral, or social convention prohibiting a particular behavior, object, or person.

tachycardia *n.* see ARRHYTHMIA.

tacit knowledge knowledge that is informally acquired rather than explicitly taught and allows a person to succeed in certain environments and pursuits. It is stored without awareness and therefore is not easily articulated. Many everyday skills are of this kind, such as the ability to recognize faces or to speak one's native language.

tactile agnosia loss or impairment of the ability to recognize and understand the nature of objects through touch. Several distinct subtypes have been identified, including amorphagnosia, impaired recognition of the size and shape of objects; and finger agnosia, impaired recognition of one's own or another person's fingers.

tactile encoding see VISUAL ENCODING.

tactile hallucination a false perception involving the sense of touch. These sensations occur in the absence of any external stimulus and may include itching, feeling electric shocks, and feeling insects biting or crawling under the skin.

tactile perception the ability to perceive objects or judge sensations through the sense of touch. The term often refers to judgments of spatial stimulation of the skin, patterns imposed on the skin, or sensory events involving stimulation of the skin (e.g., the thermal properties of a liquid).

talent *n.* an innate ability or an aptitude to excel in one or more specific activities or subject areas. —**talented** *adj.*

tapering *n.* in pharmacology, a gradual reduction in the dose of a drug in order to avoid undesirable effects that may occur with rapid cessation. Such effects may be extreme (e.g., convulsions) or relatively mild (e.g., headache, gastrointestinal discomfort). Drugs that produce physiological dependence (e.g., opiates, benzodiazepines) must be tapered to prevent a withdrawal syndrome and possible seizures. Also called **gradual withdrawal**.

***Tarasoff* decision** the 1976 California Supreme Court decision in *Tarasoff v. Regents of the University of California*, which placed limits on a client's right to confidentiality by ruling that mental health practitioners who know or reasonably believe that a client poses a threat to another person are obligated to protect the potential victim from danger. Depending on the circumstances, that protection may involve such actions as warning the potential victim, notifying the police of the potential threat posed by the client, or both.

tardive dyskinesia a movement disorder associated with the prolonged use of ANTIPSYCHOTICS, particularly conventional antipsychotics that act primarily as dopamine-receptor ANTAGONISTS. Symptoms include tremor and spasticity of muscle groups, particularly orofacial muscles and muscles in the extremities. No effective treatment is known.

task analysis the breakdown of a complex task into component tasks to identify the different skills needed to correctly complete the task. In education, for example, it entails the breakdown of a subject or field of study to identify the specific skills the student must possess in order to master it; in industrial and organizational settings, a job is broken down into the skills, knowledge, and specific operations required.

taste *n.* the sense devoted to the detection of molecules dissolved in liquids (also called **gustation**), or the sensory experience resulting from perception of gustatory qualities (e.g., sweetness, saltiness, sourness, bitterness). Dissolved molecules are delivered to the taste receptors—TASTE CELLS—on the tongue, soft palate, larynx, and pharynx. Taste combines with smell, texture, and appearance to generate a sense of flavor.

taste bud a goblet-shaped structure, 30×50 μm, about 6,000 of which occur in the human mouth. Each bud is a collection of about 50 TASTE CELLS arranged like sections of an orange. At its apex is a pore through which each taste cell sends a slender, hairlike extension studded with receptor proteins to sample the environment.

taste cell a receptor cell for gustatory stimuli. Each has a slender, hairlike extension that protrudes from the opening in the TASTE BUD. Humans have about 300,000 taste cells, although the number can vary across individuals, and there are about 50 cells per taste bud. Taste cells can be divided into four anatomical types: All but Type IV cells may be involved in taste TRANSDUCTION.

taste cortex the area of the cerebral cortex responsible for the perception of taste. The **primary taste cortex** (or **primary gustatory cortex**) is the first cortical relay for taste. It receives taste, touch, visceral, and other sensory inputs from the thalamus and permits an integrated evaluation of a chemical. Its output goes to regions that control oral

and visceral reflexes in response to foods. The **secondary taste cortex** (or **secondary gustatory cortex**) identifies stimuli as either pleasant and rewarding or unpleasant and undesirable. This information from the secondary taste cortex interacts with analyses from visual, tactile, and olfactory cells to permit an integrated appreciation of flavor.

taxonomy *n.* the science of classification or any specific scheme of classification itself. —**taxonomic** *adj.* —**taxonomist** *n.*

Tay–Sachs disease (TSD) a disease due to a deficiency of the enzyme hexosaminidase A, resulting in the accumulation of G_{M2} gangliosides in all tissues. This process gradually destroys the brain and nerve cells by altering the shape of neurons. Development is normal until the 6th month of infancy, after which there is a deterioration of motor, visual, and cognitive abilities. Death usually occurs between 3 and 5 years of age. [Warren **Tay** (1843–1927), British physician; Bernard **Sachs** (1858–1944), U.S. neurologist]

T cell see LYMPHOCYTE.

t distribution a theoretical PROBABILITY DISTRIBUTION that plays a central role in testing hypotheses about population means, among other parameters. It is the sampling distribution of the statistic $(M - \mu_0)/s$, where μ_0 is the mean of the population from which the sample is drawn, M is the estimate of the mean of the population as obtained from sample data, and s is the standard deviation of the data set. Also called **Student's t distribution**.

technostress *n.* a form of occupational stress that is associated with information and communication technologies such as the Internet, mobile devices, and social media. Affected employees become anxious or overwhelmed by working in computer-mediated environments in which there is a constant flow of new information. Technostress has significant detrimental effects on individuals' health, productivity, and work satisfaction and has been proposed as an important predictor of overall job strain.

tectorial membrane part of the ORGAN OF CORTI in the cochlea. It consists of a semigelatinous membrane in which the stereocilia of the outer HAIR CELLS are embedded.

tectospinal tract see VENTROMEDIAL PATHWAY.

tectum *n.* (*pl.* **tecta**) the roof of the MIDBRAIN. The tectum contains the superior COLLICULUS, which acts as a relay and reflex center for the visual system, and the inferior colliculus, which is a sensory center for the auditory system. —**tectal** *adj.*

tegmentum *n.* (*pl.* **tegmenta**) the central core of the MIDBRAIN and PONS. It contains sensory and motor tracts passing through the midbrain and also several nuclei, including the RED NUCLEUS and SUBTHALAMIC NUCLEUS. —**tegmental** *adj.*

telegraphic speech 1. condensed or abbreviated speech in which only the most central words, carrying the highest level of information, are spoken. Nouns and verbs are typically featured, whereas adjectives, adverbs, articles, and connective parts of speech are omitted. **2.** the speech of children roughly between the ages of 18 and 30 months. This is usually in the form of two-word expressions up to the age of about 24 months and thereafter is characterized by short but multiword expressions (e.g., *dog eat bone*).

telekinesis *n.* a form of PSYCHOKINESIS in which solid matter is purportedly moved or manipulated solely by the power of the mind.

telemetry *n.* the process of measuring and transmitting quantitative information to a remote location, where it can be recorded and interpreted. For example, a small radio transmitter may be implanted inside a nonhuman animal to measure general activity level as well as a variety of physiological variables, including body temperature, heart rate, and blood pressure. The transmitter sends signals to a receiver located outside the animal. —**telemetric** *adj.*

telencephalon *n.* see CEREBRUM.

teleology *n.* the position that certain phenomena are best understood and explained in terms of their purposes. In psychology, its proponents hold that mental processes are purposive, that is, directed toward a goal. The view that behavior is to be explained in terms of ends and purposes is frequently contrasted with explanations in terms of causes, such as INSTINCTS and CONDITIONED RESPONSES. —**teleologic** or **teleological** *adj.*

telepathy *n.* the alleged direct communication of information from one mind to another, in the absence of any known means of transmission. It is a form of EXTRASENSORY PERCEPTION. —**telepath** *n.* —**telepathic** *adj.*

telepsychotherapy *n.* see DISTANCE THERAPY.

telesupervision *n.* see SUPERVISION.

temperament *n.* the basic foundation of personality, usually assumed to be biologically determined and present early in life, including such characteristics as energy level, emotional responsiveness, demeanor, mood, response tempo, behavioral inhibition, and willingness to explore.

temporal *adj.* **1.** of or pertaining to time or its role in some process, as in TEMPORAL SUMMATION. **2.** relating or proximal to the temple, as in TEMPORAL LOBE. —**temporally** *adv.*

temporal coding a type of neural plotting of the precise timing of the points of maximum intensity (spikes) between ACTION POTENTIALS. It can provide valuable additional detail to information obtained through simple RATE CODING.

temporal conditioning a procedure in CLASSICAL CONDITIONING in which the unconditioned stimulus is presented at regular intervals but in the absence of an accompanying conditioned stimulus. Compare TRACE CONDITIONING.

temporal lobe one of the four main subdivisions of each CEREBRAL HEMISPHERE in the brain, lying immediately below the LATERAL SULCUS on the outer surface of each hemisphere. It contains the auditory projection and auditory association areas and also areas for higher order visual processing and for memory formation.

temporal lobe amnesia a memory disorder, secondary to injury of the temporal lobe (particularly medial structures, such as the hippocampus), that prevents the formation of new memories.

temporal summation a neural mechanism in which an impulse is propagated by two successive POSTSYNAPTIC POTENTIALS (PSPs), neither of which alone is of sufficient intensity to cause a response. The partial DEPOLARIZATION caused by the first PSP continues for a few milliseconds and is able, with the additive effect of the second PSP, to produce an above-threshold depolarization sufficient to elicit an ACTION POTENTIAL. Compare SPATIAL SUMMATION.

temporal validity a type of EXTERNAL VALIDITY that refers to the generalizability of a study's results across time.

tend-and-befriend response a proposed physiological and behavioral stress regulatory system that is an alternative to the classic FIGHT-OR-FLIGHT RESPONSE and that is stronger in females than in males. Tending involves nurturant activities designed to protect the self and offspring, to promote a sense of safety, and to reduce distress, and befriending is expressed in the creation and maintenance of social networks that aid in this process. Neuroendocrinal evidence suggests an underlying physiological mechanism mediated by OXYTOCIN.

tender-mindedness n. a personality trait characterized by intellectualism, idealism, optimism, dogmatism, religiousness, and monism. Compare TOUGH-MINDEDNESS. —**tender-minded** adj.

tension n. **1.** a feeling of physical and psychological strain accompanied by discomfort, uneasiness, and pressure to seek relief through talk or action. **2.** the force resulting from contraction or extension of a muscle or tendon.

teratogen n. an agent that induces developmental abnormalities in a fetus. The process that results in these abnormalities is called **teratogenesis**; a **teratomorph** is a fetus or offspring with these abnormalities.

terminal button (**terminal bouton**) see AXON.

terminal decline a rapid deterioration in cognitive abilities immediately before death. The cognitive abilities that appear to be most prone to terminal decline are those least affected by normal aging. Also called **terminal drop**.

territoriality n. the defense by a nonhuman animal of a specific geographic area (its primary territory) against intrusion from other members of the same species. Territory differs from HOME RANGE in being an area that is actively defended and from PERSONAL SPACE in being a geographic area. Territoriality is observed in a wide range of animals and is found most often where there are specific defensible resources, such as a concentration of food or shelter.

terrorism n. systematic intimidation or coercion to attain political or religious objectives using unlawful and unpredictable force or violence against property, persons, or governments. See also BIOTERRORISM. —**terrorist** adj., n.

terror management theory a theory proposing that control of death-related anxiety is the primary function of society and the main motivation in human behavior. Accordingly, awareness of the inevitability of death motivates people to maintain faith in the absolute validity of the cultural worldviews (i.e., beliefs and values) that give their lives meaning and to believe that they are living up to those standards, thus attaining a sense of personal value or self-esteem that buffers them against the frightening recognition of their own mortality.

tertiary care highly specialized care given to patients who are in danger of disability or death. Tertiary care often requires sophisticated technologies provided by highly specialized practitioners and facilities, such as neurologists, neurosurgeons, thoracic surgeons, and intensive care units. Compare PRIMARY CARE; SECONDARY CARE.

tertiary circular reaction in PIAGETIAN THEORY, an infant's action that creatively alters former SCHEMES to fit the requirements of new situations. Tertiary circular reactions emerge toward the end of the SENSORIMOTOR STAGE, at the beginning of the 2nd year; they differ from earlier behaviors in that the child can, for the first time, develop new schemes to achieve a desired goal. See also PRIMARY CIRCULAR REACTION; SECONDARY CIRCULAR REACTION.

tertiary prevention intervention for individuals or groups with already established psychological or physical conditions, disorders, or diseases. Tertiary interventions include attempts to minimize negative effects, prevent further disease or disorder related to complications, prevent relapse, and restore the highest physical or psychological functioning possible. Compare PRIMARY PREVENTION; SECONDARY PREVENTION.

test *n.* **1.** a standardized set of questions or other items designed to assess knowledge, skills, interests, or other characteristics of an examinee. See PSYCHOLOGICAL TEST. **2.** a set of operations, usually statistical in nature, designed to determine the VALIDITY of a hypothesis.

testability *n.* the degree to which a hypothesis or theory is capable of being evaluated empirically.

test analysis a detailed statistical assessment of a test's properties, including an evaluation of the quality of the test items and of the test as a whole. It usually includes information such as the MEAN and STANDARD DEVIATION for the test scores in the population used to develop the test, as well as data on the test's RELIABILITY.

test battery a group, series, or set of several tests designed to be administered as a unit in order to obtain a comprehensive assessment of a particular factor or phenomenon. For example, a researcher may administer a battery of health surveys to a group of individuals diagnosed with a particular disease to assess multiple facets of the disease.

testicular feminization syndrome see ANDROGEN-INSENSITIVITY SYNDROME.

testing effect the finding that taking a test on previously studied material leads to better retention than does restudying that material for an equivalent amount of time. Although testing is often conceptualized as an assessment tool, this finding suggests that testing (or retrieval practice) can also be considered a learning tool.

testis *n.* (*pl.* **testes**) the principal male reproductive organ, a pair of which is normally located in the scrotum. The testes produce sperm and male sex hormones (ANDROGENS). See also SPERMATOGENESIS.

testosterone *n.* a male sex hormone and the most potent of the ANDROGENS produced by the testes. It stimulates the development of male reproductive organs, including the prostate gland, and secondary SEX CHARACTERISTICS, such as beard, bone, and muscle growth. Women normally secrete small

thematic analysis

amounts of testosterone from the adrenal cortex and ovaries.

test–retest reliability see RETEST RELIABILITY.

test statistic 1. the numerical result of a STATISTICAL TEST, which is used to determine STATISTICAL SIGNIFICANCE and evaluate the viability of a hypothesis. **2.** any of the statistics relating to a test or its components, such as indices of item difficulty, item RELIABILITY, item discriminability, and so on. See TEST ANALYSIS.

testwise *adj.* describing a test taker who has developed skills and strategies that are not related to the construct being measured on the test but that facilitate an increased test score. Experience with similar tests, coaching, or the ability to respond advantageously to items that contain extraneous clues and suggestions may yield a score that is higher than that yielded by the true ability of the test taker.

tetrahydrocannabinol (**THC**; **delta-9-tetrahydrocannabinol**) *n.* one of a number of CANNABINOIDS principally responsible for the psychoactive properties of CANNABIS.

texture gradient the progressive decline in the resolution of textures as the viewer moves away from them.

T-group *n.* training group: a type of experiential group, usually of a dozen or so people, concerned with fostering attitude change and the development of "basic skills," such as effective leadership and communication. Although the term is sometimes used synonymously with ENCOUNTER GROUP, the emphasis in a T-group is less on personal growth and more on SENSITIVITY TRAINING and practical interpersonal skills (e.g., as stressed in management training).

thalamus *n.* (*pl.* **thalami**) a mass of gray matter, forming part of the DIENCEPHALON of the brain, whose two lobes form the walls of the THIRD VENTRICLE. It consists of a collection of sensory,

motor, autonomic, and associational nuclei, serving as a relay for nerve impulses traveling between the spinal cord and brainstem and the cerebral cortex. —**thalamic** *adj.*

thanatology *n.* the study of death and death-related behaviors, thoughts, feelings, and phenomena. Death was mostly the province of theology until the 1960s, when existential thinkers and a broad spectrum of care providers, educators, and social and behavioral scientists became interested in death-related issues. —**thanatologist** *n.*

Thanatos *n.* the personification of death and the brother of Hypnos (sleep) in Greek mythology, whose name was chosen by Austrian neurologist Sigmund Freud (1856–1939) to designate a theoretical set of strivings oriented toward the reduction of tension and life activity (see DEATH INSTINCT). In Freud's dual instinct theory, Thanatos is seen as involved in a dialectic process with EROS (love), the striving toward sexuality, continued development, and heightened experience (see LIFE INSTINCT).

that's-not-all technique a two-step procedure for enhancing compliance that consists of (a) presenting an initial large request and then, before the person can respond, (b) immediately making the request more attractive by reducing it to a more modest target request or by offering some additional benefit. Compliance with the target request is greater following the initial request than would have been the case if the target request had been presented on its own. See also DOOR-IN-THE-FACE TECHNIQUE; FOOT-IN-THE-DOOR TECHNIQUE; LOW-BALL TECHNIQUE.

thematic analysis a strategy for identifying, analyzing, and reporting identifiable patterns or themes within data. There are multiple phases to this process: The researcher (a) generates initial codes or categories and then collates these into potential themes; (b) reviews the chosen themes and checks that these work in relation to the coded extracts and the entire data set; (c) defines and names the themes; and (d) produces the report.

Thematic Apperception Test

(**TAT**) a projective test in which participants are held to reveal their attitudes, feelings, conflicts, and personality characteristics in the oral or written stories they make up about a series of ambiguous black-and-white pictures. Systematic coding schemes have been developed to assess different aspects of personality functioning derived from TAT stories, including motivation for achievement, power, affiliation, and intimacy; gender identity; DEFENSE MECHANISMS; and mental processes influencing interpersonal relations. The TAT is one of the most frequently used and researched tests in psychology, particularly in clinical settings for diagnosing disorders, describing personality, and assessing strengths and weaknesses in personality functioning.

theoretical construct an explanatory concept that is not itself directly observable but that can be inferred from observed or measured data. For example, a personality dimension, such as neuroticism, might be described as a theoretical construct measurable by means of a questionnaire.

theoretical distribution a DISTRIBUTION that is derived from certain principles or assumptions by logical and mathematical reasoning, as opposed to one derived from real-world data obtained by empirical research. Examples include the NORMAL DISTRIBUTION and the BINOMIAL DISTRIBUTION. Also called **reference distribution**.

theoretical sampling a strategy, often adopted in QUALITATIVE RESEARCH, in which the investigator samples new research sites, cases, incidents, time periods, or data sources to compare with those that have already been studied. In this way, he or she seeks to build a theory from the emerging data while

continuing to select new samples to examine and elaborate on the theory.

theoretical statistics the study of statistics from a mathematical and theoretical perspective, involving descriptive methods, inferences, and model building. For example, a researcher could use theoretical statistics to describe a set of achievement data and create models assessing possible predictors of achievement. Compare APPLIED STATISTICS.

theory *n.* **1.** a principle or body of interrelated principles that purports to explain or predict a number of interrelated phenomena. See CONSTRUCT; MODEL. **2.** in the philosophy of science, a set of logically related explanatory hypotheses that are consistent with a body of empirical facts and that may suggest more empirical relationships. —**theoretical** *adj.*

theory of mind the understanding that others have intentions, desires, beliefs, perceptions, and emotions different from one's own and that such intentions, desires, and so forth affect people's actions and behaviors. Children show the rudiments of theory of mind as toddlers, have a limited understanding of the relation between belief and action by age 3, and can begin to infer false beliefs in others by around age 4.

theory of planned behavior a model that resembles the THEORY OF REASONED ACTION but adds the construct of perceived behavioral control to attitude toward behavior and perceived expectations as the antecedents influencing both the intention to perform a behavior and the performance of the behavior itself.

theory of reasoned action the theory that attitudes toward a behavior and the perceived expectations regarding a behavior determine a person's intention to perform that behavior. Intentions are in turn assumed to cause the actual behavior.

theory theory a model proposing that children naturally construct theories to explain what they experience and that cognitive development occurs as they generate, test, and change theories about the physical and social world through ongoing observation, learning, and adaptation.

therapeutic *adj.* **1.** pertaining to **therapeutics**, the branch of medical science concerned with the treatment of diseases and disorders and the discovery and application of remedial agents or methods. **2.** having beneficial or curative effects.

therapeutic alliance a cooperative working relationship between client and therapist, considered by many to be an essential aspect of successful therapy. Derived from the concept of the psychoanalytic working alliance, the therapeutic alliance comprises bonds, goals, and tasks. Bonds are constituted by the core conditions of therapy, the client's attitude toward the therapist, and the therapist's style of relating to the client; goals are the mutually negotiated, understood, agreed upon, and regularly reviewed aims of the therapy; and tasks are the activities carried out by both client and therapist.

therapeutic community a setting for individuals requiring therapy for a range of psychosocial problems and disorders that is based on an interpersonal, socially interactive approach to treatment, both among residents and among residents and staff (i.e., community as method or therapy). The term covers a variety of short- and long-term residential programs as well as day treatment and ambulatory programs. See MILIEU THERAPY.

therapeutic factors factors in GROUP THERAPY that bring about therapeutic change. These include altruism, catharsis, cohesion, family reenactment, feedback, hope, identification, interpersonal learning, reality testing, role flexibility, universality, and vicarious learning. Therapeutic factors are often confused with COMMON FACTORS because both delineate effective change factors across theoretical models and techniques of therapy; however, common factors refer to individual psychotherapy, whereas therapeutic factors refer to group psychotherapy.

therapist *n.* an individual who has been trained in and practices one or more types of therapy to treat mental or physical disorders or diseases. In the context of mental health, the term is often used synonymously with *psychotherapist* (see PSYCHOTHERAPY).

therapy *n.* **1.** remediation of physical, mental, or behavioral disorders or diseases. **2.** see PSYCHOTHERAPY.

therapy outcome research research that investigates the end results of therapy or other interventions to which patients are exposed. The aim is to identify shortfalls in practice and to develop strategies to prevent or mitigate problems and improve care. See also TREATMENT OUTCOME RESEARCH.

thermoreceptor *n.* **1.** a receptor or sense organ that is activated by cold or warm stimuli. **2.** a part of the central nervous system that monitors and maintains the temperature of the body core and its vital organs. There is evidence for separate thermoregulatory regions in the spinal cord, brainstem, and hypothalamus.

thesis *n.* (*pl.* **theses**) in philosophy, the first stage of a dialectical process: a proposition that is opposed by an ANTITHESIS, thereby generating a new proposition referred to as a SYNTHESIS. The synthesis serves as the thesis for the next phase of the ongoing process.

theta wave in electroencephalography, a type of regular BRAIN WAVE with a frequency of 4 Hz to 7 Hz. Theta waves occur during REM SLEEP in nonhuman animals, Stage 2 NREM SLEEP in humans, and the drowsy state prior to sleep onset in newborn infants, adolescents, and adults. Such waves are also recorded in trances, hypnosis, and day-dreams. Also called **theta rhythm**.

thinking *n.* cognitive behavior in which ideas, images, MENTAL REPRESENTATIONS, or other hypothetical elements of thought are experienced or manipulated. In this sense, thinking includes imagining, remembering, problem solving, daydreaming, FREE ASSOCIATION, concept formation, and many other processes. Thinking may be said to have two defining characteristics: (a) It is not directly observable but must be inferred from actions or self-reports; and (b) it involves operations on mental symbols.

third-person effect a tendency for a person to expect that others will be more strongly influenced by (i.e., will respond to and take action as a result of) a persuasive communication in the mass media than he or she would be. The third-person effect generally is explained in terms of a desire for self-enhancement: People are motivated to reinforce their positive self-images and thus are unrealistically optimistic in comparing themselves to others. Also called **third-person perception**.

third-variable problem the fact that an observed correlation between two variables may be due to the common correlation between each of the variables and a third variable rather than any underlying relationship (in a causal sense) of the two variables with each other. For example, as the sales of air conditioners increase, the number of drownings also increases: The unintended third variable in this case would be the increase in heat.

third ventricle a cavity of the brain, filled with CEREBROSPINAL FLUID, that forms a cleft between the two lobes of the THALAMUS beneath the cerebral hemispheres. It communicates with the LATERAL VENTRICLES and caudally with the fourth ventricle through the CEREBRAL AQUEDUCT.

Thorazine *n.* a trade name for CHLORPROMAZINE.

thought disorder a cognitive disturbance that affects communication, language, or thought content, with symptoms that typically include NEOLOGISMS, WORD SALAD, and DELUSIONS. A thought disorder is considered by some to be the most important mark of schizophrenia, but it is also associated with mood disorders, dementia, mania, and neurological diseases. See also FORMAL THOUGHT DISORDER.

thought stopping the skill of using a physical or cognitive cue to stop negative thoughts and redirect them to a neutral or positive orientation. This skill is taught in some behavior therapies, as when the therapist shouts "Stop!" to interrupt a trend toward undesirable thoughts and trains clients to apply this technique to themselves.

thought suppression the attempt to control the content of one's mental processes and specifically to rid oneself of undesired thoughts or images. Ironically, engaging in thought suppression often serves only to make the unwanted thoughts more intrusive.

threat *n.* **1.** an indication of unpleasant consequences that is used as a means of coercion for failure to comply with a given request or demand. **2.** any event, information, or feedback that is perceived as conveying negative information about the self. —**threaten** *vb.* —**threatening** *adj.*

threat display any of various ritualized communication signals used by nonhuman animals to indicate that attack or aggression might follow. Examples are fluffed-out fur or feathers, certain facial expressions or body postures, and low-frequency vocalizations (e.g., growls). The use of ritualized threat displays can minimize direct physical aggression to the benefit of both individuals.

three-component theory see TRICHROMATIC THEORY.

three-stage model see INFORMATION-PROCESSING MODEL.

three-stratum model of intelligence a psychometric model of intelligence based on a factorial reanalysis of several hundred data sets available in the literature. The three strata correspond to (a) minor group factors at the first (lowest) level; (b) major group factors at the second level (fluid intelligence, crystallized intelligence, general memory and learning, broad perception, and processing speed); and (c) the general factor at the third (highest) level.

three-way analysis of variance an ANALYSIS OF VARIANCE that isolates the MAIN EFFECTS of three independent variables, a, b, and c, on a dependent variable and their INTERACTION EFFECTS—one three-way interaction, $a \times b \times c$, and three two-way interactions, $a \times b$, $a \times c$, and $b \times c$.

three-way design an experimental design in which three independent variables are examined simultaneously to observe their separate MAIN EFFECTS and their joint INTERACTION EFFECTS on a dependent variable of interest. Data from such designs often are evaluated with a THREE-WAY ANALYSIS OF VARIANCE.

threshold n. 1. in psychophysics, the magnitude of a stimulus that will lead to its detection 50% of the time. 2. the minimum intensity of a stimulus that is necessary to evoke a response. For example, an excitatory threshold is the minimum stimulus intensity that triggers an ACTION POTENTIAL in a neuron. Also called **limen**. See also ABSOLUTE THRESHOLD; DIFFERENCE THRESHOLD.

threshold effect an effect in a dependent variable that does not occur until a certain level, or threshold, is reached in an independent variable. For example, a drug may have no effect at all until a certain dosage level (the threshold value) is reached.

thrombosis n. the presence or formation of a blood clot (**thrombus**) in a blood vessel, including vessels in the heart. Thrombosis is likely to develop where blood flow is impeded by disease, injury, or a foreign substance. —**thrombotic** *adj*.

thyroid gland an endocrine gland forming a shieldlike structure on the front and sides of the throat, just below the thyroid cartilage. It produces the iodine-containing hormones thyroxine and triiodothyronine, which regulate basal metabolic processes, as well as the hormone calcitonin, which controls levels of calcium and phosphate in the blood.

tic n. a sudden, involuntary vocalization or contraction of a small group of muscles that is recurrent and nonrhythmic. Tics may be simple (e.g., eye blinking, throat clearing, grunting, yelping) or complex (e.g., hand gestures, ECHOLALIA, COPROLALIA). They may be psychogenic in origin, or they may occur as an adverse effect of a medication or other substance or result from a head injury, neurological disorder, or general medical condition.

timbre n. the perceptual attribute relating to the quality of a sound. Two perceptually different sounds with the same pitch and loudness differ in their timbre. —**timbral** *adj*.

time and motion study an analysis of industrial operations or other complex tasks into their component steps, observing the time required for each. Such studies may serve a number of different purposes, enabling an employer to set performance targets, increase productivity, rationalize pay rates and pricing policy, reduce employee fatigue, and prevent accidents.

time-lag design a type of QUASI-EXPERIMENTAL DESIGN in which participants of the same age are compared at different time periods. It is typically used in developmental, educational, and social psychological contexts to study whether there are differences in a given characteristic for samples of equal age but drawn from different cohorts measured at different times. For example, a time-lag study of intelligence might compare a group of people who were 20 years old in 2005 with groups who were 20 years old in 2006, 2007, and 2008.

time–location sampling a method of finding research participants in which members of a hard-to-reach target population (e.g., homeless people, migrant workers) are recruited from specific locations at which they may be found during specific time periods. Also called **venue sampling**.

time out (TO) a technique, originating from BEHAVIOR THERAPY, in which undesirable behavior is weakened and its occurrence decreased, typically by moving the individual away from the area that is reinforcing the behavior. The technique is used by teachers in schools and by parents to decrease undesirable behavior in a child.

time sampling in DIRECT OBSERVATION, a data collection strategy that involves noting and recording the occurrence of a target behavior whenever it is seen during a stated time interval. The process may involve fixed time periods (e.g., every 5 minutes) or random time intervals. For example, a researcher may observe a group of children for 10 seconds every 5 minutes for a specific 30-minute period each day, noting the occurrence or nonoccurrence of particular behaviors (overt actions). Observations taken during these periods are known as **time samples**.

time series a set of measures on a single attribute, variable, or construct obtained repeatedly over time.

time-series analysis a branch of statistics that involves the analysis of changes in a single variable recorded repeatedly over time. The data may have an internal structure that provides input allowing for the prediction of future values of the variable. Compare CROSS-SECTIONAL ANALYSIS.

time-series design an experimental design that involves the observation of

units (e.g., people, countries) over a defined time period. Data collected from such designs may be evaluated with TIME-SERIES ANALYSIS.

timing-of-events model a paradigm that describes adult psychosocial development as influenced by the expected or unexpected occurrence and timing of particular life events.

tinnitus *n.* noises in one or both ears, including ringing, buzzing, or clicking, due to acute ear problems, disturbances in the receptor mechanism, side effects of drugs (especially tricyclic antidepressants), or epileptic aura.

tip-of-the-tongue phenomenon (TOT phenomenon) the experience of attempting to retrieve from memory a specific name or word but not being able to do so. Usually, the name or word is eventually retrieved, but while on the TOT, it seems to hover tantalizingly on the rim of consciousness.

titration *n.* a technique used in determining the optimum dose of a drug needed to produce a desired effect in a particular individual. The dosage may be either gradually increased until a noticeable improvement is observed in the patient or adjusted downward from a level that is obviously excessive because of adverse effects or toxicity. See TAPERING.

T maze a maze shaped like the letter T, consisting of a start box and a stem that leads to a choice between left and right arms, one being incorrect and the other leading to the goal box. More complicated mazes can be formed by joining several T mazes in sequence. A variant of this apparatus is the Y MAZE; both are used in experiments on animal cognition.

token economy in BEHAVIOR THERAPY, a program, sometimes conducted in an institutional setting (e.g., a hospital or classroom), in which desired behavior is reinforced by offering tokens that can be exchanged for special foods, television time, passes, or other rewards.

tokenism *n*. the making of a perfunctory or symbolic gesture that suggests commitment to a practice or standard. For example, an all-White company may hire a token Black employee to give the appearance of racial diversity and inclusion in the workplace.

tolerance *n*. **1.** a condition, resulting from persistent use of a drug, characterized by a markedly diminished effect with regular use of the same dose of the drug or by a need to increase the dose markedly over time to achieve the same desired effect. Development of drug tolerance involves several mechanisms, including pharmacological ones (i.e., metabolic tolerance) and a behavioral one (i.e., a behavioral conditioning process). Also called **drug tolerance**. See SUBSTANCE DEPENDENCE. **2.** acceptance of others whose actions, beliefs, physical capabilities, religion, customs, ethnicity, nationality, and so on differ from one's own. —**tolerant** *adj*.

tomography *n*. a technique for revealing the detailed structure of a tissue or organ through a particular plane that involves the compilation of a series of images taken from multiple perspectives. Examples include COMPUTED TOMOGRAPHY and POSITRON EMISSION TOMOGRAPHY. —**tomographic** *adj*.

tone *n*. in linguistics, a phonetic variable along the dimension of pitch. In a **tonal language**, such as Mandarin or Thai, differences in tone are sufficient to mark a distinction between words that are otherwise pronounced identically. In English, tone is an important SUPRASEGMENTAL feature of speech, with different patterns of intonation serving to distinguish different types of utterance, such as statements and questions. —**tonal** *adj*.

tonic *adj*. of or relating to muscle tone, especially a state of continuous muscle tension or contraction, which may be normal or abnormal. For example, a

tonic phase of facial muscles prevents the lower jaw from falling open, a normal function. Abnormally, in the tonic phase of a TONIC–CLONIC SEIZURE, the muscles controlling respiration may undergo spasm, resulting in a temporary suspension of breathing.

tonic–clonic seizure a seizure characterized by both TONIC and CLONIC motor movements. In the tonic phase, the muscles go into spasm and the individual falls to the ground unconscious; breathing may be suspended. This is followed by the clonic phase, marked by rapidly alternating contraction and relaxation of the muscles, resulting in jaw movements (the tongue may be bitten) and urinary incontinence. Formerly called **grand mal seizure**.

tonotopic organization the fundamental principle that different frequencies stimulate different places within structures of the mammalian auditory system. This organization begins in the COCHLEA, where different frequencies tend to cause maximal vibration at different places along the BASILAR MEMBRANE and thus stimulate different HAIR CELLS. The hair cells are discretely innervated, so different auditory nerve fibers respond to a relatively limited range of frequencies. This frequency-to-place mapping is preserved in the AUDITORY CORTEX.

top-down processing INFORMATION PROCESSING in which an overall hypothesis about or general conceptualization of a stimulus is applied to and influences the analysis of incoming stimulus data. For example, in reading, knowledge about letter and word frequencies, syntax, and other regularities in language guides recognition of incoming information. Typically, perceptual or cognitive mechanisms use top-down processing when information is familiar and not especially complex. Compare BOTTOM-UP PROCESSING. See also DEEP PROCESSING.

total degrees of freedom the total number of observations in an analysis

473

minus one. For example, in an experiment in which there are 4 conditions, with 20 participants randomly assigned to each condition, there are 80 independent observations: The total degrees of freedom is 79 (80 − 1) observations. Relatedly, each individual condition has its own DEGREES OF FREEDOM as well: 20 − 1 = 19.

total effect in the study of causal effects, the total extent to which the dependent (or outcome) variable is changed by the independent (or predictor) variable, including any indirect effect through a MEDIATOR. In a simple example, if the independent variable, x, is presumed to cause the outcome variable, y, the COEFFICIENT of this direct effect, A, is the total effect. If there is an intervening variable, linked by two coefficients, B and C, this indirect effect is BC, and the total effect is $A + BC$.

totem *n.* a revered animal, plant, natural force, or inanimate object that is conceived as the ancestor, symbol, protector, or tutelary spirit of a people, clan, or community. It is usually made the focus of certain ritual activities and TABOOS, typically against killing or eating it. **—totemic** *adj.* **—totemism** *n.*

TOTE model see FEEDBACK LOOP.

tough-mindedness *n.* **1.** a personality trait reflecting the extent to which people demonstrate low levels of compassion and high levels of aggression in social interactions. **2.** a personality trait characterized by empiricism, materialism, skepticism, and fatalism. Compare TENDER-MINDEDNESS. **—tough-minded** *adj.*

Tourette's disorder a disorder characterized by many motor tics and one or more vocal tics, such as grunts, yelps, barks, sniffs, or (rarely) COPROLALIA. The tics occur many times a day for more than a year, and the disorder typically appears during childhood or early adolescence. [first described in 1885 by Georges Gilles de la **Tourette** (1857–1904), French physician]

toxicity *n.* the capacity of a substance to produce poisonous effects in an organism. The toxicity of a substance generally is related to the size of the dose per body weight of the individual, expressed in terms of milligrams of chemical per kilogram of body weight.

trace conditioning a procedure in CLASSICAL CONDITIONING in which a conditioned stimulus and an unconditioned stimulus are separated by a constant interval (called the **trace interval**), with the conditioned stimulus presented first. Compare TEMPORAL CONDITIONING.

trace-decay theory see DECAY THEORY.

tracking *n.* **1.** the process of smoothly following a moving object with the eyes or using eye movements to continuously follow a path. **2.** a type of task in which the goal is to make movements that follow a constantly moving target. **—track** *vb.*

tract *n.* **1.** a bundle or group of nerve fibers within the central nervous system. The name of a tract typically indicates its site of origin followed by its site of termination; for example, the reticulospinal tract runs from the reticular formation of the brainstem to the spinal cord. Compare NERVE. **2.** a series of organs that as a whole accomplishes a specific function (e.g., the digestive tract).

trafficking *n.* illegal transport of and trade in people or commodities. Human trafficking involves the transport of men, women, or children from one location to another, usually by coercion or by enticement through fraudulent means (e.g., with promises of legitimate work), to be forcibly exploited for the profit of others. Trafficking also refers to the smuggling of cocaine, heroin, and other illegal drugs from their point of manufacture in one location to their distribution and sale in another (i.e., drug trafficking).

training analysis PSYCHOANALYSIS

of a trainee analyst. Its purpose is not only to provide training in the concepts and techniques of psychoanalysis but also to increase the trainee's insight into personal sensitivities or other emotional reactions that might interfere with the process of analyzing patients in the form of a COUNTER-TRANSFERENCE.

trait *n.* **1.** an enduring personality characteristic that describes or determines an individual's behavior across a range of situations. **2.** in genetics, an attribute resulting from a hereditary predisposition (e.g., hair color, facial features).

trait theory approaches that explain personality in terms of internal characteristics that are presumed to determine behavior. The FIVE-FACTOR PERSONALITY MODEL is an example.

trait validity the degree to which responses to a test's items provide an accurate measurement of a personality characteristic (trait).

trance *n.* **1.** an ALTERED STATE OF CONSCIOUSNESS characterized by decreased awareness of and responsiveness to stimuli and an apparent loss of voluntary power. **2.** a state brought about by HYPNOSIS or AUTOSUGGESTION and characterized by susceptibility to suggestion. For example, hypnotized persons might accept suggestions that they cannot open their eyes or they lack sensation in a limb, or they may experience POST-HYPNOTIC AMNESIA and POSTHYPNOTIC SUGGESTION.

tranquilizer *n.* a drug that is used to reduce physiological and subjective symptoms of anxiety. In the past, distinctions were made between so-called major tranquilizers (ANTIPSYCHOTICS) and minor tranquilizers (ANXIOLYTICS).

transaction *n.* any interaction between the individual and the social or physical environment, especially during encounters between two or more people.

transactional analysis (TA) a the-

ory of personality and a form of dynamic group or individual psychotherapy focusing on people's characteristic interactions in social situations. Specifically, the approach involves (a) a study of three primary ego states (parent, child, adult) to determine which one is dominant in the transaction in question; (b) identification of the tricks and expedients habitually used in the client's transactions; and (c) analysis of the client's life to uncover the sources of his or her emotional problems.

transactionalism *n.* **1.** an approach to ENVIRONMENTAL PSYCHOLOGY that emphasizes the continuing process of interaction between a person and his or her physical and social environment. This process is characterized as an ongoing series of "transactions" in which the person's behaviors are modified by environmental factors and vice versa. **2.** an approach to perception emphasizing that, rather than being mere passive observers, people draw on past interactions with relevant stimuli in their environment to form perceptions of present situations and novel stimuli. —**transactionalist** *adj., n.*

transactional leadership a style of leadership in which the emphasis is on ensuring that followers accomplish tasks. Transactional leaders influence others through exchange relationships in which benefits are promised in return for compliance. Compare TRANSFORMATIONAL LEADERSHIP.

transactive memory system a system in which information to be remembered is distributed among various members of a group, who can then each be relied on to provide that information when it is needed.

transcendental meditation (TM) a technique for achieving an altered state of consciousness. It consists of six steps that culminate in sitting with one's eyes closed, while repeating a MANTRA, for two 20-minute periods a day. Repetition of the mantra serves to block distracting thoughts and to induce a state of relaxation in which images and ideas can emerge from deeper levels of the mind. The result is said to be a greater sense of well-being and the achievement of a state of ultimate self-awareness.

transcranial magnetic stimulation (**TMS**) localized electrical stimulation of the brain caused by changes in the magnetic field in coils of wire placed around the head. TMS is primarily used to assess the effects of electrical stimulation of the motor cortex but also is being investigated as a possible therapy for obsessive-compulsive disorder, Tourette's disorder, some movement disorders, and other conditions. **Repetitive transcranial magnetic stimulation** (**rTMS**) consists of a series of TMS pulses.

transcription *n.* the process whereby the genetic information contained in DNA is transferred to a molecule of MESSENGER RNA (mRNA), which subsequently directs protein synthesis. The base sequence of the mRNA is complementary to that of the coding DNA strand. See GENETIC CODE.

transcultural psychotherapy any form of PSYCHODYNAMIC PSYCHOTHERAPY that emphasizes cultural sensitivity and awareness, including culturally defined concepts of emotion, drives, and behavior. In the psychiatric community, the term is used somewhat more often in a sense similar to MULTICULTURAL THERAPY in clinical psychology.

transducer *n.* a device or system that converts energy from one form to another. Sensory RECEPTOR cells are an example.

transduction *n.* the process by which one form of energy is converted into another. The term denotes **sensory transduction** in particular, the transformation of the energy of a stimulus into a change in the electric potential across the membrane of a RECEPTOR cell.

transfer-appropriate processing a theory stating that memory performance is better when the cognitive processes engaged during retrieval match the cognitive processes that were engaged when the material was encoded. For example, test performance should be relatively good if both study and test conditions emphasize either semantic processing on the one hand or perceptual processing on the other, but test performance will not be as good if study conditions emphasize one (e.g., semantic) and test conditions emphasize another (e.g., perceptual).

transference *n.* in psychoanalysis, a patient's DISPLACEMENT or PROJECTION onto the analyst of those unconscious feelings and wishes originally directed toward important individuals, such as parents, in the patient's childhood. It is posited that this process brings repressed material to the surface where it can be reexperienced, studied, and worked through to discover the sources of a patient's current neurotic difficulties and to alleviate their harmful effects. Although the theoretical aspects of the term are specific to psychoanalysis, transference has a recognized role in various other types of therapeutic encounter, including counseling and short-term dynamic psychotherapy. The term's broader meaning—an unconscious repetition of earlier behaviors and their projection onto new subjects—is acknowledged as applying to all human interactions. See also COUNTERTRANSFERENCE.

transfer of training the influence of prior learning on new learning, either to enhance it (see POSITIVE TRANSFER) or to hamper it (see NEGATIVE TRANSFER). The general principles of mathematics, for example, transfer to computer programming, but a knowledge of Spanish may have both positive and negative effects in learning Italian.

transformation *n.* **1.** the conversion of data to a different form through a rule-based and usually mathematical process. In statistics, a RAW SCORE is often transformed into a STANDARDIZED SCORE for purposes of comparison. **2.** in psychoanalytic theory, the process by which unconscious wishes or impulses are disguised in order to gain admittance to consciousness. **—transform** *vb.* **—transformational** *adj.*

transformational generative grammar a type of GENERATIVE GRAMMAR based on the idea that sentences have an underlying DEEP STRUCTURE as well as the SURFACE STRUCTURE observable in speech or writing and that the former gives rise to the latter through the operation of a small number of **transformational rules** involving the movement, addition, and deletion of constituents. This approach was pioneered by U.S. linguist Noam Chomsky (1928–) as a means of supplementing the more limited analysis made possible by PHRASE-STRUCTURE GRAMMAR. Also called **transformational grammar**.

transformational leadership a charismatic, inspiring style of leading others that usually involves heightening followers' motivation, confidence, and satisfaction; uniting them in the pursuit of shared, challenging goals; and changing their beliefs, values, and needs. Compare TRANSACTIONAL LEADERSHIP.

transgender *adj.* having or relating to a GENDER IDENTITY that differs from the culturally determined gender roles for one's birth sex (i.e., the biological sex one was born with) or for one's sex as surgically assigned at birth. Transgender identities include TRANSSEXUALISM, some forms of TRANSVESTISM, and INTERSEX. Also called **transgendered**. Compare CISGENDER. **—transgenderism** *n.*

transience *n.* a feeling of impermanence combined with an anticipation of loss. In classical psychoanalytic theory, the idea that everything is transient may interfere with enjoyment and

preclude the establishment of deep or lasting relationships. **—transient** *adj.*

transient ischemic attack (TIA) an episode during which an area of the brain is suddenly deprived of oxygen because its blood supply is temporarily interrupted, for example, by thrombosis, embolism, or vascular spasm. Symptoms are the same as those of STROKE but disappear completely, typically within 24 hours.

transitivity *n.* the quality of a relationship among elements such that the relationship transfers across those elements. For example, a transitive relationship would be the following: Given that $a > b$, and $b > c$, it must be the case that $a > c$. **—transitive** *adj.*

translation and back-translation a method of ensuring that the translation of an assessment instrument into another language is adequate, used primarily in cross-cultural research. A bilingual person translates items from the source language to the target language, and a different bilingual person then independently translates the items back into the source language. The researcher can compare the original with the back-translated version to see if anything important was changed in the translation.

transorbital lobotomy see LOBOTOMY.

transpersonal psychology an area of HUMANISTIC PSYCHOLOGY that focuses on the exploration of the nature, varieties, causes, and effects of "higher" states of consciousness and experiences that transcend personal identity and individual, immediate desires. See also PEAK EXPERIENCE.

transporter *n.* a protein complex that spans a cell membrane and conveys ions, neurotransmitters, or other substances between the exterior and interior of the cell. For example, at SYNAPSES between neurons, transporters in the presynaptic membrane recognize and bind to neurotransmitter molecules and return them to the presynaptic neuron for reuse (see REUPTAKE).

transsexualism *n.* a condition consisting of a persistent sense of discomfort and inappropriateness relating to one's anatomical sex, with a persistent wish to be rid of one's genitals and to live as a member of the other sex. Those with this condition often seek to change their sex through surgical and hormonal means. **—transsexual** *adj., n.*

transtheoretical model (TTM) a five-stage theory to explain the process by which people change their health behavior (e.g., eating habits, smoking). It suggests that change takes time, that different interventions are effective at different stages, and that there are multiple outcomes (e.g., in belief structure, self-efficacy) occurring across the stages. See STAGES OF CHANGE.

transvestic fetishism a PARA-PHILIA characterized by the wearing of female clothes by a heterosexual male for the purpose of achieving sexual excitement and arousal. It is distinct from TRANSVESTISM, the nonsexualized cross-dressing by men or women of any sexual preference.

transvestism *n.* the habit, practiced by men or women, of wearing the clothes of the opposite sex but without the sexual arousal that cross-dressing serves in the predominately male paraphilia, TRANSVESTIC FETISHISM. Also called **transvestitism.** **—transvestic** *adj.* **—transvestite** *n.*

trauma *n.* **1.** any disturbing experience that results in significant fear, helplessness, DISSOCIATION, confusion, or other disruptive feelings intense enough to have a long-lasting negative effect on a person's attitudes, behavior, and other aspects of functioning. Traumatic events include those caused by human behavior (e.g., rape, war, industrial accidents) as well as by nature (e.g., earthquakes) and often challenge an individual's view of the world as a just, safe, and predictable place. **2.** any serious physical injury, such as a

widespread burn or a blow to the head. **—traumatic** *adj.*

traumagenic *adj.* describing or relating to the dynamics by which a traumatic event (e.g., childhood sexual abuse) may have long-term negative consequences, including the development of a mental disorder.

traumatic brain injury (TBI) damage to brain tissue caused by external mechanical forces, as evidenced by objective neurological findings, posttraumatic amnesia, skull fracture, or loss of consciousness.

treatment *n.* **1.** the administration of appropriate measures (e.g., drugs, surgery, psychotherapy) that are designed to relieve a pathological condition. **2.** the intervention to which some participants in an experimental design (the EXPERIMENTAL GROUP or treatment group) are exposed, in contrast to a CONTROL GROUP, who do not receive the intervention. See TREATMENT LEVEL.

treatment effect the magnitude of the effect that a treatment (i.e., the INDEPENDENT VARIABLE) has on the response variable (i.e., the DEPENDENT VARIABLE) in a study. It is usually measured as the difference in standardized units between the level of response under a control condition and the level of response under the treatment condition. See EFFECT SIZE.

treatment level the specific condition to which a group or participant is exposed in a study or experiment. For example, in a design employing four groups, each of which is exposed to a different dosage of a particular drug, each dosage amount represents a level of the treatment factor.

treatment outcome research research designed to evaluate the efficacy of interventions and to investigate the mechanism by which effective interventions produce change. See also THERAPY OUTCOME RESEARCH.

treatment resistance 1. failure of a disease or disorder to respond positively or significantly to a particular treatment, as in treatment-resistant depression. **2.** reluctance on the part of an individual to accept psychological or medical treatment or to comply with the therapist's or physician's instructions or prescribed regimens. See also RIGHT TO REFUSE TREATMENT.

treatment trial a research study designed to evaluate the effectiveness of an experimental intervention, its possible adverse effects, and other information that would contribute to the decision to use the intervention in the future. During the trial, the experimental intervention is compared with an existing one, which acts as a control. When the intervention being evaluated is a new drug, the term CLINICAL TRIAL is used instead.

tremor *n.* any involuntary trembling of the body or a part of the body. A coarse tremor involves a large muscle group in slow movements, whereas a fine tremor is caused by a small bundle of muscle fibers that move rapidly. Some tremors occur only during voluntary movements (action tremor); others occur in the absence of voluntary movement (resting tremor).

trend analysis any of several techniques designed to uncover systematic patterns (trends) in a set of variables, such as linear growth over time. Such analysis is often used to predict future events.

trephination *n.* a surgical procedure in which a disk of bone is removed from the skull with a circular instrument (a **trephine**) having a sawlike edge. On the basis of evidence found in skulls of Neolithic humans, trephining is believed to be one of the oldest types of surgery. Among the numerous conjectural reasons given for the practice is that it was a treatment for headaches, infections, skull fractures, convulsions, mental disorders, or supposed demonic possession. Also called **trepanation**. —**trephine** *vb.*

trial *n.* **1.** in testing, conditioning, or

other experimentation, a single performance of a given task (e.g., one run through a maze) or a single presentation of a stimulus (e.g., one viewing of an ordered list of three-letter words). **2.** see CLINICAL TRIAL; TREATMENT TRIAL.

trial-and-error learning a type of learning in which the organism successively tries various responses in a situation, seemingly at random, until one is successful in achieving the goal. Across multiple trials, the successful response is strengthened and appears earlier and earlier. Maze learning, with its eventual elimination of blind-alley entrances, is an example of trial-and-error learning.

triangular theory of love the proposition that the various kinds of love can be characterized in terms of the degree to which they possess three basic components—intimacy, passion, and commitment—that together can be viewed as forming the vertices of a triangle. See COMPANIONATE LOVE; PASSIONATE LOVE; ROMANTIC LOVE.

triangulation *n.* **1.** the process of confirming a hypothesis by collecting evidence from multiple sources. For example, in data triangulation various sampling methods are used, whereas methodological triangulation involves using a variety of interviews, observations, questionnaires, and other data-collection methods. The data from each source support the hypothesis from a somewhat different perspective and therefore increase confidence in its validity. **2.** in FAMILY THERAPY, a situation in which two members of a family in conflict each attempt to draw another member to their side. Triangulation can occur, for example, when two parents are in conflict and their child is caught in the middle. —**triangulate** *vb.*

triarchic theory of intelligence a theory of intelligence in which three key abilities—analytical, creative, and practical—are viewed as largely (although not entirely) distinct. According to the theory, intelligence comprises a number of information-processing components, which are applied to experience (especially novel experiences) in order to adapt to, shape, and select environments.

trichromatic theory one of several concepts of the physiological basis of color vision, as derived from experiments on color mixture in which all hues were able to be matched by a mixture of three primary colors—blue, green, and red. The YOUNG–HELMHOLTZ THEORY OF COLOR VISION is the best known trichromatic theory. Also called **three-component theory**. See also OPPONENT PROCESS THEORY OF COLOR VISION.

trichromatism *n.* normal color vision: the capacity to distinguish the three primary color systems of light–dark, red–green, and blue–yellow, attributable to the presence of all three types of PHOTOPIGMENT. Also called **trichromatopsia**. See also ACHROMATISM; DICHROMATISM; MONOCHROMATISM.

tricyclic antidepressant (TCA) any of a group of drugs, developed in the 1950s, that were the original first-line medications for treatment of depression. They are presumed to act by blocking the reuptake of monoamine neurotransmitters (serotonin, dopamine, and norepinephrine) into the presynaptic neuron, thereby increasing the amount of neurotransmitter available for binding to postsynaptic receptors. The tricyclics represented the mainstay of antidepressant treatment from the introduction of imipramine in 1957 until fluoxetine (Prozac)—the first SSRI—was introduced in 1987. Although they are effective as antidepressants, their adverse side effects and—more significantly—their lethality in overdose have led to a profound decline in their use. They remain, however, the standard against which other antidepressants are compared; no other class of antidepressants has demonstrated more clinical efficacy.

trigeminal nerve the fifth and larg-

est CRANIAL NERVE, which carries both sensory and motor fibers. The motor fibers are primarily involved with the muscles used in chewing, tongue movements, and swallowing. The sensory fibers innervate the same areas, including the teeth and most of the tongue in addition to the jaws.

trigram *n.* **1.** any three-letter nonsense syllable used in studies of learning and memory. **2.** in studies of language processing, a sequence of three words, syllables, or other items in which the identity of the first two items is used as a basis for predicting the third.

trimming *n.* the exclusion of a fixed percentage of cases at each end of a distribution before calculating a statistic on the set of data. This is done to eliminate the influence of extreme scores on the estimate.

triple blind see BLIND.

trochlear nerve the fourth CRANIAL NERVE, which contains motor fibers supplying the superior oblique muscle of the eyeball.

truncated distribution a set of scores lacking values beyond a specific maximum point, below a specific minimum point, or both.

trust *n.* the confidence that a person or group of people has in the reliability of another person or group; specifically, it is the degree to which each party feels that they can depend on the other party to do what they say they will do. Trust is considered by most psychologists to be a primary component in mature relationships with others, whether intimate, social, or therapeutic.

trust versus mistrust see BASIC TRUST VERSUS MISTRUST.

***T* score** a type of STANDARDIZED SCORE based on a score distribution that has a mean of 50 and a standard deviation of 10. For example, a RAW SCORE that is 1 standard deviation above its mean would be converted to a *T* score of 60.

t test any of a class of statistical tests based on the fact that the test statistic follows the T DISTRIBUTION when the NULL HYPOTHESIS is true. Most *t* tests deal with hypotheses about the mean of a population or about differences between means of different populations, wherein those populations show NORMAL DISTRIBUTIONS and the variances need to be estimated. Also called **Student's *t* test**.

Tukey's honestly significant difference test (Tukey's HSD test)
a MULTIPLE COMPARISON TEST that is used to test for significant differences between all possible pairs of mean values on a variable for groups of research participants. The procedure involves simultaneously comparing all possible pairs of means based on a single quantity, called the *honestly significant difference* (HSD), such that if the difference between any two group means exceeds the HSD, the corresponding population means are said to be significantly different from each other. [John Wilder **Tukey** (1915–2000), U.S. statistician]

Turner syndrome a chromosomal disorder, specific to females, marked by the absence of all or a part of one of the two X (female) chromosomes. The effects include underdevelopment or absence of primary and secondary SEX CHARACTERISTICS, infertility, and various other abnormalities (e.g., short stature, lack of menstruation). [reported in 1938 by Henry H. **Turner** (1892–1970), U.S. endocrinologist]

twelve-step program a distinctive approach to overcoming addictive, compulsive, or behavioral problems that was developed initially in Alcoholics Anonymous (AA) and is now used, often in an adapted form, by a number of other SELF-HELP GROUPS. The 12 steps in AA are encompassed in the following broad principles: Each member must (a) admit that he or she cannot control his or her drinking; (b) recognize a supreme spiritual power, which can give the member strength; (c) ex-

amine past errors; (d) make amends for these errors; (e) develop a new code and style of life; and (f) help other alcoholics who are in need of support.

twins *pl. n.* see DIZYGOTIC TWINS; MONOZYGOTIC TWINS.

twin study research utilizing twins. The purpose of such research is usually to assess the relative contributions of heredity and environment to some attribute. Specifically, twin studies often involve comparing the characteristics of identical and fraternal twins and comparing twins of both types who have been reared together or reared apart. The assumptions made in these studies are, however, never completely fulfilled, which can make the estimations of heritability open to some doubts.

two-by-two factorial design an experimental design in which there are two INDEPENDENT VARIABLES each having two levels. When this design is depicted as a matrix, two rows represent one of the independent variables and two columns represent the other independent variable.

two-by-two table a type of table used to display and analyze data for two DICHOTOMOUS VARIABLES. For example, suppose a survey of a group of 100 participants reported information on two variables: (a) gender (male or female) and (b) major in college (social sciences or humanities). The results could be shown in a two-by-two table.

two-factor analysis of variance see TWO-WAY ANALYSIS OF VARIANCE.

two-factor theory of emotion see SCHACHTER–SINGER THEORY.

two-factor theory of work motivation a theory holding that the factors causing worker satisfaction (those addressing psychological needs such as achievement and recognition; see MOTIVATORS) and the factors causing worker dissatisfaction (those addressing basic conditions, including salary and supervision; see HYGIENE

FACTORS) are not opposites of one another but are, in fact, independent factors that must be evaluated and addressed separately.

two-point threshold the smallest distance between two points of stimulation on the skin at which the two stimuli are perceived as two stimuli rather than as a single stimulus.

two-tailed hypothesis see NONDIRECTIONAL HYPOTHESIS.

two-tailed test see NONDIRECTIONAL TEST.

two-way analysis of covariance an ANALYSIS OF COVARIANCE in which there are two INDEPENDENT VARIABLES and a COVARIATE whose effects the researcher wishes to bring under statistical control.

two-way analysis of variance an ANALYSIS OF VARIANCE that isolates the MAIN EFFECTS of two independent variables, a and b, and their INTERACTION EFFECT, $a \times b$, on a dependent variable. Also called **two-factor analysis of variance**.

two-way design a type of FACTORIAL DESIGN in which two INDEPENDENT VARIABLES are manipulated.

two-word stage the developmental period, between approximately 18 and 24 months of age, during which children use two words at a time when speaking (e.g., *dog bone, mama cup*).

tympanic membrane a conically shaped membrane that separates the external ear from the middle ear and serves to transform the pressure waves of sounds into mechanical vibrations of the OSSICLES. The first ossicle (malleus) is attached to the inner surface of the tympanic membrane. Also called **eardrum**.

Type A personality a personality pattern characterized by chronic competitiveness, high levels of ACHIEVEMENT MOTIVATION, impatience and a distorted sense of time urgency, multitasking, and aggressiveness and hostil-

ity. The entire array of traits and behaviors characterizing Type A personality was believed at one time to be connected to the development of coronary heart disease, but epidemiological studies have failed to confirm that connection.

Type B personality a personality pattern characterized by low levels of competitiveness and frustration, an easygoing approach, and a lack of aggressiveness and hostility. Type B individuals typically do not feel the need to prove their superiority or abilities.

Type D personality a "distressed" personality pattern, characterized by a tendency to experience negative emotions in combination with a conscious tendency to suppress self-expression in social interaction. Type D individuals may be at increased risk of developing coronary heart disease and other chronic medical conditions.

Type I error the error of rejecting the NULL HYPOTHESIS when it is in fact true. Investigators make this error when they believe they have detected an effect or a relationship that does not actually exist. The projected probability of committing a Type I error is called the SIGNIFICANCE LEVEL or alpha (α) level.

Type II error the error of failing to reject the NULL HYPOTHESIS when it is in fact not true. Investigators make this error if they conclude that a particular effect or relationship does not exist when in fact it does. The probability of committing a Type II error is called the beta (β) level of a test.

Type III error 1. the error that occurs when there is a discrepancy between the research focus and the hypothesis actually tested. For example, a Type III error would have happened if a researcher collected data on INDIVIDUAL DIFFERENCES within a sample and determined the causes of variation but the question of interest concerned differences between populations. **2.** the error that occurs when a researcher correctly rejects the NULL HYPOTHESIS of no difference between samples but then makes an incorrect inference about the direction of the difference.

type theory any hypothetical proposition or principle for the grouping of people by kind of personality or by personality characteristics. One of the earliest is the humoral theory, which grouped individuals according to the predominant bodily fluid (i.e., blood, black bile, yellow bile, or phlegm) thought to determine their traits and which held sway in medicine and protopsychology through the 17th century and the rise of empiricism.

typology *n.* any analysis of a particular category of phenomena into classes based on common characteristics, such as a typology of personality or disease. —**typological** *adj.*

Uu

ultimate attribution error the tendency for people from one group (the ingroup) to consider any bad acts by members of an outgroup as caused by internal attributes or traits (rather than by outside circumstances or situations), while viewing their positive behaviors as the result of luck or other conditions. See also FUNDAMENTAL ATTRIBUTION ERROR; GROUP-SERVING BIAS.

ultimate explanation an account or interpretation of a particular behavior in terms of its adaptive value.

ultradian rhythm any periodic variation in physiological or psychological function recurring in a cycle of more than 24 hours, such as the human menstrual cycle. Compare CIRCADIAN RHYTHM; INFRADIAN RHYTHM.

ultrasound *n.* sound whose frequency exceeds the human audibility range. In the technique called **ultrasonography**, echoes from ultrasound waves reflected from tissue surfaces are recorded to form structural images for diagnostic purposes, such as to examine a growing fetus during pregnancy or to examine internal organs for signs of disease. Compare INFRASOUND.

unbalanced design an experimental design in which the number of measurements or observations obtained is different for each condition under study. Unbalanced designs may arise because of participant ATTRITION or other unavoidable factors. For example, if a researcher is investigating how sleep and diet influence academic performance and only 35 of the 40 college undergraduates recruited were able to participate through the full term of the project, certain data will be missing for the five people who left prematurely and the design will have become unbalanced.

unbiased *adj.* impartial or without

net error. For example, in unbiased studies and statistical procedures, any errors that do occur are random and therefore self-canceling in the long run.

uncertainty *n.* the state or condition in which something (e.g., the probability of a particular outcome) is not precisely known. —**uncertain** *adj.*

unconditional positive regard an attitude of caring, acceptance, and prizing that others express toward an individual irrespective of his or her behavior and without reference to the others' personal standards. Unconditional positive regard is considered conducive to the individual's self-awareness, self-worth, and personality growth; it is emphasized in many therapeutic approaches. Compare CONDITIONAL POSITIVE REGARD.

unconditioned reinforcement see PRIMARY REINFORCEMENT.

unconditioned reinforcer see NATURAL REINFORCER; PRIMARY REINFORCEMENT.

unconditioned response (UCR; UR) the unlearned response to a stimulus. In other words, it is any original response that occurs naturally (e.g., salivation following the presentation of food). The unconditioned response serves as the basis for establishment of the CONDITIONED RESPONSE in CLASSICAL CONDITIONING. Also called **unconditioned reflex.**

unconditioned stimulus (UCS; US) a stimulus that elicits an UNCONDITIONED RESPONSE, as in withdrawal from a hot radiator, contraction of the pupil on exposure to light, or salivation when food is in the mouth. Compare CONDITIONED STIMULUS.

unconscious (Ucs) **1.** *n.* in psychoanalytic theory, the region of the psyche containing memories, emotional conflicts, wishes, and repressed impulses that are not directly accessible to awareness but that have dynamic effects on thought and behavior. Compare CONSCIOUS; PRECONSCIOUS; SUBCONSCIOUS. **2.** *adj.* relating to or marked by absence of awareness or consciousness. Psychologists prefer increasingly to use the term NONCONSCIOUS in this sense, to avoid confusion with the psychoanalytic unconscious. **—unconsciousness** *n.*

unconscious motivation in psychoanalytic theory, all of the wishes, impulses, aims, and drives of which the self is not aware. Examples of behavior produced by unconscious motivation are purposive accidents, slips of the tongue, and dreams that express unfulfilled wishes.

unconscious plagiarism see CRYPTOMNESIA.

underconfidence *n.* a cognitive bias characterized by an underestimation of one's ability to perform a task successfully or by an underrating of one's performance relative to that of others. Compare OVERCONFIDENCE.

underextension *n.* the incorrect restriction of the use of a word, which is a mistake commonly made by young children acquiring language. For example, a child may believe that the label *dog* applies only to Fido, the family pet. Compare OVEREXTENSION.

understanding *n.* **1.** the process of gaining insight about oneself or others or of comprehending the meaning or significance of something, such as a word, concept, argument, or event. See also APPREHENSION; COMPREHENSION. **2.** in counseling and psychotherapy, the process of discerning the connections between a client's behavior and his or her environment, history, aptitudes, motivations, ideas, feelings, relationships, and modes of expression. **—understand** *vb.*

undifferentiated schizophrenia a subtype of schizophrenia in which

the individual exhibits prominent psychotic features, such as delusions, hallucinations, disorganized thinking, or grossly disorganized behavior, but does not meet the criteria for any of the other subtypes of the disorder.

unidimensionality *n.* the quality of measuring a single construct, trait, or other attribute. For example, a unidimensional personality scale, attitude scale, or other scale would contain items related only to the respective concept of interest. Compare MULTIDIMENSIONALITY. **—unidimensional** *adj.*

unilateral *adj.* denoting or relating to one side (e.g., of the body or an organ) or to one of two or more parties. **—unilaterally** *adv.*

unilateral neglect a disorder resulting from damage to the PARIETAL LOBE of the brain and characterized by a loss of conscious perception of objects or stimuli on the side of the body (usually the left half) that is opposite the location of the lesion. For example, if approached from the left side, an individual with unilateral neglect may not notice the approaching person but would respond normally when approached from the right side. Also called **hemineglect**; **hemispatial neglect**; **spatial neglect**.

unimodal distribution a set of scores with a single peak, or MODE, around which values tend to fluctuate, such that the frequencies at first increase and then decrease. See also BIMODAL DISTRIBUTION.

unipolar disorder persistent or pervasive depression that does not involve a MANIC EPISODE, a HYPOMANIC EPISODE, or a MIXED EPISODE. As such, it contrasts with BIPOLAR DISORDER. The term is sometimes used synonymously with MAJOR DEPRESSIVE DISORDER.

unipolar neuron a neuron that has only a single extension of the CELL BODY. This extension divides into two branches, oriented in opposite directions and representing the axon. One end is the receptive pole, and the other is the output zone. Also called **monopolar neuron**. Compare BIPOLAR NEURON; MULTIPOLAR NEURON.

uniqueness *n.* in FACTOR ANALYSIS, that part of the variance of a variable that it does not share with any other variable in the system. Each of the observed variables in the data set being analyzed can be expressed as a combination of a common factor shared among all variables plus a unique factor associated with a measurement error or another specific, individual source of variation.

unit of analysis in research, the group of people, things, or entities that is being investigated or studied. For example, in organizational contexts, data can be collected from employees, who in turn are part of departments, which in turn are part of the larger organization, which may have multiple sites in several countries. The unit of analysis chosen influences the methodological and analytical procedures used.

univariate *adj.* characterized by a single variable. For example, a researcher may collect univariate data by recording how many hours a day students in a particular course spend outside of class on completing their homework. Compare BIVARIATE; MULTIVARIATE.

univariate analysis a statistical examination of data for only one variable of interest. For example, a univariate analysis of study habits for a sample of college students would examine habits across all individuals without taking into account whether a particular student was a freshman, sophomore, junior, or senior. Also called **univariate statistics**. Compare MULTIVARIATE ANALYSIS.

univariate distribution an arrangement of values on a single RANDOM VARIABLE according to their observed or expected frequency. If the pattern formed follows a NORMAL DISTRIBUTION, it is known as a **univariate**

normal distribution. Compare MULTIVARIATE DISTRIBUTION.

universal grammar (**UG**) a theoretical linguistic construct positing the existence of a set of rules or grammatical principles that are innate in human beings and underlie most natural languages. The concept is of considerable interest to psycholinguists who study LANGUAGE ACQUISITION and the formation of valid sentences.

universalism *n.* the position that certain aspects of the human mind, human behavior, and human morality are universal and essential and are therefore to be found in all cultures and historical periods. Universalism is thus a form of ESSENTIALISM and is opposed to RELATIVISM. —**universalist** *adj.*

universality *n.* **1.** the tendency to assume that one's personal qualities and characteristics, including attitudes and values, are common in the general social group or culture. **2.** in self-help and psychotherapy groups, a curative factor fostered by members' recognition that their problems and difficulties are not unique to them but instead are experienced by many of the group members.

unobtrusive measure a measure obtained without disturbing the participant or alerting him or her that a measurement is being made. For example, a researcher may observe passersby in a public park from a nearby café and document their activities. The behavior or responses of such participants are thus assumed to be unaffected by the investigative process or the surrounding environment. Also called **nonreactive measure**. Compare REACTIVE MEASURE.

unplanned comparison see POST HOC COMPARISON.

unstandardized score see RAW SCORE.

unstructured interview an interview that is highly flexible in terms of the questions asked, the kinds of responses sought, and the ways in which the answers are evaluated. For example, a human resource staff member interviewing a candidate for employment may ask open-ended questions so as to allow the spontaneity of the discussion to reveal more of the applicant's qualities than a standard predetermined question set would. Also called **nondirective interview**. Compare STRUCTURED INTERVIEW.

unsystematic variance the haphazard or random fluctuation of data for individuals over time. It is one of two types of variance identified in research, the other being **systematic variance** arising from the effects of the INDEPENDENT VARIABLES studied.

upper motor neuron see MOTOR NEURON.

U-shaped distribution a graphical representation of a FREQUENCY DISTRIBUTION that is shaped more or less like the letter U, with the maximum frequencies at both ends of the range of the variable. For example, the number of people infected by the flu each year may have a U-shaped distribution by age, with those who are very young or very old having the highest frequency of occurrence.

U **test** see MANN–WHITNEY U TEST.

utilitarianism *n.* an ethical theory based on the premise that *the good* is to be defined as that which brings the greatest amount or degree of happiness; thus, an act is considered moral if, compared to possible alternatives, it provides the greatest good for the greatest number of people. The doctrine is often reduced to the single maxim: The greatest good for the greatest number. **—utilitarian** *adj.*

utilization deficiency the inability of individuals to improve task performance by using strategies that they have already acquired and demonstrated the ability to use. It may occur as a by-product of diminished WORKING MEMORY capacity. Compare MEDIATIONAL DEFICIENCY; PRODUCTION DEFICIENCY.

utricle *n.* the larger of the two VESTIBULAR SACS in the inner ear, the other being the SACCULE. Like the saccule, the utricle senses not only the position of the head with respect to gravity but also acceleration and deceleration. This is achieved by a special patch of epithelium—the MACULA—inside both the utricle and saccule. **—utricular** *adj.*

utterance *n.* a unit of spoken language, which may be of any length but can usually be identified by conversational turn taking or by clear breaks in the stream of speech. MEAN LENGTH OF UTTERANCE is considered an important index of language development in young children.

Vv

vagina *n.* a tubelike structure in female mammals that leads from the cervix (neck) of the uterus to the exterior of the body. Two pairs of glands around the vaginal opening secrete a fluid that facilitates penetration by the penis during coitus. —**vaginal** *adj.*

vaginismus *n.* a sexual dysfunction in which spasmodic contractions of the muscles around the vagina occur during or immediately preceding sexual intercourse, causing the latter to be painful or impossible.

vagus nerve the tenth CRANIAL NERVE, a mixed nerve with fibers that serve many functions. Its sensory fibers innervate the external ear, vocal organs, and thoracic and abdominal VISCERA; its motor fibers innervate the tongue, vocal organs, and the thoracic and abdominal viscera.

validity *n.* the degree to which empirical evidence and theoretical rationales support the adequacy and appropriateness of conclusions drawn from some form of assessment. Validity has multiple forms, depending on the research question and on the particular type of inference being made. For example, the three major types of test validity are CRITERION VALIDITY, based on correlation with an accepted standard; CONSTRUCT VALIDITY, based on the conceptual variable underlying a test; and CONTENT VALIDITY, based on the subject matter of a test. See also EXTERNAL VALIDITY; INTERNAL VALIDITY. —**valid** *adj.*

value *n.* **1.** the mathematical magnitude or quantity of a variable. **2.** a moral, social, or aesthetic principle accepted by an individual or society as a guide to what is good, desirable, or important.

value judgment an assessment of individuals, objects, or events in terms of the values held by the observer rather than in terms of their intrinsic characteristics objectively considered. Value judgments are frequently considered undesirable in social and other sciences.

variability *n.* the degree to which members of a group or population differ from each other, as measured by statistics such as the STANDARD DEVIATION and VARIANCE.

variable *n.* a condition in an experiment or a characteristic of an entity, person, or object that can take on different categories, levels, or values and that can be quantified (measured). For example, test scores and ratings assigned by judges are variables. Compare CONSTANT.

variable-interval schedule (**VI schedule**) a type of INTERVAL REINFORCEMENT in which the reinforcement or reward is presented for the first response after a variable period has elapsed since the previous reinforcement. The value of the schedule is given by the average interval length; for example, "VI 3" indicates that the average length of the intervals between potential reinforcements is 3 minutes.

variable-ratio schedule (**VR schedule**) a type of INTERMITTENT REINFORCEMENT in which a response is reinforced after a variable number of responses. The value of the schedule is given by the average number of responses per reinforcer; for example, "VR 10" indicates that the average number of responses before reinforcement is 10.

variance *n.* a measure of the DISPERSION of scores within a sample or population, whereby a small variance indicates highly similar scores, all close to the sample MEAN, and a large variance indicates more scores at a greater distance from the mean and possibly spread over a larger range.

variance estimate an index of variation in a population that has been calculated using a sample of cases drawn from that population. For example, a STANDARD DEVIATION obtained from the test scores of certain classrooms of students is an estimate of the deviation in the larger school as a whole.

variation *n.* the existence of qualitative differences in form, structure, behavior, and physiology among the individuals of a population, whether due to heredity or to environment. Both ARTIFICIAL SELECTION and NATURAL SELECTION operate on variations among organisms, but only genetic variation is transmitted to offspring.

vascular dementia severe loss of cognitive functioning as a result of cerebrovascular disease. It can be due to repeated strokes, a single large stroke, or chronic cerebral ischemia. It is one of the most common types of dementia. Also called **multi-infarct dementia**.

vasoconstriction *n.* narrowing of blood vessels, which is controlled by VASOMOTOR nerves of the sympathetic nervous system or by such agents as VASOPRESSIN or drugs. It has the effect of increasing blood pressure.

vasodilation *n.* widening of blood vessels, as by the action of a VASOMOTOR nerve or a drug, which has the effect of lowering blood pressure.

vasomotor *adj.* describing or relating to nerve fibers, drugs, or other agents that can affect the diameter of blood vessels, especially small arteries, by causing contraction or relaxation of the smooth muscle of their walls. Fibers of the sympathetic and parasympathetic divisions of the AUTONOMIC NERVOUS SYSTEM have a vasomotor effect.

vasopressin *n.* a PEPTIDE hormone produced in the hypothalamus and released by the posterior PITUITARY GLAND into the blood as controlled by OSMORE-

CEPTORS. It has two forms, both of which increase fluid retention in the body by signaling the kidneys to reabsorb water instead of excreting it in urine. Both forms also raise blood pressure by signaling specific smooth muscle cells to contract and narrow small blood vessels. Vasopressin also modulates complex cognitive functions—such as attention, learning, and the formation and recall of memories—and has been implicated in a range of social behaviors. Also called **antidiuretic hormone** (ADH).

vasovagal syncope see SYNCOPE.

vector *n.* **1.** a mathematical entity with magnitude and direction. Compare SCALAR. **2.** in MULTIVARIATE ANALYSIS, a one-dimensional arrangement in which the scores of a group of individuals on a particular measure are arrayed. **3.** an animal or other organism that carries and spreads disease.

vegetative *adj.* **1.** pertaining to basic physiological functions—such as those involved in growth, respiration, sleep, digestion, excretion, and homeostasis—that are governed primarily by the AUTONOMIC NERVOUS SYSTEM, which is sometimes called the **vegetative nervous system**. **2.** living without apparent cognitive function or responsiveness, as in a persistent VEGETATIVE STATE.

vegetative state a condition in which a person appears awake but lacks any self-awareness, environmental awareness, or basic or higher level cognitive functions (e.g., information processing, language comprehension and production, perception). The individual exhibits normal reflexes, circadian rhythms (including sleep–wake cycles), respiration, circulation, and other brainstem- and hypothalamus-governed functions but shows no voluntary behavior or other purposeful response to stimuli. A **persistent vegetative state** (**PVS**, or **persistent noncognitive state**) is one lasting more than 4 weeks from which there is the possibility—however slim—of recovery, whereas a **permanent vegetative state** is one lasting more than 3 to 12 months (depending on the cause) from which there is no chance of regaining consciousness.

Venn diagram a visual depiction of elements and their relations. Circles represent the elements of a set, and the union and intersection between or among the circles represent relationships between the sets (i.e., the degree to which they are mutually inclusive or exclusive). [John **Venn** (1834–1923), British logician]

ventral *adj.* denoting the abdomen or the front surface of the body. In reference to the latter, this term sometimes is used interchangeably with ANTERIOR. Compare DORSAL. —**ventrally** *adv.*

ventral anterior cingulate cortex see ANTERIOR CINGULATE CORTEX.

ventral horn either of the bottom regions of the H-shaped pattern formed by the PERIAQUEDUCTAL GRAY in the spinal cord. The ventral horns contain large motor neurons whose axons form the ventral roots. Compare DORSAL HORN.

ventral posterior cingulate cortex see POSTERIOR CINGULATE CORTEX.

ventral root any of the SPINAL ROOTS that carry motor nerve fibers and arise from the spinal cord on the front surface of each side. Compare DORSAL ROOT.

ventral stream a series of cortical maps of the visual field that flow from the occipital cortex to the temporal lobe. These maps represent nameable visual features of objects, such as color, size, texture, object identity, and the like. The ventral stream is known informally as the "what" pathway of perception. Compare DORSAL STREAM.

ventricle *n.* **1.** an anatomical cavity in the body, such as any of the ventricles of the heart. **2.** any of the four interconnected cavities inside the brain, which serve as reservoirs of CEREBRO-SPINAL FLUID. Each of the two LATERAL VENTRICLES communicates with the THIRD VENTRICLE via an opening called the interventricular foramen; the third and fourth ventricles communicate with each other via the CEREBRAL AQUE-DUCT, and with the central canal of the spinal cord. —**ventricular** *adj.*

ventriloquism effect the tendency for sounds to appear to emanate from plausible visual objects, regardless of the actual source of the sound. For example, the voices of actors in a movie are localized to the images on the screen, rather than to the speakers that produce the sound. The ventriloquism effect stems from VISUAL CAPTURE.

ventrodorsal *adj.* oriented or directed from the front (ventral) region of the body to the back (dorsal) region. Compare DORSOVENTRAL. —**ventrodorsally** *adv.*

ventromedial hypothalamic syndrome a set of symptoms caused by experimentally induced lesions in the VENTROMEDIAL NUCLEUS of the hypothalamus of a nonhuman animal. The syndrome consists of two stages. The first stage is characterized by HY-PERPHAGIA and subsequent weight gain, resulting in obesity. The second stage includes stabilization of body weight, resistance to food-getting behavior, and finickiness, such that the animal is willing to eat only easily obtainable and palatable foods. Compare LATERAL HYPOTHALAMIC SYNDROME.

ventromedial hypothalamus (**VMH**) a region of the hypothalamus primarily associated with feelings of satiety. In studies in which the VMH is lesioned, animals overeat to the point of extreme obesity. The VMH also has a role in thermoregulation.

ventromedial nucleus a group of nuclei within the ventromedial hypothalamus that receives input from the AMYGDALA and is associated particularly with eating and sexual behavior. The ventromedial nucleus traditionally has been referred to as the **satiety**

center because of its presumed dominance over the cessation of eating, but it is now known that other neural areas are involved in this function as well.

ventromedial pathway any of four major descending groups of nerve fibers within the MOTOR SYSTEM, conveying information from diffuse areas of the cerebral cortex, midbrain, and cerebellum. These pathways include the anterior **corticospinal tract**, which descends directly from motor cortex to the anterior horn of the spinal cord; the **vestibulospinal tract**, which carries information from the VESTIBULAR NUCLEI for control of equilibratory responses; the **tectospinal tract**, for control of head and eye movements; and the **reticulospinal tract**, for maintaining posture.

venue sampling see TIME–LOCATION SAMPLING.

verbal communication see COMMUNICATION.

verbal learning the process of learning about verbal stimuli and responses, such as letters, digits, nonsense syllables, or words. The methods used include PAIRED-ASSOCIATES LEARNING and SERIAL LEARNING.

verbal memory the capacity to remember something written or spoken that was previously learned (e.g., a poem).

verbal test any test or scale in which performance depends on one's ability to comprehend, use, or otherwise manipulate words.

vergence n. a turning movement of the eyes to focus on an item in the depth plane. If they turn toward each other, the movement is CONVERGENCE; if they turn away from each other, it is DIVERGENCE.

vertical décalage in PIAGETIAN THEORY, the invariable sequence in which the different stages of development (sensorimotor, preoperational, concrete operational, formal opera-

tional) are attained. Compare HORIZONTAL DÉCALAGE.

vertical–horizontal illusion see HORIZONTAL–VERTICAL ILLUSION.

vertigo n. an unpleasant, illusory sensation of movement or spinning of oneself or one's surroundings. It may arise because of neurological disorders, psychological stress (e.g., anxiety), or activities (e.g., a roller-coster ride) that disturb the labyrinth in the inner ear, which contains the organs of balance.

very low birth weight (VLBW) see LOW BIRTH WEIGHT.

vesicle n. a fluid-filled saclike structure, such as any of the SYNAPTIC VESICLES in axon terminals that contain neurotransmitter molecules. —**vesicular** adj.

vestibular nuclei nuclei in the dorsolateral part of the PONS and the MEDULLA OBLONGATA in the brain that receive fibers from a portion of the VESTIBULOCOCHLEAR NERVE and serve the sense of balance and orientation in space. They send fibers to the cerebellum, reticular formation, thalamus, and the vestibulospinal tract (see VENTROMEDIAL PATHWAY).

vestibular sacs two sacs in the inner ear—the UTRICLE and SACCULE—that, together with the SEMICIRCULAR CANALS, comprise the **vestibular apparatus**. The vestibular sacs respond both to gravity to encode information about the head's orientation and to linear acceleration.

vestibular sense the sense of equilibrium, which enables the maintenance of balance while sitting, standing, walking, or otherwise maneuvering the body. A subset of PROPRIOCEPTION, it is in part controlled by the VESTIBULAR SYSTEM in the inner ear, which contains specialized receptors that detect motions of the head.

vestibular system a system in the body that is responsible for maintaining balance, posture, and the body's orientation in space and that plays an important role in regulating locomotion and other movements. It consists of the VESTIBULAR SACS and SEMICIRCULAR CANALS in the inner ear, a portion of the VESTIBULOCOCHLEAR NERVE, and the various cortical regions associated with the processing of vestibular (balance) information.

vestibulocochlear nerve the eighth CRANIAL NERVE: a sensory nerve containing tracts that innervate both the sense of hearing and the sense of balance. It has two divisions, the **vestibular nerve**, originating in the semicircular canals, and the AUDITORY NERVE, originating in the cochlea. The vestibulocochlear nerve transmits impulses from the inner ear to the medulla oblongata and pons and has fibers that continue into the cerebrum and the cerebellum.

vestibulo-ocular reflex (VOR) the involuntary compensatory movement of the eyes that occurs to maintain fixation on a visual target during small, brief head movements. It is triggered by vestibular signals and thus does not depend on visual inputs. Compare OPTO-KINETIC REFLEX.

vestibulospinal tract see VENTRO-MEDIAL PATHWAY.

vicarious reinforcement the process whereby a person becomes more likely to engage in a particular behavior (response) by observing another individual being reinforced for that behavior. An important concept in SOCIAL LEARNING THEORY, vicarious reinforcement often leads to imitation: For example, a student who hears the teacher praise a classmate for neat penmanship on an assignment and who then carefully handwrites his or her own assignment is considered to have received vicarious reinforcement.

vicarious traumatization (VT) the impact on a therapist of repeated emotionally intimate contact with trauma survivors. More than COUNTER-TRANSFERENCE, VT affects the therapist across clients and situations. It results

in a change in the therapist's own worldview and sense of the justness and safety of the world. Also called **secondary traumatization**.

vigilance *n.* a state of extreme awareness and watchfulness directed by one or more members of a group toward the environment, often toward detecting potential threats (e.g., predators, intruders, enemy forces in combat). —**vigilant** *adj.*

violation of assumptions a situation in which the theoretical ASSUMPTIONS associated with a particular statistical or experimental procedure are not fulfilled. Because violation of assumptions introduces BIAS, the validity of assumptions must be confirmed prior to data analysis to ensure that the methods and strategies chosen are appropriate and will yield useful results.

violation-of-expectation method a technique for studying infant cognition, based on habituation and dishabituation procedures, in which increases in an infant's looking time at an event or other stimulus are interpreted as evidence that the outcome he or she expected has not occurred. For example, while a baby watches, a researcher may repeatedly return a toy to a blue box. If the researcher sometime later retrieves the same toy from a nearby red box (after a CONFEDERATE surreptitiously moved it) and the baby looks longer at that red box, it is assumed that he or she has some understanding of object permanence and was not expecting the toy to be there.

violence *n.* the expression of hostility and rage with the intent to injure or damage people or property through physical force. See also PATHOLOGICAL AGGRESSION. —**violent** *adj.*

virilism *n.* the presence in a female of secondary sexual characteristics that are specific to men, such as muscle bulk and hirsutism. The condition is due to overactivity of the adrenal gland with excessive secretion of ANDROGEN.

virtual reality therapy a form of IN VIVO EXPOSURE therapy in which clients are active participants in an interactive three-dimensional computer-generated environment that allows them a sense of actual involvement in scenarios related to their presenting problems. This treatment is currently used primarily for anxiety-related disorders, such as fear of flying.

viscera pl. n. (sing. **viscus**) the organs in any major body cavity, especially the abdominal organs (stomach, intestines, kidneys, etc.). —**visceral** adj.

visible spectrum see SPECTRUM.

vision n. the sense of sight, in which the eye is the receptor and the stimulus is radiant energy in the visible SPECTRUM. See also VISUAL SYSTEM. —**visual** adj.

visual agnosia loss or impairment of the ability to recognize and understand the nature of visual stimuli. Subtypes exist based on the type of visual stimulus that the person has difficulty recognizing, such as objects (**visual object agnosia** or **visual form agnosia**), multiple objects or pictures (**simultanagnosia**), or colors (**color agnosia**). See also PROSOPAGNOSIA.

visual area any of many regions of the cerebral cortex in which the neurons are primarily sensitive to visual stimulation. Together, all the visual areas comprise the VISUAL CORTEX. Most visual areas can be distinguished from one another on the basis of their anatomical connections (i.e., their CYTO-ARCHITECTURE) and their specific visual sensitivities. Individual areas are designated by "V" and a number that indicates roughly how distant the area is from the STRIATE CORTEX; for example, V2 refers to the SECONDARY VISUAL CORTEX, the area immediately surrounding the striate cortex.

visual cache see VISUOSPATIAL SKETCHPAD.

visual capture the tendency in humans for vision to override the other senses. It is responsible for the VENTRIL-OQUISM EFFECT.

visual cliff an apparatus to investigate the development of DEPTH PERCEPTION in nonverbal human infants and in nonhuman animals. The apparatus consists of a table with a checkerboard pattern, dropping steeply down a "cliff" to a surface with the same pattern some distance below the tabletop. The apparatus is covered with a transparent surface, and the participant is positioned on this at the border between the tabletop and the cliff. Reluctance to crawl onto the surface covering the cliff is taken as an indication that the participant can discriminate the apparent difference in depth between the two sides of the apparatus.

visual cortex the cerebral cortex of the occipital lobe, specifically the STRIATE CORTEX. In humans, this occupies a small region on the lateral surface of the occipital pole of the brain, but most is buried in the banks of the calcarine fissure on the medial surface of the brain. The visual cortex receives input from the LATERAL GENICULATE NUCLEUS via the OPTIC TRACT and sends output to the multiple visual areas that make up the visual ASSOCIATION CORTEX.

visual encoding the neural processes by which stimuli seen in the external world are converted into internal (mental) representations that can subsequently be processed and stored in memory. For example, when a person looks at a photograph, PHOTORECEPTORS in the individual's RETINA receive the visual sensory information, which in turn is conveyed to populations of RETINAL GANGLION CELLS. The cylindrical extensions of the ganglion cells form the OPTIC NERVE, which projects to the LATERAL GENICULATE NUCLEUS in the thalamus and the superior COLLICULUS in the midbrain. The sensory input reaches VISUAL AREAS in the cerebral cortex and ultimately the HIPPOCAMPUS, where it is combined with input from other brain regions into a single abstract representation. Parallel neural conversion processes occur for stimuli that are heard (**acoustic encoding**), smelled (**olfactory encoding**), tasted (**gustatory encoding**), or felt (**tactile encoding**).

visual field the extent of visual space over which vision is possible with the eyes held in a fixed position. In humans, the outer limit of vision for each eye extends approximately 60° nasally, 90° temporally, 50° superiorly, and 70° inferiorly. The extent varies with age: Very young children and older people have a smaller visual field.

visual form agnosia see VISUAL AGNOSIA.

visual hallucination visual perception in the absence of any external stimulus. Visual hallucinations may be unformed (e.g., shapes, colors) or complex (e.g., figures, faces, scenes). They may be associated with psychoses, or they may arise in association with lesions of the peripheral or central visual pathway or visual cortical areas.

visual illusion a misperception of external visual stimuli that occurs as a result of a misinterpretation of the stimuli, such as a GEOMETRIC ILLUSION. Visual illusions are among the most common type of illusion.

visual imagery mental imagery that involves the sense of having "pictures" in the mind. Such images may be memories of earlier visual experiences or syntheses produced by the imagination (e.g., visualizing a pink kangaroo). Visual imagery can be used for a variety of purposes, such as dealing with traumatic events, establishing DESENSITIZATION hierarchies, or improving physical performance.

visual masking the ability of one visual stimulus to render another stimulus invisible when presented in close temporal proximity.

visual object agnosia see VISUAL AGNOSIA.

visual perception the awareness and understanding of visual sensations that arises from the interplay between the physiology of the VISUAL SYSTEM and the internal and external environments of the observer.

visual search the process of detecting a target visual stimulus among distractor stimuli. In experimental studies, the characteristics of the target and distractors are manipulated to explore the mental operations that underlie visual attention.

visual system the components of the nervous system and the nonneural apparatus of the eye that contribute to the perception of visual stimulation. The anterior structures of the eye, such as the CORNEA and LENS, focus light on the RETINA, which transduces photons into neural signals. These signals are transmitted via the OPTIC NERVE and OPTIC TRACT to nuclei in the thalamus and brainstem. These structures in turn transmit the signals either to the VISUAL AREAS of the cerebral cortex for hierarchical processing and conscious analysis or directly to motor centers in the brainstem and spinal cord to produce eye movements.

visual word-form dyslexia an acquired DYSLEXIA characterized by difficulties related to visually analyzing the attributes of written words. An example is dyslexia associated with visual NEGLECT. Also called **peripheral dyslexia**; **word-form dyslexia**. Compare CENTRAL DYSLEXIA.

visuospatial sketchpad a component of WORKING MEMORY that briefly holds and manipulates information about the appearance of objects and their locations in space. For example, if one tried to determine which of two countries is larger or to rate their proximity to one another, this would involve mentally picturing and comparing both countries within the visuospatial sketchpad. The sketchpad is divided into two parts: the **visual cache**, specializing in information about form, color, and other aspects of visual identity, and the **inner scribe**, specializing in information about spatial location and movement representation and planning.

vital capacity the capacity of the lungs to hold air, measured as the maximum volume of air that can be exhaled after maximum inspiration.

vitality *n.* physical or intellectual vigor or energy: zest. See also FITNESS.

vitreous humor see EYE.

vocabulary spurt see NAMING EXPLOSION.

vocalization *n.* the production of sounds by means of vibrations of the vocal cords, as in speaking, babbling, singing, screaming, and so forth. —**vocalize** *vb.*

voice-onset time (**VOT**) in phonetics, the brief instant that elapses between the initial movement of the speech organs as one begins to articulate a sound and the vibration of the vocal cords. Voice-onset time has been the subject of research in adult and infant speech perception because of evidence that this continuous acoustic dimension is perceived categorically (see CATEGORICAL PERCEPTION).

volley theory the principle that individual fibers in an auditory nerve respond to one or another stimulus in a rapid succession of rhythmic sound stimuli, whereas other fibers in the nerve respond to the second, third, or *n*th stimulus. The result is that successive volleys of impulses are fired to match the inputs of stimuli, yet no single fiber is required to respond to every stimulus.

volumetric thirst see HYPOVOLEMIC THIRST.

voluntary *adj.* describing activity, movement, behavior, or other processes produced by choice or intention and under cortical control, in contrast to automatic movements (e.g., reflexes). Compare INVOLUNTARY.

voluntary admission admission of an individual to a mental hospital or other inpatient unit at his or her own request, without coercion. Such hospitalization can end whenever the person sees fit, unlike INVOLUNTARY HOSPITALIZATION, the length of which is determined by a court or the hospital. Also called **voluntary hospitalization.**

volunteer bias any systematic difference between individuals who volunteer to be in a study versus those who do not, which may potentially render the resulting group or sample of participants unrepresentative of the larger population.

vomeronasal system a set of specialized receptor cells that in non-human mammals is sensitive to PHEROMONES and thus plays an important role in the sexual behavior and reproductive physiology of these animals. In humans, this system responds physiologically to chemical stimulation and, in turn, excites brain centers, but its role in human olfaction is not known.

voodoo death a CULTURE-BOUND SYNDROME observed in Haiti, Africa, Australia, and islands of the Pacific and the Caribbean. An individual who has disobeyed a ritual or taboo is hexed or cursed by a medicine man or sorcerer and dies within a few days. The individual's strong belief in the curse is posited to cause physiological reactions in the body that result in death.

voyeurism *n.* a PARAPHILIA in which preferred or exclusive sexual interest and arousal is focused on observing unsuspecting people who are naked, in the act of undressing, or engaging in sexual activity. Although the **voyeur** seeks no sexual activity with the person observed, orgasm is usually produced through masturbation during the act of "peeping" or later, while visualizing and remembering the event. —**voyeuristic** *adj.*

vulnerability *n.* susceptibility to developing a condition, disorder, or disease when exposed to specific agents or conditions. —**vulnerable** *adj.*

V

Ww

Wada test a technique for determining hemispheric functions, typically memory and language, by injecting a small dose of a barbiturate into the carotid artery on one side of the head. This procedure selectively impairs the cerebral hemisphere on the injected side for 10 to 15 minutes. While each hemisphere is separately anesthetized, various cognitive tasks are administered; impairments on these tasks suggest that these functions are represented in the anesthetized hemisphere. [Juhn Atsushi **Wada** (1924–), Japanese-born Canadian neurologist]

wait-list control group a group of research participants who receive the same intervention or treatment as those in the EXPERIMENTAL GROUP but at a later time. Wait-list control groups commonly are used in therapy outcome and similar studies to account for the potential influence of elapsed time on treatment effectiveness.

Wason selection task a reasoning task involving four cards, each with a letter on one side and a number on the other, and a rule supposedly governing their correlation (e.g., if the letter is a vowel, then the number is even). One side of each card is shown, and the solver is asked which cards must be turned over to determine if the rule has been followed. Also called **four-card problem**. [developed in 1966 by Peter Cathcart **Wason** (1924–2003), British psychologist]

waterfall illusion see MOTION AFTEREFFECT.

wavelength *n.* the distance between successive peaks in a wave motion of a given FREQUENCY, such as a sound wave or a wave of electromagnetic radiation. The wavelength is equal to the speed of propagation of the wave motion divided by its frequency.

weapons effect increased hostility or a heightened inclination to aggression produced by the mere sight of a weapon. If provoked, individuals who have previously been shown a weapon will behave more aggressively than will those who have not.

wear-and-tear theory of aging a theory of biological aging suggesting that aging results from an accumulation of damage to cells, tissues, and organs in the body caused by dietary toxins and environmental agents. This leads to the weakening and eventual death of the cells, tissues, and organs.

Weber's law a mathematical model of the DIFFERENCE THRESHOLD stating that the magnitude needed to detect physical change in a stimulus is proportional to the absolute magnitude of that stimulus. Thus, the more intense the stimulus, the greater the change that must be made in it to be noticed. This can be expressed as $\Delta I/I = k$, where ΔI is the difference threshold, I is the original stimulus magnitude, and k is a constant called **Weber's fraction**. See also FECHNER'S LAW. [proposed in 1834 by Ernst Heinrich **Weber** (1795–1878), German physiologist]

Wechsler Adult Intelligence Scale (**WAIS**) an intelligence test for individuals 16 to 90 years of age. The current version, **WAIS–IV** (2008), has a core battery of 10 subtests that yield a Full Scale IQ score and index scores on four domains of cognitive ability: verbal comprehension, perceptual organization, processing speed, and working memory. [David **Wechsler** (1896–1981), Romanian-born U.S. psychologist]

Wechsler Intelligence Scale for Children (**WISC**) an intelligence test standardized for children of ages 6 years to 16 years 11 months. It currently includes 10 core subtests and five supplemental subtests that measure verbal comprehension, perceptual reasoning, processing speed, and working memory capabilities, yielding index scores for each as well as a Full Scale IQ. The most recent version of the test is the **WISC–IV**, published in 2003. [David **Wechsler**]

Wechsler Preschool and Primary Scale of Intelligence

(**WPPSI**) an intelligence test for children ages 2 years 6 months to 7 years 7 months that currently includes two working memory subtests, three processing speed subtests, six verbal comprehension subtests, two visual–spatial subtests, and two fluid reasoning subtests. These subtests yield Full Scale IQs, primary index scores, ancillary index scores, and scaled subtest scores. The most recent version is the **WPPSI–IV**, published in 2012. [David **Wechsler**]

weight *n.* a coefficient or multiplier used in an equation or statistical investigation and applied to a particular variable to reflect the contribution to the data. For example, a **weighted sample** is one in which different values are applied to its different constituent subgroups to reflect their representation within the larger population from which it was taken. Thus, if a population is 50% male and 50% female but the sample studied is 40% and 60%, respectively, different multipliers could be used to adjust the individual subsample results to match the makeup of the population.

weighted average an average calculated to take into account the relative importance of the items making up the average: Different values or WEIGHTS are assigned to different data points to reflect their relative contribution. For example, in examining grade point average, one might give grades A through F the weights of 4, 3, 2, 1, and 0, respectively. One would multiply the number of A grades a student obtained by 4, the number of B grades by 3, and

so forth and then divide the resulting sum by the total number of grades to obtain the student's overall weighted average. Also called **weighted mean**.

well-being *n.* a state of happiness and contentment, with low levels of distress, overall good physical and mental health and outlook, or good quality of life.

wellness *n.* a dynamic state of physical, mental, and social WELL-BEING that is the result of four key factors: biology (i.e., body condition and fitness), environment, lifestyle, and health care management. The **wellness concept** is the notion that health care programs should actively involve the promotion of good mental and physical health rather than being concerned merely with the prevention and treatment of illness and disease.

Wernicke's aphasia loss of the ability to comprehend sounds or speech, in particular to understand or repeat spoken language and to name objects or qualities. The condition is a result of brain damage and may be associated with other disorders of communication, including ALEXIA, ACALCULIA, or AGRAPHIA. [Karl **Wernicke** (1848–1904), German neurologist]

Wernicke's area a region toward the back of the superior temporal gyrus of the left hemisphere of the cerebrum containing nerve tissue associated with the interpretation of sounds. See also SPEECH AREA. [Karl **Wernicke**, who reported, in 1874, a lack of comprehension of speech in patients who had a brain lesion in that area]

Wernicke's encephalopathy a neurological disorder caused by a deficiency of vitamin B_1 (thiamine). The principal symptoms are confusion, oculomotor abnormalities, and ataxia. These symptoms are likely to resolve with thiamine treatment, although most individuals then develop severe retrograde and anterograde AMNESIA as well as impairment in other areas of cognitive functioning, including executive functions (see KORSAKOFF'S SYNDROME). [first described in 1881 by Karl **Wernicke**]

what pathway see VENTRAL STREAM.

where pathway see DORSAL STREAM.

white matter parts of the nervous system composed of nerve fibers that are enclosed in a MYELIN SHEATH, which gives a white coloration to otherwise grayish neural structures. Compare GRAY MATTER.

whole-language approach a top-down approach to teaching reading that emphasizes the reader's active construction of meaning and often excludes the use of phonics.

whole method of learning a learning technique in which the entire block of material is memorized, as opposed to learning the material in parts. Compare PART METHOD OF LEARNING.

Wilcoxon–Mann–Whitney test a NONPARAMETRIC TEST, used when data are rank ordered, to determine whether two INDEPENDENT SAMPLES have been drawn from the same population, on the basis of a comparison of their median values. The test combines the MANN–WHITNEY U TEST and WILCOXON RANK-SUM TEST into a single statistical procedure. [Frank **Wilcoxon** (1892–1965), Irish-born U.S. statistician; Henry Berthold **Mann** (1905–2000), Austrian-born U.S. mathematician; Donald Ransom **Whitney** (1915–2001), U.S. statistician]

Wilcoxon rank-sum test a statistical test of centrality for ranked data that compares the median values of two INDEPENDENT SAMPLES to determine whether they have been drawn from the same population. One combines the data points from the different groups into a single pool and ranks their values in ascending order. The ranks that have been assigned are, in turn, used to determine the test statistic, W, which is

evaluated for statistical significance. [Frank **Wilcoxon**]

Wilcoxon signed-ranks test a NONPARAMETRIC statistical procedure used to determine whether a single sample is derived from a population in which the median equals a specified value. The data are values obtained using a RATIO SCALE, each is subtracted from the hypothesized value of the population median, and the difference scores are then ranked. Also called **Wilcoxon T test**. [Frank **Wilcoxon**]

Williams syndrome (**Williams–Barratt syndrome**; **Williams–Beuren syndrome**) a rare disorder caused by deletion of a segment of chromosome 7. It is characterized by intellectual disability, FAILURE TO THRIVE, high concentrations of calcium in the blood, narrowing of blood vessels, and unusual facial features. [described in the 1960s by J. C. P. **Williams**, New Zealand cardiologist; Brian Gerald **Barratt-Boyes** (1924–2006), New Zealand cardiologist; and Alois J. **Beuren** (1919–1984), German cardiologist]

Wisconsin Card Sorting Test (**WCST**) a test that requires participants to deduce from feedback (right vs. wrong) how to sort a series of cards depicting different geometric shapes in various colors and quantities. Once the participant has identified the underlying sorting principle (e.g., by color) and correctly sorts 10 consecutive cards, the principle is changed without notification. The WCST is primarily considered a test of EXECUTIVE FUNCTIONS, particularly abstract reasoning and cognitive flexibility.

wisdom *n.* the ability of an individual to make sound decisions, to find the right—or at least good—answers to difficult and important life questions, and to give advice about the complex problems of everyday life and interpersonal relationships. The role of knowledge and life experience and the importance of applying knowledge toward a common good through balancing one's own, others', and institutional interests are two perspectives that have received significant psychological study.

withdrawal *n.* see SUBSTANCE WITHDRAWAL.

within-groups variance variation in experimental scores among identically treated individuals within the same group who experienced the same experimental conditions. It is determined through an ANALYSIS OF VARIANCE and compared with the BETWEEN-GROUPS VARIANCE to obtain an F RATIO. Also called **within-subjects variance**.

within-subjects design an experimental design in which the effects of treatments are seen through the comparison of scores of the same participant observed under all the treatment conditions. For example, teachers may want to give a pre- and postcourse survey of skills and attitudes to gauge how much both changed as a result of the course. Also called **repeated measures design**; **within-groups design**. Compare BETWEEN-SUBJECTS DESIGN.

within-subjects factor the independent variable under study in an ANALYSIS OF VARIANCE of data from a WITHIN-SUBJECTS DESIGN. This variable has multiple levels to which each participant is exposed. For example, if a researcher is interested in job performance differences as a function of work shift length (e.g., 8 hours, 12 hours, 24 hours) and has each participant work each shift length during the study, then work shift length is a within-subjects factor. Also called **within-subjects variable**.

within-subjects variance see WITHIN-GROUPS VARIANCE.

Wolffian duct a rudimentary duct system in the embryo that develops into structures of the male reproductive system (the epididymis, vas deferens, and seminal vesicles). In the female, the Wolffian duct does not develop. Compare MÜLLERIAN DUCT. [Kaspar F. **Wolff** (1734–1794), German embryologist]

word-association test a test in which the participant responds to a stimulus word with the first word that comes to mind. The method was invented in 1879 for use in exploring individual differences, and psychoanalysts later adapted it for use as a PROJECTIVE TECHNIQUE.

word-form dyslexia see VISUAL WORD-FORM DYSLEXIA.

word salad severely disorganized and virtually incomprehensible speech or writing, in which the person's associations appear to have little or no logical connection. It is strongly suggestive of schizophrenia.

word-stem completion a procedure in which participants are presented with sets of introductory letters and asked to form complete words. For example, a person given the stem *ele__* might respond with *elevate* or *elephant*. Word-stem completion most commonly is used in cognitive research on perceptual PRIMING and IMPLICIT MEMORY.

word-superiority effect (**WSE**) the finding that, when presented briefly, individual letters are more easily identified in the context of a word than when presented alone. A similar but weaker effect is obtained when letters are presented as part of a pronounceable but meaningless vowel–consonant combination, such as *deet* or *pling*.

working memory the 1974 model of British cognitive psychologists Alan D. Baddeley (1934–) and Graham J. Hitch (1946–) for the short-term maintenance and manipulation of information necessary for performing complex cognitive tasks such as learning, reasoning, and comprehension. According to their multicomponent conceptualization, working memory comprises a PHONOLOGICAL LOOP for temporarily manipulating and storing speech-based information and a VISUO-SPATIAL SKETCHPAD that performs a similar function for visual and spatial information. Both are supervised by a limited capacity CENTRAL EXECUTIVE, a control system responsible for the distribution of attention and general coordination of ongoing processes. A fourth component, the EPISODIC BUFFER, was added to the model in 2000; it binds together information about the same stimulus or event from the different subsidiary systems to form an integrated representation that is essential to LONG-TERM MEMORY storage. The Baddeley and Hitch working memory model has replaced the idea of a unitary SHORT-TERM MEMORY system.

working through 1. in psychotherapy, the process by which clients identify, explore, and deal with psychological issues, on both an intellectual and emotional level, through the presentation of such material to and in discussion with the therapist. **2.** in psychoanalysis, the process by which patients gradually overcome their RESISTANCE to the disclosure of unconscious material; are brought face to face with the repressed feelings, threatening impulses, and internal conflicts at the root of their difficulties; and develop conscious ways to rebound from, resolve, or otherwise deal with these feelings, impulses, and conflicts.

work psychology see INDUSTRIAL AND ORGANIZATIONAL PSYCHOLOGY.

worse-than-average effect see BELOW-AVERAGE EFFECT.

x-axis *n.* the horizontal axis on a graph. See ABSCISSA.

X chromosome the SEX CHROMO-SOME that is responsible for determining femaleness in humans and other mammals. The body cells of females possess two X chromosomes (XX), whereas males have one X chromosome and one Y CHROMOSOME (XY). In humans, the X chromosome carries between 1,000 and 2,000 genes, including many responsible for SEX-LINKED conditions. Abnormal numbers of X chromosomes lead to a range of disorders and syndromes.

xenophobia *n.* hostile attitudes or aggressive behavior toward people of other nationalities, ethnic groups, regions, or neighborhoods. —**xeno-phobic** *adj.*

X-linked *adj.* see SEX-LINKED.

XX see X CHROMOSOME.

XXY syndrome see KLINEFELTER'S SYNDROME.

XY see Y CHROMOSOME.

Yy

y-axis *n.* the vertical axis on a graph. See ORDINATE.

Y chromosome the SEX CHROMOSOME that is responsible for determining maleness in humans and other mammals. The body cells of males possess one Y chromosome and one X CHROMOSOME (XY). The Y chromosome is much smaller than the X chromosome and carries just a handful of functioning genes. Hence, males are far more susceptible to SEX-LINKED diseases than females, because the Y chromosome cannot counteract any defective genes carried on the X chromosome.

yea-saying *n.* answering questions positively regardless of their content, which can distort the results of surveys, questionnaires, and similar instruments. Also called **acquiescent response set**; **response acquiescence**. Compare NAY-SAYING.

Yerkes–Dodson law a law stating that the relation between motivation (AROUSAL) and performance can be represented by an inverted U-curve (see INVERTED-U HYPOTHESIS). [Robert M. **Yerkes** (1876–1956), U.S. psychobiologist, and John Dillingham **Dodson** (1879–1955), U.S. psychologist]

Y-linked *adj.* see SEX-LINKED.

Y maze a maze shaped like the letter Y, consisting of a stem that leads to a choice of two goal arms, only one of which is the correct path to the goal box. It is a variant of the T MAZE; both are used in experiments on animal cognition.

yoked-control group a CONTROL GROUP in which each participant is paired with a participant in another group; the paired individuals are then exposed to precisely the same experiences except for the specific condition under study. For example, in a study of the effectiveness of rewards on children's learning, matched individuals in the control and experimental groups would complete the same tasks under the same conditions, but only those in the experimental group would be praised for good performance.

Young–Helmholtz theory of color vision a theory to explain color vision in terms of components or processes sensitive to three different parts of the spectrum, corresponding to the colors red, green, and blue. According to this theory, other colors are perceived by stimulation of two of the three processes, whereas light that stimulates all three processes equally is perceived as white. The components are now thought to be RETINAL CONES. Compare HERING THEORY OF COLOR VISION; OPPONENT PROCESS THEORY OF COLOR VISION. [Thomas **Young** (1773–1829), British physician and physicist; Hermann von **Helmholtz** (1821–1894), German physiologist and physicist]

young-old *adj.* see ADULTHOOD.

Zz

z-axis *n.* the third dimension in a graph. It is perpendicular to both the horizontal X-AXIS and the vertical Y-AXIS.

Zeigarnik effect the tendency for interrupted, uncompleted tasks to be better remembered than completed tasks. Some theorists relate this phenomenon to certain GESTALT PRINCIPLES OF ORGANIZATION but at the level of higher mental processing (e.g., memory), rather than at the level of pure perception. [described in 1927 by Bluma **Zeigarnik** (1901–1988), Lithuanian-born Russian psychologist]

Zeitgeber *n.* a cue, such as day length, used to activate or time a BIOLOGICAL RHYTHM. See ENTRAINMENT. [German, "time giver"]

Zeitgeist *n.* a term used by German philosopher Georg Wilhelm Friedrich Hegel (1770–1831) to refer to a type of supraindividual mind at work in the world and manifest in the cultural worldview that pervades the ideas, attitudes, and feelings of a particular society in a specific historical period. A Zeitgeist theory of history stresses the role of such situational factors as economics, technology, and social influences, in contrast to the GREAT MAN THEORY of history. [German, "spirit of the times"]

Zener cards a standardized set of stimulus materials, similar to a deck of playing cards, designed for use in experiments on EXTRASENSORY PERCEPTION (ESP) and other parapsychological phenomena. The set consists of 25 cards, each of which bears one of five printed symbols (star, wavy lines, cross, circle, or square), with five cards in each category. In a typical test of TELEPATHY, for example, the cards are shuffled (usually mechanically) and a designated "sender" turns the cards over one at a time to inspect the symbol while a "receiver" attempts to guess the symbol by reading the thoughts of the sender. Also called **ESP cards**; **Rhine cards**. [named in honor of Karl E. **Zener** (1903–1964), U.S. perceptual psychologist who designed the symbols, by his colleague Joseph B. **Rhine** (1895–1980), who devised the deck]

zero-sum game in GAME THEORY, a type of game in which the players' gains and losses add up to zero. The total amount of resources available to the participants is fixed, and therefore one player's gain necessarily entails the others' loss. The term is used particularly in analyses of bargaining and economic behavior. Compare NON-ZERO-SUM GAME.

Zöllner illusion a visual illusion in which parallel lines appear to diverge when one of the lines is intersected by short diagonal lines slanting in one direction, and the other by lines slanting in the other direction. [Johann Karl Friedrich **Zöllner** (1834–1882), German astrophysicist]

zone of proximal development in the sociocultural theory of Russian psychologist Lev Vygotsky (1896–1934), the difference between a child's actual level of ability and the level of ability that he or she can achieve when assisted by, or when working in cooperation with, older or more experienced partners (e.g., adults or more knowledgeable peers). See SOCIOCULTURAL PERSPECTIVE.

zoom-lens model of attention a conceptualization of visual attention as a variably sized resource that is allocated according to interest, task demands, or other factors. Whereas the SPOTLIGHT MODEL OF ATTENTION specifies a fixed size for the focal attention zone, the zoom-lens model considers it to be malleable, that is, able to be constricted into a highly focused beam or dilated to even distribution over the entire visual field.

zoomorphism *n.* **1.** the attribution of nonhuman animal traits to human beings, deities, or inanimate objects. **2.** the use of nonhuman animal psychology or physiology to explain human behavior. Compare ANTHROPOMORPHISM.

zoophilia *n.* a PARAPHILIA in which nonhuman animals are repeatedly preferred or exclusively used to achieve sexual excitement and gratification. An animal, usually a household pet or farm animal, is either used as the object of intercourse or is trained to lick or rub the human partner, referred to as a **zoophile**.

z score the STANDARDIZED SCORE that results from applying a Z-SCORE TRANSFORMATION to raw data. For example, consider a person who scored 30 on a 40-item test having a mean of 25 and standard deviation of 5, and 40 on an 80-item test having a mean of 50 and a standard deviation of 10. The resulting *z* scores would be +1.0 and −1.0, respectively. Thus, the individual performed better on the first test, on which he or she was one standard deviation above the mean, than on the second test, on which he or she was one standard deviation below the mean.

z-score transformation a statistical procedure used to convert raw data into Z SCORES, dimensionless quantities that may be interpreted without reference to the original units of measurement. It is performed by subtracting the reference value (the sample average) from each data point and dividing the difference by the STANDARD DEVIATION of the sample.

z test a type of statistical test that compares the means of two different samples to determine whether there is a significant difference between them (i.e., one not likely to have occurred by chance). Generally, this involves comparing the mean from a sample of a population to the mean for the whole population but may also involve comparing the means of two different populations. The *z* test is based on the NORMAL DISTRIBUTION and is used when a population's STANDARD DEVIATION is known or the sample is large (greater than 30). The equivalent T TEST is used with unknown standard deviations or smaller samples.

z transformation see FISHER'S R TO Z TRANSFORMATION.

zygote *n.* a fertilized egg, or ovum, with a DIPLOID set of chromosomes, half contributed by the mother and half by the father. The zygote divides to become an EMBRYO, which continues to divide as it develops and differentiates—in humans eventually forming a FETUS. —**zygotic** *adj.*

Appendixes

Abbreviations and Acronyms

A

A1	primary auditory cortex (see AUDITORY CORTEX)
A2	secondary auditory cortex (see AUDITORY CORTEX)
ACC	anterior cingulate cortex
ACh	acetylcholine
AChE	acetylcholinesterase (see CHOLINESTERASE)
AChEI	acetylcholinesterase inhibitor (see CHOLINESTERASE)
AChR	acetylcholine receptor
ACTH	adrenocorticotropic hormone (see CORTICOTROPIN)
ADC	AIDS dementia complex
ADD	attention-deficit disorder (see ATTENTION-DEFICIT/HYPER-ACTIVITY DISORDER)
ADH	antidiuretic hormone (see VASOPRESSIN)
ADHD	attention-deficit/hyperactivity disorder
ADLs	activities of daily living
ADS	action disorganization syndrome
AEP	average evoked potential
AER	average evoked response (see AVERAGE EVOKED POTENTIAL)
AFR	alcohol flush reaction
AH	alternative hypothesis
AI	artificial insemination; artificial intelligence
AIDS	acquired immune deficiency syndrome
AIS	androgen-insensitivity syndrome
AL	absolute limen (see ABSOLUTE THRESHOLD); adaptation level
ALS	amyotrophic lateral sclerosis
AMPA	alpha-amino-3-hydroxy-5-methyl-4-isoxazole-propionic acid (see GLUTAMATE RECEPTOR)
ANCOVA	analysis of covariance
ANOVA	analysis of variance
ANS	autonomic nervous system
AP	action potential
APA	American Psychiatric Association; American Psychological Association
ART	assisted reproductive technology
ASC	altered state of consciousness
ASD	acute stress disorder; autism (or autistic) spectrum disorder
ATP	adenosine triphosphate

Abbreviations and Acronyms

B

BAC	blood alcohol concentration
BAL	blood alcohol level (see BLOOD ALCOHOL CONCENTRATION)
BAS	behavioral approach system
BCI	brain–computer interface
BCS	battered-child syndrome
BDD	body dysmorphic disorder
BIS	behavioral inhibition system
BMI	body mass index; brain–machine interface (see BRAIN–COMPUTER INTERFACE)
BMR	basal metabolic rate (see BASAL METABOLISM)
BP	*Bereitschaftspotential* (see READINESS POTENTIAL)
BPA	bisphenol A
BPRS	Brief Psychiatric Rating Scale
BSM	behavioral sleep medicine
BuChE	butyrylcholinesterase (see CHOLINESTERASE)
BWS	battered-woman syndrome

C

CA	chronological age
CAH	congenital adrenal hyperplasia
CAI	computer-assisted instruction
CAL	computer-assisted learning (see COMPUTER-ASSISTED INSTRUCTION)
CAM	complementary and alternative medicine
cAMP	cyclic adenosine monophosphate
CART analysis	classification and regression tree analysis
CAT	computerized axial tomography (see COMPUTED TOMOGRAPHY)
CBD	cannabidiol
CBT	cognitive behavior therapy
CCK	cholecystokinin
CD	conduct disorder
CF	cumulative frequency
CFA	confirmatory factor analysis
CFF	critical flicker frequency
CFS	chronic fatigue syndrome
cGMP	cyclic guanosine monophosphate
CHD	coronary heart disease
ChE	cholinesterase
ChEI	cholinesterase inhibitor (see CHOLINESTERASE)
CI	confidence interval
CJD	Creutzfeldt–Jakob disease
CL	comparison level

CLT	central limit theorem
CMHC	community mental health center
CNS	central nervous system
CO blob	cytochrome oxidase blob
CP	cerebral palsy
CPZ	chlorpromazine
CR	conditioned response
CRF	continuous reinforcement
Cs	conscious
CS	conditioned stimulus
C-section	cesarean (or caesarean) section
CSF	cerebrospinal fluid
CS–US interval	conditioned stimulus–unconditioned stimulus interval
CT	cognitive therapy; computed tomography
CTT	classical test theory
CV	cardiovascular
CVA	cerebrovascular accident
CWB	counterproductive work behavior

D

DA	dopamine
DALYs	disability adjusted life years
DAT	dementia of the Alzheimer's type
DBS	deep brain stimulation
DBT	dialectical behavior therapy
DES	dysexecutive syndrome
DID	dissociative identity disorder
DIF	differential item functioning
DL	difference limen (see DIFFERENCE THRESHOLD)
DLPFC	dorsolateral prefrontal cortex
DMTS	delayed matching to sample
DNA	deoxyribonucleic acid
DNR	do not resuscitate (see ADVANCE DIRECTIVE)
dopa (DOPA)	3,4-dihydroxyphenylalanine
DSH	deliberate self-harm
DSM	Diagnostic and Statistical Manual of Mental Disorders (see DSM–5)
DTs	delirium tremens
DV	dependent variable
Dx	diagnosis
DZ twins	dizygotic twins

E

EBP	evidence-based practice

Abbreviations and Acronyms

eCB	endogenous cannabinoid
ECG	electrocardiogram
ECT	electroconvulsive therapy
ED	erectile dysfunction
EE	expressed emotion
EEG	electroencephalography; electroencephalogram
EFA	exploratory factor analysis
EHR	electronic health record
EKG	electrocardiogram
ELBW	extremely low birth weight (see LOW BIRTH WEIGHT)
ELM	elaboration-likelihood model
EMDR	eye-movement desensitization and reprocessing
EMG	electromyography; electromyogram
EP	evoked potential
EPI	Eysenck Personality Inventory
EPQ	Eysenck Personality Questionnaire (see EYSENCK PERSON-ALITY INVENTORY)
EPS	extrapyramidal symptoms (or syndrome)
EPSP	excitatory postsynaptic potential
EQ	emotional quotient (see EMOTIONAL INTELLIGENCE)
ER	endoplasmic reticulum; evoked response (see EVOKED POTENTIAL)
ERP	event-related potential
ESP	extrasensory perception
EST	electroconvulsive shock (or electroshock) therapy (see ELECTROCONVULSIVE THERAPY)

F

FA	factor analysis
FAE	fetal alcohol effects (see FETAL ALCOHOL SYNDROME)
FAP	fixed action pattern
FAS	fetal alcohol syndrome
FFA	fusiform face area (see FUSIFORM GYRUS)
FFM	five-factor personality model
FI schedule	fixed-interval schedule
FIT	feature-integration theory
fMRI	functional magnetic resonance imaging (functional MRI)
FMS	false memory syndrome (see FALSE MEMORY)
FR schedule	fixed-ratio schedule
FSD	female sexual dysfunction
FSH	follicle-stimulating hormone
FTT	failure to thrive

G

GABA	gamma-aminobutyric acid

GAD	generalized anxiety disorder
GAS	general adaptation syndrome
GBMI	guilty but mentally ill
GIGO	garbage in, garbage out
GLM	general linear model
GnRH	gonadotropin-releasing hormone
GPS	General Problem Solver
GRIT	graduated and reciprocated initiatives in tension reduction
GSR	galvanic skin response

H

HD	Huntington's disease
HIV	human immunodeficiency virus
HLM	hierarchical linear model
HMO	health maintenance organization
HPA axis	hypothalamic–pituitary–adrenal axis
HRT	hormone replacement therapy
HSD	honestly significant difference (see TUKEY'S HONESTLY SIGNIFICANT DIFFERENCE TEST)
HSI	human systems integration
HSM	heuristic-systematic model
5-HT	5-hydroxytryptamine (see SEROTONIN)

I

IADLs	instrumental activities of daily living
IAT	Implicit Association Test
ICC	intraclass correlation coefficient (see INTRACLASS CORRELATION)
ICD	*International Classification of Diseases*
IEP	individualized education program
I/O psychology	industrial and organizational psychology
IOR	inhibition of return
IP	information processing
IPA	interaction process analysis
IPSP	inhibitory postsynaptic potential
IPT	interpersonal psychotherapy
IQ	intelligence quotient
IQR	interquartile range
IRB	institutional review board
IRM	innate releasing mechanism
IRT	item response theory
IT cortex	inferotemporal cortex
IV	independent variable
IVF	in vitro fertilization

Abbreviations and Acronyms

J

JND (jnd)	just noticeable difference (see DIFFERENCE THRESHOLD)

L

LAD	language acquisition device
LASS	language acquisition support system
LAT	Lesch's alcoholism typology
LBW	low birth weight
LD	learning disability; learning disorder
LGBTQ	lesbian, gay, bisexual, transgender, and questioning or queer
LGN	lateral geniculate nucleus
LH	lateral hypothalamus; luteinizing hormone
LLD	language learning disability (see SPECIFIC LANGUAGE IMPAIRMENT)
LOC	loss of consciousness
LR	likelihood ratio; logistic regression
LRE	least restrictive environment
LSD	least significant difference (see FISHER LEAST SIGNIFICANT DIFFERENCE TEST); lysergic acid diethylamide (see LSD)
LTD	long-term depression
LTM	long-term memory
LTP	long-term potentiation

M

MA	mental age
mAChR	muscarinic receptor
MAE	motion aftereffect
MANOVA	multivariate analysis of variance
MAOI	monoamine oxidase inhibitor
MAP	modal action pattern
MAR	missing at random
MBD	minimal brain dysfunction
MBTI	Myers–Briggs Type Indicator
MCO	managed care organization (see MANAGED CARE)
MCS	minimally conscious state
MDMA	3,4-methylenedioxymethamphetamine
MDS	multidimensional scaling
MEG	magnetoencephalography; magnetoencephalograph
MLU	mean length of utterance
MMPI	Minnesota Multiphasic Personality Inventory
MOE	margin of error
MR	mental retardation
MRI	magnetic resonance imaging

mRNA	messenger RNA
MS	multiple sclerosis
MSP	Münchausen syndrome by proxy
MTG	middle temporal gyrus
MZ twins	monozygotic twins

N

NAB	Neuropsychological Assessment Battery
n-Ach	need for achievement
nAchR	nicotinic receptor
n-Aff	need for affiliation
NDE	near-death experience
NE	norepinephrine
NGF	nerve growth factor
NH	null hypothesis
NK cell	natural killer cell
NLD	nonverbal learning disorder
NMDA	N-methyl-D-aspertate (see GLUTAMATE RECEPTOR)
NREM	nonrapid eye movement (see NREM SLEEP)
NS	not significant
NST	nucleus of the solitary tract (see SOLITARY NUCLEUS)
NVC	nonverbal communication

O

OBM	organizational behavior management
OCD	obsessive-compulsive disorder
OFA	occipital face area (see OCCIPITAL LOBE)
OKR	optokinetic reflex
OT	occupational therapy

P

PAG	periaqueductal gray
PCA	principal components analysis
PCC	posterior cingulate cortex
PChE	pseudocholinesterase (see CHOLINESTERASE)
PCP	1-(1-phenylcyclohexyl)piperidine (phencyclidine); primary care provider (see PRIMARY CARE)
Pcs	preconscious
PD	panic disorder; Parkinson's disease; personality disorder; psychological debriefing
PDM	*Psychodynamic Diagnostic Manual*
PDP	parallel distributed processing
PET	positron emission tomography
PI	prescribing information (see LABELING)
PK	psychokinesis

Abbreviations and Acronyms

PKU	phenylketonuria
PMS	premenstrual syndrome
PNS	peripheral nervous system
PRE	partial reinforcement effect
PSE	point of subjective equality
PSG	phrase-structure grammar
PSP	postsynaptic potential
PT	physical therapy
PTA	posttraumatic amnesia
PTSD	posttraumatic stress disorder
PVN	paraventricular nucleus
PVS	persistent vegetative state (see VEGETATIVE STATE)

Q

QALYs	quality adjusted life years

R

RAS	reticular activating system
RBC theory	recognition by components theory
RBD	randomized block design; REM behavior disorder
RCT	randomized clinical trial
REBT	rational emotive behavior therapy
REM	rapid eye movement (see REM SLEEP)
RI schedule	random-interval schedule
RMS	root mean square
RNA	ribonucleic acid
ROC curve	receiver-operating characteristic curve
RP	readiness potential
RR schedule	random-ratio schedule
RST	reinforcement sensitivity theory
RT	reaction time
rTMS	repetitive transcranial magnetic stimulation (see TRANS-CRANIAL MAGNETIC STIMULATION)

S

S1	primary somatosensory area
S2	secondary somatosensory area
SA	social age
SAD	seasonal affective disorder
SAM	sympathetic–adrenal–medullary axis
SAT	Scholastic Assessment Test
SB	Stanford–Binet Intelligence Scale
SBS	shaken baby syndrome
SCN	suprachiasmatic nucleus
SDT	signal detection theory; social dominance theory

SEM	structural equation modeling
SES	socioeconomic status
SIDS	sudden infant death syndrome
SIS	sensory-information store (see SENSORY MEMORY)
SIT	stress-inoculation training
SLD	specific learning disability
SLI	specific language impairment
SMA	supplementary motor area
S/N	signal-to-noise ratio
SOA	stimulus onset asynchrony
S–O–R psychology	stimulus–organism–response psychology
SQ3R	survey, question, read, recite, and review
SRI	serotonin reuptake inhibitor (see SSRI)
S–R psychology	stimulus–response psychology
SRT	simple reaction time
SSRI	selective serotonin reuptake inhibitor
SST	social skills training
s-structure	surface structure
STD	sexually transmitted disease
STI	sexually transmitted infection (see SEXUALLY TRANSMITTED DISEASE)
STM	short-term memory
SWB	subjective well-being

T

TA	transactional analysis
TAT	Thematic Apperception Test
TBI	traumatic brain injury
TCA	tricyclic antidepressant
T-group	training group
THC	tetrahydrocannabinol
TIA	transient ischemic attack
TM	transcendental meditation
TMS	transcranial magnetic stimulation
TO	time out
TOTE	test-operate-test-exit (see FEEDBACK LOOP)
TOT phenomenon	tip-of-the-tongue phenomenon
TSD	Tay–Sachs disease
TTM	transtheoretical model

U

UCR	unconditioned response
Ucs	unconscious
UCS	unconditioned stimulus

Abbreviations and Acronyms

UG	universal grammar
UR	unconditioned response
US	unconditioned stimulus

V

V1	primary visual cortex (see STRIATE CORTEX)
V2	secondary visual cortex
VI schedule	variable-interval schedule
VLBW	very low birth weight (see LOW BIRTH WEIGHT)
VMH	ventromedial hypothalamus
VOR	vestibulo-ocular reflex
VOT	voice-onset time
VR schedule	variable-ratio schedule
VT	vicarious traumatization

W

WAIS	Wechsler Adult Intelligence Scale
WCST	Wisconsin Card Sorting Test
WISC	Wechsler Intelligence Scale for Children
WPPSI	Wechsler Preschool and Primary Scale of Intelligence
WSE	word-superiority effect

Symbols

Latin

d	Cohen's d; Glass's d
D	Cook's distance; difference score
d'	d prime
dB	decibel
df	degrees of freedom
f	function (in mathematics)
f	frequency
F	F ratio
g	general factor
H_0	null hypothesis
H_1	alternative hypothesis
H_a	alternative hypothesis
Hz	hertz
M	sample mean
MS	mean square
MSE	mean square error
n	the number of cases in a particular experimental subgroup (see SAMPLE SIZE)
N	the total number of cases in an experiment (see SAMPLE SIZE)
p	probability
r	product-moment correlation coefficient; sample correlation coefficient
r^2	coefficient of determination
R	multiple correlation coefficient
R^2	coefficient of multiple determination
r_b	biserial correlation coefficient
r_{bis}	biserial correlation coefficient
r_{pb}	point biserial correlation coefficient
r_{pbis}	point biserial correlation coefficient
r_s	Spearman correlation coefficient
s	specific factor
s^2	sample variance
S^D	discriminative stimulus
SD	standard deviation
SE	standard error
SEE	standard error of estimate
SEM	standard error of measurement; standard error of the mean

Symbols

SS	sum of squares
$t_{\frac{1}{2}}$	half-life
T	Wilcoxon signed-ranks test statistic
U	Mann–Whitney U test statistic
V	Cramér's V
W	Wilcoxon rank-sum test statistic
x	a variable of interest (e.g., in research or statistical analysis)
$\bar{X}$	sample mean
y	a variable of interest (e.g., in research or statistical analysis)

Greek

α	alpha
β	beta
χ^2	chi-square statistic
χ^2 distribution	chi-square distribution
Δ	delta
κ	Cohen's kappa
λ	eigenvalue
ψ	experienced sensation (see FECHNER'S LAW; STEVENS LAW); the field of psychology or the phenomena of parapsychology (see PSI)
μ	population mean
ω^2	omega squared
φ	phi coefficient
φ_c	Cramér's V
ρ	population correlation coefficient; Spearman correlation coefficient
σ^2	population variance
σ_M	standard error of the mean
Σ	summation